Alan Cranston
Senator from California -

Making a 'Dent in the World'

Volume I

Alan Cranston
Senator from California -

Making a 'Dent in the World'

Volume I

Judith Robinson

Telegraph Hill Press
San Francisco

Telegraph Hill Press
562 B Lombard Street
San Francisco, California 94133-2314
415 788 9112

Library of Congress Control Number: 2012938011

ISBN: 978-0-692-01760-9

Printed in the U.S.A. by Patsons Press, Sunnyvale, California.

Cover photograph: Senator Alan Cranston, Majority Whip, holding 52-42 roll-call tally predicting Senate vote that rejected Judge Robert H. Bork's nomination to U. S. Supreme Court, October 5, 1987; the final vote was 58-42, close to Cranston's prediction as the "best nose-counter in the Senate." *United Press International Photo. Alan Cranston Papers, The Bancroft Library, University of California, Berkeley.*

Dedicated to American politicians who make "*politician* a term of honor, not of scorn…the noblest of man's works."

Alan Cranston, in praise of Adlai Stevenson, 1955.

Peace is the one condition of survival in this nuclear age.

Adlai Stevenson (1900-1965)

If man does find the solution for world peace, it will be the most revolutionary reversal of his record we have ever known.

George Catlett Marshall (1880-1959)

"In the First Place"

The old-timer, a lean, retired pantaloon, sitting with loosely slippered feet close to the fire, thus gave of his wisdom to the questioning student:

'Looking back upon it all, what we most need 'in politics' *is more good men. Thousands of good men ARE in.... More would come if they knew how MUCH they are needed....*

'I speak of it as a game,' the old gentleman went on, 'and in some ways it is. That's where the fun of it comes in. Yet, there are times when it looks to me more like… hand-to-hand fights for life, and fierce struggles between men and strange powers.... Still, I don't think we ought to go in with the idea of being repaid.

'It seems an odd thing to me that so many men feel they haven't any time for politics; can't put in even a little, trying to see how their cities (let alone their states and the country) are run. When we have a war, look at the millions of volunteers that lay down everything and answer the call of the country. Well, in politics, the country needs ALL the men who have any patriotism – NOT to be seeking office, but to watch and to understand what is going on…. When wrong things are going on and all the good men understand them, that is all that is needed. The wrong things stop going on.'

Booth Tarkington, *In the Arena, Stories of Political Life* (1905)

Also by Judith Robinson

The Hearsts - An American Dynasty

"You're in Your Mother's Arms" - The Life & Legacy of Congressman Phil Burton

Noble Conspirator - Florence S. Mahoney and the Rise of the National Institutes of Health

From Gold Rush to Millennium - 150 Years of the Episcopal Diocese of California,1849-2000

Contents

Introduction

This is intended to be a history of a time as well as a man who played large roles in it. It will recall events of recent history while reminding us that there is not much new under the sun. The controversies, debates and concerns with which Alan Cranston was involved from the 1940s to the 1990s still confronted the United States and the world as of 2012 – *"deja vu all over again,"* as baseball legend Yogi Berra put it. Policies to which Cranston was committed all his life – strengthening the United Nations and eliminating nuclear weapons – continued unresolved. Cranston stated presciently in 1975, "*Excessive military spending is heading this nation toward financial bankruptcy, absolute government regimentation or nuclear war – and possibly all three.*"

Cranston nevertheless had an impact on domestic and international policies both as a citizen advocate and powerful member of the United States Senate. The story also is intended to show how Congress *should* work, requiring give-and-take and compromise on all sides, and to reinforce and put in perspective the necessary role of politicians – most of them honest, hard-working, dedicated public servants – representing the will of people in a social democracy. We need reminding that the word "politic" derives from the Greek *politikos*, "*of the citizens*," that we, the people, *are* the government, that democracy is very hard work, needing the participation of all citizens.

Alan MacGregor Cranston (1914-2000) was always, it seems, headed for a political career – his other jobs, as journalist, world-peace advocate, businessman – were secondary to his goal of influencing national and foreign policies. He managed to get out of scrapes – including causing the INS wire service for which he worked to be sued by Ethiopian Emperor Haile Selassie, and being sued himself for copyright infringement by Adolf Hitler's American publisher for printing an abridged version of *Mein Kampf* – until a major one culminated his Senate career.

As his father observed of his bright, adventurous young son, "*Much of his charm lies in his spirit, but it only takes one slip to cause him and us a disaster.*"

Cranston actually was a mature and thoughtful person as a young man, not aggressively postulating but listening, thinking, refining his views. He made a point of educating himself beyond what he was taught in school, and developed ambitions and objectives early in his life. In a remarkable way he accomplished virtually all that he set out to do as a youth – became a foreign correspondent, got elected to the U. S. Senate, wrote books, plays, became an enlightened member of society. His self-education and determination in pursuit of learning shaped his future perspectives and views. One can see him evolve through his notes and thoughts, carefully written down and impressed on his brain.

He was a forerunner in many social views. His support of civil and voting rights and ways to foster world peace would be life-long themes to which he was genuinely committed, not motivated by political goals. He was early outspoken against segregation and extremist groups like the John Birch Society and consistently warned against them while being himself the target of extensive red-baiting by anti-Communists in the 1950s. He was prescient in anticipating and advocating such policies as solar and alternative-energy technologies. He also championed the value of national parks which he helped extend.

Growing up in a moderate, progressive Republican family, his evolvement into a liberal Democrat and subsequently moderate, pragmatic politician was carefully thought out.

He helped activate the Democratic Party in California after World War II in an effort to become a politician himself. Despite set-backs, he was a self-described optimist, hopeful and positive-thinking that things would get better, not only for himself but for America and the world. He also realized early that lessons could be learned from defeats.

He was an unassuming fellow, not boastful or arrogant even after rising to Senate leadership posts, which endeared him to people at many levels of society as well as loyal staff, most of whom stayed with him through thick and thin for his entire twenty-three-year Senate career, including a long-shot but no-less committed run for the White House in 1983.

Throughout his life he was a sprinter, beginning in high school, setting records in competitions and running into his late eighties. "*I want to stagger across the finish line, knowing I've done all I possibly can,*" he said of why he kept working after leaving the Senate in 1992, age seventy-eight. His mind and memory remained alert and his energy high to the end of his long life. He could quote favorite poems from memory, reciting Henry Wadsworth Longfellow's "The Day is Done" (1845) on a journey in 2000 to The Bancroft Library at the University of California, Berkeley, to which he had given his papers.

I came to realize what a direct, candid and genuinely decent man he was, far from the aloof senator whom I had perceived while a legislative aide (1969-79) to Senator Gaylord Nelson (Democrat of Wisconsin), seeing a pragmatic politician not always supportive of pro-consumer legislation. Spending time with him while preparing the biography, I saw evidence of his dedication to causes and his quiet humor. I understood why people were loyal to him for many years.

He resembled more the person whom author Wallace Stegner described in his forward to a 1980 biography lovingly written by Cranston's sister Ruth Eleanor (known as R. E.). "He has a smile that cuts Gordian knots, and a patience that, if the smile fails, can untie them. In a body notorious for show boats, he has been a work boat and sometimes a fire boat." Stegner cited Cranston's lack of pretension and exuberant energy, "even a certain boyish ingenuousness." He nevertheless was purposeful in his life: "He himself cut the clothes he wanted to wear, cut them very young and grew into them, and he wears them...with a special quiet distinction." [1]

A businessman who knew Cranston commented for a high-school student's thesis in 1986 that he had "a tremendous fund of knowledge on practically all matters and an uncanny ability to recall facts and discuss them without hesitation." Another acquaintance remarked that Cranston's answers to questions were "always very brief and very to the point. He responds directly to the question." [2]

Eleanor, whose fondness and admiration for her younger brother were unapologetic, had written, after running with him one morning in Washington, D. C., "Everyone underestimates what he can do." When she asked Cranston how he stood the demanding pace of a day in the Senate, with its numerous interruptions, meetings, quick decisions to be made, he said with surprise, "*But it's so enjoyable*!" [3]

"Alan Cranston had a passion, which these guys lack today," Democratic activist and prison-reform advocate (as warden at San Quentin penitentiary) Douglas Rigg observed. "If ever the word 'public servant' could be applied to anyone, it truly applied to him. It was an honorable profession to him, and we were lucky to have him" representing California. [4]

Republican Congressman Pete McCloskey, Eleanor's representative, told her one day in 1978 at a reception honoring retiring California congressmen, "Alan has done more than anyone in the state to restore people's faith in politics and government because he is so effective." [5]

Like San Francisco Congressman Phil Burton, Cranston's life was consumed by his work as a politician and legislator. He breathed, ate, drank, slept it. The Senate was his home and entire *raison d'être*. He would be powerfully humbled and mortified when his peers reprimanded him for taking money from accused swindler Charles H. Keating as an alleged inducement to intercede with federal banking regulators although Cranston applied the funds to voter-registration projects, not to personal gain.

The biography initially was commissioned by Cranston and his sister but the family did not interfere with the contents. It is intended to be an objective biography of a man worthy of chronicling for his influence on national and world affairs. Many of his long-serving Senate staff aides contributed to the memoir with personal recollections and observations as did congressional colleagues, campaign managers, friends and staff. The author is grateful for their assistance and candor. Cranston's papers archived at The Bancroft Library were a major source of information, along with personal papers in Cranston's possession. His son Kim and sister Eleanor also contributed to the story. Another son Robin tragically was killed by a speeding driver in 1980.

Cranston carried with him throughout his life, on a tattered piece of paper in his pocket, a credo that he aspired to emulate, written by sixth-century B.C. Chinese philosopher Lao-tzu. It began, "*A leader is best/ When people barely know that he exists*," and ended, "*But of a good leader... When his work is done, his aim fulfilled,/ They will all say, 'We did this ourselves*.'"

Mary Judith Robinson
San Francisco, California,
February, 2012

Note on Sources

Alan Cranston gave his extensive papers, covering his early life and family, professional career as an elected official in California (State Controller, 1959-67) and United States Senator (1969-93, Democratic Whip 1977-91), to The Bancroft Library, University of California, Berkeley, where they joined a large political archive. Much of the material in the biography derives from the Alan Cranston Papers (MSS 88/214c), cited as AC Papers. Other Bancroft materials include a Cranston Pictures Collection, cited as Pics, AC Papers. Cranston's personal archives to which the author was given access are cited as AC Personal Papers (those were being added to the Bancroft collection beginning in 2012). The author wishes to acknowledge assistance from the senator's son Kim Christopher Cranston as well as many people who agreed to be interviewed for the biography.

Extensive interviews were conducted of Cranston, his sister, Members of Congress, Cranston's Senate staff, campaign staff and friends. A biography of Cranston by his sister Ruth Eleanor Cranston Fowle Cameron (1909- 2008) also was a source: Eleanor Fowle, *Cranston, The Senator from California* (San Rafael, California: Presidio Press, 1980, hardcover; Los Angeles: Jeremy P. Tarcher, Inc., 1984, second edition, paperback).

Most photos and illustrations came from the Cranston Papers at The Bancroft Library. Photo credit was given and reproduction made with permission wherever known and possible to obtain.

1

"A dent in the world"

"I want to make a real dent in the world in a belles-lettres *way, or at least have a happy, Bohemian life."*
Alan Cranston to his diary, 1932.

"Ambition is probably a disease, but I have a bad dose of it."
Alan Cranston to a friend in high school.

"Much of his charm lies in his spirit, but it only takes one slip to cause him and us a disaster."
Cranston's father William Cranston to Alan's sister Ruth Eleanor, July 29, 1935.

Alan MacGregor Cranston's ancestors were nearly all Scottish. A family tree showed that an eighteenth-century ancestor, William Cranston (born circa 1720), was a shipbuilder at Leith, Scotland; another, John Cranston (born circa 1740), a "noted botanist and justice of the peace"; a third, Alexander Cranston (1753-1807), had come from Crook House Farm near Linton Church a few miles east of Jedburgh in the Shire of Roxborough. It was from Alexander that Alan Cranston descended. One of Alexander's eight children, Robert Cranston (1798-1876), was described as an "adventurous pioneer immigrant to Galt, Ontario," Canada in 1831. He emigrated because he was a second son not entitled to inherit family land. He and his wife Margaret McDougall had ten children. Alan's great-grandfather Alexander (1822-81), who was nine years old when the family emigrated, became a Canadian landowner and with his wife Marion Dickie, had seven children. One, Robert Dickie Cranston (1849-1916), Alan's grandfather, made his way to California where he became a contractor-architect and built houses in San Francisco. He married Jane MacGregor (1851-1920), whose father William MacGregor (1819-97) was born at Ayr, Scotland, and from whom Alan and his father William took their middle name. William ("Will") MacGregor Cranston (1879-1953), born at Yountville, California, was one of seven children. [1]

In a 1951 letter to Cranston's father, a Canadian relative wrote, "On the mound on which [Linton] church is built you will find a gravestone erected in memory of Alexander Cranston" and his wife Isabel Hunter. Alexander apparently was a "hind" or plowman, and "in all probability lived in one of the three stone cottages at the rear of Crook House," according to the relative's account from visits to ancestral sites. His son Robert Cranston and his family had arrived in Canada in 1831 with ten other families on the ship *Sarah Mary Ann.* The voyage took five weeks and four days. Marion Dickie's family also had worked the land in Scotland – their place was a potato farm when the relative visited. "The old farm buildings must be a couple of hundred years old and are rather shabby.... You would not enjoy living in either place," he wrote. [2]

Another bit of family lore, according to notes written by Alan Cranston, was that "Grandpa MacGregor had an uncle who married a native chief's daughter in Jamaica, and the chief gave him her weight in gold. The family disowned him. He was worth a fortune [when he died]. Grandpa MacGregor was the only heir, but he couldn't prove it because in an uprising in Scotland, all family records [were] destroyed. Finally he found a letter that would prove [it] – [but the letter was] illegible. Ruined [his] life. Finally [he] burned the letter in a stove. Two years later [they had] invented stuff [that] made old writing legible. More bitterness. Fortune (huge) went through chancery, reverted to [the] crown." [3]

The Cranstons also had nineteenth-century roots in California. Alan's mother Carol Dixon (born 1878) was the daughter of a physician, George Dixon, a leader in ventures to reclaim swamp lands in Sacramento, Yolo and Solano counties who promoted the potential riches of the Sacramento Valley in published articles. He had moved to California from Illinois and descended from early settlers in America. Investing in land and cattle interests, he lost nearly all that he owned but built up a successful medical practice despite being unpaid for many of his services. Carol Dixon attended Stanford University, which would become another Cranston tradition, where she was courted by fellow student William MacGregor Cranston. One morning in September, 1900, however, Doctor Dixon returned to his Sacramento house, ostensibly, as his wife had asked him, to fetch her. He went to his bedroom and a few minutes later, a pistol shot rang out. When members of the household rushed to the scene, they found Dixon lying on the floor before a mirror, a bullet hole through his temple. He left no message for his wife and daughters, who refused to speak of the sudden and unexpected tragedy again. [4]

There were politicians in the family, as well. Cranston's maternal grandfather, Hiram Harlow Dixon, was a Vermont state senator in 1849. An uncle of Cranston's father's, James Bolt, served in the British House of Commons from the Shetland Islands. [5]

George Dixon was the first of the family in California to run for political office but he was unlucky in politics as well as business. A proponent of "free silver" (a monetary standard using gold and silver coins to provide currency to farmers and those without access to gold), and a strong supporter of populist Democrat William Jennings Bryan for president in 1896, Dixon suffered a bitter personal defeat in a run for the state senate and was discouraged by Bryan's loss to conservative Republican William McKinley. Dixon's disappointments plunged him into periodic depressions and over six months prior to his suicide, he lost forty pounds in weight and complained of feeling unwell. A coroner's jury blamed his death on mental depression. His wife invented a story for Carol (who was at Stanford at the time) that her father had cut himself fatally while trying to remove a growth from his throat, which Carol pretended to believe. Another daughter, Grace, in time came to believe the falsehood, according to family lore. [6]

Carol Dixon had been close to her father and his loss shattered her. She did not return to Stanford, possibly because her family could not afford it – her father's only legacies were insurance policies worth $8,000 and a large Victorian house in Sacramento, one block from what later became the governor's "wedding-cake" mansion, then the home of muckraking journalist Lincoln Steffens. Carol had played there as a childhood friend of Steffens' sister and slid down its long, polished banister. [7]

Will Cranston continued at university, thanks to his father's indulging him with tuition (he had thought that he would have to pay for it himself). He graduated in 1901 with the fledgling university's eighth class, called the "naughty" one, with good grades and a B.A. degree. He had majored in law, intending to be a lawyer. That Fourth of July, he proposed to Carol Dixon. They would not marry until 1903, however, during which time the young Cranston decided to earn money by joining his brother, Robert Dickie Cranston, Junior, in their father's real estate and insurance firm, R.D. Cranston and Sons. Their office was in the Sharon Building on San Francisco's Montgomery Street. After the marriage, the young Cranstons set up housekeeping in a flat at 1500 Masonic Street near Buena Vista Park where they had views across the city. [8]

The Cranstons also were related by marriage to the family for whom Healdsburg, California, was named, through the marriage (circa 1903) of Alan's aunt Florence Cranston, a daughter of Robert Dickie Cranston, to Harmon Heald, grandson of Harmon George Heald (born 1824). [9]

Cranston's grandfather Robert Dickie Cranston, not wanting to be a farmer, had left Ontario, Canada, with money borrowed from his grandfather. He traveled to California in 1870 on the just-completed transcontinental railroad and met his future wife, Jeannie MacGregor, en route. Her family hoped to get rich by mining. Cranston got off at Virginia City, Nevada, where he worked for a time as a carpenter, helping build the Sutro Tunnel to drain water out of the gold-filled mountains. Alan Cranston counted as precious artifacts his grandfather's pearl-handled dagger and derringer pistol. Robert Dickie Cranston went on to San Francisco in 1872 when he married, although he was not listed in city directories until 1874, working as a carpenter with D.A. Macdonald & Company and living at 244 Minna Street. Two boys were born to the couple, Robert A. and William MacGregor. For the next fifteen years the elder Cranston worked with a variety of construction companies. By 1889 he was listed in the city directory as an architect and builder. He was one of the first to build large Victorian houses in San Francisco's Haight-Ashbury neighborhood, which would become a favorite destination of 1960s "flower children." San Francisco's Foundation for Architectural Heritage considered R. D. Cranston "a significant late-nineteenth-century San Francisco architect."[10]

He had a variety of partners in the construction and real-estate business, known as Cranston & Keenan in the 1890s. By the early 1900s Robert Cranston, who was trained as a physician, had joined his father, and in 1904 William joined the firm. He would start his own real-estate business, Cranston Company, the following year with George E. Belvel and Frank A. Dwyer. Robert died the same year as his father, on June 12, 1916, at age sixty-six.

Alan Cranston, only two years old when his grandfather died, was often told about him by his father and older sister Ruth Eleanor, who remembered how her grandfather loved working with tools. He built her a much-loved doll house and tree house. Some forty of Robert Dickie Cranston's houses still stood in the twenty-first century, many of them restored and valuable properties. The Queen Anne-style houses featured turrets and elaborate gingerbread embellishments, those from the early 1890s recognizable by distinctive curved cornice brackets, others for fanciful plasterwork like owls that decorated the facade. The family occupied one (at 1777 Page Street) in 1899, and it was there that Aunt Florence Cranston married Harmon Heald. Robert Dickie Cranston was photographed sitting on the steps of the house. [11]

Eleanor remembered her grandfather as a "very loveable, kind, warm-hearted gentleman. My father loved him very much. His mother was rather cantankerous and was old and ill when I knew her. She outlived him." Eleanor also remembered her grandfather's being "a big man with a gold watch chain across his vest," and giving her a ride in a wheelbarrow when she was small. He had a habit of putting his business card in newel posts of finished houses, causing restorers years later to inquire if the senator were related to the builder. Eleanor Cranston chuckled when one day in 1972 she saw one of her grandfather's houses in a dilapidated condition with a "sardonic sign" on it that read "Ronald Reagan Towers" – a commentary on the then-president's budget cuts of government housing programs. [12]

Alan Cranston obviously took an interest in his family heritage, and collected information about it, including a poem with phrases like, "The Cranston clan/ Man to a man/ Rose beyond any taunt;/ From Krag above/ Cried words of love,/ 'Ere I want, thou shalt want.../ Many a fog/ Has dampened the bog;/ The Cranston clan stands by.../A Cranston kilt/ Protects the gilt/ On California's brow,/ and Cranston's creed/ Insures her need.../ So mind your ore/ As in days of yore,/ Statesmen of old California/ From krag above/ This cry of love/ 'Ere I shall want, thou shall.'" Cranston learned that one ancestor, R. G. Cranston had been general inspector of transportation for the Atchison, Topeka & Santa Fe Railway Company. The father of another, W. H. (Bill) Cranston, wrote an autobiography, "Ink on My Fingers." In 1965 Cranston ordered a family crest on tiles from a Carmel gift shop. [13]

He delighted in a story told of a Canadian relative, Herbert Cranston, who made "a mild fortune in [19]'28," and went to Scotland in search of a family tree and "whatever ancestral glory he could track down," Cranston wrote in the 1930s in his small, hard-to-read penmanship. Herbert returned to America a few months later, downcast and reticent to talk about what he had found. "We wondered what Draculas and Frankensteins had spawned us. Father invited him to dinner one night to inquire about his treasure hunt. It took considerable probing and prodding and awesome perseverance, but our relative finally came out with it. Not a trace of the Cranstons had he found in the village where we supposedly hailed from – until he visited the sexton in the old graveyard. The sexton had scratched his head: 'Cranston? Cranston? Ah, yes! The last Cranston was hanged *lang syne*!' While father choked in his coffee, our relative summoned a note of pride to his voice, and announced that he had discovered the family motto in the town library.

'It's' [*something unintelligible*], he said proudly.

'What does it mean?' asked father, a gleam in his eyes.

'Just what is says,' said my relative, repeating the phrase, suddenly uncomfortable again.

'But what does that mean in English?' persisted my excited father.

'Well, it's really much better in Latin, and I'm just going to use it that way. In English it means, 'I shall be served before thou art.'" [14]

The 1906 earthquake and fire in San Francisco destroyed William Cranston's office at 20 Montgomery Street and the couple moved to Palo Alto where Cranston in 1908 opened the University Realty Company. In 1910 he took fellow Stanford graduate Norwood B. Smith as a partner. Their clients included wealthy capitalists and business men.

In 1907 the Cranstons were blessed with a son whom they named William in honor of his paternal grandfather. Tragically, the infant died of a rare gland infection. A daughter, Ruth Eleanor, was born two years later, on November 22, 1909. It would be another five years before a second son was born – June 19, 1914. He, however, was not named for an ancestor. His father was lying awake shortly before the birth and heard a newspaper boy calling out, "Alan, Alan." "Father just decided it was good name," Cranston said of the curious choice, and that was the one given the boy, along with the family name MacGregor. Young Alan could not pronounce Eleanor – "R. E." was the closest he could come to it. William Cranston sometimes affectionately called his son "Alan MacGregor Cranston brother boy." When he entered first grade at age six and the teacher asked everyone to give their name, young Cranston dutifully repeated, "Alan MacGregor Cranston brother boy." He also remembered "the first time I stood up," at about one year old. Eleanor would say that he "inherited Father's joyous, optimistic nature, Mother's cool judgment, the sense of humor common to both of them, and – from neither of them – a set of iron nerves." [15]

In the year of Alan's birth his father bought a twenty-acre property from an early farming family (Cox) on Fremont Road in Los Altos Hills. It had a brown-shingled farmhouse, stone fireplace and red barn for which the property was known. William Cranston planted an orchard with apples, apricots and prunes on the hill side, often photographed in spring for its colorful blossoms. Other improvements included stone steps, a water tank, small redwood teahouse moved from Palo Alto, and a playhouse. Initially the "Red Barn" was a summer retreat. Adobe Creek often flooded the road below the property, marooning them, and occasionally the basement flooded, leaving drowned mice floating in the water, which upset their mother but fascinated the children. Transportation was by horse and buggy. A black German shepherd, Zelma, was the children's constant companion, fostering a love of animals that would continue throughout their lives. A local painter depicted young Cranston and Eleanor (in a white middy dress) running up a hill above the blossoming orchards and mustard-filled field with Zelma at their side. It was a rural area with unpaved roads. Groceries were bought from a Chinese vegetable vendor who made rounds with a wagon once a week. [16]

In 1922, however, the Cranstons sold the property to Dr. C. C. Crane who moved the old farmhouse and built a chateau-style structure on the hill. The red barn, water tank and tea house remained on the site until the 1980s. The Cranstons moved to a large home on thirteen acres off Edith Avenue in Los Altos, which they would own until 1955. Once a Mexican land grant, it still had an old ranch house by Adobe Creek which bounded the property and a shed that may have dated to Spanish *Californio* days. A property marker found by the creek, and the name of a well-known Indian, Red Belt, carved into an oak tree, were favorite finds of the children. By then the family had a Marmon car (the pride of their father, Eleanor remembered) and Japanese servants who lived on the estate – a gardener, Tanaka, and a couple who worked in the house. They were like "members of the family" and the Cranstons shared Tanaka's trauma when, driving the Marmon one day across inter-urban streetcar tracks along the edge of the property, he was hit by an electric train. The Marmon was destroyed and Tanaka suffered a broken collar bone. Eleanor was touched when she found him crying in the hospital because he felt so badly about the Marmon. [17]

William Cranston named the estate "Villa Warec," an acronym for the names of family members William, Alan, R. E., Carol. It was a large property with a sprawling lawn and tennis court, fields and orchards. [18]

William Cranston later recounted how the property once had been the site of a fort for fighting Indians and home to grizzly bears who prowled local canyons. An "old timer" had told Cranston stories about growing up in the area before it was settled. An Indian road had run through it, the stream was full of trout and the hillsides with rattlesnakes. Indian burial mounds were along the creek – when excavated, they revealed skeletons, arrow heads, stone jars and bangles of abalone shell. The Cranston estate had been a ranch where rye was raised and cattle driven on a trail from Salinas to San Francisco. Among other ranches in the region was one owned by the Winchester rifle heiress, later the town site of Los Altos. In 1924 William Cranston was selling lots in Los Altos for $50 each. He would build a successful real-estate and insurance business and acquire extensive property in Los Altos and Palo Alto, which he oversaw actively to the end of his life. [19]

William Cranston had a strong Scotch-Irish sense of correctness, duty and honesty. In a short story that he wrote to illustrate a moral about taking money in a real-estate deal from a seller unaware that someone had made a bid on his property, William Cranston wrote, "Neither common nor statute law could question the transaction, and business instinct vehemently cried, 'Make the money.' Conscience whispered, ever so quietly, 'Is it a square deal?'" The brokers in the tale were contemplating buying the property themselves and quickly re-selling for profit. "I could see the piles of shining twenties [gold coins] still; it was just the amount within our grasp," the fictional young realtor says. They then called the office manager, whose "integrity had helped us over many shoals," to ask his opinion of such an underhanded transaction. From his silence, the young men realized they could not do such a thing. Perhaps autobiographical, the account was entitled, "A Glance into Crooked Street." Alan Cranston kept it in his family files. [20]

Their mother, according to Eleanor, was "always frail and very dependent" during Alan's youth. A series of nannies were tried until they found Frances Ketman. The "family just took her on from then on and she took care of Alan and me," even traveling with them overseas.

Young Alan lived a happy, comfortable, care-free life of childhood delights, fantasies and playmates. He was a nice-looking boy with freckles and brown hair. His sister called him "a rollicking, merry child, very independent, always doing his own thing. He had a *wonderful* childhood," she said. "After we moved down to Villa Warec, we were close to town, so he had a gang of friends who were *always* over, and they had track meets on the lawn and out in the field." An old shed was dubbed the "Desperate Deeds Club." A pool by a waterfall was a magical fishing hole. They could run freely through the orchard and woods. Cranston loved riding two horses that they kept. "You could go almost anywhere. There were lots of fields where you could gallop around – that was a great lot of fun." He even broke a colt before an audience of friends who "came to see me get thrown off that horse! They were sitting on top of the haystack in our field off Edith Avenue. I had never broken in a horse and wasn't sure what was going to happen, but I was quite an experienced rider. Eventually, with great trepidation, I climbed up on the horse and it didn't buck at all because I was its friend – much to the disappointment of" his audience, he recalled. [21]

But young Cranston also could be distant and not easy to get to know despite an apparent outgoingness – a combination of quietness and vivaciousness mixed with humor that was evident early. "He was sensitive, but also friendly, curious and interested in everything," but without braggadocio or arrogance, his sister felt, and he maintained an informality and lack of pomposity throughout his life. "He's very self-contained and self-disciplined," Eleanor would say many years later of his personality. It would be characteristic of him as an adult to have a demeanor of friendliness but also a very private side.

On rainy days when they played indoors Cranston and his pals hit golf balls down the long upstairs hall, caroming them off doors so that they bounced down the stairs and rolled onto a score pad on the living room rug. Cranston also had a mischievous side that manifested itself at an early age. He delighted in a steam engines that pulled local trains, "one of those big old ones that made a lot of racket and looked very powerful." He and his good friend Harry "Junior" Dutton were fond of putting pins and coins on the railway tracks bordering the estate's old prune orchard, then hiding in the brush and waiting for trains to run over them. They also put fireworks (torpedoes) on the tracks, and once moved signal flares from the track of a Southern Pacific commuter train to the that of inter-urban streetcars. When they hit the flares, the explosion frightened passengers and drivers alike. Eleanor became concerned after the boys bragged about it, swearing her to secrecy, and one day she called Alan from the train station, pretending to be the male secretary to the president of Southern Pacific. She could hear her brother's shock when he heard a husky voice ask, "Have you been putting torpedoes on the railroad tracks?" "Yes," Alan murmured. It was not long before officials of the lines honed in on the pranksters. When warned that people might be killed, Alan humbly said that he would not do it again. He would later describe his pals and their adventures humorously as "like Peck's Bad Boy and Tom Sawyer and Huckleberry Finn, so I'll never know why our mothers and fathers were astonished and dismayed" by their pranks. "We assumed it was our duty, our moral obligation and responsibility to misbehave, *creatively* – to put rocks on the railroad tracks, masquerade on Halloween, transform, *patriotically*, the weeks before and after the Fourth of July into our own version of the American Revolution, marked by rockets' red glare and bombs bursting in air!" [22]

His parents were always supportive of him – "he was the apple of their eye," especially after having lost their first son, Eleanor said. "And I suppose I was a little jealous when Alan was born because he so quickly became the center of all attention. But I was so fond of him myself that, before any amount of time went by, I was protective of him." She was told from his birth to be responsible for her younger brother whom she found "always very engaging – he had a very *sunny* nature." But as he grew older, he teased her terribly, "unmercifully about boys. I remember when I had a tennis date, and he and 'Junior' Dutton, who was his great side-kick, put the family cow on the tennis court before we came out to play. So we had to chase the cow off the court – we had a terrible time, while 'Junior' and Alan were in the bushes, laughing themselves into hysterics!" [23]

When Alan was ten, Eleanor wrote a composition about him. "He makes himself an unendurable nuisance. He has an insatiable curiosity. But when he believes anyone to be meddling in his own affairs, he has a talent amounting to genius for misunderstanding or ignoring objectionable questions." [24]

She could not help admiring his reading habits, though. He read vociferously and had "a systematic approach to books," made lists and checked off the titles that he read. Childhood favorites were Beatrix Potter's *Peter Rabbit* and other children's books including the entire set of Frank W. Burgess' *Bedtime Books* and Robert Louis Stevenson's *Treasure Island*, which he read more than once without stopping. He also liked Charles Dickens – he later collected first editions of his works – and read a good deal of non-fiction, especially travel and adventure accounts by such writers as Richard Halliburton. He wrote down quotes and poems that caught his attention, some he memorized and could recite from memory years later. He loved and read all of Mark Twain. As he grew older he was attracted to Shakespeare and George Bernard Shaw, all of whose plays he read, including the prefaces. "One book that I loved was a biography of Leonardo Da Vinci," he recalled. He also began to read about world events, "a lot of history, and biographies of political leaders like Carl Sandburg's *Life of Lincoln*. [25]

His strong father expected obedience under which Cranston sometimes chafed. William Cranston occasionally brought home treasures found in houses that he bought and sold. One such find was an American flag and pole that he erected on the hill top at "Red Barn." Alan was given his first household chore – raising and lowering the flag, with strong admonitions from his father not to let it touch the ground or leave it hanging after sunset. That was a challenge for the little boy until he figured out how to transport the flag in a wheelbarrow. A source of great amusement to the family was watching him racing sunsets to bring the flag down in time and store the wheelbarrow, following his father's orders. Theirs would grow into a somewhat adversarial father-son relationship. One of Cranston's first memories, according to his sister, was of not kissing his father goodnight as a young child, "an early clash between two very strong-willed people," as she characterized it. "Father was very dominating." On one occasion Alan was chastised and made to apologize for tossing a boy's cap up into trees as the two were walking home, "which infuriated my father," Cranston would recollect along with the boy's "funny nickname, 'Marvelous Marvin.'" As he matured, however, he had an open and apparently friendly relationship with his parents. "They were terribly crazy about him," and did not try to suppress him but were supportive parents, Eleanor perceived. [26]

"My father would argue with me some," Cranston recalled of the relationship, "tell me why he felt otherwise about politics and stuff. One very good thing they did on my part – at a pretty early age, they adopted the practice of *advising* me what they thought I ought to do about some situation, or why I should mend my ways, or how I should do it. But they didn't give orders – they gave advice, and left the decision up to me. That was very good training in decision-making, getting me to learn to make decisions at a pretty early age. No doubt," he admitted, "they were often appalled at my decisions, but they went on the theory that you learn best from experience and that this practice would develop resourcefulness." [27]

Religion was not a strong factor in the Congregationalist family who had ministers on their mother's side. "They tried to instill some religion in us," according to Eleanor, "and had us say prayers at bedtime on the sleeping porch and for a little while, had what they called Sunday-night services before the fireplace, which the nurse and hired man attended. My father read to us from the Bible." At such gatherings, Alan was encouraged to sing World War I songs like "Tenting Tonight" and "Over There." When he once forgot the words, the family stared at him, a humiliation that he later joked probably set back his "public speaking about twenty years." During World War I, soldiers were trained at nearby Camp Fremont, digging trenches in the hills and fields. The family could hear sounds of dynamite blasts from the base, which sounded like bombs or battle sounds. William Cranston was honored for service to the community as chairman of the Palo Alto War Work Council. [28]

Alan had a stamp collection from which he learned about far-away places, and liked to ride his tricycle around the house veranda pretending that he was "visiting" foreign countries. His principal source of pleasure, though, were comics and cartoons that he pasted into scrapbooks made by his mother of brown paper and string. From the age of about five, he began drawing, creating his own story lines and characters. "The funny papers, with their funny people and their funny problems, gave him a small, manageable world," Eleanor believed. He filled a note book with drawings and writings. On the first page of one he wrote, "By CRANSTON, pictures by Cranston, illustrated by the author," on another, "Alan Cranston, auther [*sic*] of Little People, Tom N. Nevers and Jo, etc." On page 105 he wrote, "Another story by Alan M. Cranston - the first one he has written, the rest are drawn - THE BEST ONE YET." Early pictures included a dog pulling a cart, windmills, a Chinese coolie carrying two jugs on a harness over his shoulder, a ship resembling a submarine with men on deck and two American flags flying from masts. Some pencil drawings were of a man with a moustache – his father's good friend, San Francisco newspaper editor Fremont Older, had one. Many drawings were careful copies of *New Yorker* magazine cartoons. An early ambition was to be a comic-book artist although Cranston conceded that his "*first* ambition was to be either an ice man or garbage man. They were friendly and got to ride around all over the place, and I thought both of those careers would be very nice," he laughed. [29]

He spent a lot of time as a child reading, drawing and writing. He designed and illustrated cartoon strips – one he called "Collegian, football season, an AL Production" – and was encouraged to be competitive, particularly by his father. Alan's record of a family "decathlon" listed results for himself, his father and mother and Frances Ketman for "breath holding" while reciting the limerick "Peter Piper picked a peck of pickled peppers" twice, the alphabet backwards and forwards, counting to 100, playing checkers, and reciting "She sells sea shells" five times each. "Most records held by Alan" with a total score of three and a half, he proudly recorded. [30]

He also wrote stories, in pencil on lined notebook pages, often with a number of chapters. They reflected what was going on in his mind, from amusement to anger to imaginative dreams, as well as his fondness for puns and double-edged jokes. He seemed to enjoy parodying people in language, especially mocking German-immigrant or African-American speech. "In Do-Do Land" by "M. Cranston" was about a boy finding a pool in the woods that he had never seen before. One story entitled "No Letter to Write" was about a student who did not follow the teacher's instructions for a class exercise to write a letter to a friend. To avoid doing the homework, the boy took a letter already written by his sister, merely changing the salutation to "Dear Friend" and hoping that he would not be asked to read it before the teacher. When the inevitable happened, he found himself stuttering through the embarrassing contents of the letter, which discussed what dresses two girls planned to wear to a party. The hapless student, named Dan Roy Smith, was ordered to "go to the princibil [*sic*]." It ended: "After school when I got out, a boy yelled 'How's your white dress?' and so on" – perhaps a parable for an actual experience. Several times he wrote, "I will not say 'I' in this story any more. Alan Cranston." Other stories were about suspenseful moments at Stanford-University of California football games, baseball and track meets. He developed a hero whom he called "Dixon," with whom he bore a close identity. "'Speedy' Dixon tak's [*sic*] first place in the...track meet," one was entitled, another, "Speedy Dixon in a new story of FOOTball – story starts tomorrow." [31]

The character Dan Roy Smith, he wrote, was created "By A.M.C., author of Speedy Dixon, Speedy Dixon Star in Do-Do Land, etc." One story began, "Well, I guess I ought to tell you who I am first. My name's Dan Roy Smith (it's not my fault). I've got a brother named Tex Baxter Smith. My brother's in New York now. I also have a big sister named Mary. She's in some college somewhere now. In the east, I think. This story all happened in about 1870. Sometime around then in California near where San Francisco is. There was a lot of woods where we lived then. One day Mother set some cookies on the table by the window and went upstairs. I saw all this from the big oak tree in our yard. As soon as she was gone, I slid down to the ground and went toward the window. But I saw that Ted had been ahead of me. Then I saw him in the barn eating them. I sprang toward him but he picked up a sword and then hit at me."

He spent hours drawing "*S.F. Call* Funnys" [*sic*]. One for December 16, 1924, had an African-American cartoon character talking in *patois* popularized by radio comedians "Amos and Andy." In the first frame, a White man says to a Black man, "Say, mush face, I got a job for you." A black-faced man says, "Job for me?" The

White man replies, "Sure, you be a prize fighter and I'll be your manager." The Black man is seen running out of the scene beneath the word "swish." "Say, kid, did you see a [Black man] run past?" the White man asks. "I didn't know what it was, it went so fast," the kid answers. The Black man reappears in the seventh frame. "Where you been all this time?" his protagonist asks. "Ben?" he replies with an exaggerated question mark. "Ben? Ah ben comin' back."

Some cartoons were colored with crayon. He drew a series called "Hut and Kut – (They'll drive you nuts)." The characters had conversations typical of ten-year-old boys, including contests over who was the tallest, the smartest, the funniest. They drove cars, got into trouble, fought and joked. Other series featured "Spud and Bud" and "Penrod and Danny," of which Cranston wrote on December 28, 1924, "The best of *S. F. Call*, This will start tomorrow!" There also were images of his sister or mother on the telephone, one saying, "Oh, yes, I wore that dress, etc., etc." There were references to being beaten in fights, loaning five bucks and trying to get it back – "This will make me strong and I can beat up Hut now." A drawing was headlined, "Tomorrow will be the great race between Fatty and Dutton," showing a plump and a slender man practicing. "Fatty is VERY FAT," the series continued in January, 1925, "There is no room to draw FAT TODAY, he is too BIG." On January 20, he scrawled across the page, "EDITOR IS SICK." One January 22, he wrote "EDITOR WILL RESUME WORK TOMOROW [*sic*]," and on January 23, "I am back again!" It was evidence of Cranston's early interest in newspapers – and of his impish humor.

A particularly long series was devoted to an African-American man called Prescription (*sic*). The series relied on *double-entendre* jokes at Prescription's expense but showed an understanding of the justice system, racial discrimination and elections. "Have you any defense?" Judge Slanters asks Prescription. "No, Sar, I don't take no fence, just a horse." "I mean, have you a representative?" the judge asks him. "Well, ah voted for Shortridge." [32]

A typed story began, "Prescription was his first name because his mother had such a hard time filling him. Johnston was his last name because his forefathers had also born that name. He was a [Black man] about twenty years old. Curly hair, dark eyes, thick lips, snub nose, that is what Prescription Johnston looked like through life. He had been in love with Lizzie Raviola (and she with him) ever since he had strained his back carring [*sic*] her books to school. One day Prescription had said to Lizzie, 'I'se gwine treat you all to chicken dinna ta night, one of Mistah Lintons, he jes got a whole new flock of chicks. I jes steal a fat one.'" But Prescription is caught in his thwarted effort to raid the chicken coop and put in jail.

"Prescription had an American friend who was a lawyer," the story continues. "He asked the jailer if he could telephone; he said, 'yes,' and showed Prescription where the telephone was and stayed there while he talked. Poor Prescription is flustered when the operator keeps asking him, "Number, please?" He gets "Mistah H. N. Hamberg" on the line and explains, "Dis am Prescription Johnston, ah was on Mistah Lintons place takin' a short cut when all a sudden he jumps out on me and says, 'I'm gwine take yo all to jail an' tell 'em that you was stealing ma chickens' – now, am dat justice? Here ah am in jail. Ah want yo all to come an' law for me. Will ya?' 'What time is your trial, may I ask?' says H. N. Hamberg, adding, "'I'm willing to come and be your lawyer free if some time you do something for me.'" There the story ended.

"What's the matter wif me, doc?" Prescription asks in a cartoon. "Chicken pox," he's told. "No, sah, ah ain't ben where I ketch it, honest." In another, a doctor asks him, "Did the other doctor take your pulse?" "Ah only missed ma' watch, so fah," he replies. "Sammy, why can't a bald [derogatory term for Black man] join a club?" says one Black to another. "I don't know." "Kase he's black-bald," the other man says, "ha, ha, ha." A Black man asks a Black woman with three children, "What's their names, Mandy?" "Dey's named after flowers – Daisy, Lilly an' Artificial." In a drug store, a Black man says, "Gimme a razor, quick." "Safety?" the man at the counter asks. "No sah, ah desires it for social use."

In some of the cartoons, Cranston demonstrated an understanding of segregation, lynching and social consciousness, albeit from the then-prevalent perspective of the times. "Were you born in Alabama?" a White man asks a Black. "Yes, suh." "And raised there?" "Dey tried ta raise me once but da rope broke." Two Black men have the following exchange about employment: "Didja ever hear bout de man in de school book dat was starvin' wif victuals in site [*sic*]?" "Ya, ah recon ah did." "He's in about de same position – he's been made de janitor ob de poultry show." A story about "A Tunge-tied" Black man began, "I went downtown and met a boy that was black all over.'" Another Black boy says, "'Don you hit that boy, he tunge tied, he can't speak right.'"

One story about his fictional Dan Roy Smith entitled "Dan's Father" began, "My father – I mean Dan's Father – came home from the German war. He was so mean to me." It continued ambivalently as to whose father he was describing.

At the end of that notebook, Cranston started a list of 166 words beginning with "aile, ailment," continuing to "eosin, epi," as if going through a dictionary to learn new words. He also attempted rhyming phrases – "1, 2, spit on your shoe, 3, 4, knock on the door...15, 16, see those hicks, 17, 18, I am aching, 19, 20, this is plenty." He had an insatiable desire to learn, which would manifest itself in hundreds of notes that he wrote to himself as he matured, ranging from lists of books that wanted to read to subjects like love and international relations.

He also learned from his parents the importance of writing thank-you letters. In a note to his Uncle Willie Sheets and Aunt Grace in 1922, at age eight, thanking them for "all the gifts you have sent me," he added, "I have nine dollars and twenty-five cents. The puppies bark and growl. Randy sings, Yama and Sena have two birds. I am going to wear glasses. With much love, Alan Cranston." In another, written on "The Red Barn" letterhead, he wrote his uncle, "Thank you for those card-board pictures, and the pin. I lost the pin.... One of the mother hens has sixteen babies, I'm going to eat my rooster for Sunday." On the back, he added, "Please send me another pin," and drew stick figures of a man riding a dog or cat. He told his aunt, "I made a damn [*sic*] in the creek. I rode a raft. I also rode a pony. We have to [two] horses. When is mom coming?" meaning his grandmother. From camp at age ten in 1924, he wrote his sister, "I read a dandy joke, here it is: young boy to another boy, 'Was your father a male man?' Other, diddo, 'No, why?' Young boy, 'Then he must have been a female man, ha, ha.' The Moon Mullens was good you sent me. Love from Alan." [33]

Eleanor, four years older than Alan, regularly sent her brother the funnies or magazines like *Boys Life* when he was at camp or away at school. She was a doting older sister who would be as close to Cranston as any one throughout his life, and he returned the loyal affection. Eleanor was sent away to boarding school for a time, so they communicated by letter during much of their youth, mostly on her part. When they were at separate summer vacation sites one summer, she said, "We were sorry when you decided not to come but we all think you showed rare judgment" in staying home to study to improve his grades. Eleanor had learned to drive by then and was anxious to get home from Tahoe, where the family regularly summered, because "I want to get on a road where I can *speed*" above twenty miles per hour without the whole family's keeping their eyes on the speedometer. "Do write to me," she ended. "You have only written once all summer." [34]

In another letter from Tahoe, she said, "I can't keep from writing to you any longer. I want you to send me something, that is if you aren't using it. The tennis courts aren't finished yet, are they? Please send me my racquet. I will return it instantly upon request.... Have I told you that Tom Mix and Buster Keaton are at the [Tahoe] Tavern? They are both great movie actors. I have been introduced to Tom Mix's manager.... Just for fun, I entered the tennis tournament over at the Tavern.... I will send you the money for the stamps it took as soon as I get it. Please write to me, Alan. I will write to you immediately when you do. This in haste from thy loving sister, R. E. C." His father added a postscript: "Dear Alan, Enclosed are 26 cents, the balance of your allowance, Father." [35]

The family were affluent and lived comfortably. Cranston went to a private school (Castelleja, where Eleanor also went) for kindergarten. "We used to tease him about it, because it was a girls' school with a coeducational kindergarten," Eleanor said. At Los Altos Grammar School, Cranston was picked up in a chauffeured Lincoln. When the boy showed an interest in running, his father had a quarter-mile track built near the family stables.

Cranston vividly remembered Los Altos (originally to be called "Banks and Braes") with its unpaved roads, hitching posts every twenty-five feet to which they tied their horses, "Mr. Fonner sedately riding to town in his horse and buggy, Colonel Austin in puttees and khaki britches, jacket and wide-brimmed World War I hat, two little old ladies from Palo Alto who drove carefully through town occasionally in their high-wheeled electric car," Pierce Arrows, Model T's, Marmons and a yellow Chalmers car. The Southern Pacific train station, morning and evening trains, "always on time; red street cars; nice, simple telephone numbers like 90 and 70J" were strong memories, along with "Jimmy Griffin going up in his self-made glider." Youthful pleasures were "riding our bikes everywhere, hiking in the mountains, playing touch football and baseball," the "endless school years, and long, long summers, catching trout in the old Indian fishing holes along Adobe Creek, exploring deep in the Frenchman's caves, bringing rattlesnakes down from the hills and turning them loose" in Gregory and Shoup's creamery "where you could get ice cream cones."

The movie theater was a frequent destination. His favorites were comedies, *Our Gang* and *Felix the Cat* short films followed by Charlie Chaplin, Harry Langdon and Marx Brothers features. "I fell madly in love with them and thought they were incredibly funny." He saw their films many times and "eventually got to know three of them. Harpo – who was totally wild – was quite a friend, and Groucho and Zeppo." Cranston also was a Boy Scout whose first building, in 1922, was made possible thanks to William Cranston's, "spiritedly, and in a style worthy of an expert auctioneer," persuading townsmen to contribute money for it. "After the scout meeting ended around nine o'clock on Friday nights, we would go up to the railway station and play games like 'prisoner's base.' I never got beyond being a tenderfoot," Cranston related (he would be a feature attraction at Troop 37's fiftieth anniversary in 1968). His first day at grammar school also was memorable. "Somehow there shot through the room full of kids that they were going to cut our tonsils out! Everybody was terrified. We didn't know exactly what that meant." He also remembered the principle, Miss Marguerite Shannon of the "red, red hair," but admitted not being a particularly good student – "I didn't apply myself, but I had a lot of fun, and many, many friends there." On one occasion "the whole class rushed to the school-room window to stare at a plane flying by." When he got to high school, he rode the inter-urban street car until he got a Chevrolet convertible with a rumble seat that "cost somewhere around $800 brand new. I kept it all the way through college." But he was not a typical boy, Harry Dutton recalled. "He didn't have a slingshot. He didn't have a BB gun. He didn't collect toads. Alan was different. A very thoughtful person – much more serious than any of the rest of us… an avid reader, very reserved" and "always for the underdog." [36]

William Cranston belonged to the exclusive Bohemian Club of San Francisco, and the Cranstons traveled a good deal in the 1920s and 1930s. They ultimately would make about a dozen trips abroad, including several around the world. In 1921, when Alan was seven, his parents went to Australia. "What a thoughtful little boy you were to write a letter for me to find in my suit case," his mother wrote him from the ship en route. "I have read it a great many times already. Yes, I hope Zelma [the dog] will smile at me when I return home, and I hope even more that you will like your teacher. I am pretty sure you will. I hope you were well enough to go to school soon after we left." She had befriended a "nice little boy on the ship, just a few months older than you," named Thor, who drew a picture greeting for Alan. She related stories about birds that she knew he would like to hear. "A few nights ago a young bird flew onto the deck, with one of its legs hurt. One of the passengers caught it.... It had a sea gull's beak and a duck's body. Four or five birds went with the ship from San Francisco; they take little trips out into the ocean and then come back to the ship to rest. Do you suppose they keep going back and forth across the ocean?" She wondered if Miss Ketman had taken him to Sunday school yet. "I think you might enjoy it," she said hopefully. Cranston would not take seriously to organized religion, however. [37]

"Probably some one will have to read this to you," she added, "but before we get home perhaps you will have learned how to read my writing. I hope you and Ruth Eleanor received the little letter which we sent back by the pilot ship soon after we were through the Golden Gate. *Much* love and many kisses from Mother."

His father reported that a young boy had been "brought on board in handcuffs by four policemen and is probably going to prison in Australia." A subsequent letter to "Dear Alan Boy" must have made quite an impression on the child in Los Altos. "The boy in chains was a stowaway and we had eight others; one of them was only a little boy in short pants and he hid in a life boat for three days until we were a thousand miles out in the ocean." [38]

From Hong Kong December 8, 1921, his father wrote, "Chinamen who carry people are chattering just below the porch on which I am sitting. Mother and I ride in their chairs and look like this" – a drawing of two Chinese coolies carrying a sedan chair. Again, animals were the subject. "There are practically no horses here. I have not seen *any* but everyone rides in automobiles, rickshaws [with another drawing] and chairs. The city is right against very high hills which go straight up to the sky. The bay is full of boats which are very queer and whole families live on them. We have had fun scrambling pennies for the children, and grown-ups also jump into the crowd and try to get the money. We liked your letter very much," he said, adding in two postscripts, "Enclosed are stamps. Please put them in Ruth Eleanor's book until you have a big book of your own," and "We are glad your chickens are doing well & that you take good care of them." [39]

Two years later, in 1923, their parents went to Europe. From Paris his father wrote Alan on a postcard picturing the Eiffel Tower, "We are at the top of this tower 900 feet above the ground. We see where the Germans arrived in 1914 when they almost reached Paris." His mother told her nine-year-old son, "I dreamed Shag [a dog] wanted to bite me when I got home. Don't you let him!" [40]

Cranston had his first taste of international travel when he was eleven. He and Eleanor were taken to Europe by their parents in 1925, sailing May 15 from San Francisco to New York aboard the round-the-world Cunard Line ship *R.M.S. Franconia*. Frances Ketman also was among the 309 passengers, as were many prominent San Francisco families. They sailed through the Panama Canal en route to Cuba and toured Panama City in motor cars. Alan Cranston would play a key role in the zone's destiny many years later. They disembarked at Havana for sightseeing, culminating in luncheon on the roof garden of the Sevilla-Biltmore Hotel. Cranston saved the menu for Sunday, June 14 – turtle soup, fish, sweetbreads and beef entrees, plum pudding and sweet pastries. He may have saved it in part for its illustrations of dashing pirates and a beautiful woman dressed in a ballooning eighteenth-century gown. [41]

The family would return to Europe three years later, in 1928 when Cranston graduated from grammar school, to see, among other things, the Olympic games in Amsterdam. One of his chums joked, "I vas hoping dat yourn ship would sink, Har! Har! To amagine [*sic*] you hollerin' around to keep the sharks away; sharks wouldn't touch your meat anyway so you need not wast [*sic*] your breath. Hope a discus hits you at [Wurm?]. Me." [42]

"It was prutty lucky you dand't get sea sick," his friend Ralph Raymond wrote, addressing Cranston as "Veesal." "I wish you were going to Mountain View High with us guy[s]," he went on. "I caught the limit in trout twice in one day and once on another day, and I caught one so big, or I mean I had him on my line but he was so beeg that he busts my line.... I've earned money enough to pay for the sword that you said you would get me if you could.... P.S. Don't forget my sword." [43]

In August, Raymond wrote, "I keep looking at the sports section all the time for news of der Olympic games.... Don't flert [*sic*] too much with the good-lookers over there. Leave a couple so ven I get rich, I go over in an airplane.... I earned forty dollars so far but remember, only five for a sword at the most because I got to save some cash for der football game coming up.... Elizabeth your girl friend I saw the other day, she bin off on a vacat.... I will try to save the funnies for you. Do they have funny funnies over thar? Or do they have such a thing as funnies? Static is coming over the radio now. Do they have many radios over there? Yours truly, old top (by Jove, I say, says der Englishman), Ralph Raymond." [44]

Cranston sent Harry Dutton a post card about "Napoleon's battle," prompting Dutton to write, "There is a slight alter[ation] to be made. 1st, I am de fellah that is leading those men to conquer Napoleon, with the flag, 2nd, youse are the fellah what's hanging onto Napoleon's horse's leg dat is kicking off. Did you bring me a souvenir? Dis is my 6th letter to you. How much does it cost you to send a letter in U. S. coin to me from France? This postal card had 90 centimes on it. I will carry out your order of beating up Ralph. He wants you to bring heem a sword. Bring him a $50.00 sword with all the 'temper' out of the steel and send it C.O.D. or collect. P. S. When you get home, let's start a paper like dis," adding that "Ralph accidentally boined up all de *Chron.* & *Exam.* Sun & daily funny papers dat was for youse." [45]

The Cranstons returned aboard the Canadian Pacific Steamship *Empress of Australia*, landing at Quebec September 7. Raymond splurged and sent a welcome-home letter via airmail. "Give the stamp to your pop with my regards. I guess you won't be here in time for the Stanford & Olympic Club game. You had better not come back to Los Altos without a sword for me. You saveve [savvy]?" [46]

At grammar school Cranston was an assistant traffic signaler but did not make the honor roll. An eighth-grade class photograph showed a grinning young Cranston with reddish-brown hair and a face full of freckles. The class included students of Italian descent and a number of Japanese-Americans, several of whom were good friends and athletic teammates. He would later remember as "very dear friends of mine" Frank Furuichi whose family ran a nursery, Isao Higashiuchi for his "straight As" and Henry Hamasaki for his "great athletic ability and sunny spirit."

Cranston at a young age got a reputation as a jokester for his verbal puns and physical pranks. The Los Altos Grammar School student publication "Chatterbox," when Cranston graduated in 1928, prophesied "that Alan Cranston will be a banker and will drive a Rolls Royce or some such." In a column of graduates' legacies, Cranston joked that he bequeathed his "bashfulness, which adds so greatly to my personality, to Tommy Moore." He contributed a limerick – "There was a young man from Maine/ Who hurdled a window pane;/ He lit on a lion in a fright,/ The man ran with [all] his might,/ and the lion with all his mane." "Can you imagine Alan C. not doing babyish tricks?" a column wondered. His "horoscope" said that others considered him "lackadaisical," his hobby was "tripping the girls," his favorite saying, "Yeh, I'll say," and his ambition, to be a dentist. His best pals, Raymond, a tall boy who played clarinet, was predicted to be a "professional humorist (terrible! Boo!)," and Dutton, a "movie magnate – spare the audience." [47]

Cranston's first effort to be elected by his peers, though, was not a success. In the eighth grade, he lost a contest to be bench monitor during recess. He was fixated by football and as a high school sophomore, went out for the team. He was small and slight, however, not a good candidate for the sport. His father had been on the Stanford track team and in the 1920s started taking Cranston to track meets as well as football games in the newly-built Stanford stadium (once when it was under construction). In his junior year, Cranston became serious about track and started competing. As he began to win, his self-confidence was bolstered, and he attributed his experience in track competitions to building his character. [48]

"As a boy in Los Altos, I watched track stars work out at nearby Stanford University," he wrote of his early interest in track. "My heroes were the great quarter-milers of the day, trackmen like Ted Miller and Bud Spencer. I dreamed that I would someday be like them. I wanted to run with the great Stanford relay teams – and in time, I did. I practiced sprinting during recess in grammar school. At first I had no endurance and feared that I would never realize my ambition. But I pushed hard at self-set limits. My endurance slowly improved. By high school I was competing in the 100-yard dash and the 440, and in my senior year I was Santa Clara Valley champion in both events. At that time, Stanford's Ben Eastman was the world's greatest quarter-miler and my idol." [49]

He was the undisputed leader of a group of boys who formed a "club" and looked to Cranston for guidance. He was a less than frequent correspondent, though, protective of spending his small allowance on postage. Letters from his pals, "Junior" Dutton and Ralph Raymond, in joking slang discussed comic strips that amused them. "What Ho! the guard, bring up number 13 of the Bawl-Out List, which is Alan Cranston," Dutton wrote August 22, 1923, when Cranston, then nine, was at Tahoe.

"Now Alan vot have youse got to say for yourszelv?... I calls you a big Chew for not wasting a postage stamp on me. You must sqeese a nickel so hard that the Indian hoots and de buffalo snorts and comes out to beat youse up!" [50]

In 1926 for the seventh grade Cranston was sent to private Tamalpais School in Marin County north of San Francisco to improve his grades and behavior, much to his personal unhappiness at being separated from his chums who went to the public school in Los Altos. "He hated it," Eleanor said. When not permitted to come home at Thanksgiving while his sister was, he was told that she had gotten good grades and he would have to stay there until he did. Dutton bemoaned the loss of his friend in a letter on September 18, 1926, Cranston's first month at the school:

"Well, Al, I wish that you would hurry up and come back, things are certainly getting dry without you.... I will force the Club to *stick together* for I do not want to have any more break-ups of the Club yet. If you are coming back over the weekend, I will make you honary [*sic*] president...you will probably be president anyway while you are there....

"P.S. If you have any suggestions about getting anything for the Club, you say so." [51]

"Dear Al, Why don't you write? Are you sick or what?" Dutton again complained in a letter addressed to "Master Alan Cranston." "And oh boy! I got some news. Your father took me to two games at Stanford yesterday. Stanford II team cleaned up on Fresno State 44 to 7 (whoopee); and in the second game Stanford beat Caltech

13 to 6. Gee whiz it was scary." He enclosed the football schedule and promised to send scores for each game. "I didn't dast hold a club meeting till I got an answer from you," he added. [52]

"I hope you haven't got home sick," Ralph Raymond wrote the same month. "We haven't had a club meeting since you left. I hope you are making good success in football. Our football team broke up. They're starting in speed ball now. The scouts have started and your dad's one of the trustees of the scouts. I haven't been riding yet because I thought you might have been joking [about being allowed to ride one of the Cranston's horses?].... There's not much doing around Los Altos. I guess it's pretty lively up there." [53]

Cranston hurt his foot playing football the next month. "Keep off your foot as much as you can and it will get well sooner," Raymond exhorted him October 6, 1926. "We haven't had a club meeting yet," he added, "I guess it is broken up until you come back." [54]

Cranston finally wrote Dutton who asked him to "send me some little souvenir, for I send you some of that 'Oh boy' and spearmint gum and every time I write to you, I send you a program of the Stanford game!... P.S. Why in the heck didn't you sign your name, I wasn't quite sure it was from you, but I could tell by your *handwriting*." [55]

"I'm awfully proud of your being on the FIRST lower-school football team," his sister wrote Cranston September 24, but she worried about his diet – something that Cranston himself one day would be obsessive about..

"That's certainly a good Beginning. Oh, you'll be on the team at Stanford yet. But I'll tell you ONE THING, Al, that is very IMPORTANT. You must eat all you can get a hold of CAULIFLOWER, EGGPLANT, OYSTERPLANT, TURNIPS, CABBAGES, SQUASH, TOMATOES, SAUERCRAUT, THE STRINGS of string beans, and the PODS of PEAS, CHARD, SPINACH, CELERY, ARTICHOKES, ASPARIGRASS [*sic*], ONIONS, POTATO SKINS, & so on. I'm only afraid you won't do it. If you are interested, I'll make out a list, these are only samples, of course. And if you are really interested, I might smuggle in to you some of the above mentioned vegetables. Let me know. However, I really am certain that the real reason you made the team is that you have only had $.05 worth of candy all the time you've been there.

"You ARE having a good time, tho,' aren't you, with all the boys, and movies, and football, and those FASCINATING little arithmetic problems, and recess, and three good meals a day, and especially-provided ACCIDENTS just for your entertainment?" [56]

He had recounted seeing an accident and a subsequent fist fight. Eleanor had more advice for her younger brother.

"By the way, you're in the seventh, aren't you? Well, when I was, we had history of the U. S., and if you have it, LEARN it ALL, if it's the only thing you do, because it will save you much more trouble than you can ever imagine, except, perhaps when you are as old as I.... Also you will forever be running across allusions to it.

"Dear old side-kick – it is because there is so little to tell you really that I am doing nothing but lecture. You need not take it all seriously." [57]

"Alandear – It's a great life if you don't weaken, isn't it?" she wrote from boarding school with news of being stopped by a vengeful motorcycle cop, "the one, you know, I told you I started to take the pistol off that day, and Mrs. Lausten's son said he would fix it up for me if he ever gave me a ticket.... I really think I shall be too nervous to drive for quite some time and if I hear a police SIREN very soon, I shall have hysterics." She confided to him about her social life, which was full of dates with Stanford students. She turned down an invitation to spend a weekend with a girl friend because Alan was coming home – "I didn't even consider it, I am so anxious to see you, Alandear! I just read your comp[osition] on the British Isles and think it is MARVELLOUS. What SPLENDID work you are going. And your handwriting is as good as lots of the boys I know. Mother said I could not write ANYMORE so goodbye and be good, Much love, R.E." [58]

Cranston was careful with money from an early age, perhaps instilled in him by his father. He wrote down expenses when away at school – "Burt, 15, Sid, 10 [loans?], dentist $10, typewriter $8, watch $3" – much as George Washington kept detailed accounts from his youth. [59]

Cranston, though, was not happy at the boarding school, away from his family and friends, and begged to be allowed to come home. His family visited him on a few Sundays, but he admitted that he was homesick. "I read somewhere that when boys go to boarding school, they want to see their families all the time at first," Eleanor wrote him in October. "but after just about a month, they begin to realize that the boys are really just as nice as those at home after all, and that there are really a great many advantages in going away to school, and they get entirely over the desire to be with their families. I suppose this will happen to you if it happens to everyone, but DON'T let it keep you from writing to me, will you, for I enjoy your letters *very* much." "You surely have plenty enough excitement," she added. "Imagine! Fires, cops, broken knees, and electrocution (you know what I mean!)" In a postscript she said, "Father was delighted to get a letter at his office." [60]

When he was sent back for another semester in January, 1927, his father personally wrote him a strong letter of admonition mixed with encouragement to take his situation like a man and improve himself. Cranston kept the letter with his personal papers in envelopes that he marked "Souvenirs."

"You first letter of the term has just come and we wish that you were continuing the good spirit which you showed during vacation and in facing the return to school.

"It is probably too soon for you to expect to see any difference between this and last term. Also you must stop and ask yourself what you have done to bring about better conditions and what you can do to remedy those which you do not enjoy.

"Thus far you have for some reason not adjusted yourself to the school environment. The reasons why you were sent to Tamalpais were because more regular life and the necessity of doing everything on time would help you both in body and mind, because your standing as a scholar was low at Los Altos and because having been sick a good deal when little, things have been made too soft for you at home. What you need more than anything else is just what you face at Tamalpais – *the necessity to make a place for yourself, winning respect and friendships where you have not your family to make it easy to do so.* You can do it because you have the powers; it is only a question of whether you are going to be strong or flabby about it.

"The easiest thing to do would be for you to return home but that would be the worst way to meet the situation. The reason why R. E. was permitted to quit was that she was in a totally different position. She had done very well at Castelleja [high school] and was sent to boarding school for totally different reasons from those which caused us to send you.

"It must be tough upon a baby bird to have to hop off the edge of a nest. It has wings, which have never been used, it has always been high up on a tree where cats and other enemies could not reach it, it has no experience in finding food for itself, its father and mother have always been protecting it. But when the time comes for it to face the new conditions, it has to hop. Naturally it would rather stay in the nest where it does not have to make a place for itself. But it would never be much of a bird if it continued unwilling to meet and overcome difficulties.

"We have been much pleased with your rating for effort, and we were even more pleased with the good sportsmanship with which you made no complaint during the Christmas vacation and went back to what seemed to you a hard job like a brave man, instead of a whining schoolboy. But we want you to continue in the same manly way.

"If you have not made friends, it is really your fault, Alan, just as it is with grown-up people who don't make friends. It is up to you to find out why you have not and overcome the difficulty.

"It will be much better for you if you return to Tamalpais after the summer vacation. Your chances of becoming a Stanford man and an athlete will be greatly increased. If you do not want to return, we probably would not compel you to, although we would be much disappointed. It is up to you….

"With love from us all,

Affectionately, Father

"P.S. We will try to visit you next Sunday." [61]

Cranston came in for both praise and advice in his father's next letter. "You certainly left no stone unturned in your endeavor to see that the Sunday excuse reached Major White," he wrote January 26. "Going after things in that way is a quality which will help you later on when you go out into the world, but one has to be careful lest it results in a feeling of antagonism when he is dealing with people other than those who love him." [62]

Whatever his failings at school, Cranston clearly was a leader and advisor to his chums, an early indication of such qualities. "Tell me if you are coming home any time between now and vacation," Harry Dutton wrote him, "for I will hold a special club meeting for you."

"I have not [held one] since you left the last time, for I keep forgetting to write to you to discuss what matters at the meetings. If you agree with any amendments that I am going to say, just check them in the enclosed piece of paper…. (1) Have club house thoroughly swept out and cleaned. (2) Have each member to hold up his right hand and say those laws that we made. (3) Have all the weeds that are in the walk leading to the clubhouse after you enter the gate hoed and raked away. (4) And I wanted to know if we should allow any more members into the club, or to put out any members that are already in that do not obey the laws, as they did last year…. (5) To have you and I think up some hard but not difficult anniciations [*sic*, initiations]. (6) And to make the club BETTER AND CLEANER.

Your friend, Hon. Harry A. Dutton Jr., Esq., Inc.

"P.S. WRITE SOON. Also send me the piece of paper so I will know what to do." [63]

Cranston illustrated a 1929 letter to his mother (on Tamalpais School stationary on which his name was imprinted) with cartoon drawings. She apparently had been sick while visiting her sister, Aunt Grace, in San Jose. "Did they use the stomach pump on you?" he asked. "We got $64.29 off of the prunes, so I'll get about thirty dollars," he added, alongside a drawing of a man on his knees picking up fruit beneath a tree. He was advancing on the football team and hoped to be picked for the first team. "You'd better answer this P.D.Q. or I will let you walk home from San Jose," he concluded. He drew his black-face comic character Prescription and a stick figure repeating one of the puns that he had thought up: "Wait for me, I'll be with you in toothaces of a lamb's tail." [64]

Cranston remained at Tamalpais for one year, then was sent to another private school, Menlo, closer to home, in 1928. The following year, apparently having proven to his father that he had made progress and would continue in that way, he was allowed to enter Mountain View Union Public High School, where he was glad to be back with his old friends. [65]

In high school Cranston blossomed as a competitive runner. He specialized in the 100-, 220- and 440-yard dash, his best event. By his senior year at Mountain View, Cranston had become a *bone fide* track star. He even had an admiring freshman attending him and bringing his warm-up clothes to finish lines. At a 1932 Santa Clara Valley High School championship meet in his senior year, he won the 100-yard and 440-yard dash, and anchored his school's relay team to win. Cranston also considered himself an "excellent" horseback rider, and "fair" golf and tennis player. [66]

His second effort at being elected by his peers was more successful than the first. He was chosen president of the Boys' League, the male student body, in his senior year. He also edited the school's paper, the *Mountain Eagle*, and its annual year-book, and regularly saw his name in print over a humorous column, "School Daze," that he wrote for the paper. The column was published in the town's weekly newspaper, the Mountain View *Register-Leader*, during the Depression when it was short of reporters. There he would find a friendly and receptive editor, Milton K. "Pop" Smith. "I typed an article [on the 1932 Olympic Games in Los Angeles] and took it over to the Mountain View *Register Leader* office," he recorded in his diary.

"'Pop' Smith barely glanced at it and said, 'Yes, I'll be glad to take it' He told me to come around Friday, the day the paper comes out and he'll pay me then. I s'pose I'll get a dollar for it. WHOOPEE!!! AT LAST I'VE SOLD SOMETHING! Am I happy." Soon after that he entered in his diary, "I want to make a real dent in the world in a *belles-lettres* way, or at least have a happy, Bohemian life." [67]

The Olympic games in Los Angles were "wonderful," even with "some earthquakes," Cranston wrote in his published account, which was filled with humorous limericks, *double entendres* and asides about dogs and film stars. "Sylvia Sydney, who[m] I sat with that day, told Claudette Colbert, seated on my left, that some big Swede was a good pole vaulter. 'He must weigh 220 pounds,' exclaimed Claudette. 'What does he use for a pole?' 'Why, that one that just won the race,' said Sylvia." Cranston ended with a limerick: "Another of Une's runners named Hill/ At the END of his race had a near spill/ For a Fin guy looked back,/ Then ran right in his track/ 'Tis an old FINNISH custom, you sill'!" [68]

In a "Prophecy of the Senior Class," Cranston portrayed his classmates in the future in a darkly humorous piece for the school yearbook, *Blue and Gray.* He placed himself in Sing Sing Prison in 1945, where he imagined hearing a San Jose radio station broadcasting familiar classmates' voices. Breaking out of prison, he "ran clean plumb to California" where he encountered his classmates in their fictional futures: Harry Dutton was an usher in a theater and Ralph Raymond a janitor who "stopped me at the door on account of my convict garb, but upon recognizing me, he came to my aid." The fictional Cranston had served in the army under the name "Private Funds." Another fellow, Jim Marshall, had been elected Prince of Wales – "England, it seemed, had tired of its former prince's falling off horses." Two girls, Alpha Rose and Esther Conner, had been elected mayors of local towns, one of whom told him confidentially that "Los Altos is growing so fast that it is expected to annex Mountain View within a year. (Oops! My life isn't worth a nickel!)" [69]

Politically, Cranston's family were moderate Republicans (his father was president of the Palo Alto Republican Club), but Cranston believed that his own leaning toward the Democratic Party was influenced by attending public schools. He had insisted on being taken out of private Menlo and sent back to public school where a variety of ethnic and social classes were represented in the student body. "I was sent to private school three times before I was out of high school," Cranston noted. "The first, which I concealed while I was running for office," he laughed, " was Castelleja, which was a girls' school in Palo Alto. I was slightly embarrassed by that, but they took boys for the first, second and third grade, then no more boys after that. So I went there [briefly] – I didn't mind that. Then I was back to Los Altos grammar school where I started in the first grade, and I had a lot of friends there whom I liked a lot. I enjoyed the public school and the mix of people there. Then, partly to get me away from Harry Dutton – because he and I were always getting into trouble – I was sent off to Tamalpais private high school over in Marin. And I *hated* it, didn't like to be away from my friends and found it was a bunch of rich kids, some of them spoiled, I felt, and I just didn't get along very well with most of them. I only lasted for a year there, and then tried to persuade my parents to put me back in public school. But instead of my going to Mountain View with Harry and Ralph, I was sent to Menlo School for Boys. And again, I didn't like it. I felt that there were quite a few too many spoiled, rich kids, and I just loved the more general kind of people I went with to public school. So…I managed to persuade them to let me go back to public school, and I went over to Mountain View. I'm sure that had its influence on me" in fostering perceptions about equality among different kinds of people in society. [70]

His experiences with people were broader than his sister's, Eleanor realized. She had spent most of her early education in private schools, graduating in 1928. Her mother took her to visit Ivy League women's colleges like Bryn Mawr, Smith and others, but Eleanor always intended to follow her parents to Stanford despite its reputation as a studious campus. "There was a saying that 'a kiss takes five minutes off your life – go to Stanford, and live to a ripe old age!'" she laughed of her perception. At sixteen, however, she had fallen in love with John "Jack" Fowle, a consulting engineer. The couple wanted to be engaged but the Cranstons were adamantly against it, at least until after she had completed her freshman year at Stanford. She did as they wished, but then married and did not return to college. William Cranston's refusal to accept his potential son-in-law made Eleanor defiant and determined to marry. The wedding took place on the lawn of Villa Warec June 19, 1929, just as dark economic clouds were about to burst over the nation. Flower petals strewn over the grass marked the bridal party path. [71]

Eleanor had an interest in creative writing, wrote poems and short stories as a young girl, and once submitted a poem to a literary review, encouraged by crusading Hearst newspaper editor Fremont Older, William Cranston's best friend – they commuted daily together to San Francisco where Older was editor of the *San Francisco Call-Bulletin*. Eleanor wanted to be a novelist and in later life took creative writing courses with Stanford professor and author-friend Wallace Stegner. She wrote two novels that she was unable to sell for publication. She finally would realize her ambition by writing a warm biography of her brother in the early 1980s. It was published when she was seventy years old and Cranston sixty-six. [72]

As a youth, Cranston began keeping notes about his life and thoughts, handwritten or typed on index-size pieces of paper and cards. Many were marked "autobiographical" and were prescient for his age. "Although the psychologists said much about the importance of heredity, I took little notice of my forbears [*sic*], although I was rather proud of a far-off relationship with Rob Roy MacGregor," he recorded under the heading "Heredity, California and Pioneers." "My family never took much stock or interest in family trees after a distant uncle made a fortune in the boom days of the Coolidge millennium and went back to Scotland to acquire a coat of arms, a motto and ancestors," he wrote of the uncle's embarrassing finds. "Sometimes I did try to attribute some of my ideals and ideas to the forbears who had caused me to be born in California, some of them unfortunate fleers [*sic*] from unemployment, low wages, and high taxation – ever moving west to find new life and opportunity. Perhaps I inherited some of my ideas of social justice from them. Others, adventurous lovers of freedom 'leaving comfort to endure the risks and hardships of a pioneer's life' – perhaps from them I inherited my disregard of physical comfort, my desire to pioneer on ahead to something greater, a greater world; perhaps their undying faith in the Golden West, in the next valley behind the next mountain…came to me as a belief in the advance of mankind. The Pacific had stopped the physical advance of adventure, but it couldn't stop the pioneering mind, which carried on." [73]

Cranston's first political memory was of Theodore Roosevelt's death in 1919. One of his chores was to go down the hill each morning to pick up the newspaper and a bottle of fresh milk that was delivered daily. "One cold morning I noticed extraordinarily large headlines on the newspaper when I went down to pick it up at the gate. I ran back to the house with it, and my parents told me the great Teddy Roosevelt had died," he recorded on cards marked "autobiographical." Eleanor remembered a breakfast conversation that morning in which her mother wondered "if Alan might ever be president." "Oh, no," his father said. "Why not?" she asked. "No, no chance," William Cranston replied. Cranston heard it and later wondered if his resentment at his father's dismissing the idea had a reverse influence by making him want to defy, or "show," his father. Cranston also cited as an early "memory of anything presidential" the sudden death of President Warren G. Harding at the Palace Hotel in San Francisco in August, 1923. [74]

"The first election I can remember anything about is that of 1928," he wrote in the early 1930s, long before he was involved in any political activities. "I was 14 at the time. Could I have voted, (fortunately – I now feel – I could not), it would have been for [Herbert] Hoover. Primarily, because he was a close neighbor; secondarily, because my father favored him. Now I was neither bright nor dull for my age, but is not fourteen somewhere around the average mental age of the American voter?... For such reasons, then, America chooses its presidents!" [75]

He had his first political experience when the newly-elected President Hoover returned home to Palo Alto in 1928. A large welcoming crowd was gathered at the yellow Victorian station as the president's train came to a stop. Hoover appeared on steps in the last car. Cranston had gauged where it would stop and raced to the foot of the steps, beaming at the president. A policeman suddenly grabbed him by the neck and pants and tossed him beyond the circle of adult notables in the greeting party. Hoover was charmed, and pictures of his freckled fan were shown on newsreels nationwide. It was, as his sister put it, early evidence of Cranston's managing to be "in the way of things happening," quoting Theodore Roosevelt. [76]

In an entry to his notes that he called "The Long-View Cycle, discovered by Alan Cranston in A.D. 1931," he mused, "At first, the infant mind thinks everything it sees is close to it, and therefore of equal importance to it. As the mind develops, it learns space relationships: the baby learns that a bee one foot off in the atmosphere is so much buzzing dynamite, but that an airplane one mile in the stratosphere is not worth looking at.... But to complete the process of mind-development, the cycle must be completed; things far away must resume their importance. To a baby's undeveloped mind, or to a drunk's befuddled mind, a fly on the nose, or in the vicinity of the nose, is much more important than an airplane bombing Berlin, or a bullet killing a duke at Sarajevo, or a dictator at New Orleans. But to the mind that has gone the complete cycle, the airplane, or the bullet, is by far the most important. Most of us go far more than *half* way around the circle, but how few go the circuit! How few of us can lay claim to an infallible long view on life." [77]

"I was close to Victorianism," he would write of moral awakenings under the heading, "Uncle Willie's un-knowledge of women's legs." "If my escape from the dogmas of western religion was fortunate, so was my escape from blind morality and Victorianism. I had many moral ideas presented to me. For a long time, I seemed to believe them all. Then one day, without being conscious of the change…I found myself abandoned of belief in a great number of them. How close I was to Victorianism, tho.' My own Uncle Willie was raised in such a household that, 'till he was near twenty, he didn't know women had legs. It was a distinct shock to him when he discovered they had. He had always seen women sort of roll across the floor with wide skirts dragging the floor, and he'd always sort of thought they led, or went on, wheels. Or perhaps he was so trained that he never thought." [78]

The Cranston parents were open-minded and the children grew up in that environment. Eleanor considered their father "an advanced thinker." Cranston believed that his father, despite his business success, "always wanted a more prestigious occupation," one reason that he had interesting friends like Fremont Older. Older and his wife Cora, also a writer, often visited the Cranstons and vice versa, despite Older's more liberal tendencies than William Cranston's. Both Olders would have a profound influence on Alan Cranston. "There were usually an ex-convict or two working on his place in Cupertino," Cranston remembered. "He had great sympathy for a guy in trouble, and went on several crusades to get people out of prison, including the Tom Mooney case," for which Older campaigned until the labor leader convicted of planting a bomb that killed ten people during a 1916 Preparedness Day parade had his sentence commuted to life imprisonment in 1918; he was pardoned in 1939. "One day, Fremont said, 'How about coming over to San Quentin with me today?'" Cranston related of a memorable experience with the great editor. "Fremont was convinced that Mooney was framed, and devoted himself thereafter to getting him out, and eventually that succeeded. Anyway, that day we went over there to talk with Mooney and every now and then, he would get very emotional and bemoaned how terrible it was that the innocent are locked up for no good reason, and said, 'I didn't do it, but they somehow proved that they thought I did, and it was an *outrage*,' and he would cry. Down the way was another cell inhabited by two McNamara brothers who had been found guilty of blowing up the *Los Angeles Times* with a bomb. In the midst of this loud bewailing, one of the McNamara brothers yelled to the other, 'Ain't you glad we're guilty?'" Hearing Mooney's side personally "made me sympathetic" to those like him, Cranston said. [79]

He also was impressed by another person befriended by Older, "a guy named Jack Black whom my father got to know. He had been a house robber, and wrote a book, *You Can't Win*. I used to have a copy but I lost it. He autographed one to my father, and wrote in it this beautiful little story. He described how on some *terribly* cold night – he said this was an example of the injustice and coldness of the world – he approached a man. 'I was freezing and starving, and along comes this man in a very obviously expensive overcoat, suit and hat, and I approached him and asked him for a dime. And this man said to me, 'You want me to unbutton my coat and put my hands in my pocket and pull out a dime for you? You're crazy,' and started to walk off. I said to him, 'The likes of you should carry around dimes for the likes of me in your overcoat pocket!'" [80]

As Cranston matured, he became tenacious about self-education, reading extensively, keeping lists of books that he thought would improve his mind and perceptions. It was part of his wanting to become a serious writer. "Picking the best passages out of books, learning to know the very best and seeking the weaknesses of the rest, is the next thing to writing them yourself. Next to creating art is recognizing it," he wrote in a note. [81]

Cranston was a lively, fun-loving, handsome young man with his freckles and dark hair. He was lean and energetic, and from an early age attracted, and attractive, to girls. In a diary that he began keeping at seventeen and continued for several years, Cranston wrote that he hoped "to marry a wonderful and beautiful woman." His first love was a grade-school classmate. She was the daughter of family friends whom the Cranstons visited for Sunday lunches, after which Cranston and the girl would ride her black Shetland ponies over the hills. Blond-haired and blue eyed, she shared Cranston's high spirits and love of animals. As teenagers they became briefly "engaged" but because they attended different high schools, drifted apart. The girl's father died suddenly and Cranston returned to seeing her. But her mother discouraged the visits and the girl became increasingly unhappy and unmanageable, according to a draft of Eleanor's biography of Cranston. He tried to interest the girl in things that he was consumed by – writing, books, travel – but it became apparent that she did not share the same enthusiasms. After devouring one of Richard Halliburton's books, young Cranston was smitten more by wanderlust than settling down. The girl would turn down other suitors in hopes of winning over Cranston. But it was not to be. [82]

Cranston grew into to a tall, slender, athletic young man, whose freckles were hidden by a regular tan from being outdoors. On a date with the same girl, Cranston was stunned when he saw that she had dyed her blond hair red. He kidded her about trying to be the actress Clara Bow. After a lively Saturday night in which her carefree wildness was evident, he told her that he did not think there would ever be anyone quite like her again in his life, a feeling that she said was mutual. "But somehow I don't think now that I'm in danger of falling in love with her again," he confided to his diary. "Time, my development, other girls, have all served as scissors on the bond. Home about eleven and studied." [83]

The next diary entry read: "Slept late, read the funnies in exactly eight minutes, deciding to waste no further time on such foolishment.... I want to learn a whole lot, make a real dent in this world."

He tried to express his fears and desires in a letter to the girl, telling her what he liked about her and wondering whether they could work out their relationship. But he had his doubts. Just after mailing the letter, he met an unusual seventeen-year-old niece of his good friend, Johnny Atkinson. "Watch out for Doris, and especially for her father," Atkinson warned. Doris was ready to rebel, and Cranston was smitten by her. Still, his previous love lingered; she replied to his letter that she would try to change her life to meet his demands. Doris Atkinson was sent to Hawaii by her father and although she and Cranston corresponded, they often were prevented from meeting. Cranston went back to the other girl. [84]

But his thoughts were on the future. He confessed to a friend, "Ambition is probably a disease, but I have a bad dose of it." Although he talked the girl out of marrying someone else, feeling that it was a bad match, the relationship was troubling to him, even if marriage were put off for several years. Finally, the girl dropped a bombshell – in a quarrel, her mother had blurted out that the girl was adopted and should show gratitude for her situation rather than cause trouble. It became clear that she craved love and affection that she did not receive at home. In spite, she took out a marriage license with the other boy and planned to wed a few days later. Cranston found himself trying to calm and thwart her impetuous action, feeling on one hand relieved that he was well out of it, on the other, protective of the needful and distraught girl. In a gesture of kindness, he invited her to stay at Villa Warec to get away from her mother. The Cranstons were surprisingly receptive, for which Cranston was grateful. All of them tried to talk the girl out of the ill-conceived marriage while realizing that for Cranston, such a union would be a disaster. But his concern for the girl made him undecided about whether he should marry her anyway. The girl ended the suspense by marrying the other boy as she had threatened. [85]

"Losing her didn't hurt as much as I thought it might," Cranston later wrote in his diary. "It ended an affair that's worried me for years, and it's left my pathway open again to a life I really think I can do something with maybe.... I hope now that she is happy."

He dated other girls and his sister saw that he would fall for them briefly but was not inclined to commit himself for the long term. He wanted his freedom. He was drawn by unconventional girls with spirit who shared his sense of adventure and punning humor. He also was attracted by handsome women. He reinstated his interest in Doris Atkinson, with whom he felt a lot of affinity, telling her the story of his ill-fated previous relationship. In a twelve-page letter to Doris, he said that she was "a wonderful girl" with a promising future but warned against her becoming "a dilettante" which "talented people are apt to do, if they don't see what their talent means.... In a word, I think the individual must accomplish something for the world – for many people besides himself – with his life.... He should try to hasten social evolution to the utmost powers, even try to control its course. It's a happy ideal; it makes one feel he's worth something." He continued,

"Do you remember when I said, 'The world is too much with you,' when the elevator was a bit slow in arriving and you were griped? I said it because you stormed when the garage was slow in bringing your car down. Money has brought things your way so easily that you may always expect things to fall as you wish.... Do you really think you could be happy, as you said, married to a fellow making $50 a week?... Forgive me...I hope this letter will help, not hurt us, so I am anxiously –hopefully – lovingly – yours." [86]

He took up with another high-school friend who was running with a "wild" crowd, telling her that if one of the boys she went out with "had to get drunk to enjoy himself, think how he must bore other people." Cranston would never be much of a drinker or tolerant of drunks himself. He fixed that girl up with a friend. He began to recognize that helping people was hard work, requiring lots of psychological diplomacy. He went back to communicating with Doris Atkinson, who lived in Southern California, although he told her, "The last thing I want is to get serious about any girl at this point in the game, and if you were nearby it would be inevitable." After a New Year's Eve date was thwarted by her father, Cranston wrote Doris that she scared him, preventing his saying what he felt. "If I once start saying those things in your presence, I'll be gone. I try to let my head rule my heart and emotions, but I'd be lost under those circumstances." The father's intervention was a blessing in disguise, he decided. "We're too young, you and I, too changing, too alive, to make ties with anything now, whether it be with ideas or persons. I'll be a different individual in two more years, and you'll be four different persons." They kept up their correspondence while going separate ways, Doris studying ballet and acting. (She once danced with the Prince of Wales at Coronado.) [87]

Women nevertheless would continue to interest, and intrigue, Cranston. In his early twenties, he posited a short-story idea about whether the world might be improved if women had more political power – what might it be like if "women take charge of the world [that] men have messed up so much, and try to make it into something – failure or success? [Women tried] to use intuition, [but were plagued by] petty gossiping – [and] monthly disability. [The concept was a] marvelous opportunity for comedy – male housemaids, etc." [88]

A poem that he wrote mixed humor with sensual innuendos and self-justification:

ODE TO MY LOVE
Too bad I'm not cereal,
Just something material –
You could swallow me whole as I am.

But I'm not,
I'm a blot
On all the hopes,
On all your ropes –
Tied to clothes and cars,
To the Mammon of Mars;
Private johns and sunken baths,
Glorious houses and primrose paths;
Golden-spooned children and for them food –
I? – I'd starve our brood.

I guess I'm a Peter Pan;
I'm sorry, but I am what I am –
I feed on life and love,
For they go hand in glove,
With happiness and joy –
I'm just a fool boy,
But I hope to help man." [89]

Cranston was disappointed when his high school grades were not good enough to make him eligible to enter Stanford, the family *alma mater*. Instead, he enrolled at Pomona College in Claremont, California. "I had a lump in my throat as I went out the driveway for the last time for some time to come," he told his diary the day he left for college in September, 1932. [90]

His father gave him a sweater and his mother slipped a letter into his suitcase, which eased the parting from home. In one of his first letters from Pomona (eight handwritten pages), he begged for news of football games, then began relating all his new adventures. "I haven't been able to read or write at all, I've been so busy. You're lucky I got time for this, but I decided I had to write now. I've had a wonderful time here so far." He described outsmarting efforts to taunt freshmen students like him by driving "way out in the country and leav[ing] them to walk home. Once we had two freshmen standing under a lamp post as decoys and about sixty frosh were behind a hedge. A car full of sophs stopped to get the two, & the whole mob of us charged out and piled in." He seemed to relish the good-natured confrontations provoked by sophomores against new students. In one *contra-temps*, "The frosh were victorious. We took the pants off every soph. It seemed funny to fight a fellow as hard as you could for a while, then when one or the other gave up, we'd shake hands & introduce ourselves." The college pranks and fun were right up Cranston's alley. [91]

He plunged into the new challenges with obvious enjoyment, undaunted by the new environment, even his roommate – "We fight badly over different subjects, but all in fun." "Our class has made a big hit with the juniors and seniors because we beat up the sophs so much," his letter continued. "One night, we captured a soph car & pushed it up on the porch of Hardwood court. The girls through [*sic*] us lipstick & we painted red 36s all over the car. Every night about 12 Norman Sears & I take our lifes [*sic*] in our hands & hike downtown by ourselves to get something to eat. Most kids don't go out unless twenty or thirty others are around, so we have a lotta fun. We get chased all around, but I haven't been caught yet. The upper classmen give us a little aid because they like us for taking the chance of going for a ride. Last night we had a treaty & went to bed early for the first time since we got here. The meals are swell here and we get all we want." Still, he ended, "It'll be swell if you can come down weekend after this."

He signed up for courses in English, French, history, biology, art and physical education. He also joined the R.O.T.C. – "got my uniform already. I didn't go out for football," but in track, he easily passed strenuous physical tests and ran the 100-yard dash in 10.5 seconds. " I sure wanted to make the best time, but I got about two hours sleep the night before, so was afraid I wouldn't." His time so impressed the coach that he "found out who I was & came around & talked to me, and Plumb, a junior who does 9.7, calls me the 'speed demon.'"

He made friends quickly and made an effort to get acquainted. "It's sure hard to remember the names of all the people one meets. I know everybody in the freshman class to speak to, practically, and a lot of the upper classmen. The student-body president & secretary, the football captain, the soph president & Plumb are especially friendly to me."

He had an open and candid relationship with his parents, evident in his letters (he wrote them faithfully once a week, sometimes addressing them as "Mother and Father," sometimes "Pop & Mom"). His uncle Willie Sheets wrote Mrs. Cranston, who had proudly sent her son's first letter from college to other family members,

"Alan's letter is one of the most amusing bits we have read in a long time – so unstudied and artless – such a happy outlook on life! Our united thanks for sharing it with us. Grace [Cranston's aunt] says the thing that impresses her most is the boy's courage. To me it is his ability to make friends unconsciously and with no effort." [92]

Of his first letter, Cranston wrote his parents two days later, "I hope it got there, it was darn long." His subsequent letters would be typed on Pomona College letterhead stationary – "Nifty letter paper, Huh? .95 [cents] a box." In that letter, he told of being "captured" by sophs when he ran into a blind alley. "They drove us way out into a semi-desert, and left us. We were talking with 'em and joking all the way up, everything that's done here is in a friendly manner." He had met another freshman who had "run the 440 in 52 or 53. Think of the swell relay team we'll have if we can get one more fellow that's even halfway decent. We ought to be able to beat every team we meet." Freshmen were required to take dates to dances "or get kilt." By his second dance, Cranston had one, "so I'm safe. I guess after tonight I'll start going to bed early." He went regularly to dances, sometimes at both Scripps and Pomona. [93]

He asked his parents to bring him, if they had copies, "Well's *Outline of History* and Robinson's *The Mind in the Making*." He soon dropped art, and reported in October that "All the people Willie [his roommate] and I were for got elected for the class offices." Cranston was not a candidate. [94]

He went into Los Angeles one day, "got some swell track shoes," and also found

"a swell second-hand book store on 7th street. It was chuck full of books and magazines, you could pretty near get lost among the stacks. I got a swell 1928 dictionary for 1.25 ($), a book of quotations for 6 bits – it's old as heck, but has all the well-known quotations, will help in English, got 5 *Pucks* that were published in 1895 – they have swell old pictures and jokes, and for $1.00 I got a paper published the day after Lincoln's assassination, telling all about it, and also for the dollar got a paper published in 1786 and another of 1800. They have ads for slaves in 'em, and everything. He had a book called 'Si Klegg put down the Rebellion.' He wants $3.00 for it, says it's very rare and he once saw an ad offering $10.00 for it, but someone beat him to it. The frontispiece shows how Si went in and came out of the war, once all covered with rolls & packages, later with only one small knapsack as he came out. He quits the war once, but the governor writes him a letter, so he joins the army again. Do you think it's the one you read? If you do think so, shall I buy it, 50-50 with you?

"Heard Lily Pons sing last night, she was sure good." [95]

His father agreed to go in on the Klegg book which Cranston, in his next letter, promised to get as soon as he could go back to Los Angeles. It was a popular fictional account of a Civil War Union army soldier with illustrations that would have attracted the aspiring cartoonist Cranston.

He went on to tell his parents how he astonished the track coach in the 220: "He didn't think I could do it this early without straining, [but] I hit 25 right on the dot, running very easily. Then he asked me what I ran in high school. I said 53, and he said I oughta do 48!!!… He meant [that] I ought to do that time next season! [Coach] Strahle said I at least ought to be as good as anybody in the frosh conference. He has me lean forward more when I run, and work my arms differently. He said my form was better than most frosh trackmen without that, tho.'"

Cranston sent his laundry home for washing, and continued to follow Stanford football – he had fifty cents riding on a game against the University of Southern California that fall – and asked for any articles that Stanford's track coach Dink Templeton might have written. Cranston's mind and heart were at Stanford but his body at Pomona, which he was glad to say was "going after track men." Coach Strahle "introduced me to a couple of high-school seniors the other day that he had down here looking over the college." Cranston also was glad to report that he got "the highest mark in the [history] class of over 70 students" but only between C and B in two other history tests. [96]

He was having no trouble getting dates with pretty girls, and candidly discussed his social life with his parents. "The formal was swell, all except having to wear a tux," he reported. "The girl I took is supposed to be the most popular fresh woman at Scripps (both with boys and girls). You know, she's the one I got the date with the night I went to the dance when you were here." A friend's play was being produced – "I'm taking a good-lookin' Scripps junior to it." He ended with what apparently was meant to be a joke about the national economic Depression: "Times are so tough, I can't tell time no more no how. When someone asks me what time is it, I can only tell 'em quarter of, I can't tell 'em what because the Depression hit me so hard, I had to lay off one of the hands." He signed it in an exaggerated calligraphy-like script. [97]

Cranston's openness with his parents about girl friends may have benefited from his older sister's paving the way. Their parents were more relaxed toward their son's friendships than hers. Cranston, in any event, "was always an amicable family member," his sister thought. [98]

Cranston lost his fifty cents on the Stanford-USC game. "Luckily I couldn't place a bet for you, Pop." While he was writing that letter October 27, he heard noise outside his room and "then there was a big knock on the door. I was suspicious, so went to our suite-mate's and looked out their door. A wastebasket full of water was leaning against our door so that if the door had been opened, it would have poured in our room. They were sure surprised when I looked out the other door. Then they worked it swell on the kids next door."

He went on to report voting results from a poll at the school on the national presidential election, revealing his preference, like his parents,' for the Republican incumbent. "In order, I voted for Hoover…. How much did we bet on the Hoibert-F. D. R. election? (I betcha I win, Pop.)." He was not shy about putting himself forward, and talked excitedly about hearing an explorer who "gave a swell talk. I went to the dinner afterwards where students were to have a chance to meet him if they wanted. I managed to get a seat next to him, the president's daughter was on his other side. So I had a good chance to talk to him. He is very interesting, and witty. In the last 31 years he has spent only 18 months outside of South America." Cranston also sent home a published article from "the first interview I ever had with anybody, written up. I was given the assignment to interview Blaisdell [former college president James A. Blaisdell] about degrees, and didn't even think who he was 'till I had gotten in his office, after arguing with his secretary for a while. I felt funny for a second when I realized who he was. He's awfully nice. He remembered the Dixon you told me to ask him about, Mother, and was very interested. He wants you to go and see him next time you're down here." [99]

In the same letter, Cranston talked about the Ku Klux Klan. "You oughta see the swell pamphlet Bill Hughes [a close friend] and I found in the street together the other day – it's the Ku Klux Klan organ. It's full of propaganda against communism and Roosfelt [*sic*]. On the back page, it has a coupon to fill out, if you're interested in the KKK, with different blanks, one asking if you're behind the Klan in all their ideas, another space to put your name and address, another asking for your phone number, and the last asking how many passengers your car holds, if any. I wonder why they ask the last two things? We could imagine all kinds of things, taking guys for rides, etc. What do you think?????"

He also had a critique for the new film, *Grand Hotel* – "I liked it. I didn't think much of Greta, or of the guy what played the part of the crook. I liked Kilengrin, or whatever his name was, the best." His intellectual curiosity was evident in his next remarks. "I was studying in the *Mind in the Making* a while ago. Do you remember the example of metaphysics of some old Greeks, in which the space was only imaginary, 'cause they couldn't conceive space when they realized nothing couldn't exist?' I must be dumb, but I stopt [*sic*] and thot for about an hour before I could figure out a logical theory against theirs." He signed off, "Slonk" – so long.

By November, he reported that he did not like French much, dreaded a forthcoming exam and tried to justify his grades, which were not spectacular. In his first year he got Bs, Cs and one D in four courses – biology (a D in second semester), English, French and history. His only As were in military training and sports. "All the first flunk slips are out, and I have at least better than D in all my subjects so far," he confessed. He nevertheless wanted to skip some classes in order to return home to see the Stanford "Big Game" (against the University of California). "I would only miss two classes, and I'm about the lowest frosh in number of cuts so far (only two)," he argued. He had gotten the Si Klegg book and "read about 40 pages, and like it. It starts like you said, Pop." It was the day that his father opened an office in Palo Alto. "I sure hope you have good luck there," he said, adding that he had "plenty of allowance" to meet his needs. As to R.O.T.C., he had to cope with learning how to shoot a gun – "It's sure a job, learning all the things we gotto do with them in drills. There is a rifle contest going on now, with medal awards. Everybody in the unit hasta [*sic*] enter." [100]

On November 9, the day after national elections in which Democrat Franklin Roosevelt defeated incumbent Republican Herbert Hoover, Cranston wrote with enthusiasm, if in partial jest, about what it portended. "Wottan election yesterday, huh? We all ate big meals last nite 'cause we knew it was the last good one we'd get.... Lotsa the bright people here, profs., etc., think that more changes in the government will take place in the U. S. than have in the last 50 years. I lost the bet on Hoover, Pop, and as you owed me $1.50 for Si Klegg, you only owe me four bits now." [101]

Cranston wrote a long column after the election, under the title "The Funny Side," which showed that he had followed it closely. He made astute observations on news accounts that clearly made him chuckle. He quoted Will Rogers' comment that both candidates might have done better if they had gone fishing during the last pre-election week because both probably regretted their final campaign statements. Cranston took note of the fact that "After all the rushing about the country by the candidates, it is interesting to note that Hoover carried New England. He didn't go there. Roosevelt got his biggest vote in Texas, Mississippi, and Louisiana. He didn't go there." Cranston also was amused by a *Los Angeles Examiner* front-page commentary about a defeated U. S. Senate candidate, Bob Schuler, who had said that he planned to keep on running. The *Examiner* – which might cause the reader to "laugh, scowl or swear" – suggested that the hapless loser "start at the confines of Los Angeles County and 'keep on running' until he gets back to Texas, whence he came." Pomona students who lost election bets were "cursing their foolishness," Cranston joked, especially one "who is starting a year's growth of beard upon his manly chin. Another poor devil is pushing a peanut from New York to Chicago with his pug nose and sheer force of gravity as the only source of motivation. In Los Angeles a bet loser was tied to a post and pelted with two dozen bad (very bad) eggs at the hands of the happy winner, who was egged on by eggcited spectators. When the eggs-itement was over, the loser said, 'Egg-ad, the yolks on me, but I'll never do it egg-ain.' What egg-regious occurrence! Hank Norman would go into politics, only he's afraid he'd flunk out of the Electoral College. And they shinny polls!!!" he continued, obviously delighted with his word play. [102]

The plight of various candidates also amused him: "In Lemon County a fellow campaigned loud and long for the office of county supervisor, lecturing in every city, town and hamlet…as well as at every farm harboring more than 100 head of livestock. But lo, on November 8, he polled just two votes, and on November 9 he was arrested for repeating! And they shoot repeaters!!!" He noted that "Certain believers in 'signs' have won large amounts of money in past presidential races by placing their stakes on the candidate whose name contained a double-O…. This device never failed," citing T. R. Roosevelt (1901), Coolidge (1924) and Hoover (1928). "Imagine the embarrassment and consternation of these [Republican] knaves when the Democrats calmly proceeded to nominate ROOsevelt!!!" To those Republicans who bet that four months after Franklin Roosevelt was inaugurated, all the banks would be closed, Cranston gleefully pointed out that "exactly four months after inauguration day happens to the Fourth of July, a national holiday!!!" and the banks indeed would be closed.

He concluded by telling a story about a "tall, gray-haired man…electioneering outside a poll in a busy section of San Francisco [who] avoided button-holing people with set expressions on their faces, for experience had taught him that their minds were made up, and that no amount of persuasion…would alter their vote." Cranston resorted to a bit of "purple prose" in describing a scene with an Irishman who "came ambling down the street, the wrinkled skin on his old face appearing as ancient parchment in the streaks of sunlight which penetrated to the depths of Market Street, his indescribable expression and the long, well-sharpened pencil tightly grasped in his strong hand, signifying his intention to vote." After considerable haranguing by the electioneer, "proclaiming the advantages, benefits, improvements, and gains which would be effected, if he, the Irishman, would only vote in favor of" the candidate's slate, the Irishman suddenly interrupted: "There's only one thing I want to know – is he a Republican, or is he a Dimocrat [*sic*]?"

Not funny, however, was the reality of the Depression on a fellow student. Cranston's good friend Bill Hughes "had to go home cause of lack of money," he reported to his parents. "We gave him a big send-off at the train tonight. He was sure popular. Just about everybody in school knew him and were sorry to see him go. I think I liked him better than any fellow I've met outside of my Los Altos bunch. He may come back here next year." [103]

His own parents, though, were worried about Cranston's academic performance. "Gee whiz?!!! You seem to think just because I said I have better than Ds that I have only Cs. I only meant that they sent out D and flunk slips, and I didn't get any. They don't tell you anything about your grades unless you are close to flunking. I don't know exactly how I'm doing in any subjects. All I know is I'm working darn hard. For the last three nites I've been up till 1 a.m. studying, and will have to do the same tonight and tomorrow night. I'm pretty sure I have a B average in both history and biology; we've got a new prof. in biology for a while, and he's sure going to make us work. I think I'm between B and C in English. Compositions that would have been As in high school are Cs here. In fact, I handed in one composition, an exact copy of an A at high school, and got a C- on it!!!!! I don't know at all where I stand in French. The first month I was sure I was flunking, and went around and asked him if I was and he said he found no fault with my work. Since then it's been getting harder and harder, and I don't know where in heck I stand. I wish I'd taken German."

On a happier note, he "had a column in the *Register Leader* for November 4th." He again begged for them to get him a ticket for the "Big Game" – "I don't care where it is" – because he was determined to go. They complied, and he got a "swell" seat, although unsure whether he would be there. "Tomorrow the crazy English prof. might say: 'There will be a test Saturday morning,' and then I wouldn't be able to come." He would not take a train "because I don't want to waste any of your money or mine. If that is the only way to get there, I won't come." The trip would not cost more than $3.00, he insisted, and would not exhaust him – he had plenty of energy, he reported. "I hafta study so darn much now that I'm used to six or seven hours sleep. Last nite I went to bed at 9:30 for a change, and from force of habit I couldn't sleep till 12. I feel swell and am gaining weight." [104]

"I meant to tell you in my last letter about the plague we had here at school, but I forgot," he continued. "They don't know what it was, they decided it wasn't intestinal flu. It might have been poison spray that wasn't washed thoroughly off the vegetables. It was swell for me; in the whole frosh dorm, there were exactly seven boys out of the 100-plus that weren't sick, and I was one of them. That shows how well I am. It lasted for about five days. One night at dinner about 1/10th of the people were there. And about every four minutes someone would suddenly jump up and run out of the dining room. Everybody would clap for them. It was sure funny. About 3/4ths of the total school enrollment was affected. Scripps had it, too, and a J. C. [junior college] nearby had to shut down for a week. We were all hoping for a vacation. The people affected were only sick for a day or two, but they were sure *sick* for that length of time." [105]

Alas, he did not get to the "Big Game." A fellow whom he was counting on to drive did not, and he had no luck hitch-hiking. But he could report that he got a B in English – "six guys did, one-half the class flunked," and no higher grade was given. [106]

Driving back to school after Thanksgiving, when Cranston and a friend reached Santa Maria at nine at night, they noticed "a lotta people leaving the first show of a theatre, and as the movie was *I Am a Fugitive [from a Chain Gang]*, we slams on the brakes and goes to the second show," the good seats "a relief after the crowded car. Around 2 a.m. we stopt at Santa Barbara for some coffee at some dump. Have you ever seen those gambling things where you put a nickel in a slot, and a derrick may, one time in a 100, pick up a prize for you? They had one there. A fella in the place that goes there often showed me how to work the thing for 1 cent, and with team work with Norm [Sear, his companion] on the electricity plug at the other end of the store, I stuck in one penny and got out a swell cigarette lighter. I sold it for six bits at school today. Good profit, huh? Norm and I stopt at one place where a guy wouldn't cash a check for us when we were hitch hiking, and showed the guy that we weren't bums, and told him what we thot of him…. I just put on my moleskins for the first time, and found the two-bit piece you stuck in the pocket 'for luck,' Mother. Thanx a lot. It was a pleasant surprise." [107]

In December he "got a job of columning on the school paper, at last, and dropped my job of reporting. The first column will appear in the edition coming out a week from today. I spent quite a bit of this aft[ernoon] writing it. After thinking it over, Mother, I think that's a good idea about giving me some money for Xmas to buy books with," he added. "I was in a book store Saturday and saw about 5,505 books I'd like to buy." He was going to hear famed Scottish baritone Harry Lauder that night – "I hope he's good." "Tell R. E. that if she doesn't write before I come back, she will die," he concluded. [108]

His column, "Quips and Slips," appeared December 14, 1932, in *Student Life* under Cranston's by-line (he identified himself as a freshman). The column was full of puns – "I'm not afeard of bars,…'cause I usta ride a bicycle an' I know how to handle bars," or "Gem from Roget's synonym book (highly recommended for English): food = 'belly timber.'" He laughed at the "frosh who got mixed up when his Scripps girl friend told him to meet her at Toll. He waited for her five hours at Bridges!" And he spoofed fellow students for their gaffs: "When we were filling out R.O.T.C. personnel blanks, some fellow piped up: 'Does nearest relation mean the one that's living nearest to college here?'" [109]

Cranston also mentioned the Klan in his first column: "There are rumors to be overheard here and there that the Klark Ku Klux Klan Klippers are soon to ride again. Lock your doors and bolt your windows, for theirs is a vengeance worse than death!!!" [110]

By the end of the 1932 term, he still struggled with French and biology "sure gets me down," he told his parents. His R.O.T.C. marksmanship was mediocre – "Only made 40 on the standing position, so don't get a medal…on my last five shots, I only scored once." "Gawd – that biology; I think I'll go join the Foreign Legion." But in a postscript, he added with great relief, at "(1/4 to 12 Mon. nite), Biology is lots betta now. WHOOPEE!!! I got one of the girls that was with us on our Thanksgiving trip to help me with biology tonight, she's a lab assistant and knows lots about it. She helped me swell so I know something about it now." He got a C+ for the course. [111]

"I think I'll get better marks next semester," he wrote home in January. He also was looking at possible fraternities, and working seriously on his running. "Plumb usually beats me in starts, but yesterday I beat him every time, and held my lead as far as we'd go – about 25 yards." His parents must have been pleased that his learning increased with new discoveries. "I spent most of the last weekend reading Dmitri Merejkowski's *The Romance of Leonardo de Vinci*. It was on a list of books that we had to read for English, and next semester we have to read it for history, so I killed two birds with one stone. It was a keen book – the best I've read for a long time. I'll be interested to see Monna [*sic*] Lisa when I go to Paris again, now that I know something about it and its artist." [112]

Another pleasure was the film *Congress Dances*. "You ought to see it if you can. I liked it as well as *Two Hearts in Waltztime* and *The Guardsman*. It is supposed to have taken place in Europe during the time of Napoleon. The acting in it is wonderful. The two pieces from Vienna – 'Live, Laugh and Love' and 'Just Once for All Time' – are played a lot in it. It has an all-German cast but is spoken in English."

His second column in *Student Life* appeared January 7, 1933. He extolled a lecture on "The Earth and the Heavenly Bodies" that he had attended, with its "truly remarkable" accompanying movies and "many clever pictures showing the courses and actions of stars, planets, and suns…through the use of balls revolving in circles, or plates spinning about." The best part was an illustration of velocity greater than light, when "the worldlings took an imaginary trip through the universe, and turned their telescopes on the earth to see how it was getting along…. They found they had overtaken the light from the earth of a decade ago, and saw a man have an accident with his horse that…happened ten years before. They turned their airship back toward the world, and as they went into the light coming from it, they saw the accident happen backwards, as a movie run in reverse appears." He also told a story about a magazine's faking an eclipse picture that a photographer on assignment had missed. "They used an electric light for the sun, and worked out a darned good eclipse. They were highly elated, but when they developed their film, they found printed across the visible part of the sun the word 'Mazda.'" [113]

Cranston's father wanted to be at Pomona for an intra-mural track meet in which Cranston would run at the end of January, 1933. Cranston warned him that he was in the midst of final exams and would have little time to see him. "Biology ex[am] was awful this morning – I got anywhere from an F to a B." He had not spent his Christmas gift on books, however. "I bet you can't guess wot I bot with my Xmas money. A pair of skis! I've tried 'em out twice already, last week up in the snow. It's sure fun; it's hard to do, but it doesn't hurt when you fall down, so it doesn't matter. I was in a keen snow storm up on Baldy last Thursday – I was never so cold in my life, I got caught out in it. First snowstorm I ever saw even. The skis I got are swell." He then boasted, "I got my first A in an English comp[osition] yesterday. It was the last paper of the semester. It was on my report of Leonardo de Vinci." [114]

By mid-February, he could send home his grades with some pride. "Wal, here's the marks you've been waiting for: Military - A; Physical Ed - A; History - B; English - B; French - C; Biology - C. Pretty good, heh? That gives me 41 grade points, and only 24 were needed to matriculate. To graduate one needs 126 grade points, so I got well over the first one-eighth." He also felt "a lot more confident of doing well" at an inter-class track meet than previously. "I'm in swell condition, I wasn't tired hardly at all, compared to last year's races. I feel I should win the 440 Sat., but of course can't be at all sure.... I haven't lost a race since I've been here, but Plumb will sure spoil my records in the inter-class. I'm hoping for a 2nd.... I finally broke 10.5 the other day, doing 10.4." He resisted skiing. "I decided not to tire myself and risk hurting myself, so stayed at school and practiced track" – he was preparing to compete in relays at Long Beach. He then related: "I've had more time for reading now, and am enjoying Mark Sullivan's book, and *The Royal Road to Romance*. I'm also reading Mark Twain's *The Gilded Age*. It's keen, too. I don't like the touches I find in it of the collaborator, tho.'... That astronomer I met sent me a paper-bound copy of a couple of books he wrote about an eclipse and astronomy. They have some keen pictures in them." [115]

"Mon Dieu!!!!!!! Did I have the scare of my life day before yesterday!!!!!!" he exclaimed in a letter March 3. The track coach had informed him that he was ineligible to be on the team because he did not have enough academic units. There had been a mistake, it turned out – "some dumb dame in the registrar's office left off a half a...record by mistake, so I was OK after all. I was sure scairt (*sic*) up to then." The coach also "made me take up boxing instead of wrestling for P. E. Says its OK if I break my nose, but my legs and arms are what's important.... [O]ther bum luck happened. March 1 I got a letter from the Santa Barbara police judge. You remember I got pinched there at Thanksgiving, but never heard from them after I sent them the ticket and a hard-luck story. Well, I gets a letter saying they haven't heard from me since their letter of Dec. 9th, (which I never got) and that if they don't immediately get the 10 bucks they asked for, they're going to issue a warrant for my arrest. I feel like waiting and seeing if they really do it, the big stiffs. If I was ineligible for track, I would, but I guess I don't want to get put in jail the day of a track meet or something." [116]

He was proving himself a real contender at track, although still a freshman. In a succeeding meet, he "just loafed" but "came out OK." To make up time as anchor in the relay, he ran "fastern I ever did before.... I wish somebody had timed me... everybody thot it was the fastest anybody had moved around a 220 curve for a long time." [117]

He was elected freshman track captain – "nobody else was even nominated. I was sure happy," he wrote in "annudder letta wit good news." "Also, my new English teacher read my last two papers in class and praised them a lot and wants me to try to sellum both. He's gonna help me if he can." The good news smoothed the way for a request: "If you can spare it, please send me somewhere around 10 dollars. I'm way in the hole becuz of all kinds fees I had to pay and becuz of that darn fine. That's sure tuff, losing your first deal because of the banks' closing, pop," he added. "I hope you can still make it. I sure got caught broke when the darn banks closed. The papers say street beggars are having an awful time, nobody has even pennies to spare." [118]

Earthquakes were another hazard in Southern California. Cranston described a series of them vividly, using his characteristic abbreviations, and gained perspective from his experiences.

"After Friday's meet, I was guzzling orange juice in the Sugar Bowl downtown when allova sudden the building got the heebie-jeebies. Bob Atkinson, who was with me, and I just sat there for the first 10 seconds, then started to walk out. A couple of other fellahs, not from school, got the idea and darn near trampled us getting out; we felt like socking them, but didn't. All the people in the town were out in the middle of the streets. A fellah driving by stopt and said, 'For Gawd's sake, what's happening?' It sure musta seemed queer to him to be driving along and allova sudden see everybody tear outa the stores. That was sure the worst shock I ever felt. Later that nite I was ata movie in Pomona and allova sudden the ceiling began to creak, the chair to shiver, and the walls to hang way out. Half the people bailed out mighty fast, altho' they were orderly. There were about three shocks while we were there. We swore we'd stay 'till the chandeliers began to hit the ceiling." [119]

He had his "first date in '33 down here, and saw *Of Thee I Sing*. It was sure good. I liked best the election returns they flashed on the screen." Another earthquake that night had frightened people away from the theater, so Cranston and his date were able to get tickets. The Sunday following he joined other students volunteering to "do relief work." "About 20 of us from school went down in the first batch," organized by the American Legion. He also would have a close call.

"I was with a fellow named Bradley, a real estate man of Claremont (formerly from the South, hassa swell accent), and some upper-classmen. I was on duty on my feet on pavement from 12 till 7 p.m., standing near dangerous buildings keeping other people away. There was only one shock while I was there, and it wasn't bad. We were in Huntington Park – I got some keen pictures of the damage. The bricks from the hotel (picture enclosed) killed the manager when she ran outside. After we were relieved, the legionnaires and their wives fed us. They were cooking in a little school house. Some of the legionnaires said this reminded them more of their old army life than anything since the real thing.

"Bradley got a pass from the Huntington Park Police Chief whom he knew, and we went down to Compton and Long Beach where the worst damage was done. Both cities are picketed by sailors and cops, both carrying guns, and it's hard to get in.... Compton was sure ruined. All the people were either living in tents in fields and parks or sleeping in their back yards. We saw lotsa families cooking their dinners out in their front gardens. I saw my first bread line there – only it was for hot soup – about a block long. Then we went to Long Beach – couldn't drive in the heart of the city, so left our car and hiked.... We walked about three miles, and saw all there was to see. Then we were too tired to walk back to the car, so we went to headquarters and pretended we were a detail just relieved. A cop drove us clean back to our car, blowing his siren, and traveling about 60-per down the streets. We reached one crossing at the same time as did an ambulance, a sailor directing traffic waved his arms frantically, but the cop just laffed, and beat the ambulance across the street by some six feet. The ambulance was going faster than 60, it looked like. I'd swiped a red bandana offen a headlight and we put it on our left lite. It made everybody think we were cops, and we went as fast and wherever we wanted.

"This morning about 5 o'clock an earthquake woke us up. No damage done. It's sure funny, fellahs go around the dorm at nite shaking beds – it sure scares the wits out of the occupants. The quake's a terrible thing, of course, but it's sure a keen way to cure Southern Cal's unemployment problem. The whole thing's been wiped out overnight down here, and the R.F.C. [Reconstruction Finance Corporation, 1932 economic recovery program] has found a really worthwhile [cause] to spend their money on. Besides better bldgs. being built, lotsa cash will necessarily be put into circulation by private concerns in the paying for reconstruction, and will thus stir things up. It was funny – I was on duty near where the Bank of America had the front knocked clean out. An old darkey came up to me and said, 'Mistah Roosefelt wouldn open de banks, so de good Lawd sho nuf done it.' I think Roosevelt's sure doing well so far, don't you? He has good ideas and is carrying them out." [120]

Cranston had begun to change his political allegiance to one that would stay with him for life.

The same accounts of his earthquake experiences appeared in Cranston's column March 18, 1933, but he changed the quote slightly for the student paper: "When an old darkey ambled along, and stared into the ruins with rolling eyes, he said, 'De good lawd sho open dat bank in a hurry when he seen Mistah Roosevelt wan't gwine to do it.'" He enjoyed pointing out "a prize boner" by the *Los Angeles Times* which carried three different photos and captions showing the same smashed car. "The hurried editor evidently failed to note that the tell-tale license number was visible in each photo!" Cranston gloated. Again, he filled his column with puns. "Song Hit: 'Buddy, Can you spare Nine Cents – I'll Take the Customary Ten Percent Cut.'" The "worst pun of the year" read: "We hope Mr. Cummings – the new attorney-general – is a short man. It's no time for short Cummings in a place like that." [121]

He also wrote a first-hand story about his earthquake experiences for the Mountain View *Register Leader* that impressed his father. "The following very interesting account of the earthquake…last month was written…by Alan Cranston of Los Altos who is a student in Pomona College and writes from the viewpoint of an 'innocent bystander' and an eye witness," the editor said in a preface to the article. It began:

"The time is 5:55 p.m.; the day Friday, March 10, 1933. The people of Southern California are following their usual habits: storekeepers are just closing up, trains are filled with people hurrying home from the day's work, mothers are calling their children in to dinner from their after-school play. Darkness is closing in on a sultry, oppressive day.

"The writer is raising a glass of orange juice to his lips in a Claremont soda fountain. Suddenly the earth shivers and shakes, an electric light hanging overhead remains stationary as the building sways back and forth uneasily, plate glass windows bend crazily, yet fail to break...." [122]

People had hurried to radios to learn what had "happened to Los Angeles with its gigantic skyscrapers," the account continued. "KFI, the largest station in Southern California, is dead. Hasty dialing locates others already telling the world of a devastating earthquake. 'Long Beach is in complete ruins,' came the first wild report, '1,000 or more killed! Hundreds killed in Los Angeles; property damage inestimable.'"

"A second shock, more violent than the first," followed, he recounted in articulate and professional prose. Seven more major shocks and countless minor ones continued through the night. "Most of the destruction lay in the falling of walls or poorly-constructed buildings.... The fact that nearly every school building in the quake area was injured, many completely demolished, seemed to point to graft in their construction," he reported. "A columnist described the earthquake as 'the first major movement in real estate since 1929,'" but "the throng of people was not an unhappy one; they were even jolly. They had survived the quake safely – what matter if their homes were wrecked?" He described "Views of cheap bedrooms of small apartment houses left suddenly and immodestly bare as the walls slid into the street," and tent cities in Long Beach "filled with homeless people. Other folks were simply wrapped in blankets, trusting California weather not to send any rain. Groups were huddled about bright fires – friends, strangers, peoples of all races thrown together by disaster." The people in the bread line "looked surprisingly merry. The few silent ones were being comforted by the cheerful." He was impressed by how people helped one another, editorializing, "Southern California people should be congratulated for the wonderful way in which they took this disaster. All those who came off easily went speedily to the aid of those hardest hit. Large sums of money were raised, even in these hard times, for aid. The quake was even looked upon as a rather unhappy, tho' efficient, solving of Southern California's unemployment problem, for it made work for thousands of men."

Back at school, although doing all right in other courses, he conceded that "French is hopeless." And "Darn it, that English prof. that liked my themes quit school and I've got now some darn teacher that makes us work like dogs." He wondered what happened "about that poem of R. E.'s you sent to the *Literary Digest* thru Mr. Older?... Didn't they accept it?" "History is the most interesting it's been rite now," he would write in April, "we're reading from a book by Randall called *The Making of the Modern Mind.* Ever heard of it? I like it so much I bought a copy." He had just about finished reading Oscar Wilde's *Dorian Gray* and was "not sure yet" whether he liked it or not. [123]

His running was improving, though. "I'm hot in the sprints rite now, I've beaten Plumb and Alf in every start this week," he reported happily. The coach "Nixon expects me to win all three races" in one meet. At another, he was warned about possible "dirty work" – the coach "had some of us practicing boxing," and one competitor "showed how to give a runner a sock in the kidneys with your fist as you pass him, in case they've done anything dirty to you. You can do it so nobody can see it, and it will knock the other fella outa the race every time." "Junior" Dutton wrote Cranston in April, "I read in the *Call-Bulletin* where 'Alan Cranston swept the sprints for 15 points.' Damned good, you old head. Keep it up & you'll make the Olympic Games yet." [124]

Cranston again talked about his dates. "The girl I took to *Of Thee I Sing* wasn't true to color. A girl I've taken out several times since then is, tho.' She's the first girl I've taken out moren once since I've been here. She's the Dean's daughter – goes to Claremont hi[gh]." [125]

But all was not well with his school work. "I'm ruint in English by getting a new teacher, gosh darn it.... [I]t took me three months to work up into the B class with the darn prof.... Then he had to go and quit school and I get still another teacher, & he gives me nothing but Cs.... What's furthermore, he had to be the one to give us our mid-semester test. In our class of 22 there were 19 Ds or Fs, three Cs and one B. Would you call it a fair test if that's the kind of marks everybody gets? I got a D- and felt lucky." [126]

Another political awakening had spurred him to action.

"Some Reds, seeing as how this is May Day, ran a red flag up the school flag pole early this morning where the Star Spangled Banner belongs, and locked the pulleys so they had to get a carpenter to get it down. They also put posters all over the campus and towns – radical stuff. By a chance remark I over heard, and by a little snooping after that, I learned two students did it, and who they were. Remember that 'KU KLUX KLAN RIDES AGAIN' poster I sent you last fall? It said also at the top, 'Communism will not be tolerated.' I remembered that and dug up one of the posters and typed a warning on it, telling the guys to watch out, that our organization would not tolerate any actions similar to those they did today, and Willie [and I] are going to stick it up on one of the feller's doors tonight." [127]

His suite-mate from the previous semester had run away from school, "taking his stamp collection and portable radio with him. Of our class of about 108 boys, he's the third so far to run away. Two of them left big bills behind. Wurt's the idea of not sending the Sunday comics no more by de laundry?" he added after just finishing "a swell pillow fight."

By late spring, 1933, Cranston was thinking about exotic travel. "Let's go to Cuba this summer instead of Mexico, it would be real interesting there now." He was tantalized by three lectures that he had attended, "all about traveling – exploring. The best one was...telling about bumming all over the world. He's stowed away on about ten different boats." Cranston obviously enjoyed films and saw a number of them, urging his parents to "See the Barrymores in *Rasputin and the Empress* if you get the chance, it's a darn good movie. I sure like Lionel." He was indulging himself in other entertainments, as well. "Norm and I went in to L. A. with exactly .03 cents in our pockets, crashed the Cocoanut [*sic*] Grove, ordered a table and everything, were down on the dance floor for over 10 minutes, and got out without paying a cent. It was a lotta fun. We got a table for four, saying we were going to meet some people at 10:30, it being 10 then. The headwaiter came around tho,' and said even if they didn't show up, we'd have to pay a cover charge for four anyway. We argued with him for about 10 minutes, while we watched Phil Harris sing, etc., and finally let him persuade us to wait out in the lobby. We saw Jack Oakie there." With his friend Willie he "pretty near bought a swell motorcycle for only $12, but some other feller went and paid $15 for it." [128]

He was up to other pranks, too. He and his friend Norm "took up a big collection of money from different frosh and bought Bob Dodge's girl a big rose corsage, without telling him," for a dance. When the victim had to admit that he had not sent it, the girl "was rather cool to him the rest of the evening. Roses are supposed to mean you're about ready to propose to the girl, so everybody stared at the corsage all nite, and…asked Bob what was the idea…. Fellahs told him nobody would go out with him any more becuz they'd think he was engaged…. It was sure funny. He didn't get sore – took it as a joke." [129]

Cranston had registered to take logic-philosophy, history, French, English, psychology and R.O.T.C. the next year. "I considered geography, but it didn't work into the program, and decided against art and astronomy because the labs would interfere with track. I think it's a pretty good course, don't you?" he asked his parents.

That letter was full of observations and dreams. He had met an older student, Peter Nekrasoff, who had been born in Siberia in 1900. He had fled Russia by stowing away on a ship and had even been kidnapped by Soviet agents. The Russian's adventures captivated Cranston, who thought of him as an "older person." His unsympathetic views of communism would educate the American college student "about how Communists weren't so nice."

"Up to Sunday I just knew him to speak to, but Sunday I lay out on the turf with him all morning, and found him to be one of the most interesting persons I've ever met. He grew up in the simple rustic life over there, then the Russian Reds began to stir things up. He was very young when he joined the White army to avoid being forced into that of the Reds. He did a lot of fighting, was promoted, then wounded, lit in a Red prison camp. He was tried for his life for treason by the Revolutionary Tribunal; the fellow before him in the court was sentenced to be shot within 24 hours. Friends, however, gained him his acquittal, provided he would study in a Red school. He thus got into the Red army, had many strange experiences – saw Rasputin in person, saw the blood on the floor where in a dark basement the last of the Romanovs were killed, deserted three times, and finally escaped to the Orient.

"He reached the U. S. as a stowaway, hid in San Francisco so he could not be deported, lying low for the five-year period, and has since been working and now is studying here. Some Soviet spies kidnapped him in S. F. once, but he escaped by jumping from a speeding car. He showed me *Chronicle* clippings telling all about it. He says even now it would be unsafe, probably, for him to return to Russia. Two of his brothers have been executed over there, in 1924. He kept a diary which he had cast into the form of an historical novel with the aid of an American friend. *Atlantic Monthly* wanted to buy it, but they want it to be first published in book form. I'm reading the manuscript of it now, and it's certainly interesting. He's been in all kinds of work – has made many fortunes and lost them again. He has hopes of some day doing engineering work in South America.

"He said nobody's ever lived until they've traveled around the world, doing this and that, anything to get money and see things, but never staying on top too long and always keeping out of a rut. I've heard so many people say that, both people who have done it and people who only wish they had, that I am sure it is right. I'll never be satisfied with my life it I don't travel about and see life in such a way. Peter says nerve is the essential thing, anyone can get anything if he has it and knows how to use it.

"I agree with you, Mother, that discretion and judgment are good things but I *don't* want them to be used in such a way as to 'temper my enthusiasm.' If discretion shows me I'd be risking my neck *too much* to go out into the world to try to see it, taking my chances along with the rest, and not knowing for certain if I'd get breakfast tomorrow morning, I'd lose my enthusiasm and settle down to a soft job and be disappointed in myself the rest of my life, even if I were well off.

"I answered an ad. and got a 3-months subscription to *Writer's Digest* for only two bits, it's a darn good magazine, isn't it? They gave me free their big year-book, too.

"Here's wot I think of making people, unless they plan to be doctors or scientists, take blankety-blank biology:

Sweet is the lore which nature brings;
Our meddling intellect
Mis-shapes the beauteous forms of things:
We murder to dissect.

Wordsworth

"I'd like to show the above to my biology prof., only I'm afraid it might make my mark lower than it already is. (Don't mis-intoipet, I've still got a C in it.)" [130]

Nekrasoff's life so fascinated Cranston that he later wrote up the story, full of fervor about the merits of American democracy – "a land where freedom has never been disestablished" – versus communist Russia. Although Nekrasoff had been a member of the Communist Party, he had "the blood of American liberality in his veins, by transfusion if not birth." Escaping, he had stowed away on a liner to America, and had been able to leap to the dock only after the ship had unloaded cargo and risen in the water so that he could drop downward. He believed that Russian communism gradually would be rejected as capitalism was injected "into the weakening, putrefying socialistic body," Cranston wrote. "If Nikita [Nekrasoff] is right, then the whole world may be in for a surprise.... The black sheep of the world flock" will have "seen the light and softly crept back into the fold." [131]

Cranston had his own economic worries, though – whether a bank in Sacramento had gone "bust with all my money? Thanks a lot for making it up for me. Wot with that and PGE [stock in Pacific Gas & Electric utility company?], I'd sure be wiped out. Willie and John Atkinson have each invested an imaginary thousand bucks in stocks; they buy and sell every day, and are going to see who comes out the best at the end. I'm in the contest, too, but I put my thousand dollars in a bank, and bet them I'd be the richer at the end of the month. From what you said about the bank, Pop, maybe I was wrong after all?" [132]

He had "been reading some of Lincoln Steffen's autobiography again," and told his parents that he would give his Russian friend a ride north when they left school. "I'll get him to stop off at Villa Warec for a couple of days if you like, because I know you'd find him awfully interesting to talk to. He's darn nice, too."

"Here's the last letter from down here for some time. Whoopee," he wrote June 6th at the end of the semester. "So youse don't know wot to give me for my boithday. Well, I do, youse kan give me a five-hundert buck movie camera, see?" he suggested. He added an athletic tidbit: "A fella made an interesting remark in the *Los Angeles Times* today – all the great Negro athletes are either sprinters, broad jumpers or high jumpers. They rarely excel at any other branch of sport. I wonder why?" [133]

During the summer of 1933, he had another story published in the *Register Leader*. It was about police dispatches which listeners "perhaps heard at the bottom of your dial as you sit comfortably before your radio of an evening." He was fascinated by the fact that in Los Altos he could hear Los Angeles police on the radio but not the nearby San Francisco police who had a closed circuit. "This does away with the surprising habit some of our bandits have of outfitting their cars with radios in order to keep tab on the police." He and his friend Norman Sear had followed an L. A. police car one night for half an hour, hoping to hear some exciting dispatch "but luck was against us. Not to be outwitted, we drove to the police station, swaggered in, and announced to the startled desk sergeant that we were criminology students and wanted a ride with the next shift of radio police." They were told that they needed letters from professors and parents to permit them to join the officers. A tour of the station, though, was exciting enough to provide material for a story. They were shown a room stacked with sawed-off shotguns and saw cops loading them for duty watching grocery stores to curb a string of robberies. A special treat was the communications center where reports on criminals were received from all over the nation, and being introduced to the radio dispatcher, one "Mr. Rosenquiz, a fat, pink-cheeked, jolly gentleman. There's humor in him to the very angle of his big, black cigar," Cranston wrote. To their delight, the boys were invited to sit with him. "According to Rosenquiz, the robber hasn't a chance nowadays, when the radio police is on the job. They have made arrests within two minutes of the crime, for when a car happens to be in the neighborhood of a robbery, it can swoop down before the thief has a chance to escape. 'Yes, sir,' says Rosenquiz, 'our record's one minute and forty-five seconds!'… Rosenquiz drones off his announcements in slow, perfect English, but when he tells us stories, he lapses into good old Americanized Irish. He gets real excited while he spins a yarn," Cranston reported, ending with, "Listen to your friend Rosenquiz tonight – he's on the air." [134]

Cranston returned to Pomona in the fall for his sophomore year. "Everybody thot I was going to Stanford, for some reason or other, so I got a fine welcome," he wrote in his first letter home September 26, 1933. "The fellers on the track team seemed especially glad to see me. [Coach] Strahle said I was the only missing link in the chain; everyone, including Plumb, is back." But there was more exciting news to report: "I got the surprise of my life in opening convocation Friday morn when my name was read off as having won the second Jennings prize in English – $25!!!!! Was I happy! It's for improvement in English composition among the boys in the freshmen class each year…. Enclosed is my check…. Please deposit it for me. It'll help me out in my liberal education next year." [135]

Enrollment in the freshmen class had dropped to about eighty men and women each during the Depression, and Cranston found the first weeks tame by comparison to his initiation to college. "There hasn't been much fighting. They [freshmen] carried our baggage in, and that was about all. Don't know wot's wrong. I've tried to stir up some excitement, and last nite some of us took a couple of fellers for rides. Later, about midnight, one of my two accomplices on the second ride was dragged outa his bed by a pile of frosh and thrown into the big fountain in the courtyard. Several people told me today that they met a mob of about ten frosh looking for me, but it's 3:30 now, and I haven't run into them yet."

His record time of 10.5 in a 100-yard dash test still stood. But it "looks like I'm going to hafta study hard this year; they sure assign a lotta work to do." Biology had brought his grade average down with a D, which he could not persuade them to change. He could get any job he wanted "on the *Metate* [the year book]," having "gotten to know the editor, Ruth Willette, a senior, pretty well. I'm not sure if I wanta work on it, tho.'" He subsequently was named one of two editors of the comic section of the yearbook, and feature editor on the college paper, *Student Life*, "one of the ten best positions on the paper!" That was more to his liking. [136]

When another earthquake struck in October, 1933, he and two pals were floating in a pool to escape a heat wave. They had climbed a fence near midnight to get in. "It was keen to float on my back and look up at the full moon above, and all the stars around it. I didn't notice the earthquake at all." He was narrowing his courses and dropped French – a new female teacher was tough. "I really want to learn the language, so have continued studying it some in my spare time. In its place I'm taking 'Elements of Sociology,' described in the catalogue as 'An introduction to the study of society.... Application of sociological principles to modern problems, such as race prejudice and movements of population, urbanization, and neo-Malthusianism, marriage and divorce, poverty and crime, child welfare, leisure time activities.' I think it should prove very useful to me, and so far like it very much." He had made a new friend, an exchange student from the University of Hawaii, Art Chung, "a swell guy, and very interesting. Funny as heck in some of his ideas." Chun, the correct spelling of his name (he was half Chinese, Cranston learned), was a feisty football player although he was small and had not played before, garnering Cranston's admiration. "Mebbe I'll ask him to come up Thanksgiving, he's got no place to go," he told his parents. He craved *Life* magazine, which he asked his parents to send with his clean laundry each week, "Also the *Readers' Digest* when you're thru with it," and "Howzabout some Sunday funnies?" He had gotten a "keen black eye" from a fracas between freshmen and sophomores which ended in a water fight with a fire hose. "Pretty near everybody in our hall got a bill for damage, but I somehow escaped. In the middle of it, I took time out and went for another moonlight swim, with Peter. We surprised four girls that were in. Sure funny." [137]

He and Nekrasoff spent one Sunday afternoon writing a short story for the *Register-Leader*. But "Pop" Smith, the editor, said "that things are so bad he won't be able to pay me for articles for a while. He liked the article Peter and I wrote, tho,' and suggested that we write three or four and send them as a series to some magazine. Seems to think they're saleable. We think we'll try. If we can't sell 'em, we'll let Mr. Smith print 'em for nothing. I guess I'll keep on writing for him once in a while anyway, it's good experience." [138]

He was being courted by several fraternities – "different frat men are always asking me to sit with 'em at dinner. It's a lotta fun" – but he chose not to go to a rush party in San Diego for one "which is noted for its illegal rushing. I was afraid to accept because I'm afraid I'd get blacklisted for a semester." He got six invitations to rush parties out of the eight fraternities on campus. He accepted those to Phi Delta, Sig Tau and Nu Alpha. "Two fellers got more invites than I," including the class president. "I was sure happy to come off so well. I'm pretty sure the Phi Delts will bid me, positive, judging by their actions, that the Nu Alphas will, and the Sig Taus have already told me they want me."

Rushing consumed his nights – "Gee whiz, I don't see how they expect a feller to do any studying around here during fraternity rushing time," he complained. He bowled with one group. "I had the best score one night, and the next to the best the other. It was good, because if there were any fellers in the frat that didn't know me, they heard I was bowling good scores, and came around and watched." His grades were improving, despite the extra-curricular activities. "I got an A, the highest one in the class, in that first psychology test. I like sociology about the best of my courses, I think. I don't like English cause the assignments are awful. The prof. can give us the boringest subjects to write upon. I think it's bad for me, I lose originality when I hafta just sit down and turn out a bunch of words without being interested in them except in so far as I make them meet the requirement and draw a good mark. Mr. Older sent me a copy of the letter he wrote to the editor in Los Angeles," Cranston continued. "It was certainly a swell one, and will serve as a perfect recommendation sometime in the future, even if it doesn't do anything for me right now. Thank him for me. I'll write to him in a few days, too." [139]

But more important and ominous events were evolving that began to command his attention and make him think about his future.

"Our sociology teacher predicts that this will be the worst winter of the last decade. He isn't cheerful about anything, including the NRA [National Recovery Administration]. Things are sure happening over in Europe, aren't they? The prof. ses 'we entered the war to make the world safe for democracy, yet have we ever been further from such a state, with such dictators [as] Mussolini, Stalin, Hitler, and Roosevelt?' If it weren't for the Olympic Games, and my wanting to get thru school by 1936, I'd like to go over to Europe a year before taking my last two years, and mosey around and do a little independent studying of conditions and affairs. I think I might get more out of my last two years if I did that. It's out of the question, tho.'" [140]

Still, he was getting anxious to move on, to see a larger world. He talked about attending the University of Hawaii as an exchange student the following year, an idea posited by Chun. In considering the matter, he assessed his strengths and weaknesses candidly. "I just laughed at him at first, but he began telling me reasons why I oughta do it, 'till I realized it would be a keen thing to do. It would certainly be an experience that would be worth a lot to me.... I'd gain an entirely different kind of education. Think of all the people I'd meet, and the experiences I'd have in their life over there." He could continue his track, might even "be a king over there" with his speeds. “As far as writing is concerned, I’d make a lot of valuable contacts and become better known in general. I’d kind of welcome a change of at least a year from Pomona anyway, and if I could get it that way, without really breaking my contacts here…without getting a class behind, and without losing any eligibility, I think it would be valuable. I get kinda tired of school sometimes, and that would be a complete change without any loss. They have some of the best professors in the world over there. It would also make my school year a lot cheaper for you, Pomona would pay a lot of the expenses….”

“If I really decided on trying for it, I’d better do so in a hurry, so as to get in on the ground floor,” he rationalized. “What do you think of the idea? Hurry up and tell me. It’d be real hard to get, fifteen tried out last year, but I think I’d have a fair chance…. The only thing that might hinder me is that my grades aren’t exceptional, but Chun says he’s going to try to impress on the committee that they should get someone who balances his studies with activities. Last year’s exchange student had a straight-A average, but little else to offer. My track and writing should help a lot…. Write and give me your views, anyhow.”

Cranston obviously was popular, and his letters home frequently discussed his friends and social life. After pressure to join other fraternities, he pledged Sigma Tau. “I had a heckova time deciding which to join…. The Sig Taus heard there was a bunch going one way, and that I kind wanted to be in the same frat as Willie, so they had a special meeting after dinner Thursday and bid Willie…I think we got the best bunch, taken as a whole, of any of the frats.” His track colleague Plumb “and a bunch of other Phi Deltas came up about midnight Thursday and tried to persuade Chuck and me to change our minds, we wavered a little, but finally stuck to Sig Tau…. It’s pretty much of a football bunch, the captain and a lotta the other players belong…. President Edmund’s son belongs …. Initiation started yesterday, we hadda go up in the cabin and work. It was the best fun I’ve had in a long time, we fooled around a lot, and most of us got paddled some.” He and Willie were paddled again the the next morning for being late getting up when their alarm did not go off. “We’re called worms at present,” and had to dig up the crawly creatures as part of the initiation which also included not smiling or referring “to ourselves with a personal pronoun. If we wanta leave, we hafta say: ‘It wants to go to its room.’ Maybe you think that isn’t hard to do. For any violations, we get paddled…. I’m third in no. of swats taken so far. I can’t keep a straight face and keep getting it for laughing. It sure hoits, but the worst is yet to come.” A week later he reported that he “didn’t get kilt in the final frat initiation. A bill for 15 bucks for the pin purty nearly kilt me, tho.’” [141]

“Thanks for the dope about seeing that editor,” he continued in the same letter, promising to do so. He then asked his mother to find a story that he had written “about stocks called either ‘Live Market’ or ‘A Venture in Stocks.’ I’d like it for several purposes pdq. It’s typed, and two pages long. Thanx. My clippings book is here.”

“Evidently neither of you think so much of the Hawaiian idea,” he went on, trying to counter concerns that they had expressed. His mother had cautioned that the islands’ hot climate was conducive to laziness and worried about other distractions. Art Chun refuted those arguments.

"He claims only certain types of people get lazy over there, and I'd be too darn busy, as an exchange student, to have any time to even think of getting lazy. Authorities would be seeing to it that I didn't play around too much. I think I'd really gain in drive.... [T]his is as enervating a climate as any right here. I've seen plenty of people come here with lots of energy and ambition, find they don't hafta study much to get by, and start sitting around or lying in bed listening to a radio all the time... I don't think sex interests could be any more dangerous there than here. I've had plenty of opportunities to 'go wrong' if I wanted to.... I don't think I've had any professors that are really remarkable enuf so that I'd think there was much chance of finding them worse elsewhere....

"I think the most I've gotten out of college comes from other than academic sides, and that would be developed more than ever if I were an exchange student.... Exchanging to any other place, Bordeaux or elsewhere, is impossible, and if I *have* an opportunity to exchange to one place, I should think it would be worthwhile. Hawaii is a real big university, and a year in such a large one might kind of balance my years in this exceedingly small one. Anyhow, write me some more answers."

Meanwhile he led a movement to improve the student paper. His powers of persuasion, if not always successful with his parents, were beginning to manifest themselves with his peers. "I got tired of the *Student Life* being such a rotten paper, it's been nothing but a bulletin board – a plain statement of facts and advertisements – and started some agitation for having a real feature page, or at least several features. At first the editor didn't like the idea, but I got a lotta people on my side and finally got it across at a meeting held last night. Starting next week we're going to have a real feature page, and I'm in charge of working it up. It's gonna be a lotta fun. That's the only part of the paper I'm really interested in. I'll probably become a columnist again! Several people have told me I could get the job of editor next semester, but I don't think I want it. For one thing, it wouldn't leave any time for anything else, and another, I'd hafta be up pretty late every nite, and it's during track season. It's worth a hundred and fifty dollars, but the heck with it." [142]

In his column – "which will appear every now and then, Lord help you," he joked in the first one November 16, 1933 – "we'll do our best to tell you of all the quips and slips and jests and gestures worth repeating, and, well, all the lowdown in general that we can get our hands on." He made fun of a student who was "reported to have written in a recent ex[am], 'Luther was condemned a heretic at the feast of worms,' and of another who remarked that 'the Constitution says that no free man shall be handed twice for the same offense.'" He also listed license numbers of students' cars that were "hidden here and there in secluded" *rendezvous* sites for dates. He ended with, "Puh-leeze don't complain too hastily about this column to Editor [Dick] Nimmons. The *Student Life* may be wasting room on us, but think of all the readers that get bored for nothing." [143]

His home-town newspaper took note of Cranston's potential, saying in an article, "Alan will make his mark as a writer before very much longer." Another mention on January 12, 1934, reported that "Alan Cranston, now a sophomore at Pomona College, has been appointed Editor of a feature page," the highlight of which was his column "concerning prominent persons and situations on the campus." It also cited three track events that he had won in the 100-, 220- and 440-yard dashes at an "all-conference meet." [144]

His forays into newspaper writing were sparked by his reading books by famous war correspondents, editors and travel writers including Richard Halliburton's *A Royal Road to Romance* (1925) and Vincent Sheean's accounts of being a foreign correspondent in *Personal History* (1935). Such reading was encouraged by Fremont Older. Cranston also no doubt was inspired by the film *Foreign Correspondent*, loosely derived from Sheean's book, directed by Alfred Hitchcock and issued in 1940 just as war was breaking out in Europe. It was dedicated "to those intrepid ones who went across the seas to be the eyes and ears of America…like recording angels among the dead and dying." It also had a heroine (played by Laraine Day) heading a "Universal Peace Party" who responded to a skeptical correspondent (Joel McCrea), asking, "What makes you think an organization like this, made up of well-meaning amateurs, can buck up against those tough military boys of Europe?" by saying, "It's the well-meaning amateurs, as you call them, who go out and do the fighting when the war comes, isn't it?" Cranston early on decided that journalism "was a very glamorous life" in which one could experience "the fascinating things that were going on in the world," and made up his mind to be a foreign correspondent. "That became, really, my first ambition." It also whetted an interest in foreign affairs and preventing wars. [145]

His desire to go to Hawaii, though, had sparked more concern at home. "Where'd you get the idea I don't like Pomona, Mother? I just said I didn't know how I'd like to spend four years in a row here. In some ways it seems kind of isolated way out here in the desert…. I'm glad, tho,' to have spent my first two years here. I don't think I could have been as well off anywhere last year as I was here. I don't know what to do next year, that darn track stuff sure puts me in a hole as far as leaving permanently. There's no use worrying about it now, anyway." [146]

He was becoming discerning about his own abilities and the quality of the teaching that he was getting. He complained that for the first time in his life, he liked "English the least of any course" he was taking. "It isn't because I'm getting bum marks, because I'm getting a B-plus average, so that does away with that theory. There's some dumb clucks in the class, and all the prof. does is spend his time trying to improve them. He suits his assignments to them – the last two weeks have been spent making outlines for articles. If there's anything I hate, it's that. This morning…he showed how to make a bibliography, and would take five minutes, for instance, to show how a quotation should be marked in a paper. I learned that, and everything else he's shown us so far, the first year of high school."

He mentioned a girl named Betty – possibly Betty Bond, a reporter on the student newspaper, whom he took to a formal dance at Mission Inn in Riverside. "It was swell, I don't think there could be a better place in California for such a dance. Lotsa people told me afterwards they thot Betty was the prettiest girl there, and I was cussed out plenty for not trading dances…. She's not particularly like anyone else you or I know. Her only fault is that she's near-sighted as ten bats. She isn't very tall, but tall enuf. She won't go out with me as often as I ask her because she says she's got a rule she won't go out with any one feller too much." She, too, was interested in writing and had composed a poem to inaugurate the student newspaper's feature section. They had seen the film *Lady for a Day* and liked *My Weakness* and Maurice Chevalier's new movie. "We also heard Lucrezia Bori, the opera singer, when she was here on the Artists' Course program last week. She's pretty good, but doesn't compare to Lily Pons. How come you didn't like *Showboat* so much, Mother? Do youse think I oughta see it when it comes south?" He did, a few weeks later, and "liked it a lot, the best show I've seen in a long time. The chorus is wonderful, I thot. I also saw Mae West's latest, *I'm No Angel*, and liked it even better than the first one she made." [147]

He had gotten an F in his first history exam, he slipped into one letter, but he had gone to see the editor to whom his father had referred him for a job interview. They "had a long talk," but "the only job he could give me would necessitate quitting school, and even then I'd have to hang around perhaps two or three months before getting on. The job would be cub-reporting. He said nearly every successful writer in America started out in that status. He told me to drop around once in a while, which I'll do." [148]

By the end of November the "history prof. sed I'm doing better. Logic has been hard as heck up to now," but "a new part starting tomorrow...should prove a lot easier." What he did enjoy was working on the feature page and writing his columns for the student newspaper. The first feature page "got ruint by a big telephone ad. that had to go on that page that day. I was pretty sore at first, but my column was printed okay, and went over swell, so I got over it." Betty's poem also was a hit, and she had been given a regular job of writing one for the page each week. [149]

Cranston's parents, however, had taken matters of his future education in hand, scotching the Hawaiian idea. Cranston sent his transcript to an official at Stanford and was "Glad to hear that he was so encouraging. It's sure lucky you know all those people, Pop. How soon do you think they'll let me know definitely? I hope sometime next week so I can clear things up down here before leaving," he wrote December 7, thanking them for the Stanford catalogue. "I think they're some darn good courses listed in it. Who is handling the journalism department now?" he asked. He recognized the name of "the feller who's been winning most of the hundreds in Stanford's fall practice [track] meets, Thoms.... I'll be in stiff competition if I come to Stanford." [150]

A week later, he could write, "I was very glad to hear everything was OK with my transcript. I got to work on the honorable dismissal right away, and will probably get it off today or tomorrow. That history professor I told you about tried to spill the apple cart, but I'm around him now, I think. When I really came down to leaving, it was hard in some ways, but I'm sure I'm doing what I'll like the best.... Telling [coach] Strahle was the hardest thing of all, but I got it over with yesterday. He showed himself to be a swell guy." As to living arrangements at Stanford, "I think I prefer to live at home for at least the winter quarter, for several reasons." [151]

That would be his last letter from Pomona. He transferred to Stanford in the middle of his sophomore year, and at last was where his family expected him to be, possibly helped by his father's ability to pull strings to get him accepted in spite of what apparently were not outstanding grades from his first year and a half at college.

Entering Stanford in January, 1934, Cranston quickly became active on campus and joined Sigma Nu fraternity. He wrote for the campus paper, but was not on dance or social committees or in such things as the drama club. He described himself as a "grind" who studied, haunted Palo Alto book stores and "was constantly in training." [152]

An early political activity turned out to be controversial. He ran a campaign for a queen of the Masque Ball, Helen Ramming, a benefit for the Stanford Convalescent home, and managed to raise a previously unsurpassed sum of $391. To promote her candidacy, he went to the extravagance of hiring an airplane to write her name across the sky. Ramming, though, had the dubious sobriquet of "bedroom eyes" and was not a sorority member. When Cranston's campaign tactics appeared to be winning, sororities put together their own candidate and managed to raise a winning $860. Cranston was criticized for his publicity stunt, which he defended in the *Stanford Daily* as having been a success. "The end justifies the means," he said, a philosophy that he would apply to future objectives. [153]

Because Cranston transferred in the middle of his sophomore year, he was prohibited, under rules, from competing in track his first year at Stanford. "I could practice with the team but couldn't compete," Cranston said of the technicality that made him ineligible for Pacific Coast Conference competition in 1934. The ruling came when he entered a Santa Barbara relay as an "unattached" athlete to get around the ineligibility. A Stanford paper reported some "opinions that it was an extremely technical [ruling], which was unfair to the athlete who might have violated the letter but not the spirit of conference rules." A University of California coach was quoted as saying, "Cranston was certainly declared ineligible on a technicality.... As far as I am concerned, I regard Cranston just as eligible as any of my own athletes. He has not violated the spirit of the rule." The set-back for Cranston would be only temporary. [154]

The Stanford track coach was Dink Templeton, a three-time Olympic team winning coach and legend whom Cranston greatly admired and was close to until Templeton's death in 1962. Cranston liked to tell how he learned from a famous San Francisco lawyer and Lowell High School classmate's of his father's, Jesse Steinhart, that Templeton might have been a notable attorney (he received a law degree from Stanford) but for his love of athletics and coaching young men. The story about Templeton's brilliance impressed Cranston: Templeton heard that the professor giving oral examinations required for law-school graduation would open a book at random, bend it back and ask a question from whatever page came up so students could never know in advance what would be asked. Templeton found out what book the professor used, got into his office and bent the book against the spine "so that it almost surely would open to that page. He then learned everything on that one page. When he went in for his exam, the professor opened it to that page, asked some question and Dink gave a perfect answer to it," Cranston laughed of Templeton's ingenuity. Templeton would have a big influence on Cranston's track career. [155]

Cranston focused on the 440, not being quite fast enough to win the 100-yard dash in college. His best 440 time was 48.3 seconds. As a 100-yard sprinter, his best time was 09.9 seconds. In his junior and senior years, 1935 and 1936, he was a member of a winning mile-relay team that competed in West Coast Relays (it finished second to U.S.C.). Cranston ran the second leg. Theirs was the fastest mile-relay team in the nation in 1936 with a time of 3:15.5. Cranston would win two letters in track at Stanford. A highlight was beating world-record-holder Ben Eastman in two out of three 440 races. Cranston always reminded reporters that Eastman was "out of his prime" at the time, but "it was a big thrill, regardless." One of his treasures was "a newspaper photo which appeared the day after I beat him. The heading over the picture read, 'When the Mighty Eastmen bit the dust.' It was a thrill I'll always treasure." [156]

At one point, it was rumored that Templeton planned to leave his Stanford coaching post to go into the newspaper business. Cranston saved the clipping, which protested that Templeton's leaving would be "an outrage," no doubt Cranston's own feelings. "[T]he man IS Stanford, when you're speaking of sports. Stories of boys who held no previous promise and who became champions under him would fill books." Little did Templeton know that one of them would be a U. S. Senator. [157]

Cranston by 1935 was laying out plans for his immediate future. Options that he recorded in his small script under the heading "After College" included travel, writing and marriage. One revealed a special interest in the 1936 presidential election, reflecting his concern that something like dictatorship might happen in America.

"1. Land in Europe as a member of the American Olympic team or otherwise. After track visit England and see how its marvelous government functions – my knowledge of Germany and Austria should already be [formulated?]; then get into Russia and see how it is ticking; then get into the Orient and look over China and Japan (this leaves South America as the one place I know little about, but I guess it can come later). This much should have taken a year. Then return to America and bum around the country for anywhere up to a year learning it inside and out. Then I should be ready for marriage and whatever line of work I seem best suited for by then. Must keep writing all this time, which should be no longer than two years at most.

"2. If I become a *great* track man, turn pro or run in the indoor winter season of '36-'37 for publicity, and keep studying all this time under 'Year-Day Program,' and write plenty. Under this plan I might have enuf dough by summer of '37 to get married and see the world with a wife (but this part of the plan is inferior to the rest).

"3. If the presidential campaign proves to be as important as the turning point between democracy & dictatorship in the U. S., stay in the U. S. to watch it, attending national conventions, etc." [158]

Cranston did make a try, in his senior year (1936), for the Olympics, which were to be held in Berlin. "I've suddenly realized how much I have to win if I can get in those Games and be momentarily famous," he wrote Doris Atkinson. A tough competitor was Archie Williams, an African-American runner on the University of California team whom Cranston barely beat once in 1936. (Williams would go on to join the Olympic team, win a gold medal in the 400, at 46.5 seconds, and become Olympic quarter-mile champion that year.) Cranston, however, failed to qualify in western regional tryouts, a disappointment that had a big effect on him. "I *should* have been on the U. S. Olympic team," he reflected years afterward. "I was good enough to be on it, but I just didn't concentrate enough. I fell short of my own mental and physical discipline and failed in my goal. I wasn't that serious at that time, for various reasons, and I just didn't make it. In retrospect – from the point of view of what I've done with my life – it was probably a good thing it happened. It was a *big lesson* to me – if you don't concentrate, you won't do what you want to do. I learned that lesson. I promised myself I would never let that happen again." It was a lesson that he would need in ways that he could not imagine in 1936. He would later write, "What I learned in victory and defeat in those athletic days served me well" for a career built on ruthless competition. [159]

It was Cranston's obsessions with girl friends and other interests, though, that prevented his making the Olympic team, teammate Bob Atkinson thought. "If Alan had concentrated and avoided feminine distractions, he would have become a world-class quarter-miler." But Cranston's exploits made him human and likeable to his mates. [160]

On the Stanford track team, Cranston met a unique young man with unorthodox political views. Lars Skattebol, a blond fellow of Nordic ancestry whom Cranston dubbed the "albino," was focused on social revolution at a young age when he already had decided to become a writer and reformer. He admired muckraking journalists. Cranston had never met anyone like him, and was greatly impressed. "Ideas flew out of Lars like chaff from a threshing machine, interspersed with wit, literary allusions and spell-binding references to his seamy past," Eleanor described him in a first draft of her brother's biography. "I became interested in issues as I went to college," Cranston said of the friendship, and Skattebol "had a lot of influence on me, in thinking about politics and reading some liberal books like Upton Sinclair's and Frank Norris' novels, and so forth. So by the time 1936 came around, I liked [Franklin] Roosevelt and what he was doing as president to help people who needed help." His father, though, turned "purple with the mention of F. D. R.'s name," and disliked and distrusted Skattebol, believing him a Communist and irresponsible. Skattebol, in turn, told Cranston, in effect, "Your friends and your folks are totally parasitical. I'm a proletarian genius who's going to shake up the world!" He kept copious penciled notes on his extensive reading in shoe boxes, a habit that Cranston adopted. [161]

"He kept me thinking!" Cranston wrote in his diary of Skattebol's amazing knowledge, boastfully exhibited in quotes that ran through his conversation about the economic Depression that had brought much of the nation to its knees. Skattebol explained President Roosevelt's government programs to Cranston, and told him about the League of Nations and disputes over national sovereignty versus imperialism. "Most vivid California memory of Ethiopian War," Cranston recorded in one of his notes. "Lars and I were climbing into the Chevie on the circle [on campus]. A newsboy rushed up with a paper about the League's voting sanctions. Lars cried: 'That's the greatest thing that's ever been done!!!'" The two began to collaborate on articles for journalism courses, Cranston's discipline complementing Skattebol's inspiration, and began to plot travel to places where they could find work as reporters. [162]

Cranston indeed was intellectually disciplined from an early age. In June, 1935, he wrote out a daily program for himself that also manifested his humor:

"9:00 a.m.	Stay in bed. ["Study memory course" was crossed out.]
10:00	Go thru quotation book.
11:00	Read "Outing [?] of Man's Knowledge" or some such.
12:00	Exercise
1:00 p.m.	Eat.
2:00	Write essay one day, short story next, part of novel next.
4:00	Exercise.
5:00	Go thru dictionary learning words (organize a system of use).
5:30	Read anything.
7:00	Eat
8:00	Raise hell & sleep." [163]

By May of 1936, his "day program" had him "get up, run mile or swim" at six a.m., read and study between 6:45 and eight, eat in fifteen minutes, than go "thru quotation book – paraphrasing, quoting, getting story and essay ideas, making epigrams, etc." At nine a.m. he would read in French, German or Spanish, then read and study in English from ten to one o'clock. In the afternoon he was to study the Oxford Dictionary, "write something," "play" between 4:30 and 6:30, eat in half an hour, then "study music" and read. At 11:30, he would "sleep and love." "Fridays and Saturday nights off, Sunday free." [164]

He also exhorted himself to "Once every six months, say July 1 and January 1, write a long paper telling what America is doing and what life is like, just as tho' I [were] writing it in 1950 to describe life in the U. S. in 1935. Touch upon politics, clothes, current interests, etc. Might write one for the world, too. Could make it [a] story – like by inserting prophecy, (as tho' writing in 1950), like: 'Abyssinia, since dead, was opposing Italy with lions.'" [165]

He laid out an ambitious reading program for himself. "For God's sake, get and read: *Political and Economic Democracy* by the professors of the university in exile, edited by Max Ascoli and Fritz Lehmana, W. W. Norton and Company," he wrote on one of his cards. "It answers such questions as, to what extent are the new developments of economic democracy compatible with the institutions of political democracy? How can economic democracy be established without destroying political democracy? How far can government control extend without undermining political freedom?" "Get quotation book," another note said, "study it in Lars' manner, picking out ones to paraphrase, to associate differently and to memorize." "Study derivatives of words…don't pick out fantastic words, but words that have meaning," "Study Fowler's *Book of Modern English Usage*," "Learn New Testament backwards and forwards, upside down and sideways" were directions to himself on other note cards. One said, "Study law – learn law to argue." [166]

Cranston's literary choices were strong novels with historic settings and political messages, often innovative in style. French literature that he checked off, presumably as having been read, included Anatole France's satirical, historical novels *Penguin Island* (which contained a chapter on the French Dreyfus Affair) and *At the Sign of the Reine Pédauque.* Rabelais and Flaubert's *Madame Bovary* also were listed. Under Russian literature, he checked *Sabine*, a novel by Mikhail Petrovich Artzybashev, condemned by the Soviets after the 1917 Russian Revolution. Under English literature, he checked Frank Swinnerton's *Nocturne*. Beside Alexander Pope's *Essay on Man* he wrote, "for Lars." He placed double XXs beside James Joyce's *Portrait of the Artist as a Young Man.* Also listed were Samuel Butler's *The Way of All Flesh* and *Erewhon.* Under U. S. A. he checked Theodore Dreiser's *The Genius* and listed James Cabell's *The Silver Stallion.* Under Chinese, he listed poetry translations by Arthur Waley and the poetry of Li Po. He put double XXs by Edward Powys Mathers' translation of *Coloured Stars: Fifty Asiatic Love Poems* (Mathers also translated the French version of *Arabian Nights*). [167]

A "list of things to know about" was categorized under "to be a good writer" and "to know vital things about what makes the world tick." "To be a good writer" required study of "religion, architecture and art, history, music, world literature." To understand what made the "world tick" required knowledge of "political & general philosophy, science (what it may accomplish), education, understand[ing] the 'personalities' of the important countries of the world." Another directive was to "Read best books supporting capitalism, and best ones attacking socialism, pdq." On the issue of religion, he asked himself to "Compile a list of reasons for a more divine belief," citing "love, existence of the world and mankind, a use for everything, desires to obtain something more than money, to achieve good that our own eyes will never see." [168]

In addition to track, his other major extra-curricular activity was the *Stanford Daily*, for which Cranston tried out in his first term there. One of his tryout articles predicted that the campus lake, "Laguanita, despite the pessimistic predictions of the past few weeks, may, after all, be filled!" The instructor wrote "Don't use ! [exclamation] point" after the opening sentence, but graded the item "A-" with a "good lively style" and "good lead," despite the mundane subject. Another tryout piece dealt with "A cure for flat tires." "An Encina youngster, so the story goes, was driving through the hills Tuesday afternoon with his Roble [Paso Robles] heart throb" when "Bang! The left rear tire had passed its days of usefulness," Cranston's lead ran. The instructor also graded that piece "A-" and dubbed it a "good feature." Cranston saved only four samples of his writing for the *Daily* but he did manage to get on the staff. [169]

An article printed in the *Register-Leader* March 2, 1934, recounted with humor his first experience crossing the border into Baja, Mexico, with two friends. "[W]e dropped off the smooth California highway onto the rough, boulder-dotted Mexican road," filled with pools of water and mud. "Charlie attempted to count the Mexicans he saw leaning on fence posts during the trip, but lost count somewhere upwards of three thousand. His investigation, however, proves rather conclusively that it is the national stance," Cranston joked. When they offered the *maitre d'* at a casino in Agua Caliente an "ancient Mexican bank note," and asked if it were still legal tender, the man "boomed in a sonorous tone: 'No, that was good previous to the third from the last revolution.'" The elegant dress of those at the roulette table impressed them. "Charlie was prompted to remark that this must be the mecca for those retreating from Hitler's Germany rather than Palestine, as is the popular belief." Just before departing for home, they put all their "wealth, amounting to the grand sum of three dollars and twenty-five cents, upon the red color" and, to their astonishment, won. [170]

Cranston would fulfill his dream to travel overseas between his junior and senior years. He was anxious to get going, writing in May, 1934,

"Imagine – I don't know where I'll be a month from now. All I know is, I'll be free as that wind dancing through the poplars outside the house, free as I've never been free before, three months to do whatever I wish, $500 to do it with, three months of adventure seeking.... A month from today, who knows?" [171]

"After dozens of trips to San Francisco, and as many phone calls, pulling all possible wires," Eleanor wrote in her biography, "he succeeded in getting a job on a Standard Oil tanker." "I'll be a sailor for twenty days – Oh, man!" Cranston recorded.

He hoped to use his correspondent skills and carried press credentials from the *Register-Leader*, which duly reported June 14, 1934, that Cranston was en route to Los Angeles "where he expected to take a boat for New York by way of the canal," from whence he would sail to Europe with his friend Vincent "Vinnie" Meyer of Los Altos, and "try to send the *Register-Leader* letters from time to time, in which he will give us some of his impressions of conditions as he finds them on the other side." (Cranston's parents also were spending the summer in Europe.) He booked cheap passage across the Atlantic and would travel through France, Austria and Germany. [172]

Cranston compiled a "Travelogia, consisting of the manuscripts, first draft, of my Journey to Europe and Back in the summer of the year of 1934, written for publication in the Mountain View *Register-Leader*." On the cover he drew a sunset over mountains and a flowing river, and quoted *The Vagabond* by Robert Louis Stevenson –

"Give to me the life I love,
Let the lave go by me,
Give the jolly heaven above
And the byway nigh me.
Bed in the bush with stars to see,
Bread I dip in the river –
There's the life for a man like me,
There's the life for ever." [173]

He sent his first dispatch from Paris. "At the moment, I am achieving one of my lifelong ambitions," he wrote to *Register-Leader* editor "Pop" Smith. "I am sitting in a dingy little room in the Latin Quarter of Paris, on the Left Bank of the Seine, writing something for publication! Writers and students…live along these narrow, twisting streets, working by day (now and then, at least) and making merry in the tiny cafes at night" – (he scratched out, "often have I seen them portrayed in movies") – "and at last, for the moment, I am one of them!"

"Vinnie and I wandered in and out of the narrow streets for hours when we arrived less than a week ago, looking for a typical, cheap hotel. After climbing countless rickety stairways, viewing numerous beds which we felt were surely already well inhabited, and haggling in broken French with ever and ever so many excitable concierges, we came upon the Hotel de la Gironde, where, on the third floor, we secured a room "*avec un grand lit*" (with a double bed), for eight francs a night, or fifty-six cents. Our abode is scarcely a block from the Seine, and by craning our necks from our window and peering down little Rue de Savoie, we can see one of the towers of Notre Dame set against the sky." [174]

"Awakened by an accordion…and by Vinnie's growls at the lack of running water in our spacious room, I joined the latter in a breakfast of six peaches at the corner fruit market. It is impossible to secure a man-sized breakfast in France," the published version continued. "I wandered up the Seine, here and there examining a book in one or another of the stalls which line the parapets of the Quais, until I came to the famous Pont Neve [*sic*, Pont Neuf], where I crossed to the Isle de la Cité, the tiny island often called the eye of Paris. Here is...where Julius Caesar and his host took over the home of the Parisii; here was built a Roman palace on a tiny island surrounded by fields and waste." His interest in history came through in other descriptions, like the fact that the bronze statue of Henry IV was made "from two statues of Napoleon which were ordered melted by Louis XVIII in one of those ironical jests which monarchs seem so often to enjoy." At Nötre-Dame de Paris, "I listened to one guide's murderous description of the beautiful stained-glass windows, and then removed myself to a spot where I could enjoy my own thoughts on the subject." He climbed one of the cathedral's towers and "wondered if Victor Hugo's Quasimodo did not once wildly ring this very" bell. [175]

He then "indulged in a little Parisian habit," drinking wine at a street cafe "and watched all Paris walk by: white men, black men, yellow men (a few); long-haired artists and ragged beggars; gaudily-painted women, and gray-haired women in black; little kids skipping along; dogs, cats and pigeons hopping." His waiter, "with the faculty which every Frenchman whom it may benefit has developed of recognizing Americans...followed the usual custom of short-changing *le Americain*." Cranston "evened the score by eloping with a roll while [the waiter] was filling another's order."

The letter ended with news that would have a major impact on Cranston's holiday, and life. "I hoped to write more of Paris, but must wait till later. This morning's papers bear news of the assassination of [former Austrian Chancellor Engelbert] Dollfuss, and Vinnie and I are leaving Paris for Vienna (we hope) late this afternoon. We were able to obtain tickets only as far as Munich in Germany, but hope to get into Austria from there. At any rate, we should see plenty of action along the German-Austrian border. All Paris is agog over yesterday's events," and many tourists were canceling trips to Austria, he reported. "Yours till Munich, and in great (very great) haste."

Dollfuss, who as chancellor had tried to keep Austria independent, had been forced from power in February by the rising National Socialist party and on July

25, 1934, was murdered by Nazis at Hitler's order. The killers had been arrested and were to be tried. Cranston got to Vienna and to his astonishment, was able to get into the courtroom when seasoned journalists were prevented from doing so. He sent a first-hand account to the local paper. "We have particular delight in presenting to the readers of the *Register-Leader* today the accompanying account of the world-famed, history-making trial of the murderers of Chancellor Dollfuss… written by one of our own 'boys,' Alan Cranston of Los Altos, graduate of our local high school," the editor wrote in a preface. The story, "which Alan has written so splendidly here, is undoubtedly the only absolutely true and unbiased report of that famous trial that has ever been printed in any newspaper in the world," and deserved wider circulation (it was reprinted in at least one other newspaper, as was a second article that Cranston sent from Vienna). [176]

Cranston boasted that his local newspaper "had more representatives…than any other paper or syndicate in the world!" by virtue of his and Meyer's "and another chap we picked up somewhere" having "inveigled our way into the court room…by various and nefarious use of" the *Register-Leader*'s business card "and a note from a UP [United Press] photographer which we got stamped by the President of Police." A *London Daily Mail* reporter told them that gaining admission to the court had taken him an hour. But Cranston had succeeded with only his hometown paper's business card "and plenty of the good ole American Boy spirit!" his editor exulted. "We hope to have more of these dandy letters from Alan in succeeding issues." [177]

"We are sitting in a tiny little room, hidden in the heart of the Landesgericht building in Vienna, where the murderers of Chancellor Dolfuss [*sic* – he spelled it incorrectly throughout] are about to be tried for their lives," Cranston's account began. "The moment is a tense one; the judges are to enter the room at any moment, and then will begin a trial which will be notorious in history from this day on." A Viennese reporter who took an interest in the two Americans whispered helpful tidbits to them – the trial would rely on rules not used "since the old days of the Austro-Hungarian monarchy" (three military and one professional judge would preside), and the verdict was assumed to be death, "carried out exactly three hours after is it pronounced." His musings were cut short by the entrance of the judges and two Austrian soldiers, between whom, "proudly erect, is a tiny, sandy-haired, nice-looking little fellow, dressed in military breeches and a prison tunic." That was Plannetta, who had shot Dollfuss, the Viennese whispered. He was followed by another Nazi prisoner, "as nice-looking as the first, equally composed, similarly as dwarfed by his guards," Cranston continued. The second man was Holzweber, "leader of the Putsch," Cranston learned. "I think that this inoffensive little chap, holding himself so soldier-like as he sits facing Plannetta, would look actually scholarly, behind those *pince-nez* spectacles, were it not for his sun-bronzed cheeks," he wrote. "His hair is curly and brown, his features are clean-cut; neither of these men is the 'hired assassin' the Paris papers described as participating in the uprising." [178]

Cranston put himself in the prisoners' places, and throughout his account, had a certain sympathy for them, possibly because he identified with their youthfulness. Both men were in their early thirties, Plannetta was Catholic, Holzweber Evangelical, according to testimony. They had been with 144 Nazis who had stormed the chancellery July 25 when Dollfuss had been shot. Plannetta was pointed out as the one who did the deed. "The Nazi nervously wiggles his fingers, and twists his face up at the ceiling, while every eye in the room is upon him," Cranston recorded. When the prosecutor demanded the death penalty, both prisoners "seemed as unmoved as anyone in the room." Cranston was astounded to learn that the defense attorneys had only been given the cases an hour before and had not "as yet, spoken a word to their clients!" The public prosecutor was "a fussy old man who evidently has his heart set on hanging the men this very night." Cranston continued to be impressed by the prisoners' coolness, Plannetta answering charges "in a clear, strong voice," now and then stating "*Das weiss ich nicht* [That I do not know]." "What a horrible nightmare this must seem to this little man who, as he stands there with his back to us, could be mistaken for a youth of seventeen or eighteen," Cranston thought. "Four feet above his head hangs a brilliant chandelier, which casts weird shadows about the room and must almost blind this little man so directly below it."

"Suddenly a bird, joyful and free, sings its last notes of the day out there in the courtyard, 'Poor Sinner's Courtyard,' where many men, charged with lesser crimes than his, have died," as Cranston described it. Plannetta, he noticed, was "apparently unmoved; no one else makes a sign, but everyone must wonder if this is the swan song for this Nazi rebel." His defense was that he shot Dollfuss accidentally "when someone jostled his arm and the gun went off." The prosecutor said no one could be expected to believe that. Next it was Holzweber's turn. He stood "like a soldier posing for a picture," Cranston related, and his replies were less faltering than his colleague's. Both men had been told by superiors "to spill no blood," Holzweber testified. The "courtroom buzzes with excitement" when Minister Emil Fey, who had been held prisoner by the insurgents, arrived (he was rumored to be a possible successor to the deposed Dollfuss). Before testifying, "a strange swearing-in ceremony takes place," Cranston wrote, in which two large candles on either side of a crucifix were lit, in front of which Fey took an oath. He revealed that the insurgents had been promised exodus to Germany if they had given up, which promise had not been honored. "Then comes sudden, intense drama as Holzweber jumps to his feet and demands of Fey, 'Did you not give us your word of honor as an officer?'" Fey slowly turned and looked "down upon the little man, disdainfully, coldly. Holzweber, dwarfed by the man he so bravely confronts, stands there, eyes blazing, like a fighting cock about the spring into action." Fey admitted that he told the prisoner "you could rely upon the agreement," at which point the Viennese reporter began to whisper excitedly to Cranston.

But the prosecutor dealt "a severe blow to the defense" by changing the line of questioning. Dollfuss' servant seemed to corroborate Plannetta's story of an accidental gun discharge. By then it was late into the night and lawyers were complaining of not having eaten since mid-day. "I wonder if Plannetta and Hozweber will not, perhaps, see the sun once more; or will the trial, already such an unusual, weird one, run on to a finish in the dark hours of early morning?" Cranston speculated. But just after midnight the trial was adjourned until the next morning. Cranston, unable to get into the crowded courtroom this time, was forced to sit in the hall "with twenty other frantic reporters, grinding our teeth and praying for a recess." A number of international correspondents by then had flown in to cover the trial. At the first break, Cranston and Meyer rushed inside, and heard the defendants condemned for treason as well as murder. Cranston noted that the prisoners were "every bit as calm today as they were yesterday, and are even less murderous looking, for their five day's growth of beard has been shaved off."

"The final defense offered for the prisoners is strangely presented, in keeping with the nature of the whole affair," Cranston wrote. Their lawyers presented weak arguments that the men were "only tools of higher-ups," reiterating the accident defense, but they were hurried along by the prosecutor. "Now Plannetta arises and in a sure, clear voice, says words which any man in a like position could well be proud," Cranston recorded: "'I may not be, in an hour; so you must believe me. I did not mean to spill blood, and I am not a cowardly murderer. I ask the forgiveness of Frau Dollfuss.' Unbelievable as it is, the little Holzweber surpasses these words, as, standing like a Napoleon and talking like a [William Jennings] Bryan, he far outdoes the efforts of his own attorneys. 'We…were only to capture the chancellery and its occupants.'" Their leaders had failed them, he said; they could have caused civil war if they had wished. "'Whatever I did, I did for my Fatherland and my people. If it was wrong, I am sorry. I am willing to take the consequences.'"

"We all sit here, hearts pounding like trip-hammers, awaiting the return of the judges" Cranston said. Holzweber's wife and Plannetta's sister "slip into the room" for the first time. "Their faces are strained, but dry." After only twenty minutes, the judges returned, followed by the prisoners, "walking like mechanical men." The prosecutor began reading rapidly, "in a harsh voice. He could as well be reading a stock market report as a court's judgment!" Cranston exclaimed. "The prosecutor literally tears through the fatal words which say that in exactly three hours to the minute, the two men standing before him shall be hanged by the neck until dead," both men for high treason and Plannetta for murder as well. "At the same moment a shovel can be heard scraping in the courtyard. Soldiers are actually erecting the gallows while the sentence is yet being read! But neither prisoner shows the least sign of emotion; a sudden, convulsive movement from Plannetta's weeping sister is the only visible evidence that a death sentence has just been pronounced." The prisoners marched "from the room, as erect, proud and defiant as ever. As I look at them for the last time, I think what a pity it is that these men must die so soon. Perhaps they have committed a heinous crime; yet they did it in the belief that it was for the best. Brave and intelligent, they could be so useful somewhere. Nazis in Germany – they might become powerful figures; Nazis in Austria – they must die."

Cranston ended the piece reflectively: "It is later. Vin and I are having our first meal of the day, steaks and beer on a little balcony overhanging the gay Ring Strasse, main street of Vienna. We look at our watches, 4:35. Little Plannetta and tiny Holzweber are dying now in 'Poor Sinners Court.'"

His succeeding piece was about "Vienna after Dollfuss' murder," on which his byline was upgraded to "Special Correspondent of the *Register-Leader*." He described their arrival in Vienna when it had been under militia curfew, how they missed the last streetcar for the night. A "very drunk Viennese – Lord knows how he escaped the vigilance of the military guard patrolling the streets" – had sent them into "gales of laughter with his hic-coughing German and tipsy stances," but had alerted them to the curfew. They next were approached by a "rigid Austrian guard, who, most politely, asked why we were sitting there" at the streetcar stop on suitcases, and whether they "contained any bombs!" They were forced to pay for a taxi to a "flop house" recommended by a "very nice Lithuanian who put his foot through" Cranston's suitcase and gave him a sardine and a pear (Cranston in another version changed the man's identity to "French artist") whom they had met on the train. At the hotel, they were "careful not to display any more money than necessary before…a couple of tough-looking mugs in ragged clothing and bare feet… Undoubtedly no one had ever before arrived at a flop-house in a taxi cab!" Cranston guarded the bags while Meyer, "with his superior German," went in search of a manager, and found himself surrounded by "ragamuffins…as if by magic" who began "hefting said bags (probably to see if perchance they contained gold bullion), inspecting my wristwatch, feeling the weight and thickness of my coat, and one fellow even endeavored to discover whether or not my shoes were well-soled!" The curious "ruffians [looked] about as tough as [boxer Jack] Dempsey must have in his hobo days." Cranston understood two questions from a "one-armed giant" – how much had his watch and the taxi cost? When he produced his passport for the concierge, the rough fellow grabbed it, found Cranston's picture and "exploded – 'Haw! Dillinger!'" The two Americans ended up in a room with five other men "whose combined snores would have been valuable to a Hollywood sound producer as a perfect imitation of an air fleet making a power dive." Their "expectations of robbery or cold-blooded murder were unfulfilled," however, and they moved the next morning to a student lodging house where they watched as "six policemen suddenly entered a student's room, searched it, and marched him off to prison – he was a Hiterlite!" [179]

They went to see Dollfuss lying in state in a "candle-lit room…buried in fragrant flowers and green wreaths," with student members of the chancellor's "dueling corps" standing at attention and women, among them Frau Dollfuss, kneeling in prayer. The funeral cortege was equally impressive; thousands of people marched, many in knee-length Tyrolean costume, following the horse-drawn hearse along with ministers who strode "with heads erect, scorning the fact that they afforded perfect targets for any sniping Nazis." The funeral mass was "one of the strangest dramas enacted to which one became almost accustomed in the weird Vienna of the week following the 'Putsch.'" The streets outside the church "presented not an aspect of peace, but of war! Machine guns were mounted on the very steps of the church, and bayonet-armed soldiers surrounded the entire building, ready to forestall any new Nazi uprising!"

From Vienna they traveled to Budapest. "This old city seems strangely peaceful to Vinnie and me, after the exciting week we spent in militia-bound Vienna," Cranston wrote in his "Travelogia" journal. "Our first evening in Budapest was disastrous. After an hour or so at a cabaret on Margaret Island, a beautiful isle in the middle of the river often called 'the glittering jewel of the Danube,' we couldn't even pay half our bill, and a fellow had to come around to our hotel next day to collect. The second night we went to another cabaret, and came off, well, somewhat better. The third night we sat in a park and listened to some distant music. Tonight we're going back to Vienna. We have discovered that even a seat in a park costs money." [180]

"Budapest is a strange city, showing queer combinations of the eastern and western influence," Cranston wrote. "The Turkish occupation, back in the centuries when America was being discovered and colonized, left an indelible mark on the city. One comes upon churches and buildings, both old and new, which are absolutely Oriental, and then upon others which would fit right along Fifth Avenue in New York. The city is cut in half by the Danube.... In Buda, it is said, people smile, while in Pest they make money. Yesterday morning Vinnie and I went on a bus tour of the city, and the guide turned out to be the same one that we had four years ago when I visited Budapest with my parents. He is a count. Having lost all his wealth and position as a result of the World War, he is forced to make his living by showing people the city he so loves. But he makes it a glorious job! He talks as though addressing parliament." The count assured him that "some day there will be a king here in this palace once more."

But new developments would put that in a different perspective, Cranston noted with prescience.

"Later in the day, we read of Hitler's ascension to the Presidency of Germany upon the death of Hindenburg and of his proposed combination of that office with the one of chancellor, an action which smacks strongly of a *coup d'etat*. I told Vinnie of Count Jackie's remarks, and we wondered if someday if it might possibly be King Hitler in the Royal Palace at Budapest. Napoleon began as a chancellor, you know.

"Much of Hitler's future depends on what he can accomplish in the next few months. There are too many rumors of dissatisfaction in Germany for them all to be unfounded, but I believe it will take something more than the events of June 30th ["night of the long knives" when Nazi storm troopers, "brown shirts," were murdered at Hitler's orders in a "purge" to appease industrial leaders, Army generals and the public] or the Austrian 'Putsch' to dislodge Hitler. He seems to me a much stronger man than many persons consider him to be. If he can survive this year, with its difficulties, economic and otherwise, he should go a long way....

"His ultimate aim must be the *Anchulss* with Austria, for this would give him countless advantages. The 'Putsch'...has been interpreted in some quarters as an attempt by Hitler to distract German attention from political and economic calamities at home.... This failed, but it has perhaps shown Hitler's hand.

"It is certain that he can make no open attempt to get into Austria for some time to come, for Austria is now openly on the defensive, and other foreign powers have shown that they will permit no *Anchluss* to take place. Thus it seems to me that no war in Europe is in the immediate offing, for Germany in Austria is the only legitimate provocation that I can see. That is now definitely postponed for some months to come, or at least until summer, for seldom do wars start in the winter or spring. Of course, by next summer the economic tension gripping the world may be lost, and with it, when it goes, should go the present danger of war." [181]

He and Meyer decided to go to Germany themselves, traveling through Bavaria where they witnessed the ritual Passion Play at Oberammergau, a moving experience for the nominally religious Cranston. The town, Cranston wrote in his journal August 1, "had been spared the ravages of plague" by preventing strangers from entering, until 1633 when a native returned from another village through a mountain pass, bringing with him “the invisible enemy.” Elders had sworn a solemn oath to “keep the Tragedy of the Passion every ten years, and miraculously, as records of the old chronicle bear witness, no one died of the plague from that moment forth in Oberammergau.” Cranston was struck by the fact that the play had been presented regularly “through times of famine and… hardship caused by war,” only interrupted for the first time in 1920 as a consequence “of the great poverty and [virtual?] starvation in Germany” after the Great War. At the time of Cranston’s visit, the town was celebrating 300 years of performances.

> “I had always regarded Oberammergau as more or less just another of Europe’s garish tourist traps. I was entirely wrong…. [T]he realization yesterday, as I witnessed the marvelous play, that nine-tenths of the spectators were native Germans who probably make the journey to the little mountain village every ten years to see the play completely altered it. Everyone, from Adolf Hitlers to princes from far-off India, comes to Oberammergau!” [182]

He was amused that natives were readily identified, both men and women, by long braids, apparently in hopes of getting parts in the play, “a marvelous spectacle.” The opening scene of Jesus entering Jerusalem “amid the shouts and exultations of the people…was something I will never forget…. When he strode into the temple…real pigeons escaped from the overturned carts, flew high into the air, and disappeared in the direction of the distant mountains. Each succeeding scene seemed to better its predecessors. The Last Supper was another which seemed really to be a reincarnation of the original…. Here was Jesus and his disciples in a scene that pen and brush have long sought to realistically paint; yet here they were actually moving about, talking and eating!”

“It is undoubtedly the seriousness with which the actors take the play which makes it so successful,” he felt. The man who played Jesus, Cranston noted, came from a family (named Lang) that had been involved in productions for “centuries.” “I will always treasure a copy of the script of the play as a sort of Sixth Gospel, adding it to the four in the Bible and *The Life of Our Lord* which Charles Dickens wrote for his children,” Cranston concluded.

These were heady sights and events for the twenty-year-old from California. He had tried to prepare himself by studying history and current events so that his accounts would be knowledgeable. He had read an article in *Literary Digest* December 31, 1931, headlined “Hitler’s astounding outburst,” that warned of his ambitions. It described him as “A slight, timid-mannered man with a Charlie Chaplin mustache” who “grabs the world by the ear to roar about his plans. What he’s going to do when he takes over control of Germany, which he promises to do soon, is the theme of this outburst from your Herr Hitler, dubbed ‘Handsome Adolf.’” The article quoted American journalists reporting on Hitler’s claim that

> “No organization in the world has such perfect discipline as the ranks of the 750,000 fighters who are inscribed in the National Socialist party proper, and they are backed by 15,000,000 voters as shown by recent elections in Germany. This

party is absolutely under my control. My will be done." [183]

Cranston had taken note.

After returning from Europe, Cranston wrote a retrospective piece, filled with verbose "purple prose." His trip had been "not by lightning express or speeding motor car, when one flashes through the quaintest of country villages without taking notice of their rustic beauty, passing under rugged mountains in dark gopher holes where nothing at all can be seen but the smoke of the steaming train up forward.... No; we have knocked about as the true wayfarer, who wishes to live to the fullest every minute of the day, and must do so by his own efforts. We have traveled on bicycles, in canoes and by that oldest...means of transportation – afoot!" They had bicycled over the Alps, lugged a canoe around "one of the ugly symbols of twentieth century progress, a power dam," not sat at home in the comfort "of the slippered hearth...wandering with Richard Halliburton's" books, viewing an occasional Pathé travelogue film, or traveling aboard "an air-cooled Pullman." What could "the inhabitant of one of those veritable houses on wheels know of the roll of the hills, the odor of the fresh-turned soil, the green, shadowy byway, the warming rays of the sun, the cooling splash of the rain? To him, a hill is a vague impediment...he frets at the slackening speed...the only noticeable odor is that of burning coal and the garlic on the breath of the fat native in the next seat (if he has not engaged a private compartment)." Cranston and Vinnie, on the other hand, had not seen merely "flashing glimpses of distant teams of oxen plodding along dusty roads, but have had to pull over into the very grass by the side of the road to allow them to pass. And we know the force of the Rhine, for its current has swept us along in its powerful grip through twisting eddies, and we have felt the chilling bit of its anger." [184]

Characteristically, he kept careful accounts of his expenses – "Sunday, August 12, 1934, Früstuck .40, Nazi outfit .9, chocolate .44, lemonade .25, abendessen 1.53, bier, zimmer 1.85." Other accounts were for stamps, "tire remedy," museum, paper, movie, map. He also kept a list of those whom he had written to: his mother and father each had four marks; he also had written Ralph Raymond, "Junior" Dutton, Mrs. Atkinson, and four girls identified only by their first names. [185]

One of their "most glorious memories" but hardest days was pushing their bikes up the Austrian Tyrol, arguing with border officials before crossing into Germany through Adolph Hitler Pass, "recently renamed, as have been innumerable passes, streams, streets and plazas in the past year in honor of Germany's new-found leader," then descending at sunset "into a long, green valley" where a blue stream flowed beside a "tiny, red-roofed town" (Hindelang) whose residents appeared, from the mountain top, more like "moths fluttering about a magnetic candle flame than real flesh and blood humans. Drinking in this heavenly scene, [we] almost believed ourselves to be God-favored sons of Adam who had been given the golden key to the Garden of Paradise. We had many such days as this, when we pedaled along with German wanderers.... Every day brought some new adventure; not a stirring, exciting adventure – the wanderer must learn to look for adventure in the commonplace, like meeting a vagabond from far-off Hamburg," drinking beer "one long night with a Nazi brown-shirt, or storm trooper," listening to "a bitter German tell, in hushed tones, of his great hatred for the Hitler regime," being "taken…for a Nazi because of a wave of the hand I had carelessly given to some fellows lying along the roadside. They had called out the customary 'God's greeting' as we pedaled past, and then evidentially mistook my return greeting for the fascist salute, for instantly it was answered with the real thing, the German 'Heil Hitler!'"

Hitler intrigued Cranston. He wondered what his appeal was, how he could have risen to power as quickly as he did, and why non-Germans viewed him so darkly when those within Germany by and large worshipped him. Cranston's political curiosity and observations were refined by his European experiences, his perceptions astute and thoughtful. On his return to the United States, he wrote two articles, "Adolf Hitler's Germany" and "Adolf Hitler as Germany sees him," both published in November, 1934, by the *Register-Leader* – "From the pen of a clear-eyed, level-headed, unprejudiced American college student" giving "a picture of the little man who is holding 60,000,000 Germans in the hollow of his hand – for a time. One of the most remarkable personages in contemporary history is presented to us here in a new light." Cranston's "keen American intelligence carried him through some mighty tight places and brought him home again all safe and sound, and ready for more adventures," another brief item in the paper stated. [186]

"'*I am the State!*' No one in history, not even Louis XIV, could pronounce those words with more truth than Adolf Hitler," Cranston began the first article. "Occupying his position by the will of the people, he rules with the power of a monarch." There were reports of "questionable voting methods" that belied Hitler's having been democratically chosen, Cranston noted, "but it is my belief, after meeting countless Germans in all walks of life…that the country is strongly behind Hitler." Four weeks in Germany and "innumerable" questions put to people confirmed that view, he said. Only one person during the first three weeks "voiced discontent, and he was a drunk fellow in a beer hall" whose perceptions Cranston discounted. Wherever he went, "'Heil Hitler' was heard on all sides, given spontaneously, not because, as all the German papers remarked one day, 'It is not the *law* that Germans greet with Heil Hitler, but it is *advisable* that the individual do so'" [emphasis added]. The greeting had replaced the equivalent of "good morning." "Everyone I met praised Hitler, proudly pointed to the large cut he has made in German unemployment, told how he has made Germans as one, and spoke of the great hopes entertained for the Third Reich." [187]

"One cold, biting night in Munich, the town where Hitler first sky-rocketed to fame," Cranston related, "I stood on a street corner for over an hour, a member of an enthusiastic, worshipful, yet jovial mob of Germans who were waiting for a glimpse of their idol, who was dining within the modest corner restaurant," *Der Bayern Haus*. People were leaning from windows expectantly, and after several false alarms of sightings, "the door was flung open and a thrilling scene was etched in the lamp light within. Hitler (in puttees and a brown shirt) was making his way toward the doorway amid a storm of cheering, and beneath innumerable arms raised in the Fascist salute – mostly only the brown-sleeved arms could be seen…. As he emerged from the doorway, the Reich's president was greeted with a great cheer" from hundreds of bystanders who shouted "Heil Hitler" three times. "It was genuine," Cranston wrote in a version composed in Germany:

"Hitler's serious demeanor could not help but make him attractive, as he bowed his head in acknowledgement of his acclaim.... A quick, short salute came from *Der Fuhrer* as the crowd pressed in, trying to touch him; then secret police cut a path to a low, open car that whirled to him through the crowd. Mounting to the running board, he raised his hand to his shoulder again, bent his head, then dropped into the front seat and was whisked away, as the people ran halfway down the block in joyful pursuit. This was barely a week after Hitler had succeeded Hindenberg, and the scene stamped firmly upon my mind the impression that Germany strongly backs her Nazi chief." [188]

"Less than two yards from the stationary car for a few brief seconds," Cranston wrote in his diary, "I saw a serious, unlined face, seemingly oblivious of the adoring crowd, as if immersed in things far away. REALIZATION IN GERMANY – if America comes to dictatorship, Herbert Hoover will be fortunate, or perhaps unfortunate, that he wrote *The Challenge to Liberty* before the liberty to challenge was lost." [189]

Although youngsters were force-fed pro-Hitler propaganda, Cranston predicted that his power would be "unlimited" as they grew "old enough to really count, if he survives 'till then." Cranston nevertheless heard a few dissenters. At Sackfingen in the state of Baden, where Hitler's majority had been less than elsewhere, walking along the main street with a portly man whom Cranston had met in a beer hall, who kept saluting others with "Heil Hitler," Cranston mentioned that he actually had seen the Fuhrer in Munich, hoping to generate "an interesting conversation." "I had tried it upon previous occasions with great success; it often made me somewhat of a hero in the eyes of Germans, many of whom stated they would have passed up a gallon of beer for such a privilege. 'Well, *I* don't want to see him,' growled my companion, and I looked at him in surprise. Calling Hitler a 'ranting maniac,' the man blamed him for alienating other nations by utterances 'like he did at Nuremberg about the Ukraine. He means well, he's sincere, but that doesn't mean he's accomplished anything,'" the man told Cranston. Hitler had spent millions of marks to reduce unemployment, but in manufacturing war materials, not houses. Cranston's companion was a carpenter, and no work had come his way and would not – unless Hitler "torments the Russians into blowing up half our homes." If he stayed in power another six months, the man offered, "'there just won't be any Germany; we'll starve – Heil Hitler!' This weird dialogue continued all the way to our destination," Cranston noticed, "my friend heaping imprecations on Hitler's head with one breath, and greeting" acquaintances with the requisite salute in the next until they reached the man's house where he and his wife greeted one another with the traditional "Gruss Gott" (God's greetings) and Cranston shared a lunch of beans and bread – "for it was bean day. One day each month throughout Germany, even in restaurants, everyone eats nothing but beans for lunch, and the money saved...is given to the Nazis to be distributed to the unemployed and the hungry." Cranston's host had been in a British prison camp during the last war because he had been in London when the Germans invaded Belgium. He had spent the four years making ship models inside bottles. As they finished lunch, a Nazi knocked at the door carrying a pail "half-filled with marks and pfennings – he'd come for the savings on the bean lunch," Cranston recorded. [190]

Even in Baden, though, "the dissenting voice was the exception," Cranston wrote, and "the rumors one hears of how a German is afraid to even whisper a negative political viewpoint is entirely unfounded. The only person I met all summer with such a fear was on the train entering Germany. He was an Oxford student, American, who had a friend who had a friend who had received a letter from a relation in Germany with several sentences, assumed to be pungent ones, clipped out by German border or postal authorities." When Cranston noticed a cross-word puzzle in the shape of a Nazi swastika, he had been told by the man creating the puzzle that he could not use it because the "sacred swastika" was forbidden "for anything so trivial." The man had "crossed out the swastika puzzle with heavy, black pencil marks [and] flashed me an apologetic smile.... Then there was a woman I almost scared to death in another town; I suddenly entered her store, and discovered her bent over an American newspaper. She almost fainted at my hasty entry, and it took her several minutes to recover her composure, even after discovering my brown leather jacket did not clothe a Nazi officer. Germans must read only German papers, all of which are under complete Nazi control." "Yes, there are dissenters in Germany," he concluded, "but so few...that even after a week in Baden, I still would believe the truth of [Hitler's] words..., 'I am the State.'"

Hitler was an "idolized leader, if a hard one – but a Fascist leader must be hard," Cranston wrote in his second article, more sophisticated and derisive of Hitler than the first. He had unified Germany and "given his countrymen new hopes," Cranston saw, although "to the rest of the world, [he] is a wild-eyed demagogue, utterly lacking in constructive ability to use his brains, if any. He took advantage of the weakness of his state to seize power, and instituted a reign of terror which has set the European clock back a hundred years. Blood drips by the barrel-full from his ten finger tips; his policy consists of nothing but, as one American magazine describes it, 'coercion by brute force.'" Why was he "idolized on one side of a river, hated on the other? The world press is probably the prime reason," Cranston stated in a candid observation. "Always searching for sensation, it has found a great subject in the brutalities of the Hitler regime. Its stories come chiefly from correspondents hoping to line their own pockets by producing a sensational story, and from refugees," whose "words cannot help but be prejudiced." "Sensation equals circulation" was the motive behind newspaper publishers who were "by interest and nature, against Hitler policies." Cranston also blamed anti-German views on the fact that it had eschewed diplomacy "which, since the War ended, has availed her naught. The present leaders, although shrewd handlers of foreign questions, are not diplomats." They relied not on tact "but dexterity" and were outcasts with the rest of the world, "but in Germany, for a change, the government is popular."

"Then there is the Jewish question," Cranston continued. "Hitler came into power with all Germans knowing it meant persecution of the Jews. He had preached it; it was one of the main pillars of his Socialist Party since its formulation in 1919. It was the equivalent of the major plank in a United States' presidential candidate's platform. In power, he and his party had to carry out the policy; undoubtedly they wanted to," believing it "an integral part of their German recovery program." The world turned against Hitler for living up to his promises, but to Germans, "He was a man of his word."

Hitler's attempt to nationalize the church, Cranston believed, had been one of the main causes for "what little dissatisfaction resides within his country," but the plan "was, from the first, doomed to failure, and will most certainly pass into obscurity." But the "'cleaning up' episode of June 30 was a mistake – a crime," as the rest of the world saw it. "In Germany it was shocking, yet perhaps necessary," Cranston related. "In a smoke-filled, noisy Munich beer hall one night this summer, a young Nazi storm trooper leaned earnestly across the table and, now and then brushing his eyes which glistened with his emotion, tried for over an hour to show me how this purge was justified. Hitler must rule with an iron hand, or not at all, until he is more firmly established, he said. Hitler has persuaded this young German, and nearly all his countrymen, that Germany is in a state of war…an economic war, and a war against oppression. In war time, traitors are shot. [Those] who died in the purge were traitors; there was no place left for them in Germany…. The storm trooper admitted that less guilty people were killed on that day by over-zealous Nazis, and lamented the fact, but in his heart, he believed the purges…justified."

"We who live outside of Germany are in an entirely different atmosphere," Cranston said. America's reliance on democracy "is one great difference; our lack of the German habit of obedience is another." Americans also did not have close neighbors with great military powers, "an important difference." "In Hitler's autobiography [*Mein Kampf*] he sets down the 'one, true doctrine' for all German National Socialists. By its very nature, it is incompatible to anyone but a German."

"The charge that Hitler is nothing more or less than a fool is not worth considering," Cranston concluded. The allegation was "heard less and less each day" because "no fool could gain Hitler's position, much less hold it. His autobiography, written in 1924 [when he was an obscure political prisoner] and in 1927…is quite obviously the work of a man of great intelligence. It is the work of a thinker and a doer who was bound…to get somewhere…. [Other nations] should bear in mind that whatever he does is done in the belief that it is the best thing for his country, a country which has been struggling to regain its feet since that black day – black for Germany and perhaps also for the rest of the world – of June 28, 1919, when the Treaty of Versailles was signed. As one German remarked, 'I am a German and I think Hitler is wonderful. If he were a Frenchman, or an American, I probably would hate him.'"

Cranston continued his discussion of fascism in another article published in the *Register-Leader*, this time with his friend Lars Skattebol, both writing separate views. Their arguments were articulate and reflected their prejudices. They prefaced the accounts by saying that they wanted to demonstrate to the public that college students actually thought about substantive matters like the impact the Depression was having on American graduates unable to find jobs. "We don't expect you to always agree with our ideas – quite often we don't agree among ourselves," they stated. Editor Smith was one who did not agree with the writers, "but at least he paid us the compliment of liking the way we string words together." Skattebol called fascism "a social disease…caused by a faulty system of economics, bolstered by fanaticism and misunderstanding, and maintained by force." In Germany and Italy, where it was festering, mechanization had caused unemployment, but so, too, had the profit-system in which "a percentage of unemployed is necessary to compete with job-holders so that employers may keep wages low enough to insure the profits which keep their system going. If there were no unemployed, this system would collapse," he believed. In Italy and Germany after World War I, he argued, wages had dropped and workers were joining organizations that advocated "social change" – the Communists or "deceiving demagogues, the Fascists" who offered "tempting economic bribes to the workers in return for the surrender of their liberties and political power." Employers were forced to either "succumb to the Communists or buy out the Fascists." Ultimately "the unemployed can be put into a war," Skattebol concluded. [191]

Cranston in his segment demonstrated a growing knowledge of political economics, the power of workers versus employers, and the need for opposing factions to compromise. He speculated that fascism could happen in America, although its people were "less emotional" than Europeans and considered "too wise and stable to be hypnotized by demagogues." He quoted popular author Booth Tarkington saying in a recent newspaper interview, "'American people would never stand for a dictator' – he evidently has already forgotten the power that [controversial, populist Louisiana Governor] Huey Long held over four states," Cranston interjected. He also quoted Herbert Hoover's condemnation of the National Recovery Administration as "'the most stupendous invasion of the whole spirit of liberty that the nation has witnessed since the days of Colonial America.'" Hoover, Cranston retorted, was "conveniently overlooking the fact that he tried the same thing with big business, on an agreement basis, in 1929, forgetting his billion-dollar subsidizing of the banks and the railroads, and his costly experiment with the Farm Board." If some naively believed that Americans would "never resort to violence and terror to preserve capitalism," Cranston pointed out that "across the bay a few months ago, men were tarred and feathered, and forced to kiss the American flag, because they refused to work for starvation wages, and tried to incite others to join their strike."

In Germany, Capitalists had promised workers a democratic share in the system to persuade them against embracing communism, Cranston argued. "But German capitalism soon found itself in a disastrous economic situation, and when that happens…it is up to the workers, not the Capitalists, to make compromises, if capitalism is to survive." Disillusioned workers had shifted to the Fascist party which "promised them many golden things," and the most disillusioned turned to the Communists. Both parties had failed the workers, and revolution was on the brink, with Communists gaining power. "There was only one thing to do – give the Fascists power, make the workers think they ruled." The same pattern had occurred in Italy, where Mussolini's Fascist party, "subsidized by bankers in New York," was attracting workers deserting the Labour Party in England, Cranston warned.

He wondered if fascism might occur in America "under a different name," speculating that "it is quite likely." The nation, after all, was "running downhill," with Democrats spending millions to bolster businesses, and Republicans campaigning against such spending. Did it "matter whether Republicans or Democrats guide us down hill?" Fascism was an alternative "knocking at our door, ready to jump in, should…our democracy fail us…. A study of how it achieved power in Europe – unexpectedly and by the most surprising methods – can perhaps show by analogy how we might wake up some morning and find ourselves in a Fascist America."

The following summer, 1935, at the end of his junior year, Cranston made another trip, this time with Stanford friend Johnny Atkinson. The week that the Pan-American highway opened, the two drove the route to Mexico City in Atkinson's Ford. They enrolled for courses at the University of Mexico, and found rooms in a boarding house for fifty-four cents a day that included three meals. Again Cranston planned to write up his experiences for the *Register-Leader*. "We expect some highly-entertaining letters from the land of *manaña*," an item in the paper read June 14, 1935. Of Cranston it said, "He is most likely to get plenty of adventures this summer, as he and a friend are planning to drive a 1928-vintage Model-T Ford all over Mexico wherever it is possible for a wheel to turn, and Alan will send us letters as often as he can." The trip indeed would be filled with personal danger and excitement. [192]

Cranston wrote observations of the colorful and different environment in which he found himself, in humorous, sometimes poignant vignettes. A list of his subjects included "The little Indian girl who wants to learn English…the silent fellow who is *almost mechanical* and pours over books with crazy geometric figures…the math prof. who learned his English at the talkies [like *G Men* or *Public Enemy Number One*], the barefoot man who bosses the girls around, the beautiful lady who lived in the next room for *one night only*, the man who would borrow our car…the little boy who collects bugs…the young feller who is wild over bull fights, the baby that cries, not to mention the parrot that whistles, the mosquitoes that buzz and itch…and the pretty girl who we think speaks English." [193]

He thought that the little boy who collected bugs had "hallucinations" – he pinned "still kicking" insects into a collection – and Cranston tried to get him to net mosquitoes in his room but he "busted a vase." The meals, little varied with rice and tortillas, "begin with soup and end with stomach aches," requiring "about a gallon of water to put out the fire." The overall impression was "quite often as horrible as the war [and gore?] photos with which [newspaper publisher] Mr. [William Randolph] Hearst cluttered up [Mexico] not so long ago." Cranston had "three great gripes: the food, the traffic situation, and summer school." Atkinson one day "almost crucified his tongue on a needle that had been lurking in the bottom of his [soup] bowl, but everything was all right when Rosa, the dark-eyed señorita who waits on us (and is really the only first-rate thing about meal time) ensured him that it was merely a typographical error – it should have been noodle." [194]

Another piece made fun of problems from not understanding Spanish. Cranston joked about trying to convey to a school registrar his desire to take the "History of the Mexican Revolution," not a course on "Mexican Art in its primitive stages," only to find himself sitting in the latter lecture the next day, unable to understand a word. [195]

"Interpreting Mexico – it's harder than trying to figure out the current trends and under-surface meanings of the New Deal," he wrote in a piece called "Altogether at Random." "In Mexico your eyes tell you one thing, established facts and statistics, another…. I've spent much of my time the past few weeks with an internationally-known newspaper correspondent who has been in Mexico since 1915," presumably Hearst correspondent Arthur Constantine, whose views Cranston characterized as "firm and dogmatic." He and Cranston occasionally met a "well-known writer who has been in Mexico since 1922, and has published several books on the country. On the surface the two men are friendly, but inwardly they have little respect for one another, and at every meeting they have an argument…. [N]o two men could have more divergent views on the same subjects. A. thinks the country should be turned over the native Indians; M. thinks its only salvation lies in the hands of Anglo-Saxons and natives with Spanish blood in their veins." Writers who had "hurried through" the country described Indians as enslaved to heartless landowners, when, Cranston said, "had they looked a little deeper, they would have learned that these Indian-slaves in nine-tenths of the cases are in reality squatters who have moved on to the land, put up their grass huts, and taken over an acre or so…to grow their corn. Lazy, happy-go-lucky, they work only hard enough to make a living, no harder. They come in droves and, once established, if the hacienda or landowner tries to put them off his land, or establishes the feudal system by demanding a [rent?], they rise up and kill him." Far from slaves, he concluded, "few men are freer." [196]

"This squatting thing is quite a habit," he continued, "it even goes on in the large cities." An acquaintance told Cranston how a group had tried to move into his large house in Mexico City, claiming to be cousins of the maid, "and seemed to consider that quite sufficient reason for their establishing themselves in the household. No one can be believed in Mexico," Cranston said, "for almost every expression of opinion is related to some very materialistic background." Most expatriate Americans living in Mexico considered the regime of [Porfirio] Diaz (longtime president until 1911), a "great Mexican period" because it had been favorable to foreign investors like rich Americans. But Indians had been exploited under Diaz' regime, Cranston felt, forced into "industrialization" that was "entirely foreign to their inherent habits of simply living and [subsisting] on a half-acre of Indian corn."

His adventures were soon to take an exciting turn, however. The southeastern state of Tabasco on the Gulf of Mexico had been dominated for fourteen years by Governor Tomas Garrido Canabal. Described by the *New York Times* as "A lusty, swaggering and witty leader," Garrido was an enemy of the Catholic church, "an ardent prohibitionist, founder and leader of the Red Shirts, a Fascist organization," the *Times* stated, "a virtual dictator [who] ran the State as he pleased. His enemies from the Right compared his regime to Soviet Russia; his foes from the Left compared him to Hitler and the late Huey Long." Garrido imposed a law requiring all priests to marry and destroyed churches, using their stones to build schools and basketball courts. His prohibitionism had destroyed Tabasco's major source of revenue, the manufacture of liquor, and replaced it with the export of bananas. He also had introduced sex education and created schools in every town, emphasizing agriculture, sanitation, anti-clericalism and sobriety. [197]

In July, 1935, a student protest against Garrido had ended with machine-gun fire from a car on the main street of Villa Hermosa, the capital of Tabasco, in which five students were killed and others badly wounded. Garrido and several of his followers were accused of firing the shots, a fact not proven.

An angry group of students in Mexico City went to the airport to meet the bodies of the slain protestors. Cranston and Atkinson were among them. In a handwritten account entitled "Dictator in Mexico," dated July 18, 1935, Cranston described the event. The account appeared, in slightly different form, as a front-page article in the *Register-Leader* on July 26. Cranston, too, likened Garrido to Long, "but unlike Huey Long, Garrido is willing to kill right and left to obtain his ends. He has passed laws which no dictator, not Hitler, not Mussolini, would dare even suggest," like those forbidding the sale of alcohol and tobacco. Garrido had become rich by levying "a gigantic tax on Tabasco's famous banana industry, and deposits 90 percent of said tax to his personal account in the Bank of Nova Scotia, in which he is reputed to possess $10 million dollars. Fanatical, aetheistical, cruel, cowardly, Garrido is never seen with less than twenty armed henchmen at his side. Machine guns are his favorite playthings." For a time, Garrido had served in President Lázaro Cárdenas' cabinet but had been ousted with others and returned to Tabasco where, Cranston said, "almost every family had watched some beloved member fall before Garrido bullets, or some precious acre of land cut away by Garrido's ruthless pen. Here and there a faint cry of protest was raised, and usually almost immediately snuffed out." The students who were killed had set up an office in the state with the intention of running an opposition candidate for governor. "They were answered with bullets." [198]

"A few hours ago I saw three of those men return to Mexico City – in ugly, black coffins," Cranston reported. "Two more dead were left in an outlying town, and three more, badly wounded, struggled from the tri-motored plane into waiting ambulances…. Had Garrido stepped from that plane, he would have been torn limb from limb, for 5,000 angry, grief-stricken Mexicans, relatives, friends, sympathizers of the dead, had waited three long hours watching the murky skies for that plane from Tabasco. The whole country is aroused over this terrible dictator's actions," and Garrido kept an airplane filled with fuel and an American pilot ready to fly him to the United States if he feared for his life.

"It seems incredible that such things can be in 1935," Cranston wrote, "but a grief-stricken Mexican mother, present at the airport this morning to welcome home the body of a lost son," exemplified the "spirit which engulfs all Mexico today." A second son had gone to Tabasco to seek revenge, and the mother had sent Garrido a message saying that if he killed that boy, she "'still had another son to send against him.' There's something wonderful in that," Cranston wrote of her spirit, "seldom seen on this earth since the days of Sparta."

"After the heart-rending scene," Cranston had followed thousands of "Gold Shirts, avowed enemies of Garrido's," back into Mexico City and gone to their headquarters, a tiny office above a bank where he found "fifty or sixty Mexicans, wide-eyed, breathless, with guns on their hips or strapped inside their pant-legs, swearing vengeance for their lost comrades, and signing a roll that would send them to Tabasco to carry on the campaign." They were "disorganized, inexperienced, young, but willing to sacrifice anything to rid their country of its blackest" tyrant – an effort that Cranston thought almost certain suicide, "but they are absolutely fearless."

"A young fellow, gun bristling on his right hip, rushed up and asked me what I wanted. I said I was from an American newspaper and just wanted to look around." Did Cranston want to go to Tabasco, the man asked? "Getting to Tabasco had been Johnnie's and my chief aim in life for three days, but we had found that no roads or trains" reached the "outlawed state"; they might get a boat from Vera Cruz but possibly not for months, and air fares were "terrible." "We had given up hope of seeing the Tabasco revolt first-hand until this question was fired at me. Our answer can well be imagined. We were stormed by excited, back-slapping Mexicans who joyously welcomed this opportunity of American companionship on their trip and the chance for the American public to obtain a fair account of their purpose from my small (but to them gigantic) journalistic pen."

"In five minutes, it was all arranged – or arranged as well as things can ever be in Mexico." The next morning, a train was to carry them, with 200 "crusading Mexicans," to Vera Cruz where they could take a steamer down the coast and up a broad river to Villa Hermosa. The students hoped to resume their campaign peacefully "but this time they go armed." The trip would not cost Cranston and Atkinson any money; they expected to stay five days and be flown back to Mexico City at reduced rates to resume summer school. "Upon our arrival in Villa Hermosa, we will, of course, separate ourselves from the Mexicans who will be in danger of being fired upon at any moment, and rush to the American consul, breaking his heart with the announcement that two American journalists are in town. No other American newspaper men are there, to my knowledge, but a Mexican correspondent who sent a stirring account of Tabasco's reign of terror to a Mexico City paper closed his article with the following pathetic remarks: 'Please forgive the inefficiency of my report, but one must move about down here surrounded by soldiers. Besides, I've been shot in the leg.'"

None of the "soldier-students" would be allowed on the train unarmed, Cranston said, but had to find their own weapons. They proudly showed off their collection of revolvers, automatic pistols, shotguns and other firearms. They had no plan of attack on reaching Tabasco, Cranston noted, except to wreck Garrido's plane and sink a ship on which he could escape by sending swimmers through "alligator-infested waters to bore holes in the ship's bottom, " an "insane idea," Cranston thought. The group also planned to arouse Indians in the jungle to revolt, hoping that the local militia would help, "yet they know deep in their hearts that they are probably traveling to their deaths. Tomorrow night we leave for Villa Hermosa," the article ended. The day for departure was Friday, July 19.

"Crowds, not big crowds, but crowds just the same, cheered us as we marched through the twisting streets of Mexico City for the train," Cranston wrote in another piece that he called "Journey to Revolution," dated July 25, 1935. "Women waved from balconies and little boys tagged along." Of the 200 or so who had said they would make the trip, eighty-four showed up at the train, including "the two Americans representing the *Register-Leader*." "This is the twentieth century," a version for the newspaper began. "I must believe that, yet somehow it is impossible. Here I am seated on a hard wooden bench on a rattly train running on rails barely three feet wide...surrounded by ugly, dusky Mexicans armed with every known weapon from long, dangerous razor blades to deadly German Luger automatics!... I go out on the platform for a breath of fresh air…. Yes, this IS the twentieth century, for over yonder I can see the headlights of a car speeding over the Pan-American highway. But I only have to turn back into the cars to make it hard to realize." An editorial note praising Cranston's article said, "We believe the accompanying story is about as good as the 'Anabasis' of the old Greek writer, Xenophon." [199]

Hearst reporter Constantine, meanwhile, was sending his own stories north with a far different "spin" from Cranston's account. Unknown to them, Constantine had filed a story saying that the two Americans had joined a revolutionary group, which translated into a headline in Hearst's *San Francisco Examiner* that read, "Two Stanford boys join in revolt in Old Mexico." Datelined Mexico City July 20, 1935, the article said the two "were part of a group of more than 100 students, Liberal and former army officers, which left here today for Tabasco to join the opposition" to the dictator. Cranston was quoted as saying, when he and Atkinson boarded the train, "We stand with the University of Mexico, even though we're only summer school students. Down with Dictator Garrido Canibal! What a lark!" [200]

"Despite rather surprising accounts which appeared shortly thereafter in San Francisco papers," Cranston retorted in the *Register-Leader*, "we had no ideas of fighting Mr. Garrido, and we carried no guns." He did write in a subsequent version, called "The Punitive Expedition to Tabasco," that "We Americans at the university summer school shared [Mexicans'] emotions. The men who had been murdered were our *compañeros*, our fellow students. It was our cause , too…. I joined [the punitive expedition], throwing my lot with my Mexican school mates." [201]

The adventure, though, would turn out to be more than a "lark." "Probably never again will such a remarkable troop be crowded into two little wooden-benched cars…sent through jungle and over mountains toward revolution," Cranston recorded. Only about twenty-four of the party were student "idealists" who wanted to "help their country, or to avenge fellow comrades. The rest were [either] job-seekers going in the hope of winning a fine job in Tabasco once they helped set up a new government, exiles going home…or out-and-out adventurers and soldiers-of-fortune." He counted twenty-six men carrying firearms of one sort or another, several with "tiny pistols that could be hidden in the palm of one hand." The others were armed only with "ready fists or long razor blades. Against Garrido and his machine guns and 12,000 Red Shirts we were throwing ourselves with but twenty-six of us armed with…machetes or razors" and a few pistols.

"As we climbed aboard the train, there was great cheering from the men, and cries of 'Kill Garrido.'" Some shouted "unintelligible oaths recounting exactly what they planned to do to Mr. Garrido and his blankety-blank Red Shirts." At the first stop outside of Mexico City, the party was reduced by one "when a mother stormed aboard our car at one end and emerged with a tearful son in hand at the other." He was replaced with a "sixteen-year-old youngster who had eloped with his grandfather's pistol. Later we learned that several such runaways were aboard, for at Vera Cruz, three of our companions were" taken into custody and shipped back to Mexico City under armed guard," on orders from "parents with less revolutionary ideas than their offspring," as Cranston put it.

As night fell, lights were lit in the cars, "bottles were passed, and the car roared with Mexican war and student songs." "Cigarettes, candy and drinks were common property in the smoky, dimly-lit car. Perfect communism, such as no radical ever dreamed of, reigned. If anyone tried to open a window, twenty hands were there to help him. If anyone started coughing, four or five glasses of water were offered. The knowledge that death may come at any moment seems to tie men together as nothing else can. Never in my life had I so rapidly made friends; after an hour on the train, almost every man in the two cars knew me by name. Warmly grasping my hand, they would say: 'If America ever has a war, we'll come and fight side by side with you.'" He noticed "five young men grasp their right hands together and slowly repeat some vow. I stumbled over to them, and learned they were representatives of the Mexican law school, and had just sworn that if one fell in Tabasco, all would stay and fight or fall 'till Garrido was dead, and if one came back to Mexico City, all would come back." At the other end of the car, older, grizzled passengers were shouting about winning "*libertad del socialismo*" with Garrido's blood. In the next car, he struck up a conversation with a bearded man who had fought with Pancho Villa "in the good old days of the real revolution. He said this was nothing" compared to what he had seen with Villa. Another young man who had worked in Stockton, California, for three years wanted to avenge his parents' being forced to flee Tabasco in 1930. "But what if you get killed there?" Cranston asked him. "Sure, what of it? I'll be there, won't I?" the man countered.

"The train rattled on and on through the night," the crowd increasingly noisy, drunk and restless. "Once a student reached inside his shirt to inspect his gun, and BANG! the thing went off, tearing a big hole in his shirt and ricocheting harmlessly along the floor. Everyone dived for the floor with the explosion, for an attack by a Garrido band was a distinct possibility, even here, far north of Tabasco," Cranston recorded. About one in the morning, he and others tried to sleep on the narrow benches. Cranston's long frame was uncomfortably poised on a bench twelve inches wide. He tucked one leg around a post to keep from falling off; his head rested on one man's boots while another slept on his foot. "Humor rides with death," Cranston wrote. An ex-barber who had fallen asleep woke up and kept asking where he was, "staring wide-eyed at the exposed pistol butts." No one had the heart to tell him, but when someone did, the man "retired to his corner, a helpless look on his face, and the rest of the group poke gibes at him." [202]

In the car full of protestors Cranston was "immediately surrounded by curious Mexicans who want to know what state I'm from, and ask to see my gun. Laughingly I show them my fountain pen and tell them I can do more good with it than with any sort of gun, as they eagerly pull long, curved machetes from their trousers, and show pistols attached to their belts."

"Being with this group certainly gives [one] more faith in humanity," his article continued. "Many of these men I would never have taken second notice of under other conditions; but now I can't help but realize that they see, all too clearly, that there is something more to life besides just living, eating and sleeping. They are going to an almost certain death; yet they're as playful and carefree as the members of the Stanford track team with which I've traveled. It's pitiful that so many of them must inevitably die; but it's men like them, who are willing to sacrifice everything they have to better their people, who keep this world turning; and as long as this world keeps on turning out men such as these, it can't help but keep on improving." Putting it in perspective, he continued:

> "Someday, when wars are forever outlawed, such men as these will be able to accomplish things in other ways. Today they must fight."

One man in particular attracted his attention. "Seated before me on a box of dynamite, precariously balanced on the narrow bench…is the most amazing man I've ever met, a "little dark man who is talking to me through an interpreter." He turned out to be a one-time Cuban medical student who had fought against dictator Gerardo Machado, and been tortured. He had lost his fingernails, two of his fingers and all of his toes, and had a bounty of $5,000 on his head in Cuba. He specialized in explosives and had joined the Tabasco band as part of a crusade against oppressive governments. "As he told his story, he gesticulated wildly with a hand grenade, one moment pretending it was a dagger, and the next holding it loosely in his fingertips. I watched it with fascination – I couldn't take my eyes from it – and when he finally drew his tale to a close, I asked him exactly what the damage would be if that little thing should happen to slip from his fingers. For answer he hurled it to the hard metal flooring! The action was too quick for my jaded nerves, but several young revolutionists gasped and threw their arms before their faces. Nothing happened. The train rolled on through the jungle." [203]

"Besides his long grenades, which he intended to distribute among us before we reached Tabasco, [the Cuban] Peraza had fifteen little round ones for his personal use, which he planned to carry in his hat. He said he had balanced them like handballs, and could throw them 250 feet. They were powerful enough to destroy everything in a radius of ninety feet. But the most amazing battle equipment Peraza had was concealed in his little brown and white shoes – ordinary enough in appearance, but actually deadly." In the spaces left by his missing toes, he had stashed fuses, cotton and acid to ignite the grenades. "I took my hat off to him as one of the world's premier revolutionists," Cranston wrote. The Cuban proudly told Cranston that the shoes alone could blow up the hated Garrido or an entire prison, should the Cuban be unlucky enough to find himself in one. Would Cranston walk up the street in Tabasco with the him, the Cuban asked? "I think of the hat full of bombs, glance at the shoes resting between mine, and realize that this man cares little whether he lives or dies, now or tomorrow, it is all the same to him, and utter a hurried 'NO.' I have some desire to live a while yet, even if I am accompanying this expedition, and what if I should get clapped into the same prison cell with those awful shoes?"

"About two a.m., a heavy-set man dressed in khaki and a broad-brimmed army hat boarded the train," Cranston's account continued. He was greeted with "lusty 'Vivas' and hearty handclasps as he strode through the car. He immediately sat down with the leaders of the expedition, who grouped around him in a manner reminiscent of our good old American football hurdles. I learned that he was General Chavez, on leave from the army. With two soldiers, he had chased us all the way from Mexico City in a little car, narrowly missing overturning several times in the mad dash. He immediately assumed command, and commenced organizing our slip-shod plans. This guiding hand of an experienced fighter was joyfully welcomed by the young students." His strategies included lying flat on the ground at the first sound of machine gun fire; when that stopped, he told the students to jump up and attack with their weapons and grenades. He admitted that some would surely die but reassured them that "Against long odds…he had won many battles by this method. He added…that we might not have to wait long to try it out, for he had heard that Red Shirts in disguise thronged Vera Cruz, and he considered it not unlikely that we would be searched and relieved of all our weapons. So at the last station before Vera Cruz, the dusky Cuban and two students leaped off the back car and disappeared in the jungle. With them went our dynamite and hand grenades, to be taken to our boat by a round-about route."

There also was fear that a Garrido spy was among the party. A friend furtively told Cranston that the suspect had been "disarmed during the night under the pretext that the general needed a gun…bullets were ready for him if he showed false colors. They had even considered pitching him from the train…but had decided to wait 'till we were at sea and then, if suspicions seemed true, throw him overboard." The man, in a long, gray shirt and tattered pants, "looked the part," Cranston said, "pock-marked and bewhiskered, viciously chewing a toothpick." He disappeared during the night. "I'll never be quite sure he wasn't done away with," Cranston wrote, "but since no one seemed to know anything but that he was no longer with us, he probably slipped away by himself."

At Vera Cruz, the group "rallied around the general and marched to the waterfront. There we were met with disappointment – no ship would take us to Tabasco." Old maritime laws had been invoked that prevented their sailing because they carried firearms and would overload the fishing boat turned coastal ferry. Enforcement of the long-dormant laws was laid to Garrido but later many thought that President Cárdenas had actually taken action "to save our lives and his own position, for if more students had been killed…all Mexico would have been after his head," Cranston surmised.

"Discouraged, we found a cheap hotel in which to establish our headquarters," turning it into what Cranston characterized as a "stronghold of some gangster outfit, as unshaven men in caps, with guns bulging from their hips and cartridge belts around their waists, lounged in the window sills or on the front steps. More than one passerby looked back in astonishment, and little Mexican children peeked at us around corners." At a nearby restaurant they "devoured a gigantic half-peso lunch in a fly-filled restaurant, and went for a swim in the warm waters of the Gulf of Mexico…. We could only go in up to our necks, for sharks abound in the tropical waters. The general promised we would sail within twenty-four hours." "My principal impressions of Vera Cruz," he added for the *Register-Leader*, "are heat, pretty girls, flies that swarm everywhere, buzzards that roost on every building, coconut trees and ash cans, and the horrible smells with which we were met everywhere we went."

There was a newspaper report that a battleship might take the rebels to Tabasco, but on Monday they learned that the ship had transported a battalion of soldiers to Tabasco. Garrido's "Red Shirts," meanwhile, had planted cannon and machine guns in trenches facing the river and planned to blow up the ship, had it sailed as planned. Another group of anti-Garrido forces, however, attacked and disarmed the "Red Shirts." "We all rejoiced over the news," Cranston recorded, "which made Garrido's days seem numbered, and went singing through the streets." More army commanders arrived in Vera Cruz, and by Tuesday evening, Garrido had been overthrown and Cárdenas had appointed a new governor. "The grizzled Pancho Villa veteran swung a seventeen-year-old student high in the air, and an idealist from the law school pounded me on the back," Cranston wrote. "Our purpose was accomplished. Several were a bit sad that they hadn't had an actual fighting part in the downfall of Garrido." [204]

"With the knowledge that our revolution was won…our expedition drifted apart," most relieved that they no longer faced death, Cranston said. Taking leave of his comrades was not "without a deep tinge of regret, for I had formed friendships and built up admiration that I knew would be in my mind as long as I lived. I had come to know those Mexicans as I knew few Americans. We rushed to the station and caught the first train back to Mexico City. Our revolution was over. It was back to school for us."

Nevertheless, he reflected, "Perhaps our little expedition had had much to do with the collapse of the Garrido regime...for the threat of our slaughter, hanging over Cárdenas' head as it had for five long days, had been a great factor in bringing about his sudden decision to act against Garrido. Shortly after the news came, I found [the Cuban] ruefully staring at his shoes. Undoubtedly he was wondering what he'd ever do with them now. In a few hours more, he had gone his way and I mine, but someday I expect to hear of him again. Hater of all dictators and champion of the down-trodden, he is bound to turn up in some future revolution, whether it is in North America or South Asia. All I have to do is watch the papers. Someday I'll read of a little Cuban minus two fingers, riding atop a revolution and blowing buildings and dictators and governments high into the stratosphere." A few weeks later rumors were "rife" that Garrido had subsumed the new governor and militia. "All Mexico believed that Cárdenas had cleansed Tabasco; now it seems likely that he either willingly or unwittingly furnished him with more tools…. Perhaps Garrido is actually hiding in the swamps, and [the new governor] Calles and [militia chief] Enriquez are really a pair of the most honest men in all Mexico." [205]

If Cranston's "revolution" had ended in an anti-climax, it nevertheless provided good copy at home. He worried that the newspaper headlines would find their way to his parents who were traveling in Europe, and cabled them from Mexico:

> "Safe in school. Don't believe anything you hear to contrary. Covered an incipient revolution a few days ago for international press." [206]

"I will breathe more freely when Alan shows up safely at Warec," his father wrote Eleanor from Austria July 29, 1935. "Much of his charm lies in his spirit, but it only takes one slip to cause him and us a disaster." [207]

"Forty-eight hours to leave Mexico! That's all we were given," Cranston wrote as they prepared to set out before the highway north was to be closed. "We tore about Mexico City saying goodbye to our friends, and were clipping our way northward along the Pan-American highway by three in the morning. At noon we passed the danger spot, hours ahead of the deadline. In a short time, a whole mountain side was to be blasted down across the highway, and after that no cars would be driven out of Mexico 'till November. We'd beaten the blast – now we'd pay no exorbitant fees to the railroad to ship our car out. We gleefully drove on down the rugged mountain side toward the little jungle village…where we'd take a ferry across the Montezuma river, and then be almost back in the States, for it's a mere 500 miles from [there] to Laredo, Texas. But we made the fatal error of stopping for some gas and a few tamales, and as a result stayed in the hot, steamy village for four days. For when we drove down to the river, we found several disconsolate motorists heading back for town – the ferry had stopped running. Its owner said the river, swollen by heavy rains back in the mountains, was too high and swift, and he would take no cars across." [208]

In reflections that Cranston wrote a year later, he mused about the violence with which Mexico's politics had been infused for centuries. His "Derelict's Diary" was a "search for…at least partial understanding of the thousand-fold forces affecting millions of people bound by birth to live under presidents and dictators, Communists and kings. In a crazy yet fascinating world, this chronicle will attempt to segregate the clashing hues of riches and poverty, of hope and despair…. It will seek elusive outlines among the ambitious and the slothful, the leaders and the led." Its "birthplace" was Mexico City, "one of the dreamiest, maddest, most fantastic cities in the world, where paradox and cosmopolitanism afford an apt baptism." [209]

"The best paid life in Mexico is a political career," he wrote in another segment, "but too often the Mexican political careerist pays with his life." A vignette recounted a conversation that Cranston had overheard at the Regis Bar in Mexico City. "An American woman tourist was trying to tell a White Mexican of Spanish blood the true story of Mexico. 'Pardon me,' he exploded, 'but…how long have you been in Mexico?' 'Since Christmas.' 'And you try to tell me about Mexico? I've been here since 1519!'" the man retorted. [210]

More of Cranston's observations appeared in the *Register-Leader* in September, 1935. He criticized "as appalling" changes made in dispatches by American "rewrite men who guessed at what they were saying, and editors who had pertinent reasons for deliberately altering facts." It made him wonder if that were a common practice – if, for example, "the various articles appearing currently in a great chain of American newspapers telling of the rotten conditions in Russia were true?" He surmised that "the writers were told what to write – I've always known that, but now I wonder if the articles even appear in print as the authors last saw them in manuscript." He had made a note of an editorial by one Harold D. Lasswell, "Propaganda Technique in the World War," that urged, Cranston underlined, "the U.S.A. to conquer Mexico," which had run in the *Chicago Tribune* (the McCormick paper that Cranston mistook for Hearst's *Chicago American*). "Fortunately, I have been writing for an independent newspaper and have been able to say what I pleased, with no fear of my stories' falling into the hands of rewrite men with radically different ideas from my own." One "well-known correspondent in Mexico [Constantine?] told me that he has been instructed never to write anything uncomplimentary about the ex-king-pin [former President] Calles." [211]

He undertook an exercise to present two versions of his Mexican observations, one as he had written it, and the other as if it had been edited for a "great chain" of newspapers. His original article began, "I have just escaped from the gastronomic perils of Mexico, and wondrously I am still in possession of a set of teeth, a stomach, and a sound digestive system." He joked about the discomforts he had experienced: a lump in the middle of his mattress which he learned to curl around, the sameness and large portions of the otherwise edible food, the benefits of siesta ("you're so chock full, you couldn't possibly walk anywhere"), the liveliness in evenings ("In

Mexico every night is Saturday night, which is much unlike America, where we are always too tired from chasing the dollar to do much celebrating except on the last night of the week"), and the traffic problems (he had been stopped more than fifty times for violations but never got a ticket because of language barriers and some policemen who stopped them regularly "became intimate acquaintances, and…just naturally gave up trying to teach us the law. We'd just wave as we'd rattle past, and they'd dazedly salute").

By contrast, the second version was a spoof that he dubbed "For people who want to be thought for" under the headline, "The Horrors of Black Mexico," and signed, "American tourist who spent seven terror-filled weeks in a land of assassination, revolution and socialism." It began: "I have just arrived back in sunny California, where it is warm the year round and where a happy, carefree people, protected since 1776 by one Constitution…live in freedom of enterprise and thought…. I think back to my recent weeks spent in dark Mexico" where "starving beggars are to be seen everywhere." He cited all the negatives that he could remember about life in Mexico. The people were "lazy and indolent" and probably "developed the siesta since they heard the country was going over to socialism. For everyone knows that it's no use working – just let the government support you."

Cranston afterward wrote in his biographical notes that the whole experience might best described with humor, pointing out that the summer school was run "after the American plan" where most students were "rich men's offspring…just looking for another happy collegiate playground." He would "describe how they dressed, in checked coats, flannels, etc. Describe 'Joe College' and how he went around in a daze, and when anyone asked him what was the matter, he'd say, 'The gal I met at the Embassy.'" [212]

Back in the United States, Cranston and Atkinson rode a freight train from San Antonio, Texas, to New Orleans. "I'm sitting on the banks of a levee by the Mississippi cooking breakfast with some other tramps," he wrote his parents on a post card. "I have only 11¢ left." From there they drove back to California. Cranston learned that his girl friend, Doris Atkinson, had gone to Hawaii in rebellion against her father, who was derisive of the boys' emulating hobos by riding freight trains. [213]

Significant national and international events in his last two years at Stanford absorbed Cranston and would have lasting effects on his future. Although he was able to stay in college during the Depression, his father's real-estate business was nearly wiped out when property values plunged. William Cranston had invested some years earlier in a site at the southwest corner of Post and Mason Streets in the heart of downtown San Francisco, one block from Union Square. The property had a large mortgage, and when the crash of 1929 struck, its value plummeted to below the rental income. Cranston was grateful to Wells Fargo Bank for not foreclosing – perhaps a measure of the respect in which he was held – and his finances gradually recovered in time. But he was unable to financially aid his daughter and new husband, whose parents also were seriously set back by the Depression, and Eleanor worked in her father's office where she gained valuable business training. Before the crash, William Cranston had hoped to become a developer but had to return to selling real estate, which he thought demeaning. "It was a great blow to his pride," said Eleanor. [214]

After a lunch with Fremont and Cora Older at Villa Warec, Alan Cranston wrote in his diary January 15, 1935,

"We were discussing Roosevelt's administration, saying what he'd done wrong. Father was doing most of the criticizing, when wise old Mr. Older, smart and alert as ever, and he's now 78 or 79, said, 'You're saying what *you* wouldn't have done, which is very easy. But suppose *you*, instead of Roosevelt, had been elected President in 1932? What *would* you have done?'

"Father thought for a few minutes, then said, 'Well, first of all, I'd disenfranchise all civil office holders and their dependents.' And Mr. Older snapped back with the perfect answer, the cleverest thing I've heard in many a day: 'If you *could* do that, you wouldn't have to.'

"We were discussing Germany. Mr. Older said, 'Hitler is a tyrant.' 'Why is he a tyrant?' I asked to draw him out. 'He's doing what he thinks right for Germany.'

"Mr. Older turned his big head, his whole body, towards me, and said, 'Why – *he kills people*!'" [215]

Cranston was greatly saddened when Fremont Older died of heart failure that same year. It was Cranston's first encounter with the death of someone close to him. "I consider him one of the greatest of all Californians," Cranston told his diary. "'Annie Laurie' [pseudonym of Hearst columnist Winifred Black Bonfils] brought tears to my eyes with one of her typical heart-tearing articles in the *Examiner* this morning on Fremont Older." He copied the entire piece, which pointed to Older's indiscriminate attraction to people who needed help, "whether a man was rich or poor, clever or dull. No, you didn't even care whether he was good or bad, not if you liked him, and you liked so many people, Fremont. Some of us of smaller vision found fault with you for that. I wonder, will it count for you or against you when you make your reckoning up there beyond the stars?" [216]

"How I loved those Sundays," Cranston recorded. "They are no more. But I can't believe that Fremont Older is completely gone; he couldn't be here one minute, so alive, so active, so alert, so kindly, and gone the next, completely lost. It just can't be." His widow, Cora Older, would be an important help to Cranston when he set out to be a journalist himself.

He continued to write for the local paper during his last two years in college, and for himself. He made notes for possible novels, detective stories and plays, one entitled "Dictator's Double." An outline for science fiction story that he made in 1936, read, "Scientist perfects machine to catch all past history, and precisely predict future." Cranston's sense of satire was evident in a mock "review" of an actual murder trial in 1935 that "played" several seasons at the San Jose Court House, each time with a different ending. Cranston (calling himself "super-drama reviewer") recommended a change in the script, again manifesting a soft spot for the underdog: the accused, Stanford University Press executive David Lamson (a "fellow newspaperman," Cranston noted), whose wife had been murdered, might "be discovered to be an innocent man" rather than guilty and hanged, as his first trial ordered. The verdict had been overturned by the California Supreme Court and a second trial was under way. Cranston also pointed out with irony that the "show" was free of charge – "its entire expenses are paid for by the taxpayers; and it is an opportunity to see a human being suffer – on and on and on!" [217]

Cranston had a rude introduction to libel laws and editorial license, however, when he saw his piece, substantially rewritten by an editor, in the San Francisco *Wasp News-Letter*, a social-commentary magazine. "Undoubtedly my article showed some small bias against Lamson," Cranston confessed in one of his personal notes, "so when the editor said it was against the laws to say anything that might influence a juror, and that moreover we wouldn't want it on our consciences that we'd put any such thing in print, I agreed to let him strike out the offending passages. So I left, and when the article came out a few days later, it was full of passages I'd never written, which gave the article a decided pro-Lamson tinge. Newspapers and magazines supposedly give the public what they want to read," he rationalized. "Every member of the 'public' to whom I showed my article went into rhapsodies over it, yet no publication but one would print it…and that one cut out its most pungent passages, and – supposedly the enemy of bias – put in lines so biased that they didn't even follow the satire form of the rest of the article." [218]

His travels, however, had fostered a special interest in international affairs. After Mexico, "the other thing that developed my interest in foreign policy," Cranston later recalled, "was that the Ethiopian war began, was fought and over while I was at Stanford. It began in my junior year and ended in my senior year. I was very interested in that. I watched the League of Nations collapse, and felt that some stronger world organization was needed." Those seminal views would grow into full-fledged ideals. He also liked Roosevelt's "reaction to Hitler and Mussolini and the Japanese war lords," and, based on his experiences in Europe, believed in the president's "interventionist policies – so that helped confirm my interest in the Democratic Party." [219]

Cranston "practiced" being a foreign correspondent by reconstructing for the *Register-Leader* an account of the October, 1935, Italian attack on Ethiopia, which he based on newspaper and magazine stories. The editor extolled Cranston's composite as "a picture of the war zone which few across the seas have equaled." Entitled "The revenge of Aduwa," it was composed as if the writer were on the scene, watching Italian "Death's Head" bombers, led by Mussolini's son-in-law, Count Galeazzo Ciano, tip their wings as they flew over troops and cavalry moving across the desert toward Aduwa, site of a punishing defeat of Italian colonists in 1896. Cranston's picaresque language described "labored, bronzed, sweating workers…stripped to the waist" building a road "in a land that had never known civilization," and was punctuated with images: "Suddenly – BANG! A puff of smoke from behind a rock…a scurry for shelter and a barrage of machine gun fire" from a sniper, a village of mud huts, fields of corn ten feet tall through which tanks cut "a path for death to march upon." The "savages" fought valiantly but were overwhelmed by Italian air power. Cranston once again seemed to be taking the side of the underdog. [220]

In his senior year at Stanford, Cranston again fell for a young woman. Dorothea Merrill was a law student who had been married and divorced. In spring the two became engaged and Dorothea was planning to join Cranston and Skattebol on a forthcoming summer trip to Europe. Skattebol and Dorothea were immediate antagonists, however, competing for Cranston's attention. Cranston graduated from Stanford in 1936 with a Bachelor of Art degree in English, although his real major was "track," he would admit many years later. He was anxious to see the world and prove himself as a writer and foreign correspondent. [221]

Soon after he graduated he wrote a long essay entitled "School versus Education," filled with cynical observations about the American educational system and urging the importance of individual freedom of thought. He apparently hoped to publish it but did not. Cranston had found himself constrained in his junior year, and was bursting with ideas that he felt set him apart. In a later biographical sketch, he credited "discussions with campus friends of phenomena of the period, such as the Depression, the beginning of the Roosevelt era and the rise of Hitler" for playing "a large part in the formation" of his ideas. He covered a number of subjects – mediocre teachers and methods, class distinctions, religious narrow-mindedness, even an early sexual experience. His international perspectives had been awakened and enlarged both by world events and by his reading and analyzing. He wrote with the candor and willfulness of an angry – or disillusioned – young man who believed that he had been enlightened. And indeed some of his thoughts were timelessly prescient. Echoes of his future voice and seeds of his beliefs could be heard. He was organizing his thoughts to face the world head on. And he was determined to educate himself beyond what he had been taught to date. [222]

The essay began by noting that all school children learned the Pledge of Allegiance to the flag from the first day of school. "We used to hurry over the last three words, and not for three or four years did we discover that 'justice for all' was not one word but three." The allegiance embodied "Great American Truths" contained in the U. S. Constitution, which were not lost, even on the slow-witted or "the red-headed kid who lived across the railroad tracks in a sulphur shed that was used every July and August to dry apricots.... His father...was in the county jail for supplying some of our parents with boot-leg whisky [*sic*]; and his mother was dead." But people like "bosses, ward heelers, lobbyists, and other men unaccounted for in the Constitution, were never mentioned by our teachers. It was as if...schoolboy patriots" would never "be incensed by the invisible government after they had thoroughly absorbed the doctrine of popular sovereignty, [and thus] would never become dangerous adults of our theoretical democracy."

"Instilled in me personally by this process was a smug patriotism that lasted more than fourteen years. All the advantages and opportunities of America's educational system were heaped upon me – and they almost buried me. While small Italians and contemporary Russians were learning that Mussolini or Stalin could do no wrong, I was learning little more than that Harding, Coolidge, Hoover, and momentarily Roosevelt, as well as the system that produced them, could commit no serious errors.

"It was in the midst of my junior year in college, early in 1935, when my teachers first timorously questioned the policies of Roosevelt, or split over them, that I became aware that there could be intelligent controversy over such things as the fundamental principles of our democracy. Then a dust-bound book inadvertently picked up from a forgotten shelf of the school library informed me that the entry of the United States into the World War [I] was a flagrant violation of the Monroe Doctrine....

"The facts shrank to insignificance beside the galling realization that my teachers had never volunteered this information; I turned to a friend with a social conscience [Lars Skattebol], 'till then merely a good competitor on the track and an excellent team-mate at touch football, and he recommended an armful of books. On the first page of one of them I learned that Jefferson, who wrote 'all men are created free and equal' into the Declaration of Independence, had been influenced by ante-dated philosophers who believed in the omnipotence of environment, and that his fellow revolutionists, considering him outmoded and a dangerous radical, had seen to it that he was conveniently absent when the Constitution was drawn to protect the rights and possessions of the commercial and propertied classes."

Cranston was further startled to learn how debate over popular election of a president had disrupted the Constitutional Convention, and that "none of the states writing new constitutions in the first days of American independence granted franchise to even half their male populations.... Shocked and dazed, I gropingly emerged from the collegiate maelstrom of pointless classes, meaningless courses, aimless education, bringing with me little more than the sad realization that I" was ill-prepared to face the hard facts of life. "Glutted with superficial convictions and common-sense platitudes seemingly intended to save me the trouble, or danger, of thinking for myself, I had an over-supply of insulated factual information and an under-supply of the understanding."

"I found myself living in a scientific age knowing nothing of science, in an international age unable to speak any foreign language fluently. Law and economics...were as unknown to me as art and music, which I had never found time to study. Uncaptivated by history professors and bored by philosophy as taught at school, I was studying literature and journalism: I would learn to write, even though I would have nothing to say.... I took over my education for myself....

"Voraciously I studied history and political theory, science and economics, philosophy and religion. I read almost a book a day, devised a filing cabinet to retain everything worthwhile that I encountered or thought, and improved my associative faculties with a correspondence course in memory training. I bought a long book purporting to outline all man's knowledge, and read it several times in succession until I had it almost memorized....

"I was convinced that my education commenced when I was a little baby.... Fortunately mine were intelligent parents who taught me quite a number of things during that period, but a baby born the same year across the railroad tracks was left completely to his own devices from the day he left his mother's breast. I can still remember the first-grade teacher's frantic efforts to teach him...that it was downright uncivilized to swallow the flies he skillfully bashed with his primer."

Cranston criticized class differences in which "golden-spooned children" were sent to private schools, dividing "my generation into two groups, the rich and the poor" – simpler than separating "the brilliant and the keen from the dull and the uninspired."

He wondered about the value of teaching "the trade-minded…cultural subjects they would never care for nor understand." There also needed to be investment in teachers, "granting them intellectual and financial independence, lack of which at present turns all but a handful of potential educators to other professions."

"Watching my schoolmates lose identity in a well-manufactured mass of 'good citizens,' I became convinced…that modern education destroys individualism." He advocated a basic "introduction to life and knowledge" through the first year of college and "a year spent at work." By then, people should be able "to chose a field for specialization." Still, he noticed that most of his classmates had not pursued work in fields that they had studied, but instead had fallen into jobs by accident.

Sex education did not escape his criticism, either. "Instead of the frank introductions to sex and hygiene, which should be presented to each child at an early date,…almost every child is introduced to this vital field by blushing parents who confusedly mumble of bees and flowers instead of humans." After making "the child thoroughly bewildered and completely self-conscious, he is sent packing off to school, only to fall into the hands of a set of neurotic, frustrated virgins who carry on with a mysterious, hushed hygiene, pointedly avoiding certain words and bodily functions." The requisite high-school biology course, dissecting mice and rabbit parts, was no better for adolescents, he thought. Noting that "a tremendous proportion of divorces are due to sexual misunderstanding and maladjustment," he blamed it on the fact that future housewives were taught "more about mice than men." "I, for one," he admitted, "learned more about life from the beautiful blond who was my field-trip partner than I ever did from my biology professor."

Religious understanding also suffered. He would not have read a word of the Bible had he not elected to take the only course in religion offered at the university, Biblical History. "Modern man [should be] given the opportunity…to select the religion most suited to his needs, or to even form a new faith." The "elder generation" was concealing the "perhaps rotting base of the world they have shaped. Are they in mortal fear that honest education would reveal the hypocrisy…of a moral code prattled but not practiced," or "expose the blasphemous fraud of their piety?" It was time for a break from tradition, he declared.

"The schools spew forth men and women utterly unequipped to face authentic life…. No curriculum offers a course teaching proficiency in graft, no study of the art of bribe-broaching is ever available." Nor were students "taught a profitable use of leisure." Sports had "become more important than ideas, and the social life of a campus more important than its intellectual activity. Only the tyrannical Red-baiters and the arbitrary minorities rage across the scene like great unthinking apes, bending evolution a bit their backward way, denying reason and truth."

A national public educational system needed to replace "today's educational paradoxes and irrationalities," which had "turned American education into a tremendously powerful propaganda weapon. [E]very teacher and every school, and every nation, holds unconcealable prejudices and opinions," he feared. "Does America follow any other course" than fascist or communist countries? "Was my generation warned that democracy, capitalism, or home-and-family were possibly defective in their present forms?"

Just before he had graduated, "the furthest-left course of a liberal sociology professor at my university was dropped from the catalogue. It had presented the wrong heroes, and had slandered the war lords, robber barons, and princes of profit customarily worshipped in the nation's classrooms." America, he worried, was "hurtling toward jagged rocks." He quoted Voltaire – "*I don't agree with what you say, but I would die for your right to say it.*" Without that credo, he feared that Americans would be goose-stepping behind Goebbels (Nazi minister of propaganda), "not only expelling liberal professors from the schools but putting them in concentration camps, not only barring radical books…but publicly burning them.… [E]ducation and democracy can never part company; education, driven downward by fear of truth, spells disaster…that can end only in demagogy and dictatorship." He concluded:

> "American education must come under the jurisdiction of the Declaration of Independence.… The schools must be allowed to seek and tell the truth, even the bitterest truth." [223]

Reflecting on his diatribe, Cranston worried that he would be seen as blaming his parents for the quality of his education. His "blast against institutions," he wrote in a personal note, should not be construed as from "a defeated idealist who chooses to blame the world and his teachers, not himself, for his frustrations. He desires to have it known that this is written from observations, not personal experiences; that he loves and admires two capable parents; that they are well-educated, never been seen to fight, fill the house with good music; that they have given him an environment [of] such happiness, contentment and guidance that he wished others could have similar ones – that they have, in brief, given him the ability to offer such constructive criticisms as the accompanying." [224]

In another piece about education called "Crimson Purge," Cranston criticized the dismissal of ten popular Harvard University assistant professors, triggering resignations of others in sympathy. "Although they were fired ostensibly because there was 'no room for promotion,'" Cranston wrote, "under-graduate observers note that a suspiciously large number of the ousted teachers are known for their liberal tendencies." [225]

Twenty-six years later, in 1962, Cranston wrote nostalgically of "The Farm," as Stanford was fondly called by alumni, highlighting those who had raised their voices about contemporary issues in the 1930s. "The Depression was on in full force.… Herbert Hoover, [class of] '95, sat grimly in the White House, challenged by Franklin Roosevelt.… One Adolf Hitler was on his way to power in Germany. His name was known only to a handful of us, but he would shape our lives and shake our world." The unsettled state of the world caused "many a '36er [to insist that] these topics be explored, criticized, taken apart, put together, turned upside down. These were the ones, in class and out, on campus and off, who made hitherto non-thinkers think.… They hammered and hammered on the anvil of our time, striking sparks… destined through us to have their influence in a world of upheaval." Pleasanter memories were "the brand new, amazing, four-lane Bayshore [highway] to San Francisco," dancing at the Palace, Mark Hopkins and "St. Frantic" San Francisco hotels to "Smoke Gets in Your Eyes" and "Body and Soul." "Prohibition came to its happy ending while [Stanford President] Ray Lyman Wilbur dourly warned that gasoline and alcohol did not mix." Happy excursions overshadowed "the drums and bugles of Hitler, Mussolini and the Japanese War Lords [who] seemed so far, so very far away." [226]

He counted himself among "the impatient ones who hoped that June, 1936, would…soon arrive so we'd be out in the world…and [realized] that the world would never, never be better, never again be quite like this." He ended with a quote by long-time Stanford President J. E. Wallace Sterling (1949-68) that reflected Cranston's views in his post-graduation essay, "School versus Education":

"Education is the prime and most abiding asset of any society. It is susceptible of manipulation, as in the police state. But when uninhibited…, when guided by a sense of responsibility to society, it is capable not only of overcoming pestilence and poverty but also enhancing that freedom which places and preserves the individual in the center of things." [227]

Cranston indeed was impatient to be out in the world and participate in events that were unfolding at the time. Little did he know how much he would become the center of things.

2

Realizing Dreams

"I was intent upon becoming a foreign correspondent, and I did."
Alan Cranston of his youthful plans.

"I believe that the end of every man's life should be to try to hasten that process of evolution, and if he is capable, even to help guide it."
Alan Cranston, "What science has given me - ideal, evolution," early observation.

Cranston set out after college intending to become a journalist. "The idea of being a foreign correspondent, wandering the world and witnessing great events, having adventures and covering the activities of world leaders, appealed to me greatly," he would later say. "It was a very glamorous life in those days. And I decided that was for me." [1]

He went East armed with hometown newspaper clippings and letters of introduction, including one from Cora Older and another from his father to an editor of a Chicago paper. His goal was to return to Europe, the place to be for an aspiring journalist in 1936. "I made a tour of all the newspaper offices in the East that my path took me near, from Chicago through New York to Boston," he wrote in a candid published letter to the *Register-Leader*. "Usually I got thrown out on my ear, but I had with me a scrapbook of all the stuff I've written for the *Register-Leader*, and every time I managed to stay in an office long enough to open it as well as my mouth, I was allowed to stay longer." [2]

No newspapers offered to hire him until Mrs. Older's letter gained a brief introduction to William A. Curley, executive editor at the Hearst *New York Evening Journal* who promised to introduce Cranston to city editor Amster Spiro the next day. But when Cranston got off the elevator at the newspaper offices, he found a hall porter fiercely refusing another man's request to see Curley. After the other man departed, Cranston asked the porter where the men's room was. "I went down to the right and stood outside the door of Curley's office 'till he suddenly burst out in a big rush, saw me, said, 'Oh, hello, c'mon in and meet Spiro.' Which I did. And the fortunate thing about all this was that I caught the city editor in an especially jovial mood – a big, tough guy, unshaven that day and looking like Al Capone. In five minutes we were pals and I was sitting on the edge of his desk." [3]

After looking through Cranston's clippings, Spiro gave him press credentials, referrals to other contacts (including editors at the *Chicago American* and *Boston Transcript* who also gave Cranston press credentials), and "authorization to cable collect from Europe queries on any good stories" that Cranston might come across. Spiro also promised "to give serious attention to a 'vagabond' column" that Cranston wanted to write "knocking around" Europe. "Imagine – a chance to write a COLUMN in a big-time paper," he exclaimed in his letter to the *Register-Leader*. "I've wanted to do that ever since, and before, I used to write that 'School Daze' column for your paper."

"Lady Luck has certainly smiled or rather had hysterics over your kid brother," he wrote Eleanor. "Then Lady Luck had hysterics again" A King Features executive to whom Spiro had referred Cranston introduced him to the head of Hearst's operations in Europe, foreign correspondent William Hillman who just happened to be visiting the office at that time. "He told me to come and see him when I got to England." Cranston eagerly took up the offer on arriving in London. "Hillman let me hang around the office to get the hang of what it was all about – it looked like a madhouse at first," Cranston wrote home. He gradually was given work, at first with no pay, then put on the International News Service (INS) payroll at $5.00 a day, working three or four days a week out of its Fleet Street bureau. [4]

"What luck!" Cranston wrote home. "Imagine my having a foreign job so soon! Most people don't get such news posts till they're aged or cynical or both." It was "the most fascinating work on earth." One of his first stories concerned preparations that England was making for possible war. He covered "such swell stories as the Richman-Merrill flight [trans-Atlantic flight of Broadway actor Harry Richman and pilot Dick Merrill, U. K. to N. Y., September 14, 1936], and the trial of MacMahon, the crackpot who threw a gun at the King." Other stories were of less import – "Soldier seeks blind girl who aided him," "Lovers have trouble getting married," "'One hoss shay' confiscated by cops," "English countryside frightened by 'thing.'" [5]

Cranston's experience as a competitive runner also came in handy. The 1936 Olympic Games in Berlin were big news when he arrived, and he proved useful in that coverage. When athletes came to London immediately after the Olympics to participate in a track meet at the Crystal Palace, Cranston was assigned to cover the event. "That led me to find a way to meet my idol," famed African-American Ohio State track star Jesse Owens who had carried away four Olympic gold medals. "I bumbed around London a little bit with him," once when Owens had a date with an attractive Austrian woman hurdler, "a blond, Valkeyrie-type," a potential scandal that Cranston did not exploit. Hitler's refusal to congratulate Owens after his Olympic wins was much publicized as a snub because of his race. Owens talked about turning professional and earning money, educating himself for a possible political career or role in which he could use his fame to improve race relations and upgrade the image of Black Americans. "I was able to get stories out of him that no one else could get," Cranston reported, and sent them off to Spiro. They were not published under his byline but parts were used in other news articles. [6]

Another scoop, Cranston hoped, was a chance to corner United Mine Workers president and legendary labor leader John L. Lewis. Cranston realized that Lewis was on some kind of special mission when he mysteriously appeared in London for four days, refusing all press inquiries about why he was there. Cranston confronted Lewis each morning in his hotel lobby but got nothing out of him. Pretending to leave, Cranston then would jump into a taxi and follow him. Cranston's fiancé, Dorothea Merrill, had arrived in London and through her he learned that Mrs. Lewis was friendly with Roosevelt's Secretary of Labor, Frances Perkins. "That knowledge started me on a chain of investigation that eventually disclosed that Perkins made a secret visit to London from Monday to Wednesday, undoubtedly to see Lewis. That gave me the story, and we beat all the other papers and news sources on it," Cranston wrote his family. "For the first couple of days it seemed like a hopeless chase, so I'm surely glad I finally got the story." [7]

Merrill's contacts would be helpful a second time when Cranston learned through her father, a timber financier, that the French *franc* was about to be devalued, possibly by August 15, 1936. The INS was reluctant to accept Cranston's sources so he wired Spiro at the *New York Journal-American*, who also did not bite. When August 15 passed without the prediction's coming to pass, Cranston was worried, but a few weeks later, the *franc* was devalued. "You were right," Spiro telegraphed Cranston, expressing in a subsequent letter "admiration for your achievement on the French money story," and promising him a job when he returned to New York. He had gained valuable respect from the veteran newsman.

His pursuit of the news did not help his personal relationship with his girl friend, however, and they quarreled. The engagement was put on hold and Merrill went back to attend Yale Law School. "It's perfectly amicable," Cranston told his parents, then in Paris. "I think we love and understand each other more than before. We just realize some of the difficulties in our way…. But I claim it's further proof that my emotions don't becloud my reason. Take care of Dottie," he ended. The two would not reconcile, though, each going separate ways in their careers.

The life of a correspondent was unstructured, as Cranston's father had feared, but Cranston defended the irregular life, pointing out that when they had assignments, reporters "had to work at terrific speed and make no errors. That's the kind of work I like," he told his father. "I certainly have my hand on the pulse of the world here. Everything that happens comes in here by phone or cable. Last night I took down [General Van Wiegand's] Spanish civil war story from Madrid over the phone on the Dictaphone and put in calls to Rome, Paris and Berlin for Hillman. That's covering territory, isn't it?" He was "having all kinds of adventures." At a fascist headquarters he found "a bunch of damn fools trotting around in black shirts and red sleeves, saluting each other and calling their big shot 'leader.'" He toured London's seedier sections like flophouses, veterans' homes, night-time dives and a pick-pockets' den with an out-of-work Communist whom he met in Hyde Park. "The people in some of the cellar holes were exactly as rough and ragged as Dickens' characters," Cranston told his parents.

He wrote up an encounter that profoundly affected him with a British society aristocrat, actress and drug addict, Brenda Dean Paul – "one of the most fascinating creatures with whom fate's irresistible magnet has ever played its sinister tricks. For two short weeks, I've been under her enchanting spell as, every night, we've wandered from one to another of the strange spots where London night life is at its weirdest." Her mind was "one of those mystical, sixth-sensed ones, dreamy yet intense, like an iceberg" with unseen depths. She told Cranston the story of her "lives," one chapter of which she related "over a carved table and a glass of ale" in Soho. Brenda, then twenty-seven, had escaped "the wracking, tearing, crazing tortures of morphine addiction," brought on by an operation and hemorrhage. Her habit had resulted in her arrest for purchasing more than the amount allowed her. "Daughter of...a future baron, it made a terrific sensation throughout London – 'Society beauty jailed as dope fiend!'" Released, she failed to appear for a monthly check on her recovery and was sentenced to six months at hard labor, scrubbing floors. Pardoned, she fled to Spain briefly until civil war sent her back to England. She told Cranston that she "had cured herself in an unprecedented way" by switching from morphine to cocaine injections, "a habit that can be broken" and had "no great physical let down," he recorded. "Addicts have tried the switch to cocaine before, but always to sniffing and sniffing is apt to so damage the brain so that it isn't capable of knowing or caring if any dope habit has been broken." As for Brenda, she was convinced that she was about the kick the habit and wanted to go on stage. "She would be a marvelous actress, she could interpret any role – she's lived them all," Cranston wrote. Her spirit impressed him – "She has the exquisite joy and anticipation of pulsing life of an unslapped child." He saved news photographs of her before and after addiction, wasted to the appearance of an old woman. [8]

The possibility of war permeated England at the time. "You can feel things are tense as soon as you get over here," Cranston told Spiro. "There are countless places war could break out. Europe was never so combustible, though people are going to be careful with their matches. No one *wants* war." [9]

While in Europe he continued the habit of writing down his thoughts and observations about life with pithy quotes from his reading on index cards or rectangular pieces of paper cut to fit a shoe box, neatly filed by subject. Those included evolution, religion, trade, world state, arms, politics, economics, capitalism (a large number of cards were in this category), communism, fascism, philosophy, love, eugenics, abnormality (homosexuality), prostitution, education (more notes were in this category than any other). Some notes were handwritten, others typed, with cites for quotes. The notes, a kind of journal, reflected Cranston's mental and intellectual evolution as he tried to put perspective on himself and his future. He continued listing "authors to read" (Stuart Chase, H. G. Wells, Mark Sullivan, Will Durant, Thoreau's *Walden*) and things "to do" ("start political-quote section in filing cabinet"). One note read, "The rapidest progress is downhill – everybody wants to get rich quick." But there was an underlying hopefulness and optimism about mankind and his own potential role in the great scheme of things. [10]

"Survival of the fittest" was the "basis of evolution, one of the most valuable of nature's inexorable laws." But when "nature is too harsh, man takes over the job" and should make it less harsh, he thought. "Undesirables can be painlessly sterilized. But this *does* take a lot out of mother nature's hands and put it in man's, and is this wise? Is man capable of assuming such a responsible position? Look at the world he runs today!" It was ironic, he observed, that just as Charles Darwin was posing his theory of survival of the fittest, scientists were "making profound discoveries of ways to preserve human life." Of sterilization he concluded, "We have yet to realize that we must use it wisely if progress is to be not a dream but a fact. Man may yet be only the last of the great apes," Cranston echoed from reading H. G. Wells. "The great ape was clever," Wells had written, "but not clever enough. It could escape from most things, but not from its own mental confusion." [11]

Those thoughts led Cranston to anthropology. One item dealt with "sexual selection," using the example of how a young lady with buck teeth might not be a "candidate for preferential mating" but after having them straightened by an orthodontist, might become desirable, only to produce, thanks to genetics, "bevies of buck-toothed off-spring." "Thus the effect of sexual selection in this [case] is to make business better for the orthodontist," the Paris *Herald [Tribune?]* of September 25, 1936, had quoted Harvard anthropology professor Ernest A. Hooton as saying. Cranston included another of his comments: "The most notable example of sexual selection is the tendency for successful male American Negroes, of whatever pigmentation, to choose as mates the lightest skinned negroid girls."[12]

"There can no *perfect* man, each falls short everywhere; we are as individuals a series of involuntary 'tries' on the part of an imperfect species towards an unknown end," Cranston summarized from bacteriologist Élie Metchnikoff's *Nature of Man.* There was "no 'perfect' dieting, no 'perfect' sexual life, no 'perfect' happiness, no 'perfect' conduct," the scientist had written. George Bernard Shaw, in his preface to *Back to Methuselah*, impressed on Cranston that "Evolution will find another creature if man isn't up to the mark." [13]

Still, Cranston wrote, thinking of his own potential, science had taught him that man, both as an individual and as part of society, "is working toward some end that cannot help but be marvelous. I believe that the end of every man's life should be to try to hasten that process of evolution, and if he is capable, even to help guide it. I would never have gained this thought from the studies of science I had in school.... I had to read *The Outline of Man's Knowledge* and see all of what man knows and has done and is trying to do, as a connected whole." "The alert and progressive man," Cranston penned on one card, "is he who refuses to accept as a matter of course those things of human society which the average man will accept." [14]

Cranston made extensive notes on man's seemingly insatiable desire to wage war and the alarming worldwide arms build-up in 1937. He particularly took note of Russia's massive military and Stalin's command to "Give me the greatest army in the world," quoted in the *New York American* March 17, 1937. "Europe to spend 13 or 14 billion $$$ on arms in 1937," Cranston recorded from another *American* article. He was disturbed by a Dorothy Thompson column in the Paris *Herald Tribune* March 11, 1937, citing "the revelation that our government is concerned with whether it can get steel from our own industries under the Walsh-Healey Act [setting minimum wages and a forty-hour week for employees of government contractors]... – all these are only straws indicating the outstanding and most important fact in the world today, namely, that an armaments race is on which has no parallel in history and... that the whole process of industrial recovery is bound up in this race. The nations indulging in this orgy of armaments have not yet paid for the last war," Thompson pointed out. Pacifists, though, Cranston noted, were expensive to incarcerate, and thus were not neutral, weakening a country's forces. [15]

"The World War was fought under the guise of making the world safe for democracy," Cranston reflected, but "today there are more absolute dictatorships in the world than for centuries before." [16]

An intriguing idea, sparking what would be a life-long crusade for Cranston, was setting up a World Council (a precursor of the United Nations concept) that would maintain armed units to be used only for police purposes to prevent war. The idea came from a 1933 Metro-Goldwyn-Mayer (MGM) film, *Gabriel Over the White House*, based on a book *Rinehard* by Thomas Frederic Tweed, which was sympathetic to President Roosevelt's New Deal programs, albeit under a dictator-like president. The film ended with a powerful plea for controlling armaments, its enlightened president saying, "Unless man's God-given faculty for utilizing the forces of nature for beneficent purposes shall surpass his vicious genius for destruction" with ever-more-powerful arms, "the race of man shall *perish* from the earth." (Cranston clearly was moved by the message, although ironically the film was produced by William Randolph Hearst whom Cranston derided. Hearst liked the concept of a strong president who could get the country through the Depression, which the film champions along with a New Deal-like "Army of Construction." MGM sent a working print to the White House for preview, promising to remove "all objectionable features." "I think it is an intensely interesting picture and should do much to help," Roosevelt wrote appreciatively to Hearst, who the following year turned strongly against Roosevelt's policies.) [17]

Cranston also wondered about the "theory of popular sovereignty – but no one knows exactly what this means" – another subject that he would address throughout his life. He read a "swell article," *Political Panaceas*, about "our imperfect Constitution" and recorded his thoughts about equality: "Politically I and W. R. Hearst have one vote apiece, but how many *more* votes and people can *he* influence? Legal equality is a mere myth – to make it real, you must have economic equality as well." Liberty meant the "right to acquire property" and "carry on a business" without the state's "interfer[ing] with you." But that right had to be reconciled "with public welfare endeavors" in which the government acts "as an umpire to make you play fair," Cranston reasoned.

He was examining the idea of a world state, writing, "States must be as free as private firms as long as capitalism exists, and thus the World State, like socialism, is impossible as long as there is capitalism." From Samuel Butler's *Erewhon* he quoted, "Property is robbery." Capitalism seemed counter to internationalism which was based on "planning, arranging nations in a way that producers [industries] are not arranged. Internationalism is the thing of the future, *it will come*," he wrote, "but nationalism may be the best thing for the present" although countries like Mexico, "with its backward Indians, would be a bad cog in a world state now." Equal states, like "equal persons, can work together, unequal can't. Is internationalism possible before all countries have been raised to a fair level of quality? Like the cogs of a wheel, which must be similar or the wheel won't turn, nations must be equal before the wheels of a world state could run smoothly." California Democratic Congressman Jerry Voorhis, in a 1937 article for *Nation*, alerted Cranston that no country could maintain itself "if it condemned a considerable number of its people to become an outcast group" or did not solve the problem of unemployment. And, as Lincoln Steffens had said, if laws were written to foster corruption and graft, there also had to be laws to protect the helpless "dumb part of our population" so they would "not be unmercifully exploited." Cranston believed that "In the World State, the individual shall not owe allegiance to the State…but to the human race, as a member of it." But "would we be happy in a perfect state, in which no evil or hardship existed?" Cranston wondered. "If so, why the adventurous spirit of man? Why do we rather read of wars and storms than peace and calms?" He made a note to study "the weakness of all world conferences – economic, disarmament, peace conferences" and "find why, basically, they failed." It would make a "marvelous book if one key can be found, other than individual selfishness and nationalism." They were seeds that Cranston one day indeed would articulate in a book. [18]

"Politics interfere with evolution," he wrote of Bertrand Russell's theory that Darwinism was "an argument for warism," with which he agreed. "By emphasizing heredity," Russell had written in *Freedom versus Organization* (1934), Darwinism "lessened men's belief in…education and substituted the conviction that some races are inherently superior to others." That led to "nationalism" and "war as a means of competition" while "the natural partner of pacifism is cooperation." "The whole point," Cranston thought, was that "we must make collective government or accept collective suicide. Our politics are decades behind our industry." Cranston quoted one observation that "the yeast of civilization – reason, intelligence, culture, humanity, knowledge – cannot be confined to the few." Ruling classes had to "resign their privilege of power and preeminence in material wealth." [19]

One significant political fact caught his attention, apparently from something that muckraking novelist Upton Sinclair, unsuccessful 1934 Democratic candidate for governor of California, had written: "Out of fifteen presidential elections since the Civil War, fourteen were carried by that party which had the biggest campaign fund." Cranston also filed a quote from Thomas Mann's "I Stand with the Spanish People," published in *Nation*, April 17, 1937: "A political man is a partisan whose will exercises restraints and limitations upon his intellect." [20]

On another card he wrote:

> "Our Great United States Presidents -
> Teddy Roosevelt was a hot-headed fire-eater, prejudiced in all his views.
> Woodrow Wilson was a coward.
> Warren G. Harding was a corrupt degenerate.
> Calvin Coolidge was meek, ignorant, 'kept."
> Herbert Hoover was incapable.
> Franklin D. Roosevelt is ???" [21]

Cranston was comparing democracy with other forms of government: "Democracy is not so much an end in itself as a means to achieve socialism. Whether it is practical is another matter." But "there's an awful lot of talking going on in America, based on very little fact." Another note observed: "Democracy is a racket – the smartest will always rule…the smartest will inevitably be able to exert more power, accumulate more wealth, get the dumbest to work for them." And "competition between political parties" was "the best method of assuring peaceable progress," although "even the politicians misuse democracy. They use it to get offices and benefits for themselves, rather than for the good of the masses." [22]

The "best methods of influencing public opinion," he wrote on a card, were either "cellular," in which many small groups, or associations, were organized to discuss issues; or "writing," an indirect method like Sinclair Lewis's *It Can't Happen Here* in which he denounced fascism. Other cards discussed unemployment – "as capitalism declines, it cannot sustain the burdens of unemployment insurance and the other social services which are then demanded of it" – and preserving large corporations while spreading out their profits – "making certain that the rewards of efficiency accrued to society as a whole rather than to a few individuals," quoted from a 1937 editorial in *Nation.* [23]

Cranston was reading about Marxism, too, balancing information from various sources. Marx's theory predicted the liquidation of the middle class as wealth was concentrated in a few companies. "Example," Cranston wrote on that card: "In 1910 ten or twenty times as many automobile factories functioned as do today. By superior technique, Chrysler, Ford, General Motors froze out these small fry. Hudson, Essex, Studebaker, etc. will soon be absorbed by these three – just watch." He noted Bertrand Russell's commentary (in *Freedom versus Organization*) that, while Marx's doctrine of class war had killed liberalism in Europe ("by frightening the middle classes into reaction"), in America, "old-fashioned liberalism still survives, and is at present engaged in a quite un-Marxian attempt at reconstruction." There were dangers in communism, though, as Upton Sinclair had pointed out (in *100%, The Story of a Patriot, 1920*), when extremists gained control, as the Reds had in Russia, proceeding "to make peace with Germany, which put the Allies in a frightful predicament and introduced a new word into the popular vocabulary, the dread word 'Bolshevik.' After that, if a man suggested municipal ownership of ice-wagons, all you had to do was to call him a 'Bolshevik' and he was done for." [24]

Cranston mused on other subjects than world affairs and economics as he wrote at night in his foreign garrets and cheap rooms. He related women and sex to the broader issues that he was contemplating. "In this boarding house where I'm staying, there are three unattached girls, all young and pretty," he typed November 9, 1936, (in Rome), under the heading, "Capitalism versus poverty – man's way, through poverty, to insure himself of plentiful easily-made women."

"One is a taxi dancer – could obviously be had. The other two are a hairdresser and manicurist – and gold diggers. They can be had, for a price. They all earn their money at their legitimate trades but they are all underpaid terrifically; can't possibly make enough to buy all the pretty things girls enjoy – clothes, perfumes, etc. They like their fun at night, too, dancing, shows and more, but they try to choose where it will be most profitable, where something may be thrown in for themselves. They have to do this, they can't get enough to enjoy themselves otherwise. It may not be called prostitution when they take flowers, perfume, perhaps a nice piece of clothing now and then, instead of money, but what is the real difference when they have to give one certain thing – not only their pleasant company but their bodies – in return? How many of them would do that if they weren't poor? How many would like a man for his money, not for himself? How many would sleep with a fat, stodgy, oldish man who has a fat pocketbook, when they could love a lean, tall, handsome youth – albeit with a thin pocketbook – if they were not themselves poverty-stricken, if they could not furnish themselves with the small amount of frills that would make them contented?

"If the world didn't operate under such a harsh system, there would be none but imbecilic or super-sexed prostitutes. So the system may be one [in which]... ugly, unattractive men make sure they shall never want. Think how it would be – just think – if the women could choose their lovers in a logical way! How much more attractive the women would be if they could think about something besides the money side. But also the men! Think how attractive men would become, how fastidious, how cultivated, if their success with women depended solely upon their cleanliness, attractiveness, wit, etc.

"It has been demonstrated that a man need not be handsome to succeed with women if he has intelligence and wit. So the unhandsome could develop that instead of doing as they do now – earning money, not developing anything else about themselves because that's all they need to [be] successful with women. How the world would be improved!" [25]

"Does a man who visits a prostitute aid or retard mankind?" he asked. "Seemingly, by contributing to an evil thing, he is helping that thing along; but, on the other hand, will the question of whether he, one man, indulges or not have any effect on the vast business? And furthermore his few dollars will at least help one poor woman have an easier time. It's the same old question, in different form, of 'What good's one vote in a vast democracy?'" He also wondered why sex urges should be considered bad, quoting one writer who justified them as making "possible the fullest flowering of the family relationship." As for homosexuality, he rationalized there were "non-physical reasons" for such behavior. It was "easier – no scandal when you live with a man, but your career can be ruined if you live with a woman" – and avoided the responsibilities of marriage and the risk of offspring from promiscuity. It also had psychological roots – "inferiority complex makes a man afraid to try to win a girl," or "run the risk of not being able to consummate a marriage with her," whereas there was less fear of "set-backs" with a man. [26]

As for feelings of superiority over other ethnicities, Cranston again quoted from Sinclair Lewis' *It Can't Happen Here* – "People are always satisfied as long as they can look down on someone." "If so," Cranston mused, "Jews should be violently anti-Negro. I don't think they are." Persecution of Jews, he recorded from a *Nation* editorial, "threatens the world's cultural heritage and the entire range of freedom for the human mind.... The fight must ultimately be made by liberal, labor, and democratic forces, willing not only to protest but to organize behind their protest their massed political and economic strength." A timely "project," he wrote at one point, would be to "visit Liberia and write up what Negroes can do by themselves." [27]

"I try my hardest to be a world cosmopolitan," Cranston wrote of his own objectives, "which means a world democrat. Only thus can one tolerate and do one's best to understand the fascist and communist and religious factions, whether and wherever they be minorities or majorities. The true democrat must understand all minorities. Hard enough in one country, it's a terrific task in the whole world." [28]

Cranston's temporary job in the INS London bureau ended after seven weeks when regular staff returned from vacation. Hillman thought Cranston might improve as a reporter "after a few rough spots are worn off," Cranston admitted in his letter to the *Register-Leader*, and suggested that he present himself to INS Rome bureau chief Frank Gervasi. "Bill Hillman advised me that if I learned Italian in three months," Cranston later recalled to Gervasi, "you'd hire me. Which you did, in December." To learn the language, Cranston watched Italian movies with sub-titles. His parents were uneasy about his going to the fascist-run country where imprisonment and other dangers for offenses to Mussolini's government were common. Beware of pick-pockets, wear a money belt and avoid Italian girls, his father behooved his son. [29]

Cranston arrived in Rome in September, 1936. "Gad, I've got a lot to do," he wrote Eleanor: "write the column, learn the language in the shortest possible time, write articles for the *Boston Transcript*, and forty-one letters." Rome was "swell," it offered many opportunities – "a chance to get acquainted with one of the most fascinating histories in the world…to learn one of the most beautiful languages, to study Catholicism and fascism from the inside," he told the *Register-Leader*. "I don't think there's any place in Europe I'd rather be, unless it's Moscow." To Eleanor he confessed, "At present I live in a heckuva dump, a cold room on the fourth floor of a *pensione* facing a *piazza*. The meals are lousy and the elevator's locked most of the time. But from a balcony here last night, I had a swell view of the comic opera of fascism." He had watched several thousand people gather in the square to listen to *Il Duce*, preceded by bands and uniformed black-shirts on parade. The speech, though, was one that Mussolini had given a year earlier announcing war on Ethiopia, this time broadcast over loudspeakers. [30]

Gervasi, himself only twenty-eight years old, and his wife Kay "practically adopted me" and fed "me pancakes – you don't know what that means 'till you're away from the U. S. for a while," he joked to the *Register-Leader*. To Skattebol, Cranston wrote that he was learning self-control from Gervasi whose ability to concentrate and absorb knowledge impressed Cranston, as did his knack of turning "sleep on and off like a light." Cranston's lack of Italian, however, was a deterrent to getting hired. After traveling around Italy for eight weeks, he was nearly broke and feared that he was not going to get a job with INS.

He was briefly considered for the Berlin bureau. Its bureau chief, according to a copy of a letter from Berlin, wrote,

> "Your suggestion of Cranston as a possibility for Berlin sounds pretty good to me. For your own information, my impression of Cranston during my brief stay in Rome was most favorable. He looked to me like a fellow who could be developed into a good newsman. I have noticed also in particular that he is not a heavy drinker…. I would be more than glad to have Cranston transferred to Berlin. I suggest that we do nothing further on this until we meet and in the meantime I am doing nothing about getting a man for Berlin myself." [31]

Gervasi, though, was short-handed and needed staff to cover such things as the imminent arrival of British King Edward VIII's lady friend Wallis Simpson. Cranston offered to help and a few days later, Hillman told Gervasi to put Cranston on the staff. He would be paid $12.50 a week – "That's about $120 a month for what it'll buy in Rome compared to California," he wrote his sister. He was assigned the "graveyard" shift, midnight to nine a.m. It was hard for him to understand Italians and with no one in the bureau to translate, Cranston found that he sometimes had little to report when Gervasi arrived in the morning because he "hadn't understood a word and didn't know what on earth had happened [or] what the story was" that had been phoned into the bureau. He confessed in a letter home, apparently written during long nights on the desk alone,

"The telephone still has me intimidated by sight and sound. I'm scared stiff it's going to bring me some excited Italian with a phony dialect – but hot news – at any moment. My informer will probably be so excited I won't know what he's talking about. Besides trying to get details, I'm ordered to get his name and number. Then hang up and on our <u>two</u> office phones make <u>four</u> simultaneous calls: first call the guy back immediately to verify and keep him busy and his line occupied so he can't call rivals with news. Also, first call London; tell them we have the report and checking on it. Call Berlin; tell them the same thing. Call Gervasi, so he [can] try to check." [32]

When he was not answering the telephone, Cranston read through twenty volumes of the *Catholic Encyclopedia* that he found in the bureau. One big story that he hoped would not happen while he was on duty alone was the anticipated death of Pope Pius XI. INS' New York headquarters had ordered its Rome bureau to "capitalize on death of his Eminence." The Associated Press was scooping other news agencies through a Vatican telephone operator who kept tabs on the pope's condition. Italians sometimes came into the INS office with tips for which they expected compensation. One turned out to be a piece of paper from a pharmacy that purported to contain the pope's urinalysis. [33]

Another person who walked into the bureau made a particularly big impression. "One day while I was working for the Hearst corporation in Rome there blows into town a guy named Lee Falk," creator of popular comic strips *Mandrake the Magician* and *The Phantom*," Cranston later recalled of their first encounter. "Journalists would inevitably call up" the bureau, whether with INS or not, "and want to chat, and one day this guy Falk calls and says, 'Can I come over and meet you guys?' I knew at once who he was: the writer of two of the most famous cartoons at that time, the most widely-read man daily on earth – those two cartoons were published all over the world, including Russia where they were pirated." For the frustrated cartoonist Cranston, Falk was a character out of his own drawings. He had a Mephistophelian face with a distinctive, narrow mustache, and his worldly, confident and sardonic demeanor attracted Cranston. For his part, Falk saw "a tall young guy with holes in his shoes, who was always hungry, frantically trying to learn Italian, sitting there in the Hearst office, dying when the phone rang, petrified that some news break would come!" Falk was in Rome on tour for King Features which syndicated his strips. "Anyway, he and I became very good friends," Cranston said. The friendship would last a lifetime. "My favorite comic strip," he wrote the editor of the San Francisco State University journalism review many years later, "is *Mandrake the Magician* by my old and good friend Lee Falk. *Mandrake* combines adventure, humor and magic – things we all need daily, including Sunday." [34]

Cranston got into a tight spot one day, however, when a story that Gervasi was holding for release was spotted by a vacationing editor from the *New York Daily News*, Russ Simontown, who dropped into the INS bureau. The story concerned Mussolini's intention to replicate Hitler's anti-Semitic policies and was based on an interview with Minister of Interior Roberto Farinacci, a fiercely pro-Fascist who had lost a hand to a grenade, reportedly while exploding fish out of water during the Ethiopian war. He wore a gloved steel replacement that reinforced his tough-man image. The visiting New York newsman had hung around the INS office telling stories. But when Cranston left the room for a few minutes, he returned to find Simontown reading the Farinacci story. Caught, Simontown quickly departed, but Cranston realized that he probably was going to steal the story. He raced down to the Western Union office in the building and found Simontown trying to send a telegram with the facts but having trouble with the Italian operator who did not understand English. Cranston put a hand on Simontown's shoulder and told him to come back to the office and explain. Simontown was determined to get the story to his newspaper somehow. Cranston offered him drinks while trying to delay him, realizing that his own career would be ruined if Simontown got the story before INS issued it.

By then, Cranston's friend Johnny Atkinson had come to Rome and gotten a job with United Press. Cranston called Atkinson and, using some Italian, asked him to come quickly to the INS bureau. They continued to ply Simontown with booze until they knew the Western Union office had closed. They accompanied him to his hotel where he again tried to telephone the story to New York, without success. Simontown then decided to go to Western Union headquarters but Cranston and Atkinson kept him going through the hotel's revolving door until Cranston was able to persuade the concierge to lock it and keep Simontown inside, making up a story that Mussolini ordered hotel doors locked at eleven o'clock. Simontown continued to try to get out, with Cranston and Atkinson restraining him each time the door was opened to let a guest in. It was like something out of a Marx Brothers' film, Cranston thought. They kept thwarting Simontown's efforts to escape through windows and other doors, finally seeing him into bed and watching him until the next morning. Simontown was furious and accused Cranston of kidnapping – Italians thought nothing of that, Cranston laughed – and at last Simontown agreed not to file the story. Cranston said that he trusted him and Simontown stuck by his word. He and Cranston later became friends, and Cranston was saved from a potentially bad predicament. [35]

He was learning from experience, though, including how to get news out of the country despite Italian censorship. The bureau staff knew that their office boy Orlando spied on them while pretending not to know English. "Our London bureau…took down our stories on a Dictaphone – and so did the Fascists," Cranston recorded in his diary notes. "Sometimes we could hear their machines – and sometimes their voices – as they listened in on our calls. Gerry [Gervasi] would be dictating a story, and suddenly break out in violent Italian, damning Mussolini and Fascist snoops. [One] time the phone went bad and every time we tried to phone the office from outside, we got Fascist police headquarters." Reporters had to work with "tremendous speed" on stories, he noted. "You had to beat U. P. and A. P. to the streets of New York, or your job wasn't worth a damn." [36]

He was amazed, and amused, by the Italians' love-hate attitude toward their dictator and their oppressed political status – they wore Fascist Party buttons while joking about it and mocking Mussolini. "Everything not forbidden is compulsory" was a favorite line that Cranston heard from the propaganda minister's lady friend. "I am busy looking at Fascism," he wrote Spiro:

"I'd read dozens of books and came here with prejudices, but some are fading away as I see causes as well as manifestations. It's a phenomenon of flat-broke countries.... I think the majority of Italians feel [that] Mussolini has done them more good than harm, and therefore support him. Rome has been on the march ever since the march on Rome, all but the fascist-educated hate the war-ism, as they hate the regimentation and spying, and loss of liberty. But they feel these are part of the only means Italy has to get anything from an ungenerous and foolish world. And they are willing to make sacrifices if *Il Duce* thinks it's necessary. But I do thank God that America is a rich country." [37]

He was struck by how afraid people were despite their outward humor, how fearful they were of being watched and caught at something forbidden. But seeing wounded soldiers and prisoners returning from war stunned him, as he told his sister.

"Saw the most heartbreaking thing of my life yesterday, soldiers coming back from Ethiopia. Gad, what wrecks they were. With horror, I watched human captives marched through the Arch of Constantine in an elaborate re-staging of the way imperial conquests were celebrated during the first Roman empire." [38]

While in Rome he wrote copious "journal" notes. A good number were under the heading "Autobiog." One read, "Apologies to all the poor people I kept awake whacking my typewriter in flimsy, thin-walled buildings late at night. I used to keep many poor Claras and Jianis and Julios awake on their beds in the next rooms. They may have silently cursed, but they seldom beat on the walls. And for my part, I rationalized it by the thought that it was really for their own good, that I was sweating over Bertrand Russell and Karl Marx and Adam Smith for them, or for people like them. Whenever I took a new room, one of my stipulations was that I would be allowed to play my typewriter all through the night if I so desired – as many men demand the privilege of playing with their girl friends through the nights." [39]

One note labeled "Lars' morbid fears stanza" recorded what his friend had written on a book flyleaf, ending, "They put away their fathers' biers/ But shoulder all their morbid fears." "Growing up in America, then wandering over Europe," Cranston wrote, "it was tragic to see my generation absorbing all the superstitious beliefs of old, shackles against progress of man. I saw Serbs hating Magyars beyond death, French hating Germans in the same way, playboys shocked at Blum's book advocating a girl's getting experience before marriage, kids my age blinded by

Catholic dogma, others doing it lip service for their families' sake – thus prolonging something they didn't even believe in themselves, etc., etc., etc." [40]

Cranston was not blind to his need to improve as a journalist. "In news work, I found myself constantly using big words to enlarge small ideas," he wrote self-critically, "and I momentarily rebelled, 'till I rationalized that I was gaining the ability to properly present the large ideas I intended to later produce." He practiced writing phrases – "a cloud-throttled moon," "some pieces of mutton in a stew that looked as if they had committed suicide in the gravy," "shadows sprawled larger and broader across the desert sands." One combination of words that he concocted and obviously liked was a "description of a big gun ready for action – 'A thirsty gun poked its mouth/muzzle into sight, panting in its passion.'" [41]

His slip-ups nevertheless provided fodder for thinking about the powerful impact of media on world affairs. One Sunday, September 18, 1937, Cranston confessed to his "journal,"

"I commit an error, which sabotages peace as Italy moves not away from war (troops to Libya and Africa), [its] press ministry slyer and slyer at denials. Gad, I've got to clamp down on my paper reading. I missed another story today, which makes two in a row after none for months. This was less fortunate than the last, due to incessant phone calls, visiting-fireman Sid dropping in, etc. On the sports page of the first edition of *La Tribuna* an obscure item told of 3,000 troops sailing for Libya tonight to 'complete' the garrison, with more going tomorrow for Ethiopia. I missed it, and it was yanked out, not appearing in the 2nd edition. Then came a query from London – N. Y. had a Reuters story of the troops, unofficial, wanted it confirmed and hit hard. I got Gervasi and then Reuters. They had first gotten it from their Naples correspondent, then seen it in the *Trib*. Gervasi gave a bawl-out, then wrote a highly dramatized story – the only way he could get the play in the papers, which would already have the plain facts from other agencies. He wrote that it was Mussolini's reply to France-Brit.'s threats and high-handed action in the Mediterranean as Italy pointed a cocked pistol at their African possessions…thus called their bluff…. He wrote (tho' he'd spoken to no officials), 'A high Italian authority bitingly declared between clenched teeth,' quote, 'We'll wake up one morning and find we can't put any motorboats out into the Mediterranean if this nonsense keeps up'…. He quoted 'controlled Italian press' in its 'withering series of editorials,' choosing the hottest quotes…. Thus he, and I, did no service to the cause of peace.

"Journalism never does create a peace atmosphere; the people want to read extras about war and danger of war, and we give it to them. I'm going to write an article someday…called 'Farewell to Fourth Estate' or 'The Press Peril to Peace.'" [42]

Cranston also was conflicted by working for the controversial but undeniably influential Hearst network, which by then was instructed by Hearst himself to fight communism. "Hearst has hired the higher intellects, thus immediately lowering them," Cranston wrote in one note; in another, he accused Hearst of "making the modern American mind" without the "owners' consent," a form of "rape," he thought. "Once I told a friend that I could justify my going to work for Hearst if the occasion ever arose. One of my arguments was the fact that Hearst won't live forever, and after his death I might be in a position to exert some influence on the future policies of his press, after the certain mad struggle for the reins had passed. 'Oh, you'd bite the hand that fed you?' said the friend. 'No,' I answered, 'I'd mend it, give it medicine.'" Hearst had ordered Gervasi not to send out stories that would offend the Italian leadership, believing that Mussolini was "a great man" who had done great things for Italy, Cranston said of orders received August 24, 1936, by the Rome bureau. Nor were there to be stories that would in any way aid the Communists. Hearst also was willing to let Italians use the INS wire to transmit stories they wanted to send abroad, telling the bureau to "Send anything they want you to send," Cranston paraphrased of the orders: "Of course, do not distort the news. If HE [Mussolini] is assassinated, send it." Hearst's close aide, Colonel Joseph Willicombe, according to Cranston, told Gervasi to "interpret" the orders rather them follow them to the letter. Hearst "is inevitably a Fascist," Cranston decided, "because he's a fanatic against communism, and fascism is the best possible weapon against it." Gervasi, he recorded, would not help Hearst get an interview with Mussolini for fear that Hearst wanted to "get dope on fascist tactics." [43]

Cranston realized that many historical figures changed political views over the course of their lives and expressed a "fear of becoming conservative" himself. "History told of so many men who started as radicals or believers in social justice, and ended among the men huddled furthest to the right. I was proud of my beginnings but fearful of what it might lead to. Mussolini's change made an impression, as did Hitler's, and the fear that Stalin had followed. [Theodore] Roosevelt's phrase about men of twenty or forty ["Every boy of twenty who isn't a Socialist should be. Every man of forty who is a Socialist is a damn fool"] was often in my mind," Cranston wrote in his autobiographical reflections. "I spent much time with the 'masses' so I'd really know them, not be like Jefferson, a Democrat partly because he didn't know the common man, and hoping at the same time that contact wouldn't make me like Hamilton, disgusted with their lives and abilities. Another reason was to keep myself conscious of their miseries. I tried to live them myself." [44]

"When we say that great men – Hitler, Mussolini, Stalin, [Jay] Gould – came from nowhere because they were paupers, or of poor, uneducated parents, we are wrong. They came from somewhere," he contemplated. "That low place in life gave them a sound foundation, a knowledge of the basis of life; the struggle up gave them force and a knowledge of realities which made them great men." [45]

Such flashes of perception led him to write, "A brilliant thought trickles into the brain, gradually permeates all the conscious cells, and we suddenly discover ourselves in possession of a profound truth we never consciously, rationally, deduced, perhaps never even knowingly searched for." [46]

He was impressed by Albert Einstein's reflections in *The World as I See It* (1934):

"How extraordinary is the situation of us mortals! Each of us is here for a brief sojourn; for what purpose he knows not, though he sometimes thinks he senses it. But…it is plain that we exist for our fellow men – in the first place, for those upon whose smiles and welfare all our happiness depends, and next for all those unknown to us personally but to whose destinies we are bound by the tie of sympathy. A hundred times every day I remind myself that my inner and outer life depend on the labours of other men, living and dead, and that I must exert myself in order to give in the same measure as I have received and am still receiving." [47]

Little did Cranston know that one day he would meet the man himself.

A particularly prescient exhortation to himself, which Cranston labeled "fear and promise if idealism turned to cynicism," read,

"As an idealist (Socialist youth), I remembered that I might (although I doubted it) become later a tough realist (Capitalist). I promised that if I became the latter, I would remember that I had been the former." [48]

Fascism and why people were attracted to it intrigued Cranston, as did Mussolini's use of Italian aristocracy. An article, Cranston thought, could explain "how I was bluffed into thinking [fascism] was good, how it makes each man think he's getting what he wants…how it hypnotizes with brass bands and stirring speeches." Spiro in 1937 asked Cranston to send him some pieces about life in fascist countries and he jotted down ideas, still hoping that it would lead to a regular column that allowed him to travel and write. He wanted to take a canoe trip down the Danube, through Austria, Hungary, Yugoslavia, Bulgaria and Rumania to the Black Sea, he wrote Spiro. "I don't know a damn thing about canoeing, but that would add to the excitement!" A "bang-up article," he thought, would be one called "Two Murders," about Hitler's head of storm troopers Ernest Roehm (who participated in a failed *coup* against the Nazis) and Italian socialist Giacomo Matteotti, both of whom were murdered by their respective dictators. Cranston would tell "why they were killed, and how" as "dramatically as possible [and] show how dictatorship requires such murders now and then, but usually they aren't of such notable men." He would describe how "Mussolini and Hitler both took complete responsibility for the acts." [49]

Another idea was to write about "the rise of radio as a political weapon, its use in the Dolfuss [*sic*] revolution, the first such use of it." He would cite examples like the "lies" broadcast in Spain by both sides, and "how the Reds learn to drown out the Fascists." One rumored incident was the death of an Italian who confessed that he was a Communist over the air waves – "a shot rang out, and there was no more." He could describe "the listeners behind doors" in Rome, "the smashing of radios, the new invention; sirens blowing on communist wave lengths – loudly – to reveal listeners; the drowning-out noise, like a train starting; the ever-changing communist short-wavers in Italy and Germany." British King "Edward's radio farewell, George VI's inauguration speech" were examples of "welding together the Empire. But you can't make people listen – Edward didn't" while Hitler and Mussolini forced "mass listenings," in Italy of Mussolini's old speeches "re-broadcast on appropriate occasions" when "every radio in the nation [is] turned on, if not from personal interest, in self-interest." He cited the Landon-Roosevelt presidential campaign in America and the "return of oratory to politics" because of the radio. One of his notes nostalgically said that he was first moved by the sound of the violin on radio in Rome. "I knew then that someday I would play the violin." It was one of the few plans that he did not fulfill. [50]

He considered writing a piece portraying Italy and Germany as communist nations. "A highly placed fascist official told me: 'Italy and Germany are the real communist nations of the world.... We are socialists who became communists when we found that asking that the rich nations divide their riches and colonies with us did not help.... We went on to the extreme of communism when we saw that our pleas...were ignored. You can get a clear view of this transition by studying the life of Mussolini, who grew from a socialist into a fascist-communist.' This can make a marvelous basis of a study of fascism, Mussolini and world conditions," Cranston said in his notes. "I can show that I am against fascism because I am against communism. But I must also admit that maybe it is because I am twenty-three, and an idealist," he conceded. [51]

A book that he had read about Mussolini got Cranston thinking about his own religious views. "Tremendously interested tonight," he recorded September 4, 1937, "in finishing George Seldes' *Sawdust Caesar*, to find in the appendix a translation of a 1904 Mussolini essay called '*Dieu N'Existe Pas*,' his first published work."

"The amazing point was the similarity of views – *Duce*'s and mine re: religion. He included the two quotes...I have most often myself quoted: Marx's (I've attributed it to Lenin) 'Religion is the opium of the people,' and the one by Epicurus saying either God wants to do away with worldly evil and can't, can and doesn't want to, can't and doesn't want to, or can.... I encountered this first in [John Herman] Randall's *Making of the Modern Mind* as a Pomona freshman in 1932, aged eighteen. It entranced and stumped me.... Thus at eighteen I was up with Mussolini at twenty-one, and at twenty-three I am ahead of him...on this point. I agreed with most of the rest of his essay.... Religion is an effort to fill mental vacuums. Surprising thing was Mussolini's attacking religion as the basis of unreasoning authoritarianism.... Yet Mussolini eventually turned to this very authoritarianism... and even made friends with the Vatican for the sake of expediency.

"I have often wondered if I, like Mussolini, would ever be willing to adopt as rigorous means as he has to achieve ends. I don't think he has really lost sight of his ends, he still works for Italy. To find that...he thought exactly as I do at the same age gives me pause to think. I must keep my ends in view, and I must remain an idealist, or a believer in evolutionary progress, and yet I feel strongestly [*sic*] that I <u>am</u> <u>not</u> going to be a mere thinking idealist, unable to act. Mussolini was unable to strike the balance between his powerful will and his ideals. I must constantly guard against a *volte face* such as his, yet I cannot allow ethics to completely negate my force." [52]

On March 1, 1937, Cranston sent Spiro eight columns. "Now it's up to you and fate," he told the city editor, but Spiro did not reply and the pieces were not published. [53]

That summer Cranston faced the prospect of running the INS Rome bureau for two months while Gervasi want on holiday – "if the higher-ups don't recall that I'm only twenty-three," he wrote Spiro. By then he had to accept the fact that he was not making enough money to live on – it cost him $44 a week to subsist (including 25 cents for baths and $10 to share a room), far in excess of the $12.50 weekly paycheck. He spelled it out to Gervasi in a letter of resignation. He realized that he had little chance of being advanced at his young age, without experience, and that his hopes and expectations of quick success as a journalist exceeded reality. [54]

Gervasi, who became a famous foreign correspondent, would remember Cranston as "a tall, quiet, lean fellow with a good mind and a quick smile" tempered by "a reserve, a reticence, a sort of privacy no one dared trespass." Still, Gervasi later confessed to Eleanor, "Alan was the only reliable, loyal assistant of the three I had in the Rome bureau of INS during those years." "Frankly, it never occurred to me back in 1935-36 when you were my assistant in the Hearst bureau in Rome that I would one day be addressing you as 'Senator,'" Gervasi wrote Cranston in 1974 when Gervasi was writing a memoir of the decade 1935-45, "though I do recall your intense interest in politics, and your grasp of the events of the time.... Since you are the only one of my several assistants who achieved real eminence, please dredge your memory." Gervasi thought well enough of Cranston in 1938 to get him an assignment to newly-conquered Ethiopia. "I seem to recall it was while the Ethiopian War was in full cry," Gervasi remembered, "and that you went to Abyssinia shortly after the Italians had conquered the country to write a series of pieces." Cranston sailed from Naples for North Africa on March 7, 1938. Shortly thereafter INS offered him a job in the Vienna bureau for $80 a week. But Cranston at last had realized his dream of being a real "foreign correspondent." [55]

"I spent four months there, sending you much copy," Cranston reminded Gervasi. "I was the first journalist other than Italians and Germans allowed to go there after Italy proclaimed victory in May of '36. I found the Italians still mopping up, and heard shooting every single night I was there." [56]

Cranston found himself in the very place that he had described from news accounts three years earlier in California. "I landed at Port Said with a bunch of Italians and kept exclaiming inwardly, 'You're in AFRICA!" he wrote Skattebol. "I bought a sun helmet. Imagine me in one of those!" He quickly perceived, as he told Gervasi, that the Italian government "was breaking its neck to give me a favorable impression of their progress in empire building. They met me at the dock, put a car and soldier-chauffeur at my disposal, and put me up in the best hotel in Massawa; drove me to the capital Asmara, threw some poor devil out in the street so I'd have a good room; gave me an immediate audience with the governor." His stories reflected the attitude that the government wanted to foster, but he soon realized that the "ultra-modern hotel in the heart of Africa, with modern conveniences," was "beginning to seem like a prison, and the precision of the dining room, though I eat there at government expense, drives me out to workers' restaurants," a letter home said. He conceded that it was "not a young squirt but INS and its 800 papers" that generated the favorable treatment he was receiving as a correspondent. [57]

There was plenty of excitement, nevertheless. A bullet "just went whistling by from the bushes" into a jeep that he was riding in. He saw a tribesman's head that had just been cut off carried into a village and stuck on a spear while natives danced before the Italian leader of the outpost to demonstrate loyalty to their conquerors. A plane in which he was being picked up tore its canvas bottom on trees as it came into land. Cranston had to wait until a native sewed it up before they could leave the outpost. [58]

As in Rome he also had to deal with censorship, provided by an assigned military escort (a Lieutenant Bertoletti). "A young censor in the branch office in Asmara almost drove this correspondent out of the empire as he thoroughly red-penciled early articles written in Eritrea," Cranston recorded in a typewritten draft for a news story. "Absolutely no military references escaped his sweeping red pencil, and he even dipped back into the last century, forbidding…the adjective 'fearful' for the defeat of the Italians at Adua [Adowa] in 1896…. I was further instructed that when the Italians marched into Ethiopia again in 1935 that it was an 'occupation,' not an 'invasion.'" Cranston was "practically imprisoned when there was slight native trouble along the road at Dessie, as it would be bad enough to have a foreigner see any trouble – if one got killed it would be utter tragedy – and eventually I was allowed to come to Addis Adaba only in a high-flying plane." He noted that one fascist leader, Marchese Catalano-Gonzago, was more liberal about censorship, "possibly because he is married to an American wife (Bostonian)," and because he realized that "strict censorship would breed animosity and anti-fascist articles" once the writers left Italy. The Adowa article, Cranston hoped, would prove to editors that "I could write picturesquely and fairly about Ethiopia." [59]

His first dispatch from Ethiopia – at the top of which he typed, "Article 1, mailed exAsmara via air March 27, 1938" – described Italian vessels unloading cargo at Massaua, "key port of the Italian empire, where men work endlessly…determined to show a world…that they can make their African empire into a paying proposition with the same amazing speed" in which they conquered it, seven months. Massaua was "springing from nothing on three islands," he recorded in his diary notes of impressions – a "big cement factory Pittsburging the sky," Muslim workers on docks "endlessly chanting…verses from the Koran, white men running the machines…swearing in the broiling heat…. Tugs, lighters, native barks make the port a maelstrom…. Acres of crated wine from Tuscany, Frascata, etc…. Men in every conceivable costume, natives in colonial uniform, women with babies piggy-back." That and other stories filed from Asmara and Addis Ababa emphasized how Italy was building up the East African colony as a "gateway to fascism's new Alps-to-Indian Ocean Empire." A quote from Italian King Victor Emmanuel III in 1932 – calling it a "tragedy" that Eritrea had been so undeveloped since Italians had been driven out at the turn of the century – was marked "censored" on Cranston's draft story. [60]

"Felt like doing some real writing," he put in his journal notes on April 5 at Asmara, "and after a visit to the gov., lit into one" about the need to "produce from East Africa. Could hardly sit through lunch waiting to get back at it, and about 3:30 had a really bang-up piece done, thinks I. Waited around interminably at the press office, and finally turned the spare time to account by translating 4/5ths of the damn thing into Italian so the lieutenant can get it done quicker in time for tomorrow air mail…. Back at the hotel after dinner, restlessness combined with inability to think up a decent subject [for another story] and the lights went off to further baffle me, so I tried the big-eyed maid for a date, but she already had one. Considered asking the brunette nurse, but the opportune moment didn't arrive, and piddling around the room looking through magazines for an idea, I suddenly hit one – the railway to Tessenei and what it may mean to trade relations with Sudan and

England. Hammered into that and kept getting new ideas, such as the catch phrase for the railway, Red Sea-to-Blue Nile, so by 1:30, with time out for a bit of coffee and air, I had a darn good article. I translated two pages before crawling into bed at 2:30. Then I couldn't sleep and read the *Reader's Digest* for a while, and then when I put out the lights, one extremely clever mosquito combined with insomnia to keep me awake most of the night." On another occasion, Cranston had a long talk with a leader of the Federation of Fighting Fascists at its labor office, one Gennari, who "gave me a welcome, then lit into me for saying his hands were 'well-groomed' in the interview which Bert [Bertoletti] submitted to him, damn him. But he wasn't sore and liked the rest of the article…and he gave me some reports to read. If he were smarter, he would be sorer. But I do think he's one of the liveliest, ablest and smartest guys I've met over here." [61]

"Ten thousand stout-hearted Italian women are today pioneering in Mussolini's African empire, sharing perils and hardships with soldiers and workers and as devoutly as they, following *Il Duce*'s famous motto, 'Live dangerously,'" he wrote from Addis Ababa June 20 after a flight in an Italian bomber that had to make a forced landing when its motor suddenly went dead. The women, he reported, were "following sweethearts and husbands wherever they wander, abandoning civilization to go deep into the malarial river belts and lowland hell holes…. Fearlessly they penetrate where threat of sudden native attack is as alive today as it was 100 years ago when American women pursued the…frontier westward. Countesses live in Abyssinian thatched tukuls and baronesses have born babies in mud huts. Women of royal blood drive into unexplored moorlands on mule back." He interviewed a leader in the Federation of Feminine Fascists, "Robust, yellow-haired Lea Balducci, vice-chieftainness of the Addis Ababa division." They were promoting a "more-babies campaign," she told him, the fruit of which would be "the best potential nucleus of permanent colonization, lacking the homeland ties of those who came here in maturity." But "the business of getting children to schools or segregating them from naked native playmates, training uninitiated native servants in the ways of pressing pants and brushing crumbs, supervising construction and organization of ultra-modern homes while still living in mud tukuls, forces every housewife to earn her bread – when there is bread," Balducci was quoted as saying. The women nevertheless expected "their husbands to put on evening clothes or full-dress uniform on the slightest provocation for a make-shift, false-bottomed society life," Cranston wrote. From his own experience, "The best-organized affair can be guaranteed to go wrong – a wall will cave in, the roof blow away, or the new native cook set fire to house and kitchen. A servant will get the giggles at sight of a monocle and hurl soup down the visiting general's shirt front…or the host will be called out" – here he wrote "censored" across "on military duty" and replaced it with "to drive a herd of donkeys off the front porch just as he commences to carve the chicken. A recent Addis Ababa cocktail party launched ambitiously on a sweltering day blew up completely when ice could not be found and drinks had to be served just below boiling point…. An over-supply of flu victims, plus too many headaches from a gala ball of the previous night, had devoured the capital's entire ice supply." The story also discussed how women rotated their few gowns for social events and avoided leaning against walls which "inevitably leave white stucco powder or multi-colored splotches of paint" on them. The best-dressed woman, he observed, was "an investor's wife, lithe and alert," who had her chauffeur carry her "through slime to save her eleven pairs of shoes." [62]

Cranston did write more in-depth articles. "I've met every big shot, and just interviewed the Duke of Aosta, the first interview he's granted since becoming Viceroy [of Ethiopia] last December," Cranston told his family. He also interviewed Italian General Attilio Teruzzi and was photographed in Ethiopia with General Ruggero Santini, commanding officer there and in Somalia. One interview, though, which he thought was a scoop, ended in a libel suit brought by Emperor Haile Selassie against the London *Evening Standard* for an INS story that appeared May 26, 1938, under the heading, "Abyssinian in 1925 intrigue with Mussolini." Cranston's official escort had arranged an interview with an Ethiopian "puppet" leader, Ras Hailu, a rich prince and former ambassador to France. Cranston was taken to his palace, given tea and fed stories. Hailu in the 1920s had been among Selassie's enemies whom he had taken with him on visits to Europe so that they could not organize a coup in the emperor's absence. In Italy Hailu made contact with Mussolini whose ambitions for East Africa already were known. Selassie had found out about it, imprisoned Hailu and then, Hailu told Cranston, had cut a nephew in half in a public square as a warning to traitors. Cranston thought that he had a big story. He couched it as an example of Ethiopian brutality and uncivilized behavior, which the Italians were fond of exploiting. The story was not censored, and soon appeared in London and New York papers as an INS dispatch. [63]

But the story had appeared two years earlier (in 1936) in the *London Evening Standard*, which Selassie had sued for libel for accusing him of such an "abominable cruelty." The newspaper had settled the suit by apologizing, stating that it was "satisfied there is no truth whatever in the story and that it is entirely without foundation in fact," and thanking Selassie for his "magnanimity" in accepting payment of costs at a time when he had "already been the victim of almost overwhelming misfortune." Selassie had fled to Britain when the Italians invaded his country and did not want to offend "the English people, for whose hospitality he feels the deepest possible gratitude," according to contemporary news accounts. [64]

In the 1936 article the emperor was alleged to have cut off Hailu's son's feet. But when the story reappeared referring to the traitor's nephew, Selassie was less inclined to magnanimity and sued again. Gervasi was furious and ordered Cranston to go back to Hailu and corroborate the charges that he had made. Cranston again visited the prince who changed his story. It was not clear whether a nephew or son had been so cruelly treated – he had so many children he could not keep it all straight, Hailu complained to Cranston. The Italians in addition did not want facts to come out about Hailu's relationship with Mussolini. Hailu indeed had participated in a plot against Selassie and had been jailed along with a nephew, one of whose shackled legs may have become infected and had to be amputated – or, according to one version, he had been beheaded. An account written in the 1930s claimed that Hailu's brother had been the hapless victim of severing. INS, and the newspapers that printed the story, had to concede that it could not be corroborated. [65]

Selassie was only dissuaded from going to court in 1938 when the *Evening Standard* again apologized, saying the offensive passage had slipped into early editions by "unfortunate oversight" and had been removed from later editions. The repetition of the allegation, the newspaper claimed, "was entirely accidental. The passage in question consisted of a paragraph" in an article that "was supplied to the [newspaper] from a source [INS] which it had always found to be thoroughly reliable." This time, however, it would have to pay a "substantial" sum to the emperor by way of compensation. The suit cost the newspaper some £3,000 and INS £15,000. [66]

"Keep your chin up, kid," Gervasi wrote Cranston. "You are now in the process of learning how to take it." Cranston received the letter on his twenty-fourth birthday, June 19, 1938. [67]

In July Cranston left Africa and returned to Rome. He had filed more than fifty stories for INS. It was time to move on – a decision that was influenced in part by Gervasi's not being able, or willing, to pay him adequately or put him on the staff permanently. "You replaced me with Cecil Brown, who subsequently became famous at Singapore," Cranston later recollected to Gervasi. But Cranston had fulfilled one of his youthful dreams. [68]

"I was intent upon becoming a foreign correspondent, and I *did*," he said of his ambitions at the time. But he also decided that journalists were "amateurs of great events (Macauley's definition)," as he wrote in his diary notes, and he had grown frustrated with the news business. "That's what griped me most about foreign correspondence – witnessing great events, almost all of them God-awful, and being there impotently. You tried to interpret, but after passing through the fascist censorship and meeting Hearst requirements, nothing of your own was left." Another autobiographical note read, "I suddenly saw the dull perspective of vagabond days that lay ahead if I continued to wander and roam." [69]

In a future job application (to the Foreign Economic Administration in Washington, D. C.), Cranston described his work with INS as requiring "intimate knowledge and reporting of every phase of Italian life – political, economic, social." He had concentrated on economic reporting, he said, to avoid censorship and expulsion. "You could expose many of the arguments of fascism in pretty subtle terms when speaking economically." He had gotten "down to the roots of Italy's import-export situation, her raw material resources, her colonial wealth, her marketable goods for foreign lands," on which he based articles "showing the fallacies of Mussolini's autarchy program, and also the madness of his imperial designs. I managed to get out a good many articles on mismanaged, badly-exploited industries," which, if better managed, "would have made unnecessary so many of the things the Fascists did." He had reported "as factually as possible." But "to do this, I had to really understand the Italian economy…and I think I did learn it," as well as the "fake 'social gains' of fascism – the handful of slum clearances, the few marshes drained – as against the actual social needs of the Italian people." He described himself as "Assistant Chief of the Rome Bureau" with supervisory duties over staff and local "stringers" who fed INS news tips. [70]

He returned to London in the fall of 1938 where he linked up with Lars Skattebol. They roomed together and jointly set out to write a book on Italian fascism and anti-Semitism. Skattebol was impressed by Cranston's sometimes near-death experiences. "Alan, in many ways, is the most remarkable guy I've ever seen,"

Skattebol wrote his parents. "Don't you dare happen to mention this in such a way as it would get to his parents but in Italy he almost died one month. He got a little cut on his hand and so much disease is running about there that this cut went on to infection, and the infection went on to almost the worst case of blood poisoning I've heard about. Johnny [Atkinson], who was with him at the time, tells me that for some time, the doctor thought he was going to lose Alan; Alan right now has dozens of scars on his left hand and arm through which the pus was drained off. He has never mentioned this to anyone; he didn't want to worry them." [71]

He went on to describe the London that he and Cranston saw, one which, as Cranston had written home, seemed almost nineteenth-century Dickensian. "Prices are much higher in London than I had any idea they'd be," Skattebol told his family. "We have to pay 2 d [shillings] (that's four of our pennies) for a single pear," and "the same for an orange from which hardly a drop of juice can be squeezed. A good grapefruit commands almost a millionaire's pocketbook. The British people are the most hideously underfed people that I can imagine; beggars are on every block and many little children beg in the streets. Alan tells me that in Italy and Germany there are no beggars in the streets, but he agrees with me when I say that there are no beggars actually begging in a prison." Plumbing everywhere in Europe was "horrible," and petrol in London cost 45 cents a gallon.

By mid-September they had completed two chapters of the book – "It isn't the same book that I came over here to help write, but that doesn't matter, does it?" Skattebol wrote home. "As Mussolini started his Jewish persecution, Alan said that he thought we ought to do our bit by writing an article on anti-Semitism in Italy. I went him one better and suggested that we write a pamphlet on it. He got furiously excited, for no apparent reason, and told us to phone him up in a couple of hours, he would consult with some others in the office and let us know definitely about the pamphlet. In the meantime, instead of doing this, he called Victor Gollancz, the biggest publisher in the world (Belfrage's publisher, Left Books, etc.) and got Gollancz excited about the project. The next day we went over to see Gollancz, and he was excited, too. We have to finish about a 200-page book by the fifteenth of October, but if it is any good at all, it is a cinch for publication. Naturally this does not mean that the Ethiopia book is finished, but we will have to wait for a month or so on that because of the great topical urgency of this other one." Cranston, Skattebol wrote, "has more clippings, books and magazines on the place [Ethiopia] than I've ever seen gathered together about any subject." [72]

The threat of war was now very real and imminent, Skattebol said. "We've been in perpetual terror here for three weeks; over there in America, you can have no idea how it feels to be expecting a bombing plane very minute. It's only about two hours flight from Berlin to here, and planes have been ready to start from both sides all this time. Air-raid drills take place here in England constantly, and the subways are being converted into bomb shelters. Every day at least twenty of the big London busses are converted into ambulances," he wrote on September 19.

At the end of September Skattebol and Cranston moved. "We've been living in a wretched dump with one bathtub way upstairs on the fourth floor and one in the basement – all to accommodate about fifty people living in this so-called apartment," Skattebol told his family. "The other day Alan happened to run across a girl on the street who had been a Stanford student; he found that her husband was here in London on a fellowship from some big middle-western university. That evening we called on them; they live in a lot better place than ours. Downstairs in their apartment is a vacated flat of a big London economics professor [R. H. Tawney], the second-ranking man at the famed London School of Economics. He, unfortunately for himself but fortunately for us, is sick somewhere in the country, so we're going to move in there tomorrow, thereby antagonizing at least half of London." [73]

But the war environment had worsened. "As I write these lines, it looks as if the planes will be over London in a few hours," Skattebol wrote his parents, "This is the most real war scare that Europe has had since the other big war. We haven't had our gas-mask fittings yet, though we're supposed to. In every block there's a big store doing nothing else but fitting gas masks on men, women and children." Skattebol described their upstairs American friends as a young doctor "and his debutante wife. They have been rushing around England cornering the silver candlestick market, profiteers to the core, apparently, as a great many people are trying to dispose of their silver during this war scare." He and Cranston had completed about seven chapters of the book and were "working hard at it every day…. Alan and I seem to make an ideal writing team, as, despite his two years in a fascist country, he has not been influenced by fascist ideas, except adversely." Each day they went into Mecklenburgh Square where they lived, to which they had keys, and ran around its gravel path. "We try for time, as Alan still has his stop watch; he holds the record now at 43.6 for the distance" (365 yards). Skattebol regretted that they did not have time to read some of the books in the flat – "it's far and away the finest private library that I've ever seen. Every old English poet is here, all the early radical writers with Ruskin, Morris, and the whole crowd of English Fabian Socialists, together with the extreme leftists, several editions of Marx's *Capital*." (The square in Bloomsbury, apparently unknown to Cranston and Skattebol, was home to other notables including Virginia and Leonard Woolf who ran their Hogarth Press from a nearby house.) [74]

On October 2, Skattebol's twenty-third birthday, he said, "The last few days have been horrible; I didn't write to you as I felt that it might blow over, which it has, though it looks as if the final conflict will be much more ghastly now that the democratic states have been measurably weakened. Just outside, in the park of which I told you where Alan and I run, they have been digging trenches for bomb shelters, ripping up the tennis courts and all the conveniences of the park. Just a little way up the street there is an anti-aircraft battery and it has been having its little games as we sit here trying to write, firing at airplanes drawing targets across the sky. On the mantle are our gas masks. Would you like a picture of us in them? The prime minister, Chamberlain, is the biggest hero the world has ever seen, but he had Hitler in full control after the mobilization of the British fleet, and yet he went there to Munich and gave Hitler all that he demanded." [75]

The twelve-chapter manuscript, entitled "Italy and Jews," relied on Cranston's first-hand experiences and information that he had gleaned from reading about fascism. "Rome's foreign correspondents were appalled," he wrote in the foreword, when the "Italian press launched a vitriolic anti-Semitic campaign" in February, 1938. It seemed at odds with Mussolini's 1929 statements to Italy's Chamber of Deputies that "fascism means unity; anti-Semitism or anti-Semitic fascism [is] therefore a gross absurdity." A 1932 book by German-born biographer Emil Ludwig quoted Mussolini as saying there were "no pure races left in Europe," and that blaming Jews for most of Germany's difficulties made them "the scapegoat." Journalists in Rome, Cranston wrote, had conspired to report all anti-Semitic fascist statements they heard in hopes that Mussolini would halt them. "Strangely enough, the scheme worked for a time." A government communiqué on February 17, 1938, refuted the government's having instituted any "political, economic or moral measures against the Jews, with the exception of cases which are contrary to the regime." Within five months, however, new anti-Semitic actions began, "clearly with government benediction." How far would the policy go, Cranston asked? "Has Ethiopia been an economic drain instead of a bonanza?" Would it be "a Jewish slave colony?" Was the policy provoked by the influx of Austrian and other Jewish refugees to Italy, or by Italy's alliance with Germany? "Can the democratic-minded of the outside world derive any long-range inspiration from anything so heartrending as another systematic Jewish persecution?" he speculated from London in November, 1938. [76]

He noted that "much Jewish blood flows in the veins of the people who live and die on the Italian peninsula, for Italy…was the first country in the west to be reached by Jewish emigrants," arriving in Rome about 139 B. C. The book examined how Italy's political, economic and international situation affected "the desperate escape-finding device of official Jew-baiting." Cranston had asked a store clerk in Rome to provide him with a budget for how he lived on the equivalent of £8 a month salary. The clerk considered himself "fortunate" because he had only a wife and child to support. His expenses included monthly dues in the National Fascist Party, the After Work Club, labor syndicate, unemployment, health and old-age insurance, plus income tax. He lived in a one-window garret room and shared a kitchen and toilet with five families. They often ate no meat for a week because food was expensive. Wounded veterans, Cranston had observed, also could not live on the meager pension they were given.

Cranston proceeded to find fault with every tenant of Italian fascism. "These people were cheering for Mussolini and for fascism, yet they cannot have been newly converted – not after sixteen years…. [M]any of them are beginning to wonder just what *Il Duce* has actually done for them. They were also cheering for fascism, but just what is fascism?" If they dissected the national symbol – "a bundle of sticks and the head of a hatchet, all bound together as an expression of unity" – they would find that the string tying it was the artisan Mussolini but "when he goes…it almost surely will fall apart…. He already is getting a bit old, and now has his girdle," his closest backers – "athlete [Achille] Starace [Fascist Party secretary and army general who proposed anti-Semitic measures], cynical [Dino] Alfieri [chief propagandist], confused [Count Galeazzo] Ciano [Mussolini's son-in-law, Minister for Foreign Affairs, whom Mussolini later had killed for treason], society-struck Edda [Mussolini's favorite and eldest child, married to Ciano]. [77]

The hatchet head was "symbolic of fascism's military might" but was "scattered and therefore weak," waging wars in Ethiopia, Spain, Palestine and Libya. Military leaders were "antagonized by fascist acts" like anti-Semitism and fighting to "support the despised Hitler." In addition, Italians had no confidence in the *lire*, which had fallen steadily. National self-sufficiency, "one of the newer fascist sticks…is a mere patch on poverty." The empire was a disaster in Ethiopia and Libya. Fascist culture was a joke, a phony new Renaissance directed by a "gangster, Farinacci," as was Mussolini's backing of the monarchy and House of Savoy. Only the Roman Catholic Church and Pope Pius XI were "openly against Mussolini's latest polices. This, then, is the fascism which the crowd cheered in October," after Mussolini returned from meeting Hitler at Munich – not with assurance of peace, higher wages, lower prices or a stronger *lire*. He had "brought them instead…a new stick…persecution of the Jews – a stick so rotten that many of the others had started to rot still further."

The British publisher, Gollancz, ultimately did not accept the manuscript for publication. Skattebol had to tell his parents on November 11, "the news is bad and so this is really a heartbreaking note to write. Altogether, this is the worst three months that I suppose I've ever spent in my life. My health hasn't been helped by the trip at all, the climate and these fogs make me feel as mean as Mama must have with her nose." He and Cranston, for diversion, had made "a little trip…to the old medieval town of Newark (after which Newark, New Jersey, is named). But aside from that…we've stayed in our apartment for most of the time, and had one melancholy idea after another hit us over the head." None had been productive, alas. "I had such high hopes on this trip," Skattebol confessed, "I suppose I have learned something that may last me for some time and be the best for me in the end, but just now I feel terrible. England is terrible, the people here are unbelievably stupid and out of touch with modern-day reality, and the worst government imaginable has ahold of the country." [78]

He and Cranston would be glad to leave. "We're coming home on the *S. S. Manhattan*, leaving Southampton on November 18," Skattebol said. "Alan and I are going to settle down in Southern California where it is warm and where living is a good deal cheaper than it is in London, and learn something about California politics, and write some plays. [Governor Culbert L.] Olson's and [U.S. Senator Sheridan] Downey's elections have come as the only good news that we've had on our entire trip to London." (Both men were Democrats and supporters of Roosevelt's New Deal.)

Cranston tried to sell other free-lance work based on his activities in Europe. "I submitted your articles to New York but Burkson and [Edmond D.] Coblentz [editor of Hearst's *New York American*] advise they are not interested at present in this material," William Hillman told him in October. At least his efforts had been given consideration. "I regret very much that I have not succeeded in placing your articles," a *Yorkshire Post* editor told Cranston in December. "I fear that at the moment Abyssinia is not topical and there is a pressure of articles on European problems which makes it difficult to promise space in the near future. Accordingly I return the articles to you with compliments and thanks. I hope you have been successful in finding a suitable post." [79]

Cranston arrived in New York in late November, 1938, rich in experiences if not income. He had cut out a quote of Mark Twain's from *Following the Equator* that he must have thought applied to him:

"We should be careful to get out of an experience only the wisdom that is in it – and stop there, lest we be like the cat that sits down on the hot stove lid. She will never sit down on a hot stove lid again – and that is well; but also she will never sit down on a cold one any more." [80]

America looked very good to him after being overseas for two and a half years. It was "wonderful to hear American spoken everywhere," he wrote home. "[Walter] Winchell had a swell maxim in his column night before last: 'Those who kick about government should try countries where the government kicks the people.' That sums up how I feel now, after escape from the dark continents across the water. Now the thing is to make sure we never do get a government that would want to kick the people." [81]

His journalistic career was struggling but he had plans, he told his parents. Skattebol, who was intent on trying to break into journalism in New York, wrote his father, "Alan and I consider that the work we are doing here is only apprenticeship as we intend to some day go to L. A. and start a rip-roaring morning paper (you know how generally foul all the papers in L. A. are but the morning papers, *The Times* and *The Examiner*). This is a great field for liberal enterprise, with the L. A. area as liberal as it is – but that's for the future." A relative of Cranston's had proposed sending him for an eight-month session to the "School of Journalism created with funds of the late Luke Nieman, former owner of the *Milwaukee Journal*," according to a note dated July 12, 1938. Cranston did not take up the offer. The *Palo Alto Times* in August reported that "young Cranston plans to write a book about his adventures as a foreign correspondent." He had "covered Italy's vast reconstruction projects in the former empire of Haile Selassie," it said, and had "lived in the former palace of the King of Kings, interviewing the Duke of Aosta, the viceroy, and traveling to every part of Ethiopia under military escort. Side adventures included such thrilling experiences as hunting elephants, hippopotami, alligators and lions.... [A]n article written by him which appeared in the London *Standard* was made the basis for a libel suit filed by Haile Selassie." [82]

With such adventures to relate, Cranston not surprisingly got some speaking engagements on his return to America. He went home for Christmas, having been away nearly three years. His father arranged a luncheon at the Bohemian Club in San Francisco where Cranston talked about his travels. He took advantage of his time in California to explore job possibilities. He drove Cora Older to Sacramento and was introduced to Governor Culbert Olson who, as one of his first acts, had just pardoned Tom Mooney. Cranston even met Mooney at a party. He next took Mrs. Older to Los Angeles where she introduced him to a number of writers. He spoke to a dinner meeting of the Adventurers' Club – it billed him as a former INS reporter "with Italian troops in Ethiopia" (he shared the program with an F. B. I. agent who had uncovered a Nazi spy ring). Cranston also was a guest at The Authors Club in Hollywood and the San Francisco Press Club. [83]

While he was in Los Angeles he met a young woman named Geneva McMath on a blind date. They were introduced by mutual friends from Pomona who thought they shared interests. She had graduated from Pomona and was then working for the telephone company. Cranston took her to a meeting of the American fascist organization called the Silver Shirts, which he wanted to observe. [84]

Cranston was using all the contacts that he could muster to find work. A news friend (and later diplomat) who had met him in Rome, Sidney Freifeld, wrote in a letter of recommendation that Cranston could be trusted implicitly, "has a facile pen, turns out respectable or Hearst English with the greatest of ease; has many valuable contacts of all kinds…from California to Europe. He is politically clean, i.e., has an open mind, with [one] bias – he simply hates dictatorships, regardless of color. Perceptibly Aryan, he has personality and charm, plus modesty. He is a hard worker with tenacity of purpose and a staying power which makes me feel middle-aged. He is not particularly on the lookout for a job as he has plenty to keep him busy, but on the other hand, I am certain is available for specific pieces of work. I can't think of anybody I would recommend more highly for gumshoe investigations amongst better elements, *ad infinitum*. On the other hand, he is a good research worker." [85]

Cranston sold some articles to the *Toronto Star* and on one occasion went to hear Theodore Dreiser – across a review of Dreiser's autobiography years later Cranston scribbled, "AC met Dreiser in '39." He worked on another book, the "Nazi invasion of Italy," and gathered information on fascist and anti-Semitic organizations in the United States like the Ku Klux Klan, League for Preservation of Constitutional Rights and the American Nationalist Party (a "Christian-front outfit," Cranston said of it). In researching the media, Cranston recorded in a memo that the head of McClure Newspapers syndicate, Richard Waldo, was reputed to have "fascist tendencies" (Waldo had said in a speech in 1939 that "it took a dictator to bring order out of chaos" in Germany, Italy and Japan). Cranston read anti-fascist works like a pamphlet by Economics Professor Walter E. Roloff, *Chickens are Nordic, too - The Nazis Condemned Out of their Own Mouths*. He met with the head of one group, the Emergency Council to Keep the United States out of Foreign Wars, Allan Zoll. "I told him I was twenty-five, unmarried and unemployed and therefore interested in any outfit keeping the U. S. out of war, also that I was to be a reporter on a forthcoming Brooklyn paper." [86]

He tried his hand at writing a play, "Realists Who Analyze, A Comedy (or it may turn out to be a Tragedy - or a Romance) in Three Acts," which began with two college students, Mark and May, "satirizing the other couples in the room, both wear[ing] self-satisfied smiles," indicating not only "approval of self but also of partner." An attempt at a novel that he called "The Death of God" dealt with beliefs. It contained obvious autobiographical descriptions of young men like himself and friends Atkinson and Skattebol: "They were almost more than typical, for they had reacted more alertly and completely to their average American lives than does the average youth; they were a bit more alive, tingled a bit more with experience and joy of the world; they had lived so much American life, felt so much of it, that they were a bit more than average." [87]

One character, whom he called Max Landon and who bore a resemblance to Cranston himself, "felt vaguely that what he really worshipped was life – experience, people, the sky, the stars. He found it a very handy philosophy, for with it he had persuaded his parents not to frown too heavily on many wild experiences that he had plunged himself into. He hoped to be a writer someday and shaped his philosophy to that purpose, arguing that he needed to do and see all things so he could vividly understand and portray them. He had spent a whole summer wandering about America on freight trains, persuading his wealthy parents that he had to live, if only briefly, a less-protected life. He hoped to turn his pen, and perhaps his actions, to helping the masses some day, and he said that to help them, one must understand them." Landon had seen death in revolution in Spain, "and when he came back from vagabonding about Europe, his family had to admit he seemed older and maturer."

Cranston wrote a number of stories and analytical articles drawn from recent experiences but had poor luck selling them. One called "Matrimonial Masquerade," co-authored with another man, dealt with the "Pygmalion" theme of remaking a woman to a man's wishes – in this case, turning a chorus girl into a musical star within six months. Another story dealt with Amster Spiro's generating stories for the *New York Journal* on slow-news days. A file marked "Rejects, '39-'40" included the titles "They Wanted Jobs," "The Dictator's Daughter," "He Who Strikes the Pope Dies," "Mussolini's Girdle," "Hara-Kira Renaissance," "Vultures Over the Vatican" (about Pope Pius XI's outcries against anti-Semitism and his death early in 1939). The first dealt with a man who had lost his job at a steel mill during the Depression. "The Dictator's Daughter" was Princess Marie Jose, Belgian King Albert I's daughter and Leopold III's sister, who had married Crown Prince Umberto of Savoy, making her a future queen of Italy. The piece (also co-authored) opened with the fact that monarchies were impotent in Europe: "Hitler, Mussolini, Stalin, Daladier, Chamberlain – none of them nobles – are the men of destiny across the Atlantic. The last surviving monarchs sit on trembling thrones. They are disregarded, while the democracies that deprived them of their power face the challenge of young and bold dictatorships." Princess Marie Jose, though, had played "a role of startling significance in the affairs of…Italy, of all places, where the emperor is openly ridiculed by the swaggering satellites of a blacksmith's son who thunders and shakes his fist, and sometimes beams benignly, as he lays down the law of the land." She had learned and secretly alerted Belgians that Germany planned to invade their country, allowing time for Belgium to prepare a defense. But a few days later, when the princess was due to deliver her third child, the doctor who had attended her previously, a Jew, was prohibited from doing so by order of Mussolini's daughter, "the headstrong Countess Edda Ciano." The two women were bitter enemies, he wrote, one anti- and the other pro-Nazi, and rivals who expected their husbands to succeed to power. Cranston sold a story about Count Ciano to *The American Mercury* in which he predicted that Mussolini's choice of heir to his dictatorship was his son-in-law Ciano, whose "singular talent" was the ability to convince "all but the most astute observers that he is a fool." Italians ridiculed his marriage as opportunistic and his habit of imitating *Il Duce* by throwing back his head. "Actually, he tilts his head back and juts his chin forward because sinus trouble interferes with his breathing, and insiders insist that to have married Edda Mussolini was in itself a master stroke." [88]

Back in New York, Cranston reconnected with Spiro who had left the *Journal* and was involved in various businesses including printing. Cranston had an idea about publishing inexpensive books like those of the British publisher who had turned down his manuscript on Italian anti-Semitism. "May I introduce Alan Cranston who has ideas about producing books cheaply on a mass scale?" a friend wrote a publishing contact. "I thought your experience…might be helpful to him, at least in knowing what to avoid." Spiro liked the idea and set it in motion. A *San Francisco Call-Bulletin* columnist reported May 9, 1939, "They will publish new books, fiction and non-fiction, at a new low in selling price – 15 cents!" But while the business was getting started, Cranston was nearly broke, unable to support himself on writing. At one point he found a rare 1883 nickel with the Roman numeral "V" but missing the word "cents" that he sold for three dollars, which briefly tided him over. [89]

Skattebol had written his parents before Christmas, 1938, that he thought Cranston would be back to New York within a few weeks, " much as this will hurt his folks' feelings. Exciting things are afoot here for us," Skattebol's enthusiastic letter reported. "At this very moment it seems that the prospects for the book company are exceedingly bright. I'm enclosing a little book that I brought home from London with me and it gives you an idea of what we are trying to do in this country." They had high hopes of finding a demand for cheap editions, inspired by the "moving force [behind] the plan," Spiro, "an ex-Hearst city editor of the horrible *New York Journal*…. It seems as if he had a vestige of conscience and finally couldn't stomach Hearst any longer." Spiro had made money manufacturing and selling games including "Auto-Bridge." Cranston and Skattebol were confidant that Spiro's network of salesmen and knowledge of "sales-promotion stunts," merchandising and circulation would put the company on a successful footing. "He has gotten printers' estimates, and finds that he can have books printed in 100,000 lots (to begin with!) and manage to sell them at a small profit (after paying the author) for 15 cents!!!!" It would be, Skattebol envisioned, "The best book scheme so far developed in the United States. All sorts of fascinating possibilities offer themselves to mind: college kids all over the country" could buy course-required books at nominal expense, amateur play societies would snap up cheap copies with wide-spaced type "and so avoid the necessity of making scripts!" [90]

Spiro, however, decided to market the paperbacks by set rather than individual copies, dooming the publishing enterprise. He then embarked on a short-lived attempt to publish a newspaper in Brooklyn with which Cranston was associated. [91]

"One rumor is that the coin [to underwrite the newspaper] came from the Repub[lican] Party," the *New York Daily Mirror* reported October 27, 1939. "Undaunted by the fact that newspapers in Brooklyn have not been conspicuously successful – a fact currently dramatized by the failing fortunes of the *Brooklyn Eagle*," another publication said, "plotter Spiro plans to start a paper with some innovations." (Brooklyn at the time was the nation's third most-populous region, fifth in manufacturing and a major port.) Called variously the *Brooklyn* or *New York Express*, the publisher was David Garrison Berger, Spiro the editor, and Cranston a member of the staff. Memos, one of which referred to a proposed tabloid called *QUICK*, said that it would carry no paid advertising, would be something like a monthly *Readers' Digest* culling news from all over the world, presented in brief format that would "have a distinct appeal to women, hence will be of circulation value." It would be a daily morning paper selling for two cents on newsstands (they hoped to sell 70,000 daily), produced economically by having a short (16-page) format and only one edition, thus saving on union payroll ("we will use no costly great-name feature writers") and distribution costs. It would be designed "to give the most complete coverage possible in the shortest space and simplest terms." There were to be "no columns of idle speculation by foreign correspondents" needing to file daily dispatches. Emphasis would be given "news disclosures and exposés, the result of independent investigation, exclusive to QUICK, and of a nature intended to correct existing evils and abuses, to defeat injustices." [92]

But there was a non-hidden agenda for *QUICK* – "It is important for the Jews of America that there be a daily newspaper to wage a ceaseless campaign against anti-Semitism," one memo read. Each day the paper would try to run a "sensational news story exposing the machinations of subversive political groups conducting un-American propaganda and seeking to disturb the relations of the United States with foreign nations. It will probe deeply into the affairs of leaders of these movements in an effort to bring to light their motives, the source from which they derive their sustenance, the strength of their following, their concealed pasts, etc." Other newspapers were doing "more harm than good by continually publicizing" anti-Jewish activities that caused people to wonder whether such intolerance "hasn't some justification," the memo stated. "Anti-Semitism in this country is not organized or wide-spread. It is localized in the vicinity of small rabble rousers…. They form spurious organizations under high-sounding names and operate in the manner of racketeers. They prey on the fears of small Gentile businessmen and get them to contribute by promising to wipe out Jewish competition" and "molest little Jewish merchants by pasting stickers on their windows and then collecting toll from them in the guise of protection money…. The only way to put a stop to this is by exposing the leaders." Other newspapers did not report such activities for fear of alienating advertisers. To be effective, the new tabloid should analyze "accusations made against the Jews and answer them with the truth." It also should appeal to "the great ignorant masses…. Thinking people don't need to be convinced, so a publication of purely intellectual appeal would be wasted," its proposers concluded. "The great majority of persons want a paper that thrills and entertains them with romantic and exciting and amusing reading." If the Brooklyn paper did that, it "should go a long way toward dispelling race hatred and unrest." [93]

Another draft of the paper's policies stated, however, that its sponsors were "not out for any one cause. This paper will not preach, will not crusade, except when we feel the Brooklyn people are as aroused as we." There would be no daily editorials "because we won't have a vital opinion every day." Instead, the paper would encourage readers to speak out in its pages, hoping to generate "all-sided discussions" among the "keenest brains in the nation and the world. We take it for granted, of course," that Brooklyn residents wanted a "paper to work for harmony among the diverse religious and racial groups that make up this community…. When we uncover unpleasant facts…we will not hesitate to speak out. It is our aim to make this paper a dynamic social instrument." The sponsors saw themselves as working in a "laboratory" for reform in how news could be presented in a "useful form." [94]

Some of the lively features they considered doing were "Al Capone's own life story (soon as he's out of jail)," "My first fistfight" by Joe Lewis (meaning boxer Joe Louis), others about life-insurance and undertaking "rackets," "fantastic murders," daily biographies of "the little people" of Brooklyn and one on George Washington Carver, "Negro slave who became a great scientist." Health issues would be addressed – "sulfanilamide, the great cure of pneumonia," anesthesia, "painless childbirth" and "marijuana madness." Cranston's interests were evident in proposed stories about "super-weapons which armies are afraid to use" and warfare under the sea," details about U. S. draft plans, the fate of British and other western Fascists, Europe after the war, and labor leader John L. Lewis' life story. There also would be stories about Broadway like "What starts night-club brawls?" and "Is Broadway capable of detecting talent?" [95]

Skattebol apparently was enlisted as one of the writer-reporters. He wrote an editorial on the dangers of college football after a Princeton ball player (Roland Wynne) suffered a leg amputation, citing the deaths of fifty boys each year and thousands of disabling injuries. "A college is a place for higher study, not professional football," he wrote. [96]

The Brooklyn paper, however, survived only one (or a few) editions before the enterprise ran out of money. [97]

At one point, Skattebol had borrowed $400 from Cranston and $50 from his father. Several years later, on American Broadcasting Company letterhead stationary, Skattebol acknowledged "the moral obligation" to both, confessing that he had lied about needing the money – "the whole story of that accident was a lie, as you have known for some time. If you were here, I would tell you personally, but this is the best I can do. I do not have the money now: Indeed, for various reasons, am very deeply in debt, some for honest reasons. The reasons for this confession are many and complicated: I know most of them, and do not think I am as much to blame as it would seem on the surface. But the main reason: It is the right thing to tell you the truth. From time to time I will send you and your dad a payment on account, until all is settled." He signed it with "kindest regards and deepest gratitude for past favors." His and Cranston's relationship, though, would not be the same after that. Cranston may have had to concede that his father's misgivings about Skattebol had been justified. [98]

Cranston meanwhile got some assignments from Seven Arts Feature Syndicate. One story received extensive play and engaged Cranston personally. Hitler had invaded Poland September 1, 1939, and by December ships were landing at New York loaded with Jewish and other European refugees. Cranston was sent to meet the Italian liner *Vulcania* and the *S. S. Noordam* to report on the sudden rise in immigration. "Mr. Cranston has been assigned to write a feature story on the refugees," the syndicate's managing director wrote the Collector of Customs January 4, 1940, asking that he give Cranston a pass on the revenue cutter meeting ships as they entered New York harbor. Aboard the *Vulcania* Cranston watched a *New York Times* reporter sympathetically interview refugees, even promise to contact a friend at Ellis Island to seek help for three Poles and a Czech in trouble for not having proper papers. "Well, this is one time we won't have to make [up?] those damned headlines about Jewish refugees," Cranston remarked to the reporter who "smiled understandingly," Cranston told his editor, Sidney Freifield. [99]

Cranston told a press agent for the Italian line that he was "going to attempt a story pointing out that many of the so-called 'refugees' are actually immigrants who would be entering the U. S. A., war or no war, Hitler or no Hitler. I added that I intended likewise to point out that not so many of these were Jews as people apparently believed." A *City News* reporter disagreed: "No, there's thousands more coming in now than ever before," he told Cranston, adding, "They're damn near all Jews. And they almost all have dough, too." Cranston disliked the man's indifference to the problems some of the passengers had, and made a point of engaging them in conversation, asking "human-interest questions." He kept "the three Poles and the Czech" busy saying "interesting things till we docked at the 52nd Street pier. Similarly, I was able to build up the story of the Swiss aviatrix, the Baroness Lisette di Kapri, by gaining possession of the sole copy of the press release she had prepared on herself and her mission. All the other reporters had to come to me for the facts, the spelling of her name, etc., and when they didn't…I had an excellent excuse to go to them with the information." [100]

Four New York papers carried stories on the *Vulcania*'s arrival but, "by concentrating on the story of the four 'country-less' refugees," missed the point of whether passengers were refugees or immigrants. Of 2,000 arrivals on two ships the same day, 200 were designated as refugees, mostly non-Jewish. "One of the main factors contributing to the success of this job was Cranston's digging up the Swiss aviatrix, to which the *Times* and *Tribune* devoted a special story…. In this case, Cranston got hold of the aviatrix and directed the newspapermen's attention to her." [101]

Cranston took a special interest in the "country-less" passengers, a beautiful young Polish woman and her husband, an orphan boy whom they were protecting, and a Czech, all of whom were in danger of being returned to Europe. The immigrants, according to Cranston's report, were a Dr. Joseph Arthur Hollander, thirty-four-year-old former head of the Polish Travel Bureau in Krakow, and his twenty-five-year-old wife Felizia who had escaped their homeland when Hitler invaded, following a refugee trail through Rumania and across central Europe to Italy. En route they encountered fourteen-year-old Arnold Spitzman whose pilot-father was believed to have been shot down by Germans during the defense of Krakow. His mother apparently had died in the bombardment of the city and the Hollanders had taken the boy under their care. The Czech was a thirty-year-old man, Mark Morsel, who had fled when a part of Czechoslovakia had been seized in September, 1938. All four were Jews. They had Portuguese visas but a Portuguese customs official at Lisbon had stamped all their passports as invalid because Poland no longer was a nation and they were refused permission to land. Their request to disembark at the Azores also had been refused, and they had been forced to continue to New York. Without valid visas, they could not even wait at the immigration facility on Ellis Island. The *Vulcania*, on which they were stranded, was due to sail for Italy the following day at noon. Cranston feared a repeat of a recent episode in which a shipload of Jewish refugees on the *S. S. St. Louis* had been turned away from Cuba. [102]

"Dr. Hollander is sure it means death, execution for him if he is returned to Italy" because he would be sent to Germany and shot for having fought with the Polish army against the Nazis, Cranston wrote in his account. Both Hollander and his wife had been outspoken opponents of Nazism, as had the Czech. Felizia was "ravishingly beautiful," Cranston reported, a candidate for a "Hollywood screen test," and she spoke "English with a delightful accent." She had been much-photographed by news service photographers "but all the papers muffed the story," Cranston reported to his editor, and none of the photos appeared in local newspapers, only two of which (the *Times* and *World-Telegram*) "even mentioned the case." Fortunately, Felizia had a brother, John Screiber, living at Central Park West, who was prepared to post bond for the Poles, who had sufficient funds, as did the Czech man, to support themselves. Cranston got in contact with the National Refugee Service which in turn contacted the U. S. State Department on the refugees' status. Felizia particularly touched Cranston with her insistence that she would jump overboard if forced to go back to Europe, which her husband reinforced about his wife's determination not to be returned. The Czech managed to impart in what little English he could speak that he was a "happy Jew," and the boy, who spoke no English, "clicks his heels, bows, and smiles shyly whenever he feels he should be saying something if only he knew this foreign language," Cranston wrote.

Cranston spent the day and night seeking help for them. He even telephoned powerful broadcaster Walter Winchell at the Stork Club around midnight, asking him to publicize the fate of the immigrants. Winchell told him, in effect, that he was going home to shave. Cranston finally got some lawyers to take up the case. He watched while they drew up a writ of *habeas corpus*, then went with them to a judge who issued it, permitting the immigrants to leave the ship. "The Sunday papers report that the four refugees who remained aboard the *Vulcania* have been admitted to Ellis Island and have not been deported back to Europe," Cranston's editor wrote on December 11. "Cranston worked for 48 hours continuously for these people, and their release from the ship is, I feel, due primarily to his efforts. Until he drew the attention of the competent agencies to their case (he was the only person aboard that interested himself in them), they were held virtually incommunicado with no chance of landing here." [103]

The Baroness de Kapri, whom Cranston also attended to, was the first aviatrix in Switzerland and held U. S. credentials as a pilot, instructor and navigator. She was "a very young woman, speaking fluently several languages, and is an old friend of the United States," her press release said. Her mission was to use aviation not as a "terrible device of destruction and death" but "for good and benefits for all." She wanted to give the Red Cross planes for a flying ambulance corps to improve its rescue operations and was planning to test and buy American planes for that purpose. Each plane would bear the names of donors to the cause, her release said, so that "every man who will be helped and saved with this plane would know to whom he owes his life." A European industrialist and pilot who had flown medical transport for soldiers in the previous war was bankrolling the initial stage of the project. On the back of the release, Cranston noted, "EMPHASIZE BEAUTY" and "speaks English." [104]

Cranston increasingly was concerned with the forthcoming war and the danger of fascism. He clipped and kept "a great column I've never forgotten" by Dorothy Thompson about "The Great Miracle of Dunkerque" when more than 300,000 Allied troops were evacuated May 26-June 4, 1940, from the French coast across the Strait of Dover after Germans broke through Allied lines and pushed them to the Channel. Thompson termed the evacuation, assisted by thousands of volunteers in private vessels, an "allegory for a strange sort of social revolution" in class-conscious Britain. "The revolutionary *élan* of national socialism falters against this new spirit," she wrote. "Day by day, win or lose, the little men of Great Britain make Britain again great, and make it increasingly impossible for any human soul to become a Nazi…in itself a victory. For national socialism will fail when no one else in the world can be persuaded to become a Nazi." [105]

A collection of observations that Cranston wrote for *The Voice for Human Rights* (published by the Committee of Catholics for Human Rights) in 1940 included one about a congressional investigation of perceived un-American activities by leaders of consumer organizations suspected of being Communists whose organizations were accused of acting "as transmission belts for the spread of communism among the middle classes." "The truth of the matter is," Cranston wrote, "that these allegedly communist consumer organizations are groups of people who have banded together to try to get a better break for their money…. If the attempt to get food more cheaply makes one a Communist, we guess we are all Communists, and should be investigated." [106]

He also worked on several plays. One called *Nuts* was a farcical mystery about which person actually was crazy. Its characters included a professor, "his dizzy, well-meaning wife, full of home tricks," a psychologist, a political scientist "fresh from London and bombings on [the Pan-American] Clipper, brusque – he may have been driven bats over there, acts odd, makes wild, yet clever, statements about the war, the future, etc." – and a career glamour girl, "mousy daughter of a prof." It opened with the psychologist asking to stay for dinner with the professor and his wife because "one of the guests, he thinks, is nuts." In the second act the psychologist fires a gun out a window, leading everyone to wonder who had been shot. One figure handcuffed himself to something stationary and swallowed the key, thwarting cops' efforts to arrest him. The police were about to haul all of the household to jail when it turned out that the psychologist was "proven to be the nut." [107]

Another play, though, was nearly produced on Broadway. Cranston got in touch with Lee Falk in New York. "I told him about my experiences as a foreign correspondent. His ambition was to add playwriting to cartooning, and he suggested that we collaborate on a play about a young foreign correspondent like me," Cranston recalled of its genesis. It was a comedy called *The Big Story*. "Lee knew how to write stuff and I didn't particularly, but I knew more about foreign correspondents and Rome than he did," Cranston laughed. "So we were able to collaborate quite well." A well-known producer, Gilbert Miller, offered to present it with actor Donald Cook as the lead. It was to be directed by Sam Levene, according to an advertisement for its pre-Broadway premier in Maplewood, New Jersey. "*Variety* predicted that it would be a big hit on Broadway," Cranston said, "but Gilbert Miller wanted us to do some re-writing, which we did, and by the time we finished, he had lost interest, and never brought it to New York. That was the end of my career as a playwright," Cranston joked. Falk would later say that the play "didn't go over too well." In retrospect, Cranston was grateful. "It was like missing the Olympics. I thought it was a good thing that it didn't make Broadway because I would have been a playwright rather than a senator!" Once again failure had turned to advantage for his career. [108]

His introduction to publishing, however, planted an idea in Cranston's head. "One day in Macy's bookstore in New York I saw a display of *Mein Kampf*, an English-language version, which I'd never seen before," he related. "I went over to look at it out of curiosity, and as I picked it up, I knew that it wasn't the real book. It was much thinner than the long book that I had read, which was about 350,000 words. So I bought it to see how come" it was abbreviated. "And delving into it, I found that it was a condensed version, and some of the things that would most upset Americans just weren't there as they were in the version that I had read, the original, in German." [109]

Why not produce a version that emphasized Hitler's design to conquer the world, Cranston thought, recalling years later of the moment when he "saw this man with a glazed look of power in his face." Most non-German editions of *Mein Kampf* authorized by Hitler eliminated much of his ranting about Jews and a German-dominated world. Spiro liked the idea and invited Cranston to his house in Connecticut one weekend to work on it. Spiro's teenaged son was startled to awaken the next morning to find not only a stranger bunking in his room but books about Hitler spread all over it. Cranston was comparing the authorized version with one that he had bought in England and an original German version that he had gotten in Berlin. [110]

In a week's time, dictating to secretaries in a loft on Third Avenue near 22nd Street in New York, Cranston put together a version with his commentaries, based on his personal observations and reading about Hitler, calling attention to the distortions, lies and propaganda contained in the authorized English-language text. One of the secretaries taking Cranston's dictation was Jewish and became concerned about being part of the enterprise. She secretly contacted B'nai B'rith's Anti-Defamation League, which sent a young man around to investigate. When he understood what Cranston was doing, he offered his and the League's help. [111]

Cranston's condensation (to 70,000 words from 300,000) was published in March, 1939, in a thirty-two-page tabloid newspaper format aimed at a mass market and sold for the nominal price of ten cents. The tabloid was emblazoned with red and black ink and large headlines announcing the subject – "Adolf Hitler's Own Book, *Mein Kampf* (*My Battle*), a new unexpurgated translation condensed with critical comments and explanatory notes." The front page boldly stated, "Not one cent of royalty to Hitler," and "Millions sold in book form at $3.00 – now for the first time in this popular edition at 10¢." Inside, readers would find hitherto "unpublished Nazi propaganda maps exposing Hitler's 10-year plan for conquest of Europe." The maps had been seized in a raid on Nazi headquarters in Czechoslovakia. On the front-page of the tabloid a cartoon showed Hitler trying to insert the shapes of Great Britain and Italy into a jig-saw-puzzle map of a Greater Germany in the shape of a swastika, exclaiming in frustration, "*Donnerwetter*! – They don't fit!" Six months later Hitler would invade Poland and launch World War II. [112]

Two other American publishers had announced early in January, 1939, that they planned to issue full-length, unexpurgated editions of *Mein Kampf*. Stackpole Sons (owned by General E. J. Stackpole, Junior, publisher of the Harrisburg, Pennsylvania, *Evening Telegraph*), planned an unauthorized translation for which they would pay no royalties on grounds that German copyright was invalid in the U. S. and the book thus was "in the public domain." Hitler, Stackpole's lawyer argued, had forfeited rights to American law when filing a second application for copyright in Austria in 1927, having joined the German Army in 1914 and given up Austrian citizenship. Houghton Mifflin publishing company of Boston, which held the book's American rights from German publisher Franz Eher, planned to produce an unexpurgated edition of an abridged version that it had published previously, the second edition to be in collaboration with Reynal & Hitchcock of New York. Houghton Mifflin claimed that the book's copyright had been validly assigned to them and served notice that they would seek damages for any other American publication as an invasion of their legal rights. Both publishers promised to give at least five percent of their profits to a fund for German refugees. Cranston and Spiro would certainly have known of these plans, described in the *New York Times* on January 2, 1939. [113]

For his version, Cranston highlighted poignant quotes from Hitler's text like:

> "The masses can only be captured by a ruthless and fanatic one-sided presentation of our nationalistic idea (Chapter VII)";
>
> "A state was never founded by peaceful economy, only and always by the instinct of race preservation, and by heroics, or by cunning (Chapter IV)";
>
> "Even as a boy I was no pacifist, and all attempts to train me in this direction were utter failures (Chapter V)."

One part of the tabloid emphasized Hitler's war aims, of which Cranston wrote, "None but the blind could have failed to discern his meaning in such expressions as the following: 'Only a potent sword can bring lost soil back into a common Reich – protest can never win anything.... War is the aim of every alliance which is not foolish and worthless.'" He also quoted extensively from Hitler's anti-Jewish views: "Was there any offal, any form of profligacy, especially in cultural life, in which there were not found some Jew? This was a devouring disease, everywhere infecting the people, worse than the Black Death of ancient times."

Cranston called Hitler "an ogre imprisoned by his hates, the quintessence of all he describes as detestable – Machiavelli, Napoleon and Capone rolled into one. Something haunts Adolf Hitler – a man whose father had been illegitimate, who could not prove his own ancestry. He eschewed meat, tobacco and alcohol. It is generally believed that he has never had sexual relations with a woman. What obsesses Hitler? Purity" of race, among other fanaticisms, Cranston believed. *Mein Kampf* he termed "illogical, unscientific, history-distorting, barbaric, apocalyptical, an appalling document in morbid psychology, an insult to the mentality of a 16-year-old child" who, on the basis of a high-school education could "refute its...warped logic. Forewarned is forearmed," Cranston ended. "Every American who has read Hitler's *Mein Kampf* has been warned!"

An attentioner to "newspapermen" at the end of the tabloid stated that the publishers were "about to launch a national weekly newspaper that is going to command attention." "Exposés, mysteries – WE WANT THEM!... We're looking for the real LOWDOWN news that's too HOT, too packed with dynamite for timid editors to handle, news that has stirring human interest appeal."

The tabloid was quickly distributed nationwide with flyers to news dealers urging them to "do your bit to STOP HITLER! by displaying prominently and promoting vigorously the sale of 'Hitler's own book.'" It was "written in much simpler language than the original, and greatly condensed so that readers need not be compelled to wade through page after page of endless repetitions and utterly meaningless ravings. Yet every important feature of the book is retained completely," the flyer read. [114]

The *Los Angeles Times* carried a brief mention of "*Mein Kampf* for a dime – a sort of *Reader's Digest* condensation of it.... Unfortunately it is rather gaudily printed, which gives it the appearance of radical propaganda, when the one convincing thing about it is the fact that it quotes Hitler's own writings.... Of course, no one should judge a man or his work on the strength of a condensation, but most of us do. Apparently what is given in this dime edition is unexpurgated and accurate. It is too bad, though, that the publishers thought it necessary to paint the lily." The two book versions were high on the best-selling list, according to the *San Francisco Call-Bulletin* May 24. "Those who don't want to pay the price are picking up a condensed tabloid edition...translated by young Alan Cranston and published by Amster Spiro." [115]

American Nazi party "Brownshirts" led by Fritz Kuhn tried to sabotage sales by tossing stink bombs at newsstands in the Yorkville section of New York City and St. Louis, Missouri. Within days, Houghton Mifflin filed suit to stop the tabloid's publication for copyright infringement. By then, only ten days after publication, more than 500,000 copies had been sold, and Cranston and Spiro were planning a second edition with changes proposed by Benjamin R. Epstein of B'Nai B'rith's Anti-Defamation League. "They have accepted my suggestions and additions, which will appear in the second edition of the publication," Epstein said in a letter requesting help in distributing the work. [116]

Spiro, together with associates, had formed the Noram Publishing Company to produce *Mein Kampf*. On July 19, 1939, U. S. District Court Judge Edward A. Conger in New York issued an injunction against Noram *et al* to immediately cease publication and distribution of the tabloid. Noram did not contest the decision – "We obviously were guilty and didn't bother," Cranston later said, "nor could we afford to contest it!" – and all extant copies were impounded. Cranston, as one of the company's employees, was indirectly a party to the judgment. Stackpole also was sued by Houghton Mifflin, and the U. S. Supreme Court in October upheld a Second Circuit Appeals Court injunction restraining that book from publication. Cranston had considered reprinting "Mussolini's lurid series published in a Milan newspaper, *The Cardinal's Mistress*," but the *Mein Kampf* lawsuit put an end to that idea. (A first American edition of Mussolini's novel had been published in 1928.) [117]

Cranston was not penalized for damages although the publishing venture soon folded. But Cranston ever afterward took great delight in the fact that, in effect, he had been sued by Hitler, considering Houghton Mifflin to have been Hitler's "American agents." The story would be perpetuated that Cranston was "the only man in the country ever sued by Herr Hitler," news reports repeated for many years. Cranston conceded that Hitler "was right and we were wrong in the case," which he nevertheless called "a beautiful example of democracy in action." His rationale for producing "a true version" to counter the "phony version" authorized by Hitler was that "the American edition left out many of Hitler's wildest, most alarming statements. It was carefully designed to lull Americans into a sense of false security. I was outraged." He and Spiro also were "outraged by Hitler's making money from his nefarious book," Cranston told author and screenwriter Irving Wallace in 1981. The half-million copies of the tabloid that were sold, Cranston believed, "helped awaken a great many Americans to how wrong Hitler was in those monstrous policies of his." He also wrote an article on the subject for the February 2, 1972, *National Enquirer*. By then a rare copy of the original tabloid, which had sold for ten cents, Cranston noted with amusement, was a collector's item for which he had to pay $50.00. [118]

Spiro, who still had an interest in the publishing business, continued to hope that Houghton Mifflin's copyright might be abrogated on grounds that it paid royalties to Hitler, thus permitting another condensation to be published. He tried to enlist help during World War II from the federal Office of Facts and Figures after Cranston went to work there. But its book-division chief told Spiro that the royalties-to-Hitler argument was "on unsure ground: In the first place, it is the government which insists that Houghton Mifflin pay those royalties, and in the second place, none of the money ever reaches Germany – what our government doesn't take in taxes, the British government seizes." But the man thought Spiro's idea about publishing President Roosevelt's war speeches "is worth serious consideration." Or, "how about a [book] on the Negro?... That certainly is one of the best [suggestions] I can give you. It is a serious problem and one that is going to cause this country plenty of anguish for many months to come." [119]

A former editor at Houghton Mifflin, however, in 1983 challenged then-Senator Cranston's account of the episode, citing "wholly incorrect" statements in a political biography which said that the Houghton Mifflin abridged edition had been "doctored dramatically." It had been the same as one published in England by Allen and Unwin, the only English translation of *Mein Kampf* at the time, Paul Brooks told Cranston, calling his tabloid a "pirated edition." Its promotional claim of "no royalties to Hitler" was "intentionally misleading," Brooks charged, "since [the publishers] well knew that Hitler never received any royalties from the legitimate edition, as this slogan implied. They were paid, of course, to the Alien Property Custodian." Furthermore, Brooks noted, Houghton Mifflin brought the suits principally to preserve "the livelihood of many other writers, including distinguished authors who had been obliged to flee from Hitler's Germany. To describe the executives of Reynal and Hitchcock and Houghton Mifflin as 'Hitler's agents' is not only absurd but clearly libelous," Brooks said. "Since these misstatements are receiving wide circulation, some correction is clearly called for." Brooks had been on the point of contributing to one of Cranston's political campaigns in support of his anti-arms policy but had reconsidered after reading two biographical paragraphs that he had found about the *Mein Kampf* adventure. [120]

Brooks' charges prompted a fast response from Cranston and his staff. "He was very pleased by the attention paid him," Murray Flander, his Senate press aide, told Cranston, "but that still leaves unresolved what we do next." They would have to modify biographical statements to delete references to "Hitler's agents." "We cannot say that Alan was sued. The defendant was the Noram Publishing Company, not Alan. And we can't even say Hitler had anything whatever to do with the suit.

He didn't," Flander argued. "I can't for the life of me figure out what we can say about this that could possibly be of any use to us," but he recommended that they "either drop the whole *Mein Kampf* story (a really painful decision); tell it, but without the law suit (which would take most of the kick out of it)"; or "get a lawyer to research court records…and try to reconstruct a first-hand version of the suit." [121]

Cranston, according to his Senate administrative assistant Roy Greenaway, did not consider important his tendency to "exaggerate" sometimes when telling stories about his past. "Alan always *knew* that he had not been sued by Hitler but by the publisher," Greenaway said, but he continued to use the story in biographical information, citing "Hitler's agents" as suing. "He had a history of exaggeration. He was always looking for a good way to tell a story, and that was an interesting way to tell that one. Murray worried about it, but Alan didn't," Greenaway said. A 1987 biographical sketch of Cranston stated that he "was sued, indirectly, by Adolf Hitler," and "forced to cease publication after Hitler's publishers sued in a Connecticut court for copyright infringement." [122]

That was the end of Cranston's journalistic career. A New York friend, Helen Gardner, after seeing Cranston on television years later, wrote a description of him in those lean years. "You were a handsome lad at that time and still are, but then you did, on occasion, hold up your pants with a rope, as I recall it, and now you are a front-line politician! I gather you are still a 'liberal' – bully for you! And running for office! You are indeed a brave soul – as always." [123]

Cranston himself wrote of that period of his life, in a letter congratulating two television reporters for winning a Los Angeles Press Club Journalism Award: "As a former news correspondent who never won anything (except a lot of good experience that has served me well all my life), I recognize the importance of receiving such an honor from one's professional peers." [124]

Asked by students toward the end of his life how he had the courage or mentality to do such things at such a young age, Cranston replied, "Maybe I didn't know better; maybe I knew that you had to deal with these issues. But I think part of it came from the self-reliance that was inculcated in me by my parents and the fact that they would give me advice…but then leave it to me to make the decision." [125]

As to why he decided to give up journalism, he said: "I became very concerned about American isolationism, the fact that there were many Americans wanting to have nothing to do with what was happening in the rest of the world, as if it weren't going to impact us sooner or later. So after doing that for a while, I decided it wasn't the life for me after all. I didn't want to spend my life writing about such evil people and their terrible deeds. I'd rather be involved in the action. So I decided to quit journalism, and hoped eventually I could get into politics and government if I could figure out how to do it." [126]

With the outbreak of World War II, Cranston would have the chance to radically change his life and career, both personally and professionally.

3

Marriage, Aliens and Army

"[W]e should not yield to temporary fears or hysteria.... Is there any good reason for adopting a measure opposed to all American traditions?"
Alan Cranston to Senator Francis T. Maloney, June 13, 1940, about an alien-registration bill.

"Unless we can control the nuclear demon, there is no defense against such an attack by determined people, sane or mad."
Alan Cranston and Lee Falk, draft for play or film, "The Bomb,"circa 1945, after atomic bomb was dropped on Japan to end World War II.

Early in 1940 Cranston took a full-time, paying job. His interest in refugees' problems had brought him to the attention of Read Lewis, executive director of a private organization called the Common Council for American Unity. It had evolved from a post-World War I Committee on Public Information known by the name of its head, George Creel, journalist and chief propagandist for President Woodrow Wilson, and was created to aid the large number of immigrants who began arriving in the United States after the war. By 1939, when the Common Council was incorporated to take over the committee's work, immigration policies had become restrictive and punitive against aliens, many of whom needed help in becoming *bona fide* U. S. citizens. The wave of immigration (foreign-born citizens then numbered 40 million) had changed the face of American demography, creating antipathy to different customs, races and religions that immigrants brought with them. "All too many Americans have not yet frankly faced and accepted the all important fact" of America as a true "melting pot," Council brochures stated. Newcomers who had become citizens were not treated "as equals," the Council stated in an announcement quoted by the *New York Times* in June, 1940, especially "non-White groups" who were "subject to economic and social discrimination." At the same time, many immigrant groups brought with them "hostilities and hatreds inherited from the intense nationalism of Europe," and had difficulty accepting American institutions and traditions. The Council's most popular publication was "How to Become a Citizen of the United States." [1]

The Council's purposes appealed to internationalist Cranston's ideologies. Hitler, after all, had boasted that America's population diversity was a fatal weakness. The Council wanted to insure that such diversity was a "democratic strength" at a time when congressional and government officials were rushing to enact new laws and rules restricting the civil liberties of immigrants, particularly those who had a hint of communist leanings. The Council produced materials for the 1,047 foreign-language radio stations and publications, interpreting America for immigrants and providing help on naturalization. Its board of directors included representatives of a number of nationalities, activists like muckraking author Ida M. Tarbell and Mrs. Jacob A. Riis, widow of the Danish-born social reformer, and James Lawrence Houghteling (a Commissioner for Immigration and Naturalization, later an official in the U. S. Treasury Department). Read Lewis, a bachelor, ran the Council with hands-on control. [2]

Cranston was hired at a modest salary, $3,400 a year (the total 1940 budget for the Council was $35,000), to lobby Congress against enacting anti-alien legislation. He also wrote a newsletter and articles for its publication *Common Ground*, edited by Louis Adamic, Yugoslav-born author of *My America* among other studies. "As Washington representative," Cranston wrote in a résumé, "I lobbied against discriminatory bills and maintained close liaison with government agencies having anything to do with the aliens and foreign-born.... That gave me extensive opportunity to acquire knowledge of the workings of government." "My contacts in Washington with members of Congress, government officials, press relations officials and newspapermen are excellent," he said in another *curriculum vitae*.[3]

At first Cranston missed the excitement and activity of the news business. He thought of himself as doing "screwy" social work although it was opening new horizons for him. He had begun to focus on a government career but needed access to a world that he did not yet know. "I still hope to get into politics someday," he wrote his sister, "and this social stuff is perfect training for that, along with the news work." That was one of the first overt mentions of his interest in politics. [4]

Cranston also registered to vote that same year, 1940 – choosing the Democratic Party rather than following his parents' Republican leanings. He had not been in the United States since he had become eligible to vote in a national election. [5]

He went to Washington on Lincoln's birthday in February, 1940, and headed for the U. S. Capitol where he watched Congress in action from the House visitors' gallery. "It was love at first sight," he later said of the moment. But he recognized that politicians had agendas that perhaps were not always in the public's interest. "Those congressional louses are going to adjourn shortly," he said in a letter to Eleanor. "They *should recess* so they could get together quickly if anyone tries to usurp too much power. But they'll *adjourn* because that way they get train fare home!" [6]

His first assignment for the Council was to dissuade congressmen from backing a bill authored by Representative John J. Dempsey, Democrat and later Governor of New Mexico, which would have permitted any person who "believes in, advocates, teaches, or advises" measures like overthrowing the U. S. government to be deported. As Lewis had written to Council supporters, "In the critical times ahead of us, unity is of the utmost urgency. Our wise and fair treatment of the alien and similar groups will be a very important factor in achieving it." Cranston was sympathetic with opposition to the bill, which allowed deportation merely on the basis of one's beliefs. He convinced Dempsey that it was excessive and unenforceable because beliefs would have to be proven. Dempsey subsequently dropped the bill. It was Cranston's first success at influencing legislation. He liked the feeling, he told Eleanor, remarking on "how easy it was for someone to show up and affect what happens in Congress," and the speed with which it could be done, if credible arguments were made for one's side. Lewis telegraphed him June 21, 1940, "Glad to get your excellent report. Congratulations on what you have accomplished." Cranston that year was nominated to membership in the American Political Science Association, and had passes to both the House and Senate chambers. [7]

He was learning to work with Congress, the players and nuances of how they related to one another, and to navigate the intricate paths that legislation had to follow from inception to enactment. Lewis was a stickler for detail and a hard task-master but Cranston tolerated, and learned from, him. An associate complained that "boiling in oil would be too good for" Lewis after he complained about a mistake in one of Cranston's legislative reports. But he redeemed himself with detailed information from his lobbying. "The hearings on Thursday almost ended in bloodshed," he wrote Lewis March 30, 1940, "with acting chairman [William T.] Schulte of Indiana threatening to hit [Charles] Kramer of California on the jaw." The bill under debate would have denied immigration papers to aliens who sought citizenship primarily to obtain relief or WPA work. Cranston was relieved to tell Lewis that it was unlikely any "of the dangerous bills will get anywhere this session." He had queried several newspapermen who corroborated that view. [8]

Lewis was pleased with Cranston's work, and kept him busy ferreting out information. That spring he commuted between Washington and New York, keeping Lewis informed. One request asked Cranston if he would learn, "In the event of war or the extension of the present emergency, [whether] the administration has any plans respecting the internment of enemy aliens or any special regulations respecting aliens. A number of groups are getting worried about the question, and it would be a good plan to find out…if anything is in the wind." It was an issue in which Cranston soon would be personally involved. [9]

Among other issues that he dealt with was whether aliens could volunteer for service in the U. S. military (they did have to register for the draft). The Council also got involved with requests to help immigrants obtain visas to remain in the United States. "Many thanks for your…efforts to speed up my case," an educator wrote Cranston in February, 1941. "How good and encouraging it is to have friends and to find them ready to bring things forward…. I am sure you will do your best to facilitate this – now my greatest aspiration. Next week I am starting my course in the Yeshiva College and Teacher's College." A physician friend in San Francisco asked Cranston's help with a German woman who had immigrated legally in 1936 but could not be admitted to citizenship under the new law because she was from an Axis nation. She worried about when she might receive citizenship papers and whether "the ruling will have any effect on funds which she has in this country." Her father was a leading banker in Germany, recently freed from a concentration camp and living in Holland; a brother was in the U. S. Army at Fort Riley, Kansas. "If there are to be exceptions whatever, I am sure that you could feel well justified in interceding for her," the doctor said. [10]

Another request for help was more dicey for Cranston. "About your Canadian pal," he wrote a friend in 1941, "I've done a little snooping, and feel it wisest that I don't do a thing about it, and the lower he lays [*sic*], the better. Communists are now deportable – those who were Communists before entry. I don't want to tell anyone here he was a Com., and don't know whether he's told anyone himself. You see that [Australian-born San Francisco labor leader Harry] Bridges now may be deported, if they can prove that he was a Communist at *any* time – the *any* time has only been in the law since the Alien Registration Act was enacted last summer. Also, [a former Communist named] Strecker has already been arrested again; his will be a test case – if he's deported, many may be thrown out after him. Until his case is decided, along with that of Bridges, your pal is reasonably safe. But there's nothing I can do, and any attempt might precipitate action against him." [11]

The Council took credit for getting the President and Attorney General to address employment discrimination against aliens, and government officials to oppose censorship of foreign-language newspapers. "Pearl Buck Speaks for Democracy," a plea for justice for African-Americans, was distributed by the Council, and she gave a much-publicized speech, "Is this Freedom's War?" at a Council dinner December 10, 1942, honoring twenty-eight Nobel prize winners living in the United States (eleven were present, including German-born author Thomas Mann, an outspoken opponent of fascism). [12]

Cranston wrote a series of articles between 1940 and 1944 for *Common Ground*, which counted among its contributors leading writers like Pearl Buck, Archibald MacLeish, Eleanor Roosevelt, Langston Hughes, Van Wyck Brooks, Robert M. Hutchins, William Saroyan, Mary Ellen Chase, George Shuster and Mann. Cranston wrote educational articles entitled "Food Follows Our Flag," "The Registration of Aliens," "Discrimination - Defense Bottle-neck," "Enemy Aliens," and one for *Magazine Digest*, "Skilled Workers Not Wanted," about the reluctance of employers to hire aliens and state laws that discriminated against employing them. "Congress has enacted no laws barring Negroes from government work," Cranston wrote in "Discrimination - Defense Bottle-neck," "but despite whatever Civil Service ratings they achieve, they find it difficult to land jobs in Washington more complex than running elevators or messages. Jews, too, are scarce in certain government departments.... Discrimination puts us in partnership with Hitler by dividing us, segregating us, turning us against one another and against America." [13]

Other articles by Cranston in defense of alien rights appeared in the *Journal of Educational Sociology* and the Jewish *Hadassah Newsletter*. "[H]aving lived under the dictatorships in Germany and Italy," Cranston wrote the Hadassah editor, "I believe I have a pretty good understanding of the way an attack upon the aliens can develop into an assault upon all minorities, [and] can pave the way to a dictatorship." "Like you, I don't want to live under a dictatorship here," he told the head of the American Jewish Committee. He hoped that his article for Hadassah would have "wide distribution, and help arouse opposition to" anti-alien bills. Putting immigration in perspective, as he had tried to do with his stories about the shiploads arriving in New York, Cranston wrote in the *Jewish Tribune* January 25, 1940, "Only half of the immigrants who entered the country in 1939 were Jewish," and the total number of aliens entering the United States had actually dropped in the previous decade. "Yet alien-baiters go on striving to convince the

American public that ever since Hitler rose to power in Germany, this country has been literally invaded by people fleeing the terrors of Europe." In *Contemporary Jewish Record*, Cranston said in stronger terms: "America's would-be dictators and their storm troopers and dupes seek to brand the alien as America's scapegoat.... They consider the voteless, often stateless, aliens the easiest group to victimize, and they know that once their persecution has set a precedent, a crusade against other groups will be more likely to succeed." [14]

He also made speeches to foreign groups, press associations and immigrant organizations. On December 18, 1940, Cranston addressed the parents' association at Girls' Commercial High School in Brooklyn on "What is Americanism?" "This group is keenly interested in the subject you spoke on and your message was very warmly received by them," the head of lectures for the federal Works Projects Administration in New York City wrote Cranston afterward, adding that he would be welcome back at any time. [15]

Cranston worked closely with groups like B'Nai B'rith, sending it alien crime statistics released by the Federal Bureau of Investigation to diffuse perceptions that foreign-born people were responsible for much crime in the United States. He and Lewis also tried to plant stories in major publications to support their cause. "Shocked as we are at the persecution of minorities abroad," Lewis said in promoting an article for *Collier's* magazine, "how many realize that some foreigners returned to [oppression in] Europe in recent years because the rising tide of ill-feeling toward aliens in the United States made it difficult for them to make a living here?" An article "showing that America has been as much of a problem to the immigrant as he has been for us, might do much toward dispelling the present ill-feeling toward aliens.... If you are at all interested, I will ask Alan Cranston, who joined our staff early this year, to talk over the idea with you, or to submit an outline or the article itself, as you prefer. He is familiar with the facts, and as an ex-newspaperman who worked abroad...with two recent acquisitions to your staff, William Hillman in London and Frank Gervasi in Rome, he should be competent to do the article for you. As far away as Ethiopia, he met a man who had lost his job in America early in the Depression; though threatened by natives and blackened by the African sun, this man found life better there, working. Bits of such personal material could well enliven the subject," Lewis hoped. [16]

Working with Congress, though, was a major part of Cranston's work for the Council. One of the House races that he especially noticed was the reelection of Texas Democrat Lyndon Baines Johnson (who had lost a bid for a senate seat in 1941). Cranston also made a point of meeting California Republican Senator Hiram Johnson who signed a pass for Cranston to the Senate chamber. He met him in the senator's Capitol office with windows that looked down over a long mall to the Lincoln and Washington monuments, a view that Cranston himself would have one day. Hiram Johnson, who had been senator since 1917, was seventy-four when Cranston visited him, a memorable moment as he lobbied his way through Congress, talking to those who could have an impact on the Council's legislative concerns. Hiram Johnson was critical and needed persuading: In the past, he had supported immigration laws that barred new Japanese immigrants to the United States and restricted their rights. He also had been a vocal isolationist, opposing

American membership in the League of Nations, something that did not win him Cranston's favor. [17]

One of the bills that the Council opposed would have deported all narcotic violators without consideration of other circumstances, like those afflicting "many unfortunate but harmless addicts whose sole offenses are minor violations," Read Lewis wrote the bill's sponsor, Democratic Representative Joe Starnes of Alabama in February, 1940. An alien convicted of a misdemeanor would have "no escape from deportation, however minor the offense, or whatever the hardship caused to his family," Lewis argued, proposing alternative language to deal with addicts. After Cranston talked to him, Starnes thought the Council's amendments were "sound" and had no objections to including them in the bill. [18]

The bill that would have deported longshoremen leader Harry Bridges, whose leftist leanings were controversial, also concerned the Council. Cranston was showing increased knowledge and sophistication about Congress in addressing that and other measures as the year progressed. "[I]t's been impossible to get a line on what may be expected to happen to the Smith bill [on alien registration]," he wrote Lewis in mid-May. "I found a friendly secretary, a Mr. Barnett, in Senator [Tom] Connolly's [Democrat of Texas, Chairman of the Foreign Relations Committee] office, however, and he's promised to give me some dope tomorrow morning. Enclosed are three of the six sheets on the labor unions here. I'll have the others corrected shortly." [19]

The Council's targets were measures that clamped down freedoms in the name of protectionism. Hitler's invasion of the Netherlands and Belgium May 10, 1940, had heightened fears in America. "The rapid change of atmosphere since that date has produced an entirely new situation on which it is important that we take counsel," Lewis wrote his members May 23. High on their list of concerns were bills that transferred the Immigration and Naturalization Service to the Department of Justice; a bill providing for deportation of aliens convicted of felonies; an amendment limiting employment of aliens as part of a civil-liberties bill sponsored by Senator Robert LaFollette of Wisconsin. The next day Lewis told James Houghteling, then with the Immigration and Naturalization Service in the Labor Department, "Things are moving so fast that it is hard to keep up with them." The attorney general was proposing wholesale registration of aliens, which Lewis argued would probably serve no useful purpose. "Only the good aliens will register," requiring expenditures of "time, money and energy which the government might much better devote to really important things.... I do hope you can persuade the Department of Justice not to rush into something on the plea of national defense," Lewis urged Houghteling. Cranston by now was savvy about how to influence Congress. Houghteling, he realized, could not "openly oppose" such measures from his position in the immigration service. [20]

For Cranston, too, things were "moving fast." "The papers are full of items about 'fifth columns' [Communist infiltrators] and the Senate spent the entire afternoon on the subject – without getting anywhere," he told Lewis in late May. It was part of debate on a proposal to limit aliens to 10 percent of an employer's payroll. Cranston perceived that one senator's agenda was "more to filibuster the LaFollette bill to death than anything else." [21]

In less than a year, Cranston had built relationships with members of Congress. He was becoming a familiar figure around committee and hearing rooms, and many members now confided information to him or at least responded to his inquiries. He felt confident enough to recommend to a staff aide that Senator James M. Mead of New York seek a "Democratic vacancy on the Immigration Committee" in hopes that he would further the Council's agenda. One of its members told Cranston that "the general attitude of the...committee was: 'To hell with the alien. He has no right to interfere in our government.' [Senator Richard] Russell [Democrat of Georgia] said that without the Dempsey [anti-aliens] bill, a Nazi could come in and advocate the setting up of a Nazi government – by constitutional means." Cranston also helped get Council backing for private bills that congressmen introduced to help certain alien groups: one introduced by Representative Kramer of California proposed re-admitting "natives of Old Russia" from Mexico without the usual immigration formalities; another sponsored by Jerry Voorhis of California canceled deportation proceedings against Hindus. [22]

Those legislators who were sympathetic to the Council's arguments Cranston particularly courted, sending them information and comments, as he did Democratic Congressman Emanuel Celler of New York about a bill (the Smith alien-registration act, H.R. 5138) that would require registration and fingerprinting of all aliens within four months. "I don't need to repeat the arguments against alien registration to you," Cranston wrote, "but these points are worth mentioning." He cited the fact that officials responsible for alien registration "Privately…admit [that] it would be ineffective and wasteful, though they do say it might serve to allay existing hysteria and so protect the alien from something worse." The bill also had worrisome provisions affecting citizens and aliens alike, which were "so broadly written as to interfere with legitimate freedom of speech," Cranston argued. One provision made "an alien deportable for membership in radical organizations at any time...no matter how long ago the membership...its duration...[or] the alien's subsequent record." [23]

Celler had written the Council that its quarterly magazine *Common Ground* ought to be on the desk of every congressman, and a Council assistant had asked Cranston if he could get Celler's permission to quote his endorsement. "You can give me no pleasanter tasks in our nation's fair capital than to ask congressmen, any congressman, if they'd like to be quoted on the back covers of magazines," Cranston replied. "As a matter of fact, I saw Celler's secretary. [Celler was in the hospital.] He said sure, go ahead, but only use the part about his thinking *Common Ground* should be on every congressman's desk…. Can I do this again for you real soon, with a senator maybe?" he added. [24]

His pleas were forcefully presented, like one to Democratic Senator Francis T. Maloney of Connecticut reminding him that "In the past, alien registration has been widely opposed as un-American." While it needed re-evaluating in light of national defense concerns, "if it will not help to detect those who are trying to undermine American democracy, we should not yield to temporary fears or hysteria," Cranston argued. There was the potential that police, "in an effort to enforce alien registration, could start questioning everyone who looked 'foreign,' or had an accent or a foreign name. This would result in the harassing of millions of native and naturalized citizens, but would it locate the alien spy or saboteur?" In short, Cranston said,

"Alien registration would not in itself identify those who should be watched or apprehended." It would instead

"lead to search and spying, open the door to exploitation and blackmail, afford an instrument for interfering in legitimate labor disputes, tend to set the newcomer apart, make it necessary for citizens to carry evidence of citizenship or face arrest as suspected unregistered aliens,...[and] subtract something from American liberty.... Is there any good reason for adopting a measure opposed to all American traditions?" [25]

"The real reason [to be] against alien registration is that it would be a divisive influence in American life, when the utmost unity is needed," Cranston concluded his arguments. It would put millions of citizens "under suspicion." "The humiliation and setting apart of those millions of citizens, with all the evils that would follow, is too high a price to pay."

Cranston was justifiably pleased when the alien-registration act, if not killed, was modified as a result of his work. He lobbied for changes in conference to reconcile House and Senate versions. "As far as I could learn, they are modifying the deportation penalty for failure to register," he wrote Lewis in June. "Celler's prediction about it's being seen to that the conferees would be anti-alien came true, all right. I had a talk with [New York Republican Representative Clarence E.] Hancock this morning, and he is all for dealing roughly with the aliens. But I think perhaps I persuaded him that the deportation provision should be somewhat modified." A few days later, he could write that the Smith bill was changed to include "a penalty only for those aliens who willfully falsify their statements when they register." "I got this from [Connecticut Republican Senator John A.] Danaher, whom I saw after the Senate adjourned...and I think I can claim some of the credit for that.... I saw [Texas Democratic Representative Hatton W.] Sumners [Chairman of the House Judiciary Committee] for about a half hour yesterday. At first he thought deportation was the right penalty, but after some discussion he began to waiver, and finally decided it was too strict. He attempted to call [then-Solicitor General Francis] Biddle to get his opinion while I was in his office, but unfortunately Biddle was out playing golf. But Sumners promised to do his best to modify the penalty if he found others who agreed with me on it – and he kept his promise. He's really a swell person, and I think I've made a friend that will be valuable in the future." [26]

Cranston also was learning tricks about how to get information in round-about ways. "I've been working with [one senator] very closely on the bill," he told Lewis. "Yesterday Murphy, the Senate legislative expert who was redrawing part of the bill, thought he couldn't tell me the new provisions. So I had him call up [the senator to ask permission to do so] – and [he] told me." The measure to deport Harry Bridges he expected would pass. (It did.) One senator had told Cranston that "after John L. Lewis' remark that FDR is in 'full intellectual retreat,' [the registration bill] is less apt to get vetoed." Roosevelt had favored universal registration, Cranston reported. [27]

An alien-registration bill was enacted and implemented in August, 1940, immediately following congressional approval. All aliens were required to register and be fingerprinted at post offices between August 27 and December 26, 1940. Estimates ranged from four to seven million aliens, most of whom were American citizens, Cranston wrote for an article on the new law (a survey in California showed that 70 percent of families headed by aliens were American citizens). About 100,000 aliens were thought to be illegally in the United States.

Although the massive registration would be ineffective in capturing spies and saboteurs, according to administrators, Congress, Cranston rationalized with sarcasm, had responded to "a wave of hysteria that swept the country after [Hitler's] invasion of the lowlands. Elderly ladies in New York started rifle practice, gentlemen in Georgia organized anti-parachute brigades, and Mayor [George H.] Lysle of McKeesport [Pennsylvania] moved to save democracy in his bailiwick with an announcement that all aliens who failed to register by the Fourth of July would be arrested on Independence Day." The "problems are endless," he continued. "A couple of years ago, an immigrant who had been here for ten years but who had stolen a chicken in Italy when he was sixteen, was deported because a neighbor had a fight with him, and informed the government of his dark past. The other day a terror-struck Russian woman visited a social agency in N. Y. and said: 'I spent five years in a Siberian prison camp because I said I believed in God. Does that criminal record make me deportable?' An immigrant woman from a western state, who entered illegally ten years ago, and now heads a $100,000-a-year business, climbed on an American Airliner and flew to N. Y. to ask a social agency how she could avoid deportation." Cranston hoped his "hurried outline" showed the "magnitude and complexity of the problem." "I know it inside and out," he added, "because I am with an agency that deals with the problems of non-citizens, and I am at present spending a good deal of my time in Washington working on registration with Solicitor General Biddle and other men in the Department of Justice." [28]

But bigger changes were about to overtake Cranston's life. The young woman whom he had met on a blind date in Los Angeles had attracted him more than he allowed to others. He and Geneva May McMath corresponded after Cranston returned to the East Coast, and he invited her to come to New York for three months to do some writing. They visited the New York World's Fair, and were photographed walking hand-in-hand on the boardwalk. In support of a Common Council position, Geneva wrote a letter to the editor of the *New York Journal* about a presidential veto of a bill that the Council had opposed. She obviously shared Cranston's views. She also had a sharp sense of irony and wit. The bill would have allowed deportation of any alien who "admitted in writing" – i.e., might have been coerced into admitting – that he was guilty of espionage or sabotage. The *Journal* had editorialized that the veto was an "aid to communism." "I disagree with the editor," she stated, "and insist that any legislation depriving the individual of his democratic right of due-process of the law is a clear aid to communism." [29]

Geneva's quick mind, dry humor, candor and self-confident maturity also were pluses in Cranston's eyes. Tall, auburn-haired with blue eyes and strong features, Geneva was striking if not movie-star glamorous. Eleanor thought her "very bright and attractive-looking." She also was two years older than Cranston, born in Berkeley, January 16, 1912, while her father, Edgar H. McMath, was getting a master's degree at the University of California. The family moved a great deal when her father changed jobs as a public school official. He had been on the faculty of the University of Southern California, a school teacher and principal of Santa Ana High School. (They lived in a house that her grandfather had built at 214 South Birch Street in Santa Ana.) Geneva had graduated from San Diego High School in 1928. She then lived at home for two years while working as a secretary and bank teller to save money for college. She saved $2,000 and entered Pomona College. When the funds ran out, she supported herself as a waitress and by typing papers for students and doing other chores (she preferred waitressing to typing papers). She had graduated in 1934, two years after Cranston had gone there as a freshman. She and Cranston had only briefly crossed paths at Pomona. "I knew him by sight but we never got acquainted," she later said in newspaper interviews. She was "idealistic" in college but not "starry-eyed." "The hard work of making my own way kept me pretty well in touch with the practicalities of life," she said with the candor for which she would be known. [30]

Geneva returned to California and Cranston wrote his parents that he was engaged, this time for real. A marriage date, though, was dependent on Cranston's fate with the military draft, which complicated matters for his future. On the day that draft numbers were drawn in Washington, Cranston had a toothache. "I read the *New York Times* while I was waiting for the dentist...searching for my own draft number," he remembered of the fateful day. His was a high number (low numbers were drafted first). But he already had decided that if it were drawn and he were to be drafted soon, they should marry immediately and he would continue his present work until drafted. [31]

At the end of October, 1940, Cranston had a requisite blood test in New York City to prove that he did not have syphilis and got a marriage license. The following week he flew to California, spent a weekend with his parents at Los Altos and drove with them to Los Angeles for the wedding. It took place at eight o'clock on a Wednesday evening, November 6, 1940, at a non-sectarian chapel on the grounds of Forest Lawn Cemetery in Glendale, Wee Kirk o' the Heather, a faithful copy of a village church in Glencairn, Scotland. John Atkinson was best man, although Lee Falk later claimed that he was, and a sister of Geneva's, Mrs. Herbert Fairbrother, was matron of honor. Geneva wore "a coat of military or soldier's blue over a dress of the same color, and looked stunning," Mrs. William Cranston wrote Eleanor who was in the East at the time with her husband. A reception followed at the McMath home in Westwood Village. The newlyweds spent their wedding night at the Miramar Hotel in Santa Monica and briefly went to Palm Springs. After returning the family car to Los Altos, they flew to Los Angeles, took a train to New Orleans and a ship from there to New York. Geneva would remember it as the first introduction to her husband's strenuous schedules. [32]

The *Daily Palo Alto Times*, gave the marriage good play, describing the groom as a man "whose career already includes three exciting years as a foreign press correspondent and the promise of success as a playwright." "All good fortune to you both," Cora Older wrote them. [33]

Geneva sentimentally wrote on three separate calling cards, "From Mrs. Alan MacGregor Cranston/ To her darling, Mr. Alan MacGregor Cranston, with love/ And to Mr. and Mrs. Alan MacGregor Cranston – may they grow and grow, through deep understanding and respect, to the height of the most profound and glorious mature love." Cranston saved the cards throughout his life. She also dutifully inducted Cranston, as a joke, into the "Married Men's Protective Association" in which she permitted her "husband to go where he pleases, drink what he pleases and when he pleases, and...to keep the company of any lady or ladies he sees fit, as I know he is a good judge," the membership card stated. "I want him to enjoy life in this world, for he will be a long time DEAD." [34]

The newlyweds set up housekeeping in a small apartment (at 317 10th Street, Northeast) on Capitol Hill in Washington. Cranston would take a liking to the location, not far from the Capitol buildings. "We're now fully settled in a perfect apartment only ten blocks from the Capitol," he wrote Read Lewis January 7, 1941. "The apartment is really nice – bedroom, bath, hallway, living room, dinette-kitchen.... In a modern apartment house, built in 1928. The phone number is LIncoln 4034-J. We hope you'll be here soon to be one of our first guests (but we have no plates yet, so don't hurry *too* much)." [35]

Cranston briefly explored other schemes with a boyhood friend, newsman Tom Crane. They conceived a plan to use American volunteers to work on merchant ships carrying war supplies to Europe and thus relieve a perceived shortage of crew on British and American vessels. Cranston tried to interest David K. Niles, an administrative assistant to President Roosevelt, and his 1943 campaign director, Senator Tom Connolly, as well as members of the Maritime Commission, but the project never came to fruition – the U. S. Maritime Commission in 1941 told Niles that it did not anticipate lacking sufficient seamen to man merchant ships. But bigger problems soon would overwhelm the nation and supporters of American neutrality. [36]

Cranston was not one of those. "I am against neutrality, or rather the idea of neutrality," he wrote Eleanor in response to her sending him a quote from Anne Morrow Lindbergh's *The Wave of the Future* (1940), which reflected her famous flyer husband's isolationist views. "I think it is non-existent in this world of warring ideas and material forces," Cranston argued with a pragmatic view into the future of a world at war.

"I favor aid to Britain now, including naval aid. If we permit England to go down, we will fight Hitler later anyway, with less chance then of defending ourselves without terrific loss. And I think a Hitler victory will mean the virtual end of democracy – or any hope of progress for many years.... More important than world trade, or rubber, is the spirit of freedom and respect for other men that characterizes America against Germany, Italy, Russia. I don't think that spirit could withstand the propaganda onslaught of a successful Germany....

"RE: the Lindbergh book, I can't see the Nazis as...on 'the wave of the future.' There is nothing new in their program.... [T]hey are going straight back to the Roman pattern – with weapons insuring that, if victorious, they should retain power far longer than the Caesars....

"The whole story of man living socially – apart from man's march in science – has been one of progressive freedom, with temporary setbacks. If this is the 'wave of the future,' we have been wrong – all of us – for some 2,000 years.

"Can you believe the Nazis don't have designs on us?" [37]

Cranston continued to work for the Common Council and was in New York at a Columbia University law professor's penthouse, drafting a bill for supervising deportable aliens, on Sunday afternoon December 7, 1941, when the telephone rang with terrible news, confirmed on the radio – the U. S. naval base at Pearl Harbor had been bombed by the Japanese. Cranston heard a plane droning over the Hudson River and wondered, as did others, whether it carried bombs. He realized that it was a moment of ending and beginning for the country. He saw soldiers and sailors at Grand Central Station bidding goodbye to family and girl friends, and remembered vividly the sight of Italy's battered soldiers returning from Ethiopia. Washington over night had been blacked out and guards were placed outside of government buildings. [38]

Cranston decided not to enlist at that moment but to try to find other work connected with the war effort. Read Lewis sent him to poet/civil servant Archibald MacLeish, Librarian of Congress and head of the government's Office of Facts and Figures (O. F. F.), which had been set up by Roosevelt to handle public information related to foreign aid. The office was expanded in the wake of the nation's entry into war. MacLeish hired Cranston (his salary nearly doubled to $6,500) and put him in charge of the office's Foreign Language Division. Geneva wrote Eleanor in January, 1942, that "If Alan hadn't had a receding hairline and therefore looked older than twenty-seven, he would never had been given that important job!" He was "delighted with his new work," she said, and happy to be associated with colleagues of the caliber of MacLeish. Geneva was pleased that the job kept Cranston to regular hours in an office instead of out and about at all times of day and night. When she expressed hope that they would "live more like other people now," Cranston grinned and said, "How do other people live?" [39]

"I was brought into the Office of Facts and Figures," Cranston said on one of his résumés, "at its earliest stages, to set up the Foreign Language Division. I planned the entire policy and program of the Division, sold it as planned to my superiors… and recruited the staff, put it into operation, and directed it." At one point he oversaw a staff of eighteen and some sixty translators working under contracts. [40]

One of his first recommendations was to improve Congress' public relations. "In two years of legislative work, I have time and again been shocked at the results of Congress' utter lack of any public-relations organization," he wrote a superior in December, 1941. "It seems to me it would be both logical and strategical for the O. F. F. to set up a special section to act in effect as Public Relations Agency for Congress." Other government agencies had publicity sections, but "Congress simply relies upon the *Congressional Record.* Each senator and representative attempts to publicize himself, and the Senate and House suffer the chaotic consequences. The resultant bad public relations combined with recent dawdling over vital bills…have badly damaged Congress and weakened America's faith in the legislative way of life." Such an office could also "insure the O. F. F. budget against congressional attack." Little did he realize at the time how his recommendations presaged his own future activities to reform Congress. [41]

He took Common Council views to his new job, arguing that O. F. F.'s efforts "to inform the foreign-born about World War II will be senseless if [they] are given no opportunity to contribute to the war effort." Cranston urged a nationwide program to break down resistance to employing them, noting that "Aliens are barred from many of the activities sponsored by the Office of Civilian Defense, and now even from participating in Red Cross work. Citizens, too, frequently are excluded if they cannot speak English fluently." [42]

Another problem was whom to arrest for disloyalty. The Justice Department had been restrained in taking action against those considered disloyal (3,000 aliens had been picked up by January, 1942), but was going after only aliens, "although there are many disloyal citizens," Cranston told MacLeish. "When the FBI arrested a few suspected citizens, [then-]Attorney General Biddle promptly ordered their release. I understand that he fears the FBI. would pounce upon many liberals if [it] were given the green light on arresting citizens. I think it would take some of the sting from the Japanese [internment] problem…if the Department let it be known that it was taking action against disloyal citizens as well as disloyal aliens," Cranston suggested. [43]

Many radio stations stopped broadcasting in foreign languages as the war progressed, particularly German and Italian stations, and replaced broadcasts with music. The reason, Cranston explained to a superior, was that American listeners who misunderstood the purpose of those stations were protesting against their continued broadcasting in non-English languages; advertisers had withdrawn sponsorship from such programs; and the stations could not always rely on the content of what they were broadcasting. Cranston proposed that the Office of Facts and Figures "take immediate steps to furnish inspiring and informative programs about America at war to stations with foreign-language audiences. It is of the utmost importance that [these] broadcasts be maintained as a channel through which the sympathy and participation of foreign groups…can be enlisted in the war effort" and kept informed. His office could prepare scripts just as it did press releases and sponsor programs for the broadcasters to use. [44]

That brought him to contact Lee Falk. Cranston now was in a position to help find war-related jobs for friends. "I have been scouting around for something for you to do," he wrote Falk at the end of January, 1942. "Would you be interested in a job turning out two or three half-hour radio scripts per week for foreign-language broadcasts within this country?... To do this, you would have to move from the shores of the [Long Island] Sound to a Washington slum; get to work at nine each morning; maybe work seven days a week; and take thyroid pills," he joked. Cranston suggested to MacLeish that they pay Falk a salary of $4,600 although there were restrictions on what one could earn outside of a government payroll (Falk was earning more than $25,000 a year from his two syndicated cartoon strips). Falk agreed and was hired as associate chief of the foreign-language division for a salary of $1 dollar a year. A congressman friend "told me to remind you about the comic drawings you said you'd send his kids," Cranston wrote Falk at one point. "If you have one of the Mandrake and one of the Phantom, suppose you send the drawings to" the children, "one of whom is named Pierre and the other Harry. If you have any other pictures to throw in, it would be a good idea if you did so," he urged. Cranston also hired a former reporter on the ill-fated *Brooklyn Express*, David Karr, as press aide. (Karr's former associations with Communist groups subsequently would be the subject of congressional scrutiny.) [45]

The Office of Facts and Figures in June, 1942, was merged with three other agencies to form the Office of War Information (O. W. I.), a large propaganda agency selling democracy to the world, as one of its promotional statements put it. Its new director was Elmer H. Davis, then fifty-three, a well-known radio commentator and newsman – "Like a stalk of sturdy Indiana corn pulled up by the roots and set down in Washington," one account said of him. MacLeish, miffed at not being named head of O. W. I., was elevated to Assistant Secretary of State for Cultural and Political Affairs. [46]

O. W. I. , like its predecessor, also had a staff of talented people, among them playwright and screen writer Robert Sherwood as overseas director (he also collaborated on Roosevelt's speeches); producer John Houseman in charge of radio programs; Harold Guinzburg of The Viking Press who directed the agency's outpost bureau; and newspaper (*Des Moines Register & Tribune*) publisher Gardner Cowles, Junior, who was in charge of the domestic branch. Historical novelist Bradford Smith, anthropologist Ruth Benedict and Asian scholar Owen Lattimore, who headed the Pacific Bureau, also were on the staff, as were editors, writers and translators from foreign-language media. (Julia McWilliams, later Mrs. Paul Child, cookbook author and TV personality, worked for four months as a secretary in O. W. I.) Cranston recruited as his assistant a Common Council colleague, six-foot-eight-inch-tall poet Charles Olson who desperately needed a job. The object of Cranston's division was to publicize and explain war activities like the draft, price controls and rationing in more than thirty-five languages, using print and broadcast media and other outlets to reach foreign-language populations in America through some 1,500 publications and 200 radio stations. The potential audience were the 22 million people in the United States who spoke foreign tongues. Cranston had not even heard of some of the languages, like Windish and Ladino. Suppressing those media outlets, according to the division's statement of purpose, "would turn those who are loyal against us – turn them to the short wave for their source of information, and make them easy targets for Axis rumor-mongers and agents." [47]

One of the O. W. I.'s strategies for propaganda was to use well-known and popular authors to carry its message. John Steinbeck wrote a book for the Army Air Force, *Bombs Away, The Story of a Bomber Team*, personal stories of six typical men trained for combat missions. Newsman Howard K. Smith, later a television personality, wrote *Last Train from Berlin*, published by Knopf in September, 1942, and former U. S. Ambassador to Japan (1932-41) Joseph C. Grew's book, *Report from Tokyo*, published by Simon & Schuster in December, 1942, helped the cause. [48]

Cranston reported his job change to the Selective Service Board, noting that he had a special "A-excepted" civil service rating for the duration of the national emergency because of "special qualifications for the particular job I am doing…to create sound understanding of our war effort and [promote] national unity among the various nationality groups." The *Stanford Alumni Review*, reporting in 1943 on the twenty-eight-year-old's new post with O. W. I., said that "Cranston has had an interesting career since he hung up his track shoes after running the quarter mile and the mile relay." [49]

Cranston was full of ideas in his new role. One was to have "Americans All" rallies in major cities with large foreign-born populations. The success of an event in Detroit in the spring of 1942, Cranston pointed out, was that many nationalities were marked for the first time as Americans, not by their nations of origin. "They were wildly enthusiastic at the Detroit rally because of their sincere desire to achieve recognition…as a group that had a material contribution to make to this nation's war effort," he told MacLeish, noting that O. F. F. had "saved the day by dispatching speakers, entertainers and assistance" to work on the Detroit program. [50]

At a joint meeting of the Italian-American Labor Council and the Mazzini Society in June, 1942, Cranston bluntly told the group, "There was a short moment in which America judged you by the fascist agents and propagandists who for a long time infested your communities. The judgment was partly justified, since during a certain period, clever agents succeeded in betraying the good faith of many of you…. It was a wild storm troubling and confusing your minds but barely touching the honesty of your heart and your love for America. Some of those agents…are still among you. The government expects you to cut them out…. America is becoming aware that your greatest sorrow is that you are suspected as a group, and that some of you are denied the privilege of serving. America is beginning to understand that the greatest need of your spirit at this moment is to be accepted, naturalized or not, as friends, as equals who ask for the privilege of serving democratic America in this war." He reassured them that the government did not intend to suppress the Italian-language media, nor "to limit the activity of loyal Italian societies." But the "beautiful language of Dante, which has been made to serve fascist propaganda and treason," was to be used in America "to express the ideals of Italian humanism." [51]

Cranston had to deal with the fact that some foreign-language newspapers were considered anti-American. When his office – which came to be known as "the little O. W. I." – felt that certain media were not serving America's war interests, it recommended that the Department of Justice take action to suppress them. The problem was deciding when the line had been crossed "between seditious utterance and legitimate criticism," Cranston told his staff, quoting the attorney general. The foreign-language press performed useful functions, Secretary of War Henry Lewis Stimson had stated, and should not be suppressed indiscriminately. But some papers "either openly or slyly denounce our Allies as selfish, undemocratic or uncooperative," Cranston said in a memo justifying action against the "worst examples" which O. W. I. hoped would "close up shop or mend their ways." Such papers tried to "create distrust of Allied victories" by nuances, calling communism "our greatest foe," criticizing "attacks upon nazism and fascism, Germany and Italy," explaining "Axis reasons for the war…. The Pole lackadaisically punching holes in bomber parts in Buffalo has been reading a Polish paper which tells him that Russia will be the only strong nation left in the world when the war is over…. The Italian housewife who cannot understand the issues of the war continues to avoid carrying out simple home-front conservation activities because the family paper keeps playing up the Italian army…and resistance of the people in Italy against the United States." Some papers were owned or subsidized by political refugees "whose first loyalty is to their native country," Cranston noted, and many carried material written by former officials of other countries. Thirty-three people had been indicted for conspiracy in the English-language press. "Like action is called for in this field," Cranston urged. [52]

One reason was that there were spies in the ranks. An Italian magazine editor had tried to slip through an article that pretended to promote U. S. war bonds, but when Cranston compared a translation with the original, the translation "concealed the fact that the article itself praised fascism." He investigated further and "found that beyond a shadow of a doubt, [Marcello Cirosi, the editor] has been and is a confirmed fascist propagandist." He had tried to pass a script onto an Italian radio station in New York but its program manager contacted Lee Falk and the script was found to be pro-fascist. The perpetrator cleverly used the word "patria" – fatherland – to promote war bonds, which confused Italians who did not know whether they were being urged to buy defense bonds to save Italy or America. Cranston had uncovered other information about those associated with an Italian Defense Bond Committee: "I now believe that over half of such committee members are Fascists," he reported. He was told to ask the F. B. I. to investigate the man in question, and Cranston's suspicions were corroborated. An executive assistant to the attorney general "personally believes that on one of [the editor's] broadcasts to Italy, he was giving the Italian government information as to the location of American defense plants," Cranston noted. The man also had "embarrassed" 1940 Republican presidential candidate Wendell Wilkie by associating him with a pro-fascist group and newspaper "to swing the huge Italian vote in New York to the Republican ticket. If [the editor] stays," Cranston feared, "our work among the Italians in this country is rendered useless. The Fascists will know that they are too strong to be controlled." He added that he believed similar situations existed in other foreign-language bond campaigns. [53]

An example of how foreign media subtly manifested views was the Italian-language radio station that played the "Victory March" from *Aida* after broadcasting a news bulletin about the British army retreating to El Alamein in North Africa. A Japanese newspaper in the Rocky Mountain area printed news of Japanese victories in large-size type, but relegated American victories at Midway and the Coral Sea to back pages. O. W. I. saw to it that the editor was no longer in a position to influence editorial policy on the paper. A German newspaper in the Midwest changed an O. W. I. release on Allied bombings of the industrial city of Essen – which stated that the bombings were so devastating that factory workers were forced to take a long vacation in the country – to read that the Reich government, in a new policy, had given the workers free vacations with full pay. [54]

Pro-Fascist groups did, in fact, still exist in America. Only a few fascist leaders had been interned by the Justice Department when the war began, and Italian newspapers, Cranston told Elmer Davis, continued to publish pro-fascist propaganda. Cranston's division had urged internment of more known Fascists and suppression of their media but "when we found that our policy would not be adopted, generally, we revised our tactics," and in an effort to promote Italian-American unity, brought together "reformed Fascists" with anti-Fascists in hopes that the latter would prevail. Cranston's office had refused to work with the Sons of Italy until it issued an anti-fascist manifesto, and had found it hard to work with the Mazzini Society because of disparate views among its members. Cranston's office was accused by socialist leader Norman Thomas of "playing the fascist game," and the socialist-anti-Communist *New Leader* magazine of "following the Comintern [Communist International] line" by favoring united nationality groups. "They fail to consider the fact that we might be simply trying to unite all Americans behind the war effort," Cranston responded. "We have at no time, anywhere, made any effort to persuade anyone to accept Communists within…the organizations." [55]

Cranston was knowledgeable about communist- and fascist-front groups and their leaders. "This organization has been and almost surely still is a communist front," he told MacLeish about the Civil Rights Federation in 1942. He advised MacLeish several times against addressing meetings organized by the American Committee for Protection of Foreign Born "since it is C. P. [Communist Party] controlled." It would "probably be unwise to ignore them entirely," though, so Cranston suggested that MacLeish send the group a message for a 67th anniversary of the Statue of Liberty, that read in part, "Today it stands for something bigger than itself, bigger than America…. It is the huge sign of the world's fight to determine whether men shall live free or slave." When MacLeish was asked to comment on the 25th anniversary of the 1917 Bolshevik takeover of Russia, Cranston cautioned against saying anything that would support the revolution, proposing to limit comments to praising the valor of the Soviet people and army in repulsing the forces of Nazism. [56]

Cranston became active in promoting special status for Italian-Americans so that they would not be considered enemy aliens. An Italian-American on the O. W. I. staff, Joe Facci, was "a very great guy who convinced me that the way to really get Italian-Americans behind the war effort was to lift the enemy-alien classification from all Italians who were not citizens," Cranston said of the germ of the idea. German and Japanese non-citizens also were classified as enemies, but Italians by that time in the war were "getting restive with their alliance with Hitler," Cranston knew, and "Mussolini was beginning to be shaky. I persuaded the attorney general to recommend it to Roosevelt and it *happened*." [57]

Cranston's efforts culminated with an announcement by Attorney General Francis Biddle on Columbus Day, 1942, that Italian aliens no longer would be classified as enemy aliens, for which the Common Council took partial credit. "We were invading Italy at the time." Cranston remembered, "and planes flew over and dropped leaflets containing the declassification information, which was recognition of Italians as friends, and that was credited with saving a lot of American lives when we invaded Italy. It shattered the unanimity and will-power of the Italian Fascists." [58]

Cranston's actions won him praise among Italians. "I learn with pleasure that you were one of the most strenuous promoters of the Biddle declaration," the secretary of the Mazzini Society wrote Cranston after the announcement. "The Society considers it as the wisest and most equitable measure that the American government could adopt." The director of the Bureau of Latin American Research sent Cranston "congratulations on the superb piece of work which you initiated and put through in connection with the treatment of Italians in this country. It was certainly a commendable achievement, and an enormous step forward in the grand strategy of political warfare." The leader of refugee anti-Fascists who became Italy's post-war defense minister arranged for Cranston to receive an award from the Italian government, the Star of Solidarity, in 1946. [59]

But a set-back occurred when Italian-born anarchist Carlo Tresca, editor of a small paper, *Il Martello* (The Hammer), was shot and killed the night of January 11, 1943, at the corner of 15th Street and Fifth Avenue in New York. The wartime blackout prevented his companion from getting a good look at the assassin (his murder never was officially solved but was attributed to an Italian gangster). Tresca, a leader in labor and radical groups, had many enemies among fascist sympathizers, Communists and the Mafia. He also was a favorite of American liberal intellectuals like Norman Thomas. Lee Falk, at Cranston's request, had met with Tresca six days earlier to discuss setting up an Italian-American Victory Council with support from many factions, an effort to bring some unity to the fractured Italian community. The murder would have far-reaching and unanticipated ramifications, however. Accusations of blame flew between factions. [60]

The O. W. I., and Cranston by association, in the aftermath came in for criticism as being pro-communist. The *New York Times* ran a story that was damaging to O. W. I., particularly Cranston and Falk. Cranston told his parents that he was "mixed up as little as possible" in the unfolding events "but every day I'm afraid it may become too much, in a classic murder mystery." The president of the Italian-American Labor Council accused O. W. I. officials of urging Tresca to accept Communists in the Victory Council. Tresca had favored participation of all factions, O. W. I.'s position. "We were advocating that *every* group that was not fascist should be in" the Victory Council, Cranston related of the episode. "It seemed sensible to get everybody – Socialists, Communists, right-wingers, as long as they weren't Nazis – and that became controversial. It wasn't easy." [61]

Elmer Davis on January 22 was forced to issue a statement refuting the newspaper story: "It has been charged that Alan Cranston and Lee Falk of the Foreign Language Division…were attempting 'to force anti-Fascists, including the late Carlo Tresca, to collaborate with Communists.' These charges are without foundation…. The fact that Cranston and Falk are being variously accused of actions favorable to both Fascists and Communists should be a clear indication that they have consistently attempted to steer a democratic middle course." [62]

Norman Thomas was vocal in accusing Cranston and his division of taking both pro-fascist and communist sides, reported in the *New York World Telegram* January 21, 1943 – a "paradox," Cranston told Davis, and "wholly untrue." "We hoped to abolish the long-established leadership of the pro-Fascists by ignoring them, but we found this impossible due to the policies of other government agencies…. Our involvement in the Tresca affair might presumably lead to the opinion that we are neither Communists nor Fascists, but anarchists." [63]

The only member of his staff to talk to Tresca in the previous six months had been Falk, "and then only once," Cranston reported. "Tresca's death has shown more clearly than any previous incident the disgraceful lack of unity in the Italian-American community…. Tresca had told us that he felt that all anti-Fascists should unite in the Victory Council until fascism is defeated." The same conflicts, he added, existed among German-Americans. "Former and current Nazis still dominate while the anti-Nazis quarrel among themselves."

Davis quickly defended Cranston and Falk. "Whether I may be able to persuade you or not," Davis wrote Thomas, "I feel that for the record I should still enter some denials, especially as the *Times*' story the other day would have carried the implication to the hasty reader that we had Tresca shot. In the first place, Lee Falk says that he was misquoted – and I believe him.... [W]e did not select the individuals or organizations who were to be represented in the Victory Council. Finally, I must repeat that our opposition to Italian fascism is not confined to Mussolini alone.... We are against them all, and in that we have the support of the State Department." [64]

"I am startled and disturbed by front-page story in Friday's *New York Times*, which contains curious attack on your organization with special aim at Alan Cranston's division by certain Italian Americans in connection with Tresca case," Louis Adamic wired Davis in a night-letter January 25. "Whole thing strikes me as too fantastic to take seriously except as a manifestation of entire tangled situation in Italian group. This outburst has certainly been coordinated by somebody and I suspect it may be some kind of maneuver within Italian unions and other organizations exploiting Tresca. Am taking liberty of sending you this wire to say I have known Cranston for several years as a thorough American who is not pro-Communist in any sense and who has been doing a most difficult job full of delicate problems extremely well.... Hope this attack will not be detrimental to Cranston and the work he has been doing and trying to do under various handicaps." To which Davis replied: "The story surprised and shocked me as much as it did you, though it was so extreme as to be ridiculous for anyone who knows the situation. This office has the fullest confidence in what Cranston and his colleagues have been doing." [65]

The matter was so hot that Cranston tried to find out who was leaking information from O. W. I. He and Davis suspected a socialist-sympathizing file clerk. "This is an entirely fictitious memo and is based on no facts," Cranston said in a note to Davis February 2, intended as bait to the suspect but harmless, if given to newspapers. "It is being sent through to Davis and to Central Files in an effort to find a leak which is getting secret information out of O. W. I." The "fictitious" memo from Cranston, marked "secret and confidential," on the subject of "Alliance between Communists and Fascists against Socialists," read, "I have a report from S. F. Rebbor that communist and fascist forces among Italian-Americans in New York, outraged by efforts of the Socialists to blame them for the murder of Carlo Tresca, are banding together to form a united front against Socialists. I have checked, and apparently this is true. There have been secret conversations between representatives of Ambrogio Donini and Generosa Pope [a loyal Fascist until Mussolini's fall, publisher of *Il Progresso* and one of Tresca's principal antagonists] on this subject." The clerk was watched, and when he picked up a carbon of the memo, wrote some notes and went to a telephone, confronted. He quietly left the agency. [66]

An aide to the *New York Times* publisher responded to Davis by saying that the Italian labor leader had changed his story and "now tells a tale different from that which he told at the start." Finding the truth was "a little tough," but "if his statement today is correct, then I think we ought to express to you our regrets that we were imposed upon in our story of January 27, to which you called our attention." [67]

It was indeed a tough job, dealing with warring factions within the United States, but Cranston handled the challenges, which gained him admirers. He also did not abrogate his political beliefs, now becoming more defined as he gained experience with people and attitudes. "At a time when 'fifth columnists' are wrapping themselves in the garments of patriotism – 'the last refuge of every scoundrel,' as Daniel Webster defined it – it is heartening to know that we have in Washington men who are true guardians of the Ark of the Covenant," the president of the Inter-Racial Press of America wrote Cranston in 1942. Cranston's address to foreign-language publishers, the man said, "reflected the true American spirit of liberal democracy." [68]

The French were not always happy with the quality of translations – "too often literal," the editor of a French magazine complained. [69]

German-language media posed other problems. "We had some reason to think that some German-language radio stations were signaling German submarines when ships left New York harbor so they could be sunk," Cranston later said. "We tried to calm them down without censorship, but some people cried censorship." The F. B. I. in early 1942 intercepted a $16,000 payroll intended to support the expenses of a New York branch of the German Gestapo. The money was deposited in the U. S. Treasury, "Adolf Hitler's unsuspected contribution to American national defense," the Justice Department announced in a press release February 25, enough to buy and equip two armored combat cars to fight the Germans. "This is the final incident in one of the most spectacular 'spy stories' to emerge from the present war," the announcement read. Thirty-three spies had been arrested and convicted of espionage. [70]

"Please stop sending me your paper as I find nothing in it to induce me to continue reading it," one Indiana reader wrote a German-newspaper publisher who became a particular problem for Cranston. "The paper was a welcome guest in my home since 1916 but not now. It is good to boost America…it is our homeland, but the Bolsheviks and the English are fighting against Germans and that is not in line with my standpoint." The paper was one of the National Weeklies, the largest chain of German newspapers in the United States, including the *Lincoln Freie Presse* in Winona, Minnesota. The newspapers had been overtly pro-Nazi before Pearl Harbor, and subsequently more subtly so. An editor had been arrested by the F. B. I. the day after Pearl Harbor, and other employees were suspected of Nazi affiliations. The Justice Department had concluded that it could not legally suppress the newspapers but repeated warnings to the publisher resulted in his agreeing to a new editor supplied by Cranston's office – one Gerhart Seger, a former Socialist member of the German Reichstag, anti-Hitler lecturer and editor of a New York newspaper, *Neue Volkszeitung*, who had escaped from a German concentration camp in 1934. The publisher, however, saw the interloper as "an F. B. I. agent," Seger wrote Cranston in 1942. "The foreman is on my side but he is naturally afraid to lose his job and therefore, when L. [the publisher] tells him to withdraw something I put in, he complies with it." The publisher next wrote an "open letter" to his readers, accusing Cranston's office of forcing the German newspapers to employ an editor "acceptable" to the government. Another unhappy reader complained that the revised *Freie Presse* smelled "like Jewish propaganda and surely will not help you in holding old loyal readers…. Did you sell out to Jews???" [71]

The weeklies' publisher, in frustration, went to Washington to meet with Cranston personally. Changes in his papers' policies had brought lots of reader complaints, among them that the new editor sounded pro-Communist, he told Cranston. He retorted that such letters were "seditious" and might be part of an organized pro-

Nazi campaign. When the publisher was asked if he would "issue everything that we send you," he said yes – "a German by nature is brought up to obey and follow instructions" – but he did not want to offend readers and loose circulation (he already had lost several thousand readers, he claimed). Lee Falk, who was present at the meeting, asked when the publisher planned to change his ways – "in 1946?" – and if he would rather offend the American people or German-Americans. It was finally agreed that Cranston's office would prepare an editorial that set forth the differences between Nazis and Germans, and that the publisher would print it under his own name. The publisher nevertheless went away angry with the pressure, and did not honor his commitment to publish what Cranston's office sent him. Cranston believed that the publisher's sympathies were "still with the Nazis," and that "some of [the complaining] letters were apparently stimulated by" the publisher himself – the O. W. I.-sponsored editor had written to a return-address on one letter and his envelope was returned, marked "no such address." [72]

The fracas was publicized in Milwaukee, home to many German-Americans, and Cranston was forced to comment on the dispute. He "bluntly charged… that the National Weeklies [chain]…was pro-Nazi and showed a 'complete lack of willingness to cooperate in the war effort,'" the *Milwaukee Journal* reported September 3, 1942. Cranston denied that the government had forced the weeklies to accept a suitable editor, who had left the job after a month in any event. Charges that Seger had "inserted Communist propaganda is nonsense," Cranston said. The publisher, on the other hand, was sowing "seeds of doubt concerning government press releases and information on the prosecution of the war" – he had described the execution of Nazi saboteurs in Washington as being "put to death like common murderers." The *Journal* reported that the weeklies were "being watched closely by government agencies and that suspension of the publications has been discussed." The publisher conceded to the *Journal* that the situation was "serious" but denied being pressured by Cranston or O. W. I. [73]

The publisher continued to withhold O. W. I. releases, however. Many of his older readers did not want to hear about the horrors going on in their fatherland, which O. W. I. fed foreign-language media. A woman hired to proofread the papers, Mrs. Charlotte Rauschenberg, was so concerned about readers' reactions to such stories that she wrote President Roosevelt in 1943. "If we [carry] articles about death-sentences for black-marketing in Germany, then some of our readers come right back with letters asking, 'What about *this* country? Did not Mayor LaGuardia ask the same in this country?'... I believe with all my heart that if we show the German-speaking people how much more successful the American form of government is… we will unite even the pessimists behind us," she said. Before going to work for the newspapers, she "was just a housewife," she added. "If I do not [run] the atrocious stories released by the O. W. I., I will lose my job and maybe my freedom?…. Kindly advise me which way I serve the country best." Cranston had to write the publisher, then holidaying in Florida, remonstrating again for his failure to carry O. W. I. releases, which he reiterated reflected "official American government policy and the policies of President Roosevelt. I am puzzled to understand – now that the Nazis are obviously losing this war – why you still persist in your efforts to aid the enemy." [74]

A more pleasant task was to assure a singing society in Detroit, whose members worried that singing German songs might be considered unpatriotic, "The loyalty of a group is not judged by the nationality of its ancestors…[but] by their demonstration of wholehearted support of the war effort." To the contrary, Cranston told them, the government did "not require that singing in German be stopped. It is a privilege enjoyed in a democracy. You can sing the beautiful old *Lieder* in German, including *Die Lorelei*, which cannot be sung in Germany because of the author's race," he wrote the Harmonie Society. [75]

After the government action benefiting Italian aliens, many questioned why Germans should not receive similar treatment. Among other ideas, the Justice Department was considering giving Germans who had been deprived of their citizenship by the Nazis or had relatives in the U. S. armed forces the same exemption as Italians from enemy-alien status. Cranston advised Davis in 1942 that "The overwhelming success of the blanket exemption of Italian-Americans from the alien enemy classification has led to immediate consideration of the exemption of loyal German-Americans." Attorney General Biddle, after all, had stated in his Columbus Day speech, "We do not forget that there are other loyal persons now classed as alien enemies. Their situation is now being carefully and sympathetically studied by the Department of Justice." Changing Germans' status, Cranston pointed out, "would be the first concrete proof that we distinguish between Germans and Nazis, that we are fighting a war of ideas, not a war of races." The matter needed study from many angles, though. The wide support given the Italian exemption indicated that Americans would be sympathetic to similar treatment of Germans – "many editorials are already urging it," Cranston noted. But there were those who feared no Germans were "completely trustworthy," and that exempting some Germans "might provoke anti-Semitism among the unexempted." One proposal in the Justice and War Departments was to set up "loyalty boards…to exempt those German-Americans able to pass rigid tests." Such boards, proponents felt, "should probably contain police representation, and…no one of German-American stock." [76]

"I cannot take any stand until O. W. I. has carefully considered it," Cranston concluded, but "Personally, I favor the loyalty-board plan," he told Davis. Elmer Davis, however, was more cautious. He feared that, while the action for Italians "was advisable" and good propaganda for America, doing the same for denaturalized Germans would have different repercussions, particularly in countries occupied by Nazis. "I am afraid that any action taken here which might be interpreted as friendliness to any kind of Germans would be a hard blow to the spirit of these peoples, and accordingly I venture to suggest that you give this proposed action a most thorough consideration from the viewpoint of its foreign as well as its domestic implications." [77]

More pleasant things happened to Cranston, some serendipitously. He went to lunch at the Russian Embassy, expecting it to be with the press attaché. But Cranston found himself "a surprise guest" at the ambassador's luncheon table. He wrote an apology for the mix-up, which he attributed to the embassy staff's failure to put him together with the press aide. "Since I had never partaken of the gracious hospitality of your embassy before, I was rather unacquainted with the arrangements," he told the ambassador. "Thus, the peculiar accident when I found myself enjoying the very entertaining company of you and your kind wife." It would not be the last time that he dealt with Russians or went to their embassy, however. [78]

Cranston proposed another "plan that may seem impossible, but which I am convinced is practical: repeal of the Chinese Exclusion Acts. The arguments for repeal are overwhelming," he told Elmer Davis in 1942. "The actual numbers of Chinese involved are minute." He estimated that repeal would permit immigration of "only 100 Chinese per year and the immediate naturalization of only 37,242 Chinese now living in the United States as permanent residents. Repeal could only be accomplished, of course, if President Roosevelt called in the leaders of Congress from both sides and sold it to them. I think that he could do this and that they could stifle the otherwise inevitable opposition." Geneva Cranston would become actively involved in pushing Congress to repeal the acts. [79]

A propaganda coup that Cranston was instrumental in bringing about was a reaction to the Germans' total destruction, in June, 1942, of a 600-year-old Czechoslovakian mining village, Lidice, whose citizens had killed a Nazi SS officer as an expression of resistance. The Nazis boasted that they had shot all the grown men, placed the women in a concentration camp, sent the children "to be given appropriate education," and razed all the buildings to the ground, thus obliterating the village forever. Americans were outraged.

"We had a meeting in the O. W. I. with the top people to discuss what we should do about this," Cranston remembered. "We figured that we ought to be able to get some propaganda value out of it. It was a terrible atrocity, and demonstrated what kind of people we were fighting. It popped into my head, why don't we re-name an American town Lidice? A big event was put on to announce it." [80]

A town near Joliet, Illinois, where more Czech-Americans lived than anywhere outside of Czechoslovakia, and where the government was completing a defense housing project, Stern Gardens, was a logical choice to be renamed Lidice. Cranston sent David Karr to promote the idea. The *Chicago Sun* editorialized that "far from being destroyed, the tiny village would be immortalized as a monument to man's will to be free." The renaming was quickly approved. In July Wendell Wilkie, the former Republican presidential candidate, went to the Illinois town to celebrate the renaming, and Edna St. Vincent Millay wrote a poem about it. "Lidice will live in the hearts of free people everywhere," the *New York Times* stated. "It will be rebuilt in Czechoslovakia. There will be a statue in its central square, honoring the men who relieved the earth of a vile beast.... We may in the meantime remember that what Hitler did to the men, women and children of Lidice he would do to those of Lidice, Illinois, or of any American town, if he could." *Pic* magazine called the renaming "The most moving and effective propaganda stunt of the war." "By no stretch of the imagination could the Nazis ever have realized what a blazing torch of glory would arise from the burning embers of a razed village," a Czechoslovakian pamphlet published in Europe exclaimed. "Not only was it a great satisfaction for us Czechoslovaks to see how the American heart responded to the horrible German act of terror but it was also a great source of encouragement all over Europe to the peoples shackled in the Hun's chains." [81]

Cranston continually had to justify support of the war to many nationalities. "You are full-fledged Americans," he told the American Croatian Congress in Chicago in

February, 1943, "yet pressure may be brought to bear on you to distract your attention from the need for American unity by urging you to take measures incompatible with your allegiance." Victory was "endangered if narrow nationalisms and bitter hatreds are reflected among Americans from their lands of origin," he warned. Such was the case with the Serb National Federation, which, Cranston told an army colonel, had "followed certain policies not in the best interests of the war effort," notably claiming that it had government sanction when members of the organization had christened an American bomber "Serbian Chetnik" with the full approval of the War Department. That had not been the case, but the group's publication, *American Srbobran*, had run a front-page story that the bomber had been so named in honor of the group – "an attempt to endorse the Chetnike in Serbia, many of whom are fighting *for* instead of *against* the Nazis," Cranston pointed out. [82]

Quarrels within the Serbian community would implicate Cranston and provoke an internal dispute at the Common Council, ending in Louis Adamic's angrily resigning from the board and magazine in 1944. A splinter group had begun its own organization and newspaper separate from the Serb National Federation. A Yugoslav/Slovenian Croatian by birth, Adamic was upset with Council positions, notably that it had "defended divisive and dangerous foreign-language papers and organizations under the slogan of 'American unity' and allowed itself to be used as a 'front' for reactionary forces." [83]

Adamic cited the Council's defense of *American Srbobran*, although O. W. I. and the Departments of Justice and State had found its editorial polices "damaging to the American war effort." The paper was anti-Yugoslav government and had defended German and Italian occupations in Croatia, Serbia's enemy. An editorial blamed Adamic and "such unwise government officials as Mr. Cranston of the Office of War Information" for condemning the group's positions. A subsequent article accused Cranston of "fraternizing with Yugoslav 'Communists' and Serb Haters." Read Lewis responded to Adamic that criticism of the paper unfortunately seemed to have pushed it "and the group it represents into an even more extreme and reactionary position." Adamic asked Cranston for an opinion on the matter. O. W. I. and Davis, Cranston said, were not in any way accusing "Serbian Americans as a whole with playing the Nazi game. But something more important is involved here," Cranston said – the suggestion that "the government remain silent while *Srbobran* continues to attack Croats and Catholics and spreads hate and nationalism among American Serbs." The situation was complex, "but it is much more. It is dangerous." Pearl Harbor, he reminded Adamic, left "all of us…no alternative." [84]

Cranston's office fared better with Slavic groups (there were an estimated 15 million people of Slavic descent in America at the time). Ten thousand people had attended an American Slav Congress in Detroit in April, 1942, including Poles, Croatians, Ukrainians and Russians. "The Communists were kept well in hand," Cranston reported to MacLeish, "but the real significance…is its victory over the Nazis…. The groups which boycotted the meeting because they believed or pretended to believe that it was dominated by the Communists suffered for their abstaining." Cranston had approved all resolutions and major speeches beforehand. He was pleased that the *Detroit News* had changed its tune from a headline before the meeting that read "Slavs battle over unity" to one afterward saying, "Slavs unite for victory." "Ukrainians proudly carried the Russian flag; Serb stood beside Croatian; Poles ardently cheered Russian speakers…distinguished clergymen sat beside Communists," the *Christian Science Monitor* observed. [85]

In 1943, however, O. W. I. became the target of congressional vitriol and controversy (led by Representative Joe Starnes of Alabama) and its budget was greatly reduced. The House wanted to end its domestic operation amid suggestions that O. W. I. was "infested with Communists" and that Elmer Davis used "Goebbel-esque methods" of propaganda. The controversy was much publicized. Republicans began to view O. W. I. as a front for Roosevelt and the New Deal agenda. Among other things, some congressmen were annoyed by the "expense and political tone of *Victory*, the deluxe glamour magazine designed to sell the U. S. to the world as a kind of Hollywood 3,000 miles square," as *Time* magazine put it. A cartoon booklet on the life of President Roosevelt, designed for distribution abroad, had further irritated Republicans like Representative John Taber of New York, who had "a low irritation point," *Time* noted. A U. S. soldier had sent Taber a copy of the comic-book biography, which the congressman called "Purely political propaganda, designed entirely to promote a fourth term and a dictatorship…. How much longer are the American people going to have that kind of stuff pulled on them?" Others on Capitol Hill, like Southern Democrat Senator Harry S. Byrd of Virginia, had been "quietly looking into O. W. I.'s wastebaskets," according to *Time*. "Each day brought rumors of reorganization, employees' rump sessions, secret caucuses. Many an O. W. I.-ster was quietly looking for another job. The house might not yet be afire, but it is smoking." Davis remained "calm as ever," defending the Roosevelt cartoon booklet as a symbol of both "a powerful nation and…land of liberty – a government information agency would be stupid not to capitalize on it." Conservative Republican Congressman J. Parnell Thomas of New Jersey, a fierce opponent of Roosevelt and the New Deal, instigated an investigation of O. W. I., conceding that, while not finding "evidence of any actual subversive activities," he had "evidence that there are plenty of people working in the place who have subversive connections. Reds, Communists, crackpots and nitwits – the place is full of them," he told the Serbian newspaper. "It's headed by the same bunch that fostered the Works Project Administration writer's project." Cranston could count himself in talented company.[86]

The Serbian newspaper relished the attacks, and particularly targeted Cranston with abuse. "It is known that one of the chiefs in the O. W. I.'s foreign-language division is a person named Alan Cranston, a protégé of Louis Adamic with extreme leanings to the Leftist press and its leadership," a columnist wrote in *American Srbobran*, June 23, 1943. "Cranston…is known to have chosen as his sources of information – and has cooperated closely with them – old-line Croatians and a few Serbian, Macedonian and Bulgarian Communists. Mr. Davis has failed to sense or realize this and thus has permitted Cranston to intimidate, besmirch and antagonize the various loyal national American groups." [87]

The budget cuts affected Cranston's division, particularly the ability to control translated materials that it put out. "We should be proud of the way the Foreign Language Division has weathered the storm," he told his "gang" in July after its budget was cut by 40 percent (from $119,525 to $70, 597). Other divisions had been completely eliminated.[88]

One House select committee chaired by Conservative "Dixicrat" Democrat Eugene E. Cox of Georgia investigated O. W. I.'s activities affecting broadcasting stations, making it a hot August in 1943 for Cranston and his colleagues. The committee alleged that O. W. I. had forced station managers to fire employees, had colluded with the Federal Communications Commission (FCC) in threats to suspend station licenses, and tried to force a pro-Russian slant to broadcasts. Some of the charges directly affected Cranston – one alleged that his division had acted without his superiors' knowledge, and another called Lee Falk "Gestapo-minded, a crackpot" who used O. W. I. for personal publicity and to secure jobs for his friends. [89]

Broadcasters presenting programs in foreign languages had agreed to sign a "voluntary code of wartime practices" to the effect that they would "faithfully cooperate with the war effort." Falk had been sent by Cranston to a National Broadcasters Association convention to urge tougher self-regulation to prevent pro-fascist material on foreign-language stations. The result was an industry Wartime Control Committee to which Falk acted as liaison for government agencies. Any suspected personnel were reported to the F. B. I. for action. In that advisory capacity, Falk had suggested that an Italian-language broadcaster on a New York station be dismissed in 1943 as suspected pro-Nazi, one of a number of people that O. W. I. effectively had "blacklisted," a congressional investigator charged. Station managers testified that Falk also had ordered them not to do business with certain advertising agencies considered pro-Fascist (Falk and O. W. I. denied making such requests to station managers although some advertising agencies were suspect). O. W. I. responded that stations were expected to police themselves for employee loyalty and ideology and that there was no "witch hunt" on its part. [90]

Cox, it turned out, had received a $2,500 fee from a Georgia radio station for representing it before the FCC in 1941, an illegal act which was reported in a publication critical of his "spite probe." Editorials ranged from pro- to con- over the congressional investigation. The *Washington Post* and *New York Herald Tribune* condemned it, the latter calling it "about as disreputable a piece of shyster propaganda as could be imagined." The *Post*, in a public letter signed by editor and publisher Eugene Meyer, called for a criminal investigation of Cox for violating ethical laws, terming the so-called "investigation" "a mockery of basic American traditions of fair play…black with bias." The *Wall Street Journal*, however, likened the FCC's leverage with licenses a form of censorship encroaching on "our liberties." The FCC defended its actions, citing examples like a narcotic addict suspected of Gestapo connections who had been dismissed from one station. Cox subsequently dropped his investigations of O. W. I. and the FCC and was forced to give up his seat on the select committee. [91]

Cranston personally came in for criticism during Congress' debate on O. W. I. appropriations in 1943, recorded in the *Congressional Record.* It was the first time that he appeared in the daily journal of Congress' activities. Davis also was criticized, accused of being a bad administrator whose multiple agencies harbored Communist employees. Cranston's "mysterious role in the Tresca affair has never been explained," Representative John Lesinski, Democrat of Michigan and leader of the Polish community, deplored in June. "The results of his costly efforts in the

Office of War Information – pardon me, War Interference," he said sarcastically, "is such that none of his press releases contain any mention concerning the activities of the exiled governments [like Poland's], even though they are our Allies and signatories to the Atlantic Charter. Insofar as Mr. Cranston is concerned, these exiled governments do not exist." The congressman went on to accuse others in O. W. I. of being Communists, citing in particular foreign-born employees, urging that O. W. I. staff be exclusively "American born, American educated, and American indoctrinated." Congressional charges of communistic penetration of O. W. I. continued, and the House Appropriations Committee released a report on the charges in July, 1943, much publicized. [92]

One account in the *Washington Times-Herald* July 29 quoted the congressional report. It stated that "Alan Cranston, chief of the foreign language division, has shown his communist sympathies by opposing bills for the registration of aliens and by supporting Harry Bridges, alien West Coast labor agitator, against whom deportation proceedings are pending." Cranston was in California at the time, but on his return, he sought help from his old employer, Read Lewis at the Common Council. "The charge is utterly ridiculous," he wrote Lewis, reminding him that they had "worked closely" with high government officials to make alien registration a success while considering it discriminatory and of questionable value. "We did not oppose it for the reasons that the Communists opposed it." As to the "charge that I supported Harry Bridges," it was "completely without basis of fact. [W]e never did any work on the bill calling for the deportation of" Bridges and the then-attorney general considered the bill un-Constitutional. "Aside from this, I never had any relationship to Harry Bridges before, during or after my employment with the Common Council." [93]

Cranston asked Lewis to write House Appropriations Chairman Clarence Cannon "pointing out these facts and making it clear that my activities…were undertaken under your direction," and the Council's purposes and activities "had no relation to communism. It would be interesting if you would learn from Representative Cannon if they have any other 'information' about my activities in this relation, since whatever it is, it is completely false," Cranston added. [94]

Lewis immediately responded with a draft letter that he sent Cranston who helped revise the version that went to Cannon, adding names of government leaders and members of Congress who were on the Council's side. "I am writing this letter on the assumption that the charges against Alan Cranston arise from his activities for the Common Council," Lewis said. The Council had "never in any way had any sympathy for communism, nor included any Communist on its Board of Directors," which counted a number of high-ranking government and public officials. He reminded Cannon that former Attorney General Robert H. Jackson had addressed the Council's dinner in 1941, and that Eleanor Roosevelt was honorary chairman of its national committee. Alien registration had been opposed by many non-Communists, he pointed out, among them Senators Robert F. Wagner, Robert M. LaFollette and George W. Norris, former New York Governor Alfred E. Smith (1928 Democratic presidential candidate against Herbert Hoover) and influential columnist Walter Lippman. After the bill had passed, Cranston had written a pamphlet that the Council issued to assist Americanization groups and aliens themselves during the registration period, and high-ranking Justice Department officials would testify that the Council's, and Cranston's, work "were of great value in helping to make alien registration effective." Cooperation between the Council and Justice Department "would scarcely have been possible if the original opposition of the Common Council…had been motivated by communistic sympathies," Lewis noted. "The charge that Alan Cranston supported Harry Bridges is without foundation in fact," he continued. "I hope that the facts stated herein may be made part of the record," and if they did not "entirely clear up the matter," he would appreciate hearing from the chairman. [95]

The red-baiting of O. W. I. continued, however, as the agency's appropriations bill moved through the House in 1943. Congressman Richard Wigglesworth, Republican of Massachusetts, inserted into the *Congressional Record* a *Baltimore News-Post* editorial of November 2 entitled "Are the Reds Running the O. W. I.?" He also pointed to articles in the communist publication *Daily Worker*, one of which was entitled "We Need the O. W. I.." "Yes, believe me, the Communists do need the O. W. I. because so many of its activities are so helpful to their cause," Wigglesworth said on the House floor November 4. Chairman Cannon, however, was now prepared to challenge Wigglesworth's assumptions. "In what respect is O. W. I. going along with communism?" he asked. "That is the first intimation I have had to that effect. There is nothing in the hearings on the subject." [96]

O. W. I., meanwhile, had been taking its case to the national media: author Robert Sherwood had met with the National Women's Press Club, and Elmer Davis had spoken to the Overseas Press Club. Republican Fred E. Busbey of Chicago, a member of the Appropriations Committee who was proud to consider himself "reactionary," again raised the issue of Cranston's activities with the Common Council, and accused Louis Adamic of being "associated with many communist-controlled front organizations," citing his opposition to Serbian partisan General Draža Mihailović, minister of war for the Yugoslav government-in-exile. [97]

The next day Chairman Cannon defended Cranston on the floor. The allegations, Cannon said, reflected "seriously upon [Cranston] and his qualifications to serve in his present position." Cannon produced a statement from the Navy admiral in charge of O. W. I. security, affirming that Cranston had been cleared by the Civil Service Commission September 3, 1942, and that nothing in the records "would warrant his termination." Cannon further defended Cranston and O. W. I. against charges that seven million O. W. I. pamphlets sent to Algiers earlier that year had no direct military connection and was a wasteful expenditure. The fact was that General Eisenhower himself had requested the materials by cable from Allied Force Headquarters and they had been shipped by Army transport. They were distributed in Algiers to French and Arabs in efforts to insure protection of Allied supply and communication lines; others were shipped to Italy at the time of the Allied invasion, carrying messages in support of the landings. "I think this pretty well establishes the military importance of such pamphlets," Cannon stated. Congressman Wigglesworth demurred that there had been no negative intentions in his critical remarks the day before, but Cannon retorted that "the inference on the part of any casual listener or reader would have been otherwise. I take it for granted then," Cannon pushed Wigglesworth, "that the gentleman has no objection to our shipping this material to

General Eisenhower upon his request." Wigglesworth had no objection. Cannon concluded by obliquely defending O. W. I.'s role: "I take this opportunity to assure the gentleman who gave this information that any forebodings which they may have entertained with reference to these matters are wholly without foundation." [98]

Busbey asked Cannon "if there was anything that I said on the floor of this House yesterday regarding Alan Cranston that is untrue." "The only thing in which we are interested here is whether or not the gentleman has any charges against Mr. Cranston," Cannon retorted, noting that Busbey had "singled him out yesterday and referred to him in a disparaging way. I would like to know if the gentleman is now satisfied with Mr. Cranston and his discharge of his official duties." Busbey would not repeat his disparaging remarks and Cannon noted for the record that Busbey could not be construed as disagreeing with the security officer's statement about Cranston's clean record. But Taber stated, "I am a little surprised at the frantic efforts the gentleman from Missouri [Cannon] is making to cover up the things that have been shown here about the O. W. I. I said that the Office of Facts and Figures was a stench. Is there anybody here in this House that would want to say it was not a stench, and that it was eliminated because President Roosevelt found that it was such a stench that he could not stand it any longer? I wonder, is there anybody who says it was not a stench?" When Cannon suggested that Taber's reasons no longer applied, he exclaimed, "Oh, no, I am not taking back anything. Everything I said about that was true."

Cranston's associate David Karr also came in for abuse from Busbey, who inserted into the House record information about Karr's having accompanied Vice President Henry Wallace on a trip. Busbey called Wallace the "Grand Exalted Smearer of all Loyal Americans who disagree with his pet theories," and pointed to Karr's having testified before the Special Committee on Un-American Activities April 6, 1943, admitting to having written for the *Daily Worker* and other communist-front publications. By then Karr was assistant chief of the foreign language division. He had told the investigating committee that "Alan Cranston…sponsored me for the position." Busbey concluded his remarks by saying that "when we hear the voice of Henry Agard Wallace, we are listening to the words of David Karr." [99]

Cranston for several years would be forced to seek endorsements to exonerate him from the congressional allegations. The former Director of Alien Registration in the Justice Department, Earl G. Harrison, said that "No organization or individuals played a greater part" in having the Alien Registration bill "thoroughly and properly understood" than the Council, "Read Lewis and yourself. I have no hesitancy in saying," Harrison added in a letter to Cranston, that concerns raised about the Council or Cranston's role were "without substance or foundation of any kind whatsoever. I have worked closely with you for more than four years now and…I regard you as a most loyal American…. I know that you are as intolerant as I am of anything that smacks of disloyalty to our form of government." The attorney general joined him, Harrison said, in feeling "a debt of gratitude both to the Common Council and to you for the work both of you have done ever since passage of the Alien Registration Act of 1940." [100]

Cranston would defend himself strongly in a letter to "Jimmie" in 1945, possibly President Roosevelt's son James Roosevelt (1907-91), Congressman from California

1955-65, a Democratic Party friend: "This business about the Common Council is the most absurd nonsense dreamable – yet it has been plaguing me off and on for several years now. Always, after a bit of wasted motion, it is cleared up to everyone's satisfaction; then it pops up a good while later from some other source." He pointed out that the Council had received annual grants for twenty-three years from the "highly respectable Russell Sage Foundation" and "for the past five years it has annually received a minimum of $25,000 from the Carnegie Corporation." Such groups "certainly would never be caught subsidizing anything red, or even pink. There are only two possible reasons why it is suspected – entirely unjustly – as being pinkish," he continued. "One is that Louis Adamic, considered some shade of red, was for a time on the board of directors." Adamic, he pointed out, had resigned and denounced the Council as "reactionary." "The other possible cause is that the Common Council, when opposing discriminatory legislation, sometimes finds itself opposing bills the Communists or their front organizations are also opposing." But that was "by no means a consistent pattern." The Council had supported bills that Communists opposed, one of which Cranston had reported on in *Common Ground*. "Oddly, this very same article has another bit that has led to my being misunderstood" – a summary of all legislation pending involving aliens, including the bill to deport Harry Bridges. "I had to mention it, and did. I took no position for or against it," which he had done on other bills, he said. The Council also had contracted to translate and distribute much of the war information put out by Cranston's O. W. I. office, further proof of its "purity," Cranston argued. "I could go on like this endlessly," he concluded, "but if this is not convincing, I give up." [101]

Elmer Davis wrote Cranston an endorsement that stated, "We in the O. W. I. have always had the fullest confidence in your loyalty and integrity. This personal judgment was formally ratified by" Civil Service Commission approval. "If my views on the subject are of any weight, I should regard you as excellent material for Officer Candidate School," he added in 1944 after Cranston had joined the Army. [102]

Before that Cranston continued his activities for O. W. I. A major issue after Pearl Harbor was the planned internment of Japanese-Americans, most of whom resided on the West Coast. Cranston was shocked by the proposal, which directly affected his family's long-time employees, and MacLeish opposed it. They and Eleanor Roosevelt, whom Cranston had met when she chaired a conference for the Common Council in 1941, tried without success to persuade the president to abandon the idea. But military advisers and others, including California Attorney General Earl Warren, prevailed. [103]

The potential for spying did exist, nevertheless. A woman friend who had worked on the Mountain View *Register-Leader* and whose family owned a store in the Salinas Valley wrote Cranston soon after the internments began, "Did you get the copies of our local daily concerned with the round-up of Japs hereabouts? I sent two which had the best yarns in them – there have been follow-ups, but only very brief stories. This morning, however, the *Chronicle* has a fine dose of Jap stuff – another beeg [*sic*] raid yesterday netted some prize fish." The woman was working to register internees.

"By the end of the week I could speak enough Japanese to make them savvy that I wanted to know 'what town were you born in,' 'what province is that town in,' 'how many years in the United States,' 'any scars or marks.' Some of them were overbearingly insolent and it was all I could do to hang onto my temper and blood-pressure, but for the most part they were almost too cooperative. Funny part of that was the fact that some of the most cooperative were the biggest fish in the sea. Some we raked into our net were ex-naval and army men, and two or three have been since found to be serving in the Imperial Army right here in Salinas! Nice thought to take to bed at night, dontcha know? They picked up one chap in Seaside (two miles from Monterey municipal wharf where the new naval base is being built now) with a whole basement full of bomb casings, guns of all caliber including submachines, and two closets full of military uniforms of the Japanese Imperial Navy and Army!

"I could rave on for pages about the set-up here in the valley, but all I will bother you with now is the fact that we got some big ones, but you should see some that got away. On paper this sounds hysterical, I guess, but the F. B. I. has a hell of a job ahead of it out here yet. There is a nice percentage of really dangerous aliens out here on the coast as yet unregistered and for the most part, I guess, in hiding. The figures didn't correspond at all with the registration in 1940. And we, who were registering, could tell that something was pretty wrong because families showed up with several members unaccounted for this time. They were too damned vague about their sons and brothers and uncles and cousins – some said, 'I don't know where they are now,' others maintained a stony silence that could mean most anything and undoubtedly means plenty, all wrong!

"We had some of the more prominent 'younger marrieds' of the Jap colony helping us with the translating, etc., and found out afterwards that they were just as slick as their elders (and in some cases 'their superiors'). So now what? Take for instance the case of that B. Priest I registered. He turned out to be an ex-copper and army man. He told me through a translator…that he had been here 'many years' but 'couldn't remember how many,' etc. I gave our chief clerk a note on the q.t. to have someone check on him. She was busy and ignored it. Come to find out, after he was raked in by the F. B. I., he was in charge of one part of the Heimushi Kai, a sort of military society directly supervised by the Emperor and his advisors. My translator later turned out to be the junior president of the 'Young Men's Association' for the valley, and it is under the supervision and guidance of the same set-up which controls, in part, the civilian arm of the Heimushi Kai! This information was given me by a newspaper editor who has been cooperating with the F. B. I. on the Jap deal here, and who is pretty much in touch with all sorts of oriental set-ups here in the valley. Some of this material was used in stories published locally and some of it was just side-meat handed out to me because he knew I was *curious* (*that's* putting it mildly!)

"Honest to God, Alan, there isn't a Jap in this entire region that I'd trust as far as I could see him. From where I sit, and I'm right on top of a potential volcano, the situation looks damned bad. Most anything could happen here most any time, and may do just that! I think that absolute martial law is the only answer for this particular part of the country. It might be inconvenient, but it would be a whole lot safer and would simplify the job for the F. B. I." [104]

She described how easy it was to drive by an army air field where a lone sentry with a field phone "didn't even use it to report my car entering the zone!... No one seemed the least bit concerned by my presence so close to so many vital 'military secrets'…but it rather bothered me." Of two inattentive sentries at a bridge leading to Monterey she wrote, "My God, I could have bombed that perch of theirs right out from under them without the slightest trouble, and been six counties away by the time reinforcements could have gotten to the scene." Most women, who were training to do auto mechanics and other civil defense work, she scoffed, "think this war is a big joke on someone a long ways from here." She asked Cranston if his division might have a job for her. "I'm sick and tired of the set-up out here. There ought to be something back there that I could do." [104]

Stories from the camps, however, affected Cranston personally, as many childhood friends and family retainers were interned. Fred Yamamoto (a school friend?), reported from a camp in Wyoming January 3, 1942, that "to start off the New Year in Heart Mountain, a man was stabbed on New Year's Day – what a gruesome beginning!!! Luckily the victim is going to pull through." Internees were permitted to work outside the camps and to join the armed forces, and Yamamoto asked if Cranston could help find him work: "In the event that you hear of any opening for jobs – most anything – I'd certainly be grateful if you could drop me a line or a postcard." Any odd jobs would help – "am eager to work and willing to learn!" he emphasized. "I'm trying to find work through the Friends Service Committee but so far nothing has turned up as yet." He also asked what was happening with the draft of American-born Nisei. "We feel that before long most of us will be drafted again. If we are, I'm hoping that we'll be able to tote guns and get into actual combat. It would lift the morale of the Nisei and at the same time make them feel a part of the war effort." He signed it "from an *American* friend." [105]

Cranston made a point of visiting two relocation centers, Tule Lake in California and Heart Mountain, to see how friends were coping with the internment. He spent three days in December, 1942, at Heart Mountain – one of the coldest on record, sometimes 30 degrees below zero. Cranston stayed with the Tanakas (Mina, Fujimiya and Kiku), the Cranstons' former gardener and his wife, and visited others who had worked at Villa Warec as well as Yamamoto and other friends from Los Altos grammar and Mountain View high schools. Cranston was appalled at the uncomfortable barracks in which they were housed in the harsh, unforgiving climate, beset by wind and snow in winter, or heat and dust in summer. Many internees were in hospital with colds when Cranston visited. Mr. Tanaka passed the time by making chairs and tables for their simple dwelling out of crude lumber that he found. There were fights between Caucasians and evacuees. The Japanese-born Issei, if somewhat resigned to their fate, feared being returned to Japan, while Nisei, who included other classmates of Cranston's like Henry Hamasaki, were angry, and felt robbed of their rightful American citizenship and the benefits of American democracy. They were not convinced by the government's argument that they had been relocated for their own good as protection against vigilantes, or that the barbed-wire fence was to keep cows out of the camp. Cranston carried his message of concern back to Washington and tried to help interned friends get permission to leave the camps or to find jobs. One project was to allow them to sell potatoes on the open market, as he told a conference on food rationing in November, 1943. It would be years, however, before he was able to do anything substantive to help his old friends. [106]

"Thought I'd be there to see you off but we're having a staff meeting and also we still have to work folding papers this afternoon," Yamamoto said in a note to Cranston. "Thanks ever so much for coming to our meeting last night. I suppose there were enough gripes presented to write volumes. Please don't think us a group of moaning individuals. We're not the only ones taking a beating, and we don't expect to be treated like little babies. But we would like for the American public to realize the peculiar situation that we're in. The best propaganda to bolster Nisei morale in camp would be to give the members of the Nisei armed forces an equal footing – send them to the front, give them something to actually fight for!" [107]

Mrs. Michi Takaki wanted "very much to apologize for the rations for dinner last night, of all times for you to be a guest and we had pork sausages. I gathered you do not like them. Perhaps you will accept a rain check to be a guest at a dinner which I hope I will be able to cook soon – I promise you I won't have pork sausages, but will have lots of mash potatoes oozing with butter. Let me know of your other choice delicacies. Your impressions of the camp here and the people," she added in a note to Cranston, "would make interesting reading – when you do write them, don't leave me out in your mailing list. Will see you someday soon in the East," she hoped. [108]

Cranston in February told her, "No, I certainly don't think that you are being coddled out there, and I am sure that if the Senate sends out a committee, they will agree with me after a night or two at Heart Mountain. The Senate committee seems to be behaving very sensibly and I think that you have nothing to fear from anything they may undertake. Of course, those who go out into war and other industries will have to face dismissal [from jobs] – along with countless Caucasian Americans – when the war is over, provided plans now under way for full employment after the war fall through. I think that responsible officials realize that measures must be taken to make sure there is no burst of unemployment after the war…. At least, if the Japanese-Americans go out and work now, they will be able to pile up savings which will help to tide them over any bad period. I never did write down my impressions of my visit to Heart Mountain in any detail," he added. "I felt it more important to try to push through some of the changes that were obviously necessary. Please keep writing to me and letting me know what you and the others are thinking, as it helps a great deal in making me understand what your problems are." [109]

He corresponded with other friends through a professor at Stanford University, sending them publicity that Cranston may have generated from his position at O. W. I. "I am sending you the enclosed clippings from newspapers in all parts of the country in the hope that this evidence of friendly feeling towards Japanese-Americans will encourage you to get 'outside' as soon as you can. We have evidence that in all parts of the country people are very sympathetic to you all. I suggest you show these clippings to others when you are finished with them…. I often look back with pleasure on the party you gave for me when I was out at Heart Mountain," he wrote Kiku Fujimiya and his wife in March, 1943. [110]

"I think that the Office of War Information will shortly issue a story of the whole relocation," Cranston was able to tell the Tanakas in May, 1943. "It should be very helpful." Henry Hamasaki and others had "gone outside," he understood, hoping that "you two will make up your minds to do this before too long. I am sure that there are plenty of fine jobs available, and I am also sure that once you get 'outside' you will find yourselves much happier and perfectly secure. I think that a number of Japanese are already moving towards Chicago, so if you go out there, you would not have to be alone. You shouldn't worry about your English. You certainly speak it well enough to get along very well." [111]

To childhood friend Katsuji Ikawa, interned at the Gila River camp in Arizona, Cranston wrote, "I hoped to see you in one of" the two camps that he had visited, "but was very disappointed to find you in neither. At Heart Mountain I did come across many of our old friends – California Ushiro, Henry Hamasaki, Tanaka, the Higashiuchis, the Feruchis, and many others. We had some fine visits together and I found them bearing up wonderfully, considering the circumstances. I wish when you have time, you would sit down and write me a long letter telling me about the relocation center you are living in. I should like very much to know how things are going, what your troubles and hopes are, and all about what you are doing and thinking." [112]

Yamamoto did join the army and wrote Cranston from Camp Shelby, Mississippi, mentioning some who resisted being drafted and signing a loyalty oath. "Did you hear about those forty-one or so Heart Mountain fellows who were misguided enough to be misled into thinking that the 'Fair Play Committee' could buck the draft? The sooner some people forget about evacuation and get the hell out of those barbed enclosures, the better off they'll be." Other interned male friends also joined the army. "The camp will be like a ghost town with so many young boys leaving for the army and others relocating back East," Mrs. Tanaka wrote Cranston from Heart Mountain, where, she added, "we have been having our ever famous dust storms at least once a day. Some nights it blows so hard that one would think the roof would fly off." [113]

Cranston traveled a good deal for O. W. I., mostly by train across the nation, and gave speeches to foreign groups, press associations and immigrant organizations. He and Geneva had an affectionate relationship filled with humor. On one occasion (possibly before leaving on a trip) he mailed her a picture postcard from the Folger Shakespeare Library behind the U. S. Capitol. It showed a statue depicting the character of Puck (in a fountain on the library grounds), beneath which was inscribed, "Lord, what fools these mortals be!" Cranston wrote on the card, as if to a third party, "Dear Toots, Be good, & watch G. for me. Feed her daily, 3 times. Bed early, teeth brushed. Love, Alan." [114]

Getting her husband to take a vacation was difficult, Geneva found. "Alan has agreed to take a week off and I hope we can go to New England when I succeed in nailing him down," she wrote a friend in July, 1942. "He has agreed to read no newspapers, English or foreign, for the entire period! He thinks I'm only joking, though. Do you happen to know of a spot in New England where one can swim (not in a pool), play golf, ride, eat, and live in play clothes? I'm afraid what we want is a spot of California within a day's ride. Do you know where it is?" She would not see New England in the summer of '42, however. [115]

Cranston later that year was sent to deal with a sticky situation in Los Angeles involving Mexican-Americans, which would require innovative organizing and political skills. There had been an increase in youth disturbances in the area and police reaction was heavy-handed. One case that garnered national attention was that of twenty-two youths, aged fifteen to twenty-two, who had been charged in August, 1942, with first degree murder for the death of a fellow Mexican in a brawl at a reservoir nicknamed "Sleepy Lagoon" that young Hispanics used for a swimming hole. The media called it "gang murder." In the aftermath, a writer in *New Republic Magazine* editorialized, "a veritable reign of police terror was unleashed." More than 300 Mexican youths had been rounded up in one raid. Axis propagandists had jumped on the issue and begun beaming short-wave radio broadcasts from Berlin, Rome and Tokyo to Mexico and South America, spreading "the wild story of racial persecution in Los Angeles," according to an account in the *Los Angeles Times*. In addition, Axis agents were using a fascist underground organization in Mexico to stir up hate against "Yankee imperialism," Mexican officials charged, resulting in an increase in violence among disenchanted "pachuco" (slang referring to people from El Paso) gangs in Los Angeles. The "pachuco" boys affected a dress style that featured long coats, trousers hitched up to their armpits with peg-top bottoms so tight that they had to be slit and zipped up. They wore broad-brimmed hats, let their hair grow long and combed it straight back in "duck tails." Their costume, and penchant for whizzing around in cut-down, souped-up hot rods garnered them the name "zoot suiters." One local sheriff told a grand jury after the mass arrests that Mexican-American youths were "biologically" predisposed to "criminal tendencies." "Fundamentally, there is nothing wrong with these youngsters," the *New Republic* editorial argued, "but, for want of a satisfactory adjustment to their environment, their energies have taken this form of expression." [116]

A Citizens' Committee for the Defense of Mexican-American Youth had been formed and celebrities like actor-producer Orson Welles had joined in advocating sympathy for the cause. Welles wrote a foreword to a booklet issued by the committee, *The Sleepy Lagoon Case*, quoting a Mexican-American. "Here's what Pete Vasquez told me," Welles wrote. "I met him at the induction center. He was ahead of me in the line. He'd been studying the clarinet and it turned out we had mutual friends among Negro Jazz musicians. He'd heard some of my broadcasts on Latin America, and he knew I was interested in what the Los Angeles papers have called 'The Pachuco Murder.'" Then quoting Vasquez, Welles wrote, "'The fellas down in our section – there's nothing bad about them, no more than anywhere else. But things are tough. There's nowhere to go – no place to play games, or nothing. If the cops catch you on the street after 8 o'clock, usually they run you in – or rough you up, anyway. If you look like a Mexican, you just better stay off the street, that's all.... I'm going into the Army, and it's all right with me.... Things'll be better in the Army, and I'm glad of the chance to fight. It makes it hard, though, for a lot of our fellas to see things that way. They want to fight for their country, all right – but they want to feel like it's their country.'" [117]

The pamphlet blamed the Los Angeles press for hyping a "crime wave" among Mexican-American youth "which was unsubstantiated by any official records." Arrest stories ran on front pages, but when defendants were released for lack of charges, there was no news coverage. The lagoon case stemmed from fights between rival gangs. But there was conflicting testimony that the man who was killed might have been run over by a car, or killed before the defendants had arrived at the site, and that they might have been misidentified with others who perpetrated the crime. Seventeen of the twenty-two boys ultimately were convicted. "These boys must be freed," the committee demanded. "This weapon of the Axis must be removed." [118]

There were larger issues involved than the fate of the defendants, as a Sleepy Lagoon Defense Committee argued in another publication, *The Sleepy Lagoon Mystery*, written by novelist and short-story writer Guy Endore and illustrated by San Francisco artist Giacomo Patri. The case was "a symbol of the struggle of the Mexican minority to free itself from a pattern of racial ostracism and discrimination which has too long prevailed in Southern California," Endore wrote. The defense committee wanted to "correct a social, as well as a case of individual, injustice," which had ramifications for U. S.-Latin American relations. The defendants, it pointed out, were "for the most part poor boys, of homes ignorant of the technicalities of the law and knowing only the simple difference between innocence and guilt, having suffered for some time not merely under social discrimination but under police terrorism." Some of the legal aid they received "wasn't too good," Endore said. And "confronted by a ruthless, unscrupulous prosecution, [the defendants] went down to a smashing defeat." The boys "happened by ill chance to be caught in a twister that was none of their making." One defendant, who had enlisted in the Navy just before being arrested, told the booklet's author, "When we were arrested, we were treated [as] if we were German spies or Japs." The introduction quoted former Under Secretary of State Sumner Welles as saying, "Unless these discriminations are obliterated…soon, the term 'good-neighbor policy' will lose much of its real meaning." [119]

Thoughtful local leaders demanded a public hearing on the whole issue. That had prompted Coordinator of Inter-American Affairs Nelson Rockefeller and O. W. I. to take cognizance of the situation and send Cranston to work with local officials to mitigate it. [120]

"He is a very able citizen and has been doing a grand job with the foreign language press and on behalf of foreign language groups," James Allen, Assistant Director of O. W. I.'s Domestic Operations, told a contact. "I am sure that you and he will talk the same language." [121]

"My first call in Los Angeles was upon Mayor Fletcher Bowron who was initially sympathetic to my mission," Cranston reported back to Elmer Davis November 28. "He became more so when I made him understand that Axis propaganda was giving Los Angeles a black eye the world over by exploitation of the local Mexican situation." The mayor made appointments for Cranston with all four of the city's daily newspapers and asked him to lay out a program for action on the problem. Cranston first convinced editors to "stop using the term 'Mexican' in connection with local disturbances, since Americans are really involved. They likewise agreed to carry positive stories of the war participation" of Mexican-Americans, Cranston reported. *Los Angeles Times* publisher Norman Chandler did "likewise – provided I would see if I could get him more gasoline for his reporters." The Los Angeles O. W. I. office got "busy digging up such [positive] stories," Cranston said. He also talked with many civic and political leaders like activist-lawyer-writer Carey McWilliams, and drew up a program that local groups approved to present to the mayor and supervisors. It was designed to involve the Mexican-American community in more civic and war-defense activities, improve programs for youths and end discrimination against Mexican-Americans. [122]

Cranston, his hairline noticeably receding, was photographed in the *Los Angeles Times* and *Los Angeles Examiner* with the group presenting a petition to the Los Angeles mayor and Board of Supervisors "seeking to counteract Axis propaganda on youthful gang warfare," the *Times* caption read. "O. W. I. sends official to make inquiries here," one headline stated. [123]

The Citizens Committee for Latin Americans, representing church, civic, labor and social interests, wanted to change conditions that led to gang warfare and to counter groups "intent on disrupting U. S.-Latin American relations by 'playing up'" gang wars, according to newspaper accounts. The petition requested more educational and recreational facilities for youths in Spanish-speaking neighborhoods, and opportunities for them to participate in defense projects through war-training schools. It also advocated Spanish-speaking attorneys as public defenders; enforcement of anti-discrimination laws; police responses "without undue emphasis against persons of Mexican extraction"; establishment of more forestry camps for juveniles on probation. It recommended opening more war-industry jobs to Mexican-Americans, Spanish-speaking personnel in federal employment offices, and nurseries for mothers employed in war work. In short, the group wanted implementation of President Roosevelt's orders relaxing restrictions on "friendly and allied aliens" who were denied full participation in federal housing projects, the National Youth Administration, defense contract work and enlistment in the armed forces. [124]

Mexican gangs, the committee argued, were "badly distorted…in the public mind" when actually "a small group of boys in about thirty gangs…fight back and forth across the county among themselves," one member told the supervisors, while more than 30,000 Spanish-speaking youths in public schools caused no problems. The problem was blown out of proportion, petitioners complained, and Axis interests were exploiting the "deeds of American youths of Mexican extraction who have been running in packs and raiding each others' parties in a manner not greatly different from the way students at local universities have recently been raiding other others' strongholds." Axis radio broadcasts to Latin America had been reporting that "local jails were overflowing with thousands…of this persecuted minority" who were in "open rebellion against violent Anglo-Saxon persecution." The allegations were exaggerated – only about three percent of Mexican youths were involved in juvenile delinquency – but the committee conceded "there may be some real shreds of truth somewhere behind them." From street-corner fist fights, the problem had worsened to youth groups provoking attacks with clubs, knives, chains, bars and even guns. [125]

Implementing the proposals "would be bad news for Hitler and the Axis, and good news for the United States and the United Nations [meaning Allies]," Cranston told supervisors. They immediately set up a committee (chosen by Cranston and two members of his group) to look into putting the program into effect, and "we took particular pains to see that a preponderance of the members were of Mexican extraction," Cranston told Davis. "The general feeling…seems to be that the program is sound…and has strong official and unofficial backing," he added. "This feeling has already seeped into the Los Angeles Mexican community and its morale is much improved." [126]

On his last day in Los Angeles, Cranston met with the district attorney prosecuting the twenty-two youths. "This is the first time in the history of Southern California that so many people have been charged with first-degree murder for the death of one person," Cranston reported to Davis. "The prominent publicity" given the case made the D. A. "easy to handle. I convinced [him] that he and O. W. I. would have a terrific problem on their hands if the trial were permitted to turn into a Sacco-Vanzetti case – as it will, if many of the kids are given stiff sentences. He eagerly agreed, said that he was personally avoiding the courtroom to keep publicity…to a minimum, and that he had decided to narrow the real case down to two of the youths." The D. A. planned to ask for a general reduction of the charges and to "tell the judge about the dangerous consequences of too stiff a verdict. I am convinced that this takes the trial out of the danger zone," Cranston said. [127]

That would not turn out to be the case, however. Three boys were convicted of first-degree murder and assault, and sentenced to life in prison; nine were convicted of second-degree murder and sentenced to from five years to life; others received lesser sentences. The trial, variously headlined as a "goon" and "Mexican hoodlum trial," received nationwide attention. [128]

Other Mexican-American youths in the wake of Cranston's visit, however, were given lesser punishment for other infractions. In one case, the judge offered two boys accused of disturbing the peace the option of ninety days in county jail or discarding their "zoot" suits and having their "duck-tails" shorn to "modern wartime style." They chose the haircuts and transformation, which the *Los Angeles Examiner* photographed from court room to barber shop under the headline, "'Zooters' get hair cut order, long locks trimmed, and OK'd by court." "These boys…will lose caste with the others," Justice of the Peace E. P. Woods said. "If others learn they may expect similar sentences…I believe they'll think twice before doing anything wrong." A friend who sent Cranston the news account wrote across the clipping that men should "get a good haircut before coming around Los Angeles." [129]

Cranston was pleased that "other projects, too many to recount, were launched during my stay," including persuading "Walt Disney to conduct a poster contest for Americans of Mexican extraction throughout the United States" after Disney returned from a trip to Mexico. It would be "a device to get all our propaganda to American-Mexicans." Cranston had gotten John Lee of the Aircraft War Production Council to help him convince Douglas Aircraft "to launch a high-powered employment drive among local Mexicans," using posters in Spanish announcing that hundreds of workers were needed in its plant. The office of Inter-American Affairs would open a local office in Los Angeles "to further good will" and give "invaluable support to the community program now under way, as Los Angeles is obviously sensitive to federal prodding," Cranston noted. [130]

"The critical situation has been overcome completely," he could conclude in his report to Elmer Davis. "All that remains for O. W. I. to do is for the Foreign Language

Division to continue its present program of war information in the Spanish language to Mexicans in the United States…and there is room for considerable expansion of it via the media of posters and radio transcription."

"I am writing to congratulate you upon the selection of Mr. Alan Cranston, who has recently…served us in a very able manner," the executive secretary of a community church group wrote Davis in December. Cranston "quickly found the right people to consult. From them he gathered and tabulated many concrete and practical suggestions as to what our community can do to improve the Mexican situation…. With the help and advice of these leaders, he put on a grandstand play before the County Board of Supervisors and the city mayor. At this grand finale, he kept in the background and made us local people 'act in the play.' We feel really indebted to you and to Mr. Cranston for his service here. I want to assure you that I shall do what I can to stimulate the community to carry out the proposals he developed." [131]

His success inspired MacLeish, after reading Cranston's report, to suggest "that the whole job you did be the subject of a magazine article on 'How a Dangerous Situation is Taken Care of by Democratic Processes," according to Charles Olson in Cranston's division. "Nice going, boy," Olson added, "prepare yourself for a real promotion the day you get back." His office was collecting "Spanish press reports on the 'curly-headed boy' – (Ed. note: <u>toupee</u>)," Olson jokingly remarked of Cranston's growing baldness. [132]

There were other positive reactions to Cranston's work. "It takes a war apparently to reveal the 'sore spots' in our society," chairman of the Sleepy Lagoon Defense Committee Carey McWilliams wrote in *The New Republic* in January, 1943. "For at least twenty-five years, social investigators have repeatedly warned the County of Los Angeles about the thoroughly disadvantaged position of its large resident Mexican population; but the community saw fit to ignore these warnings until… it became impossible to pretend that no problem existed." Cranston, the magazine piece said, had "succeeded in bringing about a noticeable change in the tone and character of newspaper reporting on the Mexican problem. For the time being, the issue has simmered down, but it has by no means died out…. While the public-relations aspect of the problem has been improved, the cultural conflict remains… and it is not likely to be removed in the absence of an affirmative federal program designed to improve the living and working conditions of resident Mexicans and to eliminate the prevalent social and economic discrimination." Rockefeller's Office of Inter-American Affairs deserved more funding, the article concluded, to improve relations with such groups. [133]

The problem, indeed, did not disappear. By mid-1943 "zoot-suit" riots were erupting in Los Angeles between Mexican-American youths and servicemen. Both groups went on forays in search of each other in what the *Los Angeles Times* termed "seething friction" over the eastern part of the city where many Hispanics lived, the servicemen taunting the "zoot suiters" by threatening to "cut those funny pants down to size" and "wake these guys up to what's going on in this country," the *Times* stated. Zooters, in turn, hurled bottles at attacking servicemen. After confrontations over several nights in early June, police arrested fifty Mexican-Americans after East L. A. dance halls were "'blitzed' by 'shock crews' of sailors, and cruising taxi loads of the blue jackets tangled with truckloads of 'pachucos' in the second night of the [city's] zooter flare-up," the *Los Angeles Examiner* reported. [134]

"The basic causes of the riots," Cranston said in a memo in June, "seem to be soldiers and sailors looking for girls, Anglo-Saxon discrimination against people of Mexican extraction, a feeling of superiority on the part of some Anglo-Saxons and a feeling of inferiority on the part of some" Mexican-Americans. "I have taken all possible steps to diminish all except the first, to create better feeling on both sides." But "a primary problem is the feeling on the part of the local Mexican population that their side of the story has not been told, that the authorities ignore them, and that their role in the war and in the local community is neither appreciated nor understood. Much of my effort, and my approach, were directed toward overcoming this apparently well-justified complex." [135]

Among steps that Cranston took was to arrange for a *Los Angeles Daily News* columnist and former managing editor, Matt Weinstock, to work temporarily for O. W. I., preparing stories "emphasizing the contributions of the American-Mexican population to the war effort" that Cranston arranged to plant in local media. He also met with Spanish-language media to discuss what O. W. I. could do to help them. Most importantly, "The first group I met with…was a body of so-called 'pachuco gang leaders.' Other officials had made no effort to get their viewpoint. Through Mexican leaders with whom I have kept in contact for some months the meeting was arranged and kept completely secret. It was attended by both boy and girl leaders. They felt that their side in the riots had been completely misrepresented in the press, that all of the blame had been placed upon them, and that the entire local Mexican community had lost whatever reputation it had. The local Hearst press had written pieces about 'free love' practices between Mexican girls and boys, etc. Several hundred of the girls were actually considering staging a parade to the office of Mayor Bowron to demand a mass physical examination to prove that they were (a) virgins, (b) undiseased. They agreed to abandon this plan, and to cooperate in a sounder project to be proposed by me. They also promised to do everything possible to avoid further riots," Cranston told O. W. I. [136]

Cranston proposed a blood-donor drive within the Mexican community – "blood that was almost spilled in the streets in clashes *with* the armed forces to be donated instead *to* the armed forces as a token of patriotism, thus not only creating real good will for the Mexican community but obliterating the idea of racial difference." The drive was to begin July 1, and was endorsed by the mayor and the Roman Catholic chairman of the governor's committee investigating the riots, all of whom agreed to request that local papers "handle it sympathetically." They did, the *Times* reporting and photographing "Mexican day at the blood bank." "There were soldiers and defense workers, business and professional men, attractive young women and dapper young men, some wearing jitterbug zoot suits, but a far cry from those who were precipitated two weeks ago into the limelight of the so-called zoot-suit disorders," the *Times* article read. [137]

Cranston also rounded up "city and county officials, church and social workers, Mexican and Negro leaders," to promote "curative action" and reduce bickering. Governor Earl Warren would be urged to promote similar programs in other metropolitan areas "to avoid…an outbreak comparable with that which occurred in Detroit," referring to race riots that summer in which a number of people were killed.

Cranston instigated the War Manpower Commission to encourage employment of Mexicans in war industries. Finally he persuaded an Inter-American Center to launch a club-house program. "Club houses are badly needed in the Mexican community to develop the best leadership among the youths and to keep them out of alleys, beer joints and trouble," he reported. The center advanced $500 "to a Mexican leader recommended by me for the experimental establishment of three club houses. Similarly, I obtained an agreement for an Orson Welles-Rita Hayworth benefit show to raise money for club houses, and a promise of $150 per month from Hollywood to maintain one club house.... In this, as in all other projects which I inaugurated...the primary aim was to place a large share of responsibility among Mexicans so as to develop a feeling that they were doing things *with* Anglo-Saxons, not that Anglo-Saxons were doing things *for* them." [138]

It would be the beginning of a long relationship between Cranston and Hollywood.

A contact at a Committee for American Unity in Los Angeles, reporting to Cranston on the new programs' progress, had joked about charges against him of communist sympathies. "With all the trouble I am in," Cranston responded in partial jest, "I will sue you immediately if you write me anything more with a sentence like this in it: 'I expect to see your picture in the *Examiner* any day now, complete with the underground press where you translate and print all your material from *Pravda.*' STOP! The fact that you switched typewriters in the middle of the letter will not make the F. B. I. any less suspicious." [139]

The frustration at setting the record straight over his role with the Common Council and O. W. I. was troublesome because Cranston had begun to seriously think about his future. He wanted to be free to express his philosophies of government, and to have an impact in some way on national policies. A high-ranking bureaucrat especially antagonistic to Cranston and O. W. I. was Adolph A. Berle, Junior, one of Roosevelt's "brain trust" at the State Department. He and Cranston clashed over how nationality groups should be used during the war. Berle sided with old-order interests in Europe while O. W. I. and Cranston were charged to unite newly-formed groups, many of whom wanted nothing to do with former leaders and governments. Thus the two agencies argued over which factions to back. Davis supported Cranston's decisions over Berle's positions. It was one of Cranston's first power struggles in policymaking. He had built his confidence to a point where he felt that he could challenge the old guard, despite his youth and relative inexperience. He and his cohorts at O. W. I., Karr later said, no longer were in awe of people like Berle, even White House aides. William Cranston advised his son to use "all the skill you can muster" to get along with people like Berle who were in more influential positions than Cranston and could cause trouble for him. Cranston, though, was feeling his strength and using counter-tactics. Berle, he told his father, was indeed a "big customer to chew off," but Cranston had inflicted "a few bites" by enlisting influential columnist Drew Pearson to attack Berle. "I spent a good portion of the afternoon with Drew," he wrote his father. [140]

But the bureaucracy at O. W. I. had become top-heavy, creating tension between new business-oriented administrators and the idealistic literary and artistic staff who had been riding high on their creative war-time activities. A number of them expressed disgust at the commercializing change in tone at O. W. I. (among them historian Bernard DeVoto of the Domestic Bureau and literary critic Malcolm Cowley) and some resigned as a group in April, 1943, including historian Arthur Schlesinger. "It was getting to be very hard on creative people," Cranston would say in retrospect. He himself applied for a job as director of the U. S. State Department's Foreign Relief and Rehabilitation Operations that same month. He also applied for a post at the Office of Strategic Services (in 1943). He was then twenty-nine years old, weighed 185 pounds and was six feet, two inches tall, his application stated. He answered "no" to questions about being a member of any political organization that advocated overthrowing the U. S. government, being arrested or having any "unfavorable incidents" in his life that might be uncovered in an investigation. He answered "occasionally" to whether he used "intoxicants." He depended entirely on his salary, he said, and had credit at several Washington department stores. Neither job came through, possibly because of the allegations about his leftist associations, and despite the fact that comments by all those contacted for an F. B. I. background check on him (in 1942) were positive. In fact, Cranston would be investigated by military intelligence in 1944, the Civil Service Commission in 1945, and again by the F. B. I. in 1946 and 1947. [141]

Geneva had replaced Cranston at the Common Council and began handling its legislative activities. She also worked on lobbying for repeal of the Chinese Exclusion Act. "Between us," Cranston wrote home, "we're earning more than a congressman!" Geneva was the Washington representative for the Common Council, a job that had paid Cranston $275 a month but for which she received $50. Her résumé said that she "worked particularly closely with the director of publicity of the Department of Justice." She spent "considerable time supplying newspaper men and commentators with material favoring American unity" behind the war effort. She also worked on another part-time job, an "airport news service" that provided wire services and daily newspapers with information on arrivals, departures and interviews of notable people passing through Washington's airport. That enterprise, which started just before Pearl Harbor, was forced to end three months later because of censorship on plane schedules for important travelers. [142]

Geneva's mother also did war work – at an airplane parts assembly plant in San Diego. She wrote Geneva that "since Dad passed" (in 1941), she had moved a number of times, renting rooms where she could find them in the war-time housing shortage. She sent Geneva one of her ration books – "you can use the two for sugar and the coffee one as I'm not using it and had a pound on hand. You can get canning sugar on your one and on mine, besides the regular allotment.... With 10 lbs. on yours and 10 on mine, you can satisfy your sweet tooth, eh?" She found the work assembling small parts for planes varied enough to be interesting – "I assembled a lot of hydraulic gauges again today. They all tell me down there that I work too hard and fast, and I do, by comparison" to other employees, she told Geneva. [143]

Geneva was organized and professional in her work. A hand-written chart of legislation before the House Immigration Committee in the 77th Congress showed that she kept track of fifteen bills between 1941-42. One bill would have required refugee physicians wishing to practice in the District of Columbia to submit proof not only of good moral character but also of American citizenship. "For Congress to approve a proposal of this sort would be most unfortunate," a memo in her files, presumably written by her, read. A shortage of civilian doctors was increasing as many were drawn into the armed forces for the war. Refugees could fill the needs. "What has citizenship got to do with competence in diagnosing a disease or with ability to cure tuberculosis?" the memo argued. One "unfounded" fear was that foreign doctors would "learn intimate matters." The Surgeon General had stated that many foreign-born physician refugees were competent and available for service in areas of acute shortages "if they could be licensed to practice." Geneva compiled a number of editorials from the *New York Times*, Boston and Philadelphia papers, advocating just that. [144]

For the Citizens' Committee to Repeal Chinese Exclusion Geneva was in charge of public relations and lobbying Congress and officials in other branches of government. She also traveled to California to "drum up support for repeal among civic leaders," as her résumé stated. The "result was virtually 100 percent support for repeal in California and a consequent switch on the part of most West Coast legislators from anti-repeal to pro-repeal position." "No one else directly related with the [repeal] committee has any legislative experience," she said of her role. [145]

She worked with such groups as the American Legion, "stressing the military and propaganda values of repeal." The fear was that veterans' groups would oppose repeal, having favored Japanese internment. Japan was using the exclusion act to bolster anti-American sentiment in the Orient, and as Allies moved to retake Japanese-occupied areas of the South Pacific, Americans wanted to avoid "the bitter experience which Britain suffered in Burma where the civilian population almost solidly supported the Japanese," an advocate argued. Getting support from labor interests and California's congressional delegation also was critical, as it had been California politicians, backed by the American Federation of Labor, who had succeeded in getting a full exclusion act passed in 1924 on grounds that cheap Chinese labor competed unfairly with American workers. But labor's position since then had reversed on the West Coast, where many Asian-Americans now were members of organized labor unions. Allowing them to be naturalized would allow for "more effective participation in the labor movement," one argument stated. [146]

Author Pearl Buck (whose popular book, *The Good Earth*, had won the Pulitzer Prize in 1931) was brought in to help with the repeal cause, beginning with a bill to permit admission of Chinese wives of American citizens. It was "a first step in dealing with the whole Chinese exclusion question," Read Lewis wrote Buck in 1943. "If the committee cannot be persuaded even to take this first step, there is less hope that they will take the larger one." [147]

The Cranstons were "marooned by measles and quarantined" that March. "I hope Alan is all right again and that you have escaped," Lewis wrote Geneva. Lewis was anxious to have her back on the job. "Who are the people in Washington that you have been in touch with who are most interested in this question?" he asked. [148]

One tactic was to enlist former President Hoover's support. The Cranstons asked William Cranston for ideas about contacting Hoover. He made inquiries of Palo Alto friends and learned that Hoover spent most of his time at his residence in New York. Stanford President Ray Lyman Wilbur and newspaperman Ben Allen were the "only two people out here who are apt to be in Hoover's confidence," William Cranston told Geneva in May, 1943. "I, myself, have no connection with either of them or with Hoover." He also recommended several other people whom they might try. [149]

Repeal bills were introduced and hearings held in May, 1943. The Common Council spearheaded the effort with a steering committee made up of "friends of China" and a publicity campaign. Geneva was assigned to work on the legislative effort full time in April, 1943. But there were concerns, as Lewis told her – "the possible complications and embarrassment involved in the wife of a public official attempting to influence legislation [on] a matter in which her husband is concerned as part of his job. That, however, is a question primarily for you and Alan. Of course, if Alan is likely to be drafted, this aspect of the question does not arise." If Geneva undertook the work, she also might have to commute between Washington and New York. Meanwhile, he asked if she would look into a bill that called for an investigation into "discrimination against Negro soldiers." [150]

Geneva was instrumental in getting valuable witnesses like retired Navy Admiral Harry E. Yarnell, who had been recalled to the Secretary of the Navy's office as Special Adviser to the Chinese Military Mission. "Please put on all possible pressure to get Admiral Yarnell there," repeal committee chairman, publisher Richard J. Walsh (Pearl Buck's husband), wrote Geneva. "In his letter to me he emphasizes the military necessity and the danger of a 'collapse' in China," which had been invaded by Japan. Geneva was successful with Yarnell and others, and her witnesses "received congratulations from all the objective onlookers. I coached each person who appeared," she told Walsh, "using red pencil on phrases like 'racial equality,' 'all orientals,' etc., and was very jubilant." Coaching witnesses, she said, "surely gives us an advantage." She lunched after the first hearing with the past commander of the Hawaiian American Legion, Dr. Min Hin Li – "I'm becoming very adept with chopsticks," she joked. "Consensus has it," she reported to Walsh, "that Pearl Buck was the best witness to appear." One group, though, the Defense Workers' League, was a bit worrisome – "they will make perfectly clear in their testimony that they voted last week not to allow any more communist members in their group," she reported. And a man who claimed to have been working on repeal for years called her, saying that he planned to bring a number of Chinese girls from a library to watch the hearings. "[O]ne of them slapped Alan's face (literally) and told him that she was a Christian and that he doesn't act like one," she added, wondering if Walsh knew or had any influence with the man. Walsh, in his testimony, produced copies of Japanese short-wave broadcasts beamed to China in March, 1943, that propagandized, "while White people are free to live in China, the Chinese cannot enter the United States." The urgency lay in the need to keep China as an ally. Japanese invaders were putting up large posters in Chinese towns urging the Chinese to cooperate with them as members of a common race, proclaiming that Americans and British were there only to conquer and exploit them, according to Walsh. [151]

By then, Geneva estimated that repeal had enough votes to be approved by the House committee, "unless something very unexpected happens." She demonstrated a thorough knowledge of the legislative process and lobbying strategies – "We wouldn't have too much trouble getting it by the Rules Committee," she believed, outlining which congressmen should carry the bill on the floor and plans to rally support from state American Federation of Labor (A. F. of L.) leaders. "We all have cause to be jubilant, I believe," she said June 2, 1943. [152]

When Congress recessed at the end of June, she and Cranston went to California for a two-week vacation. But Cranston "thoroughly enjoyed a good dose of pneumonia while there," Geneva wrote Jackson Leighter of the Motion Picture Society for the Americas in August. "He is completely recovered (thank God and sulphadiasene!), and is almost about to read the Hearst papers again. While playing nursemaid," Geneva continued to work on the repeal issue. Could Leighter help with A. F. of L. unions, she wondered? "I may try to stall" floor votes on the bill until after its convention, "if the wind is with us," she told Leighter. Cranston helped by introducing Geneva to "the people who would do us the most good" in California but after only half a day of that, "he had to fly back to Washington very suddenly." Geneva remained in California to do what she could. She was able to report success in getting repeal endorsements from the San Francisco Board of Supervisors, California State American Legion, California Department of Veterans of Foreign Wars, and other groups. An intensive letter-writing campaign to Congress, and publicity, was the next step. [153]

The repeal passed the House of Representatives in October, 1943. "Congratulations on the House vote," one supporter wrote Geneva. "You're wonderful! You're terrific! You're sensational!... Today you have made me the happiest man in the world." A proposal to give wives and children of Chinese-American citizens non-quota status failed, however, a "serious defect," backers felt. "Must America always do too little and too late on this fateful issue of racial equality?" Walsh asked in a letter to Geneva. [154]

A law ultimately was enacted in 1943 which permitted Chinese immigration to the United States but limited the annual quota to 105 and extended citizenship privileges to Chinese. Geneva was given much of the credit. Walsh congratulated her for doing "a swell job" in getting witnesses to testify. "Your praise thrills me more than you can imagine," she wrote Walsh in December from a "flu" bed. "Thank you from the bottom of my heart.... I only hope that people will long remember the time and energy you spent toward accomplishing this great gain. But fortunately, they won't. As several legislative workers and two congressmen have remarked to me, we did such an unobtrusive job that none of us became identified in such a way as to rob us of influence for future ventures. The congressmen only knew that feeling grew daily, as evidenced by what appeared to be spontaneous communications from individuals and organizations to whom they respond. To me that's the secret of success in this field and also the proof that nothing but good old American team play can make gains in a democracy." She was looking for another job, she added, and several groups had asked her to represent them. But she preferred to "work for a specific cause" rather than become identified with one group. If that did not work out, she hoped to "work for several groups with similar liberal aims.... There is no well-organized lobby for constructive immigration legislation and it's more necessary now than ever," she felt. Melding organizations with common legislative interests, she thought, would give them greater clout than operating separately. Her other news was even more important. [155]

Cranston had volunteered for induction into the army. Elmer Davis, who did not want to lose him, urged that Cranston request deferment on the basis of being essential to O. W. I.'s war work (Cranston held one of four positions at O. W. I. that was permanently deferred by the War Manpower Commission). Davis filled out a form for the Selective Service board in New York where Cranston was registered, noting that he was "directly engaged in the conduct of the war" through "psychological warfare" that O. W. I. was conducting in cooperation with the armed services in enemy and occupied countries. "The loss of Mr. Cranston's services would seriously hamper this work," Davis stated, and "it would be extremely difficult to find a replacement because of the odd combination of ability required. Maximum occupational deferment is therefore requested." [156]

Cranston's parents also discouraged the decision, his father writing that they did not share his "enthusiasm about having a soldier in the family." Cranston, however, told his superiors, "I feel that O. W. I. should not seek my deferment." His classification had changed from 3A (hardship deferment, having a wife, no children) to 2B (deferred because of occupation in a war industry), which decision he thought should be left to the Selective Service board considering "national manpower needs." He could be replaced by competent staff whom he had trained and he thought it "advisable for O. W. I. to keep requests for deferment down to an absolute minimum." Furthermore, "I am young (29) and healthy, feel that I have established an excellent division fully able to carry on without me, and therefore believe I can be fully as valuable in the armed forces. Actually," he added, "I have been planning to request induction following completion of large-scale revisions in the work of the [foreign-language] division necessitated by our reduced budget." He also had contacted his friend John Atkinson, then at the Military Police Officers Candidate School, to learn what branches of the army Cranston might try to join. Atkinson suggested that he apply for officers' candidate school with the hope of joining a military police force of occupation in an Italian sector.

Davis accepted Cranston's decision to enlist and Cranston told him, "Before I leave the O. W. I. today for service in the United States Army, I want to wish you all the success in the world. I also want you to know how happy I have been to work under you for the past year and a half. I particularly want to thank you for the real loyalty you showed at times when it would have been easier to do otherwise. I guess the real reason you backed us up so thoroughly was because you, more than almost anyone else in Washington, understand the real issues in this war. You are a swell guy. I hope we can work together again sometime." To which Davis replied, "If there is any thanking to be done, I am the one who should do it. You have done a fine piece of work in a difficult field, and I accept your departure with misgivings and regret. As for working together again – it seems to me that people who think alike on the fundamentals are working together always, no matter where they may be or what they may be doing. Thanks and good luck to you." [157]

Once Cranston notified the Selective Service Board of his decision, he was reclassified 1A, and told the board, "I would like to be inducted in the Army as soon as possible." He joined as a private, beginning service February 5, 1944. His enlistment was noted in columns in the *San Francisco Call-Bulletin*, Leonard Lyons' New York gossip columns, the *Washington Daily News* and other Washington papers, all of which cited his refusal to seek deferment. Cranston by then had good contact with columnists, Drew Pearson writing him shortly after he enlisted, "I certainly was sorry to have missed seeing you. Please let me know where you are stationed and how things go." [158]

Cranston did basic training with the 70th infantry division (Company C, 35th battalion) at Camp Croft near Spartanburg, South Carolina. Most of his younger comrades would be sent overseas. Cranston, however, would remain stateside. After only a week's training, he got measles again when it ran through the camp. "I'm in the isolation ward of the hospital with about ten other red-splotched individuals and a few other gentlemen with afflictions that seem to be 'military secrets,'" he wrote Geneva the end of February, adding, "Measles isn't the same without Geneva & Gruslinka! Particularly this kind of measles. It truly knocked me for a loop. But now I'm on the upgrade. They must have started the day I had KP – a helluva day. Steady work from 4:30 a.m. to 8:30 p.m with eight and a half minutes for lunch (timed) and ten for dinner. 'Twas my misfortune to be picked for 'outside man' – the guy who does everything that's to be done outside.... I had to fetch coal, dump garbage, unload delivery trucks, etc. (including scrubbing garbage pails inside and out with soap and water), and inside peel and mash potatoes, set tables, steam dishes, mop floors, etc.... I actually grated all the potatoes for the 250 men of Company C – in five minutes flat!" Despite a terrible cold, he went through gas chamber training – "I got my mask on so fast the tear gas didn't even make my eyes smart but at 9:30 that night, some of the boys were still crying – and not because I was on my way to the hospital." That had been followed by a three-mile hike with rifle and full field pack – "I was doing OK till then, but that floored me. When we dragged to our barracks," a fellow soldier said, "Jesus, Al, what you got on your face?" Among friends that he had made were a beer truck driver – "did a stretch in reform school but a swell guy" – and "an anti-Semitic machinist from Pittsburgh," one of "my two great admirers in the company," he told Geneva from his hospital bed. "After my spots and splotches deserted me, I got some beautiful sinus headache," he wrote a week later, "but now they're tiring of me, too." [159]

His sickness forced him to join a new group. There also was an epidemic of spinal meningitis. "I'm glad I chose measles," he joked to Geneva. All the patients were pushed to get out of sick beds. "As soon as you can stand up without falling down, you make your own bed...mop the floor every morning. For Saturday inspection, you wash windows, polish the fire extinguishers, etc. A paragraph back I had to push the chow cart down to the mess hall and back – about a half mile. It's a gigantic place. My only two [ticks?] about the army so far are: 1. Adequate care, but lousy prevention, as far as sickness and disease are concerned. Maybe it's the only system that will work, tho.' 2. Food. It's tasty enough, but not enough attention to healthy stuff. The mail service also seems to be sloppy. I haven't heard from you since my first measles letter, tho' I'm sure you've written. The first letters my parents wrote here were apparently lost."

He had contacted army officials about postings, including the chief of the orientation branch, but received only one reply, a form letter. "I wonder if I'm getting the run-around?" he wrote Geneva. "If neither works, I'll be employing my talents in the 2nd front sometime in September or October. We are ready for combat when we leave here, and will presumably be shipped overseas immediately after the furlough – that is, all except those pulled out for any kind of special service." He had to be prepared for combat duty. [160]

Lee Falk also entered the service. "He passed his physical – in the garage he used to store his car in Stamford," Cranston told Geneva, adding, "He sold his play." Cranston signed the letter, "I miss you, Love, Alan." Falk boasted humorously of his physical that "everyone present was delighted and congratulated me on my fine condition, which I modestly attribute to clean living. They said I had the finest urine they'd ever seen, and if it wasn't for the fact that I had one flat foot (a horse stepped on me some years ago), why they'd made me a major right off." He asked for details about how Cranston was getting along. "Is it tough? Does it have a future? How do you get along with your sergeant? If they get snotty," Falk added, "just remind them quietly that you…have influential friends in high places." Falk got into an orientation group, giving programs on "Why We Fight," "Nature of the Enemy," citizenship and "peace prattle." "Most of the time, we sit around in an office and read, like in the early O. F. F. days," he said, wondering whether Cranston had "gotten any leads on what you want to do in this army, and how you can go about it? Tip me off. I'm still vague about the whole business." Another correspondent was Congressman Henry M. "Scoop" Jackson of Washington, who hoped that the infantry had "not been too tough" on Cranston's feet and that he was getting along okay. [161]

Cranston was written up in the Camp Croft newspaper for his publication of *Mein Kampf* and the ensuing suit. "Private Alan Cranston, a trainee…got messed up with Herr Hitler two years before the United States started tickling the fuehrer's mustache with a bayonet," one article read. His exploits as a correspondent with I. N. S. also were reported, drawn from an interview with Cranston who was photographed in uniform pointing to a battle-front map at an orientation session. The article dwelt on Cranston's reports from Ethiopian natives about the effects of mustard gas used by Italian invaders: "Natives with whom Cranston held secret meetings told him how the mustard gas burned the skin, made them feel as though they were breathing liquid fire, finally made the victims cough up their lungs in bloody shreds." As to enlisting, Cranston told the interviewer that he "figured he'd be safer in the Army than in Washington's bureaucratic battles." He also was quoted as predicting that Germany would be defeated by the end of the year (1944) if a planned western invasion were launched that spring, but that it would take more than a year after Germany fell to "conquer Japan." [162]

Cranston, in the summer of 1944, did apply to Officer Candidate School (O. C. S.) (noting on his application that he had been in R. O. T. C. at Pomona College in 1932), and to the Army Special Services Orientation Section following basic training. He expressed a preference for working "overseas if possible." He had become a squad leader and done orientation during basic training. Public speaking was one of his talents, his O. C. S. application noted, "particularly as a government official," and "on my own, I've studied history a great deal, [and] woven this knowledge into my speaking and writing." That included a weekly column for the camp newspaper in which he tried "to develop trainee interest and pride in his branch of the service." He added that he had "studied military writing extensively while covering guerilla warfare in Ethiopia." He attended an orientation school but was in limbo as to further assignments when the Allies crossed the English Channel June 6, 1944, and began the massive invasion at Normandy that would drive the Germans out of France. In mid-June Cranston asked a friend in the orientation branch, "Can you give me any dope on my future and possibilities as far as the orientation branch is concerned?... I think I can do the most good there. But if I can't, I can make a damn good combat soldier (I'm acting corporal now) and want to settle down to being just that." Doctor Julius Schreiber, a friend who headed a section of the Army Information and Education division, made a special request for Cranston and Lee Falk to be assigned to the orientation branch, although the applications had to go through normal channels. "I don't have to tell you how much I want you to work with me," Schreiber, told Cranston. The assignment was held up and Schreiber in July made another plea to get it approved. "Private Cranston, as you know, is a most valuable man and I believe that we should spare no effort to have him picked up for us," he wrote the War Department July 3. [163]

Cranston's column at Camp Croft was called "On the Ground." In it, he displayed a sense of history, quoted from newspapers and books, and wrote what he knew infantrymen and officers wanted to hear – patriotic encouragement with a touch of humor. One column opened,

"George Washington was angry. During the debate 169 years ago on the establishment of the Federal Army – then almost all infantry – a congressman proposed a resolution limiting the army to 3,000 men. Washington sarcastically suggested an amendment providing that no enemy should ever invade this nation with more than 2,000 soldiers. The laughter smothered the resolution....

"Every day, more of the world realizes that it will take the dog-face finally to win the war. 'Battles are not won till the infantry gets there to win them,' says the *Washington Evening Star*." [164]

Cranston also tried to assuage fears of the horrors of combat. "Land mines are nothing new," he wrote in a column. "The Confederates used ground mines 80 years ago.... Smoke screens turned up first in the Bible – the miracle whereby the Israelites were protected on their march to the Promised Land. Later, Caesar used smoke in landing operations. First use of smoke in World War I came when the British burned a haystack to cover a withdrawal. Most modern adaptation came when the U. S. infantry crossed the Rapido River in Italy. We floated smoke pots down the river [which] formed a solid wall." Cranston quoted General Eisenhower's declaring that infantrymen needed "not only dogged courage and fortitude but 'a high degree of individual initiative.'" Another column cited famous lines about war, closing with Cicero: "*The only excuse for war is that we may live in peace unharmed.*" [165]

In a notebook that he kept during his army stint, Cranston wrote not only military instructions but observations like a quote from Thomas Paine's *Common Sense* (which Washington had given his troops): "*If there must be trouble, let it be in my day, that my child may have peace.*" [166]

Cranston also wrote a short story about a German and American soldier meeting on the battlefield, obviously speculating what it would be like if he found himself in that situation. "The American's finger was on the trigger of his rifle and his eye was staring down the long, brown barrel and over the blackened steel sights," it began. "It was Peyton's first contact with the enemy, yet he knew no fear…. But as he waited for the German to advance, he wondered: 'Is this his first battle, too? Or is he a veteran? Is he a cool, confident devil? A blundering fool? Anyhow, I'll kill him. For he doesn't know that I am here. Peyton tried to place the scene in its little niche in the vast war." As the German moved stealthily closer, Peyton began to wonder "about this man, now so alive, soon so dead. Did he worship Hitler? Did he fight for the Nazis unwillingly? Did he have a family? A sweetheart? Peyton thrust the thoughts from his mind – they seemed annoyingly commonplace. But the thoughts returned, and damn it all, they were human thoughts. Then he banished them once and for all for he sensed they were dangerous thoughts…. The wind felt cool and nice on Peyton's cheek, and he wondered if it was cool and nice on the cheek of the German…. A trifle had brought him a reprieve, an added minute or two of life, a few more breaths, a few more pulse beats, one more glance at the grass and the woods and the sky."

"The American looked steadily down his rifle at the stump [hiding the German], but his mind" focused on a leaf and he reflected how chance played a crucial part in saving one's life in such situations. "And now the planning of Roosevelt, Marshall, Eisenhower – all the genius of the United Nations – had been thwarted by a leaf!... In a moment, Peyton would kill the German he had come to France to kill." But the American was caught off guard when the German moved suddenly. "With his finger on the trigger, the wind returned. With the wind came the leaf – down over the rifle, hiding sights, German, all. Then the leaf was gone, and so was the German." For the first time, the American contemplated his own possible death. "All of Peyton's advantage was lost, and now he was trapped…. A leaf fluttered to his sight. Wildly he rose out of the earth…. The German fired, and Peyton fell to the ground and lay still, still as the branch and the leaf, as the wind, too, died." [167]

Lee Falk also was hoping to join the orientation branch. He was going through basic training at Camp Crowder in southwest Missouri (near Neosha), not far from where he had gone to Boy Scout camp twenty-two years earlier, he wrote Cranston in June. He had spent D-Day "doing KP – isn't that a hell of a note?" The experience was rough, Falk admitted, he loathed the Army "with a deep and boiling loathing" and had already "planned and rehearsed the cynical manner in which I shall greet my NCOs and officers after the war, when we're all civilians again. Actually, we'll probably fall into each other's arms and talk about the good old days at Crowder and get drunk, tho' that's difficult to imagine," he added. He was waiting to hear whether his play had a star and was in rehearsal. "A couple of my NCOs are Hollywood actors who haven't been in the Army much longer than I have," he told Cranston, "but they think they're playing Beau Geste, and give swell readings of tough non-coms. I hope they ask me for a part someday!" Despite the unpleasantness, Falk concluded of his army experiences, "I wouldn't have missed this for anything. It's going to be tough for guys to orient themselves to our post-war world if they haven't gone through this mill."

Another acquaintance whom he ran into at a service club was "Al Lomax – remember, the O. W. I. music guy. He's enthusiastic about everything army…finds every minute a thrilling experience. Nice fellow, but you can see that he's slightly teched." (Lomax was appreciated by his fellow soldiers for his knowledge of folk music, even recording GIs singing Black songs while drilling which the general liked so much he played the record over the camp loud-speaker. At O. W. I. Lomax had specialized in reaching minority groups, producing radio shows featuring well-known singers like Burl Ives, Pete Seeger and Woody Guthrie. He had continued a deferment by working at the Columbia Broadcasting System producing shows aimed at building relations with England. In frustration at having a script rewritten, he had resigned and was drafted in 1944. He would become famous for recording and preserving indigenous blues and American folk music, and remained a friend of Falk's and Cranston's.) [168]

Cranston expected to be sent to Officers' Candidate School when "the old bugagaboo of the Harry Bridges bill and our opposition to alien registration arose," he wrote Read Lewis in one of several appeals for letters of reference. He had just completed basic training, which he told Lewis had been hard and "hot" but "not quite so hard as I'd expected." His orders for officers' training, however, had been stopped. "I was questioned about both matters, and now – suspect – am being held here until my part in both, and the background of the Common Council, can be cleared up to the satisfaction of G2" – army intelligence. To Elmer Davis Cranston wrote, "After walking some millions of miles, mashing some millions of potatoes… and learning how to knock hell out of a target with all kinds of weapons," he had been made acting corporal in charge of a rifle squad, "thus missing the nastier jobs," he said. "Then suddenly G2 came into the picture asking questions about my nefarious past." His company and battalion commanders were doing all they could "because I worked like hell during training, but I need some help from those who knew me before I enlisted." He asked if Davis would write the War Department "stating that you have the fullest confidence in my loyalty and integrity," that "certain charges were made against me but never substantiated…that I was fully investigated and cleared by the O. W. I. Security Board…assisted by the F. B. I. and all other government investigative agencies." Cranston made the same appeal to James Houghteling, then a high-ranking Treasury Department official, Jonathan Daniels, White House administrative assistant to the president, and Earl Harrison, former director of Alien Registration. "I won't be able to leave this training camp for officers candidate school, or any other post, until this matter is cleared up," he told all of them. "The matter seems to be more troublesome than serious," he wrote Lewis, but "I am confidant I can clear it up." [169]

Lewis was sorry that the matters were still "pestering you. The whole thing is so unfair and so pointless." Lewis had been interviewed about Cranston by army investigators a month earlier but the troublesome issues had not come up. "Naturally, I emphasized that there was no question regarding your loyalty or character." Houghteling reiterated Cranston's innocence to the Adjutant General of the Army and the War Department. "I can therefore assure you that Private Cranston's activities in this connection were highly constructive and desirable. These activities should entitle him to thanks rather than criticism…. I trust that this letter may remove any obstacle to the Army's utilization of Pvt. Cranston's ability, experience and high reliability to a fuller extent." Cranston was grateful – "It was much more than I asked, and has done much to encourage my hopes that my status will soon be cleared," he told Houghteling. Daniels was glad to be a reference and to see anyone who was checking into Cranston's record. But Cranston was still waiting "for the army powers-that-be to decide what to do with me" by the end of August, 1944. Meanwhile, "they've given me the rather innocuous but certainly pleasant job of life guard at one of the camp pools. After training me to kill for many months, they suddenly put me to preserving life – and the funniest quirk to it is that they neglected to ask me whether or not I can swim!" he joked to Houghteling. (He could, but conceded that he was a "lousy swimmer.") "The trouble is," he wrote another friend, "that some of the fellows I trained with are already on their way across to France, and I feel pretty useless here." [170]

"The army didn't know what to make of me," Cranston later conceded, "and decided they didn't want me to be an officer." [171]

In the interim he was sent to Fort Leonard Wood, Missouri. Geneva drove there with him and they lived off base in cramped quarters. They spent only six weeks in the Ozarks, but Geneva later would relate with amusement how they first rented the back porch of a motel for $10 a week and shared a refrigerator with ten couples. In another arrangement, they rented a two-bedroom house with five other couples and had to take turns using the bathtub one night a week. On bath night, the husband would have to carry buckets of water from an outdoor pump and heat it on a wood stove. "I carried my sterling silver and pots and pans with me," Geneva said of their frequent moves in those days. "I felt it made each new place more like home." [172]

On his arrival, though, Cranston "got a happy break," he told his friend Schreiber in September, 1944, and was assigned to the Information and Education Division of the Army Service Forces. "I am no longer a rifleman!" In October, he was ordered to division headquarters in New York City. His salary was $840, and he rose to the rank of sergeant. In February, 1945, he was awarded a Good Conduct medal for "exemplary behavior, efficiency and fidelity." "Your devotion to duty and enthusiastic efforts have been a great contribution to the morale, entertainment and pleasure of the Armed Forces…attested by the popularity of Information and Education activities," the commendation read. [173]

His colleagues in that section included notables like cartoonist Herb Block. One day, to the surprise of both, Cranston's old Menlo School chum Ted Waller sat down at the next desk in the office at 205 East 42 Street. Waller had been involved in Japanese internment for the War Relocation Authority until drafted. After different assignments, he was ordered to the same section as Cranston. They wrote discussion outlines and trained non-commissioned and commissioned officers to lead orientation at bases around the country. One paper that Cranston may have prepared had his stamp of history in it. Entitled "Know Why We Fight," it began: "These are the times that call for healthy, wholesome and vigilant defenders of our Democracy. Let those who are cynical, pessimistic or defeatist, look into our past and…learn from Washington, Jefferson, Patrick Henry, Tom Paine and Sam Adams and Ben Franklin…. Let the soldiers know our history." Cranston and Waller traveled around the country doing the training programs, and wrote a newsletter, *Army Talk*, distributed to non-combat troops. Cranston also co-authored a pamphlet on *Fascism* that caused a "stir," a columnist reported, because it "not only told the GIs that there were American Fascists but showed them how to spot them." [174]

The Cranstons had arrived in New York in time to attend a Liberal Party rally at Madison Square Garden on October 31 for the Roosevelt-Truman presidential ticket at which Vice President Henry Wallace, Senators Truman and Robert F. Wagner (of New York), labor leader David Dubinsky and social activist Reinhold Niebuhr were among the speakers. Victor Borge, Ethel Merman, tap dancer Bill Robinson and "4-F" crooner Frank Sinatra entertained the crowd, backed by the International Ladies' Garment Workers Union chorus. They sang songs entitled "The F. D. R. Way," "Don't Break up that Team," and "Don't Look Now, Mr. Dewey (but Your Record is Showing)." One lyric ran, "How the hearts of the Nazis and Japs will quake/When the radios roar/That we've voted once more/For the Franklin D. Roosevelt way!" [175]

While still in the army, Cranston also was called on to give interrogatories in a suit brought by Victor Ridder, publisher of the most influential German-language newspaper in the United States, *Staats-Zeitung*, for having been accused of being a Nazi sympathizer. Cranston defended the man. "I sought his cooperation in lining up German-Americans behind the war effort," Cranston testified. He had suggested forming a group of prominent Americans of German descent to further that end in 1942, and had attended two of the group's meetings. He also had "mildly criticized a few articles" in Ridder's paper. "I pointed out [to Ridder's brother Joseph] that they might be interpreted as sympathetic to the Nazis. Joseph Ridder felt that this interpretation was far-fetched, and that no pro-Nazi sentiment was intended." When asked to point out obvious pro-Nazi passages, Cranston said that neither he nor his O. W. I. staff were able find any. He believed that "Victor Ridder, like some others, was for a time victimized and misled by clever Nazi propaganda" but that he was a "patriotic American citizen." Ridder, whose family would go on to build the Knight Ridder newspaper company, was grateful. "I think we worked very well together while you were in the O. W. I.," he wrote Cranston in August, thanking him for "the trouble you have taken in this matter." [176]

Geneva initially remained in Washington after Cranston joined the Army and found an interesting job, albeit somewhat different from what she planned. She went to work for Orson Welles who was active in the American Free World Association. It described itself as a "collective striving for the establishment of a world federation, a policed world, a political, social and economic order in which each individual and each nation surrenders a small part of its sovereignty and so-called liberty in order that there might be a true and genuine liberty for all men and women on the planet." Headquartered in New York, it published a monthly magazine, *Free World*. Geneva's job was arranged through the Cranstons' Hollywood friend, Jackson Leighter, Welles' partner in Mercury Productions, who, Welles wrote her in February, 1944, "tells me you are awaiting 'orders.'… Most of my time nowadays is devoted to political writing," Welles said from his Beverly Hills office, "and because I feel keenly my inability to evaluate Washington news from this distance, I am anxious for you to write me several times weekly an airmail news letter or bulletin. I read practically every newspaper and periodical with the exception of 'The Poulterer's Gazette,'" he joked, "so you will realize what I need from you. Please pay no attention to neatness or literary merit." He also would like her to research questions that he had, and would welcome her opinion on issues. [177]

"I am at your service and shall commence today," Geneva wrote Welles, while continuing "other nefarious activities (which fit in very well), and work for you on a part-time basis with a weekly salary of $50" if he agreed. "The expression of my own opinion, which you welcome, would probably be too depressing," she added. "Until I know more about what you want of me, I'll proceed with fingers crossed. I'll hope to receive many queries from you soon in order to serve you well, and also to make my assignment less amorphous." She sent him summaries of information about foreign affairs and U. S. government policies, working from their apartment at 120 C Street on the northeast side of Capitol Hill. [178]

A month later, Leighter told Geneva that "Mr. Welles is satisfied but he has commented occasionally that he would like a little more thorough coverage of Washington happenings…more frequent communications would be stimulating. I hope Alan has gotten into the branch of Uncle Sam's Army which will challenge his great abilities," he added. "If not, it is a horrible waste of mental power." Welles also engaged Geneva to be Washington correspondent for *Free World* magazine. [179]

In the summer of 1944, with Cranston away at Camp Croft, Geneva complained to Leighter of "what living alone and disliking it in abominable weather can do for one who was wacky to begin with. For a girl who's successfully hung on to gloves, birth certificates, war bonds, love letters, and other vital papers for many decades, this is a crisis!" she joked of having mislaid a tax-withholding form. She had searched her files "from Arabian oil to Zero Mustell. Then I proceeded to relive with… miscellaneous people whose beds I've inhabited since Alan went military" in search of the "important slip of paper…now known as my 'Freudian slip' because of my coy and eager embarrassment about the subject of remuneration." She finally had gotten a new form from the Treasury Department. "I'm thrilled about Mr. Welles' thinking I'm a good kid. Come August 1 (when [Secretary of War] Stimson will have disposed of Alan in some diabolical way), I'll be wanting more work." But she was looking ahead, and wanted to return to live in California. "I've quit lobbying for the moment because I want to be free to play with d'Alan part time. But as I told you, it's taken four years to sell California to Alan as a post-war base, and now that we're agreed, I'd much prefer to have him return to me there than to a gal who can support him only as a Washington correspondent or lobbyist." Cranston, "besides rugged infantry training," was writing his column "and making an hour's speech a week about the war…. He's doing a veddy [*sic*] fine job," she said proudly. [180]

Welles and Leighter in December, 1944, asked Geneva to wire them whatever she could pick up in the way of "hot news from Washington" to put in columns that Welles was about to start syndicating, "Orson Welles' Almanac." It was to begin appearing in January, 1945, syndicated by the *New York Post*. "When time permits, send along all almanac whimsies verbatim you can find," Leighter telegraphed her in December, 1944. "Orson very happy with your stuff" but thought the best system was to "stick to synthesis rather than speculation as much as possible." Welles also asked her to "kindly use a new page for each new topic, even if it's only a tiny paragraph," his secretary wrote Geneva. Welles' assistant, Loletta Hebert, told Geneva, "I enjoy reading your wires before I deliver them to Mssrs. Leighter and Welles. They sound terribly intelligent and make me feel like a stupid dud. I hope we meet one day." Welles constantly begged, "More material urgently needed" as quickly as she could get it to him to meet weekly deadlines. [181]

The Cranstons recommended a friend who also could contribute to the columns, and Cranston himself apparently was doing so while in the army. His friend sent one item about an African-American whose clearance for federal employment was held up when he was suspected of "revolutionary and communistic tendencies because he belonged to several Negro and pro-Negro groups that advocated all sorts of equality for our Black brothers. None of the government hacks who were so upset about the fellow's qualifications and philosophy of life took the trouble to read his job application, which revealed the fact that 1) the applicant is Colored, and 2) wanted [the Foreign Economic Administration] to send him to the Negro republic, Liberia." The friend was paid $5 for the item. Geneva, as Welles' representative, was to pay contributors out of what Welles paid her for material used in the columns. "If you get red hot," Cranston told his news friend, "Geneva might well find herself paying you damn near all she's receiving. If that ever really happens, you can expect to hear a loud squawk." They were "trying to pile up a backlog of material" for future columns. Welles was grateful, telling the Cranstons, "Last week's material was all very swell." [182]

Welles and the Cranstons were of like minds in their views and well suited to work together. Cranston and Welles, whose film *Citizen Kane* had come out in 1941 when Welles was twenty-six-years old, shared a mutual dislike of William Randolph Hearst or at least his policies. Welles also had produced a version of Shakespeare's *Julius Caesar* that evoked Italian Fascists. His realistic 1938 radio broadcast of H. G. Wells' *War of the Worlds*, which attracted national attention by frightening masses of people into thinking that Martians actually were attacking earth, was the kind of ironic humor that Cranston enjoyed. Welles took Democratic politics seriously. He campaigned for President Roosevelt's fourth term, was a guest at his inauguration in January, 1945, and when the president died later that year, Welles was asked by CBS radio to do a tribute to him. Welles also toyed with the idea of running for the Senate from California, which he said Roosevelt supported. It was Cranston, Welles claimed, who dissuaded him from doing so. He later speculated that maybe Cranston had not been a disinterested adviser, having his own eyes set on the prize. (In 1947 Welles briefly considered running for the U. S. Senate from his home state of Wisconsin.)[183]

In announcing his forthcoming column in 1945, Welles touted, "No ghost will write my stuff, for I'm going to say what I want to say in my own way." He saw no reason why an actor should not participate in politics, and planned to reduce his theatrical activities to one motion picture a year so that he could concentrate on the column. "Things are happening in the world today that are more important than the theatre…more exciting than anything that can be produced on the stage. Everybody with any sense knows that this is the supreme crisis of civilization and if we don't come through it, then what does the stage matter? I don't have the answers to the world's problems," he added, "and I'm not founding a new religious cult, but I do believe that if I can stir the people to debate and think about our problems, we'll find a way out. You see, I am convinced everybody should be interested in politics. If we, the Americans, lose interest, then the democratic way of life is doomed. Let's not forget that the disaster of America in the 1920s was that everybody left the practice of politics to the professionals." Among topics that he reported on was seeing documentary footage of the Holocaust, describing "The heaped-up dead in evidence, the burdened ovens." He also was going on a lecture tour. "Some people may ask why a ham actor should be posing as an authority on world affairs," he said in an interview. "The important thing is that if I make the people think, what does it matter about me personally?" A new father of a month-old baby daughter, Rebecca, with his wife, actress Rita Hayworth, Welles was asked if he worried about embarrassing questions from audiences. "I'm for it," he answered. "That's the way to find out things." [184]

Just before Christmas, 1944, the Cranstons moved to New York. In February, 1945, Geneva asked Leighter for the payment due her so that she could put down $700 to rent an apartment at 15 Central Park West "with TELEPHONE, BATHTUB, HOT WATER, MAILBOX, and other incredibly modern inventions," she told him with delight. "The minute the landlords learn that Alan is a soldier, they violate O. P. A. [Office of Price Administration cost controls], patriotism, fairness, and demand half the lease in advance." [185]

By spring Welles was asking for material that "emphasized issues rather than newsbreaks. This does not mean hot news unwanted, merely that he wants to editorialize more than report," Leighter telegraphed Geneva. "Urge you send me more leads," Welles himself telegraphed in May, "do not need stories fully developed so much as lines, angles, quotes, facts, etc. Fond regards." The Cranstons saw the column as a lively opportunity to express kindred views, and Cranston recruited John Atkinson to contribute. He sent a piece on growing anti-Russian attitudes in Britain, based on knowledge from serving as American military aide to Harold Macmillan while Resident Minister to the Mediterranean during the war. [186]

In June, 1945, Welles, who had been ill, was forced to tell Geneva, "Doctor has given me my choice between absolute quiet, which means no column, and hospital. With no money coming in, this, of course, means our deal will have to be suspended until things brighten up for me." She would continue to work for him until 1946, though, assisting with weekly radio commentaries as well as his newspaper column. "It was fun, and also gave us enough freedom to be able to afford a telephone. I did all the work and he got all the credit," Geneva later said, partly in jest. [187]

After a year and a half in the army, Cranston would ask a friend with the United Nations Relief and Rehabilitation Administration (U. N. R. R. A.) about civilian job possibilities. "I carried out my threat to escape the toils of the bureaucracy, and resigned from O. W. I.," he related, but "at the moment, I have a slight nostalgia for the bureaucracy, and wondered if you might have any good ideas." He had expected to be sent overseas, and was now disenchanted with the army posting. "I am not utterly convinced I want to get out…but I do feel I could be accomplishing more elsewhere." His successor at O. W. I., Constantine Poulos, had become "a hero in Greece," Cranston said, "Lee Falk is having one hell of a time in the army," and another mutual friend [Peter Cusick] was reportedly "the best-dressed major in England." The friend asked Cranston to fill out a federal job application as soon as possible, telling him that there was "something brewing" that might get Cranston back into government service. Would he object to assignment in Italy or Yugoslavia? His language skill in Italian was a plus. [188]

Cranston needed a letter offering him a job in order to obtain release from the army.

His army superior and friend, Julius Schreiber, wrote a sterling recommendation "for the excellent service you have rendered to the Orientation Program. Your loyalty and devotion have been outstanding. They were amply demonstrated by your voluntary passing over of opportunities for advancement in rank in order to continue with our branch where your skills and talents were vitally needed. The writing ability you displayed in the preparation of *Army Talk* was outstanding." [189]

Cranston was considered for several positions with U. N. R. R. A. that would have taken him to Europe to work on reconstruction in Italy or Germany as well as a consultant job with the Foreign Economic Administration (F. E. A.) in Washington. But War Department bureaucracy again interceded. It had "an established procedure" to relieve soldiers from active duty only if civilian employment was in the national interest. "The sergeant's [Cranston's] request will be carefully considered and if it is determined that he can render more valuable service to the Nation in a civilian capacity, discharge will be authorized," a commanding officer told the F. E. A. An impatient person might have fretted at the hold-ups, but Cranston seems to have patiently endured the delays. He must have been disappointed when the U. N. R. R. A. ultimately turned him down, saying "that there were other candidates who… seem to be a little better qualified for the current operation which we have in mind." He hoped for the F. E. A. job, and on that basis formally requested discharge in August, 1945, on grounds that the work would increase his "contribution to the national interest." [190]

But something monumental would suddenly shift his focus. Cranston was stunned by President Truman's order to drop the atomic bomb on Hiroshima August 6, 1945, and Nagasaki three days later, effectively ending World War II. More than anything to date, the events drew his attention to military power and the destruction of nuclear weapons. In a draft for an article or essay (that apparently was not published), he speculated, "There is considerable evidence that not only is the big brass – top generals, and some admirals, too – seeking to fool the American people, but that it is also seeking to fool President Truman," who had succeeded Roosevelt at his death on April 12, 1945 (less than a month before Germany surrendered). "No important scientist who worked on the atom bomb has had a talk with the president," Cranston wrote. "I predict that the scientists who really know the nature of atomic energy will make strenuous efforts in the next few days to see the president. If they fail, their efforts will end in public protests. The scientists believe that only lack of knowledge on the president's part can lead him to say that we intend to keep the secret of atomic bomb production to ourselves, when every important physicist in the country agrees that we cannot possibly keep the secret for more than five years at most, fifteen years at best. As one of the scientists said, 'To say that we will keep the secret of the atom is like saying we will keep the secret of how the world is made.'" Cranston concluded:

"Harry S. Truman was a fair to middlin' president until Hiroshima. Whether he has the vision to prevent our utter destruction in the Age of the Atom is uncertain.

"The scientists, and more and more statesmen every day, are convinced that we face the alternative of creating a world government with sufficient power to control the atom bomb, or destruction. But Truman reportedly told a visitor a few days ago, 'World government is a thousand years away.'

"The scientists say humans won't live that long without it." [191]

Cranston and Falk even drafted a proposal for a play (or film) called "The Bomb," which eerily forecast events some fifty years in the future. It began with a description of "A rapid sequence of violent terrorist acts. At the opening game of the World Series – as a high dignitary throws out the first ball – a grenade is thrown, exploding with tremendous impact; a group of officials are machine-gunned as they come out of the U. N. Secretariat building; at a state funeral, machine-gunners appear and blast the group of distinguished mourners, etc. In each incident, some of the terrorists are shot, some captured, tried and jailed." The plot concerns a "gang" of multi-national terrorists who "belong to no one group and have varied loyalties." They smuggle two black suitcases into the United States by boat and helicopter, killing everyone who observes their movements. A blackmail note is sent to the president demanding the release of terrorists jailed in the U. S. and other nations. It also demands payment of $100 million in gold bullion with "sufficient planes to carry the gold, the freed terrorists and a few prominent hostages of high rank from each nation." If the demands are not met, "an unidentified major American city will be destroyed by an atomic bomb ten times as powerful as the Hiroshima bomb." [192]

The note is considered a hoax but "kept secret while agencies investigate." Three people suspect that the murders may be connected to the blackmail threat: a coast guard officer, a woman TV newscaster and her sweetheart, a young White House advisor. A second note is sent that says "as proof of the intentions of the unknown senders, a primary bomb will be exploded somewhere." It, too, is kept secret, considered a "crank note" until an island on which one of the suitcases was smuggled and a camper shot is demolished by a bomb equal to that dropped on Hiroshima. The jailed terrorists are questioned, some tortured, but nothing is learned about the perpetrators. "No special group can be charged since many unrelated terrorist groups are to be freed." What is the source of the bomb? "Stolen from stockpiles of the U. S. A. or other nuclear powers? Fashioned from nuclear reactor material here or abroad?" Efforts are made to meet gang leaders but they do not appear. "In the U. S. A., activity is frantic…. Shall the entire country be alerted into mass panic? Shall every major city be evacuated?" The president chooses to meet the terrorists' terms. "Designated hostages, men of high rank in several countries, volunteer at the urgent request of our State Department." The "final hour approaches. Proof must be given that the bomb is de-activated." A presidential committee goes to meet the terrorists in New York City, where the bomb is hidden in the closet of a mid-town apartment. The gang hastens to the meeting with an hour to spare. But as they pass a large outdoor clock, "they are horrified to see that their watches are an hour behind. They neglected to set them ahead to daylight savings time." They try to flee but are caught on the George Washington Bridge as the bomb explodes.

"The main thrust of the latter half of this story," Cranston and Falk wrote, "is to show…the catastrophic effect of such a nuclear bomb blast on a metropolis. This disaster, outweighing all other imaginable disasters, destroys the entire city, leveling and burning it. The destruction extends far out into the suburbs…a vast radius of death and destruction. More, the huge radioactive cloud covers much of the Eastern seaboard, from Boston to Washington.... Is a message needed to follow this? It seems self-evident. Unless we can control the nuclear demon, there is no defense against such an attack by determined people, sane or mad."

Cranston would refine those concerns in a project that he had been working on during his army stint. It would bring him public attention and shape his destiny.

4

Killing the Peace and Confronting the Atom Cloud

"The world must choose now between world government and world destruction."
Flyer describing purpose of Dublin Conference, 1945.

Cranston had been writing a book, which was coming to conclusion in the spring of 1945. While at Stanford, he had watched the League of Nations fail to cope with the invasion of Ethiopia by Mussolini. He had become "very concerned about the fact that we didn't have an effective world organization to deal with such people." He also had long ruminated on the fact that only a few men in the U. S. Senate had been able to keep the United States from participating in the League after World War I. It had been President Woodrow Wilson's greatest hope that it would be the beginning of a world peace-keeping power, and the failure of the Senate to ratify the League and the Versailles Peace Treaty helped precipitate Wilson's death. [1]

Cranston had read a biography of Wilson's principal antagonist, *The Gentleman from Massachusetts: Henry Cabot Lodge* (1944), by Karl Schriftgiesser, whose book reviews appeared in national publications and whose perspectives corresponded with Cranston's. "I got so damned mad at seeing what one man could do to sabotage world peace," he told a columnist, "that I wanted to do something about it." Cranston "discovered that there was no popular book dealing, step by step, with how we lost the last peace." [2]

As World War II came to a close, another peace-keeping organization conceived by the Allied United Nations was about to be formed. Cranston, and others, worried that isolationists in Congress once again might thwart America's participation, and he decided to spell out neatly and succinctly what had happened more than twenty years earlier as a lesson in historical mistakes. He was somewhat concerned, however, that, if published, his views might be grounds for a court martial while he remained in the army. [3]

Collier's magazine rejected an article based on the manuscript, then titled "Diary of Defeat." "We've been debating for a couple of days whether we could do something with your book," the managing editor told Cranston in early April, 1945. "I read it with a great deal of interest," he added, "and think you have done a good job but it is so much off our usual pace that we don't feel we can do it effectively as an article." The Viking Press, through an agent, bought the book on condition that it be published in advance of ratifying the United Nations charter, then being drafted in San Francisco. Viking paid Cranston an advance of $1,000, half on signing the contract and half on delivery of the completed manuscript. That enabled him to hire a research assistant (Erma Fischer), and he worked hurriedly to finish the book. [4]

When sending early sections of the manuscript in April to Vanderbilt University political science professor D. F. Fleming, author of a book that Cranston had read about the League fight from the Wilsonian point of view, Cranston said, "I have put every day and night non-army moment into it since I saw you." He had made revisions based on the professor's suggestions, for which he was "in debt beyond measure." Fleming, Cranston told his publisher, was "*the* authority on the Senate and world affairs." "If you have time," Cranston asked Fleming, "I would deeply appreciate it if you would go over it. Be brutally frank in your criticism, as to treatment, ideas, even as to style of writing, if possible. I have had to do the job so fast that I know it is very spotty here and there.... I'll be waiting for your criticism, and your verdict, with very great interest." [5]

"D'Alan expects to finish the book this week," Geneva wrote Leighter about the first draft. "Veddy clever, I think – a play-by-play (like a diary) account of how we muffed the League, which should do a lot of good if he can get it published in time. It makes the most interesting reading of history I've ever seen, and though he doesn't point out the parallels, they knock you over." [6]

Cranston completed the manuscript in four months, working all night to get the last sections ready before the deadline. He went to the Y. M. C. A. the next morning to work out, and delivered the manuscript on his way to work at his army office. [7]

"The book just went to press," Geneva excitedly wrote Orson Welles and Jack Leighter, revealing. with humorous irony, her role as a research assistant and a thorough understanding of current affairs. "Viking thinks it will sell like crazy. I think it will do more to prevent muffing the peace in Congress and to get Alan in the doghouse than anything else could, she said blithely. It comes out in August – just when the Senate should feel it most. The researcher skipped [Fischer developed kidney and eye trouble], so I thought I could fit the two jobs together," working for Welles and Cranston. "But mebbe reading the very yellow pages of Hearst for 1919 all day wasn't conducive to an inspired job for you all night." She commented sarcastically on the United Nations charter convention, then underway in San Francisco. "We [meaning the United States and Congress] want a world organization to keep the peace – not a foreign organization, a strictly American one, no super foreign government to harm our sovereignty, but an effective one with no police system, no economic controls, no jurisdiction over America, etc., etc. – because we must be Americans first of all and make no sacrifices for peace.... Neither Russia nor America could take" another war. "Yet we are squaring off as if we didn't know that.... Please make suggestions if you have time." [8]

The book in hardcover came out just before Cranston was released from the Army on September 7, 1945. It was entitled *The Killing of the Peace*, "The dramatic chronicle of how the will of the people was thwarted after one World War," a subtitle read. A handful of men had been responsible for opposing the plan "to save succeeding generations from the scourge of war," Cranston wrote in his preface. The original hardcover was 304 pages and sold for $2.50. In his acknowledgements, Cranston thanked Geneva "for her fine reporting...her advice on the manuscript and her help on all the odds and ends that go along with doing a book, and for her constant encouragement – and patience." A paperback revised edition was issued by Viking in 1960. By then, Cranston noted, "all the creatures of the world live under the shadow of satellites, missiles, A-bombs and H-bombs. The day will come," he hoped, "when a plan to outlaw war will once again come before us for acceptance or rejection.... Perhaps the plan will be for disarmament enforced by a strengthened United Nations." [9]

The book revealed much about Cranston himself – his passion about world peace, his interest in the decision-making process, and in history. It also demonstrated how his thought-processes worked – carefully, with research to back up his information and arguments. While not overtly proselytizing, his point of view was obvious and his derision of opponents to the League manifest. The book also made the point that history repeats itself – many of the actions that Cranston described would be familiar to future observers of national and international policymaking.

The book covered the period between May 27, 1916, and Armistice Day, November 11, 1923. Written in 1945, when the United States was preparing to decide on participation in another international organization, the book was an expression of the thirty-one-year-old Cranston's hopefulness as well as warnings – and his prescience. In many ways, it would become his *coda* for the rest of his life. It was an articulation of his beliefs and concerns. He frequently referred people to it to understand his commitment to a world-entity and to disarmament.

In style, it was written somewhat like a murder mystery – "murder involving the lives and hopes of millions," as the jacket blurb of the 1960 edition read – building tension by recounting day-by-day events without revealing the end of the tale. The story was full of intrigue, deception, anger, bitterness, back-biting, self-serving political motives, betrayal of confidences, personal hatreds, conniving, drama – and desperation on the part of the increasingly embattled "hero," President Wilson. Cranston obviously admired Wilson, highlighting his remark, as he was applauded after addressing the Senate January 22, 1917, on the concept for a League of Peace: "*I have said what everybody has been longing for but has thought impossible. Now it appears to be possible*." [10]

Cranston had done considerable research, although the book lacked citations (it did have an extensive bibliography) and would have benefited from editing (the players were not always clearly identified). It was by no means objective; rather, a partisan statement with quotes carefully selected to reinforce Cranston's point of view (pro-League of Nations). But, as his first published book, it was a compelling read. It also evidenced Cranston's growing interest in the intricacies of American political decision-making.

The exercise of writing the book afforded Cranston an inside look at how Congress worked. His research led him to examine the *Congressional Record* at length and to track, from newspaper accounts and other sources like government records, archives and published memoirs, congressional action and debate over the League. He wrote as if he himself had been in the Capitol chambers, describing senators as if he had met them personally.

Cranston told venerable Texas Democrat and House Judiciary Committee Chairman Hatton W. Sumners, to whom he sent an inscribed copy, "A great deal of my effort went into making the life and spirit of 'The Hill' as realistic as I could, and the ways and workings of Congress as plain as I could. And you, of all people, should be able to tell me whether I succeeded or not, and where I failed, if I failed. I intended the book most of all as ammunition for the fight to build a lasting peace, and I hope that it will really do so, for the fight is far from won." [11]

The book opened with the words of Senator Harry S. Truman telling the Senate November 2, 1943:

"A small group of willful men kept us from assuming our world obligations in 1919-20, and the same thing can happen again. I am just as sure as I can be that this World War is the result of the 1919-20 isolationist attitude, and I am equally sure that another and worse war will follow this one, unless the United Nations and their allies, and all the other sovereign nations, decide to work together for peace as they are working together for victory."

In his preface to the 1945 edition, Cranston stated:

"All surveys of opinion in 1918 and 1919, and even in 1920, showed that the American people wanted to join a world organization to preserve the peace. Most of the press supported the idea, and most of the pulpit; so did business and labor, and war veterans and gold-star mothers. And so did most of the United States Senate – 76 out of 96 Senators voted for the League of Nations!

"But a little group of powerful men wanted to keep us out. They well knew the sentiment of the nation. Their leader said in 1919: 'I think a majority of the people of the country desire a League…'

"They understood they would lose in an open fight. But they conceived a subtle strategy that would fool and defeat people. The strategy was successful." [12]

The United States ended by signing a separate peace with Germany after World War I, not joining with other nations in a treaty. Cranston firmly believed that that had isolated the United States and sabotaged the objectives of the League, "an instrument that – well used and wisely perfected – could have prevented the drift toward World War II that commenced when we withdrew from the world," and sent a message to ambitious leaders like Adolf Hitler that the "world could be surely divided and perhaps conquered."

He was writing the story in hopes that it would "make it more difficult for any little cabal to do the same thing again," thus preventing future world wars.

The story began with President Wilson and Republican Senator Henry Cabot Lodge of Massachusetts sitting at the same table at the Willard Hotel in Washington the night of May 27, 1916. Both men were there to address a convention of the fledgling anti-war League to Enforce Peace. And both spoke in favor of what Lodge called "an international league or agreement, or tribunal, for peace." "Voluntary arbitration" would not work, he had said, conceding that the league had "the highest of all aims for the benefit of humanity," to warm applause. His words would come to be ironic in face of his subsequent actions as a powerful member of the Senate Foreign Relations Committee.

Wilson, who was introduced by the man whom he had succeeded, William Howard Taft, then head of the league, articulated a view that America, whether it liked it or not, was a participant "in the life of the world," and her people, he believed, were willing for the United States to join "any feasible association of nations." It was not lost on the audience that it was the first time the head of a major power had backed such a proposal. Nor that the league had been founded largely by members of the opposition political party, the Republicans.

In the forthcoming 1916 presidential election campaign, both Wilson and his Republican opponent, Charles Evans Hughes, would speak in favor of world organization, Wilson behind the slogan that "He kept us out of war!" Lodge tried to discredit Wilson's strategy as fraudulent by repeating a "tale told on a train" that Lodge had heard second-hand. He charged that Wilson had added a secret postscript to a stiff warning sent the Germans after the sinking of the *Lusitania* (in 1915), suggesting that the warning was not to be taken seriously but was meant to assuage Americans' outrage. Angry cabinet members had found out about the codicil and forced Wilson to remove it under threats of exposing the duplicity, Lodge alleged. But cabinet members and the president denied the story. In truth, Secretary of State William Jennings Bryan had proposed modifying the message to Germany, but Wilson and others in his cabinet had opposed that. Lodge, instead, was vilified in the press for "spreading stagecoach tittle-tattle at second or third hand" and disgracing his New England founding-father ancestors. Cranston noted sardonically that Lodge's proud, austere demeanor gave him a reputation among his colleagues as having a "mind like the soil of New England – naturally barren but highly cultivated."

Wilson was reelected but the aftermath of the election, in which Republicans rankled within their own party over whom to blame for losing the White House twice since 1912, set the stage for bitter differences between Wilson and Lodge over foreign policy. The concept of some kind of international organization was gaining popular support into 1917 as the frightful war in Europe raged on, and the League to Enforce Peace was growing nationwide. "League Sundays and Weeks" were proclaimed, and polls showed overwhelming endorsement of the idea. Ironically, "aging pacifist" William Jennings Bryan was the only prominent leader who opposed it. Wilson spoke openly of the need for a world authority to keep peace and urged the United States, when the war was ended, to "adopt the doctrine of President Monroe – that no nation should seek to extend its policy over any other nation or people." [13]

Such words clearly impressed Cranston, and he emphasized the intense mutual hatred that Lodge and Wilson would develop for one another. Lodge consistently had defended the Senate's powers to participate in foreign-policy decision-making, and had helped kill or weaken various treaties. By 1917 he feared that an international peace organization would abrogate the role of the U. S. Congress: If another nation refused to abide by the organization's mandates, that might force the U. S. into war without congressional input. Furthermore, since the United States would have but one vote in the proposed international body, it could be compelled to follow decisions made by smaller and weaker nations. Or the organization might interfere in domestic affairs, like ordering the United States to admit Asian or other foreign labor, a threat not only to American labor but "the purity of the race," Cranston wrote derisively of that argument. Lodge laid out other fears and objections to participating in such a world body in a Senate speech February 1, 1917.

Another visceral opponent of Wilson's was the man whom he had defeated in 1912 – Lodge's close friend, Theodore Roosevelt, who favored U. S. intervention in the European conflict, calling those who supported Wilson's efforts to keep America out of it "professional pacifists, flub dubs and molly-coddles." Throughout the book, Cranston portrayed Teddy Roosevelt as a self-serving spoiler of Wilson's peace plans. (Among other reasons to hate Wilson, Roosevelt counted the president's refusal to give the former "Rough Rider" of Cuba's San Juan Hill a military division to command in France.) Roosevelt openly admitted, as Cranston quoted, that he "abhorred" Wilson, although Roosevelt himself had spoken favorably, when accepting the 1910 Nobel Peace Prize and in a 1915 book, *America and the World War*, of the "great Powers'" forming a world league to "keep the peace among themselves" and prevent "by force if necessary, its being broken by others." Cranston noted that Lodge's and Roosevelt's "opening attacks on Wilson's idea for a League for Peace were made at the same time and were in some ways identical" before the United States had declared war against Germany.

Cranston was stirred by Wilson's concluding words when he finally had to ask Congress for a declaration of war April 2, 1917. He expressed eloquently what Cranston himself would come to follow as a political philosophy for America:

"It is a fearful thing to lead this great peaceful people into war, into the most terrible and disastrous of all wars, civilization itself seeming to be in the balance. But the right is more precious than peace, and we shall fight for the things which we have always carried nearest our hearts – for democracy, for the right of those who submit to authority to have a voice in their own governments, for the rights and liberties of small nations, for a universal dominion of right by such a concert of free peoples as shall bring peace and safety to all nations and make the world itself at last free." [14]

In January, 1918, Wilson had outlined fourteen points on which peace with Germany should be based, which included a call for "a general association of nations" that could oversee "political independence and territorial integrity to great and small states alike." Roosevelt, Lodge and others would be adamant and vocal opponents to the plan, although Germany, when it at last sought peace talks in October, 1918, agreed to Wilson's outline as did America's allies. Cranston wrote that "The plan for a concert of nations seemed to express the everlasting desires of almost the entire human race…. It had kindled a flame in the hearts of men and women in unknown corners of the earth."

Unfortunately for Wilson, the mid-term congressional elections in November, 1918, gave Republicans a majority in Congress, and by one vote in the Senate. That meant that Henry Cabot Lodge would become Senate leader and chairman of the Foreign Relations Committee, which considered all treaties.

Cranston had moments of drama in his book, notably when he described a soldier, shell-shocked and with what doctors diagnosed as hysterical blindness, listening to a pastor announce Germany's capitulation and the Kaiser's abdication in a hospital. "I could stand it no longer," the soldier later wrote. "I groped my way back to the dormitory, threw myself on my cot and buried my burning head in the covers and pillows.... I became aware of my own destiny." The soldier was Adolf Hitler writing in his memoir, *Mein Kampf.* [15]

The World War I Armistice was signed November 11, 1918, in a railway car at Compiegne Forest outside of Paris and the guns at last went silent at eleven o'clock that morning. On the same day, Cranston noted in another dramatic incident, Teddy Roosevelt entered Roosevelt Hospital in New York City.

In detailed vignettes, Cranston spelled out the actions and events that led up to the Senate's final decision on the League of Nations, President Wilson's most cherished dream, and derided its detractors, reporting that Lodge and Roosevelt, from his hospital bedside December 17 and 18, 1918, "agreed that the League could not be defeated by an open assault. So they determined to destroy it slowly, bit by bit, piece by piece…until finally even those who originally supported the League of Nations would vote against it." Roosevelt would be dead of a blood clot a few weeks later (January 6, 1919).

Describing how the opposition worked to thwart Wilson, Cranston emphasized quotes that reinforced his own views, like one from former President Taft who, although a Republican, backed the League. In an angry diatribe against Lodge and his followers, Taft wrote a friend, "It is their American selfishness, their American littleness, blinding them to the real interests of the world, that arouses me." Lodge countered, though, by drafting a statement of opposition and enlisting senate signatures to it.

Literary Digest had surveyed press opinion on the League of Nations and reported, "The majority of our papers regard the experiment as tremendously worth trying." Republican papers were among the most outspoken pro-League, Cranston noted, but Hearst, who initially had opposed U. S. entry into the war, opposed the League. [16]

Lodge got key senators to go against the League – including Pennsylvania Republican Philander C. Knox, Taft's former Secretary of State, whom Cranston described as one of the "best-dressed senators…bald, paunchy, nervously fingering his wing collar and shaking straight the crease in his striped trousers." Those who waffled came under the persistent cajoling of Lodge and his cohorts. Cranston credited them with wording a negative statement on the League "very cleverly" and telling colleagues that signing it did not commit them to voting against the League – it only put them on record as opposing it in the form that Wilson proposed. It was, indeed, a well-thought-out and clever strategy to build opposition to the concept. Lodge knew that, in fact, many signers actually wanted a League of Nations. In the end, thirty-one sitting senators and six about to be sworn in signed the declaration. Thirty-three votes ensured that the League would not be approved.

The intention was to make a public show of opposition to the Wilson plan as drafted, thus weakening its prospects for enactment and Wilson's power in general. The declaration that Lodge proposed as a Senate resolution was certain to fail if put to a vote, however, because more than half the Senate backed a league of some sort. By a deft parliamentary trick – one objection to bringing the matter up out of order would prevent a vote on it – Lodge avoided a vote. But he also succeeded in making his points. That was March 3, 1919, and Congress was scheduled to adjourn for the year the following day. [17]

League opponents particularly wanted to act on the matter before a new Congress was in place (in December, 1919). Opponents therefore decided to filibuster appropriations bills necessary to keep the government operating, anticipating that President Wilson – who was scheduled to go to Paris for peace talks during the summer recess – would have to call a special session in which League opponents hoped to kill it. But Wilson reinforced public support for the plan by inviting Taft to join him in a rally at the Metropolitan Opera House in New York City before the president sailed for Europe. Popular star Enrico Caruso sang the "Star-Spangled Banner" to a packed and enthusiastic audience, and the band played "Over There" as they cheered Wilson on his way. But two additional senators had signed Lodge's declaration and "the *New York Sun* gloated, "Woodrow Wilson's League of Nations died in the Senate." "Henry Cabot Lodge read the death warrant," Cranston wrote. [18]

Negotiations with Lodge went on via cable across the Atlantic. Wilson was urged to accommodate the critics, to which he agreed, but he believed that "No matter what I do, they will continue the attack." Lodge promised not to draft amendments if the Senate were out of session. In truth, he did not want to put anything in writing, planning to continually seek revision in the peace plan. "From the very beginning," Cranston pointed out, "Lodge had known that he would lose in an open fight." [19]

Lodge, however, continued to denounce the League, privately admitting that public opinion overwhelmingly favored its creation but without understanding it, he felt. He and Republican Senator William E. Borah of Idaho agreed that the only way to defeat the League was to force the Senate to amend and revise the peace treaty and League covenant. It now looked as if both would be approved, however. Thirty-two state legislatures had passed resolutions advocating the United States' entry into the League. A key, Wilson knew, was to keep the League attached to the Versailles peace treaty for purposes of Senate approval. Lodge's real agenda, others now perceived, was his fear that approval of the treaty and League would sweep Wilson back into the White House for a third term in 1920, Cranston observed.

The opposition organized well, though. Wealthy millionaire businessmen like Henry Clay Frick and Andrew Mellon were enlisted to financially back the anti-League campaign on behalf of the nation's commercial tycoons. Another "scapegoat" issue, as Cranston called it, was the allegation that the League of Nations gave equal rights and protections to nations dominated by "Negroes and mulattoes," as Senator James Reed of Missouri cried out in the Senate. "This is a colored League of Nations!" he declared of the inclusion of Brazil, Bolivia, Siam, Haiti and thirteen other members made up of "black, yellow, brown and red races" and "mongrel breeds." Reed's argument was that small nations had equal voting status and thus could defy League decisions over large nations like the United States with its 110-million-population. "If you erect a League of Nations, you will have taken a long step toward a declaration that American doors shall be opened to the peoples of all lands and we shall have Chinese and Japanese knocking at our gates, and along with them all the races of Asia," Reed warned. [20]

Another "scapegoat" was the fact that twenty-four of the proposed nation members were predominantly Catholic, raising the specter of the Pope's dominating the League and thus the world. It was one of several "scapegoating expeditions into fertile fields of prejudice and passion," Cranston wrote. Still another, raised by California's Hiram Johnson (who had run for vice president on the "Bull Moose" ticket with Theodore Roosevelt against Wilson in 1912), was that Americans could be forced by the British to "subdue Ireland!" As Senate debate began, another attack posed the spector of keeping 1.5 million American boys in Europe to set up the League. American destiny was about to be placed in the hands of "secret councils of Europe," Johnson told crowds at one point. All such arguments Cranston derided. [21]

He also was learning how power struggles were fought in the Senate. A key strategy was to ensure that the opposition controlled the Foreign Relations Committee. Chairman Lodge got a nine-to-seven majority by insisting that isolationist Johnson be added to it. "It is considered a Senate honor to sit on the Foreign Relations Committee," Cranston wrote, "and memberships are generally handed out as rewards for long and faithful service." [22]

The peace treaty was signed June 28, 1919. Taft later came out in support of some reservations about the League, a major break within the League to Enforce Peace. President Wilson now was "like a man in quicksand," as Indiana Republican Senator James E. Watson characterized him, "and every struggle you make will only sink you deeper." [23]

Cranston quoted a *New York Times* editorial of August 27, 1919, stating that opponents to the League were "prompted chiefly by motives of partisanship – the desire to destroy Woodrow Wilson politically," enhanced by "the fact that some of them or most of them are aspirants for the Republican nomination next year.... All the [world] Powers are put on notice that our international engagements are to be held always subject to the strifes of our party politics."

Wilson undertook an arduous cross-country trip, already unwell from stress, to take his arguments to the people, reminding them that Germany dearly wanted America out of the treaty, isolated and divided. On the day that he made those points at Coeur D'Alene, Idaho, September 12, 1919, Cranston pointed out, a band of "black-shirts" inspired by Benito Mussolini, marched across the Italian frontier and seized Fiume in defiance of the Versailles Treaty, a major bone of contention for the Italians in peace negotiations. "What [German] arms could not do" the debates in the United States were now accomplishing – separating America from other nations that backed the League, Cranston noted. [24]

Meanwhile, without a treaty or League, wars began breaking out in the Balkans and riots throughout Europe. More Americans began to fear the treaty and League's impact on their future, Cranston conceded, some on grounds that the treaty was too harsh on the defeated Germans. He quoted Oswald Garrison Villard, editor and publisher of the usually liberal magazine *The Nation*, who had joined the opposition, despite generally opposing what politicians like Lodge stood for. It was "hard…to oppose the League," Villard admitted, "for all of us had dreamed of a parliament of man."

Wilson's "last great speech of his life," as Cranston put it, was delivered September 25, 1919, in Pueblo, Colorado. He had been buoyed by the public's favorable response to his tour and carefully-made points. Cranston again had been inspired by Wilson's words:

"There is one thing that the American people always arise to and extend their hand to, and that is the truth of justice and of liberty and of peace. We have accepted that truth, and we are going to be led by it, and it is going to lead us and through us, the world, out into pastures of quietness and peace such as the world never dreamed before."

But, as Cranston dramatically added, on the same day back in Washington, Indiana Republican Senator Harry S. New was derisively proclaiming, "The President says he believes the League will prevent war.... I have seen and known people who believed firmly that a potato carried in the pocket would prevent rheumatism, that a silk thread around the neck would prevent a sore throat." [25]

Wilson suffered a stroke en route back to Washington (September 26, 1919) which generated sympathy from the public, aware that he had been willing to die for his cause. Had he died, League opponents admitted, the measure would have sped through the Senate. Lodge acted quickly by pushing through fifty weakening amendments to the treaty and League, all of which failed overwhelmingly, giving League backers a false sense of security. Many nations by then had ratified the treaty but not the League, waiting for the United States to act. Meanwhile, Cranston pointed out, Europe was restless, fascist groups and a German army (Junkers) were mobilizing.

Senate opponents stirred nationalist-isolationist fervor in rallies, particularly in the Middle West where, Cranston wrote, mobs "behaved like Holy Rollers" at mass meetings staged by the League for the Preservation of American Independence, chanting, "Freedom to defend a right, freedom to refuse to fight, freedom to mind our own business!" In pro-League rallies, women who had lost sons in the war drove anti-League speakers off the stage with rotten eggs. Polls still showed popular support for it, led by famous personalities like Luther Burbank, Alexander Graham Bell and Thomas Edison. Democrats announced that they would vote against a measure amended with Lodge's reservations, and called for compromise. Lodge refused, saying that the death of the treaty would be on Democrats,' and Wilson's, hands – a result that would not displease Lodge. [26]

In the end, Lodge won the day. Ratification of the Versailles Treaty linked to American participation in the League of Nations was defeated by the Senate on November 19, 1919. Lodge then introduced a resolution calling for a separate peace between the United States and Germany. Cranston pointed out that on the same day, the *New York Times* carried a brief item from Milan – Benito Mussolini had been arrested when police found explosives in his *Il Popolo d'Italia* newspaper office. Wilson vetoed Lodge's resolution and was upheld.

The 1920 presidential campaign pitted Republican Ohio Senator Warren G. Harding (with vice presidential running mate Calvin Coolidge) against Democratic Ohio Governor and newspaper publisher James M. Cox (with Assistant Secretary of the Navy Franklin D. Roosevelt as running mate). Moved by Wilson's sick-bed exhortation that the fight still could be won for the League of Nations, Cox made it a campaign issue. He and Roosevelt were whipped. By association, the vote also was thought to be a referendum on the League of Nations. Cranston quoted the *New York World* November 3, 1920, in what would be another prescient commentary on future U. S. presidential elections: "The American people wanted a change, and they have voted for a change. They did not know what kind of a change they wanted, and they do not know today what kind of change they have voted for." He also quoted Wilson's remark on the defeat: "The people will have to learn by bitter experience just what they have lost."

The Senate did not ratify peace with Germany until October 18, 1921, and the League of Nations did not succeed as a world-governing body. Cranston concluded his tale (written at the end of World War II) by noting, with irony, that in 1922 Americans already were beginning to worry about growing militarism in Japan; that on October 22, 1922, black-shirt Fascists overthrew the Italian government and made Mussolini Prime Minister of Italy; and on November 8, 1923, "Brown-shirted Nazis failed to overthrow the German government in a beer-hall revolt in Munich led by Adolf Hitler, Hermann Goering and General von Ludendorff." Cranston ended with the story's hero, Wilson, speaking bitter words of foreboding:

> "Nov. 11, 1923: It was after church on this Sunday, after the Armistice Day prayers for peace that a little throng of people – among them some war veterans – gathered before a home on S Street in Washington. Woodrow Wilson limped out on the front porch…. The former President of the United States haltingly said a very few words, and the very last were these:
>
> "'I have seen fools resist Providence before and I have seen their destruction, and it will come upon these again, utter destruction and contempt; that we shall prevail is as sure as that God reigns.'"

"Congrats!!!! Good Work, big boy!" Cranston's mother-in-law wrote him after receiving a copy of the book. "Nice looking job, and interestingly written. I am really enjoying it and this isn't the type of book that I pick out to read. You surely have scrapped my opinion of 'Teddy.' I'm very disappointed to learn he was as you picture him." She also liked the colors on the cover. "I once heard a lecture advising using the color of gold in packaging things – it's supposed to be lucky. Poor Woodrow Wilson," she added. "I hope they don't treat Truman that way – let's hope we learned something from the last peace attempt…. May the sale and popularity surpass your fondest dreams." She enclosed funds to "have a steak on me." [27]

Cranston inscribed and sent the book to a number of friends, some in high places. A San Francisco Democrat, Charles H. Kendrick, whose views Cranston valued – the book was dedicated to his son, killed in the war – thought it contained "a great lesson, namely that even the greatest…are not able to sell reason to confused masses, always led astray by shortsighted, passionate or egotistic individuals…. Plato said over 2,000 years ago that the age of reason will come only when myths will have disappeared…. Your book ought to be helpful in making people see that the power behind peace cannot be based on 'collaboration' between people who deeply distrust each other – and for that reason refuse to merge their sovereignties. The world, divided after the crushing of Nazi-Fascism between democracy and communist totalitarianism, is not yet ready for the 'rule of law,'" the man wrote with foresight. The setting up of the United Nations "is, at best, an armistice. At this stage, peace can be imposed only by the superior physical force of the democracies.... Maybe the atomic bomb will force this role upon the democracies...otherwise utterly unjustifiable.... We all are groping in the dark," he concluded, "some of us stealing thunders like Prometheus, but sadly lacking in moral and mental maturity." Cranston saved the letter. [28]

Nelson Rockefeller also received a personally-inscribed copy. "The book is a very timely and useful one, and should help avert a recurrence of the national isolationism which frustrated the peace settlements of World War I," he said in thanking Cranston. The Czechoslovak ambassador to the United States started to read it the day he received it. "It was early dawn when I put the book aside," he told Cranston. "Maybe you do not know that I was a witness to the happenings in the fateful days and months of Wilson's tragedy. It is a very sad book," he added in a postscript. [29]

"I am hopeful that the history of the new peace will be far more encouraging," Ohio Republican Senator Harold H. Burton, who had served with the army infantry during the war, told Cranston. "Perhaps it was necessary to go through the experience of 1918-1920 in order to make the progress which we have now made. It remains for us to make sure that we do not slip back in this critical period when a slip might well mean the destruction of humanity." Professor Fleming thought the book would "be a real contribution to the literature of this tragic period." He had written a promotional blurb that called it "a simple, clear account of the most fateful political controversy of this century." [30]

The president of the Woodrow Wilson Foundation, Arthur Sweetser, sent a letter from the *S.S. Queen Mary* en route to Europe. "I came on the steamer intending to forget all usual thoughts for a few days, turned over a few pages of your book somewhat absentmindedly, and then stuck to it till I had finished it," he wrote. "I think you have done a tremendous national service with this book." It had brought back those days "with the utmost vividness and balance, and brought out new facts," he said. Cranston seemed to have absorbed information "from all different sides, and consequently, presented a coordinated picture" as a "scientific bit of history. You have your viewpoint, of course, but the documentation is overwhelming to sustain it. I imagine you will be assailed by conventional historians for your somewhat unconventional presentation, but...I found your system of little vignettes extremely appealing." It must be a "shocking" story to "those who come upon it for the first time.... Certainly it is a chapter of our history where every American should hang his head in repentance – one which should get us away from our sense of moral superiority and lead us to a greater tolerance and understanding of the weaknesses of other nations."[31]

Cranston certainly had depicted Lodge "in a desperate light," Sweetser continued. "It makes a tragic ending for T. R.'s otherwise grand life; I had known he was bad at that time, but not so bad as your documentation shows.... But the greatest thing of all in your book, in my judgment, is the picture it gives of President Wilson. It goes far indeed to dispel the very dangerous idea which seems to me to be gaining ground that, vicious though Lodge and some of the others might have been, Wilson also was impossible in his refusal to accept any kind of reservation at all.... I never felt this to be the case at the time." Cranston's heart must have soared when he read that his book "should be the background of our policy over the years." The foundation, Sweetser promised, would try to promote it.

The book "gave me the willies," socialist and friend Harry Braverman wrote from Los Angeles. "It seems just too damn fantastic that a few men could do the job of wrecking the League so thoroughly." It told "a convincing story of sabotage perpetrated by high officials of government and supported, innocently and not, by good people. The picture is frightening. But because it is...it won't let [the reader] assume that his friends in Congress, even the best of them, can be counted on to take care of the peace of the world without constant reminders from [the] common guy," Braverman believed. [32]

Media figures like historian William L. Shirer, then with Columbia Broadcasting System, also sent congratulations. He thought the book should be "must' reading for all Americans." Drew Pearson promised to plug it as a "story of dramatic events that took place 25 years ago," writing in a column that the book "gives vivid inside details on how American hopes of peace were torpedoed in Woodrow Wilson's last years." San Francisco friend Charles Kendrick felt that Cranston was "going to go a long way in literature. You probably have the spirit of a crusader, and will use your skill in that direction. There is great opportunity for men of your character in this tremendously expanding field of public relations." [33]

Some people would not be pleased with the book, other friends said, to which Cranston agreed, "but until now none of them – nor their descendants – have said a word," he wrote one of them. "The record is so clear, and the results so frightful, that perhaps there is little they can say," he added. It was "still by no means certain that the current peace is not going to be killed, too," Cranston wrote John Anson Ford, a Los Angeles supervisor and Democratic leader. "The United Nations Charter is woefully inadequate for the atom age." He also feared that Senator Arthur H. Vandenberg, whom he had described in the book as "a large, round-faced young man...little known nationally but who, at thirty-five, was managing editor [and publisher] of" the Grand Rapids *Herald* "and a Republican power in Michigan" who had written an influential editorial against the League, might prove to be another Lodge. Cranston told a columnist that he saw danger in Vandenberg's proposal that only U. S. forces should be used to police the western hemisphere, stating, "If every country took that stand, we'd still have nationalism." [34]

Cranston's father's secretary, Lorraine Fuller, agreed with reviewers who said the book gave a "clear-cut picture...without entangling it with so many extraneous historical events that you lose the thread you were trying to follow." His parents, she said, were "so pleased with the book and so proud of the success you have achieved." "I am glad most of all that you found it more gripping than the usual histories," Cranston responded, "as that is what I tried hardest to accomplish." [35]

Viking placed advertisements for the book in the *New York Times* and elsewhere, and issued a promotional flyer about it. "Betrayal!" the advertisement screamed, "This never-before-told story is a warning for today!" It quoted favorable comments from reviewers like mystery writer Rex Stout whom Cranston subsequently would meet through peace-organization circles. The flyer advertised the book as reading "like a murder story," and quoted a review in the *New York Herald Tribune Weekly Book Review* by Gerald W. Johnson saying that it had "all the intellectual fascination of Machiavelli's *The Prince*, with immensely more emotional power," and was "full of huge, if grisly, humor," citing Cranston's description of "the paunchy Senator" Knox, in striped pants and bow tie, warning that if the United States joined the League, American boys might be sent "to the inhospitable South Pacific isles," a grim fact that had just been born out in World War II, if for different reasons. [36]

"It is impossible to read Mr. Cranston's pages attentively without being struck by the essential frivolity of American political thinking at the time," Johnson commented. A failing, however, was Cranston's not emphasizing "that the whole ghastly tragedy was enacted for the purpose of winning an election…. The shocking truth is that the people killed the peace. Lodge and the rest may have tricked them into doing it, but they did it, and they are now paying for their own folly…. [They] may be sure that some new Lodge will arise to befuddle them again. We have had our warning…. [I]t was the ordinary American voter" that killed the peace, he concluded. [37]

Cranston was delighted, and thanked Johnson for the "fine, understanding review of my book, 'The Killing of the People,'" a typographical misnomer that he repeated in several letters. "I was surprised, even startled, by the way you singled out and mentioned all of the parts of the book that I considered most important…. The 'Charles' to whom I dedicated the book died on Guadalcanal," Cranston revealed. His not emphasizing "that all this was mostly done in order to win the election of 1920" was "a point that I thought over and then did deliberately," he said. "I wanted the book to be as effective as possible right now, and I thought it might fail if it became too insulting to Republicans; and Lord knows, there is enough of that as it stands…. [Y]our criticism is…deserved." [38]

The book was widely reviewed, although neither *Time* magazine nor the *San Francisco Chronicle* had mentioned it – "and is my pop sore," Cranston told his research assistant, Erma Fischer, who had a contact at the *Chronicle*. "He has subscribed to both for years, and now angrily suspects that they have ignored it because it is not too good propaganda for Republicans. Since he is a Republican, this places him in a difficult situation and he hopefully asks me if there is maybe some other reason why they haven't review it. What shall I tell him? Seriously, can you do anything about the *Chronicle* or are they maybe sore because you have already tried to do too much?" [39]

Other favorable reviews were carried in major newspapers and national magazines like *Newsweek* – "a timely reminder of how a presidential program can be subverted through skillful, unscrupulous use of congressional machinery," its review read – and the *New Yorker*, which called it "A play-by-play account of one of the unhappiest innings in recent American history." Cranston's chronological diary-like presentation was both praised and criticized. "The drawback of the method is that it gives the reader the impression of a journey through a gallery of pictures rather than a study of a single picture," Edwin H. Blanchard wrote in the *New York Sun*. Cranston's obvious bias was stated with "conviction rather than cocksureness," though, and added to the readability. "No reader can put this book aside without the frightening conviction that a few spiteful men can wreck any peace," Sterling North wrote in the *Washington Post* and *New York Post* The *Washington Post* featured Cranston's as a book of the week with a photograph of him in army cap and uniform showing his sergeant's stripes. [40]

A review in the *Boston Herald*, however, found Cranston's use of extensive quotes without cites "a defect.... Clever, but to be read with discrimination." A commentator in the *New York World* called Cranston one of the "sentimentalists of the New Deal" who "sheds tears over the refusal of the United States to join the League of Nations" when more scholarly analysts like Columbia University professor Nathaniel Peffer, in his "courageous book," *America's Place in the World* (also published by Viking in 1945), concluded that "we should have been in perhaps even a worse case, so far as peace is concerned, if we had joined the League.... [A] ll the idealistic pacts in the world are not worth the paper they are written on, unless there is a real backing up of moral authority by money and guns," Burton Rascoe said. "Let us not allow any tricky nation to rely upon our sweet nature to take away not only our resources but our means of defending ourselves." The *Christian Science Monitor* said the book suffered "from a measure of one-sidedness" for not pointing out that Wilson, "though his was the side of the angels, stooped to the same petty methods in dealing with his adversaries." [41]

Historian Allan Nevins, who cited Cranston as "an experienced newspaper correspondent who occupied an important post in the OWI before entering the Army," said the book's diary form "loses much, but also gains something…a certain immediacy and vividness…and builds up a suspense that is lacking in topical history." Nevins also liked Cranston's punchy sub-titles that served as attentioners and kept the story moving. [42]

Other books recently had been issued on the same subject, among them *Woodrow Wilson and the Great Betrayal* by Stanford Professor Thomas A. Bailey, published by Macmillan in 1945. "It is amazing how differently two men can tell the same story," a reviewer pointed out. While Cranston blamed the debacle on "a handful of powerful plotters in the U. S. Senate," Bailey concluded that "with his own sickly hands Woodrow Wilson slew his own brain child." [43]

"Obviously, Mr. Cranston wrote his book, and his publishers timed its appearance, with the loftiest of motives," *Newsweek* book editor Karl Schriftgiesser wrote. The article was accompanied by a cartoon depicting Lodge, dubbed "The Bomb Maker," in his "irreconcilable laboratory" holding a bomb marked "reservations" in his hand. The book was "an excellent, if somewhat one-dimensional, short history of the birth and death…of the League of Nations." Schriftgiesser called Professor Bailey's version "an unsuccessful effort" to show that the outcome was due to Wilson's stubbornness. "Cranston neither twists nor turns," Schriftgiesser commented in comparing the two books. He, too, had no love for Lodge, whom he termed "a small-minded partisan politician who toyed with the aspirations of mankind in order to restore the Republican party to power." The personal hatred between Lodge and Wilson "was one of the world's tragedies," Schriftgiesser stated, and "Whatever Lodge's apologists may say in his defense, the record (as shown by Cranston and others before him) cannot be changed.... Cranston shows once again that Lodge, the Boston Brahmin, was the villain of the piece." [44]

A *New York Times Book Review* wrap-up of "books at war's end" was complimentary. "Alan Cranston's *The Killing of the Peace* has white heat in it and a sure, strong purpose," reviewer Robert van Gelder said. Cranston was in esteemed company: Other books on the list included scholarly biographies of Thomas Jefferson, Abraham Lincoln, Andrew Jackson, the men who built the Brooklyn Bridge, and Benjamin Franklin's autobiography edited by Carl Van Doren. Van Gelder may have been referring to Cranston when he described among promising newcomers "a young and startlingly capable historian," one of the authors just "mustered out of service" along with Arthur M. Schlesinger, Junior, whose *The Age of Jackson* was reviewed, and popular war cartoonist Bill Mauldin. [45]

California Democratic Congresswoman Helen Gahagan Douglas took issue with a *New York Times* statement that those who opposed the League were "liberals" and "idealists." Yes, Douglas conceded, progressives like Hiram Johnson, Robert M. LaFollette, even Nebraska's George W. Norris, had something to do with the outcome. But Cranston, she pointed out, had based "much of his case upon quotations from the editorial page of *The New York Times*." The anti-League fight in the press had been "led by Hearst and the *Chicago Tribune*" (owned by Republican isolationist Senator Medill McCormick and his brother Robert) and financed by the likes of Mellon and Frick. And, "as Alan Cranston proves beyond dispute in his new book…the same thing can happen again, with some of the very same people and forces leading us astray." The U. N. Charter would "not really breathe and live unless the Senate implements it, and unless the people of America support it with all their strength. The real fight is yet to come," she said ominously in a letter to the editor. [46]

"It is a record of how democracy went off the tracks, how [its] mechanics…were misused," a Canadian reviewer wrote. "No wonder the Senate Chaplain was said to have murmured in his official prayer every day: 'God bless the Senate. God save the people.'" [47]

Current History said the book, "flavored with personalities," exposed "the whims and political chicanery of some of" the players. A German-language Jewish weekly, *Aufbrau*, called it a "dramatic warning" of what a "small group of villains could do to thwart peace," and timely "for all men concerned about U. S. foreign policy." Editor Manfred George also congratulated Cranston for being among "progressive men…trying to prevent the abuse of a discovery [atomic energy] that could bring help and progress to the entire world." [48]

The book was a bestseller in San Francisco by the end of August, 1945, based on sales at Newbegin's book shop. The top five in fiction included James Hilton's *So Well Remembered* and C. S. Forester's *Commodore Hornblower*; in nonfiction, Cranston's was fifth behind Bill Mauldin's *Up Front* and actress Gertrude Lawrence's memoir, *A Star Danced.* [49]

The Killing of the Peace was on the *New York Times*' 1945 Christmas list of ten best books, duly noted by the *Daily Palo Alto Times*, which carried a photo of Cranston captioned, "Local boy makes good." Between the dramatic opening and closing scenes, the paper said, "are a newspaper man's terse, vivid accounts of meetings behind closed doors, congressional strategies, bitter conversations, public speeches, letters, plots, and the countless stones by which the League…was done to death." [50]

The *San Francisco Chronicle* finally carried a review by well-known literary critic Joseph Henry Jackson. He liked the fact that Cranston "let the actors...speak for themselves." Cranston must have been particularly pleased with Jackson's conclusion that, "If *The Killing of the Peace* helps Americans to orient themselves on tomorrow's parallel questions – as it most certainly should – Mr. Cranston can feel he has performed a notable service." [51]

Free World focused on the book's relevance to the "dramatic emergence of the atomic bomb, [and] its implications for the future of mankind.... It is becoming increasingly clear that a solidly integrated international organization must be established, lest the world be faced with the danger of utter destruction." The Senate's quick ratification of the United Nations Charter was evidence of the "tremendous strides made by the American people in grasping the true meaning" of the challenges. "International cooperation and world organization are rapidly becoming generally accepted concepts.... If the peace of 1945 is to be preserved, the people must maintain a constant vigil over the behavior of their representatives and governments. This is in line with one of the main lessons contained in Mr. Cranston's book." Cranston in fact would now embark on a crusade to carry those messages forward. [52]

In October he was invited to participate in a prestigious book fair sponsored by the *Boston Herald.* It would feature the "1,000 Best Books of the Year" (a special attraction was actor Frank Fay, then appearing on Broadway in *Harvey*). Cranston was singled out as one of the authors who would appear in person. The *Herald* called his "brilliant, forthright book...highly relevant to the peace problems of today." [53]

William Cranston – "at the request of my son" – entered the book in the fifteenth annual California Book Award contest sponsored by the Commonwealth Club of California in 1946. "The book was written while Alan was traveling about the United States as an instructor in Army orientation," Cranston told the club, mentioning that his son planned to return to California "to establish his home." Cranston's book was not honored, but a biography of one of its "villains," Theodore Roosevelt, was. [54]

Cranston and Geneva had moved back to their apartment at 120 C Street N. E. in Washington by November, 1945. Cranston advised his agent of their change of address "for all those huge royalty checks I expect you to start sending the day after tomorrow," a portion of which were due his researcher. To Fischer he wrote, "Don't expect anything fabulous – or anything. I haven't had any recent report on sales but it has not gone into a second edition yet. All reviews are favorable so in the end that should mean something – maybe." [55]

By February, 1946, however, Viking had decided to reduce its overstock and retain only enough copies to "handle the small orders now coming in." Cranston was given the chance to buy copies for 25 to 50 cents – he bought 125 copies, "astounding bargains," he joked. The book price was reduced from $2.50 to $1.39.

At the end of that year, Viking sent him a copy of a news article, commenting, "There's a moral there somewhere, but it's somewhat elusive." The story concerned a French interpreter seeking work at the U. N. who had been attacked on a New York subway train and beaten up by six American sailors. The victim was Serge Michel, a thirty-four-year-old former officer who had headed a counter-intelligence mission with the American 3rd Army in Europe. "Mr. Michel's troubles began at

12:15 a.m., Dec. 5, soon after he boarded an Independent subway train at 181st Street," the account said. "He was reading a book, *Killing of the Peace*, which he had borrowed from the U. N. library, and looked up casually when six sailors from the USS *Kearsarge* boarded the train at 125th Street and sat opposite him.... One of the sailors, he said in his report, got up and knocked the book to the floor. Retrieving the volume, he protested. The sailors, he said, fell upon him. They struck him on the nose and forehead and kicked his shins. Mr. Michel remembered old boxing lessons and tried to protect his head and keep his feet.... He noted that other passengers in the car looked on with indifference." Michel determined to have the attackers arrested and confronted them on the platform at the 59th Street station. A sixty-eight-year-old witness who remarked that he wished he were younger and could help Michel was knocked out by one of the sailors. A plain-clothes policeman finally halted the fight. Four of the sailors were arrested, three were sentenced to two months in the workhouse, the fourth received a suspended sentence; two of the sailors got away. [56]

A month following the book's publication, however, Cranston had embarked on another mission. He had been asked to attend a conference in the small town of Dublin, New Hampshire. The experience would turn his attention fully to the threat of the atomic bomb, and shape much of the rest of his life.

The invitation stated that the conference was "to consider how best to remedy the weaknesses of the United Nations organization." It would be held around Columbus Day, October 11 to 16, at Brook House in a picturesque village near Peterborough in the shadow of Mount Monadnock at the height of the fall color season. The invitation was signed by retired Supreme Court Justice Owen J. Roberts, who had headed an inquiry into the attack on Pearl Harbor; former New Hampshire Governor Robert P. Bass; New York attorney Grenville Clark; and Thomas H. Mahony, a lay Catholic leader and Boston attorney who chaired the Massachusetts Committee for World Federation. "We are convinced that what is now needed is not general propaganda for 'world peace'...or mere generalities about saving the world from destruction, but some severe and specific thought as to what kind of international institutions are required," the conveners said. Most of the invitees generally felt that the U. N. as crafted was "behind the times and must be drastically changed in the direction of modified 'sovereignty' and federation, if we are to have any assurance of world order." The conference had been planned before the atomic bomb "fell on Japan; but the bomb seems to confirm that the time is opportune," the invitation stated. They would discuss amendments to the U. N. Charter and how to get them adopted. The conference would be private but would issue a public statement at its conclusion. [57]

The objective, in short, was to forge a pressure group of people "convinced that the world must choose now between world government and world destruction," according to a flyer describing the conference. [58]

Invitees included many influential men and women, noted politicians, jurists, educators and businessmen. Among them were: Republican Senator Styles Bridges of New Hampshire and Democrat J. W. Fulbright of Arkansas; Congressman Jerry Voorhis of California; attorney Henry B. Cabot of Boston, chairman of a "Committee of 1,000" for international organization; two young Navy lieutenants, Chicago department store and newspaper heir Marshall Field IV, and Kingman Brewster, Junior, both still in uniform (Brewster at Yale had co-founded an America First Committee advocating isolationism and later would be president of Yale and U. S. Ambassador to the Court of St. James); Marine Corps lieutenant Cord Meyer, Junior (later with the Central Intelligence Agency); Thomas K. Finletter, former assistant to Secretary of State Cordell Hull (himself an advocate of a world peace-keeping entity) and future Secretary of the Air Force; Robert D. Smythe, one of the bomb creators; landscape architect Robert Wheelwright, a board member of Federal World Government, Inc.; the Reverend Reinhold Niebuhr and other clergymen, professors, and economists. A number of writers also were asked – among them Rex Stout; poet-professor Mark Van Doren; Clarence Streit, leader of Federal Union, Inc. and author of *Union Now*; Emery Reves, author of *The Anatomy of Peace*; editors and publishers like Brigadier General Julius Ochs Adler of the *New York Times*, John K. Jessup, editorial writer for *Life* and *Fortune* magazines, *Saturday Review of Literature* editor Norman Cousins ("who looked like cupid and seemed very young then," Cranston thought), Freda Kirchwey, editor of *The Nation*, Charles Ferguson of the *Reader's Diges*t and Donovan Richardson, managing editor of the *Christian Science Monitor*. It was a carefully thought-out mixture of senior statesmen, civic leaders and young men showing potential for leadership. Cranston believed that he was invited because his book had come to the attention of Grenville Clark, whose farm retreat was nearby. [59]

Cranston also took on the job (in 1946) of forming and directing a new Council for American-Italian Affairs, which sought to develop American foreign policy with the post-war Italian government. Allen Dulles, a wartime intelligence officer who would soon head the C. I. A., was on the board of directors. [60]

Cranston initially was skeptical about some of the participants and leaders at the Dublin conference, if not about its purpose. "It took me a while to get over slight suspicions – ignorant western suspicions of the eastern elite," he would later say, admitting that, at the outset, he did not fully trust Grenville Clark, the "blue-blood" principal player in convening the conference. "He *was* the eastern elite – a Harvard University overseer, Wall Street lawyer, representing big business. I just wasn't sure quite what his motives were in the beginning. But eventually I decided that he was a great man. His motives were perfect." He also was "utterly without guile or cunning," and "shrank from the direct use of power, having no hunger for it." [61]

Clark was heir to a banking and railroad fortune and a partner with Elihu Root, Junior, in an international law firm (Root, Clark, Buckner & Ballantine). He sat on the seven-man Harvard Corporation governing board, and was a respected bipartisan advisor to presidents and cabinet members like former Secretary of War and State Elihu Root, Senior, and Henry L. Stimson, F. D. R.'s Secretary of War, on foreign policy and national defense. Clark had persuaded Theodore Roosevelt, a friend, to train volunteers to become officers in advance of World War I (the so-called Plattsburg Camp idea), and had helped draft the Selective Service Act at the outset of World War II. In 1945 he was a vigorous sixty-four (despite heart problems), an imposing, tall, distinguished-looking New Englander with an "angry red splotch" birthmark on his face "that added still more character," as Cranston described him nearly thirty years later. Clark had declined high appointments himself but he had been an aide to Stimson in the War Department, resigning on D-Day, considering that his job was over, determined to work for peace for the remainder of his life. The Dublin meeting was his first step to prevent another war, and Clark was convinced that private citizens, rather than government officials, could more effectively pressure policymakers. [62]

In *The Killing of the Peace*, Cranston had placed Root and Stimson with League enemies, reflecting on their role when making notes late one night in the Pentagon not long after Clark had resigned as Stimson's aide. They were not heroes, in Cranston's eyes. "I just wasn't sure what Clark was up to." [63]

But Clark "took a fancy to me in the course of the meeting," Cranston said of their early collaboration. "He was sort of drawing me into being active" in the cause. "What I did mostly was run errands for Grenville Clark and carry out his big ideas. I was Clark's willing – indeed eager – junior partner in work that I looked upon as enormously significant, on assignments so compelling that it was hard not to give them priority over all else. And I viewed collaboration with Clark as a classic education, something I felt I never quite got in any school." Cranston saw the job and the one with the Italian Council as short term, however, telling John Anson Ford that he hoped "to move out to Southern California to settle there within a year." The Stanford alumni magazine erroneously reported that Cranston attended the Dublin conference in "the Irish capital." [64]

Shortly before the conference, Cranston had been reading H. G. Wells whom he had admired for years. Wells had bemoaned in an essay that the world was "at the end of its tether" and life about to be extinguished. By contrast, Clark, Cranston found, was optimistic that the world could be saved. [65]

More than fifty people turned up in response to the Dublin invitation. Most were "seasoned men of affairs," as Cranston described them, but Clark, "in a way that was typical of him, invited also some younger people of energy and, perhaps, promise." They were asked at the outset to consider the best way to improve the United Nations' mission. Should they seek to amend the charter? Or propose a union of only those nations who shared the "atomic secret" and were willing to uphold rules like the U. S. Constitution, guaranteeing individual liberty? That would exclude Russia, a "grave mistake," a tentative agenda feared. It was assumed that participants believed the new charter deficient and that "drastic and novel action must be taken to achieve a really effective international organization." [66]

In the end, majority and minority reports were drawn up. The majority report, signed by thirty, called for discarding the new U. N. organization as a means "to promote world peace and order," and called for a World Federation "with limited but definite and adequate powers to prevent war." Such a federation would have a world legislative assembly, executive body, judicial tribunals and means to enforce their judgments. A U. S. Constitutional amendment might be necessary to involve the United States in such a world government. Five minority signers – who included Justice Roberts and Clarence Streit of Federal Union – agreed with those objectives but felt that the United States should explore "the possibilities of forming a nuclear union with nations where individual liberty exists." Only a few did not agree with either report. Cranston and Clark signed with the majority. [67]

Eight specific measures were proposed, based on the fact the "implications of the atomic bomb are appalling" and there was "no presently known adequate defense against" its use. A World Federation could not only control the bomb but other major weapons, by inspection and police forces. [68]

"Whatever may have been the efficacy of the United Nations Organization for the maintenance of international peace before August 6, 1945," when the atomic bomb was dropped, "the events of that day tragically revealed the inadequacy of that organization thereafter," the majority declaration stated. "The application of atomic energy to warfare, and impressive scientific evidence as to the consequences thereof, have made the people of the world realize that the institution of war among nations must be abolished if civilization is to continue." The necessity to act was urgent – "There is not a moment to lose." World government should be limited but have authority to prevent war. It should not be based upon treaties "establishing leagues of sovereign states," as the United Nations did. Rather, it should provide minimum centralized control, allowing maximum self-government by nations. [69]

The declaration hit front pages of newspapers nationwide and generated numerous editorials. Cranston was photographed in the *Manchester Union* with conference participants, described in news accounts as "thoughtful," "prominent," "distinguished." "Dublin plan asks control of A-bomb," a *Boston Herald* headline read. The *New York Times* carried the story on the front page under the headline, "World government is urged to bar ruin in atomic war." Its article noted that eight of those signing the majority report were "veterans of the war." "[T]he atomic bomb…dominated the conference," *Times* correspondent William M. Blair wrote. "A committee headed by Alan Cranston, former Army sergeant and correspondent for 'Yank,' will lay the proposals before President Truman and Secretary of State [James F.] Byrnes." The resolutions also would be sent to the president, his cabinet, Congress, the governors of the forty-eight states and members of the U. N. assembly. [70]

Free World predicted that the meeting site, Brook House, "may someday become an international shrine. Whatever the result of this meeting may be," its coverage stated, "it demonstrates at least how deeply the necessity of world government has impressed opinion leaders in this country." [71]

One of the physicists who developed the bomb, Doctor J. R. Oppenheimer, had stated publicly that 40 million Americans in congested centers would be destroyed by one bomb, which might seem "fantastic, but the scientists who are most familiar with the weapon are alarmed the most," the *Boston Herald* editorialized. Such predictions "would have exposed them to ridicule" before the experience of Hiroshima and Nagasaki. It called the Dublin conferees "an admirable group, influenced profoundly by the possibility of" the bomb's destructiveness." A *Herald* reporter had come away "from the Dublin inn with the conviction that the two atomic bombs already exploded were merely 'rudimentary' in comparison with those which could be manufactured soon." The conferees had based "their fear…on unimpeachable scientific evidence…. It is not a nightmare that is disturbing our best minds," the editorial stated, "but a sinister, demonstrated phenomenon, laid bare by the cold light of science." [72]

Albert Einstein, the esteemed theoretical physicist whose basic science had paved the way for explorations in nuclear physics, had said in an interview for *Atlantic*

Monthly that the world no longer could postpone creating a world government to control the bomb. The "appalling, intolerable alternative" was war, "ending with one supreme power dominating all others." And Einstein, an editorial in the *Virginian Pilot* said, "is not only an abstract scientist. He is also the kind of warm and genial human being any man would enjoy as a neighbor. He appreciates the enormity of the 'menace' he describes." National sovereignty was the one great obstacle to any world-security organization. With world government, there would be no reason to wage war, the editorial rationalized, because there would be "no real opponent to fight." The urgency to control the bomb was based on the fact that, as scientists warned, "we shall not have the secret very long," it would be known in other industrial nations within a few years, and "a new-era armament race may be in full stride," the newspaper predicted. [73]

Some detractors nevertheless thought the conference a "meaningless gesture," as the Columbus, Ohio, *State Journal* put it, pointing out that the United Nations had not yet functioned as an organization, and not all participating countries had ratified the charter. The U. N. still was "at best a visionary dream of possibilities," based on the "inability of its members to see eye to eye, and the adamant determination of certain big powers to rule the roost and ignore the little fellows. Nothing that will be said or done at the New Hampshire gathering will change that." Other editorials derided the "Innocents of Dublin," "The Dublin Utopia," "A Far-off Ideal," calling it "The Wrong Approach." [74]

The *Washington Evening Star* stated that "the emergence of the atomic age has profoundly altered the character of the world. The old international society which might have been regulated by the mechanisms of the U. N. O. no longer exists." The conference had underscored the "terrible menace…unveiled on August 6 at Hiroshima," and served a constructive purpose in pointing out inadequacies of the fledgling international organization. Give it a chance, the *Star* felt. [75]

"There is a new disease which seems to be sweeping the country," Major George Fielding Eliot, a retired army officer and journalist, wrote in an opinion piece for the *New York Herald Tribune*. "For lack of a better name, we might call it 'atomic jitters.'" The "revolutionary discovery" could be "made to serve mankind." But it would "take years of hard work to find methods by which it may be controlled." The Dublin group, "after listening to scientific prophecies of what might happen to us, came to the astonishing conclusion that we should throw away our present international security organization" and replace it with world government – "shear panic, supported by very little common sense." He disparaged the possibility that Congress would approve the Dublin proposals. President Truman, however, on July 4 had himself spoken of the need for a "republic of the world," as the *Washington Post* pointed out in an editorial concluding, "The fact that the minds of men are astir with the new challenge cannot be overlooked in Congress." [76]

The conference was forced to issue responses to editorial criticism in the *New York Times* and *Herald Tribune*. Conferee Conrad Hobbs, director of the Massachusetts Committee for World Federation, defended the Dublin proposals in a letter to the *Times*. The conference "never suggested 'scrapping' the United Nations Organization," as a statement signed by twenty people headed by Karl T. Compton, president of the Massachusetts Institute of Technology, had implied. Their view was that the "shocking" Dublin declaration would "sow disillusionment and uncertainty in the minds of the American people" at the critical moment when the U. N. was being set up. Hobbs retorted that the U. N. was the most promising approach to peace-keeping then in place but "a weak reed on which to lean…in this new age of atomic energy. If the American people believe that it has in it a sufficiently stout staff, it is laboring under a dangerous delusion," Hobbs warned. "Would it not be wiser to face the facts, however disconcerting they may be?"[77]

Cranston, at the climax of heated debate between advocates of limiting international law to the Atlantic world and those (led by Clark) who wanted world law, had quoted George Washington. He chose Washington's remarks to the American Constitutional Convention at a turning point when pessimists who considered federal union an impractical dream were about to prevail at Philadelphia. "It is too probable that no plan we propose will be adopted," Washington had said. "Perhaps another dreadful conflict is to be sustained. But if, to please the people, we offer that which we ourselves disapprove, how can we afterward defend our work? Let us raise a standard to which the wise and honest can repair." The words symbolized what Clark espoused, Cranston came to realize, and Clark's high standards for overcoming obstacles would become an inspiration to the younger man. [78]

Cranston's taking the initiative and interceding in the fractious debate with an *á propos* quote impressed Clark, and he chose Cranston to chair a committee charged with convening other meetings and carrying the message forward. It pointedly was composed largely of veterans of the recent war.

The relationship between the senior statesman and Cranston would grow into one of affection and mutual respect. Cranston would later say that he did not feel closer to any other man except his father. But Clark's formality in referring to people as Mr., Mrs. or Miss caused Cranston to wonder whether he could use any other form of address with Clark. One warm afternoon when Cranston was visiting the Clark farm, the two went swimming nude in a secluded pond in the woods. "As we were dressing, I asked him what I should call him," Cranston recorded. "'An older man is usually complimented when a younger one feels at ease enough to call him by his first name,'" Clark replied. Cranston thereafter called him "Grenny." Cranston and Geneva would spend many weekends at the Clarks' old farmhouse with its fireplaces, rooms filled with books and Audubon prints, and Cranston was invited to their Long Island home and Clark's private men's clubs in New York City. Clark, Cranston came to appreciate, was a wise and thoughtful man who "instilled a sense of confidence" that he could do what he undertook to accomplish. He considered "every foreseeable" eventuality when conceiving ways to achieve world peace and law. "It was a thrill to watch his mind," which manifested qualities of both a corporate attorney and "a stern and exacting military man," as Clark posited and examined the widest array of options. He could grasp minute details while casting "his mind out beyond the horizons to the edge of infinity," Cranston observed. He picked up Clark's habit of keeping a yellow legal pad handy to jot down thoughts. Clark's capacity to instantly change tack also astonished the younger man – "suddenly dropping everything for a swim or a stroll right in the midst of a vital task facing an impending deadline…sometimes plainly to give his mind an absolute rest," as well as his heart, on orders from his doctor and pressure from his wife. [79]

Cranston began to be convinced that Clark might achieve what he set out to do and that "world law indeed would come." Some thirty years later, Cranston saw that, while Clark's vision had not been fulfilled in his lifetime, he had laid the foundations for world law, and Cranston still believed that it would come to pass. Clark's insistence on using the term "world government" had been a mistake, however, Cranston thought. "Those two words meant to others something quite different from what they meant to him," arousing "visions of a vast super-state interfering in national affairs and private lives," which Clark assuredly did not want. That was why "*closely defined and limited powers*" had been part of the Dublin declaration, restricted to preventing war. The world constitution that Clark wrote with law student Louis B. Sohn reflected those limitations, just as the U. S. Constitution limited the powers of government. [80]

After the conference, Cranston set out to enlist friends and influential people in support of the concept, sending the declaration to more than 100 people. "If you find it worthwhile, I wish you would add your name to the growing list of prominent persons who have endorsed the majority position," Cranston told John Anson Ford and San Francisco friends Doctor and Mrs. Ralph Reynolds, whom he hoped would get others to endorse it. "We are trying in a hurry to get a substantial list of citizens all over the country who will lend their names to the effort to accomplish the only thing that will prevent an atom war." [81]

"I was much interested in the resolutions that came out of the conference in Dublin," Marshall Field III (a Republican) wrote his son "Marsh" from the family-owned *Chicago Sun*. "I thoroughly agree with the majority conclusions, and you can so record me if it is of any use to your committee." Young Field's interest in moving forward prompted donations to further the cause. "From time to time now you will be getting spontaneously contributed checks in the mail to help you implement the work of our committee," Field IV wrote Cranston. "I enclose my own as one of several which I know will be forthcoming. I also enclose the first of the endorsements which I undertook to obtain." Field also suggested that the Dublin group "try to testify before the 11-man [congressional] committee recently appointed to investigate and control atomic energy." He enclosed a check for $500, for which Cranston thanked him. "I was wondering how I was going to pay my phone bill," he joked. "I'll be glad when you are closer by [at the University of Virginia Law School]...so you can help me spend the money wisely. Your father is a very welcome addition to the list," he added. Other funds had come in from Clark, and Cranston himself had gotten, among others, Raymond Gram Swing, well-known radio commentator, and Mrs. Gifford Pinchot, recent widow of the conservationist and Progressive Party leader, to sign on. Cranston wondered if Field would be willing to testify before the Senate Atomic Committee – "I think you'd be the best member of our present committee" to do so. "I don't want to do more than my share of public appearances," Cranston said, adding that Field's wife (from whom he was divorced in 1947) could expect "one of those bread-and-butter letters" from Geneva to thank them for their hospitality one weekend. [82]

When Cranston spoke at the opening session of the *Herald* book fair at Boston Symphony Hall October 15, he told the audience that he had just come from a conference attended by statesmen and scientists "with the utter conviction that we had no hope of survival unless we banded together into a world government with at least sufficient power to control the atomic bomb," an account written by Mary McGrory, a book reviewer for the *Herald*, reported. (McGrory would go on to become a widely-read, 1975 Pulitzer Prize-winning syndicated Washington columnist.) "Prophesying that the war which just ended would be nothing to the one that would start with the dropping of an atomic bomb, Cranston emphasized that such an organization must be made up of all nations with industrial power to prepare the bomb in secret," McGrory quoted him as saying. Cranston was photographed with notables like novelist Kenneth Roberts and other celebrities, including "rotund" *Chicago Daily News* war correspondent Robert Casey who "recounted hilarious stories of evading censorship on two continents." Cranston, standing next to Casey, towered over the others in the photograph. "Record crowds packed the" fair, McGrory recorded, to see "four famous stars of the stage [including songstress Sophie Tucker] and to hear noted authors discuss topics that ranged from the book-ban in Boston to trade prospects in the Far East and the future of the atomic bomb." [83]

To keep the Dublin momentum going, participants arranged follow-up meetings, like one called by Raymond Gram Swing and Norman Cousins to discuss "social and political implications of atomic energy" at the home of advertising mogul Albert Lasker on Beekman Place in New York. [84]

Other world-federation groups were enlisted to support the Dublin concept as a united front. "It seems that our ideas are 100 percent in harmony," Clark wrote Ulric Bell, executive vice president of Americans United for World Organization, Inc., (A. U.) after a telephone conversation at which Cranston was present. "Teamwork" would move the cause forward, and Cranston suggested a public announcement of unity among the various groups. Clark declined an offer to sit on the A. U. board but recommended Cranston, who joined it (as did a number of other Dublin participants). "He is keen and capable on the subject and a fine fellow," Clark said. Meanwhile, Clark was working on specific amendments to the U. N. Charter to submit to the president, Congress and the U. N. Assembly in January, 1946. Worldwide exposure would be an "acid test" of whether amendments might be obtainable. [85]

Clark sent the declaration to Anthony Eden, a member of Britain's Parliament, who had spoken to the issue in the House of Commons. "We are moving towards a World Federal Government," Clark wrote him, "and the faster we move, the better for the world." He asked Eden's support for changes in the way delegates to the General Assembly were chosen – to "weighted representation," a voting formula based on a nation's developed status rather than one-vote-per-member-country. Eden's "superb speech" on November 22, 1945, Clark said, was "a great contribution" to the cause and "encouraging beyond measure." Britain's Secretary for Foreign Affairs Ernest Bevin also had addressed the issue of world government in an "enlightened, far-reaching" speech to the Commons, and could be helpful in advocating changes in the U. N. charter. The same plea was made to Canadian Prime Minister W. L. Mackenzie King who had spoken to his House of Commons of the need for serious consideration of some form of world government. Clark wrote King that he had been "taking polls on the subject" and was "convinced that somewhere between 6 to 8 out of every 10 people are now in favor of world government." Cranston had polled an audience in Youngstown, Ohio, with similar results, and a city-wide poll subsequently was conducted of 500 families in hopes that it would "answer the question conclusively as to whether or not the people are now ready for world government," the pollster told Cranston in late December, 1945. A postscript asked Cranston, "How was the meeting with the President?" [86]

A small group, Cranston among them, had met with President Truman – the first president whom he actually met in person – December 20 for thirty minutes and had a "forthright discussion" of the Dublin plans. "The meeting with the President was surprisingly good," Cranston said. "He doesn't want to make his position known publicly until he can get prior agreement with other nations, if possible, but he does seem to have come to the conclusion that the alternative to world government is atomic warfare of undreamed violence. We all felt very encouraged." [87]

Indications of popular opinion in favor of world government would be an important asset to the cause. The Youngstown pollster hoped that British Foreign Secretary Bevin would conduct house-to-house polls in England, and had had "the opportunity to speak at some length to Mssrs. Molotov [Soviet Foreign Minister] and [U. S. Secretary of State] Byrnes about world government." [88]

Support also came from members of Congress to whom Cranston had sent the declaration. California Democrat Jerry Voorhis, (who had been a lecturer at Pomona when Geneva was a student there), put the Dublin statement in the *Congressional Record*. "The atomic bomb gives us leverage we have never had before" to advocate world government, Voorhis wrote Cranston. Democratic Representative Estes Kefauver of Tennessee asked Cranston to come and talk to him about the matter, saying, "I read your book with a great deal of interest and appreciation. You did a great job and I am sure it will serve a most useful purpose." [89]

Concern about the U. N.'s flaws was expressed in a letter possibly written by President Roosevelt's former Undersecretary of State Sumner Welles who had been dominant in designing the new U. N. as Roosevelt's principal representative. A critic of U. S. military might clothed as protecting American business interests abroad, Welles blamed the U. N.'s potential weakness on "the quarreling and bickering between the Big Three [U. S., U. S. S. R., and Great Britain] and the imperialist policies which they have been following, even before the U. N. O. is set up." If those nations could not agree, there was no possible chance of the organization's succeeding, and "people have begun to condition themselves for a Third World War." Welles, if author of the letter, feared America's foreign policies:

"Frankly, my friend, when I think of the tremendous publicity effort which we made for the high ideals with which we started World War II, and now look at the depth at which those ideals have been buried, and the policies which our country is now pursuing all over the world, I must acknowledge that I am heartsick. I am reminded again of that unforgettable morning on the apron of Lambert Field [airport in St. Louis] when we spoke of what would happen to this country in case of the death of F. D. R. It has happened." [90]

Cranston went on the lecture circuit, using a publicist to arrange appearances. "Mr. Cranston presents a forthright analysis of the prospects – dark and bright – of the atom age so suddenly thrust upon us," a flyer advertising his talk stated. He also gave "blunt warnings" about how the "people of the United States possess the power to destroy the United Nations and world peace" or strengthen it. He spoke to town meetings, clubs, organizations, any group that would listen, and was often photographed speaking in his sergeant's uniform. [91]

He became a spokesman for the Dublin declaration, often quoted by the media. He wrote a letter to the *New York Times* on establishing a regulatory U. S. Atomic Energy Commission and international authority tied to the U. N. that could "inspect, control and manage all phases of atomic energy" by treaty. His focus was an issue to which he would devote the rest of his life – the extent to which nations should keep or give up some of their *sovereignty*. A proposed treaty would ban the bomb, but the U. S. and Soviet Union disagreed over how that would be enforced. It threatened "calamity," Cranston said, because the United States and other nations did not trust "the Russian plan as sufficiently reliable to justify…ceasing the manufacture of atomic bombs or other major weapons." If the impasse were not broken, "nothing less than a great armament race, not only in atomic bombs, but in all other weapons, is impending," Cranston warned. [92]

His group urged "weighted voting" in the U. N. General Assembly. That would eliminate the power of one nation's veto. "Weighted voting" would not be based solely on population but take into account natural and industrial resources and other factors. It was up to the United States to push such a change, and to back general disarmament and "an effective world police force." There was an immediate need, however, Cranston's letter to the *Times* concluded, to cease "the shocking mutual recriminations between Russia and the United States…. People and nations can get along even if they have very different governmental, social and economic ideas," but it was as impossible for nations to negotiate as it was for individuals "if they indulge in daily insults." The U. S. needed to understand Russia and her history better, and Russia needed to understand that the U. S. was "not trying to coerce her by the atomic bomb or otherwise." [93]

A second conference was held at Princeton, New Jersey, January 11 and 12, 1946, specifically to review proposed amendments to the U. N. Charter. Kingman Brewster, Junior, wanted "to get this world-government discussion down out of the clouds of 'good causes' and noble ends to the concrete solid level of ways and means." "Hope you gave my best to Harry," he joked of Cranston's recent meeting with Truman, reminding Cranston that that there was "no 's' in Kingman." "I thought you were many Kings," Cranston retorted. In another note, Cranston said, "I would like to argue you out of going to law school." Brewster went anyway (graduating *magna cum laude* from Harvard Law School in 1948), and said that he could not participate much in person because of the demands of law school. Cranston replied that he would be glad to have Brewster's ideas at any time, particularly "because I think you and I have usually agreed," and, if not, Cranston "would like to know it, so I could examine the differences." [94]

Others shared skepticism about radical amendments to the U. N. charter but favored strengthening its authority. The editor of the *Des Moines Register and Tribune* very much hoped that the group would "exhibit the good sense not to get into slugging matches with each other. The splintering of conscientious supporters of a right cause has too often spelled futility." Cranston agreed. [95]

Representatives of Americans United, World Federalists and other groups were among those participating in the Princeton meeting. Rex Stout, who headed a Writers' Board of authors and playwrights, asked the group to review a petition that they intended to send the President of the United States. John Atkinson, still a lieutenant in the service, was among the eighty people who attended. [96]

Albert Einstein, then at the Institute for Advanced Study, participated one day at the Princeton meeting. He had made his views known in public statements, one of which was printed in the program for an "Atomic Age Dinner" sponsored by Americans United in November, 1945, whose cover had a photograph of an atomic cloud. "I can only repeat the statement I have made at various times that, in my opinion, the only way in which mankind can save itself from destruction is by the organization of a world government," Einstein reiterated. "The weapons of modern warfare have developed to such a degree that it seems probable that in another world war, the victor would suffer only less than the vanquished. As long as there are sovereign states with their separate armaments, the prevention of war is well nigh impossible." The only solution, he believed, was "a reign of law around the earth." [97]

Cranston presided at the Princeton meeting. "Now and then there would be a difference of opinion over how to express some part of a statement," he recalled, "and I'd ask for a show of hands, yes or no, to decide it. I noticed after a bit that Einstein would vote 'yes' and then 'no' on the same issue. So I asked him during the coffee break why he was doing that," Cranston laughed of the great scientist's response. "He was this *gentle* man who had produced the theories that led to the atomic bomb. And he said with this sort of embarrassed smile, 'They're such wonderful people on both sides. I just can't vote against *any* of them!'" [98]

Participants adopted proposed amendments to the U. N. charter aimed at turning it into a world-governing body with military and inspection forces to maintain peace. Changes would have abolished veto power (by making the Security Council merely an executive committee of the Assembly), barred bloc voting by national groups, and selected delegates by the formula weighing population plus other factors. That gave the "Big Three" – Russia, Britain and the United States – an initial sixty-five members apiece in the Assembly, rendering the veto unnecessary. Another change gave an International Court of Justice authority to interpret the charter. The proposed amendments were put into a petition to U. N. General Assembly members who were then meeting for the first time in London. A press release quoted Cranston and Einstein as saying "there was no time to lose." While the drafting committee felt its amendments needed refining, it decided to circulate the petition for signatures in order to get some specific proposals under public discussion. [99]

Social philosopher Lewis Mumford was concerned about "weighted representation" unless there were "equality between small and great nations." A "joker" in the proposal "restored the veto power to the Big Three" nations who "might place themselves above the law.... However weighty the political and military responsibilities of the Big Three," he noted, "we must remember that they represent only a fraction of mankind, considerably less than a quarter." He also suggested a "Chamber of Culture" dealing with "all questions of language, literature, art, religion and science" in which "equality would not be a mere fiction." Mumford would continue to be an active supporter of world government as "the only effective means of controlling atomic weapons and atomic energy." [100]

Cranston, the "youthful veteran and author," as the *Boston Herald* described him, was charged with presenting the petition at the London meeting of the U. N. Assembly. Cranston signed it although he had reservations about some of the provisions, as he told Brewster less than an hour before setting off for London, agreeing that the "important thing is to get the discussion down out of the clouds." Cranston told Clark that he hoped amendments' backers would unify behind reforming the existing United Nations. Cord Meyer had been "one of those who felt we should not work through the U. N. O. but should start from scratch by calling a world constitutional convention," Cranston reminded Clark. "We must be very certain that all who go to London give the impression that we are pledging full faith in the U. N. O., provided it is found possible to strengthen it." Indeed, an article in the *New York Times* reported that "advocates of World Government do not seek to throw away U. N. O. but to build upon it…a much more realistic approach." [101]

Clark, a devoted family man, insisted that Geneva accompany Cranston and paid her expenses to London. Orson Welles had to write the U. S. Passport office, requesting that Geneva be granted a passport as an employee for his column. "I am exceedingly anxious that she go to London for me," Welles said, "so that I may obtain accurate and up to the minute information on United Nations activities. It seems to me exceedingly important that the American people be given all possible opportunities to learn as much as possible about this vital organization." The Cranstons flew to England on a Pan-American Clipper and stayed at the Savoy Hotel in the Strand. They would remain in England after the Assembly adjourned to sound out public opinion. "Alan Cranston left for London by plane on February 7, taking with him 1,000 copies of the petition," Clark told signers. Cranston's expenses were paid by some Dublin participants, for which Cranston and Clark expressed thanks. Clark hoped that conversations with British leaders and world-government advocates would make the trip "well worthwhile." [102]

"A few days ago a plane took off from America, flew over the Atlantic, and landed at London," one news account reported. "Aboard was Alan Cranston, who had a proposal which he wished to lay before the United Nations delegates." The world, however, was "not yet ready for such an experiment in brotherhood," the Charleston, South Carolina, *Post* editorialized, conceding that the U. N. as currently composed was "hardly more…than an exalted debating society" because of the "fatal flaw," the right to veto. Few Americans, the editorial said, "would be willing to have their country's freedom of action restrained from the outside." Such a "super-state" might one day come into being after nations were educated "away from nationalistic traditions," but that was decades away. Why had Cranston "deemed it so necessary to fly to the U. N. O. Assembly," the paper wondered? "There is plenty of time ahead." Cranston's mission was widely publicized, including in his hometown newspaper, which said that he was expected back in California after his journey. [103]

Cranston worked hard in London to make contacts at the highest levels. He and Geneva had a pass to U. N. meetings, and Cranston to the House of Commons gallery. Clark was not sanguine that the Assembly would do much in that first session, however, writing Cranston February 13, "I feel pretty sure that none of our stuffy delegation will propose consideration of such amendments, the State Department being hostile or indifferent and Truman probably unwilling to push anything of the sort. Therefore it seems that the best chance lies with the British." A "British-Russian showdown, as to the Dardanelles, Middle East and Mediterranean" was likely, Clark predicted, and it was in Britain's interest to get some "machinery with which to stand up to Russia and arrange a compromise," as it had "no assurance of support from the rest of the world." He hoped that "beefy, spectacled" Foreign Affairs Secretary Ernest Bevin, as *Life* magazine described him, would "put forward something definite to that end." Clark also recommended an article by British scientist Julian Huxley in the *New York Times* magazine of February 10, "Is war instinctive and inevitable?" "It might pay to see him," Clark suggested among others to whom he referred Cranston. "You'll have plenty of people to see and I think you'll find *somewhere* some real support," he hoped. [104]

Cranston personally spoke with and presented the petition to international leaders like Paul Henri Spaak, the Assembly's first president, and a Russian diplomat five years older than Cranston named Andrei Gromyko, then Soviet Ambassador to the United States. "This very young man was on his way to power," Cranston observed. He also helped write three speeches on world law that were delivered to the Assembly by General Carlos P. Romulo, a founder of the Philippine Republic and its ambassador to the U. N. "Unless we empower it with the rule of law," Romulo argued on behalf of small nations, "the U. N. will become a hollow shell." [105]

A problem, Cranston would find, was the multiplicity of groups with differing agenda. An enthusiast for the World Unity Movement, a Corporal Kraus, wrote Cranston after reading about his mission, offering to help. "Great efforts" were underway in Britain to push world government, Kraus said. Could Cranston act as a link between England and America? Cranston spoke to one group to which Kraus brought a Communist friend – "with whom I often have fierce arguments…. He was greatly impressed by your obvious sincerity and astonished that there is in high American circles such support for a genuine world-government." Attendance at the meeting, though, was small, indicative of public apathy, Kraus said, asking that Cranston send his promotional booklet to others, including the Fabian Society. A second meeting that Cranston addressed "was the best on world government I have attended so far," Kraus wrote. But even the heads of big peace organizations were "thinking in the old Bevin-Molotov lines, as pointed out by [British author] J. B. Priestly," he moaned, thus a "pessimism and general hesitancy of them to make decisions." "As a Middle European," Kraus added, "I think that links can definitely be achieved with the Russian people, other than diplomatic, and that we will not have to wait for a Trade Union Congress to take place in two years." He hoped that Cranston and his wife were "keeping well in spite of ice, snow and coal famine." [106]

Cranston talked to members of Federal Union, an outgrowth of proposals by American journalist Clarence Streit early in the war, in a village outside of London. His host promised to drive him back to town afterward if he did "not mind arriving back at the Savoy in one of our little cars that is somewhat war weary." The audience, he added, would "not be a highly intelligent" one but would include "quite ordinary middle class 'commuters,'" both pro- and con- union, most of them conservative politically. "Therefore I do feel that you will be able to gauge the opinion of the average Britisher who rather apathetically plays such a large part in our affairs. I am sure you will be able to make your very-well-chosen remarks about Russia," he added, "as my sister, who belongs to the big C [Communist] category, is suspicious, to say the least." The meeting was a greater success than expected (several Members of Parliament were present), sparking a lengthy discussion after the Cranstons had left, and "there were many who wanted to hear much more from you. I pushed home your remarks about the necessity of the people giving their support," his host said. "My sister was most disappointed that she could not argue with you further." [107]

Actor Laurence Olivier apologized from the New Theatre for not answering a letter from Cranston sooner requesting a meeting. "I am so tiresomely busy that I am afraid this week is out of the question," Olivier said, but "Would you and your wife care to have a cup of tea in my dressing room here next Thursday week – or better still, on Saturday?" he asked. "I would so much like to meet you. I am sorry to be so unaccommodating, but my hands are tied with a bit too much on them just now!" Whether the Cranstons went to his dressing room was not recorded.[108]

Clark was elated with Cranston's report of what he was doing. "Great work, hope you can induce British government to place discussion of charter amendment on agenda for September session" of the U. N. Assembly, Clark telegraphed March 2, 1946. "Little hope our government will do so. Best hope with British.... Good luck." Clark's next step was to propose a "Committee for Limited World Government" – "Needless to say, everyone would expect you to be Chairman of the Organization Committee," he wrote Cranston. [109]

Winston Churchill, who the year before had been succeeded as Prime Minister by Labour leader Clement Attlee, had made a speech that Cranston felt would "clear the air, show the British they'd better work for nothing less than world government," he wrote Louis Sohn from London. Churchill had stated, when stepping down after five years as Britain's inspiring war leader: "Above all, we must labour that the world organization which the United Nations are creating at San Francisco does not become an idle name, does not become a shield to the strong, and a mockery for the weak." [110]

Those indeed were encouraging words for Cranston, who told Sohn, "There is a good chance now that Federal Union, pretty strong here – 50 MPs have joined, and unlike F. U. in the U. S., strongly for world government – will endorse the petition I brought over, and will also try to get the British delegation to the next U. N. O. Assembly to put it on the agenda." There were real efforts to get other British organizations, prominent people, New Zealand and Australia to "get behind the movement and take the lead" if the British U. N. delegation would not. Cranston hoped that Sohn, en route to Paris, could get something similar going in France. "Please do your best, T'would be a great step forward." Cranston, too, went over to Paris to spread the message.

Cranston also wrote a treatise that Reuters news agency publicized. He was less successful in seeing Cabinet Ministers and Prime Minister Attlee. A woman friend at Reuters, Mary Seaton, tried to intercede, assuring Cranston that ministers "were by no means inaccessible to people with serious proposals for world betterment."

She wrote a short précis of the petition that she urged Cranston to send those whom he did not see in person, and she would try to "pump" them for reaction. "You have certainly made a good personal impression on the odd Labour MPs I've sounded," she told Cranston, "which is a contrast to what they think of some of the 'crazy' American pressure-groupers who come over!" [111]

Seaton put Cranston's message into a feature story entitled "World Peace for 177 Dollars?" "Some weeks ago a young American author and his attractive wife talked the officials at a New York airport into letting them bring fifty pounds excess luggage to England," it began. "'It may save the world,' pleaded Alan Cranston. He got a dubious look, a brusque, 'It'll cost you an extra 177 dollars, anyway.'" The extra weight was from the 1,000 copies of the Dublin petition. The U. N. attracted "pressure-groupers like jam does flies in summer," Seaton wrote. "So at first Cranston encountered not a few scowls or polite evasions. But he persisted. Maybe it is something patently honest about this tall, slightly bald, smiling American; maybe he lacked the crucified…look with which other pressure-groupers queer their own pitches; maybe it was that his sponsors were impressive and that he touched a chord in hearts made apprehensive by Security Council disagreements. At any rate, Cranston achieved his conversations with a number of European statesmen, got his petition into the hands of others, and later left to continue his lobbying from Paris." He was about to return to America "with fifty pounds less baggage, a little pessimism, some hope, and much enlightenment," Seaton said. [112]

"'I believe this globe is ready for world government,'" she quoted Cranston as saying. "'Responsible sections in America, Europe and China want it. Prominent Russians I have talked with are not unsympathetic. Millions feel vaguely that it must come…. But many professional diplomats are still tied to their old, sphere-of-influence fears and traditional secrecy methods and everywhere there seems to be this insidious fear of Russia. But at least,' he grinned, 'my fifty pounds excess baggage has started a lot of people thinking.'" Labour MPs, Seaton said, were "skeptical about some points in Cranston's scheme, but in a world milling uneasily between war weariness, starvation, political disruption, strikes, under-cover diplomatic pressures" for national interests, "engendered by the fact that atom-bomb manufacture outside America cannot long be delayed, Cranston's plan deserves consideration."[113]

She emphasized the proposed change permitting individuals to vote their consciences in the U. N. Assembly. That would lead to their voting by political interest rather than national interest, Cranston was quoted as saying, "so that Tories and Republicans," rightists and Socialists might vote together, and "'do much towards breaking down the present nationalist barriers…. If this is to work at all, you must bring everyone in. It's no good barring certain countries because they are fascist, though one hopes there will be effective ways of ridding the world of fascism,'" he said. He had crossed out of her draft, "himself a Socialist." Reaction in Britain, Seaton said, included doubt among MPs that the "Big Three" ever would agree to remove the Security Council veto, and skepticism about world-government support "in the States." Still, "handing me the last copy of his petition," Cranston concluded that unless nations gave up "'the old diplomatic game,'" the world would not "'be merely in the soup. We shall be floating in eternity.' He popped a London-bought Bernard Shaw anthology into his empty petitions bag, and added, 'But I think everyone is so scared, so desperately anxious for this globe to go on, that they'll see sense in time, and we'll get World Government.'"

Cranston tried to impress Britons with the degree of sympathy in the United States. In a generic letter to editors that friends circulated to the press, he remarked on Britain's "under-estimation" of the American desire for strengthening the U. N. and controlling atom bombs. "Our first impulse was to hang onto the atom 'secret' for dear life, but American public opinion, led by our physicists, is now forcing our government to seek" such controls," he stated. President Truman had told Congress in his state-of-the-union message in January, "Our ultimate security requires more than a process of consultation and compromise. It requires that we begin now to develop the U. N. O. as the representative of the world as one society." The public was "rapidly mobilizing" for a campaign to those ends, Cranston believed. *News Review*, though, candidly reported that Cranston – an "apostle" proclaiming the "gospel of the Dublin Committee, no crank world-stater" – did "not expect U. N. O. to act on this manifesto, but hopes in the long run to rouse public opinion." The problem was that "the Russians, so far, have shown no interest" in the concepts. "They have their own idea of the most desirable State," the magazine article read – "It is called 'Socialist.'" [114]

Back in America, Cranston had to admit that "most people are very skeptical, due to American and Russian hesitancy." The U. S. had "to take the lead," he wrote a supporter. To an MP in London he asked, soon after returning to the United States, "What became of your resolution denouncing Churchill and suggesting England work toward world government? Over here, things are working slowly, but I think surely in the proper direction – provided we don't get into too serious difficulties with Russia before enough people here can be sold on the idea." He had been surprised that the English had come to accept that Great Britain no longer rated as a great power, accepting that it was outstripped by Russia and the United States. In an account for the Los Altos newspaper, he also related that food, while scarcer in post-war France, was better than the English diet, and that French hotels were warm but theaters, even the Folies Bergere, were cold. He had been overseas for five weeks and discussed the Dublin amendments with hundreds of people, Clark reported to others whom he was trying to enlist to the cause. [115]

Clark was encouraged by Cranston's mission and wasted no time in getting letters off to Secretary of State Byrnes, Senator Vandenberg, by then chairman of the Senate Foreign Relations Committee, Henry Wallace, then under pressure to leave the Cabinet as Secretary of Commerce for disagreeing publicly with Truman over "being tough with Russia," and to other influential people like financier and government adviser Bernard M. Baruch, then U. S. Representative to the U. N. Atomic Energy Commission, urging them to act on the amendments, and emphasizing that the objective was "limited" world government. Clark hoped that Vandenberg could "convert" Byrnes, "if necessary," to sponsor the plan. Baruch had stated that "There must be no veto to protect those who violate their solemn agreements not to develop or use atomic energy for destructive purposes." "I know you are always interested in solutions that really go to the heart of the matter. That is your greatest quality," Clark wrote him, reiterating Baruch's views in a letter to the *New*

York Times June 23 that was inserted into the *Congressional Record.* The *Chicago Daily Tribune* called it "the latest of the devious manipulations of Grenville Clark," a man little known in the Midwest but "one of the comparatively small number of men who have actually run the United States." It pointed to inconsistencies in Clark's having argued against costly payments to World War I veterans while head of the National Economy League in 1932, and his promoting conscription in 1940. Now, the *Tribune* sneered, Clark was promoting "the next step – the final sellout of America," forcing it to give up national sovereignty and "sign a declaration of dependence" on a world body. [116]

Actor Douglas Fairbanks, Junior, was on their side, though, telling Cranston that he was in full agreement with "the general purposes back of your organization." [117]

Cranston again went on a speaking tour for the Dublin message. He carried it to a meeting of the American U. N. delegation at Lake Success, Long Island, at the end of 1946. He also got involved with a brief move to try to locate the U. N. world headquarters at San Francisco, spearheaded by its Mayor Roger Lapham and state Attorney General Robert Kenny. Boston also was considered a possible site. Howard Leavitt Horton, who had heard Cranston talk at the Boston Book Fair, urged him to work against that option because Boston was "the very source of isolationism." Cranston agreed, and worried that a stalemate on where the headquarters would be located might result in its going to Europe. That was thwarted in the end by John D. Rockefeller, Junior's, offer to give a plot of land along New York's East River for the headquarters, where it was built. [118]

Cranston would make other trips overseas on behalf of the Dublin committee – to India where he met Prime Minister Nehru, and to Japan. Clark would articulate his views in a book written with Louis B. Sohn, *World Peace through World Law*, which advocated a world constitution and international court. It won the American Bar Association's Gold Medal in 1959. [119]

By the end of 1946, Cranston had decided to return to California. He had mixed feelings about leaving Clark, who had come to rely on his energetic *aide de camp*. But Cranston was ready to concentrate on his own future and plans – which included making money and looking into politics as a career where, he now realized, "the great decisions" affecting mankind were made. He and Clark would remain friends, frequently consulting in lengthy transcontinental telephone calls and via mail. Cranston often reflected, when confronted with conflict or indecision, "What would 'Grenny' do? How would he approach this?" [120]

"As some citizens use campaign contributions to influence the actions of government – whether for...good reasons or bad – Clark used his awesome persuasiveness and logic combined with a sure knowledge of how to reach and move the levers of power," Cranston later wrote in a tribute to Clark. "He placed at the disposal of men occupying high office the fruits of his quiet and creative contemplation." He also worried about being corrupted by power, and was careful to avoid it, Cranston noticed. It was remarkable "how little the nation knew of the part Clark played in shaping its destiny in the time he lived and worked," Cranston reflected. Clark once had told Secretary of War Stimson, who liked to deal with only one major problem at a time, that he could handle his job in four hours a day and spend the rest of the time in contemplation. That impressed Cranston, who openly credited Clark for having an indelible influence on his protégé and aspiring politician. The collaboration also introduced Cranston to many people in high or influential places, from famous authors to heads of state. [121]

It was while working with Clark in 1945 that Cranston came across a poem that reflected Clark's attitudes and behavior. It was by Chinese philosopher Lao-tzu, born about 604 B. C. Cranston would try to be guided by the 2,000-year-old message, conceding that it often was hard to do so as a politician seeking reelection and needing public recognition. The words, though, described Clark perfectly, Cranston thought.

> "A leader is best
> When people barely know that he exists,
> Less good when they obey and acclaim him,
> Worse when they fear and despise him.
> Fail to honor people,
> And they fail to honor you.
> But of a good leader, who talks little,
> When his work is done, his aim fulfilled,
> They will all say, 'We did this ourselves.'" [122]

As to a similar influence on his own philosophy, Cranston would later say in an interview:

> "When I think back over the books which have inspired me and influenced the way I've tried to live my life, one that comes to mind is Louis Fischer's magnificent biography of Mohandas Gandhi. I can think of few leaders whose wisdom and teachings have greater relevance for a time when so many of us are giving serious thought to the abuse of power and the ever-constant threat of nuclear warfare [1981].... Gandhi's attitude toward power is indeed a humbling one: 'Banish the idea [to] capture power, and you will be able to guide power and keep it on the right path.' Fischer's own words about Gandhi are worth reflecting upon: 'Power gave him no pleasure; he had no distorted psychology to feed. The result was a relaxed man.'" [123]

Before returning West, Cranston became involved in a political campaign in California and tapped his friends to help financially.

"I hate like hell to write you this letter, debated it some time, decided I should anyway," he wrote Marshall Field IV in October, 1946. Will Rogers, Junior, son of the popular humorist, was running for Senate against incumbent Republican William Knowland, and "having a rather rough time," Cranston said. "The boys in California who adhere to the C. P. [Communist Party] line are very strong, and are refusing to support Bill [Rogers] because he does not adhere to the line. By attacking him, they have confused the issue and deprived him of the support of many good liberals who under normal circumstances would be helping him get elected. It's a critical race, for California is one of the few states not already decided one way or another.... A few thousand votes in California, Massachusetts, Kentucky and Montana will decide whether the Republicans or the Democrats rule the Senate." [124]

A key concern was that if Republicans controlled the Senate as well as the House, they would enact a succession bill that would make Republican House Speaker Joe Martin President in the event that something happened to President Truman. "[T]he race is important because Rogers has a good voting record in the House, and is making his campaign on behalf, pretty much, of the things I think you and I are agreed on, whereas Knowland (appointed to succeed Hiram Johnson when he died) is campaigning on this slogan: 'KEEP THE ATOM BOMB SECRET' – with absolutely no enlightened discussion of what else we must do.... Republicans have poured dough into California, and Knowland posters, loudspeaker, radio hours are overwhelming. Meanwhile, deprived of the support he is entitled to expect, the Rogers campaign badly needs help for some dynamic, last-minute work." If Field and anybody he knew would rush checks "payable to 'Eddie Cantor, Trustee,'" Cranston would wire Rogers' headquarters that they were on the way – time and money were very short. Whether or not Field helped, Rogers lost the Senate race (Knowland served until 1958).

Cranston also communicated with Lee Falk, who had tried to buy a house in California. "Natcherly you couldn't find an adequate homestead without enlisting the aid of the Cranston Realty company, you fathead," Cranston joked. "We plan to move there as soon as the United Nations covers the ground I'm here to work on," he wrote October 31, 1946. They hoped to be home by Christmas. "We will drive out in our brand new 1946 Nash! – equipped with the screwiest gadgets, each of which boosted the price another 99$99 above the O. P. A. ceiling, all legally, of course. We plan to live around San Francisco at first, probably Los Altos till we find a place of our own." He wished that Falk would join them. "Ain't it lovely there?" Cranston said. [125]

Falk meanwhile had gotten married. Al Lomax was "sore as hell at you for not telling him" and promised "to make up a dirty ballad about you." Lomax, Cranston reported, was "spending all his time on Peoples' Songs (an outfit, you know) and it apparently is growing and thriving." Meanwhile, would Falk help with the Rogers campaign? Knowland was "a louse and a Republican," and Rogers the "guy who, when a member of the House, took a swing at one Representative E. E. Cox, who then proceeded to pull Bill's hair." Cranston's offer to help with fundraising in the East had been minimally successful. "Haven't had too much luck, tho've raised some," he told Falk, reminding him that he (Cranston) had an "almost religious attitude toward your millions...appreciating but declining your generous offers to lend me $ whenever it appeared I might need some, etc., but that California campaign is so crucial that I hereby ask you if you're willing to make a contribution." Rogers, he added, "had a voting record in the House like you or I would have."

A few months later, Cranston set off across the country to begin a new career that might let him prove that point.

William MacGregor Cranston, Alan's father, 1900. Born in 1879, he grew up in San Francisco, graduated in Stanford University's eighth class, 1901, and became a successful real-estate businessman. *R. H. Furman Photo, San Francisco. Alan Cranston Papers. Courtesy of The Bancroft Library, University of California, Berkeley. All photos are from same source unless cited otherwise. Credits where known are given.*

Carol Dixon Cranston, Alan's mother, 1900. Born in 1878, she was the daughter of a Sacramento physician. She and William Cranston married in 1903.

Cranston's grandfather and grandmother, Robert Dickie Cranston (1849-1916) and Jeannie MacGregor Cranston, Virginia City, Nevada, about the time of their marriage in 1872.

Houses built in the 1890s by Robert Dickie Cranston, early developer of San Francisco's Haight-Ashbury neighborhood, showing cable car to western San Francisco that ran from Market Street to Golden Gate Park via Ellis Street, 1892. *M. Le. Bunn & Co. Photo, San Francisco.*

Alan Cranston, age 10, and sister Ruth Eleanor ("R. E."), age 15, at Los Altos home, 1924.

SOMEBODY IS ALWAYS TAKING THE JOY OUT OF LIFE.

"WE'RE HUNGARY GIVE US SOME TURKEY IN GREECE"
"I'M SORRY BOYS, BUT I CAN'T SERVIA"
"THEN GET THE BOSPHORUS"
"NO. I DONT WANT TO RUSSIA BUT YOU CAN'T RUMANIA."

A.M.C.

Grammar school graduation portrait, 1928.

Cartoons by Alan Cranston, 1924, when ten years old. He was passionate about comics throughout his life and drew his own as a child, relying on *double-entendre* jokes, early evidence of his impish humor. "Prescription" was a favorite subject in a series that showed an understanding of the judicial system and racial discrimination. He also did a daily newspaper with cartoons called "Hut and Kut – (They'll drive you nuts)."

At Pomona College, 1932-34, which Cranston attended for his freshman and one semester of sophomore year until accepted by Stanford.

Cranston at Stanford track practice, 1936, with coach Don E. Liebendorfer, later historian of the Stanford athletics department, who inscribed the photo, "Al Cranston and the last Republican to whom he spoke a kind word." *John M. Reed Photo.*

Cranston wearing one of two Stanford letters that he won for track in which he excelled as a 440-yard sprinter (he graduated in 1936), with his father William Cranston.

"Villa Warec," an acronym for family names William, Alan, R. E., Carol, childhood home of Cranston. A large property with lawn, tennis court, fields and orchards on thirteen acres in Los Altos, it was owned by the family from 1922 to 1955, later sub-divided. Once a Mexican land grant, it had an Indian's name, Red Belt, carved into an oak tree, a favorite of young Alan. The family had a Marmon car and Japanese servants who lived on the estate; Cranston would try to help them when they were interned during World War II.

Page Six

Adolph Hitler's Germany

By ALAN CRANSTON

"I AM the State!"

No one in history, not even Louis XIV, could pronounce those words with more truth than Adolf Hitler, leader of modern Germany. Occupying his position by the will of the people, he rules with the power of a monarch. Never before has a man held such a position.

The statement that Hitler rules "by the will of the people" may be challenged, for one constantly hears reports of questionable voting methods in Germany, but it is my belief, after meeting coutless Germans in all walks of life during this summer, that the country is strongly behind Hitler. Certainly the voting methods aren't as rank as those adopted in Italy. There, I am told (the statement lacks verification) the voter has his choice of two boxes

From the pen of a clear-eyed, level-headed, unprejudiced American college student, we have here a picture of the little man who is holding 60,000,000 Germans in the hollow of his hands—for a time. One of the most remarkable personages in contemporary history is presented to us here in a new light. This is the first of two articles by Alan Cranston on Hitler and his activities. The next article will appear in an early issue.—Ed.

ed for the Third Reich.

A POPULAR IDOL.

One cold, biting night in Munich, the town where Hitler first skyrocketed to fame, I stood on a street corner for over an hour, a member

dirty rat—Heil Hitler!" (this to another passing friend) "he may mean well; guess he does; but he isn't doing it. Any man can cut unemployment by his method; why, he's spent millions of marks to cut the unemployment by four million. Hasn't thrown any work my way, either. That loud mouth—Heil Hitler" (another acquaintance) "—that loud mouth has the whole world down on our ears. Shouts into the radio about uniting all the Germans in Europe under one flag. No wonder our diplomats—ha! ha! diplomats—stand alone at foreign conferences. If that damned Hitler fellow stays in power another half year there just won't be any Germany; we'll starve—Heil Hitler!"

And so this wierd dialogue continued, all the way to our destination, with my friend heaping im-

One of several articles published by Cranston's local newspaper based on reports sent from his 1934 travels in Europe while an undergraduate at Stanford University. Mountain View, California, *Register-Leader*, November 16, 1934.

Cranston as seaman on oil tanker, working his way to Europe in summer, 1934. He saw Hitler in Munich and wrote vivid newspaper dispatches about the Vienna trial of two young Nazis who assassinated former Austrian Chancellor Dollfuss July 25, 1934.

Cranston in Ethiopia, 1938, with Italian commanding General Ruggero Santini (his daughter married a relative of Mussolini). While a foreign correspondent with International News Service in Rome, Cranston saw Mussolini and covered the aftermath of the 1936 Italian invasion of Ethiopia, later writing, "I was the first journalist other than Italians and Germans allowed to go there…and heard shooting every single night."

Cranston in fedora during his years as a foreign correspondent in Europe, 1936-38.

Lee Falk (1911-99), author of King Features popular comic strips "Mandrake the Magician" and "The Phantom," created in the 1930s. A life-long friend of Cranston's, they co-wrote plays including (circa 1940) *The Big Story* about a foreign correspondent, produced in 1975 in Palo Alto. Falk worked as an advertising executive, owned theaters, produced and wrote plays. In World War II he served in the Office of War Information with Cranston. *Bender Photograph.*

A dapper Cranston with Italian army officer, Rome, 1938.

Cranston, unidentified location, with cartoon character Mickey Mouse on window as "The Sorcerer's Apprentice" in Walt Disney's film *Fantasia*, 1940.

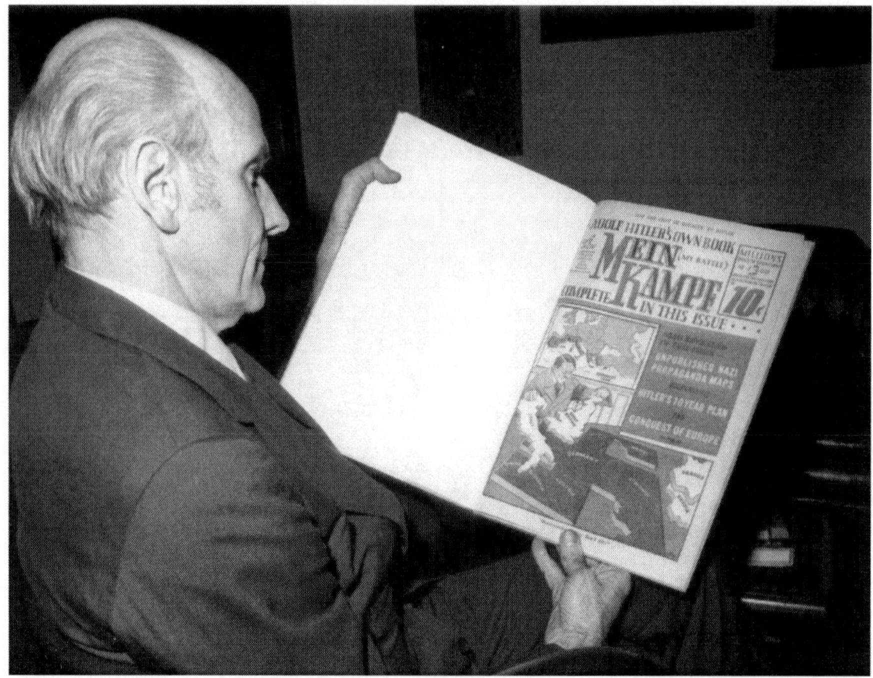

Cranston with 32-page tabloid edition of *Mein Kampf* (*My Battle*) that Cranston and friends published in 1939, highlighting sections removed from U. S. book version, stating, "Not one cent of royalty to Hitler." It sold 500,000 copies at 10¢ each until stopped by Hitler's publisher for breach of copyright. Cranston delighted in perpetuating the story that he was the only man in America ever sued by Herr Hitler, considering the publisher his "American agents." *Phil Brennan Photo for National Enquirer, February 29, 1972.*

Cranston with his first book, published in 1945, which he wrote while in the Army. *The Killing of the Peace* was a "dramatic chronicle of how the will of the people was thwarted" after World War I by a handful of senators opposing U. S. entry into the League of Nations. A paperback revised edition was issued by Viking in 1960.

Cranston in Office of War Information (O. W. I.), 1943, where he headed the Foreign Language Division (1942-44) until enlisting in the Army. O. W. I., in which many famous authors worked, was the government propaganda agency selling democracy to the world, according to its promotional statement. Cranston oversaw a staff of eighteen and some sixty translators. His wife Geneva wrote Eleanor Cranston Fowle that "If Alan hadn't had a receding hairline and therefore looked older than twenty-seven, he would never had been given that important job!" *O. W. I. photo by Douglas Hayes.*

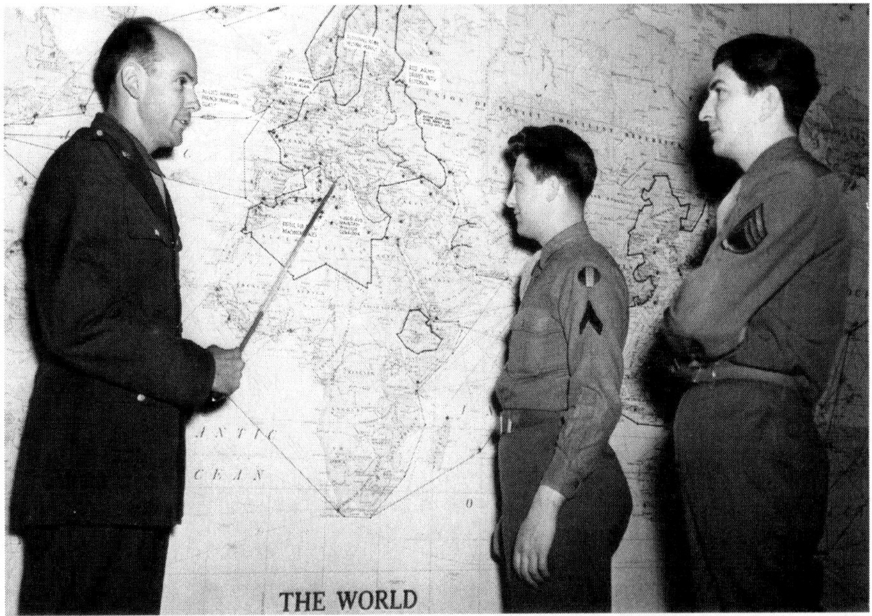

Cranston doing orientation during World War II Army service (1944-45). He joined as a private, rose to sergeant and did basic training with the 70th infantry division at Camp Croft, South Carolina. Most of his younger comrades would be sent overseas, but Cranston remained stateside, working with the Information and Education Division of the Army Service Forces. *Steve Piazza Photo, U. S. Army Signal Corps.*

Cranston with Geneva McMath (1912-85), newly engaged, on boardwalk at New York World's Fair, 1940. They married in 1940, divorced in 1977 (she suffered a stroke in 1969). During Cranston's war service, she worked (1944-45) for Orson Welles, corresponding for his monthly magazine *Free World* and syndicated column. She also worked as a lobbyist to repeal the Chinese Exclusion Acts.

Alan and Geneva at a New York club ("Cinderella"?) about the time of their marriage.

With first son Robin, wearing an "S" for Stanford, probably at a track meet, 1949.

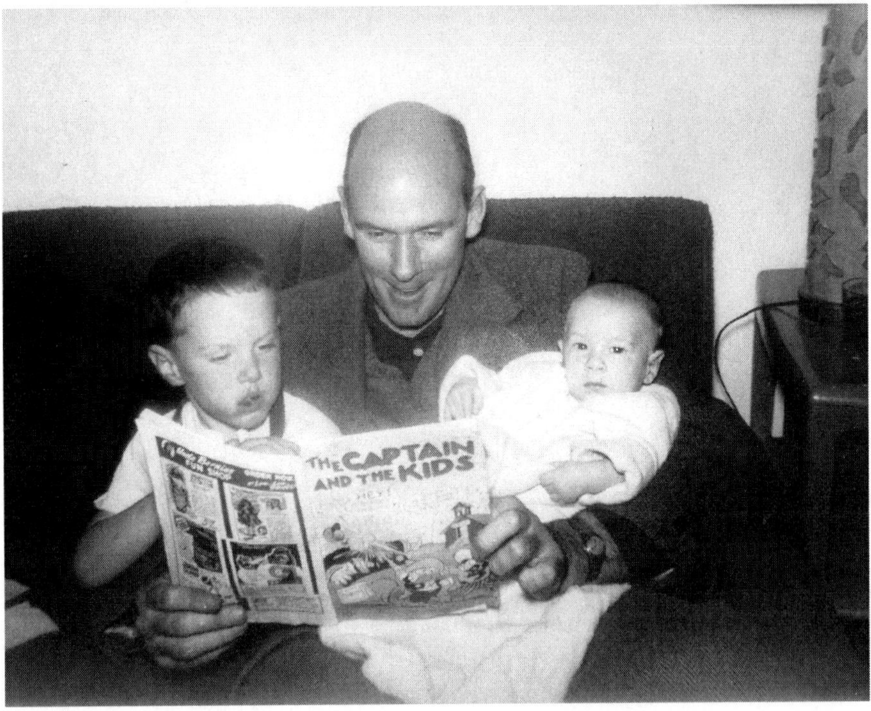

Cranston reading comics to his two sons, 1953 – Robin, born 1947, and Kim, born 1951.

With Eleanor Roosevelt with whom Cranston worked to strengthen the United Nations charter in the 1940s while an advocate with "blue-blood" attorney and public servant Grenville Clark who convened a Dublin (New Hampshire) Conference of private citizens to promote a world-government entity. *Tom Vano Photo, Clift Hotel, San Francisco.*

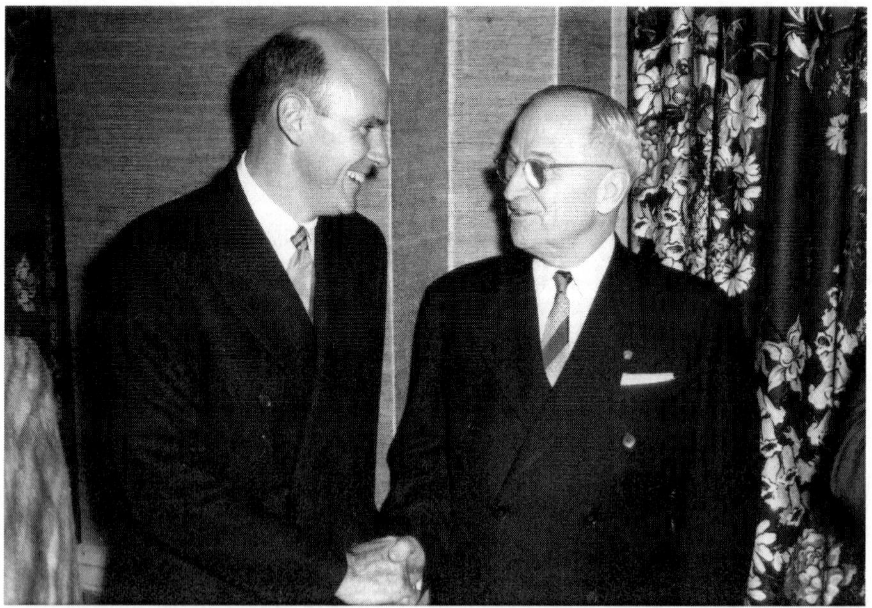

With President Harry Truman in San Francisco, possibly when he delivered address to opening session of United Nations founding conference, April 25, 1945. Truman was the first president whom Cranston met in the White House – December 20, 1945, for a "forthright discussion" of world-government proposals. Truman had expressed support of the concept and Cranston admired him but was stunned by his order to drop the atomic bomb on Hiroshima and Nagasaki in August, 1945, starting Cranston on a life-long anti-nuclear-weapons crusade. *George Shimmon Photo, Palace Hotel, San Francisco.*

Cranston (second from right) promoting World Federalists, which he served as Northern California chair (1947-49) and second national president (1949-52). He remained committed to world government and a strong United Nations throughout his life, despite attacks on Federalists as left-leaning and abrogating national sovereignty.

Cranston's campaign for state controller, 1958. Robin (left) was eleven, Kim, seven. The family often campaigned together. Cranston's reputation for helping re-build the Democratic Party was the impetus for his first elected office.

5

World Government and Red-baiting

"We demand world government not because we believe man is about to become an angel, but because we know darn well he ain't."
Cranston describing United World Federalists' support for world government, 1947.

"I am enthusiastic about Alan because I feel certain he has a career in politics. He has the stature, the homespun qualities, the community-mindedness of a politician. He can become one of the best."
Raymond Gram Swing to Eleanor Cranston Fowle, April 25, 1952.

Cranston had realized that there was more to participating in world events than reporting them. "Part of the reason that I left foreign correspondence," he later said, "was that, as great as the experience was – the opportunity to learn about the world and witness great events and interview famous people – what I basically was doing was covering the beginning of World War II, the events that led to it, Hitler and Mussolini. I decided that I didn't want to spend my life writing about such evil people and their evil deeds – I'd rather be involved in the action. So I came back to America, intending to get into politics, if I could, and into elected office. But it took quite a long time to get there." [1]

His next step after leaving the army was to settle in a community and explore possibilities for realizing that political goal. He and Geneva traveled slowly across the country in their new Nash, "taking it extremely easy, sometimes making less than 200 miles a day, driving as much as 30 miles out of our way to superb eating places recommended by Duncan Hines," Cranston wrote Grenville Clark in February, 1947, from "Somewhere in Tennessee" on a lecture tour. "Christmas Day found us in the middle of Kansas, and all restaurants closed. At about 4 in the afternoon we were starved, and I stopped at a farmhouse and asked for a glass of milk for Geneva. The people insisted we come in and do away with the remains of their still warm Christmas dinner, and so it all turned out wonderfully. We left in a blaze of (Kansas) glory when I presented them with a copy of my book." [2]

They returned to Los Altos and rented a house "made of mud! It's an adobe, very Mexican-like, sitting on a hillside with a beautiful view of the bay," as Cranston described it to Clark. "It's in the middle of an almond orchard which was blooming white when I left. The place has never been made exactly livable, but with a lot of hard work, it is becoming so, and I, of course, instructed Geneva to have everything in order by the time I return. It's wonderful for both of us to be out of apartments at last. We got a dog – a shepherd – at once. One problem is the bit of adobe that comes off every day, leaving a thin coat of yellowish dirt on everything. I suppose the whole house will vanish one day, like the one-hoss shay collapsed." To his landlady, Cranston said, "My wife and I are delighted to be moving in, and we are having a wonderful time arranging furniture, planting the garden, making use of the spare adobe bricks, and so forth. We had no hope of finding such a place when we left Washington." "Our house is over near R. E.'s, back of the old Isenberg place, near where the be-damned saddle turned over with me one day," he wrote his old school chum Ralph Raymond in July. "We love the joint, have a year's lease." They also planted a large vegetable garden. "We have 10,001 tomatoes redding at this moment," he told a Washington, D. C. friend late in the summer, "corn, radishes, onions, watermelons, muskmelons, chives and mint. Also sunflowers. We keep bees and grow almonds," he bragged. [3]

Cranston considered starting the magazine that he had dreamed about over the years, but it would take "a large amount of capital, and people are terrified of new ventures until they know a bit more about the 'recession,'" he wrote Clark of his hopes. "I spent much time on the mag. idea," he told Raymond. "Finally concluded I couldn't raise enuf $ to make it a safe risk to go ahead with other people's $." He would write Falk in August, "Yes, the magazine is shelved. Then turned down an opportunity to go into an existing mag. And next week go into above-indicated firm," which he humorously called "Cranston Real Estate Entrepreneurs and Ideas, Inc., Ltd." He hoped to concentrate in time "on low-cost housing. I'm convinced there's a great opportunity…which most people in the business are completely overlooking in their scramble for bigger things," Cranston told Clark. Real estate and housing would be "a very fertile field in ever-more-crowded California for the next few years," he believed. But that career was not to be "for life. You're certainly right about the difficulty combining making a living with other activities," he added. Meanwhile, he had been "doing quite a bit of lecturing in western states" on world-government issues. [4]

He and Geneva also took a vacation at Lake Tahoe. "We've spent three weeks up here chasing a fish," he quipped to Falk, "also wonderful sun-bathing, etc. My father and mother came up, bringing their huge police dog, Ajax. We brought our small police dog, Duffy. Ajax and Duffy hate each other. Other day they staged a fight on front lawn to horror of fellow guests and management [of Tahoe Tavern]. Harry Braverman and wife come up tomorrow for a few days. I saw the whole Wallace crowd out here when H. W. [Henry Wallace] came. There's a slight chance Henry might carry California in the Democratic primary next summer. Is he universally considered nuts in the East, tho'?" [5]

In his description of the dog fight to Raymond, Cranston said, "Pop and I finally stopped them with a convenient hose to which a sprinkler was attached and from which torrents of water emerged. Pop fell on his head once, emerged with a bum knee. I got a chewed finger…. Only Duffy, whom we were theoretically trying to rescue, emerged unscathed." Duffy would be a long-time, much-photographed member of Cranston's family. "One of our favorite sports in California," he told

Raymond, "is taking dog Duffy to the new drive-in theatre down on the Bayshore back of Paly [Palo Alto]. He is mad about Mickey Mouses. Loses interest in features after about 15 minutes, when he eventually loses track of the plot." He added a query: "Did ascorbic acid work for you?" apparently referring to treating colds, an indication of his life-long interest in healthful food and remedies. "Throw out the Repooblicans!" he added with a "Pome: Senator Taft/Is a horse's aft." [6]

His big news to friends, however, was "Cranston, Jr., due in October!" He "is thriving with Geneva at the moment," he told the Raymonds. To Clark, he said, "You can see that this move to California is a real revolution. We're excited about it – but you should see my mother and father!" [7]

Cranston brought new dimensions, ideas and energy to his father's established real estate business, "somewhat to the discomfiture of Father and his secretary of thirty years," Eleanor would write of the activity that accompanied Cranston's return to the fold. Cranston himself thought that he both "surprised and pleased" his father by joining the business. "Your pop, Ralph, signed a paper for my real-estate license, saying he'd known me 55 years," Cranston joked. "I didn't let him read it, of course. Some small print in it also signed away their house and all your earnings for the next 99 years." [8]

Cranston did undertake building moderately-priced housing. "Finally! The home you've wanted – at the price you can pay!" one advertisement promised. The ranch-style homes could be "Yours in 60 working days!" and were built with "workman-like construction." Two- to three-bedroom homes ranged from $7,800 to $10,200, plus the cost of a lot ($900). Federal Housing Administration (FHA) and veterans' loans were available to help buyers. [9]

Cranston also built houses for investment, including several for his mother-in-law, May McMath who saw them as future legacies for her daughters. In 1948 Cranston told her, "We've sewed up the lot, and have a home planned for it which is a real honey – Geneva agrees it is the best we've planned yet. I'll make you a bet that we do at least twice as well on this next one as on your first one." Mrs. McMath had worried about the risk of such investments if there were another war. "What with Truman and Marshall disagreeing…and Russia acting as it is, it looks now as if we could be sending some calling cards in the shape of bombs most any time." If there were war, there would be a demand for newly-built houses, Cranston predicted, adding, "We sell about 25 percent of our homes to vets." [10]

Cranston also was building – partially with his own hands – a house for his growing family to occupy, with help from Ralph Raymond and Mel Hawley who soon would be elected a county sheriff. "It's really going to be nice," Cranston wrote McMath. "You'll love to visit us in it." By then the Cranston family also had puppies. A menagerie was starting that would grow in size. [11]

Cranston was proposed for the exclusive Bohemian Club in 1948. Its criteria for membership included some form of creative talent and the club asked Cranston for a sample of his work as a playwright so members could "form an opinion of his ability in this direction." "After thorough consideration, the Jinks Committee has decided that the election of Alan Cranston as an Associate member is unlikely," the club decided a few years later. "We all agree that Mr. Cranston is an outstanding young man and I believe it is the private opinion of the members…that he would be a desirable Bohemian; however, his particular qualifications are not presently in demand so far as the Associate list is concerned." The club needed musicians, it told his sponsor, and also was uneasy about Cranston's having business that took him to the East Coast regularly. Perhaps he should apply for regular membership, its secretary suggested, regretting "any disappointment you or Mr. Cranston may feel in this connection." [12]

Cranston's other activities still concerned Grenville Clark's pet project, world government. Six organizations in 1947 had merged to form United World Federalists (U. W. F.) whose principals included many people associated with the Dublin Conference. It was headed by a war hero who had lost an eye, Cord Meyer, Junior, a former Marine Corps captain awarded the Purple Heart who had served as aide to Harold Stassen at the U. N. founding conference in San Francisco. The new organization's board included Clark, Norman Cousins, Harper Brothers publisher Cass Canfield, author Carl Van Doren, and radio personality Raymond Gram Swing. Albert Einstein, U. S. Supreme Court Justice William O. Douglas and actor Douglas Fairbanks, Junior, were among a prestigious national advisory board. Eleanor Fowle wrote the text for a promotional cartoon booklet called *One World (Maybe None)* – it traced mankind's warlike tendencies from apes hitting one another with sticks and stones through the development of gunpowder to the atomic bomb. [13]

Cranston had written Clark in 1947, "I volunteered to do anything out here that they wanted, but haven't heard a peep out of them.... I don't know how it may seem to you back East, but out here I see almost no signs of progress...in the world-government field...despite Gallup polls showing that the American people now believe war is likely before too long. Nobody seems shocked at the inadequacy of the U. N. and the need...for Truman and Marshall to bypass it.... Something has to be done to get the alternative before the people in a way they can get their teeth into." As a Constitutional amendment authorizing the United States to enter a world government was unlikely, Cranston thought that "the next best thing is a simple resolution" passed by state legislatures, which already had occurred in Massachusetts at Clark's instigation. "It would at least help focus attention" in debates on the subject. "It is difficult to be patient, isn't it?" Cranston added. [14]

Cranston soon was enlisted to form U. W. F. chapters in California. His first successes were in Los Altos and Palo Alto, where community leaders were happy to join. One of those was Republican Assemblyman Robert C. Kirkwood of nearby Saratoga who, unbeknownst to Cranston at the time, would be a future political opponent. Cranston was made Northern California Chairman of the Federalists and traveled nationwide lecturing. He even visited San Quentin Prison on San Francisco Bay, talking to a group called "The Seekers." "Your interest in our group, and in prison problems generally, is very gratifying to all of us," its secretary thanked him, adding that they were "in full accord with the...ideal of peace and world government." [15]

Cranston had met again with the Philippines' U. N. delegate Carlos P. Romulo who was ready to "start the fight" again for charter reforms at the next U. N. Assembly session "and thinks our strength will be much greater." Cranston confided that he was drafting an article over Romulo's name for *Collier's* magazine. "This is just between us," he told Clark, but "I think too many people learned that I was writing

Romulo's U. N. speeches. As you see, you managed to involve me so deeply in the world-government business…that I haven't yet been able to untangle myself the least bit," he added. "When I get back to California (March 15) I am, however, going to look into the matter of also making a living." [16]

In his lectures he reiterated the arguments for a strong peace-keeping entity. "There are those who say that the course we advocate is unrealistic or idealistic." Such "adjectives were employed a century and a half ago by those who thought the vision of the United States of America was a great but idle dream…. All the history of man has shown that there can be no peace without justice, no justice without law, no law without government to enact, interpret and enforce that law." [17]

The federalists, however, were continuously having to justify their stance. "We demand world government not because we believe man is about to become an angel," Cranston explained in his talks, "but because we know darn well he ain't." [18]

He quoted or paraphrased ancient Greek philosophers like orator Isocrates (436-338 B.C):

Let the leaders contrive to put an end to our present troubles. The treaties of peace are insufficient for their purpose…. We stand in need of some more durable plan, which will forever put an end to our hostilities, and unite us by lasting ties of mutual affection and fidelity. [19]

He reminded audiences that "4,000 treaties of alliances between nations were in existence in 1939 – the year that Hitler launched World War II…. And there is not a shred of evidence that war is an effective means for dealing with the specific foe we face – communist imperialism." Even if communist countries like the U. S. S. R., China and their satellites were destroyed, communism might continue because it was "an idea, and ideas survive even the mightiest bombs." It nevertheless would be "dangerous and demagogic" to "abandon our arms, renounce our alliances, and trust to the good will of our fellow humans for peace, freedom and security. I certainly do not propose that we do so. I am not a pacifist. I recognize the need for great American military strength as long as we face the threat of aggression from communist or other dictatorships. But I do say that we must refuse to surrender, abjectly and totally, to the tides of the arms race. I believe that we need a policy of peace to match our policy of power…. I believe we need enforceable world law." [20]

He carried with him, typed on a crumpled piece of paper, words of Demosthenes speaking to Athenians in 351 B. C. about war with Philip II of Macedonia, which had relevance for the atomic age:

Shame on you Athenians for not wishing to understand that one must not allow oneself to be at the command of events but must forestall them….

Never a fixed plan, never any precautions, you wait for bad news before you act. [21]

He also used his appearances for fundraising. "For those of you who may still suspect that we Federalists are soft in the head, we are now going to demonstrate one facet of practicality – it takes money to carry on our movement," he would joke.

He hoped that "hard, cold logic" would touch listeners' hearts and induce them to invest in "man's last, best hope" for the future. [22]

But the Federalists had to defend themselves against attacks that "world government means world communism." A Federalists' pamphlet, *Inside the Straw-man, the Truth about the Attacks on World Government*, urged critics to "discuss the facts, not distort them," and emphasized that, by its bylaws, "U. W. F. will not knowingly admit or permit as members persons who are Communist or Fascist or others who seek to overthrow…or weaken the United States, or to change its form of government by other than by Constitutional means." [23]

A "globalist glossary" that Cranston quoted humorously characterized differing views: A "maximalist" knew "what would be *good* for the people better than they do"; a "minimalist" knew "what the people of the world *will accept* better than they do"; a "partialist" wanted "to have a federation even if nobody else is in it"; and a "universalist" believed "that no nation should join a federation until all other nations have done so." [24]

Cranston helped draft a radio program to be broadcast one Fourth of July. Listeners were urged to wire suggestions to the "United Party of the Nation," a group formed by members of both American political parties to advance the anti-war agenda. [25]

He told Ralph Raymond that he was "spending too much time on world government," but boasted of "recent headway – about 10 senators from both parties introduced a bill in Congress calling for a U. N. amendment to make it strong enuf to keep the peace. Early next year we hope to get a vote on it. Am also messing with the Democratic Party," he added." [26]

"I wish there were a million more fellows like you with vision and the ability to put the idea of world government over," Raymond replied. "If worse comes to worse, you can never condemn yourself for not having tried." In another note, Raymond commented on Cranston's small, hard-to-decipher handwriting. [27]

But Federalists still had to cope with charges that their proposals might help communism take over the world.

Senator Glen H. Taylor of Idaho, a liberal who ran for Vice President on the Progressive Party ticket with Henry A. Wallace in 1948, had agreed to introduce a world-government resolution in Congress. Cranston offered to tout it in a speech in Taylor's state, noting that he now had cosponsors "in contrast to your lonesome authorship of the bill two years ago." But Taylor had to admit that he was having "difficulties obtaining bipartisan and broad sponsorship," although several thousand letters that he had sent to interested people had resulted in thirty members of Congress calling to say they were "flooded with mail urging that they back the proposal." [28]

Back in California, Cranston was meeting with important politicians like San Francisco Mayor Roger D. Lapham – he wanted to learn from Lapham's political experience. "Your present occupation is bringing you up against a lot of forces and problems I've had some experience with, but not enough – yet – and I'm more than a little interested in your reactions, judgments and decisions," Cranston told him. [29]

To Clark, who had decided to write a memoir, Cranston wrote of his former ambitions: "I once thought that if I decided to be an author to the exclusion of most other activities (which I decided against), I would like to tackle three biographies:

[Republican presidential candidate Wendell] Wilkie's, [F. D. R.'s Secretary of War Henry L.] Stimson's, and yours. That's an odd list for a good Democrat like the undersigned, isn't it?" [30]

He told Clark in August, however, "I'm not planning on doing any writing… for several years, but am keeping on lecturing, and hope to help build an effective branch of U. W. F. out here." He had gone on its executive committee and still was hopeful that the U. N. charter could be altered, particularly from one-vote-per-nation to the "weighted" version proposed by the Dublin conference. "I think it's important to get across the idea that, unfair as the present system is to us [the United States], it's even more unfair to Russia. I've been stressing this in talks to all sorts of audiences." But it was hard to "get these fine points across to an America roused by" a growing anti-communism mentality. "If we fail, I'm going to be a bit uneasy about any citizens I persuade to invest in property so close to San Francisco and the nice bomb target at the Sunnyvale air base," he mused. [31]

Cranston spoke out forthrightly about the dangers that he feared. "Allen [*sic*] Cranston, chairman of the United World Federalists of San Francisco, last night attacked the Big Five veto power under the United Nations Charter," the *San Francisco Chronicle* reported in September, 1947, of a talk to 200 people attending the first local organizing meeting at the Fairmont Hotel. The present system of representation was "tantamount to California's and Nevada's having equal weight in the United States Congress," Cranston said, reiterating a point that he frequently made – there had been only 268 years in the previous 4,000 in which there had been no war on earth. [32]

Cranston also participated in radio debates like one in San Francisco discussing "Which path toward world government?" in which young British Labor M. P. Henry C. Usborne took part. Usborne and 100 Members of Parliament advocated an international People's Convention, made up of one delegate for each million of the world's population, to create a world constitution. Many in U. W. F. were skeptical of the idea because communist nations would be weighted heavily against the United States in numbers of delegates. Cranston argued that "It is entirely impractical and unrealistic to place any of our hopes for peace in an organization which can function only when people agree, as witness the U. N. What is needed is an organization which can function when people disagree, as witness the United States of America." [33]

Cranston turned down Clark's offer to get him "back to lobbying at the General Assembly. I wanted very much to do it, but I've really gotten going at my plan for some intensive $-pursuing out here, and, as you know, my hope is that I can buy some freedom to be put to good use in a few years hence. I'm in a low-cost-housing project which cuts under the market by two and three-thousand dollars, and thus far it's going wonderfully." He had managed, though. to raise $627.84 to send a revised petition to the U. N. Assembly, timely at "a terribly tense period." Some in Congress and others wanted to "drive Russia from the U. N. or to compel Russia to submit to our dictates…. That is no real step in the direction of world government," Cranston felt. [34]

To move the concept of world government forward, Cranston advocated getting state legislatures to act, starting with the original colonial states' introducing a model resolution to that end. His language for such a resolution was based on the American justification for *federal* government – "to perform certain functions that states could not perform." An international governing body would act when "governments cannot perform a supreme task" like preventing war. [35]

He had just been elected state chairman of U. W. F. in California, "which doesn't amount to much, as it's been more or less impotent out here," he admitted to Clark, but he had found an eager co-worker, Edgar Osgood, to help activate the forces. Cranston ended the letter, dated October 9, 1947, "Geneva just now advised me not to seal the envelope, so that perhaps, when I mail it in the morning, I can add a note advising whether it is Robin MacGregor Cranston or Candace Cranston. The event is about that close. Geneva is fine, meanwhile."

The event occurred on November 1, 1947. Robin MacGregor Cranston was born at 6:26 in the evening. "Hereby transmit proxy from Robin MacGregor Cranston, new world government convert who arrived this evening from Geneva, pledging his fortune of seven and half pounds to British parliamentary plan. Robin has inside information. Geneva perfect condition. Love, Alan," Cranston telegraphed to his sister, who was attending a world-government convention in St. Louis in his stead. "Hurrah, hurrah, Robin shows fine sense of time," Eleanor wired back, adding that the convention had adopted the concept of balanced representation and negotiations with Russia, "as suggested by Grenville," and that Cranston had been reelected to the Council for Limited World Government. The birth was noted in local papers, and Cranston saved three front pages for that November 1: the *San Francisco Chronicle*'s was dominated by a story of "All 18 on Alaska airliner dead"; the *San Francisco News* headlined "Gaels out-galloped, Notre Dame wins," and "Man O' War dies," while the *Palo Alto Times*' headline read, "Truman advisers ask return to wartime inflation control." [36]

A friend who worked at *Collier's* magazine wrote a tongue-in-cheek letter to the infant, to "tell you about the family you inadvertently fell into. Your parents are large, healthy, amiable and illiterate. They toil, they spin, but they do not communicate" with friends regularly. "Your father has a plan to save the world but he never has a stamp. They will keep you there on display until the novelty wears off and then I don't know. Make the most of it while you have their interest; they are fine, upstanding…people, and may be shamed into cherishing you. At the first sign of weakening, however, get in touch with me and we will pasture you on the ranch." [37]

By June, 1948, Cranston could report to his landlady that "Rob," who bore a strong resemblance to his mother, was about to walk, was getting into things and was "covered with adobe and spiders." The Cranstons hired a young girl, Trude Hoffaker, as a baby sitter. Geneva's mother sympathized with her daughter's being house-bound as a new mother, remonstrating to Cranston a year later how "Geneva was looking forward to [getting out one night] with much interest – she has been so tied down this winter, and not well either and Robin not doing too well, that it has been rather bad for her. A gal can get very tired staying home day after day, fussing with a cross baby, doing dishes, diapers, meals, beds, etc., etc., constant repetition. It is a most trying time in a gal's life – I wonder how they can look pleasant sometimes. It is such a feeling of freedom when the babies are started to school and the mother isn't so tied down. Glad it's all over for me. That's one of the penalties of being a mother. I haven't decided yet whether it's worth it – rather pessimistic view, eh? In my brighter moments, I'm sure it is, because my girls mean so much to me now, when I have nothing else. We never know what these youngsters will mean to us in later life." [38]

Cranston now was actively promoting the World Federalists. Its first president, Cord Meyer, toured California in 1948. The national Chamber of Commerce's "outstanding young man of 1947," he had authored a book, *Peace or Anarchy,* that U. W. F. sold. Cranston slipped an announcement of Meyer's talk at Palo Alto High School onto the bottom of an advertisement for Cranston Company homes. [39]

An early recruiting meeting in Los Altos, Cranston wrote a friend, "turned the town upside down." It had been hosted by a school board member and Stanford University Chancellor Doctor Ray Lyman Wilbur. One tactic was to stage a mock atomic attack, which was done at Palo Alto High School. "U. W. F. officers emphasized that it's only make-believe," the local newspaper reported, "because they want no recurrence of the mass hysteria caused by Orson Welles' *Men from Mars* radio show." A student organizer of the high school chapter, Allyn Kreps, co-wrote the script. Like others attracted to the movement, Kreps would become an admirer of Cranston's and play a part in his future career. [40]

Cranston's recruiting activities got considerable press attention, including from popular San Francisco columnist Herb Caen. When a Freedom Train traveled through Palo Alto in January, 1948, carrying the Declaration of Independence, Cranston used the opportunity to make a comparison to the current world situation. It had taken forefathers "more than ten years to discover that thirteen separate colonies, with no common government above them, could not make secure the unalienable rights of man" – they had "as much trouble as the United Nations today." In time, major California newspapers would editorially endorse the Federalists' message and messengers. "They number some of the most realistic minds in the community," the *San Francisco Chronicle* stated, "bankers, corporation presidents and directors, highly successful attorneys. And yet they are enlisting in a program which sometimes seems as visionary as the colonization of Mars," it cautioned. But there was no viable alternative. "What is all-important is that there shall be such movements, that men shall be seeking the answers while there is yet time to find them…. United World Federalists is just as good a banner as any under which" to discuss the issue. Send them a check, the editorial concluded, there was "everything to gain and nothing to lose." "People are plain scared over this dangerous U. S.-U. S. S. R. tension," the Palo Alto *Mail-Dispatch* reported of Cord Meyer's appearance in April, "just as you expect two stiff-legged dogs circling and growling at each other to suddenly have a go at it…. What is your church, lodge, P. T. A. or club doing specifically for world peace?" the paper asked. [41]

The Los Altos *Town Crier* joked, though, that while Federalists feared for the future, "Allan [*sic*] Cranston, a leading figure in the U. W. F. movement, claims that the pumice stone blocks used in homes he is constructing are guaranteed to last a full 200 years. Wonder if he's got some inside dope?" [42]

Cranston did have a plan for getting political backing for Federalists. He raised $8,000 to donate to political candidates who endorsed the U. W. F. program. One of them was Republican Kirkwood who was running unopposed for reelection to the California Assembly. The funds subscribed at a meeting at Cranston's home to hear U. W. F. director Upshur Evans "places Los Altos in the lead among California towns and cities backing world government," one news account reported. The strategy would serve Cranston well in the future. Kirkwood, in a letter to Cranston with the $6.00 membership fee, said that he was "in full accord with the aims and views of the" Federalists, and would be glad if they wanted to use his endorsement. He also offered to work with Cranston on a Constitutional amendment to reinforce American participation in world government. Cranston promised to announce the assemblyman's position in a press release. Kirkwood soon would be helpful in the Assembly. [43]

Fundraising efforts were not always successful, however, and Cranston was getting experience at it. He admitted to a chapter chairman that "funds can be raised…only after the most careful ground work" like that which he had done in Los Altos. Pleas did not have to be made to only selective groups. "I have seen vast amounts raised in meetings open to the public for far less worthy causes," he said. "Of one thing I am certain: There are some people who will subscribe funds in public meetings, under group psychology, who will give nothing, or far smaller sums, if privately approached." Cranston had been accused by one woman at an organizing meeting in Oakland of trying "to bully the members of the audience into pledging" monthly amounts to the new chapter. [44]

He also found wealthy supporters who were sympathetic, including members of the generous and liberal San Francisco Jewish community like philanthropist Jesse H. Steinhart and Ben Swig, owner of the Fairmont Hotel. Steinhart had subscribed $3,000, and $6,000 in pledges followed, including $500 from Swig. [45]

Cranston participated in a "town meeting" broadcast July 27, 1948, with Republican Senator Wayne Morse of Oregon acting as moderator, debating the question, "How should the United Nations progressively establish international law?" Clarence Streit, the *New York Times* correspondent and advocate of worldwide "union," challenged the Federalists' position as weak. "Mr. Cranston and his United World Federalist supporters have been doing their best to make people forget" that such a union, unlike the U. N., would have unlimited powers to enforce international law. Nations could not "make the long trip around [the U. N.'s] 'Cape Veto' as quickly as they can in my friend Cranston's mind. Federating the democracies requires no U. N. decision, and consequently, Russia cannot veto it," Streit argued. [46]

"I have not come here to argue with Clarence Streit," Cranston retorted. "We share the conviction that world government is necessary if the world is to survive. We differ only as to method." Less-than-*bone fide* democracies ought to be permitted to join such federations, Cranston said – applause greeted his statement that excluding such nations was like excluding Mississippi from the United States. Cranston reiterated stories of people's fears about the bomb – "I know a practical businessman who is trying to find out which bank west of the Rockies has the deepest safety deposit vaults." A senator, he added to laughter from the audience, had proposed amending the Constitution to provide for electing two vice presidents and forbidding one of them ever to go to Washington in case it should vanish in an atomic cloud. National sovereignty, though, made it impossible to enforce control over the bomb. "International law as we know it sufficed to drive the Captain Kidds from the seas, but today, in our search for security, we are not greatly concerned with pirates," rather, with "jet-propelled rockets carrying atomic war heads…radioactive clouds bearing drops of death…invisible armies of lethal bacteria. At present, the United Nations Assembly can only make recommendations; it cannot write laws…. Can you imagine order in the smallest town or the largest nation if there were no laws, only recommendations; if thieves were given a veto over the police; and if murderers could refuse to go to court?" "You've struck some hot argumentative sparks," Senator Morse said of Cranston's points.

When one panelist, Utah Judge Reva Beck Bosone, argued that existing international law had in the past thwarted aggressors, Cranston asked, "Is it common practice in Salt Lake City to refer to the police force as the town bully?" More laughter from the audience. It was public opinion, not police, she said, that enforced laws. "It's the police force plus public opinion," Cranston retorted. What was needed was to elect people to office who were committed to world government. Streit and Bosone, he concluded, "hold that we must get peace in order to get world government. I hold that we must get world government in order to get peace," which garnered more applause. [47]

"Suppose the United Nations ran Los Altos?" was the title of a skit that Cranston wrote to illustrate the weakness of the United Nations. It had a "crook" stealing groceries while an "outraged citizen" protested, "*Hey! You can't do that! That's not nice! That's my dinner*!" "*How you gonna stop me*?" the thief asked? The citizen would take him to court and it would send him to jail. "*Listen, bud, I need dis' stuff in my house. The court's got nuttin' to do with my house*," the crook replied in jargon reminiscent of Cranston's youthful cartoons. "*You have witnessed a demonstration of the powers of the World Court*," a commentator explained, which had no powers over individual nations, only "*a sort of gentlemen's agreement*." "*I ain't no gentleman*," the crook told the citizen, shooting him and stealing his money in a second scenario. In a third, to demonstrate the Security Council's veto stalemate, the crook started to carry off the citizen's wife to protests that he would report the matter to the council. "*I veto that!*" the crook exclaimed. [48]

Cranston privately confessed to enthusiastic Federalist Harris L. Wofford, Junior, "at the moment…the only thing we can put over is *limited* world government," although he still held out hope for "*unlimited* world government" one day. Cranston had sent Wofford his book. "Some day I hope to write another," he said, "but not for a long time, I am afraid." Wofford, then at the University of Chicago, had founded Student Federalists and would work together with Cranston for many years from that time forward. [49]

In 1948 incumbent President Harry Truman was opposed by Republican New York Governor Thomas Dewey. "I'm not too sold on Dewey," Cranston's father wrote a friend, "and would have felt that our pockets had been picked except for the nomination of [Earl] Warren," California's Republican governor. William Cranston, although a Republican, apparently shared his son's concerns about the volatile state of the world. "The chief count against Dewey," he said, "is danger internationally. [John Foster] Dulles is apt to be Secretary of State and he has indicated a belief in things such as cartels, which lead to war." Alan, he added, had gone to the Republican National convention, although his plane had been delayed by mechanical difficulties and "after leaving the airport, made a forced landing in a field." His father was confident that his resourceful son, who had gone without any hotel reservation or ticket to the convention, "probably obtained both. He met [Harold] Stassen and Mrs. Warren in his first hour there (after sleeping in his traveling suit)." [50]

Cranston, who had gone to the convention to gin up support for world federalism, sent an account to a Palo Alto paper portraying delegates making secret deals over the presidential nomination "in a hotel room with the Dewey men." Stassen, Cranston wrote, seemed "to be the popular man, as Wilkie was in 1940, but the regular Republicans are prepared…to stop the popular choice." Stassen he described as "tall, erect, smiling with assurance, the most relaxed of all" the candidates," while Dewey, "the front-runner, strides through his hotel lobby with an air of vast confidence, but his movements are quick, tense, his glances sharp and darting. Taft, who simulates ease, has eyes that are deadly tired, and sagging shoulders. Senator Vandenberg seems a bit lonely, while his supporters wonder if he has played his waiting game too long." Or, Cranston wondered, would they nominate Eisenhower? Cranston's impressions were of "trading, dealing, grabbing arms, stalking in hotel lobbies, whispering, shouting, proposing, elbowing, tripping, pushing, roaming the convention floor." [51]

Cranston at that time concentrated on getting both political parties, and ultimately state legislatures, to endorse the resolution urging the United States to call for and join a world-government organization, and his lobbying efforts began to pay off. "World government entered the realm of practical politics in the United States with startling speed this summer," he could say in a newspaper report in August, 1948. "At Sacramento a week ago, the Republican and Democratic parties both wrote world-law planks into their state platforms." The same had occurred with both parties in New Jersey and Maine, and with one or the other party in seven other states. One example of the attention the subject was getting was the announcement that "the Chance Vought Division of the United Aircraft Corporation…is moving its entire aviation plant and at least 1,500 families from Stratford, Connecticut, to Dallas, Texas, in order to be in a safer area in the event of atomic war!!" Cranston reported. A small step within the U. N. also was encouraging: a "Little Assembly" meeting at Lake Success, New York, in 1946 had approved, 19 to 7, a resolution favoring a conference to strengthen the charter. The U. S. delegation had led opposition to it. But, Cranston related, "The U. N. at last has a police force – consisting of 49 men carrying unloaded revolvers, now on duty in Palestine." An opinion poll showed that "very close to a working majority of [Americans] seem convinced that world government is desirable." U. W. F. membership in California had quadrupled in 1948 – the state was second only to New York with twenty-three chapters and more being organized. [52]

Cranston had gotten his old friend Ted Waller hired as U. W. F. legislative representative in Washington. Harris Wofford, who was doing research at Hoover Library at Stanford, with his wife Clare Lindgren also were active in Cranston's legions. Cranston hired Clare to be director of the Northern California Federalists in 1948. "She loved working for Alan," Wofford said in reflecting on their long friendship. Waller had been in Russia as chief of a U. N. Relief and Rehabilitation Administration program. "I often wondered what the current chapter in the Cranston saga is turning out to be," he had written from there. "Are you getting to be a senator or making money?" When he returned, Cranston had recommended him for the U. W. F. job, remonstrating that he would "oppose any steps towards world government which contemplate leaving out the Russians. We must negotiate – not fight – with the Russians." [53]

The U. S.-Russian "Cold War," however, was growing ominous. Cord Meyer had found in Washington "an hysterical conviction that the next war was imminent," and told Clark that he believed Secretary of Defense James Forrestal was "now the strong man…directing policy" in favor of aggressive action. "Some very large and dramatic undertaking is necessary if we are to reverse the drift of events," Meyer warned in March, 1948. [54]

The undertaking for U. W. F. would be a petition to Congress and the president, signed by many veterans, especially those with name recognition like famed cartoonist Bill Mauldin. Clark asked Cranston to help write the petition. Clark felt that "the vital thing is to get Truman-Marshall-Lovett-Forrestal-Leahy-Bedell Smith *out*," referring to members of Truman's cabinet in the State and Defense Departments and the Ambassador to the Soviet Union (Smith). "Almost *anyone* would be better; couldn't be worse for world government and pushing us into war – not soon maybe, but pretty [scary?] if they had four more years along present lines. Are you rooting for Wallace?" Clark asked Cranston. [55]

Cranston said that he would "assume some of the burden of getting" the petition going although busy in "local business, local politics (primary June 2), and local U. W. F.," he told Clark. As tensions tightened between the two super powers, Secretary of State Marshall had demanded that the Russians act through the U. N. which they had rebuffed, prompting Cranston to say, "Our government obviously knows – though it won't admit it – that the U. N. cannot be used for great purposes at present." In any event, a petition should be bipartisan, Cranston stressed, so that whoever became president in 1949 would be inclined to heed it. [56]

The petition was to call for a "Citizens Committee to explore the prospects for a settlement with the Soviet Union." Cranston was honored to be considered for the committee, "provided it doesn't take too much time outside California – where the problems of home building are manifold," he told Clark. [57]

By the end of 1948 Cranston was being congratulated for his organizing and political skills related to the U. W. F. "You have succeeded wonderfully in inspiring the sort of practical and yet idealistic persons upon whom the movement now rests," an activist wrote him. "In my time, we were mostly crack-pots and undoubtedly scared the doctors, lawyers and engineers away, or rather, never attracted them." The writer was cynical about the future, though, predicting war within a year in which communism would "win the world" unless Federalists rallied public opinion to pressure the White House to curb the U. S. military and appoint a Federalist Secretary of State. Events overtook the petition effort, however. [58]

Cranston privately admitted to fellow Federalist Charles "Chuck" G. Bolte, American-born British army officer who had lost a leg at El Alamein and founded the American Veterans Committee, then at Oxford as a Rhodes scholar, that he feared the movement in the United States was not taken seriously by policy-makers in power. "I am not slamming Cord. I do not mean to say that he is not considered respectfully, but nonetheless, Marshall, Dulles, etc., must have the same opinion of Cord and a great many others of us as Bevins must of Usborne and other British Federalists – '*nice, sincere young men with an idea that sounds nice but can't be done*.' When I was in England early in 1946, Usborne certainly influenced M. P.s numbering closer to 100 than five." Cranston wanted to know their strength in England now and in other European countries before going to a national U. W. F. convention. Bolte agreed with Cranston's assessment. "Nobody who carries any weight takes WG [world government] seriously," he wrote from Oxford. Usborne had lost support in England and "his Parliamentary group has dwindled to a very considerable degree." Part of the problem was dealing with Usborne – "He is, like all messiahs, obsessed by his idea, determined to carry it out in his own way with a minimum of interference, and largely indifferent to suggestions or objections." [59]

As to Usborne's plan for a People's Convention, Cranston subsequently told Waller, "I am not precisely 1000% sold" on it, although he thought it had "great propaganda value" and "might give us a great boost." The perception that Communists might dominate such an approach had to be faced. "If we are going to start retreating every time a Communist appears, we might as well quit right now." [60]

Waller complimented Cranston for crafting a resolution on the Russia-U. S. situation at the 1948 U. W. F. convention in Minneapolis that November. "We owe you a real debt of gratitude for that." Cranston thanked him, protesting that another compliment – about his participation on a panel – was not deserved. "I was lousy," but "the one regarding the resolution is accepted; it *is* good." [61]

The Federalists needed to refine their mission, Cranston and Clark realized after that convention. "I strongly agree that a careful restatement of the 'limited' approach to world government would be useful," Cranston believed. "There has been a preponderance of propaganda for the 'unlimited' idea," and U. W. F. leaders needed to be persuaded to change tactics. [62]

Cranston was focusing on a more pragmatic approach – getting state legislatures to endorse world government. "I think such resolutions serve a mild purpose," he told Clark. They laid the groundwork for seeking a Constitutional amendment requiring the United States to participate in such an entity, and provided a rallying point for public participation. "It would be a lot easier to get people in all the states working on this than on any other project we have thus far had," he surmised. "It would have most of the virtues of the People's Convention idea, minus its drawbacks," he told Meyer. [63]

Cranston was enthusiastic about the challenge, clearly enjoying the strategizing, which he outlined in a long "confidential" letter to Waller in January, 1949. It was "concrete political action – the first *real* local job we have had, apart from supporting (without endorsing) candidates for Congress…. This will give U. W. F. the greatest organizational shot-in-the-arm it has ever had…. As states take this action, it will serve as solid notice to peoples in other lands that the people of the U. S. are taking firm steps in the direction of world government." The approach got around the Constitutional requirement for two thirds of both Houses of Congress to approve Constitutional amendments. If two thirds of states called for a Constitutional Convention, Congress would be forced to call one. Cranston urged keeping the strategy "among ourselves for the time being" so as not "alienate Congress." He was confident that enough states would act to force its hand. [64]

Waller in turn got Cranston involved in James Roosevelt's political ambitions for Congress The Democratic National Committeeman wanted "a man in Northern California who could be relied on" as part of a "super brain trust to guide party policy-thinking in California. He put great emphasis on political maturity and discretion." Cranston then was on the Stanford Democratic Council in Palo Alto. [65]

He went to Sacramento well prepared to get his resolution through the legislature. He managed to get some "muddled-up language" replaced in the Assembly Rules Committee, which reported it out "favorably (after considerable rumpus)," he told Clark. "The great difficulty is that most of the legislators have no idea what we're doing, didn't even know what we were talking about at first. Some are learning fast, and in the Assembly of 80 there are now 10 who talk our language, and 35 more who have said they'll vote for it." Cranston was "confident something will be passed." The *San Francisco Chronicle* was giving the resolution "superb support – ran an editorial favoring" the resolution and giving it "good news coverage," as were "most of the other papers. Beyond question, it is proving to be a great educational device," he was glad to say. [66]

The favorable coverage resulted because Cranston had won over *Chronicle* editor and general manager Paul C. Smith, who in turn reportedly contacted the most powerful lobbyist in California, Arthur "Artie" Samish, asking him to help get the resolution through the legislature. "What's world government?" Samish had asked. He soon learned. Cranston himself had met Samish once on a plane flying from Burbank to Sacramento, and he became involved in pushing the resolution. [67]

Samish had become infamous as a lobbyist in California, calling himself "the guy who gets things done." He boasted that within two weeks he knew what a legislator's every needs were, including what he liked on a baked potato. *Collier's* magazine in a 1949 article dubbed Samish "The Secret Boss of California." Among his major clients were beer and liquor interests. Waller jested, in a letter marked "personal and confidential," "Is it true that during the period of your interest in U. W. F. you have been on the payroll of the California Brewers' Institute? Is it true that Artie Samish is Chairman of the Political Committee of U. W. F. Northern California? These are, of course, questions which I should be able to answer to the satisfaction of the Senate Investigating Committee." [68]

The world-government resolution was approved unanimously in the State Assembly March 24, 1949, and in the State Senate a few days later by a vote of 23 to 9. California was the first state to urge an actual Constitutional Convention. Cranston, who had testified for the measure, was given credit along with Clark for making the "California plan" the core of U. W. F.'s national strategy (together with the continued effort to get Congress to approve a world-government resolution). There had been no organized opposition to the resolution, which had moved with great speed through the legislature despite cries that it was "un-American" because it would weaken U. S. sovereignty. "We succeeded mainly because the opposition was caught off balance," Cranston reported to Waller, "and before it had time to organize, we had accomplished our purpose. I can see how tough it is going to be in some states," he added, "but our experience here doubly convinces me…that we have here a mechanism that will enable us to gain terrific strength across the country, if the job is tackled intelligently." The U. W. F. financial drive, though, "has not worked too well thus far." Waller agreed "that it has now been demonstrated that the Constitutional amendment project is a potential source of terrific strength." They should take advantage of the momentum and plan a "major offensive on this score in 1950 and '51." Several other states had approved similar resolutions, including Maine and Connecticut. [69]

Cranston had orchestrated the legislative accomplishment, and was justifiably proud of it. "I did it mainly by getting to know the two powers-that-be and working with the sort of people you'd think wouldn't be interested." The leaders were both Republicans – Assembly Speaker Thomas A. "Tommy" Maloney of San Francisco, who had sponsored the measure, and Harold ("Butch") Powers, President Pro Tempore of the Senate, later lieutenant governor. Cranston sent Clark a transcript of the debate, which he had taken down in long-hand in the assembly gallery. "Much of the ground covered at Philadelphia a century and a half ago, and in the League of Nations fight in the Senate," he delighted in telling Clark, "was gone over again at Sacramento – all the traditional arguments were brought up once more. Fortunately, our opposition was not skillful, and so didn't make the effective fight that could be made against the amendment project." [70]

Cranston showed considerable knowledge of lobbying and the legislative process, as well as vote counting, which he obviously enjoyed describing in detail to Clark. U. W. F. had sent postcards to all members of the legislature, asking them if they would support the resolution. "About one-third, thinking, if they thought anything, that it would be a meaningless memorial – not binding in any way – replied that they would. There were no negative replies." Then they sent a questionnaire to all U. W. F. California members, asking them to contact their state legislators. To a question of whether they knew their representative, one woman replied, "Yes, I know my Senator rather well. He is my husband." Cranston had gotten himself "smuggled in" to a Junior Chamber of Commerce cocktail party for San Francisco legislators, where he had cornered Assemblyman Maloney and arranged to discuss the resolution the next day. "Tom is a happy-go-lucky-seeming bird, but actually quite efficient on his job; above all, a slick and skilled politician. He decided the resolution would be good for Maloney – peace and all that – and agreed to sponsor it in the Assembly at once. We learned that in the Senate there were two key men – if you had them, you had the Senate." One had been a candidate for governor (George Hatfield), the other President Pro Tem Harold Powers. [71]

"I called them both long distance. No luck" with Hatfield who was "quite deaf, uses an ear phone." Powers at first referred Cranston to his own senator, "a fairly potent man named [Beryl] Salsman (as you saw, he gave perhaps the finest speech)." But Cranston pursued Powers, offering to go to where he lived in Northern California (near the Nevada border) to talk with him. He was "a cow-country senator – a real rancher, with several thousand head of cattle, thousands of acres, living way up in Eagleville," about as far from Los Altos as Dublin, New Hampshire, from Washington, D.C. Powers told Cranston that if wanted to come all the way up there, he would talk to him. "So the next weekend, Geneva, Robin, Duffy (dog) and Diana (dog) piled in our car and drove to Eagleville. Found [the senator] a clear-eyed, handsome, forty-fivish rancher. We sat in his study for an hour, while Geneva,

Robin and the dogs played outside in the snow and looked at the cattle. This was one of the most hopeful incidents in all the time I've spent on world government." The senator knew "almost nothing about the U.N.…but just knew darn well that something is badly wrong in the world, and saw another war brewing. In that one hour, he completely accepted the idea of world government – and stuck resolutely to it from that moment on. He by no means realized what a scrap he was getting into, but as the opposition began to appear, later, he got stronger by the moment. He had absolutely no constituent pressure – we still don't have a member in his county. As we left his ranch, I remarked, 'I'd have been awful mad if we'd driven way up here, and then you'd said world government was the worst idea you'd ever heard of.' He laughed: 'I'd sure have told you right off if I didn't agree with you.'"

Others in the U. W. F. organization helped rally legislators, as well. A glitch occurred when Maloney, who at first wanted to grab all the attention to himself by being the sole sponsor, had the legislative counsel's office re-write the resolution, watering it down to "a simple memorial…concerning international affairs." Geneva and U. W. F. volunteer Bob Walker, who were lobbying for the measure in Sacramento, alerted Cranston, and other legislators began to clamor to cosponsor it "because of the constituent pressure they'd been subjected to. Maloney, somewhat surprised at the commotion, agreed" to have them join as cosponsors. "To the utter amazement of Geneva and Bob, sitting in the gallery, 29 members, out of a total of 80, rose and surrounded Maloney, and signed the resolution," Cranston reported to Clark. "Maloney, too, was flabbergasted. This was a tribute, most of all, to Bob Walker's superb organizational work. With that, the resolution was on the map, and got considerable publicity. Maloney, to his surprise, found that the resolution was going to get much more than the mild goodwill publicity he'd anticipated."

"Well, everything sailed smoothly and fairly rapidly for a time," Cranston continued in his report to Clark. "I moved up to Sacramento, and we settled down in an auto court with perhaps the oddest arrangement for lobbyists seen there or anywhere. We left Diana, one of our huge Shepherd dogs, with my mother and father. But we took Duffy, our first love. He stayed in one room, with Bob Walker and me. Geneva and Robin stayed in the adjoining room, together with Geneva's mother, whom we imported from San Diego to baby sit. And so we buckled down to work." The legislative drafters agreed to "tell Maloney they'd made a mistake – we told him that for historical and other reasons, it was imperative to return to the original language." That was done, but it complicated the process because the amended version was not what the cosponsors had signed. "I'm convinced that most of them never found out about the change until after the resolution had gone over to the Senate," Cranston gloated. He had been the only witness to testify before the Senate Rules Committee, and had to justify the revision. Senator Powers kept referring to its objective as a "world court" – "he really seemed to overlook that it went further and set up a whole government." Cranston, Geneva and Walker talked to every senator they could "get at." Opposition began to surface. One man told Cranston, "I'm an isolationist – what are you going to do about me?" The U. W. F. realized that it had to mount constituency pressure. "An attractive young couple flew to Sacramento from Modesto in their private plane to tell Senator Hugh P. Donnelly [of Turlock, a leading opponent], for whom they had ardently campaigned (as Democrats), about the resolution. He advised them that it was the worst proposal that he had ever heard of. They came to our motel headquarters deeply upset, preparing to go home to organize to defeat him in '50. 'Why,' said the girl, 'he talked worse than a Republican!'" Cranston recounted. [72]

By then, the *San Francisco Chronicle* had praised the resolution editorially, and several lobbyists were giving U. W. F. "some invisible help," Cranston continued. But not without *quid pro quos*, he found to his amusement. "One member of the legislature said to us, 'I'll vote for your world-government bill. Now how about you getting all your members to support my bookie bill?" Cranston again was called to testify before the Senate Rules Committee, which began to discuss how to bring the matter to the floor. One sponsor finally protested, "'I think this had better stop. This is the first time I ever saw the committee discuss Senate floor strategy with a witness, after his testimony.' So I cleared out."

A significant part of Cranston's work was counting how legislators might vote, something that he would master in a future arena. He had prepared "dope sheets" with "17 almost sure-fire Ayes," nine likely Nays and five or so unknown votes. Twenty-one votes were needed to adopt the measure. "A day or so before it came up in the Senate, we discovered that the Senate secretary, Joseph Beek, was a member of U. W. F. He was delighted to discover the resolution, and we were delighted to discover him. He commenced lobbying four doubtful senators, including his own," and became "an invaluable source for technical advice on Senate procedure." Cranston and his allies had prepared notes with "impressive quotes and sound arguments" for supporters to use in floor debate, and enjoyed watching many of them studying the tip-sheet at their desks. Senator Powers referred to it from the presiding officer's chair while writing his speech. He "did a good deal of stumbling" at first, which was worrisome, "couldn't even remember the name 'Security Council,' and had to thumb hastily through the [notes] to find it," Cranston wrote of the scene. "The opposition piled onto him, and our hearts sank. But then [Beryl] Salsman, [Richard] Reagan, [Burt W.] Busch and [Thomas F.] Keating did their superb jobs, and our hopes rose from the clouds of seemingly inevitable defeat to some optimism." [73]

"It was one of the longest, tensest debates the Senate had seen in a long time, and drew the complete attention of the Senate" and those watching from the gallery, Cranston told Clark. "Something nice happened when [Senator] Mayo demanded that the resolution be read in full so it would be plain that it was a binding Constitutional step and not just another meaningless resolution. Joseph Beek "leaped from his desk, rushed across the floor, fighting his way through scattering pages, to grab the resolution, and read it himself…slowly and beautifully, stressing all the right words, completely unlike the drone usually employed in such circumstances – he was almost reverent, everyone hung on his words, and the points [were] driven firmly home." When the roll was called, the resolution barely received the required twenty-one votes. That did not diminish the satisfaction in the gallery where Cranston and his friends "exchanged handshakes," and "got a happy grin from Powers on the floor."

It was not over, however. A lobbyist blurted out, "Wait, you haven't won yet." Donnelly was making a motion to reconsider the vote, "and to our horror, it was granted." The U. W. F. forces would spend another ten days working "under increasing pressure," sending wires and letters to legislators. "The opposition made some headway – a Sacramento paper ridiculed the resolution; it was rumored that the [American] Legion and V. F. W. [Veterans of Foreign Wars] were against it; the D. A. R. [Daughters of the American Revolution] in their state convention passed a resolution opposing world government; one senator [whom] we had counted among the sure 17 deserted, on the grounds this was a federal and not a state problem. Each day, the opposition requested another day's delay," which was granted, giving it more time to organize. Cranston and company made sure that their "strongest friends" were on the floor each day as the hour approached for the reconsideration vote. "By the time the second debate came, we felt that every politician in the state knew something about world government. Powers was really beginning to know the subject…and even Maloney, who almost had a fist fight over it in the Senator Hotel, was beginning to talk the language of world government." In the end, only three opposition leaders spoke against it. "Our side made a demonstration of strength by making a point of order ending debate, the roll was called, and we won again, by a lesser margin, but a sufficient one." Donnelly again tried to sabotage it by calling for absentees. "The great doors of the Senate were locked, so no one could leave, and only senators could enter. After a dramatic 40 minutes, Donnelly gave up, picking up only a couple of votes, and we had finally won. One of the most heartening things about the whole affair was that, apart from the good publicity and general strength and prestige the world-government movement gained by the victory," Cranston concluded, was that many legislators had become converts to the cause.[74]

Cranston had made an impression on many of them with his forthrightness and organized approach. "I remarked to many on the effectiveness of your presentation," Marin County Senator Thomas Keating wrote Cranston after his testimony before a committee, "and I must take this opportunity of telling you that I thought it was one of the finest I have heard made before a Legislative Committee. It was complete and dignified and did great credit to the United World Federalists. You were a perfect representative under difficult circumstances."[75]

Minnesota Democratic U. S. Senator Hubert H. Humphrey touted the California action in a U. W. F. press release April 7 as a "heartening sign. It indicates the true desires of the American people and should be encouragement to those who are seeking a stronger world order." Republican Governor Earl Warren sent copies of the California resolution to other states, urging similar action, and to President Truman and members of Congress. The *Chicago Tribune*, however, owned by ultra-conservative Robert R. McCormick, whose editorial policy was decidedly isolationist, disparaged the action in California, "notoriously the land of cults and fads and screw-ball political and social schemes," citing the fact that California hogged "the water supply from the Colorado River, a motive which hardly jibes with the One-World principle of surrendering selfish sovereignty." Other states might retaliate by using "California as an outlet for excess Asiatic populations, or divert the Colorado to" irrigate Mexico. Warren could not be expected to mitigate such effects – "After all, he was Tom Dewey's running mate, and both of them have successfully kept it a secret to this day what they were running for or about." The newspaper would be relentless in its criticism of U. W. F. policies.[76]

Cranston had to defend the U. W. F. position against critics who feared that a world government would put the United States in a vulnerable position if forced to disarm. Federalists, Cranston wrote the *San Francisco Chronicle*, accepted that the United States had to defend its people and territory against aggression, and were on record in favor of preparedness, the Marshall Plan and the North Atlantic Pact (predecessor to NATO signed in 1949), while believing that such a pact would be of limited duration and would not solve the fundamental problem of preventing war. Meanwhile Federalists went forward with their efforts to get other states to pass similar resolutions. [77]

There was opposition to overcome. *Common Cause* magazine carried "quite negative articles" on the proposal that needed rebuttals, and Cranston hoped that Clark could "draw [Secretary of State Dean Acheson] into a good correspondence." [78]

There was positive action in Congress, however. Ninety-one members introduced a House resolution asking that the government work for the establishment of a world federation with "powers adequate to preserve peace and prevent aggression through…enforcement of world law." The *Chicago Tribune* again was critical and derisive, calling it "*the great illusion*." "Before Americans seriously consider subjecting themselves to rule by such a world government," an editorial warned, "they will wish to take a careful look at the types of countries and governments" with which they would join – military dictatorships in Latin America and the fascist one led by Generalissimo Franco in Spain, semi-socialist states like Britain and France with its "powerful communist minority," communist China, African colonies that "would bring to world government a race problem far more acute than anything we know here." The paper conceded that without Russia and its communist satellites, "a federation of powers would be as useless as the present United Nations." [79]

In the course of working with Congress, Cranston first encountered the new congressman from Southern California, Richard Nixon, who in 1947 had defeated, in a nasty, duplicitous campaign, Cranston's friend Jerry Voorhis. Already known as conservative, Nixon would be a plus if added to the roster of sponsors, Cranston knew. At a hearing held by the House Un-American Activities Committee (HUAC), he decided to send Nixon, a member of the committee, a note. It read, "Alan Cranston, president of the United World Federalists. May I see you for a moment?" Nixon looked at it, made an ugly face, crumpled it up and threw it away. [80]

Cranston was optimistic, though, after his recent state success. "Our experience in California did away with my remaining doubts," he wrote Norman Cousins, who had sent a "heart-warming wire" of congratulations, "and I now know that we have found a mechanism for developing the strongest peace movement the nation has yet known." [81]

He pitched an attention-getting theme to promote his cause – cutting taxes. "A 6-feet-2 former Stanford University athlete yesterday told San Franciscans how to cut their taxes by 80 percent," the *Chronicle* reported in August, 1949. "The method is limited world government." War, Cranston argued, cost every American citizen 78 cents out of each dollar paid in taxes. It was an argument that he would use in future. [82]

The Federalist movement, however, coincided with the increasingly strident Red-baiting of Wisconsin Republican Senator Joseph R. McCarthy, who "made the Red scare into a potent political weapon," a political writer noted. (McCarthy ultimately would be censured by the Senate.) The Federalists' position in favor of a peace-keeping body was construed by conservatives as giving up U. S. sovereignty to non-American powers, although Federalists favored policing only disarmament. [83]

"I find myself snorting in derision at the announcement by Drew Pearson of the un-American Committee's next project – flushing out Italian Fascists in this country," a friend wrote the Cranstons in 1947. "Would like to hear Alan's comments on this.... [T]he country is belly-full of their attempts to stir up hysteria over communist infiltration.... I don't know how it is in California, but I bet the witch-hunt is growing strong out there, and as you can well imagine, the atmosphere in Washington is one of fright and tension. We know people whose [telephone] lines are being tapped (in one case, the telephone company even told one of the victims, when he complained of the bad service he was getting), and of course it's an old story that you take note of who sits at adjacent tables in restaurants and cocktail spots before you say anything that might be misinterpreted." [84]

"I'm told you've become something of a factor in California politics," Amster Spiro wrote Cranston, "presumably because of that compulsion of yours to battle for the underdog? I suppose you're battling all the local McCarthyites – sandwiched in between your building of earthquake-proof dwellings and having a barrel of fun out of it, as usual?" [85]

Cranston spoke forcefully against Red-baiting in testimony before the State Senate Judiciary Committee in June, 1949, when the world-government resolution was threatened with recision.

> "I appear before you to oppose Senate Joint Resolution 36 [to rescind the measure], and along with it the whole dangerous, vicious practice of witch-hunting – of calling 'Red' or 'Communist' anything or everything someone may dislike. For that has been the tactic of the backers of [the resolution] in their effort to rescind Assembly Joint Resolution 26.
>
> "Those who seek to pin the label 'Communist' upon every person or cause they oppose for any reason whatsoever are unwittingly playing the communist game. They drive many good Americans from countless worthwhile causes....
>
> "I charge that those who shout 'Communist' at every new solution proposed for today's political, social and economic problems are disloyal to democracy. It is nothing less than treachery to give the Soviet Union or its communist agents here credit for every decent impulse that arises on the American scene. To do so belittles the creative capacity of free minds in free men.
>
> "If every honest, intelligent effort to deal with the manifold problems of the 20th century is indiscriminately labeled 'communist-inspired,' eventually the underprivileged, the insecure, and many more will say, 'communism can't really be so bad, after all.'
>
> "There is no greater treason to democracy than this. There can be no greater service to Moscow." [86]

By then, twenty-two states had adopted resolutions in favor of world government and the congressional resolution had 102 House sponsors and nineteen in the Senate. President Truman had sent a public message to U. W. F. the previous year, saying, "From time to time, the increasing activities of your organization have come to my attention, and I must congratulate you on the patriotism and high sense of historical destiny that inspires your work." That may have been the result of a meeting that Cranston arranged – his second with the president since 1945. Cranston took a group that included Norman Cousins to discuss World Federalism and the need to strengthen the U. N. "We had a very good talk with him," Cranston later recalled. [87]

Even Republican Senator Robert A. Taft had praised the "high sense of patriotism which inspires every member of your group with whom I have talked." "Will any American citizen with any faith in our democratic institutions believe for one moment that the Communists are so strong and efficient, and the elected representatives of the people so easily duped, that all this activity in…states and in the national Capitol is a communist conspiracy?" Cranston asked in his testimony to the state committee. "Actually, the facts would seem to indicate that the opposition" to the state resolution "and to world government in general is communist-inspired." He could make "a rather convincing" case for that point, but it would force him "to resort to the witch-hunting tactics which are so subversive to all things American." Opponents, he argued charitably, were "patriotic, well-meaning Americans" who "have simply failed to come to grips with the facts of life in the twentieth century." They even had circulated an attack upon war-decorated Cord Meyer in an effort to squelch the state resolution. [88]

They were resorting to innuenda and clothing "themselves in legislative immunity," Cranston charged. U. W. F. would counter such attacks with "charges of libel," if necessary, he threatened, to clear its name. [89]

Several California state senators, however, switched their position from pro- to anti-world government. "Possibly you were influenced by the loose charges of communism made in and about the Senate," Cranston wrote them, enclosing his testimony documenting the "solid and patriotic nature of the world-government leadership." One senator, H. R. Judah of Santa Cruz, changed his position to support, telling Cranston that he did not worry too much about American sovereignty under a world government. "The menace of war which is continually hanging over us is a frightful thing and any move to eradicate it should be backed up by legislative bodies," Judah wrote Cranston. At the time, there was hope that Russia, whose people, Judah said, were "really slave laborers," would implode in its own revolution. "In such a case, the carrying out of the World Federalists' plan would be much easier." [90]

Heartened, Cranston replied, "Frequently we are amazed by the rapidly growing strength of the sentiment in this country for this program." [91]

But Cranston had to defend the U. W. F. locally when a Palo Alto woman, in a letter to the *San Jose Mercury Herald*, angrily charged that Federalists would be sent to a Paris conference at taxpayer expense and world government would supersede local laws. "Actually, the United World Federalist proposals are extremely conservative and highly limited," Cranston rebutted to the editor, and would leave "all power not lodged in the world federal government…to member nations." A world government "would not write our traffic laws any more than the U. S. government" did for states, he ended in exasperation. [92]

Cranston's work on the California resolution nevertheless made him a prime candidate to lead the national U. W. F. Ted Waller sounded him out in April, 1949: "If a), Cord were to definitely abandon any thought of another term, and b), there were to be a clamor for your services, would you consider the job? PPS. They loved you in Denver. They say, 'A[lan] was a fine U. W. F. man, full of gusto, artful in skirting the tough problems." [93]

"I am rather horrified at the idea," Cranston replied, "because I'm leading the good life in California, enjoying it, and getting on. It would sure interfere with my personal plans, and also, anyone who brings up Robin in N. Y. for a while, instead of in California, should be shot. However,…if the clamor was sufficient to give me opportunity to [correct]…some of U. W. F.'s ills…as a condition of my acceptance, I might be willing to consider the thing." [94]

The organization indeed was plagued by internal disagreements over its mission and tactics. "If we are going to significantly influence American foreign policy, we must expand, not destroy, our rapport with the people who are now in power," Waller advised. U. W. F. could not be "all things to everybody. We have got to stop being intimidated by one-man minorities on the executive council" and the "nauseating illusion that we can afford to work with everybody who is for world government." [95]

On the matter of Cranston's possible candidacy for president, Waller reported "there has been only one negative note. It is to the effect that the candidate tends to be impetuous and to act with too little consultation and insufficient planning. If we are serious about this proposition (and I think we should be), then I submit that this criticism (in which there just might be a tiny nugget of validity) should be met implicitly in advance," by getting support from "respected and accepted brain-trusters."

Several other people were being mentioned as possible presidents, and there was "also a little anti-Cranston talk based on the impression that before the last Assembly, you were in league with the People's Convention boys and this is at best an evidence of instability." Cranston reiterated that he had tried to "prevent a schism in the U. W. F. over the People's Convention." Waller, too, had received criticism that Cranston tried to counter, reinforcing support for the job that Waller was doing in Washington. [96]

Taking the post was not an easy decision. Eleanor and Geneva felt that it might be a beneficial move if Cranston wanted to build a reputation for future political purposes. On the other hand, the organization had fiscal problems, and the movement enemies, all of which could turn the job into "a personal calamity," as Eleanor put the options. Even U. W. F. leader Upshur Evans, who was urging Cranston to accept, told him ominously, "Only an ass would take the job, and he must face the fact that it could ruin his career." [97]

Cranston's father also gave advice on taking the job. He drew a line down the middle of a page, and listed the "pro" and "con" arguments. Under "pro" he cited "business and political contacts which might be important, potential opportunity to lobby in public interests, interesting life in Washington, work for which you are especially suited." The "con" list was longer: "May mean a five-year delay in principal objective [of earning money];...the smear [referring to allegations of association with communism]; limitations on working and writing for world government ["and other causes," Cranston himself added]; loss of developed skill in public speaking; less in touch with property interests; leaving California" – under which William Cranston listed, tongue-in-cheek, "less outdoor life, less Stanford football, not good for children, having to wear city clothes, away from family and contacts, high cost of living, etc." He concluded by citing whether Cranston wanted a business or political career, advising that he "should [be] learning more about real-estate investments." Cranston starred the points he thought critical – the last was not among them. [98]

By the end of May, Cranston would tell Clark that "after a good deal more thought, after some long talks with Cord...and after your letter, I've decided I should be available if the conditions are satisfactory." He wanted it to be a maximum two-year stint to make it worth moving his family back East, and to encourage new leaders to take the job. It was as good a time as any for the family to move for a short period, and Cranston told Clark that he had enough income "leeway to give us some sense of security" against the low salary that he would receive. He hoped that he would be able to get Clark "on the phone almost at will" for advice and help, and agreed that putting the organization on a sound financial footing was priority. "I wish I could stay here [in California] and do it, and Geneva raised the same point; but I don't think it would work, any more than you do," he conceded. [99]

"As for politics," he revealed, "I could be the Democratic candidate for Congress in this district in the next election if I wanted to be. But the plain fact is that I would almost certainly be licked, as would any other Democrat. For this is a real Republican stronghold, with no sign of imminent change. To run for Congress, or any other office, I almost certainly would have to reside in another district. It would be as easy, perhaps far better, for me to move after the N. Y. stint, if it comes. Although I'm on excellent footing with the party leadership at the state level, running for anything more than Congress is of course not presently in sight. So here, too, the U. W. F. thing seems not to be minus; and perhaps here it could turn out to be plus."

He now considered the prospect "challenging...and something I'd rather like to take on. One of the great advantages of my returning to N. Y., if I do," he added with wry humor, would be that long-distance calls to "Dublin #1," Clark's telephone number at his farm, "will be much closer at hand."

In June, 1949, Cranston was chosen by the U. W. F. nominations committee as the presidential candidate. Waller asked him to send "some documentary evidence of the nature and coloration of your activities while you were with INS in Rome and with O. W. I. here.... We have a little preventive medicine to do, nothing serious, but I am the stitch-in-time boy." [100]

Waller meanwhile was working on the congressional resolution which had no force of law but encouraged the president to explore options for world government. The Senate Foreign Relations Committee had appointed a subcommittee specifically to consider the resolution. "This is far more than we had hoped for on the Senate side," Waller told Cranston. Having ninety-one House members from both parties co-sponsoring the measure "could scarcely have been imagined a decade ago," the *New York Herald Tribune* editorialized, and "even today seems astonishing for its boldness." The *San Diego Union* also editorialized favorably, quoting British poet Alfred Tennyson who had envisioned a "Parliament of Man, the Federation of the world." [101]

But a chief House sponsor of a competing Atlantic Union Committee resolution – proponents of an Atlantic pact composed only of democratic nations – cried foul. Republican Walter H. Judd of Minnesota telegraphed Waller to "register strong protest against unmistakable and unjustifiable implication" that the U. W. F. was advertising its "carefully defined and limited" resolution as "equivalent to world government." The misleading promotion "may well be disastrous to hopes of getting favorable action" on anything in Congress, he said, asking, "Is your group more interested in fireworks for itself or real progress toward workable world organization to prevent war?" When one sponsor withdrew his name because he felt the Federalists endorsed "a socialist-planned economy," the *Christian Science Monitor* retorted that "the chief strength of the World Federalist movement has been that it has cut across divisions of right and left, and drawn both conservatives and liberals in support of its ideal of limited world government.... The wisest Federalists have seen the error of attacking the U. N. rather than seeking to strengthen it gradually... and the congressional resolution did no more than set an ideal for American foreign policy to aim at." Socialists, it commented, were "the chief obstacle" to that goal. [102]

Cranston had used his acquaintance with Estes Kefauver, who had backed the Atlantic Union resolution, to lobby on the Federalists' side in the Senate, to which the Tennessee congressman had been elected in 1948. "I was delighted to follow your great victory," Cranston wrote him with personal interest. "I hope that you are writing [a] book...so that others can find out how to repeat the process elsewhere." He was "very pleased" to find Kefauver "interested in...paving the way to world government.... It is certainly going to help the Federalist movement get ahead to have you in the Senate." [103]

Kefauver, though, introduced the rival resolution in that body. He argued that all avenues should be considered, pointing out that approaches to date had been piece-meal – economically through the European Recovery Program, politically with the North Atlantic pact, and militarily with a rearmament program. "Meanwhile...there are whispers of a new atomic enigma to be solved," Kefauver stated. [104]

Cranston also congratulated newly-elected California Congresswoman Helen Gahagan Douglas, the attractive former actress and singer, on her "magnificent November victory." Cranston, while still in the army, at her request had counseled her on running for office in a meeting at the Hay Adams Hotel in Washington. Now he was "writing to say that I hope you will find it personally and politically possible to run for the U. S. Senate in 1950. If you do, I want you to know that I am prepared to do anything that will help." Cranston was looking ahead, not only for Douglas but for himself. "At the moment I am concentrating on United World Federalist activity, but I am also active in the 8th Congressional District of the Democratic Party. I am program chairman of the Palo Alto-Stanford Democratic Council." By then, there were 3,000 U. W. F. members in twenty-six chapters in Northern California (with similar figures in Southern California). [105]

In the summer of 1949, Cranston was chosen unanimously as the second president of the Federalists, succeeding Cord Meyer who had been forced to retire by "fatigue," one article said. Cranston cabled his parents in Florence, Italy, "ALOFT," family code for "arrived safely," to which his father sent congratulations, tempered by regret that the younger Cranstons would be moving away. Cranston also would quit the family business, which was sold to a longtime friend of William Cranston's, Edward Ames. [106]

Norman Cousins sent warm words: "I started out to write you a note of congratulations a moment ago, but tore it up when I realized the congratulations ought to go to everyone around this table [the U. W. F. Executive Council]. You've got a real team behind you. Put it to the test." Cranston would need all the help that he could muster. [107]

The change was publicized in national media and local publications like the *Stanford Alumni Review*, accompanied by photographs of a nearly bald Cranston looking older than his thirty-five years. "When the war ended, a young Palo Alto contractor wrote a book called *The Killing of the* Peace. Alan Cranston, the author, considered his preoccupation with…peace in our time sufficiently important to… do more about it than just write a warning book…. [T]his fortnight he found that his grave concern…had led to a full-time job," the California magazine *Fortnight* reported. Cranston, it said, while a correspondent in Europe in the 1930s, had become convinced that isolationism was a direct cause of war, and that only authoritative world law could reach beyond national borders to secure peace.[108]

"He is a massive, square-jawed young American, casually dressed," a profile of Cranston in the U. W. F. monthly publication *World Government News* began. "By his slightly receding hairline, you would judge him to be in his late thirties. If you are introduced, you get a strong handshake, a brusque but friendly smile, and no small talk. Meeting him, you might assume that here was a practical, ambitious young businessman, or a successful college coach, or possibly an up-and-coming newspaperman." Cranston's "clean-cut, 'American boy' looks" no doubt had helped him obtain entry to the Dolfuss trial, the writer, Bennett Skews-Cox, executive director of the Northern California U. W. F., said of Cranston's foreign-correspondent experiences. [109]

He "is a practical man, a voracious reader with a prodigious memory," and a liberal, Skewes-Cox continued. "His attractive and equally dynamic wife, Geneva Cranston, calls him 'an almanac of sports statistics…from the year 1890 on.'" She added that he "loves people more deeply than anyone I've ever known," and "never notices whether they are Christian, Irish, Jewish, Scotch, Negro, Japanese, Canine or Female." "Two German shepherds and his cyclonic two-year-old Robin (on whom his father dotes) complete an energetic household for Mrs. Cranston, herself an active and intelligent Federalist." Cranston himself, for a profile in *Current Biography*, added to his list of hobbies movies, the comic strip *Blondie* and political anecdotes. That profile said that Cranston was "considered a forceful speaker."[110]

Cranston was credited with championing the state resolution plan for a Constitutional amendment. And "Delegates to the national U. W. F. convention in Minneapolis last year will recall his humor and good sense," Skewes-Cox wrote. Cranston also was "an excellent administrator blessed with the ability to effect compromise among his co-workers," assets that would be needed to forge unity within the diverse organization. [111]

Cranston optimistically predicted that a change in the U. N. toward world government would come about by 1955 "at the very latest." That would be the tenth anniversary of the U. N.'s founding when it was to consider calling a conference to revise its charter. He also anticipated that 1950 elections would send more pro-U. W. F. representatives to Congress. As its president, he would continue to push for more states to adopt the Constitutional-amendment resolution. "It's 1955 or bust," he said in an interview with the *Daily Palo Alto Times*. "The local man has given up all [other] interests to promote the United World Federalist cause," the article said. As to national sovereignty, he had decided that the world no longer had those rights. "Tojo [the Japanese prime minister] made the most important decision in our lifetime when he pulled the string that caused Pearl Harbor. Bang, we were in the war. Where was our sovereignty then? If Mr. Stalin chose, he could with one puff blow our sovereignty to bits again by plunging us into war." U. W. F. welcomed opposition, he added, confident that its ideas would stand up as the best options available. Communists, he emphasized, were firmly in the opposite camp. [112]

U. W. F. numbered 50,000 members nationally when Cranston took over as president in October, 1949. *Newsweek* magazine called it "the nation's biggest world-government group." Even before he was officially president, Cranston was pushing for annual dues of $5.00, urging New York members to vote for it as not only "necessary for the success but possibly for the survival of U. W. F." [113]

The Cranstons had been living with his parents while the house on Hilltop Road in Los Altos was under construction and would not occupy it until his presidential term ended. Faced with finding a place for his family and "small dog" (Duffy, the German shepherd) to live in Manhattan, Cranston asked the New York director of U. W. F. if he would run a notice to members that might lead to a three-bedroom apartment "if possible around Washington Square near the office." He could not pay more than $250 a month. In the end, the Cranstons found an apartment at 1 Lexington Avenue next to Gramercy Park. Eleanor wrote in her biography that by amazing coincidence, Lee Falk had chosen the same building and moved in the same day as the Cranstons. Geneva, besides being a new mother, found time to ghost-write a book, the subject of which she carefully guarded from reporters. [114]

Cranston's tenure as U. W. F. president would be marked by a constant need to refute charges that the organization had communist ties. A particular nuisance was Myron C. Fagan, a Hollywood gad-fly who had worked against the U. W. F. resolution as director of the Cinema Educational Guild. Fagan described himself as a former producer who had been "black-balled" by the Warner and Mayer film studios for his persistence in exposing communists in Hollywood. According to a report on un-American activities in California, Fagan had been a playwright and producer in New York until going to Hollywood in 1920 where he worked for Pathé Pictures as a writer-director. He had written plays, one called "Red Rainbow" about the threat of domestic communism, which, the report said, in 1945 had been so opposed by pro-communist elements that he was unable to raise money to produce it. He had produced one play in Hollywood called "Thieves Paradise" in 1947; its leading man, Howard Johnson, had been harassed by telephone to the point of a nervous breakdown, forcing the play to close. It reopened under sponsorship by a group of women's organizations. At one performance Fagan made a curtain speech naming 100 prominent people in the motion picture business as communist sympathizers. [115]

The Cinema Educational Guild, formed in 1949, issued booklets, letters and circulars about communism. Fagan had relied on the California legislative Committee on Un-American Activities for his information on infiltration in Hollywood. Its report, however, pointed out that Fagan continued to slander people who might have quit alleged subversive organizations, a fault common to similar "unofficial" groups who did not have the facts and thus caused "an enormous amount of harm." Fagan misled the public by claiming to have access to "official" files. Many of his publications, the committee report stated, contained "erroneous," "self-serving" and anti-Semitic statements. In short, "Mr. Fagan may well be one of the nation's outstanding experts on matters theatrical, but that does not necessarily qualify him as an expert in the field of counter-subversive intelligence," and much of his smearing was "sheer nonsense." [116]

Fagan had sued U. W. F. of California along with the *Christian Science Monitor*, CBS news commentator Chet Huntley and the Anti-Defamation League of B'nai B'rith for libel in 1950, then brought charges against his lawyer, which the California Bar Association dismissed as unsubstantiated. The suit claimed that a broadcast by Huntley slanderously accused Fagan of bigotry, anti-Semitism and cooperation with the Ku Klux Klan. Fagan dropped the suit with prejudice (meaning that he could never bring suit against the defendants again for any of the charges).

Fagan charged that U. W. F. had railroaded its resolution through the legislature and was "controlled by known 'reds' and 'pinks,'" calling delegates to the founding Ashville meeting – Albert Einstein, Serge Koussevitsky, Raymond Gram Swing, Thomas Mann, Carl van Doren, Rex Stout and Elmer Rice – "active members of various communist and front organizations." Student chapters of U. W. F. were "stooges" drawn by the idealistic "promise of no more wars," Fagan said. [117]

Future U. S. Congressman Don Edwards, then chairman of the Palo Alto Federalists, strongly denied Fagan's charges, calling them "ridiculous" and his appearance in Palo Alto presumptuous. Edwards backed his case by showing newspapers Jew-baiting pamphlets, including one written by Fagan, "Red Stars over Hollywood," all mailed from the same postal box as one used by anti-Communist agitator Gerald L. K. Smith of Tulsa. [118]

"An all-out on slot on the U. W. F. is getting under way in Los Angeles, seemingly engineered almost entirely by former 'American Firsters' and people who have gravitated around" Smith, Cranston wrote Harry Braverman. Pressure was being brought on members of Congress who had sponsored the world-government resolution, which Cranston noted was giving Los Angeles Republican Congressman Donald L. Jackson enough "cause for alarm to do us great damage in the House Foreign Affairs Committee." Cranston asked Braverman for advice on how to approach the congressman "and the best ways to bring pressure to bear upon him." [119]

HUAC member Richard Nixon was asked by the Republican State Central Committee chairman to furnish a committee report on U. W. F. "In checking with the committee staff," Nixon responded, "I have been informed that the United World Federalists has not been cited as a communist-front organization by the committee, the Federal Bureau of Investigation, or the Attorney General. As far as I can determine, no investigation of the organization by any of the afore-mentioned groups is contemplated. You are welcome to make this information public, if you so desire, since it represents an official report by the committee staff to me." [120]

Cranston's first act as U. W. F. president was to testify in October, 1949, before the House Foreign Affairs Committee on the world-government resolution. He would not dwell on the consequences of World War III, he began: "I am sure that efforts have been made by experts to scare the members of this committee" about atomic, bacteriological and other weapons of mass destruction. "I would like to talk to you, as a businessman, about the consequences of the present preparedness program and the arms race." He couched his testimony in economic terms, arguing that the high cost of military expenditures was detrimental to the national interest. "Today, payment for past and preparation for future wars consumes almost 80 percent of the tax dollar," the Marshall Plan for rebuilding and arming western Europe was causing a $2 billion deficit in the U. S. balance of payments, and national debt lowered the value of the dollar, he pointed out. [121]

He emphasized U. W. F.'s conviction to strengthen the United Nations. Other nations, though, were waiting for the United States to take the lead. The existing U. N. could not "be relied upon to execute the worldwide inspections and controls which must be an essential element of any plan for armament control." He quoted from George Orwell's *Animal Farm* – "All animals are created equal, but some animals are more equal than others" – to illustrate the need to revise representation so that nations had voting power proportionate to their economic and other assets. "What is envisaged is a government, federal in form, *like our own*, reserving to its various members all powers not specifically delegated to the world body. This is *not a proposal* for the *abandonment* or *sacrifice* of American sovereignty. Sovereignty is the business of doing something yourself, or, with others, choosing representatives to do for you certain things that you *cannot do alone*." [122]

It all sounded very plausible and convincing, and Cranston would argue the point throughout his life, tenaciously defending it against charges that America would lose its sovereignty.

He also reiterated that communist nations *opposed* world government and had disbanded such organizations in Poland and Czechoslovakia. Republican Congressman Jacob J. Javits of New York thought U. W. F.'s the most practicable approach because it was limited to a plan to prevent war, which helped Cranston's cause. [123]

Cranston's appearance before the committee brought disdain from right-wing newspapers, which tainted him by dredging up his O. W. I. associations. The unfriendly *Chicago Daily Tribune* snorted that "With a minimum of publicity, a new leader of the largest 'world-government' group in the United States has emerged on the public stage." It reminded readers that while "No direct communistic affiliations were attributed to him, he was named in Congress as a supporter of Harry Bridges, leftist labor leader, and an associate of Louis Adamic, a member of numerous communist fronts." The old allegations were cited, bordering on libel, including Cranston's association with David Karr, accused of reporting for "Drew Pearson, smear columnist," and Robert Sherwood, labeled "the leftist dramatist." [124]

The *Washington Times-Herald* derided U. W. F., "an outfit dedicated to the extinction of the American republic," for trotting "out a retreaded New Deal war-time propagandist as its new president and mouthpiece. It is a rather remarkable fact that the government goes out of its way to prosecute leaders of the Communist Party for seeking the overthrow of the United States, but that leaders of movements which would achieve the same result in a different direction are given a respectful audience by congressmen." Its advocates were "pretty silly people" who would render the U. S. a minority under a world constitution "drafted by the backward masses of China, Russia, India, and states of that order." [125]

Cranston apparently was undaunted by such antipathy, confident of the rightness of his mission, and traveled across the nation promoting it. He and Albert Einstein drew a large crowd at Princeton University (Cranston noticed that Einstein was doodling during the presentation). He spoke to Rotary (of which he was a member) and women's clubs, Chambers of Commerce, whatever and wherever groups would hear him. [126]

In California, Cranston's immediate family were a supportive part of his "team." Eleanor and Jack Fowle both were active Federalists – Jack chaired the Los Altos chapter (of which state Senator Robert Kirkwood was a member, something that would come back to haunt him). Eleanor was a delegate to the national executive council, and wrote tracts promoting U. W. F.'s ideals. [127]

Critics and Congress, though, would not leave U. W. F. alone. In 1950 Cranston again would be before Congress, defending the Federalists to the House Un-American Activities Committee. U. W. F. had offered full cooperation to the committee, whose information consisted largely of media accounts, none of which were incriminating for communist alliances. To the contrary, a 1950 article, "The World-Government Plan" in *The Worker* communist magazine, called the idea "a reflection…of the aspirations of American foreign policy to dominate the world." U. W. F.'s hierarchy, author Frieda F. Halpern complained, was "as fine a collection of the monopolists, military men and anti-Soviet careerists as can be found anywhere…both very 'respectable' and most obviously non-radical." Cranston was among those whom the committee biographed, noting references from detractors (principally Congressman Fred E. Busbey) and the fact that Cranston's name appeared in an investigation of the Federal Communications Commission by a Select Committee in 1943. The HUAC report added of Cranston: "It should be further noted that, according to the *New York Times* of February 26, 1950, page 7, Alan Cranston, president of the United World Federalists, Inc., denied a charge that his organization 'stinks of communist government' and stated that Communists are barred from membership in his organization." "I could furnish you many speeches of mine in which I said unpleasant things about the Soviet Union," Cranston told the congressmen at one point. [128]

A U. W. F. researcher, Margaret "Peggy" Dudley, helped gather information to exonerate it, especially to counter the *Chicago Daily Tribune* charges. She found no evidence in congressional records that the House Appropriations Committee had criticized O. W. I.'s foreign-language division as furthering Soviet interests, telling Cranston in January, 1950, that she was "tired of spending evenings in the Library of Congress" but was "glad to help in any way to combat this horrid disease." [129]

Cranston issued a long statement refuting the *Tribune*'s allegations. Attacks seeking "to give the impression that I am a Red" were the same as those used by the un-credible Myron Fagan and his associates, one of whom was "an acknowledged Ku Klux Klanner. For the sake of the record, I will here set forth the facts concerning the allegation made in the McCormick press as it has joined hands with the Hearst press in violent opposition to world government," Cranston said in a rare bit of vitriol. [130]

But the charges continued. A teacher in northern California, Fern Bruner, was accused of being subversive by a San Francisco radio commentator in 1958, citing her membership in U. W. F., which he called communist-dominated. Bruner was discharged and sued for reinstatement and damages. The State Senate Committee on Un-American Activities in California testified on her behalf, pointedly stating that it had evidence U. W. F. was *not* a communist front. Bruner was awarded $55,000 in punitive damages. Her attorney, Gardiner Johnson, a candidate for State Chairman of the Republican Party that year, said the verdict indicated "that the American people will no longer tolerate this kind of attack," and the *San Francisco Chronicle* said of the decision, "It will, we hope, halt the careless, the ignorant, the vicious public accusation of subversion against innocent and loyal persons and point up the advisability of carefully investigating such accusations before they are put into print or on the air." The legislative committee further exonerated U. W. F. by saying in a 1961 report that it was "an example of an organization, liberal in nature and non-conformist in objective, that has been unjustly accused of being a communist-front organization."[131]

A high school Federalist in Palo Alto one day mentioned to classmates that her father had been an attaché to the Russian delegation in 1945 when the U. N. was being formed at San Francisco. The next morning her family found outside their house a set of phonograph recordings of the Russian Red Army chorus. "We did not know if the gesture were anti-Communist or pro-Communist," Joanne Peterson Sonnichsen remembered, but it was "disquieting. Those were very disquieting years. I understood the fear that people were coming after you." She would still "believe in world peace through world law" a half century later. It seemed "the only way we were ever going to get a handle on this terrible situation. And because Alan Cranston was head of the Federalists, I respected him." [132]

Cranston found that he had to defend the Federalists wherever he went, turning the criticism back on its strident opponents. "The Daughters of the American Revolution and Veterans of Foreign Wars are being misled into the camp of the Communists in their opposition to world government," one newspaper quoted Cranston as saying. He had to make his case during a fourth effort to rescind the U. W. F. resolution in California (of 22 similar state resolutions, only Georgia's had been rescinded in 1950). U. W. F. could hardly be called a communist front, Cranston frequently noted, when Radio Moscow dubbed its leader Cord Meyer "the fig leaf of American imperialism." Cranston appeared confident and smiling broadly in photographs accompanying news accounts of his talks. [133]

He personally tried to intercede for his former O. W. I. colleague in the Foreign Language Division, Joe Facci, who came under suspicion in 1951. "Apparently the wolves are after him again," he told their former colleague Jerry Spingarn, asking him to "poke around in the State Department" to "learn what they're trying to do. He is absolutely not a Communist. He hates all dictators violently. He is simply a typical, Italian anti-Fascist, with the most heart-felt democratic sentiments, as his emotional letter makes damn well plain. The wolves got after him once in O. W. I. I was told to fire him. I flatly refused, declaring I'd resign before doing so, or if it was done over my head, and make as much racket as I could. At that time, the wolves had not yet started after me, my bargaining power was high, and he was saved, because there really is no substance to any charges against him. I'll go to the limit in vouching for him." [134]

But Cranston had to tell Facci a few weeks later that he should not expect immediate help from that end. Facci, then in Mexico with a U. N. E. S. C. O. rural education program, had had his passport taken by U. S. authorities. Cranston advised him to "write a simple letter to the State Department," asking why. "Do not go into any of the arguments…or other matters which you did at such length in your previous letter. I am afraid that they are so swamped and under-staffed that they simply won't plow through such letters." He also advised Facci to get legal advice from the organization with which he was working. Cranston believed the action would not affect Facci's American citizenship, and he also could cross the U. S.-Mexican border without a passport. The matter was still unresolved by February, 1952, when Cranston told Facci, "It seems to be impossible for Douglas [meaning Supreme Court Justice William O. Douglas, a member of the U. W. F. board?] to intervene…. The fact is that the State Department is terrified at present by the activities of Mssrs. [Joseph] McCarthy and McCarran. Justice is particularly hard to find in this election year." [135]

Cranston himself had to contend with another outspoken Red-baiter, Joseph P. Kamp, author of an anti-world-government book, *We Must Abolish the United States*, and editor of the *Awakener* (1932-35), popular with Nazis. Kamp had been cited in 1944 and served a four-month prison term after conviction in 1948 of contempt of Congress for refusing to tell the House Committee on Political Expenditures who his associates were in a Constitutional Educational League. Cranston pointed out that D. A. R. leader Grace Brosseau had written an introduction to one of Kamp's books. [136]

Kamp, Gerald L. K. Smith and other pro-Nazi sympathizers were "poison-pen pals of the U. S.," *Time* magazine bluntly charged. "In sum, their messages are incoherent, self-canceling and wildly contradictory. But their common purpose is the big smear." The "pince-nezed" Kamp's "touch is far from subtle," *Time* stated disdainfully; "he fans anti-Semitic feelings by picturing prominent Jews who are supporting Ike." [137]

Kamp's followers went so far as to circulate a handbill in Los Altos that tried to smear Cranston. The handbill, which called for rescinding the world-government resolution, stated that Cranston moved "in communist circles" and his friends were "fellow travelers with communist sympathies. Alan Cranston may not be a Communist, but [Assembly Joint Resolution] No. 26, of which he is sponsor, is a plan by the Soviet Union to take over the United States from inside." [138]

A refutation was distributed in Los Altos, surprising Cranston's father and family. "The person attacked is well known locally," it read, "so that little damage can be done to his reputation. The cause to which he is devoting himself, World Federation, however, could possibly be injured." It quoted from a 1950 *Look* magazine article that called Kamp "a greater nuisance than the crude Gerald L. K. Smith" because he "has succeeded in deceiving a greater number of important people regarding his real nature and true purpose." *Look* cited a "record of anti-democratic propaganda" beginning in 1933, used by Nazi news services, which "finally got him into difficulties." His Constitutional Educational League in 1942 and 1943 comprised groups indicted for conspiring to undermine the morale of the armed forces. Gossip columnist and popular broadcaster Walter Winchell publicly had branded Kamp a Fascist, for which Winchell had been castigated by Kamp in a "vicious pamphlet." A substantial part of the League's income came from some 500 industrial organizations and wealthy individuals who shared his agenda, *Look* reported. [139]

The anti-Kamp handbill had been delivered by a local man in the Los Altos business district and San Jose. At first the Cranstons and Fowles thought it best to ignore it because the person handing it out was "known to be a crackpot" and "might resort to violence" if provoked, William Cranston told his son, and decided to publicize their own refutation. He also suggested "a libel action against Kamp" might be useful. "Naturally, we have been upset over the situation, but believe that you will be taking it in stride and having a long-range view rather than seeing the immediate difficulty." [140]

Cranston did take it in stride and went on another nationwide speaking tour. He added germ-warfare to the list of fears that should concern people. The United States and "at least one other country," presumably Russia, had the new weapon, he announced in San Diego. The arms race and its terrific cost was a prominent theme as he reminded audiences that Lenin thirty years earlier had predicted that the United States would spend itself into destruction – and "There is some reason to believe that we are now doing so. We are spending $15,000,000,000 on the arms race, and $16,076,000 on the United Nations – less than New York City spends to dispose of its garbage." But Federalists were not a pacifist group, he stressed. In fact, it urged the House Appropriations Armed Services Subcommittee to approve a military funding bill, recognizing that "until the threat of aggression is stopped, there can be no alternative" to such "tremendous expenditures." [141]

Cranston also continued to work with United Nations officials in support of the U. W. F. goal – to strengthen rather than abolish it. Deputy U. S. Ambassador to the U. N. Ernest A. Gross wrote him in appreciation for "the real assistance that you have given to the State Department and which you gave to me personally while I was Assistant Secretary of State for Congressional Relations in connection with obtaining support on the Hill for legislation affecting international organizations." The ambassador pointed out, however, that some congressmen who had co-sponsored the world-government resolution were not supportive of actual legislation to build an international organization like the U. N. Gross hoped his letter clarified some of Cranston's "troubles and doubts" about the ambassador's view of U. W. F. "Your constant and patient helpfulness is too greatly valued to permit me to remain silent in the face of any possible misunderstanding of my attitude, which I think you know from our personal association," Gross wrote. [142]

In October of his first year as U. W. F. president, Cranston received the Italian "Star of Solidarity" award for his work to exempt Italians from enemy-alien status during the war, news of which his proud father sent him, asking that Cranston translate the Italian so that a news release could be issued announcing the award. "Perhaps it is not too late to have your new honor listed in your biography in *Who's Who* for 1951," he added "with congratulations and love." Cranston was photographed receiving the award from the Italian Consul General in New York. [143]

He also got a mandate of support from U. W. F. members who overwhelmingly affirmed their goal of worldwide federation, not a partial federation if Russia refused to participate. A group of delegates to the fourth annual convention proposed adopting a "realistic" plan that could operate without Russia. Cranston rallied the convention by calling that a "dangerous doctrine" designed to sell the federalist movement to doubting members of the public.[144]

As war in Korea worsened at the end of 1950, Cranston told his membership that world federation remained "a valid objective" and a stronger U. N. was needed more than ever. "Federalists who have battered their enthusiasm against public apathy must redouble their efforts," he wrote in a Christmas message. He was encouraged by membership renewals that U. W. F. was getting as the war expanded. [145]

The California resolution, however, was rescinded in 1950. Its chief opponent, who successfully pushed through the recision, was a conservative assemblyman who would carry a grudge against Cranston for many years, Bruce Reagan. In addition, there was an embarrassing revelation that a U. W. F. leader in Palm Springs had forged names on forty-nine telegrams from her chapter, which Cranston had to admit at a legislative hearing. [146]

The *Chicago Tribune* did not let up its anti-federalist campaign, and wherever he spoke, Cranston had to defend the organization against communist taint. U. W. F. severed relations with a World Movement for World Federal Government after it invited a group accused of having communist backing, Partisans for Peace, to join. On another controversial issue Cranston personally backed President Truman's "firing" of General Douglas MacArthur during the Korean conflict, calling it the "only thing he could do," which "quite possibly saved the United Nations from destruction." He added in a public statement, "I imagine we're in for a wild time with the general coming home now. Something reminiscent of the America First days, only more violent," he predicted. At the same time, U. W. F. was undergoing internal conflicts, over which Cranston had to preside. "I wouldn't be surprised if President Cranston – after a shake-up or two – will return to the quiet and peace of his Los Altos estate," a detractor wrote a local newspaper. [147]

Eleanor Fowle was worried about the perception that U. W. F. was being infiltrated by Communists, particularly youths who were "moving in on it" and might take over. She wrote Cranston in July, 1951, "You're lucky I don't have time to give you my violent views on the student question. Have got a lot of the inside dope on it and am horrified at the N. Y. radical contingent in the leadership.... The new Communist Party line about affiliating has had some surprising results already, according to Fritjof" Thygesson, a Los Altos student activist whose mother was a friend of Eleanor's, "and Wally Stegner," author and Stanford professor of creative writing. [148]

Even President Truman found himself defending a Federalist whom he had named Secretary of the Air Force, Thomas K. Finletter. The Veterans of Foreign Wars had complained that Federalists advocated a reduction in U. S. armed forces for purposes of international policing. Truman responded with characteristic no-nonsense candor. "It seems to me that if you veterans would spend more time trying to find out the good points of a man in public office, instead of trying to tear him down, it would be much more help to the country," he wrote V. F. W. Commander Clyde A. Lewis, who released the letter to the press. "There is not a better or more able public servant than Finletter," Truman continued. "All this howl about organizations a fellow belongs to gives me a pain in the neck. I'd be willing to bet my right eye that you yourself and I have joined some organizations that we wish we hadn't. It hasn't hurt me any and I don't think it has hurt you any." [149]

A more positive event was one in New York in February, 1951, when prominent members of U. W. F., the Writers' Board for World Government, presented a star-studded show, "The Myth that Threatens the World," arranged and directed by musical librettist Oscar Hammerstein II – a founding member of the Federalists – with a supporting cast from Broadway hits *South Pacific* and *The Happy Time*. Rex Stout was master of ceremonies introducing supporters like actor Ralph Bellamy, playwrights Russel Crouse and Robert Sherwood, Massachusetts Congressman Christian A. Herter, and Brigadier General Telford Taylor, chief U. S. counsel to the Nuremberg war crimes trial. Cranston was among the speakers and described the beginnings of U. W. F. [150]

Cranston was not universally popular within the organization, it turned out, and when his term as president was about to end, there were opponents to his reelection. Eleanor, who attended national meetings, reported inside gossip and internal fights to her brother. After an executive council meeting in July, 1951, she wrote Cranston from the "City of San Francisco Streamliner" en route back to California, "There was one more Myth that Threatened U. W. F., disseminated by the people around New York, the only one you had no chance to refute – the myth that you couldn't be reelected. (Bennet [Skewes-Cox] urged me to persuade you not to run because, 'having taken a partisan stand, you couldn't be a unifying influence.' He…persuaded quite a few people of this." Even Cord Meyer had come to think that Cranston could not be reelected. Eleanor loyally told her brother, "It's your responsibility, fighting spirit, and unwillingness to compromise that are the elements of greatness, but Leviticus [actually Matthew] says (though I know you will love me quoting the Bible), '[They] who live by the sword will perish by the sword.'… You've made such a *tremendous contribution to the movement*, I know you can accept the present disappointment. It'll work out for the good of you *and*, later on, the movement, believe me. *It's too bad,* though…. I know there will be people advising you to knife them [opponents] back, so I'm going to advise you not to, most strongly. A year of skillful consolidation may be what U. W. F. needs. There mustn't be further divisiveness – there's just too much else to do." [151]

"You've done a *magnificent* job," she continued. "I was more impressed than ever before, and a spell of relaxation and thinking is essential now," she advised, adding, "It'll be *wonderful* to have you in Los Altos and Geneva and Robbie and Duffy, and the family and neighbors are going to be delighted. Please let me know if there's anything I can do to help get things ready for you. Lastly I do appreciate the opportunities all this has brought me, more than I can tell you. The new policy statement" that she and another person had drafted, "was accepted with only minor revisions by the whole committee and the assembly. So I experienced the realization of every Federalist's pipe dream!" of having influence. People were "terrifically enthusiastic and busy discussing plans," she concluded. "You don't need to worry about momentum after *that* convention!"

Cranston acknowledged that Eleanor had "analyzed what happened accurately," adding, "I can quote the Bible right back at you: 'An eye for an eye, a tooth for a tooth.' Actually, however, I am acting with restraint." [152]

In another letter, Eleanor wrote, "I've been trying to think of things all day that are good reasons for belonging to the World Federalists. I know you have thought of all these, but they can't be said too many times, and just in case you may have forgotten one of them, here are the arguments that mean the most to me." The first was: "There will always be problems but w. g. [world government] offers a mechanism for solving problems and meeting change peacefully instead of by violence." Another was Cranston's point that military costs could go to more constructive purposes. "Many of the men who enlisted and fought in the first war now [realize] the uselessness of that war," she noted. "If war comes again, one of the causes will be our own apathy." [153]

Norman Cousins meanwhile had put himself forward for president, but after Waller talked with him, Cousins seemed "unquestionably loyal to your candidacy," but wanted to be considered in future. "Is it possible that the anti-Cranston movement could become strong enough so that the issue will be...whom to have in your stead? It seems to me possible that the boys put up Cousins as a stalking horse...and would then rush in with somebody" else. "Maybe we ought to keep Cousins' theoretical candidacy alive until more information is at hand," he suggested. [154]

The Cranstons planned in any event to move into their new house in California, which had been rented in their absence. "Its' *extremely attractive* – aren't you lucky to have built it?" Eleanor wrote in July, 1951. "The outlook from all the windows is lovely. And I love the corner fireplace." Everything looked in good shape. Help, though, was "mighty scarce." [155]

The U. W. F. executive council, however, "decided I should be president for one more year," Cranston wrote Rex Stout in September, 1951. The second term was "under what I deem to be ideal and, indeed, mandatory circumstances – I am now firmly implanted in the beautiful hills of Los Altos and only need to come to that place called Manhattan for six weeks or so." Cord Meyer, in congratulating him, said, "As far as I'm concerned, that is by far the best solution. I rather suspected it would happen after a talk with Norman Cousins." (Cranston went on to serve a third term, through the summer of 1952.) In the same note, Meyer identified an important donor – Marian Javits, wife of Republican Congressman Jake "Jack" Javits. [156]

Such contributions and memberships were crucial, as the organization was "in an extremely tight cash situation at headquarters," Cranston reported to Stout. "This is not good and is partly due to the summer of uncertainty that we have just endured and also to the various rows that have been going on, all of which have, I believe, finally been settled." He asked if the Writer's Board could advance $1,000 against fundraising efforts. "It would be of immense and perhaps life-saving help to us at this time." [157]

One disaffected member, Ada M. Field, told Cranston that she would not renew because she had "become convinced that U. W. F. has departed so far from its original" concept of "just and universal world government that it is no longer a sound organ through which to work for that goal. When military action in Korea confirmed the exact criticism which U. W. F. had rightly made of United Nations' limitations…U. W. F. not only did not rise to the challenge but reluctantly (sometimes enthusiastically) said, 'Me, too.'" They were strong words, and Cranston responded that U. W. F. had not changed its long-range goals. "It is the belief of most Federalists that until world government is achieved, our country must be defended by other methods and it is for this reason that we supported the use of force against the communist aggressors in Korea." [158]

But the rival Atlantic Union Committee "ruffled the feelings of [U. W. F.] when, in its annual report, it commented pointedly that the Federalists had suffered recent losses in membership, financial support and congressional backing," the *New York Times* reported under the headline, "Report shows Federalists in decline and evokes detailed denial." Cranston retorted that U. W. F. membership stood at a steady 40,000, but conceded that it had a deficit of $19,000, which it was reducing. The Atlantic Union report added that failure to end the Korean conflict had "disheartened those who had put their faith in the United Nations as the sole means to maintain peace." It had been a hard year for all peace-seeking groups, but the Federalists remained "an effective and well-organized group," the report stated. [159]

Cranston continued to lobby Congress to further the U. W. F. agenda, telling Ohio Republican Senator Robert A. Taft that he thought there was "considerable common ground between your views and those of us who are convinced that the United Nations must be strengthened." Taft agreed to meet Cranston to discuss "American foreign policy."[160]

Cranston wrote Grenville Clark in the fall that the family was happy to be back "in that superior place, California, in our own house, with Robin delighting in the freedom of fields and orchards after the concrete of Manhattan, and a new member of the family on hand – Kim Christopher, who arrived fifteen days ago. All concerned are doing beautifully." California now was "home base." "We had to race with the stork all the way back," Geneva said in interviews, "so Kim would be a native son," and "keep the family's all-native-Californian record intact." [161]

Kim was born September 26, 1951, weighing six pounds, thirteen and a half ounces. Robin would be four years old that November 1. Kim bore a strong resemblance to his father, inheriting the same freckles as a boy. [162]

By April, 1952, Waller, who had taken an additional job with the American Book Publishers Council in New York, had decided that it was time to leave U. W. F., "partly because of the drift of things in U. W. F. and partly because of my preoccupations elsewhere…. I'm afraid I am not cut out to be a passive member of a mass organization." [163]

President Truman again praised U. W. F., commending it on its fifth anniversary for "steadfast support of the United Nations in its work to improve world conditions and preserve the peace." Cranston in 1952 could report to members that the movement had become significant internationally: Pope Pius XII had declared world federation to conform to the doctrine of the Catholic Church; a parliamentary conference of Federalists had met in London; the idea was gaining currency within the U. N.; and "the present plight and hopelessness of all other courses" portended favorable action on the resolution in Congress. National elections that year offered an opportunity to get U. N. reform on political platforms in time for its tenth-anniversary review in 1955. He also could tell audiences with pride that "in less than four years, we have built U. W. F. into the largest organization in the United States devoted to foreign policy," including 5,000 student members. Cranston delighted in noting that the Harvard chapter had posted a notice of a meeting "to establish a world government" and "the public is invited," which *New Yorker* magazine reprinted with the comment: "The public damn well better be invited." [164]

Cranston became involved in the 1952 presidential race, demonstrating considerable insight and perspective on the political scene in California. He offered to help populist Senator Estes Kefauver, whose investigations of organized crime had gained him a national reputation. "I'm a native, on good terms with all factions of the Democrat Party there, and just made an effort to assess the trends through talks with the political editors of San Francisco and Los Angeles dailies, top elected officials of the party, widespread county and district leaders, and others who are politically knowledgeable. There is a great interest in you as the potential standard-bearer, in all sections of the party," he told Kefauver.

San Francisco, he added, was "the scene of one of the sorrier scandals" – possibly referring to Kefauver's 1951 investigation of Artie Samish, whom Kefauver famously derided as "a combination of Falstaff, Little Boy Blue and Machiavelli, crossed with an eel" – but Cranston thought that "those who are in hot water over internal revenue and other matters are fascinated by the thought of embracing you and your anti-corruption atmosphere and thus publicly purifying themselves." Many were afraid to embrace Kefauver "because they can't afford to offend Truman," Cranston confided, but they would be receptive if Truman withdrew or Kefauver got "him on the run." Many "impartial and unprejudiced observers," including some prominent figures behind Truman, believed that the senator could "carry the California primary" if he put on a vigorous campaign. "The powerful attraction of your candidacy both to forces above all taint, and to forces thoroughly tainted, is a remarkable paradox," Cranston felt. He added that he would be happy to keep Kefauver informed as he met political leaders "on my almost constant travels." He also suggested that the senator, a principal sponsor of the American Union Committee resolution in Congress, make "some careful remarks re: the U. N. and enforceable disarmament in a way that would inspire a great many of our 40,000 U. W. F. members to vigorous efforts in your behalf, yet in a way that would neither offend you're A. U. C. friends nor incite the D. A. R. and the V. F. W." [165]

Kefauver took up Cranston's offer of help and by spring Cranston was addressing him as Estes, suggesting a way in which he might attract U. W. F. and other support "without in any way drawing fire from the isolationists and nationalists. I refer to disarmament. The Democratic Party is extremely vulnerable on the matter of war and peace" because the U. S. had entered both world wars and the Korean conflict under Democratic administrations, a theme that the Republicans were touting. Democrats should identify themselves as the party of peace, Cranston recommended, "laying great stress upon the internationalist traditions of Wilson, Roosevelt and Truman," and backing disarmament through the U. N. "There is abundant evidence that the candidate who hits this hardest will win a very great response – all the opinion polls indicate that foreign affairs, war and peace" were of most interest to voters. A national magazine had asked readers what headline they most wanted to see. "Eight out of ten favored: WAR ABOLISHED FOREVER," Cranston noted. He even drafted remarks that Kefavuer might make to that end, which Cranston was happy to circulate and publicize. [166]

But Cranston's strategy backfired. Kefauver found himself having to deny that he supported the World Federalists. He qualified his position by saying that he would support any reasonable proposal for world peace. He did say that he had "never supported and always opposed the World Federalist idea and [its] resolution in Congress," favoring the Atlantic Union version. "You cannot unite democratic nations with communist nations any more than you can mix oil and water," Kefauver's statement to the press said. The U. W. F. resolution never came to a vote of approval by both Houses of Congress. [167]

Cranston, as part of his U. W. F. efforts, tried to promote publication of another book that he hoped to author, "Peace on Earth - How?" Chapter headings included "No Peace on Earth," an indictment of American foreign policy; "The Sword and the Bible," on compromises to the U. S. defense program; "Pride and Prejudice," outlining opposing positions. "The truth is self-evident," he wrote in the first chapter, "War now dominates America. It invades every home every day. It mocks the tomorrow of all our hopes and cherished dreams, and the tomorrow of our children." (The book was not published.) [168]

During his last year as U. W. F. president, Cranston worked hard to bring new ideas to build the organization financially, emphasizing education as a part of its activities. He proposed an advertisement that would attach famous names to the movement, ranging from Albert Einstein to actor Douglas Fairbanks, Junior. Eleanor Roosevelt was helpful in publicizing the cause through her column, "My Day," stating in one, "I know what the United Nations is trying to do. I cannot claim that it always succeeds, but would like as many people in the United States as possible to feel that they really understand the program, and are able to sort out truth from falsehood." But keeping wealthy donors, like a St. Louis shoe store owner, was sometimes frustrating. Charles B. Edison told Cranston that while U. W. F.'s ideals were widely accepted, it was "timid," failing to adopt "bold, striking plans" to force political parties to back them. Edison could not "continue to make financial sacrifices to maintain" an organization that did not sell its ideas forcefully," although he still hoped that under Cranston's leadership it would. "Is our country to be forever bound to Teddy Roosevelt's policy of 'speak softly and carry a big stick?" Edison moaned. [169]

Cranston defended what he had done: "We have made a great deal of solid progress organizationally during the past year by doing important but unglamorous work… inside U. W. F. and outside with other organizations," he told Edison, adding, "I would like to see us undertake some more powerful and attention-getting projects, too, but I am very much opposed to launching them unless funds are in sight to insure that they will not collapse for want of resources." [170]

Indeed, U. W. F.'s finances did improve somewhat: the $30,000 deficit from 1950 was eliminated by 1952 and a modest surplus of $1,700 showed on its books. [171]

In his travels Cranston took every opportunity of becoming acquainted with local political leaders, pitching the world-government platform. Frank Church, who was considering running for Congress, entertained Cranston on a speaking trip to Boise, Idaho. Cranston told him "how wonderful it is to find someone as capable as you taking such an active part in our work." Senator Adlai Stevenson, a major presidential candidate, hosted Cranston for a weekend. "Do feel free to call on me at any time if you wish to speak of disarmament in any greater detail," Cranston said in thanking him. He sent Stevenson a proposed plank for the Democratic Party to consider. "A good many party leaders" seemed to agree "that it would be constructive to get something along these lines into the platform." His suggested language read in part:

> "Our arms and alliances have purchased us some time.... They cannot purchase lasting peace. For as Talleyrand said, '*You can do anything with bayonets except sit on them.*'
>
> "It would be folly for us to resign ourselves to engaging in an everlasting arms race....
>
> "We cannot allow America to become a permanent armed camp, forever under the dark shadow of catastrophic war, with our children wearing dog tags to school day in and day out as they now do in New York and San Francisco." [172]

Cranston honed political skills during his tenure as U. W. F. president. He often urged members, like one at Los Alamos, New Mexico, to contact their congressional delegations in support of the world-government resolution, and to remind members of Congress that the Soviet Union itself, at the Dumbarton Oaks Conference, had proposed giving the U. N. an air force and authority to close military bases of small nations. [173]

By then Cranston was giving serious thought to entering politics himself, but he had to decide whether to continue working for the likes of U. W. F., possibly as its legislative director in Washington. Waller and Cranston even had discussed relocating into low-population states like Nevada or Montana and running for the U. S. Senate. Cranston, however, had begun to fix his eye on the prize in his populous home state. The two also considered starting a lobbying firm with enough business clients to underwrite advocating for good causes. In the end, Waller went into book publishing. One candidate for Waller's job was an ambitious radio news reporter from Missouri who had been covering Capitol Hill. Cranston offered to pay him $10,000 a year but Walter Cronkite turned the job down. [174]

In a candid letter to Eleanor Fowle in April, 1952, Raymond Gram Swing wrote,

> "I am going to tell you – quite privately – that I hope Alan doesn't take the U. W. F. legislative job in Washington for two years. This sounds like heresy... and ingratitude to Alan. Whatever it is...I want to see Alan anchored somewhere where he can rise on the tides of his own effort in his own community to political

eminence. That is why I am so elated when I hear that he may go into politics. That is what going into politics means to me….

"I suppose I have an ingrained distrust of 'causes.' They are very important, and they are part of American techniques. But they are not careers. And once one stays too long in a cause, that becomes his career….

"I am enthusiastic about Alan because I feel certain he has a career in politics. He has the stature, the homespun qualities, the community-mindedness of a politician. He can become one of the best. And it is infinitely better to serve a community than to serve a cause….

"There is now no hope of getting more than the limited WG [world government] that would come from genuine total disarmament. That is the most to hope for in our life time…. But I don't believe U. W. F. will be willing to work simply for this goal…. I don't believe Alan could possibly become the difference between success and failure in this development. So I believe he doesn't need to sacrifice his chances of a career outside the cause."[175]

It was one of the letters that Cranston saved.

Swing was not the only U. W. F. leader who had become cynical about its objectives. Publisher Harper Brothers chairman Cass Canfield asked to be replaced on the executive council in 1952, telling Cranston, "I must admit to the feeling that World Government is now such a distant aim as to make me disinclined to devote time to organizational work in U. W. F." He would be glad to help "on specific projects like Rex Stout's plan in connection with the Advertising Council." His decision was "the result of much thought and soul searching over the past week." [176]

A more positive supporter, birth-control advocate Margaret Sanger, sought to link her Planned Parenthood movement with U. W. F., asking Cranston – who she said was "much loved in" both the U. S. and India – to lend his name as a sponsor of a population conference in India. Cranston had to decline, citing U. W. F. policy of not aligning with organizations except those designed to strengthen the United Nations, although he was about to go to India on a special assignment for Grenville Clark. [177]

As Cranston's term wound down, he was praised by his colleagues. His successor, Norman Cousins, told Cranston that "all Federalists are in your debt for making it possible for the new president to take over an organization that is at last free of factional disputes, pettifogging and personal animosity." Cousins had only just learned "how close we had come…to being on the skids, and the more I learn about U. W. F., the more impressed I am with the rebuilding job you have accomplished." [178]

The forthcoming 1952 presidential elections, in which Adlai Stevenson, not Kefauver, would face General Eisenhower, augured well for the Federalist viewpoint, the editor of *The Federalist* thought, asking Cranston to write an article about both candidates. Cranston demurred because he now was "working hard for Adlai" in California and in good conscience could not write an objective piece. He suggested that the magazine run separate articles about the candidates by Federalists who supported each one, preferably members of Congress. [179]

Grenville Clark, the patrician advisor to presidents, also took action in the campaign. He telegraphed Eisenhower from a campaign train (sending Cranston a copy), urging with "no hesitation" that "Nixon leave the ticket" as Republican vice presidential candidate. Nixon, who had beaten Jerry Voorhis in 1946 for a congressional seat and been elected to the Senate in 1950, had been found to have received $18,000 personally from supporters. Clark joined many Republicans in urging that Nixon be dropped from the ticket. "The admitted facts illustrate a practice subject to such grave abuses that it cannot be condoned," Clark wrote. To retain "Nixon would put you in a false position and largely nullify the corruption issue. It is impossible to estimate the effect on votes of Nixon's retention or retirement. It is better to be guided by what is right in the interest of high standards in government and trust the people." [180]

Nixon was left to defend himself and did so in a nationally-televised spontaneous statement, presenting himself as humble, self-made, rising from poor circumstances (his parents ran a grocery store in Yorba Linda, California), claiming that he had not used the money for personal reasons but for political activity, and that his Senate salary ($15,000) was modest. He even itemized his personal budget, noting that his wife "Pat" had no mink but "a respectable Republican cloth coat." He had received as a gift, he admitted, a cocker spaniel whom his six-year-old daughter Trisha named "Checkers," and "regardless of what they say about it, we're going to keep it." He then proceeded to attack his Democratic opponents (Stevenson, vice presidential candidate Senator John Sparkman, Truman and his Secretary of State Dean Acheson) as soft on communism while praising General Eisenhower, on whose decision Nixon's future rested. Nixon remarkably stayed on the ticket and with Eisenhower was elected in 1952, serving two terms. Cranston, watching the wily Nixon's career from close proximity in future, would see Clark's warnings born out. [181]

After leaving his post as U. W. F. president, Cranston continued to travel and lecture. The anti-world-government forces also continued their assaults, including one that misconstrued a professor's statement that some Americans equated world government with hauling down the American flag and defiling it. Cranston attacked back. In a letter to the *Palo Alto Times* in 1953, he called Gerald L. K. Smith "America's would-be Hitler" and Kamp and the like "demagogues." Even President Eisenhower, he noted, had wired U. W. F., "I commend your organization for its dedicated concern for a lasting peace and its steadfast support of the ideals of the U. N." [182]

Eisenhower's Secretary of State John Foster Dulles had made a speech before the American Bar Association urging revision of the U. N. charter, asking for public reaction. Federalists were urged to write him appreciative letters. Cranston did so, congratulating Dulles for his "statesmanlike speech" advocating changes to "make possible enforceable disarmament. I had not been aware of the fact that the State Department, under your leadership, had already committed itself to seeking charter review in 1955. It is a sign of greatness in you that, despite your part in the original shaping of the charter, you have no hesitancy in stating the obvious need for change. It is my very deep feeling," he added, "that international trade can never reach anything like its potential place in the world until the ever-present threat of war is done away with." Dulles replied that the issues "should be thoroughly aired in widespread discussions among the American people before final policies are adopted." [183]

Despite his busy schedule, Cranston found time to review books, something that he would do periodically throughout his life. His reviews appeared in the *New York Times*, *Political Science Quarterly* and other newspapers and magazines. The books generally dealt with political topics and Cranston invariably incorporated his own voice into the reviews. *Handbook of Politics* by Lowell Mellett (a former newspaper man who had spent six years as an aide to F. D. R.), Cranston wrote, was "based on the premise that the most important thing to do in any election is to throw out the bad office holder – even if his opponent is no better. The book should be in the hands of every conscientious citizen – even those who do not share Mellett's liberal viewpoint.... He explains why you learn more from the votes that a congressman casts for bad bills than for good bills." A "careful" biography of Adlai Stevenson (*The Politics of Honor* by Kenneth S. Davis), Cranston noted, praised "his repeated refusal to say and do things that would violate his deeply-held principles" even though he was "told time and again that if only he'd do so, he'd surely reach the White House." If the author went "a bit overboard in his praise of Stevenson," Cranston, by then considering running for the U. S. Senate himself, said that "all who knew and admired him will be forever tempted to do likewise." Another subject dear to him was the State of California (as expressed in a review of *Southern California Country* by Carey McWilliams), which Cranston extolled as "the incredible land of upside down, where Mark Twain fell into a river and came out all dusty, where there are two springs and two summers, where boomers sell the climate and throw the land in, boasting, 'We're not boosting California for all she's worth, because, sir, no man knows what she's worth.'" [184]

In a review of nineteen-year-old Student Federalist Harris Wofford's *It's Up to Us*, Cranston described the origin of the author's involvement: "One night when he was fifteen, Harris Wofford, Junior, tossed aside his Latin and algebra books, tuned in 'Mr. District Attorney' on his radio, and got into the bathtub. The thriller went off the air, and to his disgust, Wofford was compelled to listen to a forum on a United-States-of-the-World versus world destruction. Young Wofford emerged from the bathtub a confirmed Federalist." He established a student chapter at Scarsdale High School and a Federal Union office in his home. "So many boys and girls swarmed in every afternoon to confer, mimeograph, type, that Wofford's grandmother had to turn off her earphone," Cranston wrote of the memoir, which author Clifton Fadiman had called "naive." "The book is not naive," Cranston retorted, although Wofford opened "himself to attack" by advocating more power to world government "than most supporters" thought possible to prevent war. "Alan saw a draft, and was a good adviser to the book," Wofford would later say. [185]

Cranston revealed his considerable knowledge of national economics in a review of *The Coming Crisis* by Fritz Sternberg, which discussed the potential for another Depression once the post-World War II boom was curtailed by a lack of consumer spending. Sternberg, Cranston said, had devoted "too little consideration to the possibility...of an effective trust-busting drive" to break up business monopolies. "The fact remains," Cranston wrote, "that an effective assault upon monopoly, led by a coalition of Americans drawn for varying reasons from right, left and center, is possible and could drastically alter the present economic state of the union." It was early evidence of his attention to business policies and interests. [186]

Much of what Cranston thought and did during his three terms as U. W. F. president would refine his ideologies for the future. He would carry the same messages forward from different podiums and on different fronts for the rest of his life. He also became knowledgeable about fundraising during that period. And the contacts that he made in business and political circles would serve him well.

Cranston's association with the Federalists, though, would be used by political opponents for years to try to taint him, but he turned it to advantage. "It used to be that one of the worst things his opponents could say about Alan Cranston was that he was a 'one-worlder,'" an article noted in 1983 (when Cranston, then a Senator, was running for President of the United States). "I've always been proud of my Federalist membership," Cranston would say. The attacks, rather than hurting politically, actually helped, he thought, "because I could show the voters the importance of world law to American prosperity and safety," he said in a 1981 Federalists fundraising letter. "Those of us who became active in U. W. F. shared a deep concern for the fragile nature of world peace and the threat to that peace from nuclear weapons," he told a constituent in 1984. [187]

"One of the Federalists' more noted members was Ronald Reagan," Cranston also liked to remind people of the actor's, and future president's, association with U. W. F. [188]

Cranston, though, by 1953 was nearing forty and had decided on a personal agenda. He set the stage for his next career move by establishing a base from which to consider becoming a politician himself. A *Palo Alto Times* reporter who looked to Cranston for newsworthy quotes and information wrote him many years later, "It seems I thought a young Los Altan named Cranston might possibly have a political career ahead of him." His prediction would come to pass. [189]

6

'Politician' - a term of honor, not of scorn - the noblest of man's works

"By '58, if not sooner, I'm confident we'll make this a real Democratic state – something it's never been. I'm having a hell of a lot of fun in the process."

Alan Cranston to Ted Waller, July 17, 1954, on Democrats' success in primary elections.

"[B]etter an elected controller than a defeated senator."

Helen Myers, Democratic Party activist, to Cranston prior to his decision to run for elected office, October, 1957.

Cranston went back to work with his father and on résumés listed his position from 1952 to 1958 as "real-estate broker" with a salary based on sales commissions. He helped manage family properties in Los Altos, Palo Alto and San Bruno. In 1952 the Cranstons built a commercial structure on Los Altos' Main Street to hold three businesses. [1]

The intention was to compete with a proposed shopping center that Stanford University planned to build on property less than a half mile from University Avenue, the main shopping district where William Cranston owned property. He and his son quietly began to seek citizen opposition to the large-scale mall. "This move, if carried out, is a very serious threat to all property owners in Palo Alto," William Cranston stated in a draft letter that Cranston sent his mother-in-law, May McMath, in June, 1953, asking if she might get others to write the *Palo Alto Times* registering concern about the shopping center. "It threatens to reduce values on University Avenue by 30%," Cranston senior feared, which would reduce the ability of those merchants to pay city taxes, shifting the burden to residential property owners. He also worried that the shopping center might fail and cause financial "disaster for Stanford University," which he, his wife, Eleanor and Alan had attended, and "perhaps some of our grandchildren will attend." [2]

Cranston, as chairman of the Los Altos Business Property Owners' Committee, also became active in promoting parking for the business district, circulating petitions to the City Council in 1954 favoring a multi-story lot to hold 500 stalls. The project included installation of new sewers to replace septic tanks. Sixty percent of property owners had to sign the petition before the projects could begin.

By spring of 1955 all the largest property owners had signed, but when the petition was presented to the city council, two property owners withdrew their signatures. Some on the fringes of the district felt that they would not much benefit from the project and were reluctant to sign. [3]

Cranston had to call on all his lobbying skills and convince hold-outs that those who would benefit the most would pay the highest assessment, making the plans "completely equitable." He put his persuasive and negotiating talents to work, and by May, announced that "differences had been ironed out" – the petition would be recirculated and resubmitted. "Los Altos' triangle parking district effort, derailed a few weeks ago by objections of some State Street property owners, is back on the track with a more ambitious plan than ever, according to Alan Cranston," the *Daily Palo Alto Times* reported. The following spring the parking plaza was approved by the city council after a public hearing attended by more than 200 people at which protests were heard. Many wore lapel cards reading, "I favor the parking plaza," no doubt one of Cranston's strategies. "They were in the majority," a news account noted. The garage by then had been expanded to accommodate 1,000 cars and the entire project, including new sewers, was estimated to cost $1 million. It had taken two years to convince merchants of the need for parking for the district's survival. The mayor "denied vehemently that any deals or commitments had been made to sway protestants," the *Times* reported, but "commented that 'This thing is not going to be ramrodded down their throats.'" [4]

A principal objector was a Baptist Church whose directors promised to drop their protest if their assessment were reduced. Another property owner wrote Cranston, "In watching your career from afar over the years, I noted that you were always activated by high principles and a spirit of justice, thus I turn to you in our dilemma. We are heartily in favor of a parking plan for Los Altos, but in our individual case, it causes undue hardship on our small and static income." The plan would cut off thirty feet of their rental property and partly demolish the house, depriving them "of even the small rental" income they received. A $100 monthly assessment also "would entail a great hardship. Will you please devise some way to ameliorate this trying situation?" Cranston had to respond, "Frankly, I am not sure that there is any just alternative to what is proposed. However, every opportunity will be given to you to present your views" at the Mayor's Committee on Parking. "I will do my best to attend that particular meeting, and I trust that an understanding – the fairest possible – can be reached by all concerned." Whatever the result for the hapless property owners, the project went forward, although the assessments were protested by the Los Altos Board of Realtors into 1957. Friend and Sunnyvale *Standard* newspaper publisher Joe Houghteling, introducing Cranston at a political meeting, joked that he was "a man who attends to everything – from Los Altos sewers to world government!" "I sort of led the way to creating the parking plaza in Los Altos," Cranston later would say, converting the business district into a shopping center "after a long, protracted, difficult struggle." The following year, Cranston was surprised when presented a "Stake-in-Los-Altos" award by civic leaders at a "victory" dinner dance to celebrate completion of the parking plaza. Cranston was photographed smiling broadly, sharing "amused appreciation" for the "gag gift in recognition of his leadership in the project." [5]

But Cranston's major interests lay with renewing the strength of the state Democratic Party. Democrats in California had been losing elections for many years and needed a new infusion of energy and organization. The Young Democrats (YDs) had helped by building membership in Democratic clubs, which grew within the state and nationwide after the war. Party leaders emerged from the Central Valley to the Bay Area. They included Lionel Steinberg, a liberal valley farmer – the first large grower to sign a contract with farm-workers' union organizer Cesar Chavez – who became president of the renamed California Federation of Young Democrats in 1949; and an ambitious young attorney, Phillip Burton, who had formed a strong club in his home town of San Francisco in 1950 and was actively seeking an opportunity to run for office. Burton in turn was a "guru" to up-and-coming YDs in Los Angeles like Howard Berman and Henry Waxman (both of whom, like Burton, would serve in Congress). [6]

Steinberg, chairman of the YDs' 1949 convention, planned a "somewhat novel program," telling attendees like Cranston that previous conventions had been devoted to "wrangling over obscure points" and "neglected the important problem of winning elections. This convention is to be less a debating society and more a school in how to win elections." Panels would deal with "precinct organization, how to get workers and money, farmer-labor cooperation, how to get representative participation." Two-hundred and fifty participants were expected, including honored guests like San Francisco district attorney (1944-50) Edmund Gerald (Pat) Brown, national committeeman James Roosevelt, American Federation of Labor (AFL) state president Jack Shelley (a future congressman and mayor of San Francisco), and former Congressman Will Rogers, Junior. The objective was to have each club identify "what it is going to do to replace Republicans" with a goal of setting up 100 YD clubs with 10,000 members.[7]

But factionalism threatened to disrupt the convention even before it began. Some Northern California members accused it of being an unauthorized "rump convention," which Steinberg refuted. Fresno County YDs president Frank Snyder hoped that "nothing will for a moment deflect the attention of the Young Democrats of California from the objective – the election on the 7th of November, 1950." [8]

The 1949 YDs meeting was seminal for the club movement, and did in fact push the Democratic Party to organize better for campaigns. Some clubs traced themselves back to EPIC groups – "End Poverty in California" – started by Upton Sinclair for his gubernatorial campaign in 1934. [9]

As the federation of clubs grew, particularly during the 1952 presidential campaign of Adlai Stevenson which spawned Stevenson clubs, Democrats began to realize that they might regain power in the state. Party chairman, State Senator George Miller, Junior, of Richmond, and others in the "club movement" decided that they needed a strategy to generate party loyalty and make it a viable organization for fielding candidates. A long-time problem was that candidates could cross-file in primaries to win nominations in both the Democratic and Republican Parties. And although official party endorsements were prohibited before primary elections, Republicans had an unofficial organization (the California Republican Assembly) that made such endorsements. Democrats had elected only one governor in the twentieth century – Culbert Olson in 1938 – and had not controlled the state legislature since 1890.

Both U. S. Senators were Republicans, as were 19 of 30 U. S. House members in 1953. Moderate Republicans like Governor Earl Warren and State Controller Thomas Kuchel (of Anaheim) had been elected in large part because of support from Democrats. In 1952 conservative Republican Senator William F. Knowland (owner of the *Oakland Tribune*) had won both party nominations, leaving Democrats with no senatorial candidate. Miller, Burton, Cranston and others realized that by eliminating cross-filing and making endorsements, Democrats might regain voters. [10]

They hoped that presidential candidate Stevenson might revitalize the party in California in 1952. Cranston admired his intelligence and ideals and was involved in his campaign almost fulltime. He formed a Stevenson-Sparkman Club in Los Altos and instigated precinct work that had not been done before in the county. Cranston referred to himself, in a review that he wrote of a biography of Stevenson, as "an avid and active supporter." [11]

The election, though, went to the popular post-war general, "Ike" Eisenhower. California Democrats were desperate.

A few days after the election, Cranston was on his way around the world on a Pan-American airliner to assist Grenville Clark in a study of disarmament sponsored by the Ford Foundation. He was to interview political leaders in India and Japan on "what it takes to establish a meaningful peace," he wrote his old Pomona friend, the Russian émigré Peter Van Norden. "It was torturous to pass over and stop briefly at the airport at many other European, Middle Eastern and Asian lands…locked up in quarantine…so that my impression of many a strange and far land is of an airport very similar to the one in Des Moines, Ioway [*sic*], or Oshkosh." In India he talked with Prime Minister Jawaharlal Nehru and Gandhi's son as well as the leader of the "Untouchables" but saw "none of the fabulous scenery, except the Taj Mahal." He also met with political and business leaders, parliamentary members of the Congress Party, chairmen of all opposition parties except the Communists and "an erstwhile terrorist name Guha. The Indian leaders all seem to feel that we don't have any concept of their honest efforts to stay out of foreign entanglements – just as *we* did for 150 years," he wrote Norden. "They think that we place too much emphasis on guns, and not enough on economic needs in Asia. The living conditions of the millions in India is beyond comprehension." [12]

The purpose of the trip was to gather information, not see the sights, but he particularly wanted to see devastated Hiroshima. He sought advice from a Japanese Federalist who told him how to get there (eighteen hours by express train from Tokyo). Japanese U. W. F. members and elected parliamentarians were anxious to hear him lecture, his contact said. [13]

While in India, Cranston "by sheer accident, stumbled upon some beautiful handicraft copper and brassware they make over there – trays, goblets, plates, cups, ladles, and so forth" that he imported for sale in gift stores. Geneva told an interviewer that she had asked him "in a semi-serious nature" to bring home some copper for Christmas, which he did, "enough to start a business." That occupied his time along with real estate, he told Van Norden, but his principal activities were in "Democratic politics. California has always been a Republican state, but many of us are taking steps that may make it a Democratic state at long last – something that seems vitally good for the welfare of the nation, since we are presently represented in national affairs by Nixon and Knowland, than whom there are few worse (except McCarthy!)." [14]

In January, 1953, George Miller called a conference at Asilomar on the Monterey peninsula to discuss "What's Wrong and What's Right with the Democratic Party in California." Cranston led a panel on precinct organization and was "extremely enthusiastic about" a possible pre-primary convention at which candidates would be endorsed. At a club convention in Fresno that year, more than 500 delegates voted to create a new entity like the one the GOP had. The California Democratic Council (CDC) was born. Cranston's organizing skills were recognized, and he unanimously was elected the CDC's first president (he would be re-elected annually until resigning in December, 1957). Phil Burton's Polish-born wife, Sala, would be a vice president; Joseph L. Wyatt, Junior, a Pasadena attorney, was elected secretary and would succeed Cranston as president. Cranston subsequently agreed to chair one of five committees that Miller created to get the party moving on its objectives – the Committee on Coordination and Integration of Clubs in Communities and Counties. [15]

Initially the intent was to create a state organization with delegates from county and state central committees who would make pre-primary endorsements. As sort of an after-thought at Asilomar, the state central committee decided to let *clubs* send delegates to the state party convention. The clubs at first did not have delegates, and the CDC was not organized originally to be a vehicle for clubs. Its objective was to broaden the party base and "give all Democrats a voice in party affairs" through the new "league of volunteer clubs," as Cranston described it to Drew Pearson in 1957. [16]

There was a rival group, however, Dime-a-Day for Democracy (DDD), headed by two Los Angeles delegates, Elizabeth Snyder and Del Smith, which created tension at the Fresno meeting. They were organized largely to back Congressman Samuel Yorty of Los Angeles, who saw that the CDC was going to be too liberal for his taste. Another detractor was Los Angeles activist Jesse Unruh, who was wary of the growing volunteer YD movement and club members. Unruh headed a rival faction of more moderate-to-conservative Democrats that he had built up, beginning as a student at UCLA. Unruh saw the club movement as a nuisance to his political machinations, and would be a long-time antagonist to it. [17]

Cranston, a trademark yellow legal pad with notes for his speech in hand and mindful of the differing factions, made his points forcefully to the crowded assemblage at the California Hotel in Fresno. "We are gathered here to do all within our power to end the stranglehold Republicans have held for too long upon politics in California.... We have had only one Democratic governor in the twentieth century. The state legislature for longer than anyone can remember has been controlled by the Republicans – and/or Artie Samish." Only one Democrat held statewide office – Pat Brown, who had been elected attorney general in 1950 when moderate Republican Earl Warren was governor (1943-50). Republicans held 111 of 162 state elective offices – "all of this in a state in which there are almost a million more registered Democrats than Republicans, approximately three million to two million." The CDC was the best way to try and end that stranglehold, he urged. He also addressed the desire for power by right-wing Republicans like Richard Nixon. "Our country is challenged...to seize the initiative from communism by developing policies capable of meeting human needs and aspirations...by democratic methods...and to resist those who would embrace totalitarianism in the name of combating it," Cranston concluded. "Though Alan's personality was low-keyed and relaxed," his sister would write of the moment, "he had become a surprisingly effective platform speaker, displaying a knack with words and exuding assurance and optimism" that attracted a loyal following. [18]

Cranston now was in a leadership position to be quoted by the press. He "commands a key unit in statewide party reorganization maneuvers," noted the Palo Alto reporter Robert A. Bernstein, who had seen into the future, and "freely predicts a significant Democratic upswing in the 1954 battle of the polls. But the 39-year-old Los Altan says he personally will not seek any of the public offices that he expects to fall from Republican control. At least not this year." [19]

As an unofficial organization, the CDC was not prohibited by law from endorsing candidates and it began to do so vigorously. As one of its leaders put it, the CDC "completely revolutionized the party in California. It made it viable and the state Democratic Central Committee sank into a well-deserved oblivion." The CDC became for all intents and purposes the party organization and its pre-primary endorsements were essential to a candidate's election. The party also was reinvigorated with grassroots volunteers who walked precincts, licked envelopes and worked telephones during elections. Membership in clubs grew from fewer than 1,000 in the 1940s to more than 5,000 in the early 1950s (it would reach some 70,000 dues-paying members in the 1960s). One of the educational tools that they used was a film to stimulate club members, "The Political Saga of John Doe," for which the CDC charged a $15 fee. [20]

One of those who would become extremely active in the new entity was recent Korean War army veteran (1952-54), Roy F. Greenaway of Fresno. He had won an American Legion National Oratorical Contest in 1947 while at Roosevelt High School, and attended the University of Chicago (1947-51) on a $4,000 scholarship that he won in the contest, receiving a B. A. degree in English (he was a member of the Big Ten debate championship team in 1950). He had been drafted in 1952 for the Korean war and served in Japan. Now he was working on a Master's Degree in linguistics at Fresno State. His thesis would be an analysis of philosophic assumptions by top linguistic grammarians of whether or not there was a universal grammar. His association with the CDC, and with Cranston, would shape the rest of his life. [21]

Cranston's election as CDC president was heralded in newspapers as a "first step toward a much stronger Democratic Party in California" aimed at statewide victories in the 1954 elections. It was the first time since 1926 that the party would make pre-primary endorsements. Newspapers also noted that the CDC had approved a policy against communism or any other totalitarian threat after a dispute over how far to go in taking such a stand. [22]

Cranston, who was chairman of the Los Altos Democratic Council and a member of the state Central Committee, also became chairman of a Santa Clara County Democratic Council that he helped form, and in 1953 the party established an office in San Jose with a full-time executive director. "Out of power but not without hope," the *San Jose Mercury* reported of the first party headquarters in "local political history" in an off-election year. It would be supported by annual pledges, of which $3,000 already had been collected, Cranston said. But Cranston himself surprisingly was defeated in a bid the next year to be returned to the Central Committee. He was involved in other activities, though, that would give him visibility, possibly at his own instigation. Attorney General Pat Brown appointed Cranston to an Advisory Committee on Crime Prevention. "I'm most grateful," Cranston told him of being appointed, "particularly for doing so at the last minute after your plans had more or less jelled. The deplorable condition of our Santa Clara County jail, and my past experiences in cooperating with the Department of Justice on minority problems make me much interested in the very important work you are undertaking in the field." [23]

His personal life, too, was full, exemplified by the amusing address that a friend used to "Ye Alan Cranstons - (Copper, politics, speeches, real estate, poultry, canine psychiatry, parent-children relationships, excellent food, articulate conversation, etc.), Hilltop Drive, Los Altos." The boys were thriving, Cranston told Van Norden, "at present singing 'Davy Crockett' and pretending to shoot bears and kill Indians" as he was writing. "Life is really very pleasant out here," he continued. "You'd never know Los Altos – it has grown immensely since the days when you visited us here. About a year ago, I visited Pomona for a day. It is still much the same," with the same football coach. Cranston signed the letter, "Your old friend." [24]

The boys required Geneva's full attention in those years, and she in turn needed her husband's. She wrote Cranston in December, 1952, that "Rob had a nightmare" and she had to help "snap him out of it." Cranston asked to be excused from Santa Clara County jury duty in April, 1954, sending a doctor's letter stating that Cranston's wife was "to have surgery at Palo Alto hospital" and it was "in the best interests of all concerned" if he were excused. [25]

But a great sadness occurred in 1953. William Cranston had been ill for nearly a year with leukemia. Cranston had sought advice about treatment, but his father deteriorated and on August 26, he died at seventy-four. Obituaries, which pictured him with a favorite German shepherd, lauded him as "a pioneer in the development of Palo Alto…prominent for many years in real estate and insurance activities" with "extensive land holdings in Los Altos and Palo Alto." He was buried at Alta Mesa Cemetery. "I feel an extremely deep sense of personal loss," family friend Doctor Ralph Reynolds wrote the Cranstons. "To me he was a fine and faithful friend, one in whom I have often confided and in return received confidences, an advisor in many ways and from whom I always received deep affection in the sense that it exists between men." William's death had not been "a tragedy," he mused; "tragedy lies in failure, disillusionment and sorrow. The slow deterioration of old age represents tragedy – or at least great pathos. The person who starts out with bright ambitions and illusions and who settles into mediocrity represents pathos. On the other hand, a life is perfectly complete, no matter what it is like, if it is successful, happy, useful, full and well-rounded. Bill's life did not represent failure or mediocrity in any sense of the word…. He had the love of his whole family, the respect of his fellow men and the reward of leadership in his community. We miss him sorely." [26]

"I shall always remember your father as I saw him one morning standing at his front door," a neighbor wrote, "he was dressed in excellent tweed, his dog by his side, and his face fresh and relaxed. The expression 'perfect country gentleman' flashed through my mind, and I have thought of him as such ever since." To Eleanor a friend said, 'It must help you to know you always gave your father much pleasure and companionship as well as satisfaction in your ability to comprehend and discuss matters of interest to him. You must be very proud to have had a father who was able, and had the inclination, to give people the understanding and assistance he has given me. Devotion of time and thought to solving wisely the overwhelming problems of another person is a rare gift.... Would you please share this note with Alan as it applies to you both? He brought so much pleasure to his father's life." Cranston saved the letters. "That's one of my regrets – that he never knew I got to be a senator," Cranston later said of his father who had indulged his son's desires to follow his own path and given him such good advice, but did not live to see him succeed in his dreams to be a politician. [27]

Villa Warec was sold shortly afterward, on condition that it be developed in an environmentally sympathetic way to preserve the landscape, creek and country atmosphere. The site was sub-divided under the direction of a landscape architect who "designed a beautiful plan," Cranston said of the project, and a number of single-family homes were built on the estate surrounding the Cranston house, which remained. When William Cranston's estate was distributed to heirs in 1957, it was valued at more than $203,000. [28]

Cranston went back to politics, now consuming most of his time. He got his mother to change her registration to Democrat – "after Father died," Eleanor noted. One of those whom Democrats had hopes of unseating was U. S. Senator Tom Kuchel who had been appointed to fill out Nixon's term when he resigned to become vice president. "He is cagey," former California Assemblyman and government economist Dewey Anderson wrote Cranston from Washington about Kuchel, "but, unless I miss all the signs, once he [holds] his seat for any length of time, we are going to witness a reactionary performance that will put Bill Knowland's in the shade for good." Democrats, Anderson felt, needed to field a strong contender immediately if they wanted to make an "effective campaign next year" (1954). (Anderson had been an alternate California delegate to the 1952 Democratic National Convention.) Television was becoming a major source of advertising for political campaigns, and raising funds required an early start, he warned, otherwise they would "never see the substantial sum…needed to run a traditional campaign through the press, radio, TV., etc." Although the "likelihood of electing a Democrat is so slight that while we must fight as deadly earnestly as possible," there was "great value in putting up a highly qualified man who can…help our people" realize "what democracy really means, regardless of victory or defeat." [29]

"I wish very much that you'd supply chapter and verse on Kuchel's performance in the Senate," Cranston replied. "We could do a great deal with it. The state is presently thoroughly in the dark as to what sort of a senator he is.... No spade-work of any sort is being done re: a candidate to compete with him. You are mentioned more than anyone else as a possibility." On the other hand, "A great deal of spade-work is being done to form a more effective Democratic Party in the state. George

Miller is encouraging all sorts of forward-looking efforts. There is a good chance that during the fall and winter, a statewide organization somewhat analogous to the Republican Assembly will be formed," Cranston said of the potential CDC. "All factionalism is well in hand – everybody is truly working together," he was glad to report. [30]

In early 1954, Cranston happily told Ted Waller, "Yes, I'm having the time of my life with the California Democratic Council – referred to by the Hearst press itself as the 'largest and most all-inclusive Democratic organization in the history of California.'… If we survive [a pre-primary endorsing convention] united, with good candidates, as I believe we will, we'll be in business as never before, and cross-filing will no longer bedevil us to the degree it has in the past. My present role is to do all sorts of fair and just things that disprove shouts that the convention is rigged. Actually, it isn't rigged, and couldn't be." [31]

Cranston indeed was happily driving an old Mercury station wagon all over the state, building the party and organizing groups into the CDC. [32]

The 1954 endorsing convention would be the first ever held by the CDC. It turned into a feisty event with arguments over whom to endorse, particularly for the U. S. Senate race. Cranston approached General Omar Bradley and Robert Maynard Hutchins, former chancellor of the University of Chicago who recently had resigned and started a think-tank in Santa Barbara. Both had name recognition, but both declined. Los Angeles Congressman Sam Yorty could almost taste the elevated position, but he was not universally liked, considered too conservative by liberals. State Senator George Miller, still a respected CDC leader, refused to endorse Yorty as did most delegates from Northern California. Cranston tried to appear neutral, telling Yorty that if he were endorsed, he would support him. But the dapper former assemblyman, once considered liberal and pro-labor, had shifted his positions to pro-military and other stances aligned with Republican ideologically. Yorty retaliated against his opponents by insinuating that their concerns over McCarthyism, civil rights, federal aid to education were radical, left-wing, even "Red." He even wrote F. B. I. Director J. Edgar Hoover in June, 1955, "You will recall our conversations relative to 'communist' infiltration of Democratic clubs here in California. Cranston will try to prevent infiltration. But has Cranston been cleared?" Yorty's outcries backfired on him and further angered his detractors. University of California political science professor Peter Odegard was nominated as an alternative to Yorty and enthusiastically endorsed. That posed the problem of a possible intra-party primary in which the well-known Yorty would have the edge. Throughout the night, pressure was brought to support Yorty, which Miller and other party leaders reluctantly agreed to do. Odegard, after long consultation with Cranston privately, withdrew his candidacy. The CDC endorsed Yorty. But it had been a bruising forum. [33]

Dewey Anderson sent Cranston (and possibly all CDC delegates to the 1954 convention) a letter stating: "There can be no victory for the Democratic Party in California in 1954, nor for that matter in any future year, unless its candidates for national and state offices are true-blue liberals standing on a platform that reaches to the very heart of the economic and social programs which the government must tackle and solve if we are to experience prosperity and growth at home and peace abroad. No compromising with expediency, no attempts to look as conservative as possible, will wean away from the reactionary Republicans their supporters, or appeal to the silent and unorganized mass of voters whose ballots are so often decisive." [34]

Cranston himself was approached to run for some statewide office that year, but he still felt that he was not ready nor the timing good for him to succeed in a political race. His role as organizer and prodder would serve him well, he knew, if he ran in the future. [35]

Following the CDC meeting, Cranston received several congratulatory notes for his handling of the fractious group at Fresno. State Superior Court Judge Stanley Mosk of Los Angeles said, "I cannot resist writing you a fan letter to express commendation for the splendid manner in which you presided. It was a delight to see your firm, yet courteous, handling of the speakers and delegates on this occasion for which there was no precedent. I am fortunate to do as well in Court – even with the power of contempt plus a burly bailiff!" Cranston told Mosk in reply that it had been "a lot of fun to help make the convention work as well as it did," but he had hoped to present Mosk as one of the seven endorsed candidates. "The whole convention was in many ways a personal triumph for you," Odegard wrote Cranston. "It certainly has done more to restore the soul and sinews of the Democratic Party in California than anything that has happened in recent years." Cranston replied with appreciation, "although of course the greatest thing about Fresno was that it was a team job involving literally hundreds of people." [36]

He could tell Anderson in May that the CDC had made "some remarkable progress" but "we'll find out for sure come June 8," a primary in which he expected "a good percentage of our statewide candidates" to survive. He was pleased to report that "For the first time in ten years, we have a candidate for every statewide office. For the first time in the memory of man, no statewide Democratic candidate has a strong Democratic opponent. For the first time in memory, we have a candidate in every congressional district," only five of whom faced primary fights compared to nine Republicans who did. One district had no Republican contender – San Francisco where Jack Shelley was running for Congress. The CDC planned to distribute 1.3 million copies of a tabloid listing all Democratic candidates. "Of all this, we are proud," Cranston said. [37]

Not everyone was happy, though. "It's typical of the be-damned political situation out here to get…mud slung at you when you happen to differ with someone," Cranston wrote another friend in Washington, attorney Jerome H. (Jerry) Spingarn, who had tipped him to some negative views. Nevertheless, Cranston said, "We're making headway politically here in an organizational sense that will pay big dividends eventually. But $ and the press are making things tough for our statewide candidates." He still anticipated "some gains in Congress and the state legislature." [38]

One tactic was to put out a "Memo for Demos" in June, but that, too, annoyed some party "old timers," like Dr. W. B. Townsend of Colton. CDC interference "split the party in this county [San Bernardino] badly, also gave the Republicans a senator," he told Cranston in a terse letter. Townsend also complained that "A group of four Jewish boys who have never been active before (backed by [Democratic

National Committeeman] Paul Ziffren), are about to gain control of the county organization." [39]

Cranston was correct in his assessment of Democratic gains in the June primary, however. Yorty and all CDC endorsed candidates won nomination. "We did achieve some remarkable victories," Cranston could tell Spingarn, "but have a long way to march by November." Richard Graves' race for the governorship was the toughest, but Cranston expected that Yorty might win and that Democrats were "a cinch for significant gains in the state legislature." Cranston projected congressional winners in districts where endorsements narrowed the field to one Democratic candidate. "By '58, if not sooner," Cranston euphorically told his old pal Waller, "I'm confident we'll make this a real Democratic state – something it's never been. I'm having a hell of a lot of fun in the process," he added. At the end of the year he would be named to a Democratic State Central Committee group to consider by-law amendments among his growing number of party leadership roles. [40]

Interestingly, though, he failed in an election for membership on the Santa Clara Democratic central committee that he himself had set up, and was called an "also-ran" by his local paper. [41]

Odegard summed up the 1954primary: "Although cross-filing is not yet dead, I think it is dying, even though its ghost may haunt us for some years to come. Thanks to the adoption of Proposition 7 requiring party designation on the primary ballot; thanks to the Fresno convention…; thanks to the quality of the candidates… and above all to the California Democratic Council, which made all this possible, we shall go into November with virtually a full slate of candidates on the ballot for both major parties. Thus, for the first time in nearly forty years, the voters of California will have a real choice among men and measures at a general election." [42]

In the general election, however, all the hard-fought Democratic candidates lost, including Yorty. Only incumbent Democratic Attorney General Pat Brown was reelected. It was a set back. But Cranston was not daunted. [43]

He was hopeful that former President Truman might attend the 1955 CDC convention. He should appear on a Saturday, Cranston reminded Paul Ziffren, because "I know that he has a rule never to speak on Sunday." The report of the CDC's first year "might be of use to you in approaching Harry," Cranston hoped. Other party leaders were working on Senator Hubert Humphrey, and Cranston asked Ziffren to try to get a "Hollywood figure" to address the convention. "The prime purpose of the event is, of course, to lower and, if possible, eliminate our deficit; and we are going to be extremely rigorous about expenses," Cranston told Ziffren. Fundraising, Cranston could see, was to be an ongoing problem facing the party, with which he would be constantly involved. [44]

Geneva also found herself in the press spotlight as Cranston gained public attention. "The charm and friendliness of Geneva Cranston is only to be surpassed by her immense interests in the many, yet versatile, accomplishments of her husband, Alan," a *Palo Alto Times* article read in 1954. She was invariably portrayed as "the other half," the homemaking helpmate and "secretary." "Her husband's work [has] been of utmost importance to the vivacious" Los Altan, the portrayal read. Of her own work as a lobbyist in Washington, Geneva said, "It was fun…and I loved every minute of it…. Constructive lobbying – making one's wishes known to the legislature – gives one the knowledge of democracy" and how the system works. "You have to believe in what you're doing in order to put over what you're thinking," she was quoted as saying of her work to end discrimination against immigrants. During the war years when Cranston had been in the army, she confessed that she "didn't want to be bothered with anything domestic" in the homemaking area. But after the birth of her sons, she felt it important to devote as much time as she could to them. "One parent should be home all of the time." That allowed her to be "Alan's unofficial secretary," answering "at least 50 telephone calls a day, greet[ing] visitors, and contact[ing] people whom Alan hasn't time to call during the day." Geneva was "almost as politically minded as her husband," and during elections was his "follower, attending many meetings and conclaves with him." Geneva said that her interest in politics had begun with her political science major at Pomona. Now, "people want to know how I carry on" at such a hectic pace. Women needed to be involved, she felt. "If we want democracy to prevail, both men and women must work together. Nowadays, with the government getting larger, foreign affairs more important, the threat of McCarthyism getting larger," it was important for mothers to play a "part in world politics" to influence "how the future will be." It was vital also that both parties were active to prove democracy stronger than communism. The writer concluded that Geneva was "as competent in her work as she is in her speech." [45]

"Geneva is a very jovial person," the writer added, "and she has a way of putting over her tales" with wry humor. One related how the entire family had traveled to Salt Lake City on a copper-selling excursion. They stopped to buy chocolate ice cream cones en route, and when Cranston arrived at the shop where he was to transact his business, the shop owners, seeing the car and chocolate-covered children, "thought he was part of a vagabond troupe – not a serious-minded businessman. Anyway he made his sale."

Cranston's association with O. W. I. resurfaced that same year. In November, 1952, he had been subpoenaed to appear before a congressional select committee on the war-time massacre of thousands of Polish intellectuals and army officers in the Katyn Forest where they were being held prisoner in Russia. He was called to testify on whether O. W. I. had brought pressure during the war to curb Polish-language broadcasters in the U. S. who blamed Russia for the massacre. "I was somewhat baffled as to what anybody thought I had to do with *that*," he told Ted Waller in July, 1954, "but appeared on my way to India. It turned out they were investigating why the O. W. I., from Elmer Davis down, seemed to think the *Nazis* massacred the Polish officers there, when it later seemed to turn out that the *Russians* did it (apparently the Russians really did). In the course of the examination, I was asked the $64 question, and swore under oath I never was and wasn't then [a Communist]. Everything went very nicely, and friendly-like, and nobody's bothered to bother me since. I assume this had something to do with my being omitted by" a 1954 Senate Internal Security subcommittee inquiry into suspected Communists in the Army Information and Education Division. Cranston had told the committee in 1952 that government war-time policy was to discourage media attacks on Allied unity, including ally Russia. He was spared appearing at the 1954 inquiry. Information later corroborated that the Russians had in fact perpetrated the grisly 1940 massacre of the cream of the Polish officer corps, revealed from war records that contradicted previous Soviet claims that Hitler's Gestapo agents committed the killings. (The Stalin secret-police massacre, which occurred before Germans invaded the region south of Smolensk in 1941, soured Soviet-Polish relations thereafter. Only in 2010 did Russia's parliament issue a resolution taking responsibility for the 1940 murder of 22,000 Polish officers in Katyn forest, over the objections of the Communist Party, which continued to deny a Soviet role in the massacre.) [46]

Cranston's émigré friend Peter Van Norden was in the hospital about that time. Cranston wrote a letter to cheer him. "Be sure to get back on your feet. The hospital is no place for a feller like you. I've missed our old-time talks together," he continued, "and have wanted an opportunity to particularly hear what you think of the course of events in your one-time Russian homeland. It's hard to figure out exactly what is happening there, and who is really the boss now, isn't it?" [47]

The CDC, Cranston was proud to report, now was the largest Democratic organization in the state's history, and the 1954 election had resulted in Democrats' "running better than in any elections since 1938. We are now the strongest we have been in the state Senate since 1939, and the second strongest in the history of the state. I have not run for any office myself, but probably will sometime in the future," he revealed. "I don't have any idea what office it will be when I do run. I enjoy politics immensely, and, as you know, always hoped to get into it."

Cranston attributed Democrats' success to the club movement of which CDC was the central body. He also perceived the momentous, and historical, importance of what he was involved with. In his "President's Report" published in *The California Democrat* in 1955, he called the CDC the "symbol, the spirit, the soul – and the solid structure – of a new and bold experiment in democracy. The experiment is significant because it is taking place within the oldest political party on earth and the only nationwide party in the United States, the party that has directed the destinies of our nation for an even 100 of our nation's 166 years, the party that today commands Congress, a majority of the governorships and the allegiance of a preponderance of the people." Significantly, it had the "full participation of all party leaders in "what will soon be the most important state in the greatest democracy on earth, at a time when democracy is everywhere under assault – at home by those who doubt the ability of the people to govern themselves, abroad by Communists who hold half the world in thralldom." He identified the CDC with Thomas Jefferson's vision of a political party "by and for the people. We Democrats of California are in the vanguard," he exulted. The party's spirit was carried by Adlai Stevenson, who was about to make another run for the White House. Stevenson, Cranston said, was resolved to make "*politician* a term of honor, not of scorn," to restore it to its rightful place as "the noblest of man's works." A measure of the new vigor in California was that Democratic clubs, after Stevenson's 1952 defeat, "skyrocketed" from 75 to more than 400 in 1955. A "great strength" was that men and women were attracted to the party "by principle rather than by patronage." [48]

But there were brambles in the newly-tilled fields – some California Democrats still did not "trust the people" to govern, and opposed the CDC. "Aghast at the growth of the clubs, fearful that they will fall into 'bad hands' and run amuck," Cranston warned, "they would retreat from free and open conventions to the comfort of their beloved smoke-filled rooms, where the manipulations of the few replace the mandates of the many." The pointed reference was to the ambitious, aspiring politician, Jesse Unruh. Cranston urged loyalists not to be swayed by such people. He also inserted warnings about corporate control being consolidated into a few companies ("abetted by the Eisenhower administration"), and the continued testing of weapons that might "bring down upon us disasters surpassing those of war itself." But the bottom line for California Democrats was to elect Democratic senators in 1956 and 1958, and to help Stevenson get into the White House.

Sam Yorty continued to be a thorn in the party's side from the liberals' point of view. Cranston made it clear that Yorty would be subject to the same rules as other candidates at the 1955 convention – allowed five minutes to address the audience. "I'm sure that your experiences in the '54 campaign will enable you to be most helpful to us in our efforts to plan effectively for the future," Cranston said as diplomatically as he could in his invitation. "Thanks for the above," Yorty wrote at the bottom of Cranston's letter, which he returned, adding, "Five minutes is not much time for the statewide candidate who got the most votes." [49]

The United Auto Workers wanted time on the agenda to talk about a strike against a Kohler Plumbing plant in Sheboygan, Wisconsin. Cranston had to tell them "no" but they could distribute literature at the convention. [50]

The 1955 convention, CDC's second, had to prove that the entity was viable. In thanking Ziffren afterward, Cranston said that he had done "more than any other single person to dispel all danger that anyone could label the convention 'rump' – our major hurdle." The CDC came through with a "a sounder dues structure, better by-laws, a solid political program approved by the delegates after very mature debate, an excellent slate of officers, and a good deal more of value. We now have more than $10,000 in the bank!" Cranston delighted in saying. [51]

National figures sent endorsements that further reinforced CDC's credentials. "We Democrats should be carefully reviewing actions of the present [Eisenhower] administration and I am glad you Californians have begun the process," Senator Kefauver telegraphed. "My recent hurried trip through parts of California convinced me you have great opportunity for furthering the cause of liberal democracy," Minnesota Senator Hubert Humphrey's telegram stated. "Let us quit defeatist attitude and get victory spirit in the air. All it takes is hard work and willingness to work together for common cause," he urged delegates. National party chairman Paul Butler showed up in person. "Your presence itself was a very great source of strength to us," Cranston told him, "and your warmth, your understanding of what we are trying to accomplish, and solid advice, combined to make your visit one of the most productive events within the Democratic fold in our state in many a moon." It was a coup for Cranston to get such national endorsements and attention, both professionally and personally. [52]

New York Governor Averill Harriman, a star of the national party, stressed the need to get a Democratic majority in Congress "to pull the president out of the holes his own party is continually getting him into." Harriman would make a campaign appearance in California in January, 1956, telling Cranston it had been "pleasant to be at [San Francisco restaurant] 'Trader Vic's' with Democrats who have played so big a part in the recent progress of our party in California." [53]

California Democratic Congressman Clair Engle of Red Bluff also had taken notice of the CDC's potential influence. "I am very anxious in the months ahead to establish a close liaison with the Democratic Clubs in my District," he wrote Cranston before the 1955 convention. "It is important, I believe, to have closer cooperation between the Democratic congressional delegation and the party organization in California," he said in a letter that he instructed be sent by "personal stamp," not franked as official House business. [54]

Cranston had invited the president of Aerojet General, former Secretary of the Navy Dan Kimball, to address the convention, an early indication of Cranston's building acquaintances with industrialists who could help bankroll campaigns. (Kimball had pioneered a program in his company that encouraged employees to make voluntary contributions to the party of their choice, which Cranston liked as a way of ensuring campaign funding without requiring large sums from corporations or individuals). They had dinner with Pat Brown and Dore Schary, vice president of MGM Pictures, and Kimball agreed to chair a campaign committee for Richard Richards' race for the Senate in 1956. Cranston became active in raising money for Richards, calling on his friendships with U. S. Senators like George Smathers of Florida and Stuart Symington of Missouri, members of the Democratic Senate Campaign Committee. Senators Wayne Morse and Richard L. Neuberger of Oregon and recently-elected Senator Frank Church of Idaho attended a fundraising lunch in San Francisco in October, 1956. San Francisco hotel owner Ben Swig hosted a luncheon for Pat Brown at the Fairmont, from which Cranston sent $500 to the Stevenson campaign that included checks from his sister, brother-in-law and mother. Swig afterward told Cranston, "It is good to work with you on this committee. It seems as though you and I think pretty much alike on a great many things." Theirs would be a long mutual friendship. Cranston urged Swig to personally call people who in 1952 had switched registration from GOP to Democrat in order to support Stevenson because they disliked Nixon and Joseph McCarthy. [55]

Cranston also was grateful for the organizational skills of young Roy Greenaway in making the convention a success. Greenaway was a full-time high school teacher at the time, but as Fresno County Democratic Council president, was charged with running the convention. The CDC had no money or paid employees, and had to rely entirely on its 50,000 members to keep it going (Greenaway had about fifty helping him with the convention that year). Starting months in advance, they organized everything, staying "up all night" the Friday before the 3,000 delegates convened, "with mimeograph machines, doing bylaws, platforms, committee reports, a big managerial job," Greenaway said of the demanding task. [56]

Among other details, Greenaway had told Cranston that Fresno people thought $3.75, even $3.50, too high a price to pay for dinner. Cranston replied that it was "impossible to go below $3.50," they were "too deep in red ink." Afterward he told Greenaway, "The arrangements were beyond doubt the best we have ever had.... I hope that your remarkable talents will now be devoted to spreading the club movement throughout your county into the communities where there aren't effective clubs." Greenaway also was active with the California Foundation of Young Democrats (1954-56), and would be a future vice president of CDC (1957-60). He in turn told Cranston, "I was quite impressed (as were many other Fresnans) with your ability and personality. I have heard many compliments paid to you by the local people since the convention. I enjoyed working with you and hope to see you again soon." He offered to help with the 1956 convention, saying, "I think I could contribute to it." He subsequently organized the conventions in 1956 and 1958-60, all in Fresno – except in 1957 it was held in Long Beach. "I was putting pressure on the City of Fresno to build a new convention center – and they *did*!" he laughed of why theirs was held elsewhere that year. He and Cranston would work together more closely, and for far longer, than either could anticipate at the time. [57]

Cranston asked Fresno Congressman B. ("Bernie") F. Sisk if he might have Cranston's report to the convention printed in the *Congressional Record* and distributed, at taxpayer expense, using his postal frank. Sisk declined, after giving the matter "sympathetic consideration…. I do not believe this to be advisable," Sisk said, having considered "the over-all picture" for "the welfare and advancement of the Democratic Party." Similar mailings, he perceived, had "demonstrated that citizens generally resent the use of *Congressional Record* reprints and particularly the franking privilege for distribution of partisan literature. Even though the reprint shows 'not printed at public expense,' many people feel that this is campaign material at tax cost. I personally feel that the possible bad effect of such mailings is greater than any benefit which could be realized," but, he added, "I am anxious to cooperate with you in any way I can." [58]

Cranston understood, but realized that "the CDC and clubs still have a long way to go in establishing a sound working relationship with the congressional delegation." At home, however, things were looking even better for Democrats: two Republican assembly seats had become available, reducing that body to the lowest number of Republicans since 1944 while the State Senate had the fewest Republicans since 1938. Cranston believed Democrats could capture the Assembly in 1956, and the state Senate in 1958. "It's obviously of the utmost importance that we be in command of the state legislature in 1960," he noted to Sisk, "so that, for the first time in this century, we can do the redistricting. It's now estimated that eight new House seats will come to California after the 1960 census." Cranston was not alone in perceiving the importance of redistricting. One of his colleagues in the early building of the CDC, San Franciscan Phil Burton, would have a hand in that exercise with a skill rarely matched in any state. [59]

Cranston, meanwhile, was honing a talent of his own that would become legendary – vote counting. He also was looking well into the future. After checking historical records, he learned, for example, that State Senator Richard Richards of Los Angles had received more votes in his previous election than what was "cast for any winning presidential candidate through and including both of Andrew Jackson's victories" in 1828 and 1832 – more than 600,000. That was because Richards represented L. A. County, equal to 40 percent of the state, prior to reapportionment based on one man, one vote. Would Richards keep his ears attuned to possible openings for other California Senate seats that Democrats might win, Cranston asked? "We really have a chance to approach that magic 21 mark in the next elections if we take full advantage of every opportunity," he hoped. [60]

Cranston was the honoree at a dinner in Fresno that October to which Sisk sent a telegram citing Cranston's "fine and unceasing work which has contributed so heavily to the growth and success of the Democratic Club Movement throughout California." [61]

Congressman Jack Shelley was another politician who offered opportunities for control of a major bloc of Democrats. "I've been delighted to hear vague rumors in San Francisco that you *might* reconsider your position re: the mayoralty race," Cranston wrote Shelley in July, 1955. "I don't profess to be a great expert on San Francisco politics, but from all I hear, [George] Christopher is not yet proving to be the formidable candidate that many thought he would be. There seems to be a great deal of feeling that a better man would walk away with the race – and a broad consensus that that better man is you…. A victory in San Francisco…would pave the way to great victories in '56 and '58." [62]

Christopher, a moderate and popular Republican, was more formidable than many thought, however, serving two terms as Mayor of San Francisco (1956-64) – the last Republican mayor as of 2012. Shelley did not run for mayor in 1955, having stated at the end of 1954 that he would not be a candidate, and believing that "it would be unwise and a little foolish…to get into the fight now on a hastily conceived draft idea." Shelley also had made commitments to other candidates and it would be "embarrassing" to change his mind now. [63]

Shelley, however, had a heart attack in November, 1955. Cranston wrote him of seeing the "black headlines," but saying that perhaps it was "a blessing in disguise" and that now he would live "twice as long" by slowing down. Shelley blamed his attack on "overwork and strain." Cranston could not resist talking politics, reporting that the CDC organizing committee now had "greater good-will and understanding on all sides." A son, Kevin, was born while his father was recuperating in the hospital. (Kevin Shelley would have a political career of his own, as a San Francisco Supervisor and Secretary of State.) [64]

Phil Burton, who had lost an assembly race to a dead incumbent (William Clifton Berry) in 1954, was building support for a second run from predominantly Democratic, pro-labor San Francisco. The CDC, he knew, could be invaluable to him and all Democratic aspirants. He suggested that it keep "tabs" on Republican office-holders and let "key Demos, clubs and LABOR UNION LOCALS" know if they had "bad" labor records, fodder for Democratic candidates. Like Cranston, Burton wanted to know all the facts about a district – registration figures past and present, election results over time. That way they could assess which districts were "safe Republican, safe Democratic, or marginal, and what steps" might be taken to shift them to the Democrats, focusing on districts needing "special attention." The two aspiring politicians would be part of a formidable team that included a silent partner. Burton's letter bore the typist's initials "sg" – presumably Sala Galant, Burton's wife by her maiden name. She was on the Democratic central committee board, and would prove to be an astute political operative in her own right. [65]

Cranston's knowledge of history prompted him to write *Time* magazine boosting Adlai Stevenson's candidacy for president in the summer of 1955, likening him to George Washington, a self-effacing candidate for such great responsibility. "Even after all the states had voted that he be the first president, George Washington refused to declare his willingness to serve, vowing instead reluctance 'to quit a peaceful abode for an ocean of difficulties, without that competency of political skill, abilities and inclination which is necessary to manage the helm.,'" Cranston noted. [66]

In November, 1955, after Democrats won a special State Senate election in Santa Barbara, "an overwhelmingly Republican District," Cranston told Jerry Spingarn, "We seem to be set to carry California overwhelmingly for Stevenson in the primary." [67]

To his old Dublin conference acquaintance, Marshall Field IV, Cranston related that while involved "in two totally unrelated businesses – real estate and importing – I am actually spending almost all my time on Democratic Party activities." The CDC, with its 400 clubs, had led to "some unprecedented victories.... Virtually all organized Democrats in the state are for Stevenson, and I'm confident we'll carry our state's primary for him." [68]

Assemblyman Augustus "Gus" Hawkins of Los Angeles, a light-skinned African-American, also was encouraged, expecting "a real Democratic victory in 1956 if we continue along our present lines. Needless for me to say that much credit is due your very able leadership of CDC and personal integrity," he told Cranston. [69]

The hopefulness that Democrats in California, and nationwide, felt for that 1956 presidential race was enormous.

A rival for the presidential nomination, though, was Senator Estes Kefauver, and some CDC activists thought "it would be a mistake *not* to invite" the senator to address the 1956 convention. "After all, this convention is a convention of Democrats, not a Stevenson convention as such," Harold F. Taggart told Cranston in response to a poll of CDC's leadership. Taggart also urged that CDC stick to a voted decision not to endorse a presidential candidate. "We do not want to see the club movement break up into factional groups supporting one or the other candidate. A Democratic Club should be conducted in a manner that will permit Democrats who support different men for president and vice president to belong and become active," Taggart urged. [70]

Cranston, who had lobbied Kefauver while U. W. F. president and helped him in his 1952 presidential bid, told him, "Immediately following announcement of your candidacy, I proceeded to poll the CDC executive committee, as I indicated to you I would, and I am now most happy to extend to you a cordial invitation to address our convention on February 5 in Fresno. There is a rapidly growing consensus of opinion," he had to add, "that there should *not* be a presidential endorsement" by the CDC, which was formed to endorse "contests against cross-filed Republicans." [71]

Stevenson also was invited to speak to the convention, although Cranston found that some rank-and-file members were not sanguine about that invitation. "There are some who would rather Stevenson did not come to a CDC affair," Cranston wrote one, Ben Held. Cranston had not brought the matter before the full board, wishing "to delay their knowledge of the invitation, thus reducing their opportunity to block it," and, in the event that Stevenson declined, to "avoid publicity if possible." Both presidential candidates attended the 1956 CDC convention. "I don't see how the appearance of Stevenson – and Kefauver – can be anything but good from our point of view," Cranston felt. [72]

Despite dissension in the ranks, "California Democrats will go into their state convention at Fresno next month with at least an outward appearance of unity," a political writer reported in January, 1956. CDC and Dime-a-Day for Democracy

(DDD), largely a fundraising group, were still vying to be the unofficial party endorser of candidates, and DDD felt that CDC was trying to control the party. But they worked out an agreement to prevent double or conflicting endorsements, especially for the forthcoming U. S. Senate primary. The compromise proposal from CDC was to add delegates from districts that had elected Democrats. DDD president, former Governor Culbert L. Olson, however, took exception to the requirement that such districts had to have elected national or statewide candidates, arguing that CDC did not adequately represent many Democratic districts in California. [73]

Cranston apparently negotiated agreements that somewhat mollified the disparate group, for which he was congratulated. Congressman Engle called it "the biggest assemblage of Democrats I have ever seen in the State of California," and complimented Cranston on "a fine job managing" it. The convention received national press and television coverage, and its large attendance of some 1,500 delegates gave it the atmosphere of a national nominating convention. [74]

Cranston again was "indebted" to Greenaway for his help, and would try to get him into the Democratic National Convention at Chicago. "Alan *did* get me in, as an alternate delegate. I was the youngest member of the California delegation, twenty-eight years old," Greenaway acknowledged. [75]

Stevenson's praise after the CDC convention was a boon to its goals. "I don't participate in local primary controversies," he said, but the convention "impressed me a great deal." It was "evidence of increasing political activity by people who have no axe to grind, who pay their own way, who have no hope of jobs or patronage or political preference…. I don't know that I have seen anywhere a better and more reassuring illustration of it than I saw in this meeting in Fresno." [76]

Still, Cranston found himself having to assure party members that the convention represented "all elements of the party," he told Paul Ziffren in March. Yorty, now the former congressman, had determined to run again in the Senate primary, this time against State Senator Richard Richards. Cranston agreed with Ziffren that "from here on, the best treatment for Yorty is [to be] very silent." Quietly, anti-Yorty forces would try to sabotage his campaign. [77]

"Do your best to offset the impressions that Sam Yorty is trying to create," Cranston urged Clair Engle with whom he was working on elections in his district. Engle wanted to distance himself from some candidates on a slate card to be sent to Democratic voters in Butte County. Cranston was happy to oblige. "I assure you again that we'll do nothing in your district without your consent." His association with Engle would have important ramifications for Cranston's future. [78]

Yorty continued his attacks on the CDC as left-leaning. "Frankly, I'm getting damned tired of the implication that the CDC is communist-stacked and -controlled," another CDC leader told Cranston. "I choose to believe, as you do, that it's a damned fine organization representing the true grass roots in California, and the Democratic Party that we all believe in. I don't mind arguments back and forth in the true democratic fashion, but this kind of stuff is getting under my skin," attorney John E. Thorne complained, enclosing articles from the *San Jose Mercury* and *News* about a Yorty visit to the area. "It seems to me high time that someone took him on with a damned fine law-suit to make him either put up or shut up." [79]

Yorty knew that this time he could not expect to receive the CDC endorsement.

In a dramatic moment, he mounted the convention platform and angrily withdrew his name from consideration, saying that he did not recognize the convention's legitimacy, calling it a closed, boss-run conspiracy against other Democrats. The crowd jeered back but the short, dapper politician delivered a defiant, bitter speech charging that "this convention is wired, stacked, rigged and packed! The professional politicians of the CDC have become so power drunk that they're determined to… control the convention." That further enraged delegates and Cranston pounded his gavel and shouted for order. "Let 'em boo!" Yorty told him, then marched out followed by more jeers. Yorty was repudiated, Richards was roundly endorsed, and $50,000 quickly raised on the floor to set his campaign in motion. That prompted more contributions from people who now saw that the CDC could back its nominees with money. [80]

Yorty went on to run in the primary anyway, and filed suit to stop circulation of a party pamphlet supporting Richards. Cranston was named as one of the defendants along with the CDC and Roger Kent, vice chairman of the Democratic State Central Committee. Yorty later dropped the suit but kept the grudge, and further alienated Democrats by trying to court, or emulate, Republicans. Prior to the Fresno convention, he had held a press conference that backfired because of his evoking Nixon. That "explains why Sam didn't get a single S. F. vote at Fresno – the praise for Nixon," Cranston told Ziffren. Yorty had tried to identify himself with Republican Governor Goodwin "Goody" Knight in the 1954 gubernatorial race against Richard Graves, and in 1956, "he hopes to slate up with Eisenhower as well as with Nixon," Cranston saw. [81]

Yorty's attacks against Richards included a challenge to "clear up his attitude toward communism." In a speech at San Jose, a pro-Richards supporter demanded that Yorty either prove or terminate his "innuendoes of communist tendencies" on the part of Richards, accusing Yorty of "Nixonian" methods. Richards in 1952 as an attorney had signed an American Civil Liberties Union (ACLU) brief involving Constitutional issues in the case of fourteen Communists then facing federal charges. The brief, which Yorty quoted, held that the defendants were not dangerous enough to warrant being prosecuted. [82]

Another of those whose careers would rise in 1956 was Assemblyman John McFall who was running for Congress from the northern San Joaquin valley. "Johnny McFall is off and running in the 11th, and we're sure to hold his Assembly seat," Cranston reported to Engle. Democrats had "an excellent prospect of taking over the state legislature, a good chance" for five State Senate districts, and might pick up two congressional seats (including the one for which McFall was running). "Unless something totally unforeseen happens," he said, Richards would "wallop Yorty in the primary" for U. S. Senate, and give incumbent "Kuchel a real run for his money in November." Democrats were "contesting more seats than we have in a political generation," Cranston boasted. [83]

Richards did beat Yorty in the primary, as well as Kuchel who cross-filed. Richards got 53.3 percent of the vote, a measure of CDC's effectiveness. The result had given "Kuchel the biggest scare any Republican incumbent senator has had in a political generation," Cranston wrote Drew Pearson. [84]

Richards was very grateful for Cranston's help. The CDC's 1956 primary work was a "landmark in Democratic political history in California," he wrote Cranston, and the party could "look forward to unity and success, based on a healthy and ever-widening base." (Yorty in 1961 would be elected mayor of Los Angeles, garnering the sobriquet "Saigon Sam" for his hawk position on the Vietnam war.) [85]

Cranston also stood by his CDC colleague Phil Burton in his campaign for the Assembly when the San Francisco Democratic County Committee refused to endorse Burton in 1956. "He remains one of the Democratic challengers most likely to oust a Republican incumbent assemblyman," Cranston said in a letter to voters as president of the CDC, despite the fact that Burton's opponent was the man who had helped Cranston move the World Federalist resolution forward in the state legislature a few years earlier, the sixty-seven-year-old former stevedore-turned-Assembly Speaker Tommy Maloney, who was thought invincible. Thanks to dogged precinct work by club volunteers, including Burton's younger brothers Robert and John, Burton eked out a victory over "unbeatable" Maloney by 811 votes. Burton resigned as a CDC director when he went to the Assembly. "If we achieve all that we should in 1958, a great deal of the credit will have to be shared with you," Cranston wrote him. "I do count on you to be very close to the CDC in the years…that lie before us and we will count upon your help in a great many ways." Burton would rise to become one of the state's, and Congress,' most powerful and influential politicians. [86]

Another successful Democrat who subsequently would go to Congress was Los Angeles Assemblyman "Gus" Hawkins. "Congratulations on scaring out all the opposition in your district!" Cranston wrote him after the CDC convention. Any assistance that Hawkins could lend in the Los Angeles area would be helpful, Cranston said, admitting that he was "not quite so familiar with the situation" there as in the rest of the state. To Carlos Bee of Hayward, who also would serve in Congress, Cranston said after the June primary, "Congratulations on holding your seat in such a pleasant way!" [87]

Indeed, the primary gave Democrats "fabulous" results, as Cranston told Engle. "Not a single Republican defeated a Democrat in our own primary anywhere in the state! Democrats defeated Republicans in ten Republican primaries," and twenty-five seats were "already won – three in Congress, nine in the Senate, thirteen in the Assembly." "I am sure that in many instances these results are directly attributable to the political activity of the California Democratic Council," Engle said. [88]

Twenty-year veteran Congressman Harry R. Sheppard of San Bernardino County also was impressed. "I am of the firm belief that the Democrats in California are finally awaking to their obligations as Democrats and voters," he wrote Cranston after the primary. Although long ahead in registration, that advantage had been eroded by a "large segment of Independents." The CDC seemed to be driving those voters to the Democrats. "It has been a long time since the prospect of success for our Party in the state has been so encouraging. Keep up the good work!" incumbent Congressman Cecil King told Cranston. Los Angeles Assemblyman Charles H. Wilson, another who would go to Congress, told Cranston that he "went right to work following the primary to see what could be done to help in those Assembly districts…that have a good Democratic majority." The Democrats were motivated statewide. [89]

The CDC was gaining attention and viability with a number of national politicians.

Senator John F. Kennedy would campaign for Stevenson in California, writing Cranston, "You are certainly doing a terrific job out there, and it was a real pleasure for me to go out and do what I could. The spirit and enthusiasm which I found in Democratic ranks throughout California augurs well for November 6. I hope that you will look me up whenever you are in Washington." [90]

Cranston's overriding interest in 1956 was the election of Adlai Stevenson. At the Fresno convention, Cranston had presented him a bound volume containing more than 2,000 pledges of support by California Democratic leaders. The CDC also threw a 56th birthday party for the presidential contender with a cake shaped like the White House, and volunteers ran a whistle-stop campaign train through the valley, harkening back to Truman's winning style in 1948. [91]

"I know I can count on your continuing assistance to achieve our common purpose – the victory of the Democratic Party in November," Stevenson wrote Cranston, adding, "I am honored to know that we shall be working together to that end." "Now after three years of Republican misrule, deadly drift in our foreign policy, weakening of our national defense, give-away of our natural resources, indifference toward our farmers and working men, government *of*, *by* and *for* big business," Stevenson told voters in rhetoric that would be echoed repeatedly over the years, "we face a new fight – a fight to make the American people aware of the dangers confronting our nation." He was concentrating on California in hopes of winning a large bloc of electoral votes, and did well in the June primary, beating Kefauver by 600,000 votes. Kefauver withdrew and endorsed Stevenson. Charles Wilson credited the win to CDC "effectiveness," which had overwhelmed anti-CDC "dissidents." [92]

Pat Brown was state chairman of the Stevenson campaign and asked Cranston to serve on the campaign committee. Cranston was so anxious to help Stevenson that on one occasion he preempted McFall at a testimonial dinner for him and had to apologize. "My enthusiasm for Stevenson carried me away…and I was horrified when you had to cut down the superb speech you were giving." It probably had helped McFall, though, "for people always resent the bird who speaks too long, namely me, in this case. And they rally around whoever is victimized, namely you." McFall was not bothered – it probably had kept him from putting his foot in his mouth, he replied. [93]

Cranston's sons were part of the political world from childhood, and "a lot of funny things happened" as a result of their involvement, Cranston recalled. Stevenson spoke at Palo Alto before a cheering crowd of 1,000, predicting a new era in which the "quality of life" and a "more lively concern for the mind and spirit" would be priorities for Americans, blaming the Eisenhower administration for "indifference to intellectual growth and academic freedom." Stanford professor and author Wallace Stegner introduced him, and Cranston, grinning broadly, was photographed with Stevenson at his campaign bus, holding a skeptical-looking four-year-old Kim on his shoulders with eight-year-old Robin at their side. "I was shaking Stevenson's hand, and a photographer was there to take a picture. Kim's looking around, and the photographer said, 'Kim, look at Stevenson,' and Kim said, 'Where's Stevenson?'" But the boys were an attractive subject for the media. Herb Caen reported in his gossip column, "Baghdad-by-the-Bay," that Rob had been with his dad and Attorney General Pat Brown at a political meeting in Sonora in Gold Country. "While the politicos were having their session, Rob wandered around Sonora, keeping his eyes and ears open. He returned to whisper to Pat: 'I've got news for you, Mr. Brown. There's plenty of gambling in this town!' The result was bannered in Monday morning's headlines: 'State agents raid Sonora gambling clubs,'" Caen joked. [94]

Cranston would attend the national convention as a delegate for Stevenson. Senate Majority Leader Lyndon Baines Johnson sent "personal congratulations" with rallying words. Despite "razor-thin majorities" in both Houses of Congress, Democrats had had legislative successes – an increase in the minimum wage, the first major expansion of Social Security since its inauguration, drastic revision of farm policy. But unity in the party was essential for its future, he emphasized. [95]

Cranston afterwards told national committeewoman and Los Angeles delegate Carmen Warschaw, "One of the most fascinating and – sometimes – pleasing things about that convention was the opportunity it provided to see who stood where when the chips were down – and how long they stayed there. I was delighted to note, repeatedly, that you were among those who stood firmly on things that seemed to me to count." [96]

Raising money for candidates, though, was a continuing challenge for Cranston as head of the CDC. It could not afford to give any to candidates who were sure of election, nor to those whose odds of winning were low. "It was hard for us to make this tough decision," a CDC memorandum stated, "but we believe that Democrats generally will agree that it would have been wrong to have passed out equal checks of $60 - $70 to all nominees." Only candidates in races where Republicans received no more than 55 percent of the primary vote got funds. McFall, whose district was targeted by the GOP (he was elected to Congress nevertheless), and one other congressional candidate, got $500; one state Senate candidate fitting the formula got $400; and four Assembly candidates, including Burton, got $300 each. [97]

"I have been deeply engaged in fundraising for Dick [Richards] and it is working very well in California," Cranston told Waller just before the election. "We are obviously very close to Kuchel but need a bit more muscle for the remaining days of the campaign if we are to win." In a recent Field poll, Kuchel had 45 percent to Richards' 43 percent, with 12 percent undecided. It was the closest a Democrat had been in a Senate race "in many, many years." Drew Pearson had reported that Republican leaders had warned Eisenhower that Kuchel would lose unless "Ike" campaigned in California. "Three days later, the White House announced that Eisenhower" would do just that, and Vice President Nixon had admitted at a press conference, "There is concern about the senatorial race." It was considered a toss-up by *Newsweek* magazine. "All of this and a great deal more leads us to believe that Richards can win," Cranston said with hope that Waller could raise some money back East. [98]

Richards, though, would lose the election to Kuchel and return to the State Senate. His defeat was blamed, in part, on his being identified with liberals who advocated recognizing Red China when virulent anti-Communist advocates were calling for "containment" of the "Red menace." Cranston's help, Richards said, had "been tremendous and your ability unmatched. I shall never forget your confidence, and your friendship. Now, what can *I* do for you?" he added in a postscript. [99]

Kuchel, however, would not fulfill the forebodings that Dewey Anderson had expressed earlier, turning out to be a moderate-to-liberal Republican senator. He would serve until 1969.

Stevenson's overwhelming loss to Eisenhower a second time was equally heartbreaking for Democrats. "More than ever, it is necessary for people like thee and me…to build up an effective opposition to the Republican Party," U. W. F. associate (Truman's Air Force Secretary) Thomas Finletter wrote Cranston. "I had thought that when this election was over, I would call it a day on politics. But now, as of two days after the election, my reaction is precisely the opposite. It is absolutely indispensable for the Democratic Party to provide the most powerful and searching opposition to this administration that we can." They were rallying words for the disappointed Cranston, who agreed. "There should be great opportunities for us in the years ahead and we must do our very best to take full advantage of them." [100]

"Well, what do we do now?" Waller asked. "Suggestions please," Cranston replied. [101]

He regretted an invitation to honor Governor Olson November 8. "I am afraid that if I left home that soon after the election, on anything having to do with politics, I would never be allowed to return," he wrote, a reference to Geneva's complaining about his chronic absence from the boys, who now were playing Little League baseball. [102]

Despite the Stevenson debacle, Cranston could tell fellow Democrats at the 1957 CDC convention that they had made "incredible strides in four years." Two new California Democrats were elected to the House in 1956, and Democrats had made gains in the state legislature which they might control for the first time in the twentieth century. There now were 500 clubs with 40,000 members in California. Republicans, meanwhile, seemed "on the verge of civil war," divided into factions behind conservatives Nixon and Knowland versus the moderate Knight, affording Democrats "unprecedented opportunities" to field "the strongest statewide ticket in many decades," Cranston believed. "We must move on to new thinking but not neglect old battlefronts," he warned delegates, referring again to his favorite theme: "We must refuse to surrender totally to the tides of the arms race. It is our responsibility to seek a policy of peace to match our policy of power. This is the most important matter upon the agenda of mankind." [103]

He alerted Drew Pearson to what the CDC had done in the state in the past four years, hoping to give it national publicity. "We set out to form clubs, man the precincts, and make endorsements in primary elections – to end the Republican practice of capturing our own primary nominations under California's odd cross-filing laws. The results have been phenomenal." In 1954 every CDC-endorsed Democratic candidate for statewide office had won a primary for the first time since 1914. In 1956 no Republican won a Democratic primary, and Democrats won several Republican primaries. By 1957 the percentage of Democrats versus Republicans in state elective office had changed dramatically – in 1953 Republicans held 112 to Democrats' 50 offices; in 1957, Republicans had 88 to the Democrats' 74, and Democrats controlled the State Senate for the first time since 1890. [104]

Pearson put the news into a column, and Cranston thanked him "for the very nice things you said…. It has been most helpful out here." It also had brought responses from "long-lost friends from all over the map – one from as far away as Mexico City. I didn't know you appeared in Spanish!" In return for the favorable press, Cranston offered to see what he could "do to clear your air problems in California." [105]

Cranston was re-elected CDC president and went back to work on state politics. He urged Glenn Anderson, CDC vice president and former chairman of the Democratic State Central Committee, to "give careful attention to getting a good number of minority and labor appointments on committees." [106]

But he kept up his interest in international affairs. When a populist anti-Communist uprising occurred in Hungary in October, 1956, suppressed brutally by the Soviet Union, Cranston issued a statement of outrage. He publicly proposed sending United Nations' volunteer observers into the country, despite the communist government's official refusal to permit them. "The eyes of the world would be on this mission of peace and humanity," he said, and if the Communists attacked a clearly-marked, unarmed plane carrying U. N. observers, arrested or expelled them, he predicted that "they would offend virtually every nation on earth." Even the "mere announcement by the U. N. that the mission was to be undertaken," he thought, "would end the brutal strife and bloody slaughter in Hungary." But, as an editorial pointed out, the U. N. still did not have the authority or force of a world-governing power. Cranston's statement condemned the Republican administration for its policies: "It is incredible and intolerable that under [Republicans], the U. S. has acted through the U. N. against our friends England, France and Israel for the use of force in Egypt, but has failed to act against the Soviet Union for their use of force in Hungary. This is a blot on the American record that must be expunged – most of all because of our part in encouraging patriots to revolt in Hungary." [107]

Cranston also traveled through southern states (Texas, Mississippi, Alabama and Georgia) on a fact-finding trip in 1957 when bitter disillusionment among African-Americans was rising, as were civil rights leaders like the Reverends Martin Luther King, Junior, and Ralph Abernathy of the Montgomery, Alabama, Improvement Association. Cranston met with them and leaders of the National Association for the Advancement of Colored People (NAACP), White Citizens Councils, Ku Klux Klansmen, political, church and media leaders. He also visited a bombed Black church and two ministers whose homes had been dynamited. [108]

He gave an impassioned report on the trip to the Western Democratic Conference in San Francisco early in 1957. This time his remarks were inserted into the *Congressional Record*, thanks to Congressman James Roosevelt, who referred to the "freshness" of Cranston's approach. "I went to feel the winds of freedom blowing there," but found the South "a place of paradox, surprise and contradiction," Cranston said. [109]

"I asked a Ku Klux Klanner if he thought subversive elements were at work in the South. 'Well,' he said, 'there's one outfit that's infiltrated down here like a thief in the night and is going around stirring things up – the F. B. I.'" [110]

"The Negro has made great gains," Cranston felt nevertheless. Some were small and unobtrusive, like a North Carolina League of Women Voters chapter that opened membership to Negroes, and a Mississippi medical society that admitted a "colored physician." But "Negroes are losing hard-won ground." Eight southern states had enacted laws to circumvent the 1954 Supreme Court school-desegregation decision, and none had begun desegregating. The Reverend King had "achieved incredible results" and "touched the southern soul at its tenderest spot." His mimeographed "Integrated Bus Suggestions" nevertheless, after a boycott resulted in another desegregation ruling, warned: "*Do not deliberately sit by a white person unless there is no other seat. If cursed, do not curse back. If struck, do not strike back, but evidence love and good will at all times*."

But "Negro after Negro" blamed the Democratic Party for "strangulation of their rights" by compromising on the issue, notably voting rights. "A cold, silent stare by an election official has turned many a Negro from the polls," Cranston stated. A White Citizens Council leader frankly told him, "We're playing for time, *ad infinitum*. We'll think up a trick to keep the Negro away from the polls or out of school."

Cranston proposed taking "the federal election process out of the hands of state governments" and setting up a Federal Elections Administration. That would "let southern legislators off the hook," ridding "us of our Eastlands [a reference to Mississippi Senator James Eastland], while liberating able southern" members of Congress "who refuse to rabble-rouse" but feared it "political suicide to treat the Negro like a full-fledged citizen under present circumstances."

"Politically, as Democrats, we can no longer play fast and loose with human rights without being hurt badly in national elections….. We know, as Americans, that our nation is desperately hampered in world affairs by our treatment of the Negro race. We know, as human beings, that it is inhuman, immoral and unjust for us to do anything less than the most we can for those who are denied their freedom." [111]

Cranston's suggestions anticipated the federal Voting Rights Act of 1965 by eight years, and much of what he proposed would become law. His proposal for a Federal Election Commission, as it would be called, was endorsed by the CDC a month after he delivered the speech. He sent it to key members of Congress who were pushing for reform, including Senator Wayne Morse of Oregon, whom he had met on a town-meeting radio program in 1948 and invited to address the CDC convention (Morse regretted). Cranston also sent the proposal to Representative Emanuel Cellar of New York, a strong advocate of civil rights and chairman of the House Judiciary Committee, and Senator Hubert Humphrey, telling them there were precedents for federal takeover of elections where voters were disenfranchised. "I am going to read every word of it," Humphrey promptly replied, "Thank goodness that someone is doing some constructive thinking." Humphrey added that he had an aunt living in Los Altos (at 715 Fremont Avenue, Mrs. Harry B. Humphrey). "If ever you are around that neighborhood, why don't you stop by and say hello? She is a dear and wonderful woman." (Cranston and Kim one day would live on the same street.) Cranston told Humphrey that he would look up "Aunt Harry – I trust she is a Democrat?" [112]

He hoped that the senator "might find it productive" to "tackle" the election-rights issue. Humphrey did, with characteristic fervor. He introduced a bill embodying Cranston's proposals, and would become one of Congress' leading proponents of civil-rights reform laws. Cranston sent an analysis by Stanford political science professor Alfred di Grazia to aid in drafting legislation. One of the professor's suggestions was to call the oversight agency the Federal Election Commission (not to be confused with one established in 1975 to enforce campaign-finance laws). Cranston also sent the report to civil-rights leaders like King and Abernathy, soliciting comments. "Those of us who stand amid the desolate midnight of injustice are given new hope in the emerging daybreak of freedom and justice when we know that such persons of good will exist in the nation," King replied. [113]

Cranston also sent a copy to Drew Pearson, calling it a "proposal designed to secure the vote for the Negro." Gus Hawkins, then in the California Assembly, told Cranston that he concurred with his "fine proposal on civil rights." [114]

New York Senator Herbert Lehman, though, was not sanguine that federal commissioners would be either Constitutional or effective. If seen as carpetbaggers, they would increase rather than diminish "local opposition and intransigence." "You have put your finger on what is obviously the most difficult matter," Cranston replied. But a Federal Election Commission would "circumvent the court-house gangs and [political] machines…whose political existence depends upon barring the Negro from the polls." [115]

Cranston also thought the Republican administration's civil-rights proposals should be supported as "a step forward" with "some chance of passage in this session of Congress." But they did "not go far enough to be truly effective," he told a skeptical Pasadena woman. "They leave the burden on the Negro to go before hostile officials in the effort to exercise their Constitutional right." [116]

Cranston by now had formed a plan for his own future. In January, 1957, he told CDC vice president Glenn Anderson that, while it had been "wonderful to play a part in the great gains the Democratic Party has made in California in these past four years," he was reluctant to serve another term as CDC president. "I do not wish to stand in the way of" new leadership," and "I might conceivably be a candidate for public statewide office in 1958." He had let it be known that he was available for the U. S. Senate nomination, but said that he would accept the CDC presidency once more if that were the general will of the party. [117]

Pat Brown, meanwhile, did not think that the party was achieving its potential, even with the new organizing efforts, a backhanded slap at the CDC. "The Council of Democratic Clubs [Brown's preference for a name] is a good organization, but in my opinion is not reaching anywhere near the number of Democrats that it should reach," he told a Southern California activist. "If this job were properly done, California would become a Democratic state in 1958." Brown himself did not feel dependent on the CDC for support, having already proved himself the only Democrat popular statewide. His staff were never enthusiastic about the CDC. Brown "didn't even know what the initials CDC *meant*," Greenaway said of Brown's indifference to it, which angered CDC backers. [118]

Cranston, though, recognized the value of getting Brown's backing when "many Democrats in office didn't *like* the CDC because they got there without it. They thought, 'Why do we need all these volunteers running around?' As Jesse Unruh put it, 'The trouble with a volunteer is, you can't *fire* him!'" Brown, Cranston saw, "was a perfect collaborator for CDC. Having grass-roots volunteers working with a guy at the top of the heap was a very strong combination." [119]

A few weeks after writing his denigrating letter, Brown's name topped a plea from party leaders urging Cranston to consider another term as CDC president. "Five years ago the political effect of the clubs was localized and isolated," it stated. "We do not underestimate the contribution of any individual or group when we single you out as the person most responsible for today's standing of the CDC in the eyes of political leaders everywhere.... We are not aware of your plans for the future," but, they implored, "Please finish the job you have so ably begun." It was signed by twenty-one Democratic leaders. The party could not afford to lose him was the message. [120]

"I want to thank you from the bottom of my heart for joining with so many others in that letter," Cranston replied to Brown. "I am proud to have your support and look forward to working with you in the future to achieve our great end – the transformation of California into a Democratic state in 1958. I hope that a part of that process will be the election of one Pat Brown as governor, but I will, of course, devote all my energies to your support for whatever office you choose to seek." Brown could not afford to lose Cranston as a political friend. [121]

The pressure for Cranston to continue as president was heavy. The CDC received letters and club resolutions from all over the state urging him to carry on the job. Cranston said that he would accept re-nomination but stressed that it did not imply commitment to Richards for the 1958 U. S. Senate race in which both were interested. Cranston also told clubs that he "had great reservation as to whether" he should serve again, but in view of the numerous requests, agreed to do so "if it is the will of the convention." [122]

The convention keynote speaker in 1957 again was a national figure, particularly on agricultural issues – Senator Albert Gore of Tennessee (father of future Senator and Democratic presidential candidate Al Gore). His appearance, though, would cause a small controversy prompted by his southern accent when some attendees thought Gore used the word "nigger." "It was unfortunate indeed that you and others understood me to use the word," Gore retaliated. "I assure you that I did not. I readily acknowledge that I did not adequately pronounce the 'o' [in Negro].... This occurred, I assure you, without intent to offend but rather as the natural result of environmental and of colloquial inflection. In my area, for instance, we always pronounce piano as 'piana' but never, that is, if one is educated, as 'pianer.' With me, the same has been true with the word Negro. The polite and correct pronunciation, maybe I should not say cultured, is 'negra,' never 'nigger.' Of course, I know the correct pronunciation and, after this episode in California about which you write, you may be sure that I will pronounce it correctly. It does occur to me that those who insist upon tolerance from others might consider being tolerant, or at least understanding, of the errors of other persons." [123]

Cranston told Gore, in thanking him for "making that long trip to be with us last week in Long Beach," that he had more to say "in regard to that *word*," but regretfully could "not put it in a letter. Actually that whole problem died a rapid death and everyone seemed to have forgotten it by Sunday." [124]

Senator Paul Douglas of Illinois had been asked to be keynoter, in part because he was leading Congress in civil-rights efforts, but he was not able to attend. California

Democrats were "proud" of his leadership on the issue, Cranston told Douglas. [125]

Cranston publicly attacked Senator Lyndon Johnson for helping to weaken civil-rights bills and called on him to resign as Majority Leader. Speaking to a Democratic club meeting in Los Angeles County, and sounding like a politician himself, Cranston said, "If the Democrats were led in the Senate by a man who would fight for what most Democrats want, the civil rights of millions of Americans would now be protected. Senator Johnson's remarkable skill is of great service to certain of his Texas constituents, but it is of great disservice to the Democratic Party. I have been warned that to criticize Johnson might injure my potential Senate candidacy, but I think it vitally important that at least one Democratic leader in California say publicly what so many have been saying privately about him. Senator William Knowland, Republican leader in the Senate, must share the blame with Johnson for weakening the civil-rights bill," he added. Cranston took Johnson to task on two other major issues in a CDC press release. He accused Johnson of favoring a natural-gas bill that would increase the cost of heating, and an oil-depletion allowance that would raise Americans' taxes "to make up for the special favors handed to a few multi-millionaire oil drillers in Texas and elsewhere." [126]

In another release, Cranston called for a food and fiber bank "to save American farmers from catastrophe and American foreign policy from collapse. The farm program of scarcity and controls has failed from the day Henry Wallace [FDR's Secretary of Agriculture] started plowing under pigs to the day Ezra Benson [Eisenhower's Secretary of Agriculture] began plowing under farmers," he told a party gathering in the central valley. "It's immoral and suicidal to pay American farmers not to produce food in a hungry world threatened by communism." He recommended depositing agricultural surpluses in an international bank for distribution to needy nations where people fought "a losing struggle to survive on barren soil by prehistoric farming methods." The idea, he noted, was under serious consideration in Washington, a response to worsening depression among American farmers whose income had dropped seventeen percent since 1952, resulting in farmers' debt of $3 billion and a doubling of foreclosures. Cranston indeed was sounding as if he were running for office. [127]

He also made public statements against nuclear testing and radiation fallout in 1957. "I am grateful, as I'm sure many others are, for your courageous statement on the need for an end to nuclear testing," a member of the Quaker Friends Committee wrote him. "I wish more Demo. leaders would 'catch up' to you on this and other foreign policy issues." Cranston replied that he was "catching the dickens for this from the Knowland-owned *Oakland Tribune* and other Republican newspapers." California Democratic Congressman Chet Holifield was chairing hearings on the subject of radiation fallout. "You are getting a fabulous press throughout California and performing vital business for all humanity," Cranston wrote Holifield. "I was thinking the other day about the battle that you, Helen Douglas and others waged along with Brian McMahon to place the Atomic Energy Commission under civilian rather than military control," he added. "I shudder to contemplate what the consequences would be, had you failed in that vital struggle." [128]

Cranston urged the California legislature "to deal with radiation dangers. We in California are doubly exposed to radioactive fallout because of the proximity of the U. S. tests in Nevada and the prevailing winds carrying contamination to us from Russian tests in Siberia. We can't stop bomb tests by ourselves, but we don't have to lag behind so many other states in regulating other sources of radiation.... California shoe stores still use x-ray fitting machines, for example, although these devices have been outlawed as dangerous in many states. It is senseless to pile needless radiation on top of what Californians already receive from fallout." He urged creation of a commission to regulate all radiation-producing devices and those licensed to use them. He also charged that G. I.s exposed to ARC lights were made sterile. [129]

In addition to his own possible agenda to run for office, Cranston saw the potential for a Democrat to win the 1958 governor's race. Goodwin Knight, a genial but somewhat ineffectual governor, had succeeded Earl Warren after his appointment in 1953 to the U. S. Supreme Court. Knight expected to have an easy reelection in 1958. But there was a spoiler in the works. Senator Knowland had presidential ambitions, and thought that being Governor of California was a logical step to that end. Cranston's sister described Knowland as "dark, brooding, barrel-chested 'Big Bill'" whose defense of non-communist, nationalist Chinese got him labeled the "Senator from Formosa." His announcement in 1957 that he was leaving the Senate at the end of his term the next year complicated things for Republicans. [130]

"Alan's heart leapt when he heard the news," Eleanor wrote of the opportunity that suddenly appeared. Cranston seriously began conferring with colleagues, and the possibility of his running for the Senate or some other office began to get press attention. A *New York Times* account called the "energetic" Cranston an "active but undeclared candidate," although Senator Clair Engle, the "picturesque member of Congress from California's second district," was "eager to go after the senatorial nomination," assuming that Pat Brown ran for governor, not the Senate. [131]

Brown was the obvious Democratic gubernatorial candidate. He had an unbroken record of wins (seven years as San Francisco's District Attorney, two terms as state A. G. since election in 1950). In 1954 he had been the only Democrat elected to statewide office. A warm man with an ingenuous quality of honesty and directness, the bespeckled Brown was popular, astutely maintaining a moderate political position. Brown felt confident that he could win reelection as attorney general and the race for governor was dicey. Cranston, though, saw that Republicans were losing popular ground nationally thanks to recession, civil-rights battles and Russian space successes with "sputniks" that troubled people. California also was being invaded with new residents and under Republicans, was in the "red" financially. But no Democrat wanted to announce until Brown's decision was known. Cranston began to boost him. [132]

In a widely publicized CDC speech in July, 1957, Cranston boldly predicted that "the winner of the inevitable knock-down, drag-out Republican battle for the governorship of California next year will be a Democrat – Attorney General Edmund G. Brown. By all the logic, lore and law of politics, it is too late for either Governor Knight or Senator Knowland to avoid one of the biggest and most destructive intra-party wars in the history of the state.... One will be knocked out in the primary, the other dragged out in the general election." Another inducement to Democrats was that Congressman Engle had said that he planned for run for Knowland's seat if Brown ran for governor. Brown continued to hedge about his decision, finally blurting out, in what became a familiar pattern to the media of saying more than he intended, "If anyone thinks I'm going to let Knowland and Knight take this state by default, they're mistaken!" When Cranston saw Brown making that statement on television, he smiled and said to friends, "The die's *almost* cast." In early September, Brown – appearing uncharacteristically nervous, Cranston noticed – formally announced that he would run. [133]

What did it augur for Cranston's future, many wondered? Ted Waller, then head of the bibliophiles' Grolier Society in New York City, asked him about his prospects. "There've been developments favorable and developments unfavorable, and the odds remain about the same re: making the race – 50-50," Cranston told him. [134]

By September, 1957, Cranston's friend Jerry Spingarn was offering advice about his political future: "I should like again to encourage you to accept a minor spot on the ticket if a major one is not available.... In the event that you are elected, you will have an excellent opportunity to tour the state frequently and get your name and face well known." Cranston appreciated his "words of wisdom" and revealed that it looked as if he would run for controller – "actually an important job in California, second only to the governorship in terms of administrative responsibility, but nothing will be firm and fixed until we have our endorsing convention January 10-12, [1958]. If I do wind up going for controller, I will probably have no serious Democratic opposition." At the time, Cranston expected that incumbent controller Robert Kirkwood (appointed by Governor Warren in 1953 to replace Kuchel when he went to the Senate) would run for the Senate. [135]

Helen Myers, a Los Angeles party activist and first vice president of the CDC in 1954, sent Cranston a long letter outlining her thoughts about his future as well as the CDC's, which she thought strong but "not yet decisive. We haven't been in business long enough for that. Perhaps our greatest weakness is that we do not have enough elected Democratic officials who are obligated to the club movement." Brown was "the most electable" Democrat but lacking "principles about party organization." As to Cranston's running for Senate, "I know that you come closest to representing what our volunteers want in a candidate. But Clair Engle wants it, too," and already had the backing of powerful people in office and with money. He had a long record of public service and was "a good campaigner in an earthy way," if he had "only recently discovered the party" and "might easily forget it," she joked. "But under the circumstances, I do not think it would do you any good personally, or the party, to buck Engle." Furthermore, she reiterated, the Republican opponent for the Senate probably would be Pat Hillings who would have "Nixon's and the *L. A. Times*' support.... Hillings is a nasty little guy, cast in the Nixon mold, and his will be a dirty campaign. There'll be no lofty debate on the leading issues of the day with him, so let Engle take him on in his tough, fighting bantam-cockish way." [136]

Myers believed that Cranston could get CDC endorsement for controller. "And this is no mean plum. I can think of any number of old pros licking their chops to get a crack at it." It would give him "a chance to acquire experience," important if he wanted to move on, as well as "a power base – and there is quite a bit of power there.... While you won't be able to resolve the H-bomb problem from the position of controller, think of all the other advantages. You would stand a better chance of getting elected, and better an elected controller than a defeated senator."

While most people associated Cranston with his interest in "international problems and peace," Myers pointed to his being "one of the most efficient administrators in politics," a "talent not to be minimized." In a handwritten postscript she recommended that Cranston not "publicly back away from the senatorship until you're darn sure you have the support of some important people" for the controllership, "because your chief bargaining power is your ability to split the convention."

She had "set forth a most logical case," he conceded, "both from the party's point of view and from my personal situation. Betwixt us (and I suppose you may by now have heard something of this), I've told Clair that I won't contest with him for the Senate. If he fails to generate support, and falls on his face, I've reserved the right to get back into the picture. But I'll do nothing to disturb him, and will remain occupied elsewhere if he stays out in front – as he obviously is now. I haven't made a final decision to do so, but will probably go for controller," he confessed, thanking her for her "frankness and perception." [137]

Cranston confided to Dewey Anderson that Pat Brown was "scheduled to announce his candidacy for governor in Los Angeles on October 30. I am almost surely going to switch to the race for state controller in the interests of preserving the very wonderful harmony we now have in California at this moment of colossal Republican division."[138]

As word got around, others communicated with Cranston. "I was very glad to hear last night that you are probably settled in your decision to enter the controller's race," newspaper publisher Joe Houghteling, who had been publicizing Cranston's speeches, wrote him. "I think that in this year, both your personal career and your contributions to the Democratic Party are best served by such a choice. If you win this office – and I believe there is every probability you will – you will have behind you one of the essential qualifications for even higher office – the demonstration by an election victory that you are a vote-getter on a statewide basis. Best wishes on whatever you choose." "I am glad that you feel that I am making a wise decision," Cranston replied. "I will be seeking your advice and assistance before too long." [139]

"I wanted to run straight out for the Senate in '58," Cranston later said of what was then in his mind. But "I had to go through a stepping stone." He had not run for the legislature in his home district because it was predominantly Republican and it would have been "very tough to win a congressional or assembly seat as a Democrat. That was one reason I didn't do it – a tactical reason. The second reason was that I was more interested in world affairs than local-type things that you worked on in the state legislature. And you had more impact in the Senate than in the House." From working on *Killing of the Peace*, "I knew a lot about the Senate. I'd worked around it when I was lobbying on immigration and naturalization matters for O. W. I. But mainly the Senate dealt with the issues I was most interested in, namely, world peace, democracy around the world, and world organizations." [140]

"I could have gotten the Democratic nomination in 1958 because of the CDC," Cranston firmly believed. "Engle knew I could get that and he didn't choose to run against the CDC. So if I had run, he would not have run, and I would have gotten the nomination. But whether I'd win the general election was questionable. Pat Brown wanted a tried politician who had won elections to run with him. He decided that he'd like Engle better than me and urged me to run for controller. He said to me one day, 'You're side-stepping the local step that most people take, of being first a mayor or maybe in the Assembly or the House. You're going to a statewide office first off. That's ambitious and fine, but how about trying state controller instead of U. S. Senate? If you'll go for state controller, I'll do all I can to help you.' So I acceded to his wishes. I didn't want to jeopardize the governor's race by *my* ambitions. So I stepped aside, although I knew I could get any nomination that I wanted because I was so strong through the CDC at that point." Engle admitted that he probably could not get the CDC endorsement if Cranston ran, but he frankly told Cranston that he did not think he could win the senate seat. At a swimming pool gathering of Democrats in Bakersfield, where Engle made the pronouncement, he later recalled, "Alan sat there braiding and unbraiding his long toes while I told him what would happen to him if he ran for the Senate." [141]

Controller was the second most powerful administrative post in the state, and, as Myers and others pointed out, an excellent place to gain valuable experience. So after conferring with Brown and his key advisers, and with top fundraisers like Elinor Heller, Democratic National Committeewoman and long-time Regent to the University of California, who made it clear that Cranston would not receive the kind of money needed for a Senate race, Cranston agreed to run for controller. He accepted that he would have to bide his time before running for higher office. [142]

"Alan's too nice, and hides his disappointment well," Geneva was quoted as saying of his acquiescing to the party's wishes, as his sister recorded of a family discussion at Hilltop house. But Cranston was not unhappy about his decision. Now forty-three years old, his dream of long standing was about to become reality, if at a lower scale than he had envisioned. Nor did he blame Pat Brown for helping thwart his first effort to run for high office. "I didn't hold that against him at all," Cranston said in retrospect. [143]

Roy Greenaway believed that Cranston was overly optimistic about getting the CDC's endorsement for a senate race against Engle, and not facing realities. Engle was not popular with the CDC because he voted to appease conservative constituents, but neither was Cranston that popular nor well known. Greenaway thought that he probably would not have gotten the endorsement. [144]

Cranston formally announced for controller at a press conference in Los Angeles December 4, 1957. He had done some historical homework on the controller's office and hoped to break a 68-year Republican hold on it. Not since 1890 had a controller won by election, he pointed out. Most had been appointed by Republican governors when incumbents retired or died. (Kuchel himself had been appointed controller in 1946.) "I will show the voters why the Republican Party has so carefully kept the controller's office from public scrutiny," Cranston pledged. "I do not suggest corruption in the conduct of the office. I do suggest contempt for constitutional government in the way the office has been filled and its importance concealed." He pointed out just how important the controller was: He oversaw all public spending, sat on numerous boards and commissions that affected nearly every aspect of life in California, and had "more influence on tax policy than any other man in the state." Cranston promised to simplify tax forms, cut red tape, make the system fairer, and encourage the "lowest tax rate consistent with the public welfare. As a member of the three-man State Lands Commission, I would fight the senseless prohibitions barring the people of the state from camping, hiking, hunting and fishing on lands they themselves own." He also "would seek maximum protection of the peoples' stake in tidelands oil and tidelands recreation." As a member of the state Water Projects Authority, he would acknowledge the "need for providing adequate water for both north and south, with special privileges for neither," a volatile issue in California when the south was draining water from northern watersheds. [145]

A biographical description touted Cranston's CDC record. "Early in 1952, a tall, lanky, ex-track star hurtled into California's political picture and with his appearance began a bold, new experiment in democracy." He had brought "tremendous administrative capabilities, catalytic energy, and most important, a plan for organization. Within two years, the Democratic Party sprang to life.... His plan achieved in the short span of two years what other Democrats had been trying to accomplish for a decade – stop embarrassing losses at the polls" when Democrats outnumbered Republicans by one million. They now were "a formidable foe to Republican 'cash-and-carry' politics." [146]

Cranston, no stranger to the importance of media in a campaign, thanked *San Jose Mercury-News* political writer Harry Farrell "for the fine coverage the announcement of my candidacy received in your paper." It did not mitigate Farrell's sometimes negative reporting about Cranston, however. [147]

Cranston's mother by then had accepted that "that's what I intended to do," be a politician, and was supportive of his decision to enter the public fray. "She became a Democrat in mind, if not in" registration. "Actually, an odd thing – my father was registered Democrat although he was really a Republican. In the early part of the twentieth century and on up to CDC days, the Republicans were better organized than the Democrats. They would field one candidate, Democrats would field many, without any discipline. And the single Republican would invariably beat an assortment of Democrats because of cross-filing. With no party label for candidates in primaries, you couldn't tell by the ballot who was a Democrat and who a Republican. But there was always one Republican and five or six Democrats, so the Republicans would always win. My father registered Democratic so he could help that process by voting in the Democratic primary for a Republican," Cranston laughed of the irony. "And my mother did the same thing under his advice." [148]

As Cranston had predicted, Republicans were in disarray. The man who succeeded Nixon to the House, Southern California Congressman Patrick J. (Pat) Hillings, predicted that Knight, pressured by the conservative wing of the party, would quit the governor's race and run for Senate. Knight denied it, and as Cranston later put it, "took to a sick bed in Sacramento," then mysteriously disappeared in late October, 1957. He was found in seclusion at a ranch in Arizona. By then, the plot was being followed closely by the media. Pat Brown blatantly wrote an open letter to Knight that read, "The power elite of the Republican Party who are dictating to you say that you are going to Washington next week as the savior of Republican unity in California. If you do, it will be to seal a bargain born of treachery." Harry Truman even joined the fray, stating, "There's an under-the-table deal to push Knight out of the way – and authorities ought to look into it." Knight did go to Washington a few days after Brown's letter, and after meeting with President Eisenhower and

Vice President Nixon, announced that he would quit the governor's race and run for the Senate. The press dubbed it the "Nixon-Knowland-Knight switch" to "rig" the elections for the state's highest offices. "The big-money boys dried up Knight's campaign-fund sources," the *Los Angeles Examiner* stated in an editorial November 5, 1957, and with "other pressures…forced the governor to abandon his reelection intentions." "The truth is, and who is there to deny it, that a few willful men pulled the strings and Goodie Knight, unlike the late and great Hiram Johnson, did not have the courage to tell them to jump in the lake," the *Santa Barbara News-Press* stated. "Poor Goodie! What the boys have done to him!" The revelations sat poorly with some Republicans. One leader in Los Angeles deplored Knowland's conduct as "reprehensible," and Assembly Republican leader George Milias called it a "smelly deal." San Francisco Mayor George Christopher in disgust jumped into the Senate race. Polls had shown that either Knowland or Knight could beat Brown, but the polls began to shift. Cranston, campaigning statewide for himself and the party, joined in denouncing Knowland and his "right-to-work" theme as "the right to work for nothing or less." [149]

Controller Kirkwood had himself hoped to run for the U. S. Senate. Within an hour of learning Knowland's decision, Kirkwood had declared himself a candidate. But when Knight announced that he would run for the Senate, Kirkwood saw no option but to seek reelection as controller. (Assemblyman Luther Lincoln, who had announced his intention to run for controller, withdrew from the race in Kirkwood's favor.) [150]

Kirkwood was a formidable opponent. Handsome, with a wife and four children, he had proved a strong vote-getter. He had beaten his 1954 Democratic opponent George Collins, Junior, by nearly 400,000 votes. In that campaign, a pro-Kirkwood group called "Citizens for Good Government," on a flyer aimed at attracting Democrats, quoted Adlai Stevenson as saying, "If the voters of this nation ever stop looking at the record and character of candidates, and look only at the party label, it will be a sorry day for democracy." Kirkwood's record was touted as more moderate than Collins.' [151]

Kirkwood identified himself with "the great Eisenhower movement of New Republicanism." The would-be contenders also were acquainted, and Cranston personally liked the Republican from Saratoga, in the same county (Santa Clara) as Cranston's residence. The two men were more alike than different – both were attractive, in their forties (Cranston was forty-three, Kirkwood forty-nine) with families, both had attended local public schools and Stanford. And Kirkwood had openly been a World Federalist. That was considered a potential liability and did not escape press notice. "One of the issues that persons close to Kirkwood expect to crop up in his campaign is his former affiliation with the United World Federalists, which several years ago was accused of being communist-controlled," Farrell reported, pointing out that Kirkwood had "belonged for four years before the Korean war," and had "answered prior criticism…with a statement that he checked the organization with the F. B. I. and the House Un-American Activities Committee, and found the organization untainted." A 1950 photograph of Kirkwood at a panel discussion on world government with Cranston, Jack Fowle and others, was republished and circulated in a political pamphlet to show Kirkwood's association with "questionable" company, as the Los Altos *Town Crier* put it. "Our loveable, local lads questionable?" the paper joked. "That's not worthy of an answer." Cranston himself admitted to having the same nagging fear of being tainted: "I was always expecting that the Federalists' activities would be brought up in the campaign because U. W. F. was controversial." But the fact that Kirkwood had signed up as a Federalist while Cranston was national president "nullified that issue." For fellow Federalists, Cranston's leadership was a plus – "Cranston was the only politician I voted FOR," Joanne Peterson Sonnichsen remembered. "I had a good feeling about him – and not as the lesser of evils, but as someone who stood up for his beliefs. Because he was head of the Federalists, I respected him." [152]

The 1958 CDC convention promised to be a tug of war – a *Los Angeles Mirror-News* political editor called the group "raucous." Brown, the only one unopposed in his bid for the state's highest office, was endorsed by acclamation, although a few "noes" were heard from the rear of the cavernous hall. "'The chair hears no noes,' chairman Joe Wyatt decreed without batting an eye, and that was it," Farrell recorded. Delegates cheered Brown to the strains of a catchy new campaign song, "Our Pat Brown." The forty-six-year-old "short, wiry…peppery" Engle (Farrell's description) won endorsement after a scare in which the liberal Peter Odegard was rumored to be gaining support. Odegard and another contender, Kenneth Hahn, joined to make Engle's endorsement unanimous after pulling out of the field. "If it's ever suggested in the press of this state that Democratic nominations are arrived at by backroom machinations, I want to sign an affidavit that this has been a democratic process and a real tough fight," Engle said afterward. [153]

Brown said that he hoped he was "physically, mentally and spiritually up to the task you have given me." He urged the crowd to register fellow Democrats and promised to campaign in every district of the state. Engle promised to conduct "the hardest, fightingest, sluggingest and roughest Democratic campaign in California history." [154]

Cranston resigned as CDC president, now himself a candidate seeking endorsement. But he had a challenger – the 1954 nominee for controller, George Collins, a diminutive hunchback and much-respected liberal whom Cranston knew and admired. Collins (who had given up his Assembly seat to run for controller in 1954), had been the only state assemblyman to vote against internment of the Japanese. Now he charged that Cranston had been offered the nomination as a "swap" to get him out of the Senate race. Cranston's endorsement "came as an anti-climax to the Brown and Engle endorsements," Farrell wrote. Grinning, Cranston went to the stage followed by his family, whom he introduced. "These are my sons, Kim (six) and Robin (ten), the best two precinct workers in California, and my wife Geneva who, thank heaven, loves politics," he told the crowd. In his acceptance speech, he called on Democrats in 1958 to "dispose of men like Knowland and mice like Knight," and ridiculed Republicans for the "Nixon-Knowland-Knight nightmare." He would conduct a "slate-minded" campaign that backed all CDC endorsees, adding that he would discuss not only state but foreign, economic and farm policies among other national issues. After Cranston "bested him," as Farrell put it, Collins added his endorsement to make it unanimous, but the contest caused a sore rift between Collins and Cranston. [155]

The convention also backed trade with Red China, a controversial stand; opposed right-to-work laws; called for easier farm credit, fair-employment-practice laws, and repeal of the 1952 McCarran-Walter Immigration Act. One resolution "deplore[d] the broad mandate given to the House Un-American Activities Committee," demanded that "it be reformed" and urged "clearing the climate that has beclouded the work of America's scientists and the progress of technology." Other resolutions dealt with federal aid to education, mental-health programs and treatment for narcotics addicts, even monitoring disarmament, clearly a Cranston proposal. [156]

After the convention, a Los Angeles newspaper bannered, "Amateur politicos battle professionals to a standoff in Fresno." It had been marred by discontent expressed by State Senator Robert I. McCarthy of San Francisco who refused to allow his name to be put up for nominee to attorney general (Superior Court Judge Stanley Mosk was endorsed for the race), and assailed the convention as "a rubber stamp" of nominees that contravened the state's primary law. Cranston's name would appear on the party slate with Engle, Brown and Mosk, former Assemblyman Glenn M. Anderson of Hawthorne for lieutenant governor, certified public accountant Bert A. Betts of San Diego for treasurer, and attorney Henry P. Lopez of Los Angeles for secretary of state. The CDC was satisfied that Brown might win, but the convention ended "with considerable misgivings about the vote-getting capacities of the rest of the ticket," political writer Clint Mosher reported in the *San Francisco Examiner*. Brown's personal popularity and Knowland's unpopularity for advocating right-to-work legislation were keys to that race. Pat Brown announced that he would run "as a lone wolf" independent of the slate in the primary. [157]

Cranston took to campaigning with vigor, and his family frequently joined him up and down the state "when they could," he remembered, "when it did not interfere with school or whatever." Despite cross-filing, Cranston was not fearful of his chances. He cross-filed, as did Kirkwood. "I was quite confident," he said of his first run for public office. Among campaign literature, he circulated the *Congressional Record* reprint of his voting-rights speech, prominently noting at the top, "Not printed at government expense." [158]

He would use very few television advertisements – "it just was just beginning to come into its own and wasn't used that much then." It also cost what were considered staggering sums – as much as $500 for a ten-second spot. A friend with a Los Angeles television talk show that broadcast after midnight offered to give Cranston some free exposure, but there was a catch: a contract limited guests to discussing contact lenses, the product of the advertiser who underwrote the show. Cranston did not wear lenses but he wanted to go on the air. Whatever he did, his friend exhorted Cranston, he was not to say the word "Democrat." With his fondness for puns, Cranston was ready when introduced and asked to identify himself. "I'm Alan Cranston, and I'm running up and down the state making contacts and jumping in front of lenses!" Billboard advertisements, too, were expensive. Cranston would have only a few, some on flat-bed trucks so they could be moved (including one in East Los Angeles), that simply read: "*Elect Alan Cranston – First Democratic Controller since 1886!*" [159]

He concentrated on making personal appearances, driving with his family or friends in their dusty Mercury station wagon to virtually every county of the state.

Geneva often drove while Cranston worked on speeches in the car. A two-year-old German shepherd, Roy, was part of the team (he had been sent to obedience school in preparation). Cranston was always conservatively dressed in a business suit, white shirt and dark tie, not the casual garb that he generally preferred. An unexpected adventure occurred one day in June at Long Beach where Cranston was to speak to the Veterans of Foreign Wars. The family was hurrying down the sidewalk to the convention hall when Kim, now six, saw a red metal box on a post with a tantalizing lever. He pulled it as he went by. Suddenly Robin exclaimed, "Kim just pulled a fire alarm!" Sure enough, as they entered the auditorium, they heard sirens approaching. Admonished, the now-frightened boy cried, "I thought it said *free*! I thought I'd get bubblegum." Cranston in exasperation thought the firemen would never believe that story. Geneva more practically worried that people would think it was a publicity stunt. Veterans who escorted Cranston to the podium were impressed, thinking that he had a police escort. Cranston watched as confused fireman waved hoses from three fire trucks, part of the audience jumped up and left, and the commotion drowned out his opening remarks. Geneva took the boys to a rest room where they hid until hearing the trucks depart. Kim feared that he would be arrested, and for some time any reference to the boy's being a "veteran campaigner" had a double meaning. [160]

Cranston himself liked campaigning, and it showed in his ever-smiling face, trim and energetic figure. Along with the myriad of appearances at factory gates and special events, county fairs and coffee "klatches," he made certain that he courted the media. His outspoken attacks on the "Nixon-Knowland-Knight nightmare" began to get coverage. Brown came in for constant praise, by contrast. Cranston's only opposition in the primary was Republican Kirkwood, thanks to cross-filing, and no Democratic candidate for controller had won election in the twentieth century. Cranston rarely encountered Kirkwood but frequently ran into his wife Jean who jokingly urged Cranston not to campaign too hard. [161]

As the campaign got underway, staff critiqued Cranston's style and themes. They thought that he should emphasize the importance of the controller's role, but Cranston kept talking about issues and the Democratic Party. "Would you shoot me if I suggested toning down some of your jokes?" one aide asked. "I think the warmth of a good joke is fine to open meetings and speeches, but I am concerned and so is Teddy" Mueller, his Los Angeles campaign manager. "Jokes are tough, because they can have the opposite effect on people," the aide, possibly his Northern California manager Marta Teilhet said, adding, "You are an outstanding speaker, and there are few that can beat you when you express your sincere feelings. There is a truth and sincerity that rings through to people that cannot be beat." [162]

Cranston did make a point of educating people about the importance of the controller's role as second only to the governor's. He pledged to open all the boards that he sat on to public meetings. That got press attention. He also would see to it that a variety of ethnicities were appointed as tax appraisers – under Republicans, there were no Hispanic, African-American or Asian appraisers and only one Jew. Cranston called it a "country club" and promised to change it to provide equal opportunity. [163]

His principal piece of campaign literature was a simulated currency bill, reminding voters that the controller dispersed $15 million of the public's tax money every day. It had an oval picture of Cranston in the center. The other side listed the boards on which the controller sat, and facts about Cranston – "Native of California…married, 2 children," and summarized his work experience. [164]

A memo to campaign operatives laid out "Suggestions for Planning and Executing a Visit to your Community by Candidate Alan Cranston." Joining parades was "useful only if he is in a thoroughly decorated car, covered with his cards, bumper strips and other identifying material. Do not put the candidate in the reviewing stand." Appearing at factory gates was "OK only with a loud speaker or careful advance" notice of his visit; spending time at county fairs was "useful only if there is a booth, well-decorated, and the candidate is at all times accompanied by people who can introduce him to people as they pass by." A "Sample Perfect Day" started with a local Cranston-committee meeting, media interviews in the morning, afternoon visits with leaders from business to labor, dinners with potential contributors plus a speech to a union or some other organization. "Make certain that you know the hours when the paper is being put to bed," the memo noted. "Nothing is worse than to interfere with these people when they are trying to beat a deadline. In any event, keep Cranston on the move!" [165]

A particular strategy was to line up support in professional and business communities like lawyers and small businessmen. Cranston hit on one subject that attracted their attention – filling out forms and paying taxes. He sympathized with the fact that they had to collect sales taxes and promised, in a four-point program, to simplify the job for retailers, establish an appeals panel in the Board of Equalization (responsible for collecting taxes) and a dispute-resolution plan. He then got merchants to distribute his ideas to colleagues in a letter that described Cranston as "not only a successful businessman but…a top executive…in the federal government…. His background in financial affairs qualifies him superbly to deal constructively with the great problems facing us." In talks Cranston would say that "merchants are unpaid tax collectors" who "should be treated by the Board of Equalization with the respect…for the burden they carry in collecting the sales tax." [166]

"I have been getting incredibly fine reaction to proposals that I have been making" with the letter to merchants, he told campaigners. "If you can persuade a local retailer in your district to sign and mail these – in his own envelope if possible – to other local retailers, I am convinced we'll pick up much strength. Thanks fifteen million times!" [167]

The approach worked. "Our retailers letter has made quite a hit and more than 6,000 have already been sent out," Mueller reported to Cranston backers. Committees were formed to round up backing from realtors, Nisei and Chinese-American organizations, ex-F. B. I. agents, accountants, veterans, labor interests, even sportsmen. He got a letter of endorsement from two retired Los Angeles police officers, and political science professor Dean R. Crisap at San Jose State College, a neighbor of Cranston's, sent a letter of support to a group of professors. [168]

The same approach was used with attorneys who were asked to send a similar letter to colleagues. It read, in part, "Alan Cranston will approach his duties from the standpoint of the taxpayer and businessman and give us a long overdue impartial and sensible administration of this important office.... [H]e will reverse the trend of diminishing state solvency.... I would consider your support of him a personal favor," attorneys were urged to say. [169]

Republicans who backed Cranston were encouraged to do the same thing, and a form letter praising him read, "I am a lifelong Republican who has almost always supported Republicans, but this year I am supporting a Democrat Alan Cranston for state controller. [He] has demonstrated a notable ability to carry imaginative planning into bold and effective action." It cited in particular his "almost single-handedly" transforming "the entire business district of his home town of Los Altos into a shopping center, saving property values in a community where he has substantial investments." The letter denigrated Kirkwood for failing to act effectively to end scandals in the state treasury or to invest surplus state funds. "The clear-cut contrast between these two men as to what has been done in the controller's office and what should have been done...leads me to support Alan Cranston," the letter concluded. [170]

Other issues that Cranston addressed included helping needy people on fixed incomes, civil rights, public higher education for scientists (America was in a space-race with the Soviets), and purity of elections (he deplored a "spoils" system that rewarded backers with juicy jobs like diplomatic posts). [171]

He proposed another four-point program – an approach that he took for a number of problems – to compensate mountain counties for providing water for irrigation and power needs to lowland areas. That got good press in the Sierra Nevada regions, where he would meet local officials in a cafe like the "Blue Bell" in Placerville. Cranston pointed out that his proposals were analogous to what Congressman-now-Senate-candidate Clair Engle had done in federal water-project legislation. Cranston "took his opponent, incumbent Robert Kirkwood, to task on several points," the Placerville *Mountain Democrat* reported, "accusing him of siding with the favor-seeking Pacific Gas & Electric (PG&E) company in a recent vote" and "running away from the issue apparently because he was afraid of losing a few votes in the lowland counties." Cranston explained that his water program "would satisfy all parties." The vote to which he referred had been on a Kirkwood-sponsored bill that Cranston said gave private utility companies like PG&E a $40-milllion tax windfall. "This shocking piece of legislation hangs over the head of every homeowner, businessman and farmer" by effectively taking tax revenues out of the "pockets of California property owners." [172]

A favorite subject was what the controller could do to protect the state's scenic beauty. Cranston would be "zealous in guarding" such resources, he stated in speeches. As a member of the three-person State Lands Commission, which negotiated tidelands oil leases and oversaw state properties, he promised to "to protect the sanctuaries of serene beauty and the wonderful playgrounds that are the glory of California's coast. We must obtain the maximum revenue for the people of the state from tidelands oil, but we must be careful not to exploit one natural resource at the expense of another." It was an early hint at what would become one of Cranston's legislative themes.[173]

All of this was done with typewriters, carbon paper and messy, blue-tinged mimeograph machines; advertising was principally a few moveable billboards and radio interviews; campaign workers were dedicated volunteers. There were no computers, skilled public-relations agencies or political professionals preparing slick television spots that glossied up the candidate.

Cranston resisted all publicists' efforts to identify him with "Lamont Cranston," fictitious hero of the popular radio drama, "The Shadow" (ironically once played by Cranston's friend Orson Welles), prompting *San Francisco Examiner* columnist Dick Nolan to quip that Cranston "refuses to consider any Shadow issues." [174]

One leaflet reprinted newspaper articles favorable to Cranston, highlighting his stances. It included his call for Lyndon Johnson to resign as majority leader; his warning that Nixon was preparing for the White House in 1960 and had "stabbed in the back every top Republican leader in California"; and one blasting John Foster Dulles for banning U. S. newsmen from communist China, saying that freedom of the press applied only to publishing, not gathering, news. Cranston termed it "the most subversive utterance by a Secretary of State in American history," making it "impossible for the American people to know the facts about the most populous country on earth." Other clippings cited Cranston's attack on the Eisenhower administration for failing to halt inflation: "We must disprove that fateful forecast of Lenin's that America would spend itself to destruction." Other clippings publicized his call for Russia and the U. S. to reach agreement on ending atomic bomb tests. [175]

Not all of Cranston's press was favorable, however, and he had to prove his political mettle. Early in the campaign, a *Chico-Enterprise Record* editorial called him the "rider of the purple phrase and bell of alarm," like Shakespeare's *Macbeth* making "'sound and fury, signifying nothing.'... Many Democrats refer to him as an exponent of 'irresponsible' elements of the party." Democratic Attorney General candidate Robert McCarthy took "a dim view of Cranston's campaign tactics," fearing that they would backfire on the party, according to the editorial, which quoted McCarthy as saying, "Buffoonery of this kind goes a long way toward explaining why Democrats have put so few men in public office in California in the past twenty years." "We think Democrat McCarthy hits Democrat Cranston right on the boil on his nose," the editorial concluded. "California voters are too sharp to swallow such fishhooks." [176]

Another small-town newspaper, the Willows *Daily Journal* lambasted Cranston's charge that Eisenhower and Nixon had concocted a "planned recession" for political advantage, dubbing it "exaggeration and unconfirmed gossip." Cranston had opened that speech with a joke about Eisenhower's hurrying to finish a golf game before returning to Washington after it had been bombed. "Unbecoming," the paper said. "Mr. Cranston is an intelligent man," it conceded, but "how can he possibly believe some of the baloney he's throwing around?" The commentaries, both from rural areas, were a measure of conservatism in the state. [177]

Cranston found that he had to defend himself. He wrote a long letter to the editor of the Willows paper, saying that he had not been questioning Eisenhower's loyalty. "A great thing about America and our democracy and our freedom is that we can joke about the most serious political matters." Cranston also defended his attacks against Kirkwood for mishandled state funds and lost investment opportunities, saying they were thoroughly documented. In a backhanded way, he complimented the paper, defending its right to express opinions, reminding voters of his background as a newspaperman covering fascist regimes, and reiterating his pledge to open to the press and public all meetings of boards that the controller sat on. California newspapers were by and large "fair and unbiased in their political reporting," he said. "Even if they weren't, I would oppose any and all restrictions on their freedom." [178]

On a positive note, the A. F. L. and C. I. O. had endorsed Cranston. His proposal for a simpler income-tax form had gotten wide press attention, as did the fact that F. D. R.'s former physician, Admiral Ross H. McIntyre, was chairing the Cranston committee in San Diego. [179]

But polls showed that the race had a large number of undecided voters. "We are a long way from feeling secure about Alan's election," Teddy Mueller had to say, urging workers to concentrate on getting out the vote. "One vote per precinct could win this election!" Cranston had studied Kirkwood's election track record. In 1954, when he had defeated Collins by a margin of 54.7 percent to 45.3 percent, a shift of 185,000 votes would have defeated Kirkwood (among nearly four million cast in the controller's race). [180]

Soon after he was nominated Cranston had sent every club member – numbering 50,000 – a letter asking for $l to aid his campaign. "I do not want to be dependent upon big contributions," he told them. "If I can rely on each of you for one dollar, then I'll be over the hump…. A dollar bill and a three-cent stamp on the enclosed envelope will start me on my way." A cartoon – reminiscent of Cranston's childhood drawings and apparently by his own hand – accompanied the plea. It showed a bald man scratching the back of his head speculating on campaign expenditures from media advertisements to bumper stickers, each with a price tag attached. It was captioned, "*When a feller needs a friend.*" At one point, Cranston remarked that it had cost $50,000 to elect President Lincoln in 1860, $50 million to elect Eisenhower in 1956. [181]

But there were "only a few pennies in the till and here come the PRIMARIES," a memo from Northern California director Marta Teilhet told fundraisers with exhortations to generate donations. "Sad, but shockingly true, we just haven't received enough MONEY to carry on the kind of pre-primary campaign that will elect Alan as state controller." They had "a good start" with $3,000 from club members but it was "not enough for a real campaign. We are hollerin' HELP!" They were budgeting campaign materials "for *minimum* expense but *maximum impact*." The campaign, indeed, was a lean one. [182]

Raising money would be a constant headache. Small sums were just as welcome as big ones. "I paid my $800 filing fee in 800 one-dollar bills," Cranston told potential contributors, "symbolic of the nature of the support my campaign is based upon." He enclosed a bumper strip "with high hopes that you will put it on your car…. Each one traveling up and down the streets and highways equals at least a $50 contribution," he hoped. [183]

One person who was meeting fundraising targets was field-coordinator Irwin J. Nebron, a Ventura attorney and chairman of the Ventura County Democratic Central Committee, who joined the campaign in July, 1958. He raised money "by asking!" he was touted as saying in a staff memo. The S. F. Bay Area coordinator was a rising party activist named Rudy Nothenberg. [184]

The primary budget for the first five months of the campaign was $146,000.

Cranston spent the bulk of his time in Southern California, where there were the most votes and he was least known. [185]

Republicans, however, were running scared. Kirkwood was quoted in the *San Jose Mercury-News* as saying, in answer to a question about whether Republicans could carry all state offices, "We'll have a heck of a time doing it. We've been making it awfully hard on ourselves. I think we can – but it's a little too early to say we will." Cranston, his staff noted, had "been campaigning constantly, speaking, visiting newspapers, courthouses, city halls, union conventions" up and down the 800-mile-long state. [186]

A week before the primary, Cranston allowed a local reporter to join a Sunday family outing. It had been planned "meticulously" weeks before by the boys "in anticipation of their dad's next 'day off,'" a news account read, with a photograph showing Cranston sitting on the engine of a toy train in Los Altos' Shoup Park with Geneva and the boys on board. "A tall, prematurely balding Los Altan, whose long legs have been striding California almost without letup since January, came home last weekend to relax," the story related. "His 'holiday' schedule went like this: Ten a.m. – read funnies aloud; 11 a.m. – build a fort; 1 p.m. – submit to being thrown in a swimming pool (fortified with soda pop and hamburger); 3 p.m. – test Shoup Park's new playground equipment and wade up Adobe Creek, pants legs rolled high; 4 p.m. – home for Wide Wide World's humor program on TV; 5 p.m. – foot race over Stanford University's greensward; 6 p.m. – take car-full of small boys for hike over Black Mountain; etc., etc. Least winded at bedtime was 43-year-old Alan Cranston. He was modest about his stamina, grinning that he's been 'in training' for months. It was a humorous understatement from the man who's confidently aiming to upset a 68-year-old political tradition." [187]

Geneva also was the topic of press coverage, often revealing her sense of humor. "Mrs. Alan Cranston is probably the only candidate's wife who had to arrange for a 'rat sitter' while she was out helping her husband" campaign, a *San Francisco Examiner* profile of her began – the boys had thirty-four hooded rats as pets. The number had been reduced to the original pair "after making a generous contribution to the Junior Museum," Geneva joked to reporter Mildred Schroeder. "But the unusual is the typical in the Cranston family," she wrote, "and the tall, blue-eyed [candidate's wife] wife admits she loves it." Schroeder observed that Geneva's "quizzical right eyebrow inched up under the tiny veil of her feathered hat as she talked" about her own varied career before marriage. "Recalling how she worked her way through Pomona College, the good-natured brunette listed such jobs as waiting tables, baby-sitting, bank-tellering, typing and even one engagement as a night-club singer." But there was "one department in which she confesses she can't keep up with her husband. 'Alan can get along without sleep – he averages about five hours a night for months during the campaign – but I can't.'" [188]

Cranston and Geneva went to Los Angeles' Biltmore Hotel to await primary returns on June 3. It became evident that Cranston and most other CDC-endorsed Democrats had won their nominations (Mosk's over Robert McCarthy was in doubt although Mosk eventually won). After the primary, based on the total number of votes received in both parties, Brown had a big margin of more than 600,000 votes. But Cranston's and Kirkwood's totals were alarmingly alike, giving Cranston a mere

3,571 margin. Cranston was "terrified by how badly he had done in the primary," Greenaway remembered, particularly in Fresno. "So they pushed the panic button." Over lunch at the Fairmont Hotel in San Francisco, Cranston asked Greenaway to chair the next election round in the San Joaquin Valley. That would turn out to be an important decision. [189]

Cranston put on a brave face publicly, saying in a post-primary statement, "I am deeply grateful to those whose votes have put me in the strongest position any Democrat has held since 1886 as a candidate for controller." A subsequent press release noted that he had won more votes in the primary than any candidate for controller in the state's history, and more votes than each of the national presidents from the founding fathers through Franklin Pierce (1852), although his opponent, Kirkwood, had spent more than twice as much money. [190]

Cranston went back to campaigning, reminding audiences that the last Democratic contender to be elected had run in the year that the gasoline engine had been invented (1886). He added to his campaign materials a cartoon depicting the last Democratic controller as a bearded antiquary. It made for good media copy. He continued to warn Democrats that they faced "the most vigorous, ruthless and rough campaign we've ever had" from Republicans fearful that California might go Democratic, ominous for the GOP in the next presidential campaign. Cranston hit the Republican ticket hard, charging them with "contradictory and confusing statements about whether we're knee-deep or neck-deep in red ink," and the need "for a whole new team in Sacramento." [191]

He denigrated slick advertising, accusing the GOP of hiring "professional hucksters" to sell their candidates, "using methods learned in selling soap, marketing candidates as they would a soft drink." Speeches were designed to "avoid displeasure," candidates projected as "a father who knows best and can do no wrong. But the American people are going to develop a 'buyer's resistance' against this kind of political campaign," he predicted. "There will be a repulsion of ghost candidates who fail to meet the voters face to face and refuse to discuss issues…. They will elect candidates who tell the truth, no matter how painful," he hoped. His own campaign, he said, was devoted to explaining the vital function of the controller's office. [192]

He also made a point of speaking to the African-American community. Blaming criminal tendencies on inherent characteristics was "one of the worst libels against the Negro people," he told a "Man of Tomorrow" group in San Francisco. "Those interested in improving the conditions of life of minority people should work for an end to job discrimination, housing discrimination, and any form of second-class citizenship." His appointments would "reflect a true representation of all the people," he promised. Eisenhower's suggestion to slow school integration showed "an appalling lack of knowledge of the real situation. Perhaps the president's advisors have failed to inform him that the Supreme Court laid down no timetable for school desegregation." [193]

Kirkwood actually gave Cranston "the only real issue that Alan, as a liberal, had against" his opponent, Greenaway noted, allowing him to establish credentials with African-Americans. Joseph B. Williams, a six-foot-five-inch-tall Black attorney who was Phil Burton's San Francisco law partner and a leader in the civil-rights movement, had organized a Black Forum of some 150 members. "We invited Kirkwood for luncheon – we wanted to hear what he had to say. Somebody asked him – I think it was me - if he would appoint a Black person as an inheritance-tax appraiser. And of course his answer was, 'This is not the time for that.' He didn't think people would be happy to have a Black appraiser coming into their homes at times of bereavement. *Bereavement*!," Williams laughed scornfully. "So we took the statement down. And when Cranston came to make a speech, I told him what the guy had said, and that all *he* needed to do was to say that he was going to appoint some Black people as appraisers. So he made a speech, danced around, and finally made that statement before a totally Black audience. We mailed the statement to all Black newspapers in the state, so they would know that the Republican just wasn't for *us*." [194]

But Williams was not happy about Cranston's giving short shrift to a big dinner that Williams organized for Cranston in San Francisco's Chinatown and paid for himself. "I knew that a lot of people didn't know about the job of controller. I told Cranston that we were going to have 200 to 300 Black people there. He showed up for about five minutes, got up and thanked me, and walked out." [195]

Another issue that gave Cranston good publicity was the revelation that Pacific Gas & Electric Company (PG&E), the state's principal power utility, had submitted deceptively-high property tax estimates in order to "dupe the people of California," as he put it, into supporting a partnership with a federal Trinity River hydro-electric project. Cranston contended that the true taxes would be half of what PG&E had alleged it would pay the state. He jumped on the issue as one that the controller oversaw, accusing his opponent of failing to analyze the figures, so "I felt it my duty to do so." Newspapers in the affected area, the agricultural valley, publicized the story. [196]

Campaigning grew vicious between some contenders, producing memorable insults. Knowland called Brown a "two-faced Santa Claus" or "Buster Brown," a children's book character. Knight described Engle as a "wisecrack at the end of a cigar," and mocked Engle's short stature as misrepresented on his billboards. "Up in the mountains where I come from," Engle retorted, "they measure a man from the neck up." Even Cranston was not immune – a Woodland paper called him "bird-brained." When he attacked Kirkwood's record on keeping track of state-owned lands, Kirkwood denied the charges as "cobweb claims." In other attacks as the campaign was closing in on election day, Cranston got tougher on Kirkwood. "My opponent calls himself the state's top financial officer – but this is hardly a claim to fame in an administration that has put us deeply in debt and mishandled our money." Cranston was "ignorant" of how government worked, Kirkwood retorted. "For several months my opponent has been taking a correspondence course in state government by scanning reports issued by state agencies. He continues to demonstrate, however, that he has failed do his homework" and lacked qualifications for the office. Cranston rejoined that Kirkwood was "either ignorant of his official responsibilities after five years in office, or else is trying to deceive the voters by attempting to cover up errors of his sloppy administration." [197]

Cranston got a taste for attacking his opponent as the race tightened, and his statements and releases grew stronger. He also had a "spy" at the state GOP convention, who gave him inside information. [198]

Cranston and his family meanwhile were photographed with the Democrats' slogan mounted on a broom to "sweep the state in '58," the boys neatly dressed in blazers and bow ties, Geneva in smart suit and hat. [199]

A major campaign tactic was to suggest that Kirkwood was getting funds from his appointed inheritance-tax appraisers (ITAs) who did not have civil-service job protection and thus were not prohibited from engaging in political campaigns. The charge had come from one of Cranston's backers, a former screen writer turned savings-and-loan tycoon, Bart Lytton, who liked to keep the opposition off guard. Jesse Unruh described Lytton as "a mad genius – in equal parts." Cranston sent a carefully worded letter, on his personal letterhead, to all 119 appraisers appointed by Kirkwood, some of whom were Democrats, saying that if he (Cranston) were elected, as now appeared possible, he would try to be fair and impartial in the selection of appraisers but he would not expect them to back him in elections, implying that Kirkwood had. The letter, which was quickly leaked to the press, read in part:

> "The fact that I have not accepted the help so generously offered…by some of you…does not mean that I will not want experienced help in my conduct of the controller's office….
>
> "I simply feel it best that you…refrain from taking an active part on either side in the present campaign for controller, regardless of political affiliation.
>
> "I wanted to write you in this vein as soon as I became a candidate, but felt that such action on my part might seem presumptuous prior to the primary." [200]

"Looking forward to seeing you in January," the letter confidently concluded. One appraiser whose office had displayed Kirkwood posters quickly removed them. Others felt that campaign activities had to be curtailed in the wake of Cranston's letter. It got both good and bad press. "Appraisers given 'no-politics' hint," the Watsonville *Register-Pajaronian* bannered in a front-page story. "California inheritance-tax appraisers – principal local representatives of the state controller – have received polite letters of 'advice' from the non-incumbent candidate. The jobs are considered political plums," and while not particularly lucrative in small counties, "in large counties they represent fat, fulltime jobs," and "in practice, many appraisers act as unofficial local campaign managers for the controller. Whether Cranston's letter constituted a threat, a warning, a statement of policy or friendly advice was not clear. Appraisers were left to draw their own conclusions." [201]

The Ventura County *Star-Free Press*, under the headline "Letters better not sent," remonstrated that Cranston's "admonition to Mr. Kirkwood's appointees not to thump for their boss is ill-advised and self-defeating…. The implication is that a lot of tax appraisers will be out of jobs if Cranston is elected." It wondered if Cranston would make the same demands of appointees in a reelection bid, should he be elected. "We doubt it." It would not be the last that Cranston heard of the politically-charged appraisers issue. [202]

Cranston again had to respond to press criticism. He admitted to having been offered campaign aid by several appraisers. "After considerable pondering, it seemed wisest to graciously decline these offers because to accept them might complicate" choosing "the most competent men" to serve in the posts, a letter to editors read. "What I failed to anticipate, however," was that the letter "would be interpreted by the present appraisers as a sign that they would all be turned out of office if I were elected. This misunderstanding…led these strategically placed, well-to-do and highly respected men to begin opposing my candidacy actively. I was in a dilemma. Silence would hurt my candidacy unjustly…. I chose to write personal letters…explaining my decision." Refraining from all such campaign aid made the playing field more even, he felt. "I still believe that my course was a correct one." [203]

The biggest coup of the campaign for Cranston came a month before the election. Pat Brown, against his advisers' wishes to keep him separate from other candidates, "wholeheartedly" endorsed Cranston, crediting him with being "one of those most responsible for the re-establishment of the two-party system in California" and "the resurgence of the Democratic Party. Over the many years of our friendship," Brown wrote in a carefully-worded letter, "you and I have worked closely together on many matters. I hope that we will be given the opportunity to work together in Sacramento. You have rendered invaluable service to the public and to me" through service on Brown's crime-prevention advisory committee. "I have the greatest confidence in your ability and your integrity, and I believe the people of California will show on November 4 that they share that confidence. I hope that everyone who votes for me for governor – Democrats and Republicans alike – will vote for you for controller," it stated, in full knowledge that the letter would be made public. A campaign flyer was designed that included a photo of Brown clasping hands with Engle and Cranston, who towered over both men. Brown also sent a fundraiser, Prentiss Moore, to help Cranston – "as kind of a reward for his not running for the Senate," Greenaway said. "That was Alan's big problem, he couldn't raise money." Cranston described Moore as a "savvy, daring guy to have on your side." [204]

Brown himself, in a promotional biography, was characterized as "a warm and friendly man who has been in public service for fifteen years," and "distinguished himself…both for his astute talents as the chief law-enforcement officer of the state and his personal qualities as a man." His friends ranged from valley farmers and lumber jacks to business and civic leaders, it said. He had gotten his nickname during World War I when he pitched the sale of Liberty Bonds, closing appeals "with a fervent 'Give me liberty or give me death,'" resulting in being dubbed "Patrick Henry" Brown. Now fifty-three years old, the San Franciscan had graduated from the University of California Extension Division and San Francisco College of Law, passing the bar in 1927. His wife Bernice was the daughter of a police captain. The couple had four children – Barbara Casey, 25, Cynthia Kelly, 23, Gerald Brown, Junior, 19, and Kathleen Brown, 12. While practicing law, Brown and other young attorneys had formed an Order of Cincinnatus to work for good government. Brown had first run for office (the assembly) as a Republican. He had lost and in 1934 changed his party affiliation to Democrat. He also had lost his second political try – for San Francisco District Attorney (in 1939), but when he ran for the same post in 1943, he was elected. "He has always attracted first-rate associates," the biography stated, one of the reasons for high performance in the offices that he headed, "and he is frank to attribute his success to these friends." [205]

Another unexpected boost held some irony for Cranston – an endorsement from prominent Republican San Francisco attorney John Francis Neylan, one of William Randolph Hearst's former publishers and legal counsel, who had served as Governor Hiram Johnson's director of finance. Neylan was a close friend of William Cranston's. As a Regent of the University of California, Neylan had led a militantly anti-Communist effort to require faculty to sign a loyalty oath in the late 1940s. Now, reminding people that the state controller was watchdog of the treasury and auditor of tax funds, Neylan said that Cranston had the "integrity and courage" to "restore the office to the dignity and importance it formerly enjoyed." That had credibility with the conservative business community. [206]

In addition, State Senator Robert McCarthy, who had been critical of Cranston, had come over to his side. But *San Francisco Call-Bulletin* political columnist Jack S. McDowell mocked the turn-around. It "sounded a mite strange, coming from the man who publicly scorched the tail feathers of the California Democratic Council a short while back," calling it "'the hot-rod set' of the party." "I have endorsed Cranston for controller, *period*," McCarthy tersely told McDowell. But Cranston's announcement quoted McCarthy as saying that Cranston was "far more qualified than his opponent to serve as California's chief fiscal officer." Pressed by McDowell, McCarthy said that he had never uttered "a word against Kirkwood or his abilities." When McDowell read more of Cranston's release to McCarthy, "a sort of gasping noise came over the telephone." "I didn't say any of those things," McCarthy told McDowell. "They must have been manufactured in Cranston's headquarters, because they sure didn't come from me." It "must have been the work of political hob-goblins," McDowell joked of the Halloween release. [207]

Cranston still was not doing well in Fresno and the agricultural valley, and the *Bee* newspapers, whose chain covered the area, had come out for Kirkwood. The Cranston committee sent a desperate letter to Democratic voters begging for support. "Alan did not carry our county in the primary as did most of the other Democratic candidates," the letter reminded them, inexplicable after Fresno County had been one of only three in the state to vote for the 1954 Democratic controller candidate (Collins). And the opposition had "dollars to spare." [208]

Cranston also was dogged by old skeletons coming out of closets. Literature began to appear with the mark of trouble-maker Joseph Kamp, calling Cranston a Communist. "Our opponent's forces are distributing a vicious smear article about Alan, written by the discredited hate-monger, Joseph P. Kamp," campaign directors Teilhet and Mueller told coordinators. He had been denounced by "most California newspapers as a right-wing smearer after his writings were brought to California by Mrs. William Knowland in a desperate but vain attempt to discredit Pat Brown," they said, referring to a *New York Times* story that Helen Knowland had distributed 500 copies of the Kamp pamphlet until her husband asked her to stop. Cranston's staff urged campaign workers to circulate the Kamp exposés to counteract the smear wherever it was being circulated. [209]

United Auto Workers president Walter "Reuther as Governor [an allusion to supposed influence over candidate Brown] is bad enough, but Cranston as comptroller would be even worse!" Kamp's pamphlet "Headlines" said. "Read the TRUTH about Alan Cranston, published some seven years ago." It reiterated charges that the world-government movement and its national leader had "a record which literally reeks of communist contamination." It cited among "fellow-travelers" Louis Adamic, "who recently committed suicide," quoting a book about Yugoslavia that called Cranston a protégé of Adamic's. "Cranston's curious past affinity for Communists and their propaganda line may not make him a Communist," the pamphlet stated, but it was "an added argument" to "stop-look-and-listen" to what World Federalists and Cranston proposed. [210]

A newspaper editorial took up the line, saying, "The World Federalists are not all parlor pinks and left-wingers, for their movement has attracted numerous well-meaning, idealistic persons." Cranston, whose attendance at the University of Mexico "in the mid-thirties, when it was a favorite haven for Reds," also was suspect, as was his work for the "communist-front organization, the Common Council for American Unity." His O. W. I. job and Army orientation work, writing a fact sheet that was "so pro-Soviet that it aroused a storm of protest in Congress," were dredged up. "It is fantastic that a man with such a background should be the Democratic candidate for state controller," the editorial concluded, "striking evidence of the influence which left-wingers have exerted on Democratic Party councils in California. Unless the voters wake up to this man's record, the next controller…may be a top promoter of the movement to submerge our American government and national sovereignty." [211]

Hearst reporter Carl Greenberg of the *Los Angeles Examiner* dug up old clippings about Cranston's exploits in Mexico and asked him, "What were you doing in that Mexican revolution in 1935?" [212]

Cranston held a press conference to denounce the smear campaign as "Republican cannibalism," blaming Kirkwood. "People opposed to my candidacy are circulating a magazine published by hate-monger Kamp," he said, declaring that he would not answer Kamp's "lies and distortions" until Kirkwood "stated whether or not he welcomes Kamp's help in his campaign" and repudiated "this obnoxious material. These unconscionable tactics could not be used without Kirkwood's knowledge and consent…. If Kirkwood wants to team up with Kamp and Knowland to form a new KKK, I will have plenty to say…. It is well known that Kirkwood himself was a member of U. W. F. and sponsored a U. W. F. resolution in the state legislature," along with former Senate leader Harold Powers, now running on the Republican ticket for reelection as lieutenant governor. Powers had been on the U. W. F. state advisory board in 1949-50. Kirkwood remained silent, and Cranston worried not only about the effect of the attack on himself but on the gubernatorial race. [213]

Brown, in fact, also was being smeared, and had accused Knowland of accepting support from Kamp (Knowland in turn accused Brown of having "gangster" ties). Brown called on Nixon, who attended a GOP rally in San Francisco, to intervene against distribution of the pamphlets. "It's now almost certain…that the 'Red' issue will be raised once more against the Democratic ticket," Washington correspondent Ruth Finney reported in the *San Francisco News*. "One GOP committee has a former F. B. I. man scrutinizing candidates, and records of the House Un-American Activities Committee are being combed…. It seems certain that an effort will be made to raise a doubt in voters' minds. If the campaign shapes up this way, the legions of anonymous telephone callers, used before in Southern California, may be called on again." The reference was to the Nixon-Helen Douglas race. "If there are any real Communists on either ticket, they, of course, should be exposed, but no politico has a license for baseless innuendoes or far-fetched maligning," the Ventura County *Star-Free Press* editorialized. [214]

Cranston's aggressive refuting tactics backfired in some quarters. *Mercury-News* political writer Harry Farrell accused "the tall, balding Cranston" of "one of the nastiest charges hurled by anyone" in saying that Kirkwood "was condoning a smear campaign against him." Cranston "used such terms as 'unconscionable rumors' concerned with his former status as national president of the United World Federalists. In short, the smear Cranston complained of might be nothing more than a shadow," pointing to the fact that both candidates had been Federalists, causing some people to wonder why Cranston was concerned. The allusion to a shadow, of course, was to the radio program's Lamont Cranston. [215]

Kamp, however, had a highly-placed, if unwitting, ally. Vice President Nixon had written Governor Knight in March that "a mutual friend of ours who is a strong Democrat" had suggested that Cranston's O. W. I. job had been gotten with help from Communists," which "Congressman Busby claimed in a congressional speech." Using the charges against him was "both legitimate and can be very effective," Nixon confided to Knight. [216]

In mid-October, a letter to the *Los Angeles Times* was circulated citing "Mr. Cranston's very questionable background." It referred to his attendance at the University of Mexico when it "was crawling with theories of communist incubation." It was signed by three Southern Californians. [217]

Just a few days before the election, Cranston's sympathetic publishing friend Joe Houghteling wrote an editorial in the Sunnyvale *Standard* denouncing Kamp as a "screw-ball" who was "attempting a smear against Mr. Cranston, a respected and patriotic citizen of this county. We trust the public reaction against these evil documents will be as outraged as it was when the *New York Times* first revealed that Senator Knowland was utilizing material from this source in his campaign." [218]

Cranston's staff knew that getting out the vote was crucial at the end. And despite the smear, Cranston told his workers that he had "a renewed burst of enthusiasm for the campaign." [219]

Republicans also were rallying to get out the vote. "If we fail in this vital task, California may fall into the hands of Democratic administrators *completely lacking in qualifications for the vastly important positions they seek*," a GOP memo to its leaders stated October 29. Kirkwood, it quoted *Call-Bulletin* reporter Jack McDowell as saying, was "highly intelligent, efficient, fair and without a smidgen of smudge on his integrity." Cranston, by contrast, had "No experience or training in state government, finances or taxation," according to the GOP memo. To date, it added, "no California daily newspaper has endorsed Cranston." [220]

It was true that Cranston had not been endorsed by major papers. Kirkwood had gotten the *San Francisco Chronicle* October 20, 1958, and the *Los Angeles Times* prior to the primary (June 1, 1958) as well as a number of small newspaper endorsements. He also had been endorsed by one of Cranston's local papers, the *Palo Alto Times*, and the San Rafael (Marin County) *Independent Journal* (May 29, 1958). Cranston was endorsed by the *Santa Barbara News-Press* and the *Los Angeles Sentinel* African-American paper. [221]

By then some polls showed Kirkwood as a seven-to-five-odds winner over Cranston. [222]

But Cranston still was not pessimistic. A note to his campaign workers read, "From the very start, there was one state office that many people said no Democrat could win – the one the Republicans have managed to hold for 68 years. It took the primary and now the general [election] – more than a 'Democratic trend' – to prove them wrong.... Now the Republicans are desperately fighting to hold at least one office [the controller's]. Republican money and backing have poured in these last days to try and keep my opponent in office.... Now we are up against the final push for the one and only thing that counts – to get out every vote." [223]

An important component of his style was to thank his staff, as he did in the note to workers, and to send thank-you letters to supporters, quickly and gratefully. "Be careful of Cranston," a campaign worker, Tom Sanders, told Ann Alanson when she started working at Democratic headquarters. "He writes thank-you notes for the thank-you notes, and he'll have you doing it." "That's how he operated," Alanson saw. "It was a hallmark of his early career." [224]

Early on election night, Cranston was trailing while Brown was winning by huge margins, and Engle was beating Knowland. Kirkwood's lead continued as the night wore on. There was a brief moment of relief when, thanks to Cranston's San Francisco County chairman, Tom Feeney, some returns were recounted and Kirkwood was found to have been wrongly given 10,000 votes. The Cranstons went to bed, uneasy and depressed, not knowing the final results. To fill time and divert themselves the following day in San Francisco, the family went shopping at the Emporium department store. Among toys they got for the boys was one for Robin that neither parent could put together. Things seemed to be going downhill. They went to see the film *South Pacific*, but Cranston was restless, and went out to check more returns. When he came back, Mary Martin was singing "Happy Talk." Things were looking up, he reported. It would not be until the next day that final tabulations were known. [225]

To their relief, Cranston appeared to have won by 31,000 votes (among some five million cast). Pat Brown also had won, and for the first time in the century, Democrats controlled the legislature and all major statewide offices except for secretary of state (won by Frank Jordan, not related to a future police chief and mayor of San Francisco). Cranston's lead was due in part to a big turn-around in the Central Valley that Greenaway helped orchestrate, increasing Cranston's percentage more than in any other part of the state. [226]

The Cranstons returned to their Los Altos home. "Alan put a symphony on the record player, and we sat by the fire," his sister recorded. "Geneva poured coffee from her copper pot while the boys ran in and out, shouting excitedly. Roy, their German shepherd, barked at their heels.... [W]e talked about the move to Sacramento, and read the stacks of congratulatory telegrams." [227]

But the election would not be officially declared won for a month, during which Kirkwood did not concede and talked about asking for a recount. Cranston's managers sent out another memo to "Constant Cranston Campaigners" asking them to find out from county clerks exactly when votes were certified and to check tally sheets to see whether party totals seemed unusually inequitable. If predominantly

Democratic precincts received a majority of Republican votes, they might be challenged. "Sometimes a transposition of the figures, made in error, can be responsible for a great loss of votes." [228]

Kirkwood continued to hold out while admitting that he probably had "a pretty slim chance" of retaining office. Cranston was showing a lead of 67,000 votes three days after the election and before all absentee ballots and votes in Orange County, which Kirkwood expected to carry, had been tallied. Cranston had factored in absentee votes and figured on getting enough to solidify his win. Both men concurred that, while contentious, theirs had been the cleanest of the campaigns. Cranston called Kirkwood "a strong and gallant opponent who has my admiration and respect." [229]

Kirkwood went duck and pheasant hunting in Colusa County in mid-November (which he had won by 569 votes), telling a local newspaper, "We'll just have to wait and see." But by Thanksgiving, the race still had not been decided. Cranston's lead had dropped to 57,000 votes. He made a trip to Sacramento nevertheless, and talked with Kirkwood to discuss the functions of the office while "just poking around" the capitol, a news report said. Kirkwood was not giving up because "the gap in this race is closing." Kirkwood was getting 65 percent of the absentee votes, and his aide believed that Cranston's margin had dropped to only 25,000. [230]

On December 3 it was reported that Kirkwood was seeking a recount after Los Angeles County added more than 10,000 votes to his total, further narrowing Cranston's margin to less than one vote per precinct. [231]

Finally, on December 10, Kirkwood called Cranston. "The phone rang in the kitchen at Hilltop Drive," Eleanor wrote. "It was Kirkwood. Geneva had been washing dishes. She gave the phone to Alan…. After a moment he looked at her, raised his eyebrows, wrinkled his forehead and nodded his head vigorously. 'That's good of you,' he said. 'You fought a great campaign.'" Kirkwood had told him that he would not pursue the matter any longer. [232]

Cranston had won by 31,523 votes, and had spent $379,046 to Kirkwood's $234,567. Kirkwood would be named to head the San Francisco Public Utility Department. [233]

"HALLELUJAH! We've really won!" Cranston's managers exclaimed in a memo. "Alan is officially the new controller. Kirkwood conceded today! Isn't life wonderful! Merry Christmas - Happy New Year! Thanks 'Fifteen Millions'!" Cranston was ecstatic. But Geneva was daunted by images of their future life, which promised continuous campaigns, living in the public eye, relocation of household and family. It was their eighteenth wedding anniversary. [234]

"We have been apart too much," Geneva told a reporter as she prepared to sell the Hilltop house and move to Sacramento. "'It is more important for the children to be with their father than to worry about changing schools,' she said decisively" of the disruption the family faced. [235]

Cranston was sworn in a week early, December 29, 1958, at the Los Altos town hall by Associate State Supreme Court Justice John Wesley Shenk, a friend and neighbor, in order to officially meet with the state Board of Equalization the next morning. His mother, wife and children, friends and supporters watched the swearing in. He named Irwin Nebron as chief deputy state controller. The state's new Democratic leaders had an average age of forty-eight. They had been toasted in song by film star Judy Garland at the party's victory dinner in Los Angeles. [236]

One telegram to Cranston after confirmation of his victory simply read, "Phew!" It was signed by "Charter members 'Cranston for President Committee.'" [237]

Lee Falk joked that Cranston's new title was "obviously taken from the works of George Orwell or Lewis Carroll."

"What do you control? Thought? Morals? Traffic? Weather? Butterfat content? Yourself? It's the kind of thing one would expect in that state of make-believe out there. 'Let's have a controller.' 'What'll he do?' 'We'll figure that out later. But let's have one, because it sounds so gruesome!'

"If you're not ashamed to admit what kind of a mess you've gotten into out there, write me about it.... Of course, I'm telling none of our mutual friends here about it. I have a vision of you striding the windy shores near Los Altos, ordering the waves to stop, and shouting, 'You *must!* I am the Controller of California!'

"Do write and tell me how you got into this sad condition. I'm certain Geneva and the children are standing by you staunchly....

Worriedly,
Lee Falk" [238]

7

Triumph and Defeat

"Your reputation for honesty and integrity is and should be beyond reproach."
Pierre Salinger to Cranston, apologizing for Senate primary campaign attacks, April 21, 1965.

"This is the first letter I have dictated since taking office," Cranston wrote his mother January 14, 1959. "I am sorry I haven't been able to write to you (and to others) sooner, but as you can imagine, I have been swamped. The office is beautiful, and I hope you will come up soon to look at and at me in it." [1]

The office indeed was grand. It was directly across a marble hall from the governor's on the southwest corner of the Capitol. He could see the Senator Hotel across the capitol grounds, where as a boy his family had stayed en route to holidays at Lake Tahoe. He also could just see, at the corner of 12th and L Streets, the site where his Aunt Grace Skeel's Victorian mansion had stood and where his parents had married in 1903. [2]

"It is wonderful to be here in Sacramento where I am finding the responsibilities and duties of the office extremely interesting and challenging and the legislative processes fascinating," he told the Democratic State Central Committee secretary. To committee member Elinor "Liz" Heller he wrote, "It gives one a little sense of accomplishment to see so many Democrats here after all the work that we have done together in the vineyard." [3]

Soon after the election Brown invited the Cranston family to meet with him at a hotel in Palm Springs for a working vacation, where they were photographed together in bathing suits by a pool. Robin and Kim had a playful water fight in the pool and Cranston worried about their harming the governor-elect. He thanked Brown candidly for supporting him, and Brown genuinely told him that he was glad to have Cranston as part of the new administration. They agreed that fulfilling their policy goals would be hard slogging. [4]

Brown also warned Cranston to be careful in making appointments, particularly inheritance-tax appraisers, which were prone to charges of political patronage. Cranston accepted that patronage was an inevitable part of the mix, repugnant though it was to some. He already was being besieged by people seeking such appointments. But, as Brown reminded him, the fact that Cranston's win had been so marginal meant that he was vulnerable to attacks and criticism from the media,

Republicans, even Democrats. Cranston would have to keep his image clean and make himself better known if, as Brown knew, he wanted to run for the Senate. [5]

The inaugural ball in January, 1959, was a show of glitch by the triumphant Democrats. A ballroom was decorated with gold-satin-lamé canopy, cherubs and urns spilling ivy and gold roping, huge ice replicas of the state capitol, a bust of Governor Brown with the state seal and historic flags while a fifteen-piece orchestra played and officials were formally announced. A serious and quiet attendant, Eleanor observed, was twenty-year-old Jerry Brown, the governor's son who had to get permission to leave the Jesuit seminary where he was studying for the priesthood. Geneva wore a full-length green satin gown with a matching stole that draped across her shoulders and attached to a "mermaid" train, described in detail by the *Sacramento Bee*. She had lined the stole with foam rubber to keep her warm, causing it to bounce against people, something that she joked about afterward to a friend. [6]

The Cranstons purchased an old ranch house on seven acres in the northern suburbs of Sacramento at 3825 Thornwood Drive, fifteen minutes' commute from the Capitol. It was a square, two-storey, white clapboard house with crumbling stables that once had housed race horses – which they dubbed a "Currier and Ives" barn – bordered by a creek called "Chicken House Slough." Oak trees separated their property from sub-divisions crawling through the ranch's original olive orchard. The place would become famous, or infamous, as the Cranstons' "Animal Farm," taken from the title of George Orwell's political satire. But on the Cranston farm, people and animals got along together. Cranston at one point listed its residents as 39 chickens, 21 ducks, four cats, two goats, one dog, one lamb, an old mare horse named Lady which they had bought for $25, a sow pig, occasional frogs and "scads of birds." Roy, the German shepherd, was "really part of the family," Geneva conceded, with "a persuasiveness in peacemaking that would bring Mao Tse-Tung and Andrei Kosygin running to the conference table," a reporter wrote of his leaping between fighting cats or other animals and "snarling them into a ceasefire." Roy often appeared with other pets in annual family photos for Christmas cards. The same reporter asked whether the Cranstons ever considered eating some of the barnyard animals. "That would be like saying which child should we eat for Easter!" Geneva exclaimed, "eyeing the visitor with much the same skepticism that a white hunter might view a suspected cannibal." [7]

The white sow, named Snowball – "the good pig in Orwell's book," Cranston noted – grew to 700 pounds. Rob caught her as a piglet in a greased-pig contest at Los Banos in spring, 1961, and brought her home in the back of the family station wagon. She was given full reign of the property and sometimes wandered into the house living room, guests remembered vividly. An aggressive rooster named "Cassius" had to be penned in, though, after developing a habit of attacking Cranston as he ran around the property for morning exercise. Geneva liked to tell reporters, fascinated by the visual and human interest of the controller's urban farm, how one of the goats, Captain Billy Kid, saved Mary the lamb from several wild dogs by jumping a fence and running to the house for help. The goat, who was house-trained and wandered inside, had been acquired when the family was at an auction in Roseville in the nearby foothills. "A man drove up in a pickup with all these tiny goats and happened to say, 'They'll be good eating for Easter.' That was all Kim needed to hear. He bought the goat for $3." It liked to climb ramps that Kim had built to a tree house in a large oak from which the goat often startled visitors. [8]

Those were happy times for the family. Cranston himself planted 700 eucalyptus and other trees to shield the farm from urban sprawl. Kim at the age of nine found himself farm manager. Feeding the animals required pet food by the case, sacks of chicken mash and bales of hay each month. He had several regular customers for fresh eggs, which helped defray expenses. [9]

At first, Geneva spent time watching legislators at work. Described in a *Sacramento Bee* story as "a tall woman in tailored clothes with a fresh, outdoors look about her," she told the reporter, "I don't know how the housework is ever going to get done. I just can't stay away from the legislature. I loved it when I was in Washington, working with the Congress, and it's just the same here." She "was enthusiastic" about living on a "farm" in the middle of urban Sacramento, saying "Alan relaxes best by working outdoors and working at home with the children seems better than golf or something like that." Cranston, she said, was tearing down "a sort of barn that's obstructing our view." No longer a career woman, her life now was centered on her children, she said. The boys had been "wonderful about the campaign and taking part in what interests *us*." Both had had birthdays during the campaign but did not want a party without their father, so they had held off until Christmas week for their parties. It was "only fair to be active in *their* lives" now, she felt. "One has the feeling that she attacks each activity – farming, being motherly, watching legislators and being political – with equal zest," the reporter concluded. Eleanor saw that Robin paired off with his mother, Kim with his father, on whom he was quite dependent, she thought. [10]

In time the Cranstons built a modern ranch house that Cranston and Geneva designed. It had a glassed-in living room with a central fireplace where guests could put their feet up after dinner. The horse and sow, who were constant companions, could often be found gazing through the window from outside. "It's real togetherness," Geneva said in interviews. Cranston also was the only state officer listed in the telephone directory. "We get some pretty interesting calls," Geneva related of unhappy taxpayers who knew that Cranston was the chief tax collector. [11]

Halloween was a special family celebration, which delighted Geneva with her penchant for imaginative pranks and letting-go. Kim recalled to his aunt for her memoir of Cranston that they created a "haunted" house one year. The living room resembled a Charles Addams cartoon with a neighbor dressed as a hag who cackled when someone approached her rocking chair. Geneva wore a witch's outfit and "ran around scaring people." Irwin Nebron offered visitors red Kool-Aid drinks from a bathtub filled with dye to look like blood. "Even I didn't take any," Kim said of the ghoulish image. The state controller was dressed as a hobo in torn pants, old shirt and shoes with several days growth of beard on his charcoaled face. He greeted children towing a garbage can and grunting. Kim, followed by neighborhood children looking for treats, suggested that they might be in the can, whereupon his father grabbed him by the feet and tossed him into it. A pillow kept him from damaging his head while Cranston dragged the can into the kitchen. Kim was heard to howl and his father reappeared with a large knife and a piece of raw calves' liver in hand. "At that point, the kids dropped their candy and ran!" Kim recalled of the realistic scene. "You're crazy if you go into *that* house!" they shouted to other children coming up the driveway, dropping their bags of candy as they ran away. It was all "great fun," Kim remembered. The next Halloween the neighbor children showed up with water balloons. [12]

The boys sent their parents cards and notes, Kim writing on one Mother's Day card,

> "Your candy is sweet
> I love your spice
> And you're very neat
> And you're very nice.
> I heard a bird
> I saw a bunny
> One thing I know
> You're my honey." [13]

Robin for a fifth-grade essay wrote an account of how they acquired the horse. Numerous misspellings got him a C- grade, but his father lovingly kept the essay.

> "About one month ago as soon as my father came home he jumped out of his car and ran over to our stables, and came puffing up to me and said still out of breath, 'Robin, a man named Assembly Alan Miller ask me down at the capitol if he could bring his hourse here. You and Kim could be the stable boys. You can ride the hourse and will be payed $1.50 a week.'
>
> "Oboy, I yelled and went running off. A few hours latter a 1959 golden Imperele [came] with a big horse traler hook on the back. I took a look…and saw a buitfil Arabin horse. Its name was Rowitize. A few minets latter I was rideing him and I still do every chance I get. I gallop, trot and walk him almost every day. And it's a lot of fun.
>
> The End" [14]

The boys had chores to do and on one occasion, Robin explained in a note why he had neglected one. From an early age, both boys called their father by his Christian name.

> "Dear Alan,
>
> "The reason I didn't do the lawn is that when I started to do it, around dusk, 3 toads started hoping around in the grass and all I could catch was one – the others hid. But I will cut the lawn, the first thing tomorrow morning. Robin" [15]

Robin's spelling did not improve and in an English class essay describing his father, written when Robin was fourteen, it was so bad that the teacher wrote across the top, "You would not do justice to your father with this kind of spelling," giving him a C grade. If the story lacked in spelling skills, it still provided a candid view from a son.

"This person is 47 years old. He is about 6'2" tall and weighs about 202 [pounds]. He has lived in Sacto [*sic*] 3 years, Los Altos 40 years, New York 1 year and has traveled about 2 years. He has gone around the world 2 times and has been in all the European countries, northern and southern Africa, the West Indies, Mixico [*sic*] and Hawai [*sic*]. His favorite sports are watersking [*sic*], skindiving, swimming, track, football, and baseball. He went to Standford Collage [*sic*] and graduated in flying colors. He then went into the real estate busness [*sic*] with his father. After that he started a copper importing business until he got interested in politics and became chairman of the California Democratic Club. In 1959 he was elected to the office of California State Control [*sic*]. He is easy to get along with and makes friends with practically everyone he meets. He is especally fond of children. (My father)." [16]

A few years later, Cranston wrote the Fowles that "Rob seems to be doing much better at school this year – we hope, [but] no grades yet. Kim is doing his usual superb best." [17]

On the job, Cranston initially was overwhelmed by the "mammoth bureaucracy" that he would have to confront, telling his sister that he thought it unresponsive to both citizens and their elected leaders. Civil-service bureaucrats tended to ignore new arrivals and carry on as they were accustomed to doing. Cranston was permitted only two staff appointments of his choice – his chief deputy Irwin Nebron and a press aide, Dick Walton. The controller relied on more than 500 civil servants as well as staff on seventeen boards and commissions of which he was a member. Even his personal secretary (Eleanor MacArthur, cousin of a *Palo Alto Times* columnist, Henry MacArthur) was a previously-appointed civil servant as was another deputy (Ralph McCarthy), both of whom stayed on with Cranston and proved to be compatible and loyal aides. Over time Cranston would gain respect for experienced staffers who maintained institutional memory and expertise through political changes, although he regretted that talent could not be more easily rewarded and incompetence removed. [18]

Infighting and power struggles surfaced early. In the first week, Cranston was asked by Democratic Lieutenant Governor Glenn Anderson and Republican Bert Levit, whom Brown had appointed his director of finance, to support each for chairman of the State Lands Commission. Cranston expected to back his party associate, and so told Levit. Cranston also expected to chair the Franchise Tax Board. Brown tersely told him, however, that Levit would not support him for the tax-board chairmanship unless Cranston backed Levit for the lands-commission slot. It was agreed that Levit would get it and that Anderson would succeed him when Levit retired later that year. [19]

A few years later, Nebron was upset with Cranston sufficiently to offer to resign as his deputy. "I have always believed that a great public figure should, especially at a potentially significant turning point in his career, hold no mental reservations whatsoever about the loyalty, ability or integrity of those subordinates whom he has gathered around himself," he wrote Cranston. Such reservations "can only have a weakening effect upon all concerned.... Therefore, I at this time unconditionally tender my resignation to take effect at your pleasure. To be associated with you has afforded me the opportunity to witness government operating as I believe it should.... If I can ever be of some help in the future, you can count on me." [20]

Nebron nevertheless stayed on the staff. "Irwin resented anybody else who was close to Alan," Eleanor said of what may have prompted Nebron's pique, including her, especially when she became chair of the State Democratic Women's committee.

Appointing inheritance-tax appraisers (ITAs) would turn out to be one of the job's most controversial functions. One appraiser gave Cranston inside "dope" on how the system worked, reinforcing that ITAs had been expected to contribute to incumbent Kirkwood's campaign. "I was personally happy to see you" elected, the man wrote, "despite the money spent to defeat you. Now it is up to you to clean house of all the state inheritance-tax appraisers. We all worked against you, and paid handsomely to do it." Appraisers did "very little work," he revealed. "We sit in on hearings, usually before a deputy state controller, when the value of the estate goes over $200,000. Otherwise we just sign routine appraisal reports. You can do without any of us." He warned Cranston that pressure would be brought "by some business firms and labor leaders to keep some of the boys," and confided the names of two Los Angeles appraisers who had led opposition to Cranston. He also noted that the editor of the *Sacramento Bee* had a brother who was an appraiser. "Do not hesitate to replace all of us," the man concluded. He signed it, "One of the boys." [21]

Cranston solicited advice from probate attorneys. One, Martin E. Rothenberg, said that because the system had been run out of the public eye by Republicans for more than seventy years, it came as "a great surprise to many people to learn the facts" of how it operated. In some counties, where one appraiser might provide service and another be "lazy," judges rotated assignments, which Rothenberg recommended adopting statewide. Another problem was fairness in compensation. In counties where wealthy people lived, appraiser fees were higher than elsewhere, leading to charges that such plum appointments were politically-based. "Some method of equalizing compensation should be adopted," Rothenberg suggested, adding that "all of the present appraisers who supported Kirkwood fully expect to lose their positions, a political fact of life." [22]

Cranston's first appointments fell into that category, starting with defeated Democratic Secretary-of-State nominee Henry P. Lopez in Los Angeles County. "The appointment tends to re-establish an old pattern for state appraisers' jobs, which recently have come under attack as the last important patronage in California politics," a news story stated, citing Cranston's other ITA appointments: his campaign treasurer, Orange County lawyer Claude Young; prominent Los Angeles attorney and community leader George L. Thomas, one of the first Blacks named to the job; and Democratic lawyer Richard Vaughn of San Diego. In time, he would appoint Roy Greenaway and Prentiss Moore, who had helped Cranston win election; Pat Brown's brother Harold; civil-rights activist Joe Williams; and the wife of an AFL-CIO lobbyist, Mrs. John Despol. Other friends or supporters who got ITA jobs included Alan Parker, CDC treasurer, and John Strahan, husband of CDC vice president Virginia Strahan. Cranston increased the number of appraisers in Los Angeles from 19 to 22, adding 35 new appraisers to the 125 previously in place. His rationale was that it reduced appraisers' fees without increasing costs to taxpayers. The legislative auditor in 1959 had estimated that appraisers statewide received more than $1 million in commissions for valuating estates, most making about $40,000 a year. Money could be saved by abolishing appraisers altogether and turning the job over to civil servants. Political writer Harry Farrell called it the "last major stronghold of the spoils system in California government." The *San Francisco News* ran a series exposing the fact that some judges favored friends with appraisal work and that some appraisers sub-contracted the work out, depriving estates of fair-market values and the state of income. To counter the criticism, Cranston decided to publicly report appraisers' annual earnings, never before done, which did not sit well with appraisers. [23]

Although "fairly leisurely about getting rid of Kirkwood's appraisers," as Farrell put it, Cranston honored his pledge to change the make-up of the appointments, naming the first women appraisers in the state's history as well as Blacks, Hispanics, Asians and Native Americans. But the appointments were continually debated and Cranston was constantly pressured to favor people with them. "For every appointment you make, you create a hundred enemies, and one ingrate!" bemoaned Governor Brown who faced similar problems. One of Cranston's proposed changes created unforeseen repercussions. He planned to replace a Sonora dentist with a young attorney as appraiser in Tuolumne County in the Sierra Nevada foothills. Cranston was to ride a horse as honorary marshal in the annual Mother Lode Round-Up Parade the day before announcing the change, and with his family went to Sonora where Cranston's Aunt Jessie Patton lived. Decked out in western gear and a large cowboy hat, Cranston noticed that the family seated next to his in the grandstand waved more enthusiastically than any others in the crowd, as if "they were long-lost friends," he thought, wondering who they were. It turned out to be the existing appraiser and his wife who had made a point of being friendly to Aunt Jessie. They invited the Cranstons to visit them in Columbia, a well-preserved Gold Rush town. Cranston demurred, although he took the family to see the picturesque site, hoping to avoid the appraiser. As they drove into the village, they met his wife. She reiterated her invitation to visit her home, promising historic memorabilia. Cranston reluctantly acceded, pressed by the boys who delighted in the Gold Rush curiosities in the house. To their astonishment, however, Robin discovered a stash of matchbooks labeled, "Elect Bob Kirkwood as Controller." The appraiser was mortified, the wife distraught, protesting that she just used them to light fires, and the Cranstons made their exit, with mutual apologies all around. [24]

Cranston was confronted with a dilemma: if he replaced the appraiser, he would be accused of political punishment. He put off the decision for several months. He joked to Democratic National Committeemen Paul Ziffren, "I am counting on you to furnish me 5,000 tickets to the Democratic Convention! The least I can do is give one to…lifelong Democrats…qualified to be appraisers whom I will not yet have appointed by the time of the convention." [25]

One who was not happy with Cranston's slowness to act was Joe Williams, Phil Burton's law partner. Burton had to pressure Cranston to appoint Williams. "People said to me, 'Joe, you spent your whole time helping get this guy elected – think he'll give you an appointment?' We *never* heard from him, so Phil got on him, and couple of other people got on him. Phil leaned and leaned," Williams recalled. "*Finally* he called me up and made the appointment – reluctantly. He didn't do it because he loved me. Then he decided that he was going to appoint some Black conservative from Oakland. We got on him about *that*, so he ended up appointing another Black man, the head of the NAACP in Oakland, who later became a judge." [26]

Cranston also had to quickly learn the nuances of government budgeting – controlling expenditures while raising revenues to cover them. The Brown administration had come in facing a $100-mllion state deficit. As controller Cranston had to warn Brown that the "unprecedented overall indebtedness" required urgent "budgetary revisions." Brown called for higher taxes to pay for services needed by the increasing population. The new revenue would help refill the state's general fund and balance the budget. But Cranston also recognized that such proposals were not always popular and looked for other ways to raise revenues. The oil-rich costal tidelands were one resource. [27]

One of his first controversies on the State Lands Commission (which controlled state-owned mineral resources) was the fate of Long Beach, which was sinking, thanks to years of oil drilling that undermined the city. The naval shipyard also had caused geological problems and was threatening to move out. On a tour of the area, Cranston saw Navy officials walking on docks that were knee-deep in salt water, a yacht club that had sunk some forty feet behind a dike holding back the ocean, and other damage estimated at some $90 million, compounded by the conflicting interests involved – oil companies, the city, state and federal governments. [28]

Cranston was outspokenly impatient with Long Beach for failing to address and solve its problems, and pledged that the Lands Commission would be "rigorous and vigorous in carrying out a policy of preventing further damage" by prohibiting "further drilling that might cause subsidence." Ultimately the legislature approved aid to pump water underground to replace extracted oil and repressurize the foundations of Long Beach. For Cranston it was a "unique opportunity to learn about resources" like oil, he said, and he asked for funding for a researcher to help him understand the state's oil-leasing policies. He had campaigned on seeking more dollars from state tideland oil production by "royalty" instead of "bonus-bidding" from private companies in order to make the system more open and fair. He helped engineer new arrangements with oil companies to lease state-owned tidelands and pay the full value of oil. Cranston chalked up experience dealing with "some of the hardest, shrewdest businessmen in the world," he said of the negotiations. He learned to deal with corporate personalities in order to understand the game of bidding and ruthless competing that went on between rival companies for use of the state's oil resources. His role, he knew, was to protect the public interest, "since the public owned the oil." He also looked at other ways to increase state revenues, like raising the one-cent-per-acre grazing leases on state lands. [29]

Cranston stood firm in favor of a Lands Commission prohibition of oil-drilling platforms on state leases within one mile of shore in certain areas, notably off Santa Barbara (prescient, in light of a 1969 oil spill in its channel). At a public hearing in 1960, he said the commission was "well aware of the great beauty of the coastline and considers it a natural asset to be protected." There were then 30,000 acres under lease in that area and the state was considering leasing another 50,000 acres for oil drilling. [30]

And therein lay the rub. The state needed money, the oil was out there, how to get it without defiling the environment on land and sea? Cranston had to reassure people that drilling could be done without that happening, telling Orange County audiences that it merely involved sending barges offshore, drilling a well and piping the oil out. But a local columnist derided Cranston's argument that offshore drilling was "painless," portraying him as "swallowing quickly so he wouldn't drool as he hopefully eyed the Orange [County] coastline." Once the well was drilled, Cranston said, there was nothing to indicate that an oil well even existed – merely a buoy which could be removed if dangerous to shipping. He was asked whether pressure for drilling might lead to repeal of the 1955 Cunningham-Shell Act that prohibited drilling in state-owned tidelands south of the Santa Ana River and Huntington Beach. "There's no suggestion at the present time that any change be made," Cranston "quickly averred." But offshore oil was a resource that could help pay the state's bills, he reminded audiences. [31]

The commission ultimately set up the Tidelands Oil Company with money put up by oil firms to explore off the California coast. [32]

During his reelection campaign in 1962, Cranston became chairman of the Lands Commission and announced that his immediate objective was "the earliest possible resumption of development of the Wilmington oil field" off Long Beach, believed to be one of the richest sources of oil in the West. The promise of $500 million from the field would relieve the cost of a new state water plan. In the previous three years, the state had reaped more than $66 million from the coastal oil resource, and interest in exploiting it was mounting. Again he stressed that the commission would "see to it that no tidelands oil development injures the beauty and recreational value of our shore." (Four oil platforms in Long Beach Harbor were cleverly disguised as "islands" by a landscape architect to mitigate the argument against them as eye-sores.) Cranston also opposed dredging and mining off Palo Verdes. [33]

There were antiquated matters to address, too, some of them amusing. Interest had not been paid on an obligation made in 1899, he found. And there was $2,806 still sitting in a war-bond fund established in the 1850s during the Gold Rush to finance expeditions against troublesome Indians. "*Does anyone have an old Indian war bond to cash in?*" a newspaper headline joked, "*Paleface keep wampum in reserve*." The then-new state had sold the bonds to raise quick money and petitioned Congress for reimbursement to provide for the common defense, Cranston explained of the unexpected find. "It seems improbable that anyone will ever again present an Indian war bond for payment. But we shall keep the account intact on the off-chance that the bonds may yet turn up" for redemption. "The tragedy is," he added, "that most of California's 20,000 Indians were of peaceful persuasion. Not many – except for perhaps Chief Jose Rey of the Chowchilla Tribe and Chief Winnemucca of the Washoes – could justifiably be called 'hostile.' Many of the others were unfortunate victims of irresponsible adventurers who would create an Indian 'war' where none otherwise existed – and finance it at government expense." [34]

He also found 500,000 acres of state land left over from acreage that the federal government had given California when it became a state in 1850. The lands would be sold to the public, Cranston told a realtors convention. Other surprises came from bank vaults that held a myriad of treasures from gold coins to a set of embalmed Siamese twins. Another unexpected task surfaced when outgoing Governor Knight complained that he did not like his official portrait and wanted one in which his eyes followed viewers. Cranston had to withhold a $3,000 authorization until the legislature decided whether it wanted to pay for a second portrait of Knight. Cranston also appealed for missing pictures of five former controllers to put in a gallery of all who had served since 1849, telling reporters that he enjoyed doing historical research and the serendipitous finds that resulted. The item got wide press coverage. [35]

A guilt-ridden person sent Cranston an anonymous letter enclosing $30 "to cover the cost of food I ate and some medicine I used and any other item I used" while working at a state hospital. "I am trying to make my peace with God," the letter said. [36]

Cranston personally delivered a retirement check to the oldest teacher in California on the occasion of her confirmation by the Episcopal Bishop of Los Angeles at age 104. Born in Iowa in 1858, Miss Kate Hukill had begun teaching in 1877 and had retired in 1923. [37]

Cranston himself practiced fiscal restraint in using his perquisites – Capitol garage mechanics reported that his official car's battery kept running down because he did not drive it. He said that he wanted to conduct business from his office, not on wheels, and did not know what to do with the car. (He did jot notes on the merits of various kinds of cars at one point, apparently considering buying one for Robin. A "Corvette" he decided was "too powerful" and expensive to repair.) [38]

The controller also sat on a Board of Control originally set up to hear taxpayer grievances. Franchise Tax Board chairman Bert Levit invariably was unsympathetic to claimants and the three-person board generally denied claims, to Cranston's discomfort. He flinched when Levit actually berated claimants for taking up the board's time, or refused to see merits in their claims. Deciding that it was not a good place to spend his time, Cranston designated his deputy to represent him on the board. [39]

He would take action, though, when a somewhat unorthodox claim came before it. An African-American laborer, accused of murdering his girl friend in 1958, brought a wrongful-conviction complaint after another man subsequently confessed to the murder. The defendant, John H. (Tennessee) Fry, who consistently maintained his innocence, had been convinced by his public defender to plead guilty of involuntary manslaughter and sentenced to San Quentin prison. Six months later, another woman was murdered and the killer confessed to both. Governor Brown pardoned Fry in June, 1959. But Fry pursued redress, although no one had ever collected damages for pecuniary injury in the Board of Control's history. Cranston ordered a full investigation that included a hearing in San Francisco where the murder had occurred. The board finally voted to award Fry $3,000, and the legislature raised the amount to $5,000. But Fry's claim was based on his loss of earnings, so the question arose as to whether the compensation was taxable income. Cranston shepherded the matter through the Franchise Tax Board, as well, and Fry was not taxed. The story sparked news commentaries about the two men "rather far apart in life's station. The wheels of justice…grind slowly, but every once in a while there's a spark in somebody that ignites a fury against injustice, and the wheels…not only start up but move with comparative speed…. Although he has weightier problems on his mind, like keeping track of most of the state's financial transactions, Cranston pressed" on, with the result to Fry's benefit. Cranston's prodding also led to a change in board procedures to have full hearings on such claims in future. [40]

Another complainant was not so fortunate, nor so innocent, it turned out. William G. Bonelli, a former member of the Board of Equalization, had been indicted in 1954 for liquor-license bribery. Once a political science professor at Occidental College, member of Phi Beta Kappa honorary society and the Sons of the American Revolution, he had fled to Mexico and was fighting extradition. Now sixty-two, he wanted to get the state pension due him for government service, $445.45 a month. He applied for it from an "aristocratic" Mexican prison cell, where he spent seven months. Newspapers were loud in mocking the request from "a man on the lam." Cranston asked attorney general Stanley Mosk whether Bonelli were entitled to receive the pension while an out-of-state fugitive, and when Mosk ruled that he was not, announced that Bonelli would get checks "over my dead body!" He had made "a mockery of the concept of public service," Cranston said. If Bonelli wanted his pension, he could "come and get it," headlines blared of Cranston's challenge. He also threatened to sue Bonelli for illegal liquor-license gains. His pension by 1959 had accumulated into thousands of dollars, and Bonelli kept up the public *contre-temps* with defiance and sardonic insults to the state. His $10,688 pension ultimately was held in abeyance while he was a fugitive. (Cleared of tax-evasion charges in 1966, Bonelli still was trying to get his pension by appealing to the State Supreme Court.) One effect of the publicity was to make Cranston's name well known throughout the state as a good guy protecting the public coffers. Such favorable publicity, Pat Brown had pointed out, was important to a politician's future career. [41]

Despite the Democratic sweep of top state offices in 1958, there was warfare within the party. Brown's principal adversary was Los Angeles Assemblyman Jesse Marvin Unruh, now a giant of a man in his late thirties popularly dubbed "Big Daddy" – his surname meant "unrest" in German. He had worked his way up through the Democratic Party from his years as a student at the University of Southern California (class of 1948) where he had organized veterans (he had served with the Navy in the Aleutian Islands in World War II) and been the center of left-wing challenges to traditional fraternity domination of campus government. He was elected to the Assembly in 1954. En route to becoming the powerful Assembly Speaker in 1961, Unruh had shifted to the moderate wing of the party. Political writers made much of the Unruh-versus-Brown-Cranston antipathy, contrasting Cranston, the healthy track star, with the gluttonous Unruh. [42]

Unruh had gotten powerful, in part, after helping the savings-and-loan industry escape adverse legislation in 1957-58, for which he received campaign contributions, much of which he had given to other legislators, thereby gaining their appreciative loyalty. He also dispersed money from lobbyists to fellow candidates in need. "*Money is the mother's milk of politics*," Unruh was fond of saying, and "*if you can't take their money, eat their food, drink their booze and vote against 'em, you don't belong here*." [43]

One pundit wrote a poem satirizing Unruh, entitled "My Heart belongs to Daddy."

"I used to be in CDC
I dined on a hamburger patty.
But I had no strain in
In my last campaign.
Now my heart belongs to Daddy….
Sorry, Alan, Glenn and Paddy.
Though you know that I love you all,
Still, my heart belongs to Daddy….
At Frank Fats' his banner unfurls…
Calls for votes…for booze…for girls.

Stand on principle all you please,
Still my heart belongs to Daddy….
So go ahead,
Pretend he's dead,
Cheering and calling him fatty.
I'll get my kicks in '66
'Cause my heart belongs to Daddy." [44]

As a way of trying to change his "boss" image, Unruh nevertheless had helped to elect Brown in Southern California by paying college students $10 to do precinct work on election day, and had been rewarded with the chairmanship of the important Ways and Means Committee that controlled financial legislation. In that position, Unruh would be pivotal to Brown who decided that reorganization of his top-heavy executive branch of government was essential. (There was not room for the governor's cabinet to meet in his office.) Brown appointed a commission to draft a reorganization plan, in the course of which the controller's office necessarily was affected. Republican Assemblyman Milton Marks of San Francisco reintroduced a long-discussed plan for a Finance Department that would take tax functions out of the controller's office, abolish the Franchise Tax Board and strip the Board of Equalization of many duties. Unruh surprisingly backed the Marks proposal when it came to his committee. His objective, he said, was to strengthen the governor's office, on which he had his own designs.

Cranston saw the ploy and the effect that the new department would have in stripping his office of responsibilities. He argued that it over-centralized power. But when he and other officials appeared to testify against the bill, Unruh pointedly kept them waiting. When permitted to speak, Cranston made the point that changes would not save but *increase* costs, put authority in *appointed* rather than elected officials, and curtail protections against fraud and the public interest. "There is no virtue in mere bigness," he stated of the plan, which was more likely to create red tape than streamline government business. "It would be needless folly to increase the cost of collecting taxes and diminish the voice of the people…when we are asking the people of California to pay higher taxes," he argued. Others, like Board of Equalization chairman Paul Leake, worried about giving the governor "the powers of a tyrant" in fiscal matters. Unruh, who had characterized Brown as "a tower of Jell-O," wondered sardonically if opponents to the plan, including many Democrats, feared the present chief executive would become a czar, as San Francisco Assemblyman Edward Gaffney suggested would happen. [45]

The centerpiece of debate became the controller's role. Other proposals were considered, including one that Brown quietly backed which would cut the controller's responsibilities and transfer some of his staff to other departments. A *San Francisco Examiner* cartoon depicted red-tape-plagued taxpayers conceding that they liked their "*old* octopus best." Cranston now was pitted against Unruh. Deputy controllers Ralph McCarthy and Irwin Nebron urged Cranston to fight what clearly was an initial effort to dismantle their department's authority. Cranston did fight, knowing that it meant angering Unruh. [46]

In October, 1959, after nine months in office, Cranston announced that his auditors had saved the state about $1 million by finding exorbitant or illegal claims and improper charges against the public treasury. A *Sacramento Bee* writer said that while "not announced as a direct counter-attack on the…proposal to take auditing powers away from the controller's office, that was its inevitable effect. The guess in political circles…is that the elective controller, though an ardent booster of his fellow Democrat, Governor Brown, will not be among those cheering for the reorganization committee's plan to shift the auditing functions and most other duties of the controller's department to a new and broadened state finance agency under an appointive administrator." Cranston argued that auditing should be in the hands of an independent elected official. (He identified eight such efforts in the previous quarter century to abolish or strip the office of authority.) He defended auditors as "good investments" – they paid "for far more than their salaries with the savings effected by their sharp-eyed practice of spotting errors." There also was a "subtle benefit" – the "deterrent" of removing temptation to cheat the state. [47]

In the end, Cranston's side prevailed and Unruh, as predicted, was infuriated. "He took it as a personal affront," Cranston would recall of the humiliating defeat in Unruh's own committee. "You sure took the governor's pants off in my committee," he growled at Cranston in the underground garage of the El Mirador Hotel when the two met. Cranston knew that he had made a long-time enemy who would not soon forget the humiliation. He told his sister that, in retrospect, it had been a mistake to challenge Unruh on what was a relatively unimportant issue, particularly as he came to realize that Unruh considered himself a student of government organization. [48]

Assessing their relationship, Cranston admitted to a visceral enmity between the two at the height of their disputes. "Unfortunately it seemed to become that," although they did make peace in later years. Unruh was easy to dislike, but "he was also easy to like – he was very popular with some people. He had an interesting personality and an irresistible sense of humor – and he was a *very* skillful politician, and politicians enjoy that capacity in another politician," as Cranston described his long-time adversary. "Even when he had me most upset, I couldn't help but admire his immense political skill. We were mainly driven apart by his scorn for volunteers, and the fact that I was number-one volunteer in the state, organizing the CDC," he laughed. Unruh "saw it as a barrier to his ambitions. He wanted to be governor, and he felt that the CDC would never endorse him for governor. And the CDC endorsement was tantamount to winning the nomination for quite a few years. So it was just a *natural* problem between us." Unruh did have "one odd characteristic," Cranston said of negative aspects to Unruh's personality. "He liked using force, bashing people. Rather than try to *persuade* you to do something, he might prefer to *force* you, just for the pleasure of using force." He also "could be very charming," witty, amusing and quick-thinking on his feet. [49]

Cranston subsequently reorganized the controller's office, reducing its civil service rolls by moving people to other positions without replacing them in the controller's office.

His office also simplified the state income-tax form, as he had promised to do. An editorial said that "the fact that it's printed on a card is a convincing indication that it must be an improvement on the old state form.... Controller Alan Cranston deserves credit for arranging early use of the form." It would "do away with only the drudgery – not the pain – of paying state income taxes," Cranston conceded, because the new tax law required more taxes from high-bracket taxpayers. He worked on tightening tax-evasion laws as chairman of the Franchise Tax Board, and overhauled the State Board of Equalization (all-Democrats for the first time in its 80-year history) with a new plan to review employee responsibilities. [50]

By the end of the year, Cranston could proudly report that the state had "rediscovered fiscal responsibility – the downward trend of an entire decade was reversed in a matter of months. We have steadied a rocking boat," he boasted of the Brown administration. [51]

Brown after his first year in office was compared to Governor Hiram Johnson's 1911 progressive regime for the amount of liberal legislation that had been enacted. They included fair-employment and fair-housing laws, a minimum wage, prohibition on cross-filing, tax reforms and increases that balanced the budget, a master plan for higher education, a smog-control bill, agreement between north and south over water resources, and creation of a Consumer Counsel to look after consumers' interests in the marketplace. With Unruh steering many of the bills, the legislature also abolished literacy tests and loyalty oaths for state employees including university professors. Brown now was a nationally-known figure, and Cranston was happy to be riding on his coattails. [52]

California in 1960 had the biggest budget of any state in the union, but population was predicted to double in twenty years, from 15 to 30 million. How to keep the budget balanced without unduly raising taxes became the subject of Cranston's speeches. "Every Monday, California absorbs what amounts to a brand new city of 9,000 persons," he told audiences. "We have a staggering task in keeping pace and still being able to render the services needed." In other talks Cranston cited the fact that the University of California would have to double its facilities by 1970 to handle the increasing number of students. The state was moving toward being the most populous in the "democratic world" and would have a vital impact on other nations because of its industry. And while the Brown administration planned to balance the budget in its second year, dangers for the future lay in Cranston's favorite theme – the arms race. "Unless we find a way out of [it] and into an enduring peace, all that we believe in will be lost," he warned in 1960, reminding people that 80 cents out of every dollar went to defense. [53]

California also was suffering from a national recession. Unemployment was high, the general fund was low, taxes could not be cut. Brown's popularity began to drop, even behind Nixon as a possible contender for governor. Brown, disheartened, seriously considered not running again. Speculation on that possibility put Cranston forward among other Democrats who might run – Glenn Anderson, Stanley Mosk and Unruh. [54]

But while the boat had been steadied, there was a turbulent swell ahead. Brown, who philosophically opposed capital punishment, had stayed the execution of a man whose name would become as well known as the governor's. Caryl Chessman was on death row after conviction for robbery, kidnapping and rape. Jerry Brown, still in seminary, had influenced his father's decision. Cranston saw the compassion in the move but instinctively worried about its political ramifications. He spoke in defense of Brown's argument that the death penalty was unfairly administered and not a deterrent to crime. But the public was deeply divided on the issue. Brown went further and asked the legislature to ban the death penalty, angering many who resented being asked to vote on the controversial issue. Unruh, his aides reported, was so outraged that they had to keep him in his office until he cooled down. Brown, after all, was not up for reelection until 1962, but legislators had to face voters in 1960. Brown's stay ended and Chessman was executed in the gas chamber on the eve of the primary, May 2, 1960. "It proved to be the beginning of Pat's downfall," Cranston would reflect. [55]

1960 also was a presidential election year. Brown himself was considered a dark horse candidate in the event of a deadlock between John F. Kennedy, Adlai Stevenson, Senator Stuart Symington or Lyndon Johnson. Brown begged California delegates before the National Convention to "stand together and not let our party become involved in divisive internal difficulties. A Democratic split would be just what Nixon and the Republicans need most this year in this critically important state.... [I]t is most important that our delegation stand solidly together for the June 7 primary and not splinter among national candidates at this time," he wrote party leaders. Cranston loyally heeded the call to remain uncommitted publicly prior to the convention, but he told students backing Stevenson that Kennedy appeared to have the strongest support in California, with Symington "running a hard race." While he promised to consider Stevenson, Cranston subsequently told Clarence Heller, a party leader in San Francisco who was working hard for Kennedy, "I have a very high opinion of Jack, and it is rising still higher very rapidly. I am not yet quite ready to commit myself, Clary, but I wouldn't be surprised if I were with you before this thing is over with." He hedged to others who were backing Johnson and a group from the high-rent Sea Cliff section of San Francisco urging that former Ambassador to India, Connecticut Congressman Chester Bowles, be the party's nominee. "Frankly, I have always had it in the back of my mind that it would be wonderful if he emerged," Cranston wrote "Sea Cliff Democrats." "I have known him ever since I became acquainted with him while he was Ambassador to India in 1952," and, he added, he would have dinner with Bowles that evening in Los Angeles. "If Chester Bowles doesn't win the nomination himself, I am quite confident that he will be very prominent in the conduct of foreign affairs in the administration of either Jack Kennedy or Adlai Stevenson," he predicted. (Bowles got one-half of a delegate vote from the California delegation; he served as Democratic platform chairman in 1960, was named Under Secretary of State in 1961 and reappointed Ambassador to India, 1963 to 1969.) [56]

When the delegation convened in June in Sacramento, it had the unpleasant task of trying to depose Paul Ziffren as a national committeeman, a move led by Governor Brown. Ziffren had come out of Chicago "boss" politics and built a lucrative legal practice in Hollywood and Beverly Hills. Smart, charming and a leader of the liberal wing of the party, he had become a national committeeman in 1953 (for backing Kefauver who selected Ziffren after winning the California primary) and was close to national party chairman Paul Butler (also liberal and a supporter of Adlai Stevenson). Ziffren had been associated with the CDC from the outset and had many loyal followers. He and Cranston had always been friendly but Brown, closer to the establishment side of the party, was cool to Ziffren who was conspicuously absent from Brown's gubernatorial campaign. Elected Democrats in California and nationally, notably Senate Majority Leader Lyndon Johnson and House Speaker Sam Rayburn, also were antipathetic to Ziffren who had allied himself with Butler's attempt to set up a policy advisory council. They complained that Ziffren got publicity but failed to raise money for the party. He had gained notoriety in 1954 by withholding national campaign funds from Congressman Jimmy Roosevelt because of his marital problems. Knowland, as a campaign tactic, had jumped on the anti-Ziffren bandwagon by trying to link him to a Chicago mob figure who had been murdered three years earlier, hinting that mobsters tied to Democrats were moving into California. Ziffren also was associated with a construction company (Enterprise) under investigation by the Federal Housing Administration for fraud. The Knowland attack backfired, according to *News-Call Bulletin* political editor Jack McDowell, ironic since Knowland had mistakenly assumed that Ziffren was close to Brown. By 1960 Brown wanted to get rid of Ziffren, who made no secret of his liberal views. [57]

Cranston took Geneva and the boys to the Democratic National Convention in Los Angeles, which would be volatile. Brown staged a successful "coup" in which Ziffren was replaced as national committeeman by Attorney General Stanley Mosk. Greenaway, watching from the audience, saw that Brown, sitting on stage, took notes on how everybody voted. "Talk about intimidating!" Greenaway thought of the governor's tactics. Cranston generally went along with Brown, even though he was more aligned politically with Ziffren, and Greenaway suspected that Cranston voted against him.

Cranston also found himself in a hard place between presidential contenders that included Governor Brown running as a "favorite son." Cranston's personal preference was Stevenson. But the nomination would be bitterly contested by California Democrats. Liberals and CDC volunteers had been insulted when the Boston-bred Kennedy forces suggested that party operatives expected to be paid. There was a "big revolt" against that, Greenaway said. "We were proud of being volunteers. So the club movement said, 'We don't want to have anything to do with Kennedy.' I and others think that J. F. K. caused the end of the volunteer movement in California. It had been non-partisan, with no political machinery, and people were not accustomed to getting paid." Brown privately was "100 percent for J. F .K." and withdrew himself from contention, allowing his backers to vote for their choice. Most CDC rank-and-file Democrats, though, were for Stevenson. Cranston was expected to vote for him, but he was afraid to go against Brown, so he announced that he would vote for Kennedy (Nebron announced for Stevenson, a compromise they worked out). [58]

Cranston kept careful tallies in pencil of votes by each state delegation, writing on his yellow legal pad at one point, "need 761." Despite Brown's backing of Kennedy, the delegation remained divided (junior Senator Clair Engle voted for Symington), a measure of Brown's lack of control over it. The California delegation ultimately gave Stevenson its support but Kennedy would get the party's nomination. Brown and Cranston both would campaign for him. Kennedy would win that November but lose California to native-son Nixon by 35,623 votes. A show-down between Brown and Nixon in the 1962 governor's race loomed as a real possibility, although Nixon denied such aspirations. Cranston continued to warn audiences that Nixon would be Brown's likely opponent. [59]

With that in mind, Cranston and other Democrats tried to find ways to discredit Nixon. Cranston was a friend of *Long Beach Independent Press-Telegram* publisher Herman Henry "Hank" Ridder, who had received information about a loan made to Nixon in 1956 while vice president to bail out his family's business, Nixon's, Inc., which was in financial difficulties. The money, $205,000, was given by Howard Hughes' Tool Company to Nixon's mother Hannah M. Nixon. Ridder passed the information on to Fred Dutton, Governor Brown's campaign manager in 1960 and Assistant Secretary of State in the Kennedy administration, and to Cranston, asking that it be passed on to Attorney General Mosk. Ridder needed help from state and federal agencies to corroborate facts before exposing the story. [60]

According to an affidavit from an accountant, Phillip Reiner, Nixon's, Inc. was "then insolvent and could not qualify for any business loan." Hughes made the loan (secured it by a trust deed) through an intermediary, attorney Frank Waters of Los Angeles, who gave the money to Hannah Nixon. She then loaned $165,000 to the family company "but the books did not disclose any entry for the remaining $40,000," Reiner testified. He was sent to meet a representative of Hughes' interests "on a street corner at Wilshire Boulevard and Flower Street," then driven to Whittier to examine the Nixon company books "as a favor for the Nixons." Nixon's brother Donald then asked Reiner to get Hughes' attorney to put "the rest of the money in escrow." Reiner reported that Nixon's was losing more than $5,000 a week. At a meeting at Hughes headquarters, attended by executive vice president Noah Dietrich, a committee was set up "to oversee the affairs of Nixon's, Inc.," and Dietrich asked attorney Waters to "call Dick and inform him of this decision," according to Reiner's statement.

By April, 1957, the vice president had approved dissolution of the management committee, and Reiner was told to inform others that Nixon "should not be named in [a] letter to a Hughes employee, and that the term 'Eastern division' [a dummy name for the Hughes company] was used as a device to conceal the identity of Richard Nixon," the affidavit said. Hughes' attorney then told Reiner that "'it would be a good idea' to get the name of Hughes' operative (Frank Waters) off of the $205,000 trust deed between him and Hannah Nixon because of a law suit and legislative investigation of certain oil leases in the Los Angeles harbor tidelands in which Waters and Dietrich were parties. The deed was reassigned to Reiner and back-dated. Hughes' lawyer, Reiner said, "made it clear to me that the purpose of the assignment was to conceal the true nature of the transaction." Reiner did as he was asked, and when he received a check payable to Hannah Nixon's account, Reiner was told that it was rent money ($797) from the Union Oil Company station on the Nixon lot in Whittier. Reiner received other checks through 1958, and was told that "when Dick comes to the West Coast," Hughes' people would discuss with him conveying the Whittier lot before the end of the year "to establish a capital gains situation" for Hannah Nixon "to be offset by taking a bad-debt deduction for her $165,000 loan to Nixon's, Inc." Reiner received the deed to the Nixon lot, which he turned over to Hughes' attorney. Tax ramifications stemmed from the fact that Reiner reported the money received, $14,290, as income on his 1958 federal and state income tax returns. In 1960, however, he paid the sum over to Hughes' attorney. Reiner added one other tidbit:

> "In the fall of 1959, at the [elite Los Angeles men's] Jonathan Club, [Hughes' attorney James J.] Arditto was asked if he thought Richard Nixon would be a candidate for president in 1960, and Arditto pointed to me [Reiner] and said, 'If he does, this man's name will become a household word all over the United States,' and in this context Arditto referred to me as 'Mr. Goldfine.'"

The reference was to a 1958 scandal that ended with the firing of Eisenhower's friend and White House Chief of Staff Sherman Adams. It stemmed from gifts to Adams of a vicuna coat among other things from Boston textile manufacturer Bernard Goldfine, who was being investigated for Federal Trade Commission violations; he was cited for contempt of Congress for refusing to answer questions about his relationship with Adams. Nixon falsely claimed that he had the unpleasant task of telling Adams to resign. [61]

"We do not need any additional information to make a good story," Ridder told Fred Dutton in April, 1961, "because the single fact that Mrs. Hannah Nixon is still the owner on record of the property is astonishing enough." Reiner had been "used as a stooge" by Hughes' people, Ridder said, hoping to get Reiner to cooperate in the story by asking for a refund of the taxes he had paid since he never owned the property and had paid all the income back to the Hughes company. "This request for a tax refund will be a reasonable and proper start for both the state and federal tax agencies to look into the entire matter," Ridder hoped. "The basic facts remain unchanged. The deal was a phoney…. The money is still either a bribe or a gift, depending upon how polite you want to be. Unless this story is fully investigated and brought out, Nixon will run for Governor of California and probably be elected." Ridder would be glad to discuss it with the U. S. Attorney General, the president's brother, Robert F. Kennedy, which Dutton could arrange. "I recognize all the difficulties of breaking the story, such as bringing poor old mother into it, but, after all, poor old mother was brought into the picture by the Nixons originally." [62]

If Reiner could not be persuaded to file for a tax refund, Ridder told Cranston, "we will have to think of some other move to open up the necessary avenues for finding out what actually happened in the transfer of cash and the payment or non-payment of taxes." Ridder and his wife, he added, had voted Cranston and Geneva "our favorite houseguests."

A week later he told Cranston, "It becomes increasingly clear that at some point, necessary and appropriate governmental inquires should be made" to corroborate what the newspaper had dug up. "Otherwise it would be embarrassing for us to break the story and suddenly discover that there were a lot of loopholes. Our plan is to break the story jointly with the McClatchy papers in California, the *Washington Post* and some national magazine and also possibly with Drew Pearson, since he broke the story in the first place." Any "undue delay" might make it possible "for some of the information to be brushed under some convenient rug." He wanted to know if there were serious interest in taking action on the part of government officials. Reiner did agree to seek the tax refund in order to trigger a tax investigation in California. Ridder hoped to "track these matters down before any additional steps are taken to conceal the facts." [63]

The loan was among other fodder that Democrats were gathering on Nixon for a possible 1962 gubernatorial campaign attack. Cass Canfield sent Cranston a three-page list of intellectuals in California who might rally against Nixon. It included writers Wallace Stegner, Aldous Huxley, Ray Bradbury, George Stewart, Mark Harris, Mark Shorer, newspaper columnist Art Hoppe, architectural writer Allan Temko, and nuclear physicist Edward Teller. Cranston also considered writing an article about Nixon. One note for the article read, "lack of character and conviction, perhaps not evil, but not good." [64]

The Hughes loan, which was not repaid, would dog Nixon for years. He blamed revelations about it on his losses for president against Jack Kennedy in 1960, after Drew Pearson revealed it one week before election day, and for governor against Pat Brown in 1962. In that campaign, Nixon erupted in San Francisco's Chinatown after opening a fortune cookie in a public ceremony and finding a message reading "What about the Hughes loan?" It had been planted by political-prankster Dick Tuck.

Cranston meanwhile was riding high amidst conjecture over his own future. The Willows *Daily Journal* had changed its tune and by 1961 was editorializing that Cranston was "scrupulously thorough," and had high employee morale in his shop which was run "efficiently and economically, to the great advantage of California's taxpayers." The paper gave Cranston credit for "tact, plus firmness on matters of conviction" that had earned him respect from his department and the "cooperation and admiration of legislators." He again was being mentioned as a possible U. S. Senate candidate, while his frequent appearances around the state as a party speaker prompted political writers to suggest that Cranston might even challenge Brown for governor. Republicans were taking note of the rising politician. [65]

In a column for a Democratic newsletter in January, 1961, Cranston reported that in two years as stewards of California, Democrats "produced a catalogue of legislation that has blazed new trails, dislodged vexatious stalemated issues, and implemented California's predestined role as America's greatest state." The record might be attacked by opponents but it could not be "downgraded," he said, comparing it to progressive Hiram Johnson's for "pioneering accomplishment." Democrats could pitch it in 1962 with "no apology." There was much yet to be done "in the fields of education, social welfare, public health, natural resources, labor-management relations, but the governor is not without ideas," Cranston said with enthusiasm. Even the water controversy had been resolved – one issue on which Cranston parted from Brown – "but few things that are daring and visionary are ever achieved without a certain amount of contentiousness." The fact that the state now was on a solid fiscal basis refuted "the myth so assiduously cultivated by the opposition that Democrats cannot manage the people's money." Governor Brown called their legislative program "responsible liberalism." Cranston called it "sensible liberalism." [66]

Cranston no longer was "an unknown," a Long Beach columnist wrote in October, 1961, although his identification with the CDC "led many businessmen to look warily on him as a leader of his party's ultra-liberal fringe. They were surprised after his election [in 1958] to discover that he was a competent administrator." Among his major reforms in the controller's office was installation of a $1-million computer with a data-processing system, one of the most modern in the world, Cranston bragged, saying that it would save money and pay for itself in five years. [67]

Geneva, too, was getting more publicity, although "being a wife and mother to her husband and two sons is much more important than being 'Mrs. State Controller,'" a feature story stated in 1961. She was pictured weeding the yard by the pool in a profile to show her down-to-earthness. Rob now was fourteen, Kim, ten. Both went to public school in Sacramento, and Geneva cited as her principal activity working with parent-teacher groups and raising bonds for the school district. "It's one thing for Alan to be involved with schools in his job – and the children are proud of him – but he works on *his* level. My work is for *them*, on their level, and it is important." Asked how the move to the state capitol had changed her life, Geneva said that it hadn't except that they entertained more than in the past, particularly during the legislative session. "This, perhaps, is the most interesting part of being the wife of a man in political office," she said of her sociable nature. "I've been able to meet so many interesting people from all over the state." Everyone in Sacramento wanted to "meet everybody else," which made life "like a grand tour of the state while staying at home." She preferred having small groups to their house. "I like to cook, but I can't do well for a huge crowd, so we have groups of six or eight for dinner, and in this way we really get to know our guests." Asked if she always did her own cooking, she answered modestly, "Oh, yes." Eleanor Fowle, who was present at the interview, interceded, "She won't tell you what a really capable hostess she is, or what a marvelous cook." (Among those whom she entertained was Mrs. Orville Freeman, wife of the U. S. Agriculture Secretary.) She also did most of her own housework. To a question about whether her husband's work kept him away from home a good deal Geneva answered, "Yes and no. I try to keep life as peppy as possible when he's away. But when he returns, there is plenty of excitement, especially for the boys." She admitted to belonging to the PALS Club (Protective Association for Lonesome Souls), a non-partisan group of officials' wives that met socially during legislative sessions. [68]

One newly-married couple, Jack and Vicki Tomlinson, who received an invitation for dinner remembered being surrounded by "all kinds of animals – and, if you looked carefully enough, there'd be a couple of humans, too. The highlight of the evening was this huge pig, Snowball, who had free run of the house, so you'd be sitting there and Snowball would sort of cruise by!" Geneva and Cranston said little at the dinner table, they noted. [69]

In another interview, Geneva confessed that the last person she wanted to look at her checkbook was her husband, who left the bookkeeping at home to his wife. She repeated a joke about the controller's electronic machine that issued some 17,000 checks: It automatically locked when all the money in an account was expended and would not unlock until a new deposit was made. Men often asked where they could get a similar machine for their wives, she told a reporter. [70]

Geneva candidly called herself an "odd sort of candidate's wife" because her first priority was looking after the children's interests. "I don't want them to grow up allergic to politics," she said in an interview with the *News-Call Bulletin*. Her boys led "an interesting life in a very political family," she felt. "They read newspapers, they're concerned about China and India and Cuba. They meet interesting people at home. And they have fun riding horses in political parades." Of negative things that they heard about Cranston, she said, "We've told them it's part of the game. Your opponent can't be expected to say nice things about you," she shrugged. [71]

Friends like the Tomlinsons, though, noticed that political life was taking a toll on Geneva and her health, and that "Alan's driving ambition really seemed to have some drastic effect on his family." On one occasion, the Tomlinsons were asked to pick up the boys and take them to a reception. One of them had pants on that were six inches too short. Vicki showed him how to lower the pants below his waist so they "at least didn't show all of his socks." Vicki thought that Geneva felt "isolated" and was unhappy at being left alone much of the time. Other political couples, the Tomlinsons noticed, had similar experiences when an intelligent wife found herself left at home with children. Cranston staff also felt that Geneva was privately bored, angry, frustrated and lonely. [72]

Despite rumors to the contrary, Cranston made it clear that he would run for reelection in 1962. Republicans were reluctant to field any one against him, finally choosing a sixty-one-year-old savings-and-loan executive, conservative Assemblyman Bruce Reagan of Pasadena, described in press accounts as "blue-eyed, silver-haired, and dapper." Reagan this time was the little-known candidate for controller. [73]

Cranston was nominated unopposed and endorsed by the CDC convention in January, 1962. "First, let me introduce three of the best precinct workers in California," he said in accepting – "my wife, Geneva, and sons Kim and Rob." After the convention, Cranston wrote Eleanor, then in Greece, that "all troublesome resolutions were blocked, tremendous speeches by Ted Sorenson of the White House and Hubert Humphrey. Dick Richards was endorsed for U. S. Senate," as were all incumbents "without any problems at all. I gave 22 speeches in 24 hours!" [74]

All had not gone that smoothly, however. The CDC had approved a resolution to abolish the House Un-American Activities Committee, which would be used against CDC adherents, but voted down a resolution for fall-out shelters. Delegates had even booed President Kennedy's special counsel Sorenson for proposing a national shelter plan. [75]

In his formal announcement, Cranston called his term as controller a "priceless privilege." In addition to handling the state's "vast financial transactions," he wanted people to know that he had "dealt with the problems of individual citizens with the same care and dispatch as matters involving millions of dollars…for I serve not only the public, but each individual." He had begun a habit of jotting people's questions and concerns in a notebook when he met them at events. He cited among other accomplishments his role in "opening a new tidelands oil field off Long Beach which is expected to produce as much as a billion dollars for the state." [76]

Cranston's campaign activities ranged from milking a cow to barbeques. At an event to register voters, he was photographed lending his back to a man filling out the form. (Registration had dropped since the 1960 presidential year although the state population had increased by about one million. And even though Democratic registration was down by 300,000, and Republicans by only 83,000, Democrats still had a three-to-two majority.) A breakfast fundraiser in Pasadena featured movie stars Shelley Winters, Mercedes McCambridge and Barry Sullivan. Cranston used his award from the Italian government to attract voters from that community. A Stanford classmate wrote other alumni, "We can be very proud of the job our classmate is doing and I hope you'll let him hear from you with your vote for him on November 6. Let's keep Alan in office." Cranston's honorary reelection chairman in Marin County was ironic in light of later events: He was San Francisco State University professor and semanticist S. I. Hayakawa, whose expertise in "clarity and communication" were "indicative of the direct and open approach" that Cranston advocated "between the people and the officials they elect," a press release stated. The two men would face one another on opposite sides of the aisle some years later. [77]

When a friend and neighbor, political activist Ted Baer, asked Cranston why he put in such long hours and traveled so exhaustively, Cranston blurted out, "Because when I stagger across the finish line, I want to know that I've been everywhere and done everything that it's humanly possible for me to do." [78]

In Barstow he told locals about being booted off a freight train while a college student during the Depression, which the local paper touted in a headline about his appearance before the Chamber of Commerce. Substantively, he could brag to business leaders of putting $125 million that had been lying idle in checking accounts into investment and interest-bearing accounts that had earned the state an additional $65 million. He also had reformed how state bonds were sold, using competitive bidding rather than selling through a syndicate. [79]

His campaign flyer emphasized his accomplishments and pictured him with well-known party leaders like John Anson Ford as well as the family, using that year's Christmas photo showing Kim blowing a trombone and Rob holding pet cats. It touted his simplifying tax forms, regrouping property taxes from utilities, building up the State Teachers' Retirement Fund, and making possible a program to buy televisions for state colleges. [80]

Rallying the African-American vote and assuaging warring factions within the Democratic Party were additional challenges. One African-American campaign worker, San Francisco party activist and federal Civil Rights Commissioner (in the Kennedy administration) Aileen C. Hernandez, in a "personal and confidential" memo to Cranston, urged that he "mend some fences" with pro-CDC factions and "do some P. R. work in the Negro community." That was based on conversations with people like Joe Williams. He had cited "discontent" among CDC Democrats with Cranston's appointing six "anti-CDC" people as appraisers and the fact that Williams' own appointment resulted in "much hassling" when it "should have been a clear-cut decision." Cranston's problems were compounded by the fact that some in the party resented CDC control in Los Angeles and San Francisco, notably under the direction of Assemblyman Phil Burton. "I can recognize your reluctance to deal *through* P. B.," the memo said, "but I think we can overcome this with some effort." Cranston needed to cultivate people who felt left out, like Joe Williams who was "sensitive to problems" in the party structure. He could "be useful to the campaign," particularly with the African-American press and community, Hernandez believed. "I think you can get maximum cooperation out of Joe simply by doing what comes naturally – seeking his advice in areas of his own expertise and making him feel really important to your campaign," she said. She also was helping build relationships with the Hispanic community. Mexican-American Ed Roybal's campaign for Congress in Los Angeles that year was uniting Black and Hispanic voters throughout the state. From Williams' perspective, Cranston did not take Hernandez' advice, but others like Ann Eliaser observed that Cranston always "bent over backwards" for the African-American community. [81]

As a further warning, the June 5 primary results were worrisome. Although Cranston was uncontested and led the Democratic ticket in 25 of 58 counties, Democratic turnout was lower than in 1958. There also were fears that Bruce Reagan would be better financed than Cranston and would campaign aggressively. Primary votes for both candidates were close: Cranston had received 1.7 million votes to Reagan's 1.4 million, even though Cranston had spent ten times what Reagan had in the primary - $94,768 to Reagan's $8,788. Reagan was "a determined opponent," a Los Angeles columnist said. Reagan also accused Cranston of misleading voters regarding the state's finances. "Hard work and enthusiasm on everybody's part will be needed to carry Alan to victory in November," an appeal to voters from Cranston's campaign warned. Cranston played up his association with President Kennedy and groups like attorneys who backed him – more than 1,000 in Los Angeles had formed "Lawyers to Reelect Cranston."[82]

Cranston celebrated his forty-eighth birthday June 19, and his office staff surprised him with a party. Geneva and the boys joined them, Kim entertaining the group with magic tricks. [83]

One event on the campaign trail was frightening, however, and nearly cost Cranston his life. While taking an afternoon swim break in late October off Hermosa Beach, he was caught in a sudden riptide that carried him and a campaign worker, Robert Ginsberg, 150 yards out to sea. They did not realize that they were in danger at first. A news account incorrectly said that Cranston had been on the Stanford swim team and was "an excellent swimmer," but a lifeguard had to take a rescue buoy and swim out to the men. It took ten minutes to tow them to shore, and all three were swept under waves. "We could have been in real trouble out there," Ginsberg was quoted as saying. The lifeguard had just rescued another man, which Cranston had observed before starting his swim. Eleanor, who was also at the beach, had chosen to nap and "slept all through that episode. Alan came and woke me up and was chagrined that I hadn't been worried about him," she laughed of the recollection. "I remember it vividly. There was a lot in the papers about it." Cranston played down the danger and went back to speech-making, telling reporters that he had been swimming often, sometimes three miles from a Manhattan Beach pier. [84]

After he sent a personal note to a reporter in Pismo Beach, along with a copy of *Killing of the Peace*, Cranston got a back-handed compliment. Compared to "baby-kissing…prevaricating, mud-slinging" politicians, Bob Frantz wrote, Cranston was a "Ph.D. – a genius in the field." Cranston's note, addressing Frantz and his wife by their first names although they had only met once at a speaking engagement, thanked Frantz for "nice words" with hope that Cranston would "always merit" the reporter's "friendship and good will." That was "the way to win friends and voters," Frantz wrote. "What Mr. Cranston did not know was that we, confirmed Republicans, voted for him four years ago. He was the only Democrat to get our vote then and, like as not, he will get it again. This man has done a fine job in Sacramento, despite the obstacles." Frantz added that he thought Cranston would do an even finer job under a Republican governor. [85]

Cranston sent out postcards with a photograph of the family just before the November election and got lots of responses, pro- and con-. One person wanted to know who paid for it. A pundit sent Cranston a cartoon drawing of an overweight, slovenly man with a days-old beard, cigarette hanging out of his mouth and a glass of whiskey in his hand. Thanking Cranston for his postcard, the man "thought you would like one from me. State vocational guidance counselors suggest that I go into politics – since I am hopelessly inept in working for an honest living. What do you think?" "I agree with the vocational guidance counselors," Cranston wrote back. "Anyone with your sense of humor stands a good chance of success in politics." Another wrote him that the color photograph of his family and pets "struck a familiar chord with me because I love well-cared-for and loved pets. The pigeon in your wife's arm completed the picture of warmth and family strength." Cranston would be the only person the writer would vote for "because I am not an informed voter – no interest whatsoever," and "next time, I'll vote for you for governor!" [86]

Nixon, as Cranston had predicted, did run against Brown in 1962. Nixon's vitriol energized the waffling governor who decided to fight back, touting his administration's accomplishments. Cranston was one of Brown's biggest private and public boosters. Nixon, Cranston predicted, would draw out Democratic voters. Senator Kuchel again would face Richard Richards, but Kuchel had to beat a right-wing challenger, Lloyd Wright, for the Republican nomination. Wright's campaign chairman, Cranston and others noted, was actor Ronald Reagan, a former Democrat turned Republican. Cranston himself received a Kuchel campaign card sent to his former Los Altos Hills address, an indication that the moderate Republican was seeking votes from Democrats. [87]

The Brown-Nixon fight, however, made news because of the negativism. Brown played up Hughes' secret loan as indicative of Nixon's behavior. But Nixon would pull out all his old stops, leading one political writer to call 1962 "the year of the smear." [88]

One night at an event at a private home in Hollywood, Cranston was approached by a woman who asked to talk with him in the garden. Confessing that she worked for an advertising agency handling Nixon's campaign, she gave Cranston an envelope, then hurriedly left. When he opened it in the privacy of a locked bathroom, Cranston found original photographs of Pat Brown with a little girl whom Cranston recognized as a Laotian cerebral-palsy victim. Brown was bent over her with his palms held together in a traditional Buddhist greeting. The picture had been taken in the Assembly chamber for a cerebral-palsy fund drive. But the envelope also contained a composite photo that replaced the child with Soviet Premier Nikita Khrushchev, to whom Brown appeared to be bowing in reverence. An image of left-wing labor leader Harry Bridges was inserted in the background. The made-up photograph was intended for a pamphlet accusing Brown of being a communist sympathizer in the same way that Nixon had tried to insinuate Helen Gahagan Douglas and Jerry Voorhis. [89]

Cranston gave the incriminating material to Brown's public relations man Harry Lerner, and when the pamphlet appeared, Brown countered by revealing the doctored photos and the duplicity of the charges. But Brown was worn down by Nixon's tactics, awaking one night in a strange motel to fears that Nixon had put a woman in his bed – until Brown's wife Bernice rolled over.

Nixon and Cranston met once, on a hot day before a parade in Los Angeles. After exchanging a few words, Nixon unexpectedly thrust his finger into Cranston's chest and blurted, "You're not sweating!" "I felt as though I had been stabbed," Cranston related to his sister. A *Palo Alto Times* photograph of Nixon shaking hands in Cranston's home territory showed signs in the crowd reading, "*Viva* Alan Cranston - State Controller" and "Governor Pat Brown." Cranston was asked several times to look into Nixon's tax returns from his position on the tax board, once by a newspaper publisher and again by a man saying that he represented Brown. Such things had been done by candidates trying to unearth exploitable information in other campaigns, Cranston knew. The temptation was great, worried as he was that Nixon was a national threat, but Cranston refused the requests. He even got the Franchise Tax Board to approve a resolution ordering staff not to give board members information about tax returns unless instructed to do so by the full board at a public meeting. [91]

Nixon attacked the CDC during the campaign and singled out Phil Burton, who was running for Congress, as one Democrat who especially should be defeated. Burton retaliated by accusing Nixon of "distortion and dishonesty" and "shabby opportunism" for comparing the CDC with "right-wing John Birch fanatics," challenging Nixon to a debate, which never took place. The attacks further cemented Democrats' like Burton's and Cranston's hatred and distrust of Nixon. [92]

Other red-baiters also came out of the woodwork in 1962. One who falsely claimed to have been an undercover F. B. I. agent, Karl Prussion of Los Altos, put out a full-page political advertisement under the headline, "Candidates not qualified to combat communism," and a booklet playing on the letters CDC – "California Dynasty of Communism." He targeted three state leaders – Governor Brown, Attorney General Mosk and Cranston. "The Communists in the United States have chosen California as their pilot area to become the model Soviet State," Prussion's attack stated. "Subversives in California" were pushing "left-wing centralized hierarchy" to "control the individual and the family from birth to death. (THIS

IS COMMUNISM.) The inroads they have made are appalling...particularly in politics." While conceding that he did not imply his targets actually were, or sympathized with, Communists, Prussion said of Cranston, "During the winter of 1952, at a...meeting of the Communist Party, it was revealed to all comrades that 'One Worlder' Alan Cranston of Los Altos was preparing to form a new organization consisting of California Democratic Clubs [*sic*] (CDC)." By 1954, Prussion claimed, the CDC was full of "communist sympathizers, socialists, collectivists, liberals" who were guiding the Democratic Party "through hidden identity." Cranston was denigrated for his role in a "pet" issue – repeal of an amendment to the state world-government resolution that reserved the right of the United States "not to submit to a world court those issues that were wholly internal." He also associated with Democratic candidates whom Prussion accused of being communist sympathizers. "Why does not Alan Cranston rid the CDC organization, which he founded, of subversives?" Prussion asked. "I believe that Alan Cranston is naive on the subject of Communists and their machinations and therefore he does not qualify for state office!" [93]

Cranston's notes alongside the charges read, "twisted," "arms talk, '64," "forged telegrams" – and were checked "T[rue]" or "F[alse]." Eleanor noticed, however, that Cranston generally seemed unperturbed by the attacks.

The smear booklet prompted a question to Nixon on the national television program "Meet the Press." Nixon repudiated it, but Republicans found themselves having to deny that the booklet was tacitly sanctioned by them. Caspar Weinberger accused Democrats of manufacturing the smear issue, even of producing a bumper sticker that read, "Is Brown pink?" in order to "make silly charges of this kind." But Democratic state chairman Eugene L. Wyman retorted that his campaign workers had gotten the booklet at Republican headquarters in downtown Los Angeles and Beverly Hills, and that it was handed out at a Republican State Central Committee meeting (a CBS television news team had filmed people buying the booklet at Beverly Hills headquarters). "Either Mr. Nixon condones this type of campaigning or he has no control over his party," Wyman declared. Kuchel carefully stood apart on the matter, stating that "Whatever a person's views on Pat Brown's record, he is a good, loyal American as far as I'm concerned." [94]

The Democratic State Central Committee sued to have the booklet squelched and in late October, 1962, a Superior Court Judge ordered distribution of it to stop pending a hearing the day after the election. The party also sought $500,000 in damages for the false assertions that defamed and libeled the three candidates. [95]

Another booklet made even stronger charges against Cranston. "Is Alan Cranston mentally immature on the subject of communist machinations and, therefore, being duped?" it read. "Or is Cranston deliberately collaborating with the Communists?... Let us eliminate this man from his present position of authority and trust." It mocked Cranston as a "collectivist egghead" who was serving "the cause of world socialist government." Of the CDC it said, "The many thousands of Communists in California do not stay home evenings reading Marx and Lenin; they are in the CDC working for the Leninist objectives!" [96]

In retaliation, the CDC in the last two weeks of the campaign issued a "special bulletin" that accused Nixon and his strategist Murray Chotiner of doing "anything to win." "There is just one final answer to Chotiner-Nixon – the ballot box," it stated, reminding voters of Nixon's dirty tricks in all his previous campaigns. Nixon had admitted that he was counting on Democrats to stay away from the polls. "A fighting-mad bunch of Democrats up and down the state can" get out the vote, the CDC urged. Last-minute Republican mailings dealt "in fraud and deception in varying degrees," it warned, citing one that purported to come from a "Committee for the Preservation of the Democratic Party" that illegally used the party's name to solicit money. It actually came from Nixon headquarters. Another mailing claimed to come from "Democrats for Nixon." "YOU are the best answer to slurs against Democratic club members. Your neighbors know and respect you and will reject Nixon's slanders when you stand up with the truth," the CDC stated. "Point out the lie and misrepresentation in the Republican campaign." There already was evidence that it was backfiring. "There is no question that the average voter will react with revulsion to these tactics if he is made to understand what is going on." The "indignation and outrage" that people felt might end "this insidious nonsense," if people voted their consciences. [97]

Cranston's brother-in-law, Jack Fowle, was personally attacked by a man named Wendell L. Reich who sent a letter in April, 1962, to residents of Los Altos Hills. It opened by calling them "privileged to live in a lovely residential community" typifying "the rewards of personal accomplishment under the…spirit of free enterprise and freedom." Reich had been running for city council but was withdrawing because he said that he could not remain in an area that harbored leaders like Fowle, Los Altos Hills mayor and city councilman, who belonged to the American Civil Liberties Union (ACLU). Reich enclosed a leaflet accusing the ACLU of being communist-infiltrated. "I recently attended a lecture by a former member of the Communist Conspiracy [Prussion], a counter-spy for the Federal Bureau of Investigation, who reported a close association between the Communist Conspiracy…and the ACLU," Reich stated. "It was pointed out in this lecture that members of our city council (one of whom is running for reelection) are members of the ACLU. John Fowle…at that meeting identified himself not only as a member but also as an official of the ACLU…a matter of very serious concern." Reich hoped that voters would let their "consciences be" their guides when casting ballots and "vote for candidates dedicated to OUR way of life." [98]

The Fowles contacted a leading San Francisco attorney with Democratic ties, William K. Coblentz, to see whether Reich could be sued for libel. "While it is true that you have a cause of action for libel," Coblentz told them, "I would recommend that suit not be filed for the following reasons." He cited the fact that the ACLU had defended Communists, thus the defense might "obscure the issues to such an extent that a jury may well feel that you have not borne the burden of proof in suing" or "been libeled, inasmuch as there was some question concerning the ACLU" and its involvement with "questionable causes." Coblentz also worried about putting Fowle on the witness stand: "My feeling is that a good defense lawyer could propound such questions to you as to put you in an extremely embarrassing position as well as obscure the main question to the court." It might also be a lengthy trial, and any judgment would likely be nominal, far less than their legal costs. Accusations that people were Communist could easily be disproved, but Fowle's case was more complicated, Coblentz concluded. [99]

Fowle resorted to countering the accusations with leaflets supporting the ACLU and quoting a 1960 letter from President Eisenhower congratulating the organization on its fortieth anniversary and defense of civil rights. "Our people – and our neighbors overseas – are not blind to the fact that prejudice and economic discrimination still continue to deprive some Americans of guarantees provided by the Constitution and laws of the United States," Eisenhower's letter said. "It is good to be reminded that the members of the [ACLU] and the overwhelming majority of my fellow citizens are working together in this field with steadfast vigor and understanding." Fowle stated that he was "proud" to be a long-time member of an organization whose purpose was "to defend the American Constitution and Bill of Rights." [100]

Bruce Reagan also used the anti-Communist issue in his campaign materials. One political advertisement was headlined, "Veterans! Wage war again! Support anti-Communist and anti-left-wing state officials." Reagan blasted the CDC, citing his opponent's presidency of it, for taking "vicious, radical and subversive" positions like advocating abolition of the Un-American Activities committee and the loyalty oath, and favoring admission of Communist China to the U. N. Reagan also linked Cranston to Artie Samish, recalling his involvement in the Federalists' state resolution in 1949, and accused Cranston of building a "personal political machine" with ITA appointments, including one to a garbage collector. There had been "bad blood between these two men ever since" Reagan led the successful legislative fight to rescind the Federalists' resolution, a Los Angeles columnist reminded voters in August, 1962. [101]

Cranston declared that he disagreed with the CDC resolution to abolish the House committee. "I have not always approved of congressional investigative procedures," he said, "but I recognize the right of Congress to conduct – within Constitutional limits – investigations to obtain facts upon which to base legislation." He also had beaten back the CDC resolution calling for diplomatic recognition of Red China and admitting it to the U. N. (Cranston later qualified his position by saying that he "would not object" to trade with communist countries like China in "non-strategic" materials.) Governor Brown and Senate candidate Richard Richards also differed from the CDC on the issue. Although Cranston was being attacked by hard-core liberals, a minority in the party and largely Young Democrats, for seeming to move to the center politically, he remained extremely popular with the CDC, which was not, as Republicans charged, captured by the left of the party. [102]

Cranston continued to defend the CDC while putting its stands in perspective. Some of its controversial resolutions, he told a reporter, might better have been forgotten, "but it does not mean that an organization like the CDC is not healthy for democracy. The CDC has been vastly misrepresented and distorted by its opponents," he said in an interview for the *Sacramento Union*. [103]

In fact, Cranston was becoming more pragmatic in his politics. He had authored an anti-Communist plank for the 1962 Democratic Party platform. He described it to newspaper publishers after the party's convention in August as committing to a positive, rather than negative, stand on combating totalitarianism. In what sounded very much like Cranston's voice, it stated:

"Our belief in freedom compels a total rejection of the totalitarian philosophies, including communism and fascism. The contest between [those] and our democratic way of life is one between two wholly different approaches to the meaning of life. We believe in a form of society which places its highest value upon individual dignity. We totally reject a form of society in which the rights of men are sacrificed to the state. We believe the policies of totalitarian governments are sterile, unsound and doomed to failure. In time and with our help and guidance, those people now living under such governments will reject the intellectual prisons in which they are confined and will choose the eternal principals of freedom.

"It is our duty as Americans and our solemn obligation as part of the family of man to prove that a democratic society can meet the challenges of the 20th century, can fight vigorously against illiteracy and poverty, can provide means so that equal rights and opportunities are provided to all." [104]

Attorney General Mosk, however, made statements implying that the Federalists were a "subversive organization," causing Cranston and Don Edwards, a candidate for Congress in Santa Clara County, to ask state party chairman Roger Kent to intercede. Kent in turn asked a leading Federalist to talk to Mosk and "urge that he not slander the organization for his own sake and also for the sake of Cranston, Edwards and other Democratic candidates who might have been members or might be members." [105]

Cranston had to fight off other negative attacks. One month before the election, someone sent the *San Diego Union* a letter accusing Cranston of "setting an inheritance-tax trap for husbands and wives who come to California from another state." The allegations had to do with community property acquired elsewhere and brought into California, and with legislation enacted in 1957, before Cranston took office. The law had been changed in 1961, permitting conversion of such community property without being taxed. "In truth, Controller Cranston had absolutely nothing to do with the legislation to which reference was made," another letter to the *Union* editor said. [106]

He did get more favorable press, however. "The man behind this mountain of money is no cold-eyed calculator," *Los Angeles Herald-Examiner* columnist Mike Jackson wrote of the controller. "He's genial, articulate, with nothing in his background to suggest his present position…. I am not qualified to speak of Cranston's financial abilities. I just happen to like him as a person." Jackson cited his track record – "he was in good enough shape to beat his kids, Kim, 10, and Rob, 14, in a daily 330 race along the sands" of Manhattan Beach – and the fact that Cranston once had drawn cartoons and been a foreign correspondent. "He has been around and knows the score," Jackson wrote. "He does not give off the standard political platitudes." His menagerie, Jackson joked, "pose more problems than the whole State of California. The pig is fed oats. Dog steals the oats. Pig steals the grain from the horse. Cats eat the dog food and the hamster got out of its cage to chew up the draperies." The senior Cranstons take it all in stride, he wrote, sitting quietly "while son Kim asks you riddles and son Rob tells you 'sick' jokes." Cranston himself was the kind of person Jackson liked to be around – "easy-going, informed, humorous. He does not take a solemn stand on the soap box. He will talk about Mel Durslag [*Herald-*

Examiner sportswriter], Harpo Marx, Danny Kaye and William Faulkner. He has a professional's interest in newspapers. I never knew a tax collector could be that kind. But, then, Alan Cranston is the only one I have met." [107]

Cranston, in calling on newspaper editors and publishers, was quick to say that he was not a doctrinaire CDC-er, noted Lee Ettelson, former editor of the *San Francisco Examiner* who was visiting newspaper editorial boards on Cranston's behalf. That made an impression on those with pro-Republican views, especially when they learned from Cranston or his aides "something of Reagan's bed-fellows." The objective was to keep newspapers from endorsing Reagan, even if they endorsed the rest of the GOP ticket. Many papers, like the *Santa Rosa Press Democrat*, were "quite bitter about Pat [Brown], who has some fences to mend there, as you had," Ettelson reported. Some papers were upset with Cranston's replacement of long-time tax appraisers. In the case of the Santa Rosa paper, however, editors rescinded their planned endorsement of Reagan after hearing more about him. Even so, Ettelson said, "you seem to have a lot of fence-mending to do in many communities, for they all, with few exceptions, regard your first appointments as purely political and, of course, you are regarded as a bit to the left in many places on account of the CDC. The latter is a problem, as it always is…how to keep up the liberal tradition without having the organization taken over by the ultras. Indeed, the Republicans are having the same problem on the other side of the fence." But if Cranston seriously planned to run for higher office four years hence, he "had a problem and it should be worked out systematically and surely," Ettelson urged. Cranston needed to win the confidence of "many Republicans" and to win "back Democrats who felt slighted and abused." Meanwhile Ettelson would call on more newspapers, but "until the World Series is over, it is impossible to get appointments with people whose mind is on 'higher' things!" In particular he would try to see Scott Newhall, editor of the influential *San Francisco Chronicle* – which had not endorsed Cranston previously – and "pour some poison down the well." [108]

Ettelson also hoped for success with the otherwise pro-Republican paper in Santa Cruz but despaired of the Monterey paper's endorsing Cranston. "The paper is sore at you because you made a speech there telling how much the Brown administration had cut taxes and they claim the cut was one-twentieth of the tax *increases* made by the administration, [and] they don't like your extreme liberalism, as they call it, specifically your relationship with the CDC. [They] said that some of the stuff, particularly on disarmament, could not have pleased the Kremlin more if the Russkies and had written the resolutions." (Cranston was campaigning on the fact that the Brown administration had managed to reduce taxes for two straight years, despite the costs of the state's incredible growth, and planned to do so again in 1963. "Our tax cuts have not been huge," he said, "but since increases in 1959, the trend in California has been downward.") Brown, too, was out of favor with many publishers and editors. In Monterey they were angry at his Highway Commission's proposal to add freeway interchanges and increase the unemployment tax. "Altogether it was not a pleasant half hour" that Ettelson had spent with the Monterey paper's staff. [109]

Cranston would get more newspaper endorsements in 1962 than in his first race – twenty-five, compared to the mere five dailies that backed him in 1958. He now had credibility as a state official. The *San Francisco News-Call-Bulletin* thought his handling of ITA appointments had been "watchful and responsible." The *Examiner* credited him with "fine stewardship, invaluably husbanding public resources" and "protecting public interests in oil lands." "His restrictions on excessive earnings of part-time inheritance-tax appraisers, and his appointment of a larger staff of full-time appraisers at fixed salaries, brought order out of chaos in a long-neglected field of state business," it said, and "he deserves reelection." The *Palo Alto Times*, which had endorsed Kirkwood in 1958, reversed itself in 1962: "The surprise is not that Cranston's performance has reflected his intelligence and energy. We recognized those qualities in him four years ago.... Rather, the surprise is that Cranston, whose pre-1958 interests seemed to lie in other directions, has found the controller's work so challenging and satisfying." The *San Francisco Chronicle* came through, giving him endorsements from all three dailies in that city, which prompted a press release citing other major papers who favored Cranston: the *Los Angeles Herald-Examiner*, *Long Beach Press-Telegram*, even the normally conservative *Sacramento Union* as well as the McClatchey-owned *Bee* papers and the *Riverside Enterprise*. A number of normally Republican papers endorsed him, like those owned by Dean S. Lesher in Contra Costa County and Merced, and Orange County papers including one owned by the Scripps family in San Diego. He was the only Democrat that some papers endorsed. He also received strong labor support, endorsements from San Francisco's *China World* and African-American *California Eagle* which stated in an editorial, "He wiped out a color line that barred Negroes from positions as state inheritance-tax appraisers," three of whom now held such jobs. [110]

In the last few days of the campaign, Lee Falk joined Cranston on the campaign trail. "We're trying to get the pygmies to vote for him, too," Falk told reporters in Eureka where the two were photographed together, Cranston grinning broadly, in the Humboldt *Standard* newsroom. They were touted as "old friends and former play collaborators" dating back to World War II days. It was Falk's first trip to California in fifteen years. Normally he prepared his story-lines for the comic strips every day, but he had been "so busy chasing Alan" that he had not had much time to work. He delighted in telling newsmen how the *Phantom* strip had been a morale booster in Norway during the war when the Germans were trying to convince Norwegians that the United States was being destroyed. "They would look at *The Phantom*," which was being smuggled in, "and know that the Germans were lying. 'Phantom' became a password for the Norwegians" for a time, the only assurance they had that America was not being bombed, Falk said in an interview. He told how children in remote places like an Italian village, Estonia and the Yucatan jungle were devoted to the comic strips, which Falk called the "folk literature of the world, and for many their only contact with literature." Cranston's campaign took a back seat when the mustachioed Falk visited newspaper offices with him. He had used himself as the physical model for *Mandrake the Magician*, he told a *San Francisco Examiner* reporter. Falk "found politicking fun but exhausting," he confessed, although "almost everything I do winds up in one of my strips," and the campaign experience might, too – in a non-partisan way, he emphasized. "That, even for the hypnotic Mandrake or the ingenious Phantom, will be a neat trick," the *Examiner* reporter wrote. [111]

Eleanor, too, was active in the campaign, hosting fundraising events for her brother and other Democratic candidates. As the mayor's wife, she even helped take minutes of town council meetings. Politics were "discussed around our house all the time," she said for a feature story about her in the local Los Altos newspaper. She fielded "about 100 calls a week" and had to install a private line for personal use because their listed number was constantly busy with people calling for the mayor's help on various matters. Eleanor also served on the boards of a family-service agency, the League of Women Voters and the local Democratic council. But by 1962, both her children were grown, and she and Fowle wanted to "live more simply." Because she and her husband were known to be generous to the party and candidates, "we had to develop our defenses against appeals for help of every sort," she confided to Cranston. But while pulling back on contributions, they were always willing to help Cranston whenever he needed it. She also offered to help by baby-sitting, cooking "or whatever." She confessed that "the only way we get to see you these days is politically." Prior to a luncheon for forty women that Cranston was to attend, she told him, "Most of them will have heard you before" and "a few are friendly Republicans. An appropriate theme, I should think, would be interesting inside stuff about the state government and...the value of effort[s] toward better government. But you'll know what to say. I'm *so* glad you are coming! The funny thing is that most of them are like me and just like to hear your speeches over again." [112]

In the end, Californians reversed their 1960 presidential leanings and defeated Nixon in 1962 by some 350,000 votes. In a televised statement, he unwittingly referred to running for "president of California," and, unshaven and haggard-looking, his eyes swollen and words slurred, announced the morning after the election that the press would not have "Nixon to kick around any more, because, gentlemen, this is my last press conference." Cranston was among many who hoped that would be the case, calling Brown a "great governor and a giant killer who ended the political careers of Nixon and Knowland." Brown reportedly told President Kennedy, when they laughed about it afterward, that Nixon was "an able man, but he's nuts." Kuchel again beat Richard Richards for U. S. Senate, but incumbent Democrats had all been reelected to statewide offices. One Republican winner who received a large vote was high-school teacher Max Rafferty as Superintendent of Public Instruction. The other big headline the day after the election read, "Mrs. FDR dies" – she was seventy-eight years old. [113]

Cranston, however, led the ticket in votes with astonishing numbers that added fuel to predictions about his future. He received more than three million votes, 1.25 million more than his opponent, and carried every county except Orange. He could boast that he got the highest total and margin of any state official in the nation that year, indeed, even in U. S. history. He had won more votes than New York Governor Nelson Rockefeller and a bigger margin than its Senator Jacob Javits, both Republicans in another high-population state. Cranston also had beaten Brown's 1958 record of three-million-plus votes, and gotten three times the votes given another gubernatorial possibility, Attorney General Mosk in his reelection. Cranston had spent $390,655 and ended with a debt of $12,901. [114]

Cranston also was winning friends with normally conservative groups. "I note with more than passing interest the fact that you were the leading vote-getter," the publisher of the *Sacramento Union* wrote Cranston immediately after the election.

But "the bitterness of the campaign distressed me," he continued, "and we have suffered some of the repercussions. One was from extremists who could not understand our endorsement of you as being consistent with our own integrity and… not inconsistent with our political philosophy." Nevertheless, he added, "I look forward to our getting to know each other better during these coming years." [115]

"I'm not at all surprised at your victory" or large vote count, Joe Williams wrote in a conciliatory note. "When you shake hands with about half of the public in the state, you are bound to reap the harvest. Sis [Williams' wife] and I hope to be active in your campaign for governor in 1968," but "please tear this up – I wouldn't want anyone to think that I was putting ideas in your head. Congratulations again for showing them how." [116]

Cranston and Geneva went to Hawaii after the election where Cranston attended a National Association of State Auditors, Controllers and Treasurers meeting. He had been the organization's president the previous year. While there, he met with Democratic Senator-elect Daniel K. Inouye.

There now was considerable speculation about who might succeed Brown four years hence, with Cranston high on the list. "The would-be successors to Pat Brown may be sailing on political collision courses which foretell a bloody battle in Democratic ranks," wrote Harry Farrell. He likened the potential Democratic clash to the Knowland-Knight-Nixon "smash-up that ripped California's solid Republican organization to shreds" in the mid-1950s. Unruh was most often cited as a contender for the governorship. "Who, then, stands in his way?" Farrell asked rhetorically. "Alan Cranston, for one." Cranston still was thought to prefer being a U. S. Senator, but the fact that a fellow Democrat (Clair Engle) held the seat next up for election (in 1964) meant that it was unlikely Cranston would run until Kuchel's seat came up in 1968, far into the future. Unruh and the CDC still were at odds, not only because Unruh disdained what he considered a leftist faction that "spoke with a loud voice, though not necessarily a commanding" one, as Farrell described it, but also because the CDC cut into Unruh's own personal power structure within the party. Unruh had set up a rival organization called – ironic, given his antipathy to unpaid volunteers – the Democratic Volunteers Committee. As Speaker, he had life-or-death control over legislation. Cranston's influence with the CDC was the reason that Unruh wanted to curb Cranston's power by taking some of his domain away, notably making appraisers government employees. "To strip Cranston of his machine would enhance Unruh's position mightily," Farrell pointed out. [117]

Voters may have been rewarding the controller "for a job well done," Capitol News Service reporter Henry MacArthur wrote. But Cranston's vote tally, despite his being listed fourth down the ballot (which some voters tended to ignore), gave Cranston considerable edge in the gubernatorial speculation. MacArthur noted, though, that Cranston's opponent, unlike other Republican candidates, had not had the benefit of high-powered public relations help from such firms as Whitaker and Baxter, which had handled GOP candidates for attorney general and lieutenant governor, probably contributing to the tighter races for incumbents Mosk and Anderson. On the other hand, "Much also goes to [Cranston's] pleasant personality," and the large number of newspaper endorsements that he got. His relentless campaigning throughout every corner of the state also had given him name recognition. He had gotten support from Republicans "because they were happy with the way I handled their money," Cranston surmised in interviews. *Sacramento Bee* political writer Herbert L. Phillips noted that Cranston had "stood on his record and refused to be needled into debates or other personal campaign exchanges which might have provided a welcome voter audience for his challenger." [118]

The CDC by then had grown so powerful that Unruh tried to render it useless by curbing its endorsement powers. In 1963 he introduced two bills to "purify" the election process. One gave county and state party *committees* the authority to choose nominees for *special* elections (an effort to deny Phil Burton nomination to run for Congress in San Francisco). The other bill, the Truth in Endorsement Act, required all pre-primary endorsements from *unofficial* or volunteer organizations like the CDC to carry a disclaimer that they were not from the *official* party. Governor Brown and Cranston countered by pushing a different election-reform package which called for detailed accounting of campaign contributions. The Unruh bills (handled by his "henchman," Assemblyman Tom Bane of North Hollywood), however, were moving through the legislature. Cranston joined an outcry against the "get-Burton" bills, calling them "inconsistent in their belated efforts to create an image" of election purity, and accusing Unruh and Bane of killing the governor's "workable bill" for "one that no one in the legislature can vote for." The measures deprived voters of the right to pick candidates, they argued, permitting back-room deals by a handful of committee "bosses," making "a mockery of the democratic process," as Burton, fighting for his political future, put it. In addition, Bane introduced an amendment to enforce rigorous reporting of campaign expenditures, particularly for ITAs. Obviously directed at the controller, the Bane measure made violators subject to $500 fines or six months in jail, and removal for those in public office. [119]

But cries of "foul" finally carried the day for the "purity" bill. In an Assembly closed-door caucus June 5, 1963, Democrats overrode their leaders and amended it to benefit Burton. The *San Francisco Chronicle* called it "Defeat for Boss Rule." Unruh's bill on endorsements, however, was approved by both houses of the legislature. Again, Cranston opposed Unruh, arguing against the bill and urging Brown to veto it. He did, further angering Unruh. [120]

The CDC also was reassessing. Liberals in it no longer treated Cranston as their standard-bearer, accusing him in January, 1963, of pushing a man for CDC president who "doesn't have a liberal bone in his body, whose courage is measured by commitments to the establishment, and who can be counted on not to rock their boat." Was Oakland city auditor Martin Huff "what the CDC needs?" its newsletter *The Liberal Democrat* asked. Cranston was falling into the "establishment" mode of trying to "keep the CDC alive – but not kicking." The real bug-bear was Jesse Unruh. "And if Unruh is to be stopped, a lifeless CDC would be of no value.... We are surprised that Cranston doesn't see this," an analysis said. "This is not the time to call in a mortician. CDC is not yet dead. Liberals should start moving for the leadership post." Among those put forward were Roy Greenaway, CDC regional vice president Toby Osos of Los Angeles, party activist (and future San Francisco chief administrative officer) Rudy Nothenberg – and "don't count out Paul Ziffren of Beverly Hills" who, although dumped by Brown and Unruh as national committeeman, "has leadership abilities, independence and financial resources to give the time to the job of re-building CDC." Greenaway was "the favorite of the liberals," but if he left his appraiser's job, he would have to "worry about eating." "We are disappointed in Cranston's analysis of CDC's future role – although not surprised," the newsletter concluded. Cranston did push his candidate and was "licked," a labor newspaper reported after the 1963 CDC convention in April. The tugs-of-war reflected power plays by potential governors, but Cranston was praised for having "enough good sense and good grace to…say the organization had a right and a duty to be free from political domination." That kept the CDC from being "dominated by a political machine," which could not "push a dedicated, grassroots party organization around." [121]

San Francisco Examiner columnist Dick Nolan was amused by the antics of the CDC "because it makes Pat and Jesse nervous. They never know just what this organization of mavericks is likely to do next. [Both] are vote counters. Their minds click madly like adding machines in reverse every time the leftward leaning CDC lets out another rebel howl." The governor and speaker, Nolan jested, would be happy if they could keep the organization "in a dark closet somewhere, to be taken out only at election time, when the dismal chores of precinct work must be done, and manpower is needed to do it. Picture the consternation of Tweedlepat and Tweedlejess," Nolan continued, when the CDC "considers that the cause of peace might be served if the United States quit testing nuclear weapons" (the CDC skirted the issue in the end). Brown and Unruh wanted to remake the CDC "in a more respectable image," Nolan wrote, and keep it from bringing up "all those bothersome bigger issues" beyond state matters. To Unruh, who "understands money" and wanted to bring the organization to heel like a dog, "the dratted mutt persists in behaving like a tramp, foraging as best it can out of the two-buck, five-buck garbage cans…of little contributors." Nolan argued, with prescience, that the CDC was important "to all Americans" as a "pocket of resistance in a war against blandness in public affairs" that would put both major political parties "squarely in the middle of the road, with little to choose between them beyond the haircuts and TV styles of their nominees for office." Such blandness was un-American, he joked. What was so radical about stopping nuclear testing, he asked sardonically? "It might even be thought of as a moderate proposition, one extreme being a suggestion that the United States pursue peace by out-and-out disarmament as an example to the world. The extreme on the other side would be the proposal that we quit horsing around and initiate a preventive war right now by blasting the Soviet Union with everything in the arsenal. Somewhere between extremes solutions lie. It is the function of political parties to offer contrasting philosophies for free choice. The CDC, I submit, is somewhat more American than Pat Brown." Cranston no doubt smiled when he read that column. [122]

Cranston and Unruh now were described in news accounts as rivals in "semi-open warfare." There was an unabashed anti-Unruh move at the CDC convention when "party professionals suffered a sharp setback at the hands of liberal elements." Unruh was continuing to try and weaken Cranston's power by making ITAs civil servants. By then there were some 140 appraisers under Cranston's aegis. Harry Farrell wrote that appraisers became "fanatically loyal to their leader," and Cranston enjoyed such loyalty now. Without them, Farrell speculated, "Cranston would have a much harder time mounting an effective campaign against Unruh [for governor] in 1966." [123]

Cranston generally backed Brown's agenda. "I did my best to support Pat," he told his sister. He disagreed in 1963, however, opposing a withholding tax on wages and found himself "on the hot political griddle," as one reporter put it, with the Assembly Democratic caucus after speaking out on the issue. Cranston also "was sharply criticized for supporting the right of the CDC to endorse candidates running against party incumbents" in primaries. Two assemblymen, Robert W. Crown of Alameda and Mervyn M. Dymally of Los Angeles (a future congressman), called Cranston on the carpet for "splitting the party." To the press asking if he had been taken to task, Cranston replied, "That's not the way I would express it." [124]

Cranston had opposed withholding state taxes since 1960, arguing that if the state continued effective enforcement of tax-collecting, there was little need or advantage in doing so. He maintained that it would cost as much to manage the withholding revenue as might be collected from tax evaders, that it added an extra burden to employers, and that only about $3 per-taxpayer was lost through evasion, less than $500,000. Cranston's independence as an elected auditor gave his arguments credence. The *Chronicle* congratulated him on "a sound position" and "strength of character in resisting heavy pressure to switch it." The legislature and governor should listen to the him, the paper editorialized. A related cartoon depicted Cranston as Revolutionary War naval hero John Paul Jones standing on a ship declaring, "Surrender! I have not yet begun to fight!" as Brown's ship, flying a withholding-plan flag, sailed along side. [125]

By May, 1963, political writers were tasting blood among Democrats, one describing the situation as a "powder keg." Party leaders were hardly speaking to each other, Carl Greenburg reported in the *Los Angeles Times*, and "It will be a rare day when you see the state controller, Alan Cranston, strolling out to lunch with Jesse M. Unruh, the powerhouse speaker of the Assembly." There were rumors that the Kennedy White House would downplay Unruh's role as state liaison in favor of Brown. The reason was that a number of Democrats were unhappy with Unruh's grip on "their collars." Unruh, who was sensitive to his "boss image," kept saying that what he did was for the good of the party. "He's watching his step," said Greenberg, "And the hawks are watching him." [126]

Cranston was keeping an eye on his own options. He continued to be a popular speaker around the state, often "fiery" with "a sense of humor and a sense of devotion," a *Fresno Bee* reporter wrote. "He believes in athletics, in giving good advice to the youth of our state and in humility, as was evidence in his short, informative talk" to a B'Nai Brith student Athlete-of-the-Year banquet in Fresno. Cranston at forty-nine still looked trim and fit, and maintained a regular exercise program, circling his house two or three times on a home-made 523-yard track at 6:30 every morning. He called it more of a "small cross-country course." He then swam the length of his 50-foot pool two or three times underwater without coming up for air. He got to the office by 8:30. "It gets rough at times," he confessed in the *Bee* interview, "but it keeps the body and mind alert." He made some forty trips a year to Los Angeles for meetings, and traversed other parts of the state. [127]

"If there is anyone in the capitol building today who could walk fifty miles without collapsing, it probably is Cranston," Charles "Chuck" Hurley, city editor of the *Fresno Bee*, told a reporter assigned to cover Cranston's appearance at the Fresno sports event. "He doesn't smoke, is a very mild social drinker (never at lunch), and does lots of calisthenics – even in his hotel rooms when he is traveling. I've seen him do 100 side-straddle hops…and not even breath very hard afterward." He added that Cranston "enjoys all sports, especially the '49ers [San Francisco football team], but he is a track nut first and foremost, I would say. He attends as many meets as he can squeeze in." Hurley subsequently worked for Cranston as press secretary in the controller's office (and later for Phil Burton). [128]

Cranston's mother, now eighty-five, was frail, and Cranston took Robin to see her in September, 1963. "What a delightful visit we had the other day," she wrote. "You and Robin looked so well and happy. I was only sorry that Geneva and Kim did not come." She gave Cranston the address of a Canadian relative and some postcards that she had saved for the boys to enjoy, including one of the Grand Hotel Panorama at Les Boissons in the French Alps that she had sent to Cranston in 1923. She also was giving them some of the family silver. "I hope Geneva was pleased with the silver bowl and spoon. How about the six individual nut dishes and salad fork and spoon?" she asked, adding, "Your house is alone so much that these things may be safer with me, but if you really want them now, you can have them; also the beautiful table cloth and napkins, which were made for us in Florence." Her wobbly condition made her "dubious about going to Sacramento" to visit them. But she felt "well off really for a woman of my age, so I should not complain." Of two gifts that they had brought her, apparently made by the grandsons, "The pressed flower card is beneath the glass on my bureau and the sweet little gentian pin is precious. They are mentioned in the Bible, so think how long the flower has been on earth." [129]

In July and August, 1963, Cranston took his family to Europe for nearly two months. He wanted to relive some of his own youthful experiences with his boys, now fifteen and eleven. It was Cranston's seventeenth Atlantic crossing, including his 1952 round-the-world trip for the Ford Foundation. The family flew to London, rented cars and toured twelve countries by car, train and plane, from Scotland to Greece including Lichtenstein, Monaco and the Vatican in Italy. Cranston wanted to prove that advance reservations were not necessary and that Europe was inexpensive. "We lived and ate on $5 a day per person," he related with pride in interviews on his return. "You can get fabulous meals for 75 cents and $1.25." They stayed in moderately-priced hotels and guest houses. [130]

Cranston's personal "trip list" showed his attention to minute details and his penchant for traveling light. It included the guide book *How to See Europe on $5 a Day* and John Gunther's *Inside Europe* (1936). Other items on the list, carefully checked off under columns marked "packed" or "ready," included one tweed jacket, one pair of slacks, a summer suit and raincoat, two white shirts and two neckties, three sports shirts and one sweater, two pairs of shoes (one suede and one soft), a pair of shorts, four pairs of socks, three of underwear and swim trunks. He planned to "buy in Europe" a light bathrobe, hat, beach cap and still camera. He would take a movie camera, vitamin C tablets and "Stewart's formula vitamins," medicines, two international driving licenses, health certificates and traveler's checks. Geneva

("G get") was to procure soap, a plastic bag for dirty laundry, extra passport photos and a Bank of America credit card. All of the family clothes were to fit into three light suitcases. Also on the list were notes to "leave wallet items" and turn "off sprinkler." [131]

Traces of Mussolini still existed in Italy, he reported on his return, but none of Hitler in Germany. They had seen the site of the chancellery building where Hitler had committed suicide, describing it as "a weedy field in the middle of Berlin." Most of Europe was "a happy, hopeful and increasingly prosperous place," Cranston felt, but Berlin was in stark contrast, the western sector still war-scarred, the eastern, "a grim and tense place." The Cranstons had gone into east Berlin through the wall at "Checkpoint Charlie," which took two-hours to clear through Russian officials. They were allowed to wander as they pleased once through the wall, and Cranston was encouraged by signs of increasing freedom of speech. But they watched east Germans building the wall taller and thicker while guards armed with bayonet rifles stood at the ready to prevent attempts at defection. The family also met two relatives in Scotland and found traces of Cranston ancestry. In Rome they had breakfast with Governor and Mrs. Brown. [132]

Cranston told reporters, who photographed the family unpacking their bags at the end of August, that California and Governor Brown were well known in Europe, and that President Kennedy was "a very popular figure because of his efforts toward peace. There is a feeling that the strong stand of the president in the crisis over Cuba, followed by the test-ban treaty, greatly increased the prospect for an enduring peace." [133]

He came back to face a scandal related to a planned world's fair at Long Beach. Concessionaires reportedly were being asked to pay "juice money" to officials in order to participate, and Cranston's name was among Lands Commission members allegedly involved. The commission had to approve any expenditures from tidelands oil revenues if used for the fair, under rules that such money met a "state interest." Cranston asked a district attorney's office to investigate rumors that bribes were being solicited and that a tape-recording existed naming Cranston and other officials (including Lieutenant Governor Anderson and Finance Director Hale Champion) as putting pressure on prospective concessionaires. [134]

Cranston transcribed a telephone conversation in which he discussed the rumors and problems in planning the fair. Manager Fred Hall had been going behind people's backs, arranging funding without an executive committee's knowledge and "name-dropping," telling people that "Cranston's office will be able to swing these tidelands funds, don't worry about it." Ridder, Cranston's Long Beach publishing friend, was quoted as saying of the mismanagement, "Clean out the mess." Cranston's informant had discussed the problems with Eugene Wyman, Unruh and others, and told Cranston, "I don't like to see your name bandied about." Cranston asked whether other funding options were being explored if the tideland money did not come through. His contact had consulted an underwriting firm, but it did not want to proceed with the current managers of the project. [135]

The district attorney tracked down the "mystery" tape recording – and was embarrassed to find that it came from an investigator in his office who was trying to get the security-guard concession for the fair. The D. A. concluded that the tape contained no evidence of criminal offenses or wrongdoing by any public officials. But other problems plagued the fair, including questions about the legality of its financing. [136]

Fair proponents wanted to pledge a share of oil revenues assigned to Long Beach as security to underwrite the fair. At a Lands Commission meeting, Cranston emphasized that it had not considered financing of the fair to date, although the fair's management was acting under assumptions that the commission would approve oil-revenue funding. A ballot proposition even had been approved by Long Beach voters authorizing investment of such oil revenues. That had prompted the commission to ask the attorney general for an opinion on the legality of using tidelands money for such purposes. Cranston angrily warned that fair managers were implying that commission approval was a certainty. "That is far from the truth." Furthermore, he said, an audit of the fair's bookkeeping revealed "certain highly unsatisfactory conditions" that were "of deep concern to us." Cranston was serving "public notice that this commission has not only *not* approved any financing plans of the Long Beach International Exposition, but that it feels there are critically important questions of legality, management and public policy yet to be answered." [137]

The Lands Commission ultimately approved letting contracts for use of tidelands-oil revenues, although Hale Champion told a state senator that he and Cranston had been "very reluctant to proceed with approval of the Long Beach matter." But the commission felt that further delay would cost the state substantial sums of money. If the bids were unsatisfactory, however, or new information came to light that use of the funds would be detrimental to the state, the commission could alter its course. New York was a rival for a world's fair, which was held there in 1964-65. [138]

A new challenge – and opportunity – was about to appear on Cranston's horizon. Senator Clair Engle in August, 1963, had been diagnosed with a brain tumor. Exploratory surgery showed it to be inoperable, and the fifty-two-year-old senator was unable to speak and partially paralyzed. He underwent radiation treatments at Bethesda Naval Hospital to shrink the tumor. The possibility was real that his seat soon would be available. [139]

By October Unruh was willing to make a deal if Cranston's job became open. The speaker's political power was greatly reduced when he tyrannically defrocked all Republican legislators of their committee assignments at the end of the 1963 session. Now he was seeking a sanctuary, "a quiet job away from the blistering he is receiving from both Republicans and the California Democratic Council," one reporter wrote. If Unruh stepped down, though, some Democrats warned that it would be "catastrophic" for President Kennedy's reelection campaign in California in 1964. With the "extra-legal" CDC guiding the party, it would "return to the individual baronies and duchies of the past," a California congressman feared. Most of the Democratic California delegation, with four or five exceptions, were on Unruh's side, and the current tug-of-war was "causing the seemingly insensitive and indestructible Unruh a great deal of distress." But Unruh reportedly was ready to step down as speaker in exchange for Cranston's job. Cranston, it was widely thought, wanted to be appointed to Engle's seat, should it become open. That was not outside the realm of possibility because Cranston, like Engle, was from northern

California, and tradition held that the state's two senators should represent both ends of the state (Kuchel was from Southern California). Cranston also felt personally close to Engle, and hoped that he might recommend Cranston to succeed him. [140]

Brown for his part wanted to keep control of his party and chair the Kennedy reelection campaign. But Engle and his wife and former secretary Lucretia (Lu) were not ready to say that the senator would retire. Brown was cautious in his conversations with Cranston about a possible appointment to replace Engle, warning that whoever got it would have to stand for election in 1964, when Republicans would fight hard to regain the seat.

Cranston confronted Brown at a Democratic reception in Sacramento in September. The two were discussing options in a corner of a room at the Senator Hotel, Brown complaining that he was under terrific pressure. Cranston finally blurted out, "You know, Pat, you owe me a Senate seat." He had always considered that he had an edge on the post because of agreeing to bow out in 1958. Brown still would not commit himself, wondering aloud whether Cranston would like to see Unruh as controller if Brown appointed Cranston to the Senate. Cranston had to admit that was not a prospect that he relished. The tense exchange would haunt him, as he wondered whether he had over-stepped the mark with Brown.

As it developed, Brown was thinking about the Senate job for himself, and was feeling Cranston out about releasing Brown from his 1957 commitment to pick Cranston if an opening came up. "He laughingly said no," Brown later told interviewers. [141]

Cranston had to keep his options open. He was getting good press and political writers began to cite him as a likely replacement for Engle. Although Cranston had "always had one foot in foreign affairs and one in the political life of California," a Beverly Hills columnist wrote in October, "he has brought excitement and glamour to his office and has consistently shown his prowess as a vote-getter." He had "hewed to a very strict and careful line of independence of thought and action" so that "no claim of empire-building" could be "laid at his doorstep." Cranston had "gained strength" while the CDC was not always the dominant party machine. [142]

Stanley Mosk, however, might be a formidable primary opponent in a Senate race. A *San Francisco Examiner* headline October 9, 1963, read, "JFK wants Mosk - if Engle must quit." If Engle did not actually resign, there would be an open primary, possibly pitting Mosk against Cranston, a "battle of Democratic Giants." The two men would be evenly matched, both popular vote-getters with CDC support. The "state financial operations have never been sounder," the writer pointed out, and Cranston had been given wide approval from both parties. His entry "into the mire of the California World's Fair" had given it "closer scrutiny. He won his point and his political strength was well demonstrated." Cranston was described as a "a tall man, carrying his baldness quite well" with "a strong physical image. He is affable and energetic." If he were pitted against someone like Mosk in a party foray, he would be "up to his ears, and that's pretty high for such a tall man." [143]

Cranston continued his statewide appearances, that October speaking to the show-business celebrity Friars Club in Beverly Hills, talking more like a national politician than a state exchequer. In November, anticipating the 1964 presidential election, Cranston pitched hard for Kennedy's reelection and blasted potential Republican nominee Barry Goldwater. If he were elected, Cranston warned, it would "be the greatest change in leadership in the history of our nation." He urged California Republicans not to back Goldwater in a primary, believing that California would be a key state in the election. He had analyzed the states and feared that the Midwest and South probably would go Republican – with the possible exception of Texas, which Kennedy was about to visit with that in mind. Cranston told the crowd that Nixon's apparently wanting to run again was "unbelievable." He also asked the audience to consider the impacts of poverty and over-population on the world, pointing out that only one of twenty children born in a single day (numbering 200,000) that year would be Russian or American – half born in a dictatorship and half in a democracy. The rest faced lifelong hunger and illness in lesser-developed nations. But, he added, he was convinced that half of American families or individuals lived in poverty or on the brink of it, "invisible" to the more affluent. "We are facing the possibility of becoming two Americas – rich and poor, hopeful and hopeless," he said.[144]

In October Cranston wrote the Fowles, then on holiday in Ireland, "No change in Clair's condition. All signs indicate I'm in front if there's to be a succession – so naturally, all rivals are firing at me. Meanwhile, great maneuvers are under way to grab the controllership. Unruh wants it. I don't think he'll get it." President Kennedy, meanwhile, had settled the power struggle in California by naming Mosk and San Francisco District Attorney Tom Lynch – described by one reporter as "as close to Brown as his morning shave" – to head the president's reelection campaign, a slap at Unruh. [145]

But the reelection was not to be. The young president tragically was assassinated November 22, 1963, while on a political trip to Dallas. A pale, frail and semi-paralyzed Engle attended the funeral in a wheelchair. When State Democratic Chairman Eugene Wyman tried to ask Engle what his plans were, he was told that a decision would be made in January. Two conservative Republicans quickly announced that they would run for the seat – San Francisco financier Leland Kaiser and former dancer-actor George Murphy, a Hollywood film executive active in GOP politics for twenty-five years, former state chairman and two-time delegate to national conventions. [146]

At the end of November, 1963, a Ventura County weekly magazine featured Cranston in a cover story authored by him and entitled, "The Watchdog of State Funds Tells His Trade Secrets." Photographs showed him with his family, riding a palomino horse in western garb at a political parade, and the boys feeding pigeons in Venice's St. Mark's Square. Cranston opened his article by quoting Lee Falk's letter after the 1958 election, wondering what a controller was and did. It was not quite as Falk had joked, but Cranston said "it certainly has its moments." He had become most impressed by the extent to which the job affected the day-to-day lives of Californians. He also had come to realize that California, now the most populous state, would soon be the most influential in the nation, "beyond any doubt," in "the greatest democracy on earth." "If we govern ourselves wisely and well…we will be setting an example of self-government at its very best" and "give new strength to the cause of freedom throughout the world," he concluded. "It's a challenge, isn't it?" [147]

A good friend, San Francisco real-estate financier Louis R. Lurie (he and his son Robert purchased the San Francisco Giants baseball team and Lurie backed Broadway theater productions), had been operated on for cancer in 1963. Cranston sent him flowers in a cart-shaped vase drawn by a donkey, telling Lurie that he had donated money in his name to the Damon Runyon fund (of which Lurie was western director). Lurie wrote back that mutual friend George Killion, head of American President Lines, had said of Cranston, "That's the guy for the United States Senate!" Lurie (who had had a heart attack in 1939 at age fifty-one) also enclosed some "Rules" that would qualify hard-driving executives for "full membership in the Coronary Club and a permanent vacation trip to the Mortuary." They included: "Work evenings, Saturdays, Sundays and holidays. Don't let any personal consideration interfere with your job.... Do not eat restful, relaxing meals – always plan a conference for the meal hour and take telephone calls throughout lunch and dinner.... Don't take short vacations, if any.... Do not delegate any authority or responsibility to subordinates – carry the full load yourself.... Pay no attention to your blood pressure or any other ailments – hard work will take care of everything.... Pick a quarrel over any and all trivialities and do not hesitate to enter any quarrel that's going on, even though it's none of your business." It was signed, "Louis R. Lurie, Coronary Thrombosis Expert." He must have thought that Cranston would benefit from the advice. [148]

Cranston visited his mother in January, 1964, and brought her a check paying interest on a $10,000 loan that she had made him. She looked forward to another visit the next week, and hoped that they could "have a game of chess. I fear it will be a very short game, for you will trip me very soon, I am sure," she wrote Cranston. An article in the *Christian Science Monitor* about California politics she noted was "strongly in favor of you." But, she added, "Unruh does keep himself before the public pretty steadily. I suppose there always is a man like him in politics and it's a great pity. It is astounding that they appeal to so many people. Is this great influx of humanity into the state going to lower our standards even more?" She had heard Cranston in a broadcast interview – "We had a great time getting the right channel... but managed to do so just in time. Your voice is excellent over the air and you answer questions very clearly. I am one out of a good many who think this, so it is not only maternal pride," she said. She signed it, "Yours smilingly, Mother." [149]

One of Cranston's first political acts in January, 1964, was to honor a commitment to endorse Phil Burton for Congress. "Last spring, we worked very closely together in opposing legislation introduced in the Assembly which would have fostered boss rule in California politics," Cranston wrote Burton in a formal letter that honored his pledge, if somewhat unenthusiastically. "Immediately subsequent to that collaboration, I agreed to support you for Congress – upon one condition – in the event that Jack Shelley was elected Mayor of San Francisco and a vacancy occurred in the 5th [congressional] district. The event has occurred – Jack Shelley is now mayor, and you are a candidate in a special election. The condition has been met: Your are the endorsed candidate of the Democratic Party, and I thus support you, as I support all endorsed candidates in partisan elections." [150]

Cranston and others felt that Burton, in effect, had "forced" Shelley to resign his congressional seat to run for mayor, thus creating the opportunity for Burton to run for Congress (which he did successfully), and the relationship between Cranston and Burton was always stand-offish. [151]

But Engle surprised everyone on January 6 by saying that he planned to seek reelection. His wife invited high-ranking party officials to their home on Capitol Hill. Cranston was among those anxious to learn Engle's real condition. Elizabeth "Libby" Rudel Gatov, Kennedy's former U. S. Treasurer and a national committeewoman, spoke for the group. Leaving the Engles' house on New Jersey Avenue, Gatov grimly told waiting reporters that she could not imagine Engle's being able to wage a campaign. While he looked better than she expected, he had trouble conversing, and often laughed in a strange way for no apparent reason. There would be a contested primary, she predicted. Cranston shared the sadness at the senator's condition. Pat Brown also tried to see Engle, hoping to persuade him not to run if too ill. Mrs. Engle refused to let the governor see her husband, implying that Brown wanted Engle to resign in order to appoint a replacement. Brown and the Democratic State Central Committee then demanded a public medical report on Engle's prognosis. Engle would have party support "only if the full medical facts about his illness and ability to campaign" were released to the public. The same kind of disclosure made by President Eisenhower at the time of his heart attack would avoid "the widespread confusion and concern now being evidenced" about whether Engle could continue serving or campaign effectively. When Engle's doctor refused to release the information, Brown announced that the race was wide open. Engle did appear in the Senate twice after that to vote on key bills of President Lyndon Johnson's programs, but it was obvious that he was frail. One arm was in a sling, the other clutching a cane. [152]

Cranston announced at a CDC directors' meeting in Fresno January 19 that he would run for the Senate if party officials decided that Engle should not seek reelection. "Never have I known so many to be so acutely and inwardly torn by… this tragic situation," he said. On one hand, there was loyalty to a "conscientious public servant" and friend, on the other, an obligation to insure strong leadership for California. He even wrote Engle, urging him to authorize his doctor to make public a medical report, saying that he would support Engle if it indicated he could run. "I'm sorry to see you've joined the ranks of the saliva testers," a response from Engle said, referrinig to Mrs. Engle's saying disparagingly that she had "been pouring tea for a parade of saliva testers" making cold-blooded and ruthless efforts to get her husband out of the Senate. The words sounded more like her than the once-friendly Engle, and Cranston told Eleanor that he instantly lost any hesitancy about running after reading that letter. Eleanor sent him a note saying, "Ain't all this exciting?" She and her family were ready to "drop anything any time to help. Such devotion must be deserved!" [153]

She got busy arranging appearances and publicity for her brother, to which he responded, "It would be fine if I could talk to that peninsula manufacturers' association sometime *after* the primary…. I have some reservations about a CDC article at this time…. If you could push the idea of a *Sunset* [magazine] story on the animal farm, it would be most helpful." But there was another possible hurdle. Polls began to show that Mosk and Congressman Jimmy Roosevelt had leads over other likely Senate candidates, who now included, besides Engle and Cranston, Glenn Anderson, Assemblyman Byron Rumford of Berkeley, and government economist and former Assemblyman Dewey Anderson. [154]

The 1964 CDC convention in February at Long Beach promised to be a showdown. More than 7,000 club members showed up, excited about the Senate race and anxious to show strong opposition to Unruh's efforts to disempower the organization. Mosk had behind-the-scenes backing from the Unruh forces, although he had publicly denied any help from "Big Daddy." Roosevelt was a serious contender with charm and a voice that reminded people of his father. Cranston and his backers won a first round when the convention agreed to make a single endorsement for the Senate rather than endorse all contenders. Cranston also now had the backing of the governor, which rankled other hopefuls. Brown had personally called county central committee chairmen on Cranston's behalf, and forty-eight of the fifty-six chairmen did endorse him. But holdouts included chairmen in populous Los Angeles and Sacramento Counties. Brown quietly dropped "publicly from the Cranston bandwagon," the Long Beach newspaper reported. Still, Cranston was seen to have the inside track to a Senate appointment if the seat became available before the election, even though, as columnist Herb Caen wrote, the CDC was "looking snideways at its fair-haired boy…since he ducked the civil-rights issue on a TV interview," a reference to his reaction to a CDC resolution on the controversial Rumford fair-housing act prohibiting discrimination, which opponents wanted to repeal. It was a "losing issue for Democrats," Greenaway remembered. Unruh equivocated on it as if favoring repeal; Greenaway, still an inheritance-tax appraiser, was "hassled" by other ITAs for publicly attacking Unruh, and the matter was touchy for Cranston and his Senate hopes. "Cranston did not fire me," said Greenway, and was always supportive of fair housing. "But then he was looking to a Senate campaign and nobody knew what would happen." [155]

Engle was among the nominees at the convention and a prearranged telephone call was put through to him. His responses were halting. When CDC president Tom Carvey asked, "When will you be out to see us in California?" there was a long silence. Then Engle was heard to say, "Well, it's problematical," followed by the strange, cackling laugh. "Senator, we all love you. God bless you, and get well," Carvey told him, to more silence over the line. The crowd applauded, many were in tears. Roosevelt followed with a fiery speech and liberal agenda that ended with a standing ovation. Mosk was not endorsed or nominated. Cranston's principal opponent now was Roosevelt. [156]

Cranston, though, had the advantage of a coterie of CDC colleagues who spent the night politicking on his behalf. The next morning he garnered 53.4 percent of the endorsement ballots (1,197 to Roosevelt's 727 and Engle's 281). A *Los Angeles Times* headline read, "Engle spurned, Cranston given CDC support." With Geneva by his side on the platform, a lei of white carnations around his neck, Cranston said that his exhilaration was tempered by the sad situation surrounding the incumbent Engle, and he predicted a tough, hard fight. But he was closer than ever to his dream of becoming a United States Senator.

Coincidentally, on the same weekend, at a dinner for Stanley Mosk in Los Angeles, White House press secretary Pierre Salinger was assuring guests humorously that *he* had no intention of opposing Mosk if he were to run for the Senate. The next week, Mosk, feeling pressure from Brown (who later admitted that he had urged Mosk not to enter the primary) and claiming financial reasons, decided not to make the race. There were more titillating reasons for his dropping out that would be revealed in later years (concerning his girl friend), but Mosk's public statement said, "I am unwilling to impose on my personal friends" or to "accept obligations" implied by "contributions from those who are not motivated by friendship" to raise the $600,000 that he estimated he needed for a primary contest. "This factor disturbs me and must be of concern to thoughtful members of both parties." [157]

The following night, Roosevelt called Cranston to say that he would support him and do anything he could to help his candidacy. (He did campaign for him, often with Greenaway.) Libby Gatov came out for Cranston soon afterward. Cranston's formal filing for the race in San Jose was a sentimental family event that included, besides his wife and sons, his 85-year-old mother, his eighth-grade teacher and grammar-school principal, Miss Margaret Wibel, some fifty friends and relatives. Asked by a reporter if he would accept Unruh's support, Cranston exclaimed to laughter, "I'd be startled to receive it!" Brown subsequently issued a statement saying, "Alan Cranston has the vigor, the vision, and the ability to carry on for Clair Engle and California. His experience in fiscal and foreign affairs equips him uniquely for the Senate." Cranston, a *Christian Science Monitor* article read, "entered the primary as one of the most-liked Democrats in the state." His likely Republican opponent George Murphy disparaged the CDC endorsement as "political extermination" of Engle "by Alan Cranston and his henchmen." [158]

Cranston quickly announced that, while happy to have the 70,000-member CDC endorsement, he would not let it dictate his stands, stating, "I intend to make my own decisions on issues." He gave the press a lighter subject by stating that he had "decided to stay bald," telling reporters after a wig-maker suggested that "a headpiece has a softening effect on one's countenance," "I don't want to deny the Birch Society the privilege of calling me an egghead." The *Sacramento Bee* in a drawing compared Cranston's appearance with and without wig, noting his "high brow." [159]

Another news account noted that Cranston may have appeared to have "suddenly vaulted from a relatively obscure state office to competition for" the high office of senator, but that was part of a long-term plan – he had "set his sights on the Senate some years ago." [160]

Engle was still a potential candidate. He issued an angry statement accusing Governor Brown of trying to "bury" him. "But I will not be buried.... I didn't oblige him by dying. Like Caesar, I feel this is 'the unkindest cut of all.'" Brown believed that the statement had not been written by Engle, although an Unruh ally, Assemblyman Tom Carrell, said that he had seen Engle dictate it. Engle's administrative assistant and press secretary resigned immediately after the statement was released, saying that Mrs. Engle and a secretary had drafted it and issued it without the staff's knowledge. By then, Engle was able only to indicate votes in the Senate by putting his hand to his eye (for "aye") or to his nose (for "no"), and the Senate had told him that his aides no longer would be permitted to speak for him. His wife denied that she was interested in running for his seat, but Sam Yorty now made noises about challenging Cranston, assuming that Engle would not run. Cranston began campaigning, avoiding talking about Engle's health and hoping that the other potential candidates would fall by the wayside. [161]

He did talk about his views on issues. "I am keenly aware that the taxpayer's dollar must be handled with infinite care, both at home and abroad, in order to inspire confidence that money spent on needed programs is money spent well and efficiently," he said. He backed President Johnson's civil-rights bill (signed July 2, 1964), favored school desegregation and the Rumford fair-housing act in California. (He again had met with civil-rights leader Martin Luther King, at a realty board banquet in California.) On another issue, Cranston attacked the American Medical Association for making a deal with the tobacco industry to sabotage new cigarette regulations in exchange for votes against Medicare, a plan to provide health insurance for seniors then being considered in Congress. [162]

But there was about to be an unexpected ringer in the fray. On March 19, just one day before the deadline for filing a candidacy, Governor Brown got a call from the White House. Press secretary Pierre Salinger had continued in the job with President Johnson, but, like other Kennedy staffers, was not comfortable with his new boss, whose style and preferences differed from Kennedy's. Salinger, who had been born in San Francisco, told Brown that he was flying to California that night to file for the Senate race. Brown was stunned. He tried to persuade Salinger to run for a congressional seat that was open in San Francisco. Salinger was intransigent. He had made the decision over a period of several months, he later told reporters, first telling presidential aide William Moyers (on March 12), who relayed the news to President Johnson. "Well, there's no better place than the Senate," Johnson reportedly told Salinger, then asked what the filing fee was. $450, Salinger thought. Johnson wrote out a check for that amount and wished him well. It was a mutually convenient arrangement, observers thought. Johnson was glad to be rid of a powerful Kennedy aide, and if Salinger were to win, Johnson would benefit from Kennedy coat-tails when they ran on the same ticket in California. Cranston concurred that Johnson probably wanted to get rid of Salinger and that his leaving was a relief to the president. Prior to making his decision, Salinger had consulted with Robert Kennedy (who was rumored to be considering a similar move to run for Senate in New York State), Mrs. Jacqueline Kennedy, Unruh, Mosk and others in California political circles. [163]

Cranston was equally astonished at the turn of events, relayed to him by Hale Champion. Both knew that Salinger would be very hard to beat in a primary because of the Kennedy association. As presidential spokesman for four years, Salinger was as well known as the late president, who called him "Portly Pierre" for his large girth (he had refused to take exercise or go on 50-mile hikes during the Kennedy "New Frontier" fitness fad, endearing him to those who shared his views). He was amusing, irreverent and professional in press dealings. Cranston also detected the hands of Unruh and Mosk in the turn of events – they would put their support behind Salinger, he knew. [164]

Cranston issued a statement gently rebuking Salinger. "I welcome him into the race, the more the merrier," he said, adding, "I don't think Salinger's entry will materially affect the campaign. He might be an expert on the Washington scene, but not on the California scene." Brown announced that while Salinger was "an able young man and an old friend," he would stick to his commitment to Cranston. [165]

But the June 2 primary was only nine weeks off. Salinger certainly could be tainted as a carpetbagger – his voting residency for the past three years had been Virginia and he had been out of California for nine years. He also had no experience as an elected public official. Cranston had worked with Salinger in the Kennedy presidential campaign in California and the two had visited in Washington before Kennedy had been nominated. Cranston had had to decline an invitation to dinner from Salinger, but knew that had not caused the interloper to run against him. Cranston was genuinely angry about it but could do nothing other than redouble his campaigning efforts. [166]

Salinger flew to San Francisco the night before the filing deadline, arriving at 4 a.m., and by noon had rounded up the requisite seventy-five signatures to qualify him to file. "I have come home to San Francisco, the place of my birth, to announce my candidacy for the United States Senator representing California," he said at a press conference at the Fairmont Hotel on San Francisco's Nob Hill. He denied that he had "succumbed to the urging" of friends. His action was self-inspired, he said, based on the feeling that he could "better serve the interests of California than any of the announced candidates. There is no question that the lateness of my candidacy means that many of my friends in the Democratic Party are already committed to another candidate," he conceded. "I shall not try to change those commitments." As to his eligibility as a non-resident to enter the race, he was confident that he met state constitutional requirements although he could not vote in his own primary. "I once said that I would not walk fifty miles. But I plan to walk many times fifty miles, through every community in this state, to tell the story of my qualifications," he said. It would be "a vigorous campaign," he predicted. [167]

The thirty-eight-year-old Salinger once had worked as a reporter for the *Chronicle* – in a series under the alias "Peter Emil Flick" he had gotten himself thrown into jails to investigate conditions, for which he won an award and praise from Governor Earl Warren. Salinger relished the attention of news colleagues, raising his thick eyebrows and chewing on a characteristic cigar for colorful effect. "He oddly resembled a baby disguised as a cartoon politician or an old-fashioned political boss," Eleanor Fowle thought, recording that he smoked twelve cigars a day and derisively was dubbed "a walking smoke-filled room." News accounts described him as "195 pounds of confidence…wrapping the mantle of the slain president around him." "He has to get rid of that cigar and the wisecracks," a Democratic party leader was quoted as saying. *Chronicle* editor William German told Salinger, who had asked over lunch how to win, that he ought "to shave more often." Another Democratic leader called the primaries a "circus" with Salinger playing "a mean piano" for the Democrats and George Murphy tap dancing for the Republicans. The contrast of the hefty Salinger to the lean Cranston, the "fat and the fit," was a newsman's delight. A *Life* magazine article showed Cranston and George Murphy doing athletic activities, running and playing paddle-tennis respectively, while Salinger was seen flubbing a drive trying to bend over his protruding stomach at a Palm Springs golf club. He did lose thirteen pounds in five weeks during the campaign, *Time* reported. [168]

Cranston was further disturbed, however, to see that, standing beside Salinger, was political consultant Don Bradley, executive secretary of the Democratic State Central Committee, with whom Cranston also had worked on the Kennedy campaign.

Bradley, a long-time personal friend of Salinger, was considered the most effective Democratic campaign manager in the state: He had managed Brown's 1962 race in northern California, and Engle's in 1958. Bradley denied that he would manage Salinger's campaign, telling the press that his boss was for Cranston. But the obvious alliance was another blow below the belt for Cranston. In addition, a former assistant state labor commissioner and the first African-American to hold a high position in the White House, Salinger's assistant press secretary Andrew Hatcher, had quit at the same time to help Salinger. Many who opposed Cranston also had joined Salinger, *Washington Star* political commentator David Broder noted, calling the controller a "formidable rival" if a "somewhat colorless liberal" who "commands a personal political task force composed of his" 140-plus inheritance-tax-appraiser appointees. Many top Democratic officials, Broder reported, "are privately discomfited by Mr. Salinger's belated entry in the race," and "cannot honorably renege on their commitments to Mr. Cranston." One person who had not joined Salinger was Glenn Wilson, a top party fundraiser with the savings-and-loan industry. Wilson wrote former YD president Richard Nevins that reports of his helping Salinger were "not true." Nevins sent it to Cranston. Salinger meanwhile kept stressing that he was personally devoted to Pat Brown and was not challenging his political influence. Salinger's campaign would be adversely affected if the public viewed his candidacy as an effort by Mosk and Unruh to depose Brown. [169]

There still was a chance that Salinger's name would not appear on the primary ballot. Attorney General Mosk was seen as the person who had counseled Salinger that his candidacy would be legal. Mosk was "bitter over the...manner in which his own ambitions were thrust aside by Alan Cranston," one newspaper editorialized. (Other events would surface many years later, implying that Cranston had played a dirty trick to discourage Mosk's candidacy.) Republican Secretary of State Frank Jordan refused to put Salinger's name on the ballot, but the State Supreme Court overrode him. "If Salinger wants to be a senator, let him return to Virginia and run against Harry Byrd!" State Senator George Miller, Junior, sniffed, referring to the well-entrenched senior senator. [170]

After the court decision, Cranston again said that Salinger was welcome to run in the primary – "It's certainly going to be a lot livelier with him in it, and will give the Democratic Party a broader choice." Democrats, though, would have to decide whether a man who had been out of the state for nine years was the one whom they wanted to represent them. "I am fully convinced that I will win," Cranston added, "and I am fully determined to conduct my campaign in a manner that will strengthen, not divide, the Democratic Party in California." But Salinger quickly jumped ahead of Cranston in polls (by 33 to 21 percent in a Field poll), with Engle far behind. Bradley did take on the Salinger campaign and brought a team of professionals with him. Geneva thought that Cranston was up against "a stacked deck," as Eleanor recorded of the growing number of obstacles he faced. Brown, described in a *Life* magazine story as "privately furious," announced that Bradley's decision severed their relationship and "in no way reflects any change in my full support of the candidacy of Alan Cranston," given "before Mr. Salinger's last-minute announcement. I believe Mr. Cranston to be better qualified and prepared to represent California in the U. S. Senate." The State Democratic Party now was divided. The British *Economist* called the *contra temps* "potentially explosive." It looked ominously like a Democratic replay of the Nixon-Knowland-Knight debacle. A Lou Grant cartoon depicted the lanky Cranston and portly Salinger in a boxing ring in a "bare-knuckle brawl" while a Democratic donkey covered his eyes in shame. Cranston, who saw Salinger's candidacy as more harmful to Engle than to himself, kept warning audiences that infighting could give the election to a right-winger like George Murphy or Leland Kaiser. To reporters' questions of whether Cranston thought Salinger's decision had been long-planned, Cranston snapped, "It was an impetuous decision." He also thought that it would be hard for Salinger to build an organization before the primary. [171]

Cranston accused Salinger of running on publicity rather than issues, and of leading a power play "to seize control of the party from the working Democrats of California." He kept reminding people that Salinger's only experience was as a public-relations man. "California voters won't be swayed by Salinger's slightly-clad 'P.S. [for Pierre Salinger], I-love-you' cuties," Geneva told a *San Francisco Chronicle* reporter, a reference to Salinger's campaign slogan and buttons reading "Sweethearts for Salinger." Cranston's "appeal lies much deeper," she said. "I heard the comment that people would be taken in by the razzle-dazzle and that candidates who talk about issues would be considered dull eggheads," she continued, "but now I think Alan's chances look marvelous." [172]

He did emphasize senatorial-type issues like world peace and the national economy in his campaign talks. "We must first work to solve the problems of war and peace or we might soon not have anything for which to work," Cranston told a $6-a-plate Democratic dinner in Santa Maria as he launched his primary campaign. As to the domestic economy, "We must work to erase the fears of automation, to retrain those unable to find employment or displaced by automation." He warned Southern Californians not to build their economy solely on defense spending. "I will work to make sure that California receives its share of the defense dollar," he said, "but at the same time, I look toward the day when it is not necessary to spend so much of our budget on defense." Those were the issues that would engross him as a legislator. [173]

To Salinger's call for a debate, Cranston retorted, "I wish Mr. Salinger would make up his mind. He says in one breath that he agrees almost entirely with my positions on national and international issues, and in the next breath, he wants to debate them with me." The only subject that Cranston thought debatable was Salinger's "apparent desire to reapportion the U. S. Senate with three seats for Virginia and one for California." If Salinger disagreed with any of President Kennedy's or Johnson's policies, which Cranston supported, a debate was welcome, Cranston said sardonically. [174]

The family rallied to help Cranston. Jack Fowle raised money for television ads, Eleanor rented a car and drove around California attending teas and coffees for her brother, their mother clipped newspapers. Eleanor was a "secret weapon," one reporter wrote of her help for Cranston. "If modesty and enthusiasm can win elections, he's a shoo-in," a profile in the *Santa Rosa Press Democrat* said of her visit to the newspaper. Eleanor had "enchantingly tried to uncover all the voting assets that her brother might possess while countering all questions detrimental to his campaign." She had cited family roots in nearby counties – their paternal aunt had married

Sonoma resident Harmon Heald and their father had been born in Yountville (Napa County). When she was asked about Salinger's lead in polls, she quickly reminded reporters how misleading they could be – Nixon was shown beating Brown 59 to 41 percent in 1962, and Truman losing to Dewey in 1948. "Shall I go on?" she demurely asked the editorial board. "The attractive, grey-haired housewife seemed too quiet and proper to be cast in the role of a politician's campaign assistant," the reporter wrote. Geneva also was touring the state, considering that the boys, now twelve and sixteen, were old enough to manage without her all the time. In the past, "I stayed home and worked on precinct lists and made cake and coffee," she said in a *Chronicle* interview. "But now I am having a wonderful time, talking with interesting people and wishing I could stay longer with them." Indeed, she did seem to enjoy campaigning, and did "very well," frequent traveling companion Ann Alanson Eliaser said in restrospect. "She had a wonderful personality, was very gracious and generous with people, and outgoing. She was a great and giving person," and a real asset to Cranston. It amused Geneva that while she was actually enjoying campaigning, people said to her, "Oh, you poor thing, it must be awful for you." She admitted that Kim was the one who was upset at first about the prospect of moving to Washington. Cranston "made his first and only campaign commitment to Kim," promising that they would take all his animals with them. "Frankly, I am very interested to see how Alan accomplishes the move," she added wryly. [175]

There were light moments, though, like the time the campaign staff met at "Animal Farm" to take stock of what to do next. "We were all sitting around this circular couch when Snowball the pig came in and wandered around," campaign worker Thomas (Tom) G. Moore, Junior, remembered. Hale Champion exclaimed, "What kind of a campaign is this? We can't have a meeting without taking care of a pig!" But Cranston "really brightened up when the pig came in, he suddenly came to life," Moore laughed. [176]

Dan Kimball, former Secretary of the Navy, was Cranston's state chairman and former Kennedy Treasury Secretary Gatov was active in the campaign. The CDC sent four million registered Democrats Cranston literature. His slogan and buttons read, "AC to DC." But he was challenged to take positions on what some newspapers called the "far-left views of his most ardent supporters, the California Young Democrats," turning it into a left-versus-right political contest. Both candidates would accuse each other of right-wing tendencies, while conceding that they agreed on most issues. [177]

Cranston went to Washington in April to appear at the National Press Club, a move "to counteract the legend that he was a worthy but colorless politician, fated to lose to Salinger in star-gazed California," columnist Doris Fleeson wrote, saying that Cranston "attacked his election problems with lucidity and a light touch." Another columnist, George Dixon wrote that while Cranston might be considered a "dry-as-dust fellow" in California, "in Washington he turned out to be a bit of a comic." Salinger's appearance at the Press Club had filled the auditorium, but Cranston delighted reporters with his self-deprecating humor. "The political news from California is, as always, strange and wonderful," he began. "Even I find the current situation confusing, despite my familiarity with our Western tribal customs…. Our primary already is producing the antics most of you have come to expect of the

Wild West. Where else, for example, could a man run for the Senate in an election in which he is not even eligible to vote?" While he addressed the problems that California faced with its rapidly growing population ("No wonder the freeway we open today is running at capacity tomorrow"), and ways that government could help, Cranston also jested about the contest in which he found himself. "It is only coincidence that…Pierre is short, stout and hirsute, while I am long, lean – and almost always on time…. In the present circumstances, Pierre represents the campaign of personal publicity, combined with touches of show business, which has sometimes been successful in California – although not very often…. It isn't often that somebody...does his campaigning at events like the Academy Awards dinner." Asked why young girls seemed to be attracted to Salinger, Cranston said that it was "just another example of news management. How can you fight a guy whose program is 'Love and Lunch?'" he said of Salinger's "sweethearts." A reporter asked why there were "so many 'nut' organizations in California?" Because "there are so many people coming from other states," Cranston snapped back. As to the Republicans, Cranston said that Murphy "is looking for answers to today's problems in some century behind the one inhabited by Barry Goldwater." [178]

Washington Star columnist Mary McGrory called Cranston "a lean, intense intellectual" who spoke dispassionately and logically. Cranston had told her, "It's glamour versus organization, and we're leaving all the glamour to Pierre." But when *Newsweek* also used the word "colorless" to describe Cranston, a fan wrote the editor: "Any candidate who promises his twelve-year-old son that, if elected, he'll transport the family's animals – one horse, a pig, one goat, one dog, three cats, 60 pigeons and 30 chickens – to Washington can't be 'colorless.' Unlike the usual concept of a controller, Cranston has wit and a sense of humor that he isn't afraid to use in his speeches. It's a joy to listen to him speak; he's intelligent, literate and lucid. Although I am not a Democrat, he's been getting my vote – and that of other Republicans, I suspect," Elena Bell of Ukiah wrote. [179]

"I'm the candidate who lives and works in California," Cranston told audiences. He even likened Salinger to Nixon: "Both came back to California after many years away and promptly misjudged the leadership and direction of the Democratic Party." Polls now began to look better for Cranston. The AFL-CIO and 500 labor leaders endorsed him, as did major papers, Salinger's former employer the *San Francisco Chronicle* and the *Sacramento Bee* among them. All of the Democratic congressional delegation, including Phil Burton, backed and campaigned for Cranston, and Robert M. Hutchins, now president of the Center to Study Democratic Institutions at Santa Barbara, signed a statement supporting him. [180]

Cranston went after media coverage in ways that offered photo opportunities. He was pictured milking a cow and hugging his mother on Mother's Day. One photo showed him handing a refund check for recreational-boat gasoline taxes to a comely Sacramento woman seated in the stern of one, reminding "Miss Allison Espey that his office refunded $224,198 to 9,049 boaters last year." His position against ill-considered "bulldozer" development brought a favorable editorial in the *Chronicle*. "California's primary has suddenly acquired merit," it read. "It is refreshing…to find a decent respect for esthetics and natural grandeur, open space and recreational areas creeping into an election campaign. It would be comforting if more candidates…

would recognize the existence of what is one of the most important domestic issues of the day, and take a stand on the side of the vanishing and irreplaceable natural resources that are being recklessly sacrificed to the bulldozer and cement mixer," the editorial stated. [181]

Cranston was portrayed as "uneasy with small talk" in a *Los Angeles Times* interview headlined "'Egghead' senatorial candidate, basically idea man, shuns trivia." Making small talk with supporters "comes hard" to Cranston, Richard Bergholz wrote. Unruh called Cranston "an IBM machine," recognition that the controller "has a mind that runs through facts and ideas with sometimes startling speed." There was "about him a pervading image of an intellectual liberal" who frequently changed his talks from the prepared text to his own words. But "even his best friends concede he isn't loaded with charismatic appeal for his listeners." Cranston also admitted to chafing under the "managed life" of a candidate, being told when to get up, when to eat, where to go, what to do. He nevertheless obviously enjoyed the give-and-take of press conferences. He had "boundless energy and stamina," Bergholz said, "and sometimes considers it a wasted day if he hasn't worked both ends of the state within an 18-hour period." [182]

Salinger retaliated by portraying Cranston as "the eager tax collector who'd make a fine mortician." Touting his White House experience, Salinger was fond of saying, "I looked down the nuclear gun barrel with John F. Kennedy" during the Cuban missile crisis. He knew how to get through doors to influential people, he bragged. "It is one thing to get in the door," Cranston retorted, "it is another thing to know what to do when you're inside." Salinger sent out four million postcards with a picture of Kennedy and the legend, "In his tradition." [183]

Engle withdrew from the primary race after a second operation in late April. Cranston, according to a poll, would gain the most from the withdrawal while Salinger was expected to get backing from conservative Democrats. Cranston openly said that the coming primary was between liberal, grassroots Democrats and Unruh's political machine, and about "the nature and future of the Democratic party's leadership in California." The stakes indeed were high for more than the candidates: Governor Brown's control of the party and the possibility of his being chosen as a vice-presidential nominee by President Johnson were at risk if Salinger won. [184]

Brown indeed was worried, because, despite his previous experience, Cranston was considered somewhat inept as a candidate. Brown aides like astute Finance Director Hale Champion warned Cranston that he did not have "anything resembling a campaign structure, even though he thought he did," according to one who worked for Cranston, Jack Tomlinson. Cranston was relying on CDC volunteers and his appointed ITAs as "the crux of his campaign organization. The Brown people pointed out that this was hardly enough, and that he needed to have some experienced political types, operatives, if you will," Tomlinson said. One of Brown's press aides, a highly-regarded speech writer, was lent to set up a Cranston office in San Francisco. Tomlinson also was "loaned" from Brown's office to be an advance man for Northern California. Cranston was "desperate and needed some soldiers and Brown was willing to loan him some," believing that Cranston was not a great campaigner and had "self-made" problems, Tomlinson reflected. But when he walked into Cranston's San Francisco headquarters at 950 Market Street, a "sleazy" location, Tomlinson was "almost struck dumb by the receptionist," a beautiful young woman who had been working for the Democratic Party, Vicki Greenlee. The two immediately were attracted to one another, and before the year was out, would marry. [185]

Tomlinson's first sight of candidate Cranston had been at a reception for the press to meet him. "We arrived early – Alan had already arrived, and was sitting over in a corner of this rather large room, reading the *Wall Street Journal*. I'll never forget it," Tomlinson recalled. Brown's press aide "grabbed my arm and said, 'Go over there and get that ass-hole on his feet.' Well, easier said than done! As it turned out, Alan Cranston at that point had few, if any, hand-to-hand campaign skills. He was not a room worker, he didn't like it. During the course of the few months of that campaign, getting him to call people, especially regarding fundraising, was a real arduous task. He was a really smart man – smart enough to know that doing that was really *awful*, but he couldn't quite bring himself to get over the hurdle and play the game. As he evolved over the years, he certainly learned how to do that – in spades," Tomlinson saw.

Salinger's entry, though, was a "*shock*, to say the least, to everybody." When Don Bradley took "a whole operation of Democratic loyalists" to the Salinger campaign, Cranston was "truly outgunned, in almost every way," Tomlinson believed. Cranston also was "outgunned by Salinger personally, who was a good campaigner, good hands-on guy at almost any kind of event." Tomlinson, who arranged Cranston's appearances and traveled with him, found him to be "stand-offish and aloof, the kind of person who would listen and not comment when suggestions were made." That made him difficult to work with, but Tomlinson noted that he "was *quick*, very quick *mentally* – no question."

Some campaign workers joked about the "confederates, confidants and companions" whom Cranston selected to accompany him. Tomlinson and others believed that Irwin Nebron "had *no* concept of campaigning" and was ill-suited in such a job. Nebron and Cranston were "highly suspicious – paranoid is a better word – about spies, so they communicated by having rendezvous" in out-of-the-way places. "You'd be roaring down a highway on the way to Modesto or somewhere, and Cranston would say, 'Pull over there' at some rural gas station so he could call Irwin on what those two thought was a secure line. These calls were constant," Tomlinson remembered with humor.

Lee Falk also showed up again – "an advisor without portfolio." "His job was to whisper in Alan's ear how everybody was screwing him," as Tomlinson remembered. "And Alan must have believed what he heard, or at least, *liked* the 'phantom,' because he kept him around, and the guy would travel with us from time to time and bitch about the accommodations." Falk's presence and influence irritated campaign staff, who joked that Cranston's paranoia was the result of either "Lee's influence – or too many story lines in the comic strips." But it was obvious that Falk "was kind of reassuring to Alan," Tom Moore realized. "Alan liked having Lee around, he made him feel comfortable because they had been friends for a long, long time. He tried to be helpful but he didn't know much about political campaigning." Still, Moore found Falk "a good storyteller." He always had attractive women on his arm, and helped raise money for the campaign. Eleanor thought that others (particularly Nebron) were "jealous of the closeness" between Cranston and Falk, calling him her brother's "closest friend." [186]

The campaign turned nasty in May. Salinger charged Cranston with "dirty politics," accusing his campaign of planting a false story in a Southern California valley paper intended to show that Salinger was against the Rumford fair-housing act. But four California congressman immediately afterward rallied to support Cranston (Representatives James C. Corman of Los Angeles, D. F. Sisk of Fresno, John J. McFall of Sacramento and Jeffrey Cohelan of Berkeley). Cranston kept asking Salinger to admit that Unruh was one of his chief backers and strategists, which Unruh kept denying publicly. "Every political writer in California knows that" the speaker "is working around the clock to defeat me and the working Democrats I represent," Cranston told the San Francisco Press Club. [187]

A law suit was filed May 15, obviously driven by the Unruh forces, seeking an injunction to prevent distribution of a Cranston brochure. The issue was whether an "unofficial" disclaimer were required on the material citing CDC's endorsement of Cranston, pursuant to the Unruh-sponsored bill that required such disclaimers for non-official party organizations. A judge refused to grant the injunction, a victory for the CDC and Cranston. The CDC issued a statement that the law and the suit were efforts to "embarrass CDC, an attempt to muzzle its operations and to intimidate its freedom of expression." Billboards reading "California Democrats for Salinger," after all, bore no visible disclaimer. [188]

Inevitably charges erupted that Cranston was putting a strong arm on his appraisers for money. Cranston called them false and slanderous. "I have made no efforts to raise funds from my appointees," he said. "They have been under no pressure. Some contributed to my campaign, and some did not," he admitted. Some appraisers, however, felt "forced to contribute," and with cash, not checks, as Greenaway found out. [189]

Cranston announced that he had no objection to eliminating appointed appraisers. A derisive editorial in the *Santa Rosa Press-Democrat* noted that only seven ITAs were professional appraisers; others included such people as a "social planning consultant, press agent and fruit shipper." [190]

Two former appraisers, however, admitted publicly to having given Cranston money, telling the press that in effect they had "bought" their appointments with political contributions. One of them, John C. O'Keefe of Azusa, said that he had been "directed" to contribute $2,000 to Cranston's reelection fund in 1962, and had quit the job after that. In fact, O'Keefe had resigned in January, 1962, when embarking on a run for Congress. In his resignation letter, O'Keefe had thanked Cranston for "the excellent treatment" rendered him, and an "enjoyable, fair and impartial" relationship with Cranston personally. "All of your actions toward me have been more than complimentary and satisfactory.... If there is anything we can do to assist you in your campaign in our congressional district, we will be more than pleased to do so," O'Keefe had written. But in a sworn affidavit to the State Senate Rules Committee just two weeks before the primary, O'Keefe stated that Cranston had "literally sold inheritance-tax appraiser positions."[191]

"The fact is, that appraisers' jobs are not for sale, have not been for sale, and will not be for sale in the State of California," Cranston responded. "The fact of a political contribution is not a ban to any office…nor should it be. That Mr. O'Keefe contributed to my campaign has been a matter of public record for six years." [192]

Another appraiser, who claimed to have rescued Geneva in a 1956 boating accident in which four other people drowned, was paraded at a press conference at Salinger's Los Angeles headquarters ten days before the primary. Edward J. Soehnel, a San Bernardino real-estate man, said that he had agreed to give Cranston contributions for his 1958 race if assured of an appraiser appointment. Soehnel's sworn statement said that Cranston, in reply to the request, had said that he would consult Soehnel before making an appointment for the county. Soehnel made a second contribution, and was appointed in 1959. But Cranston fired him in 1964 "for unethical conduct," Cranston said, after learning that Soehnel was an officer in a corporation that purchased property that he had appraised. Soehnel coincidentally also had declared support for Engle. Soehnel admitted to the press that no one had told him that he "must" make a contribution to get an appointment.

The boating accident had occurred after Soehnel reportedly had been asked to inspect a beach property for Cranston. On a tour of the Southern California shoreline, sea swells in a cove swept four people overboard from a small boat. Soehnel said that he saved Geneva, who was holding Kim, from also going overboard. "I almost drowned," Kim recalled, "Mom was holding me while waves came over the bow. Robin was OK." Kim did not remember a man's saving his mother, though. Cranston called Soehnel's charges "ridiculous – I've talked to no appraisers about money, nor will I." Cranston then issued a defensive statement through a spokesman, saying that the attack actually reflected the "evil of the system in which people contribute to all candidates. If you want to read into a contribution a promise of reciprocation, then it's true of all candidates, including Jesse Unruh." [193]

Cranston called on Salinger to repudiate the attacks, and admit that Unruh was "now calling the shots" behind the scenes "to defeat me." Salinger indeed had the backing of Unruh's Democratic Volunteers Committee. But Salinger relished the accusations, which reached a pitch shortly before the primary. Unruh joined in the attacks, calling the ITA-appointee system among the "most corrupting influences in California politics today" while continuing to declare that he was neutral – "or maybe non-belligerent might be a better word" – in the primary contest. "I want to stay out of that nest of snakes," he told a press conference. To which Cranston countered, "Unruh's attack…would be amusing were it not also deceitful and totally dishonest." It bore "no relationship to the truth," and Unruh himself had "consistently taken political contributions from inheritance-tax appraisers," Cranston noted. "Is Salinger tarnishing Unruh with the same brush with which he is trying to smear me?" Cranston asked. To questions as to whether Unruh himself would take the controller's job if offered it, the speaker answered, "With the inheritance-tax appraisers stripped out," as he proposed, "it's a nothing job and nobody would want it." [194]

A Republican State Senator, Jack Schrade of Del Mar, introduced a resolution in the legislature calling for an investigation of whether Cranston had pressured appraisers to pay kick-backs to his campaign fund in order to keep their jobs. The resolution (Senate Resolution 140) accused Cranston of practicing "Eastern machine political techniques," and cited cancelled checks confirming donations to his 1958 and 1962 campaigns. It also alleged that ITAs had been "called upon to perform political duties as a condition of their continued employment," like hosting cocktail parties and fundraising events, turning the controller's office into a "patronage political machine." The investigation was sidelined by Cranston supporters in the Senate (it refused to let the resolution be printed), but the Assembly reactivated it, serving notice on all 148 appraisers that their books might be subpoenaed and asking the controller's office to release gross incomes of appraisers (it already released net incomes, after expenses, which Cranston had instigated). But Schrade charged that appraisers were padding expenses to make net incomes look low. Cranston responded that he would welcome an investigation of charges that appraisers had been forced to contribute to his campaign. But he questioned whether he would get a fair hearing from the partisan legislators who were Unruh's closest associates. As to releasing gross-income figures, he believed that would violate individual privacy. No controller before him had released even the net income of appraisers, primarily because no law required it, but Cranston had done so because he thought it in the public interest. [195]

Cranston issued a statement saying that Schrade had not "produced a shred of evidence" that the controller was "guilty of the slightest wrongdoing," calling Schrade's resolution "the gutter politics we have come to expect of this irresponsible Republican." State Senator James Cobey of Merced, an attorney and valley chairman of the Cranston campaign, called Schrade's allegations a "collection of junk" and "an incredibly obvious political hoax" from "an extremist Republican from San Diego, using material from" Unruh associates (including O'Keefe) whose candidate of "is facing defeat by Controller Alan Cranston." Unruh's "guise of non-belligerence is now completely gone," Cobey bluntly stated. "I've never seen such an unsupported attack on an elected official in my life. It would be laughed out of any court in the state." To discredit O'Keefe, Cobey released his praising letter to Cranston, noting that O'Keefe had failed in his congressional bid, had supported Unruh's 1962 campaign and been fired from a job with the Democratic State Central Committee for "unsatisfactory performance." [196]

Unruh admitted at a news conference May 21 that he had encouraged O'Keefe, whom he knew, to give his documents to Schrade. A draft statement in defense of Cranston said that his opponents were "trying to make a scandal of what is a well-recognized fact in practical politics in this country, from the presidency down…that political appointees are expected to contribute to the campaign of the man who gave them their offices…. However, any appointee who feels that a request for campaign aid is a strong-arm tactic should resign immediately and say why he has done so," a reference to O'Keefe's six-year delay in complaining. Whether the statement were issued was not clear. But Cranston did issue a press release May 22 which said, "These appointees did not lose their interest in politics the day they were appointed any more than…appointees of the president, the governor, state legislators or any other elective officeholder…. I consider it a tribute that some appraisers now are working for my election to the United States Senate, even though it could possibly result in their replacement by my successor." A list of his contributors had always been a matter of public record, he noted. [197]

A number of appraisers, in fact, had contributed to Cranston's campaign, and some were not happy about it. "We were *forced* to contribute," Joe Williams recalled with bitterness. "He made us each pay him $3,500. He shook us down for that." The contributions nevertheless were legal. One campaign aide remembered that ITAs' names were on the list of people whom Cranston was expected to call to solicit money. [198]

Cranston's patience by the end of May had been stretched, and he sued Salinger, Don Bradley and the two former appraisers for libel and $2 million in damages, charging them with "conspiracy to make false, malicious, and defamatory statements to influence the outcome of the primary." Cranston hoped that voters would "see the smears for what they are – the wild and irresponsible charges of a losing candidate." He was suing Salinger because he had "encouraged and circulated this libel against me." Salinger quipped that "the suing season has opened approximately on schedule. It will last until about 7 p.m. on June 2, when the polls close." [199]

Cranston's suit and Salinger's charges came under respective headings of "bluff" and "baloney," one editorial read. That the controller had received contributions from his ITAs should not come as a shock or surprise – every previous controller had benefited in the same way. And, the editorial added, Cranston, Kirkwood and Kuchel were all fine public servants. While there might be a better system, the State Bar Association in 1963 had concluded that California's was better than systems in many other states. "In any event, Salinger's sudden discovery of the long-established appraiser system is hardly a basis on which to choose the Democratic nominee for U. S. Senator," the Redding paper concluded. Other editorials took the same line, the *Palo Alto Times* reminding voters that Cranston had "democratized the appraiserships by increasing the number of posts, limiting the maximum earnings, naming minority members, giving the appraisers special training…and establishing a code of ethics for them. Despite the smear attempts," it concluded, "Cranston's honor remains unsullied." [200]

Red-baiter Myron Fagan also resurfaced, issuing another of his broadsides, this time harassing all three Democrats (Cranston, Salinger and Engle). Engle's voting record, it read, had been "100 percent left-wing. Salinger's background reeks of socialism, if not outright communism – as does his mother's [she had been a French journalist]. But of the three, Cranston has the most malodorous background of socialism, treasonous one-worldism – and frenzied support of communism." [201]

There was another bit of bad publicity when it was revealed that Tom Moore, newly-named executive assistant to the state director of mental hygiene and one of Brown's inner circle, was working for Cranston. Although the department said that Moore did not take the campaign job until June 1, a Republican assemblyman charged that his extra-curricular work short-changed mental patients. The assemblyman's office had been told, when it called the department to inquire about a patient, that Moore was "down in Los Angeles running the Cranston campaign." [202]

Republicans "kept trying to get the press to make an issue about people in state employment who were detached periodically to work on campaigns," Moore recalled. "I was just one of the more conspicuous ones, because I'd come from the Brown campaign against Nixon." Until Salinger had entered the race, "it was kind of assumed that it would be a walk" for Cranston. But he had never campaigned in such a competitive environment. "I don't think his previous campaigns prepared him for what he had to do to beat Salinger. Salinger was a *pro*, and had put together a real rough-and-ready operation in *very* short order, apparently raised a lot of money, and they were on the road. I traveled with Alan, I was his traveling press. I also helped him make money calls, which in the beginning was very hard to do. He was very reluctant," Moore remembered. "The way we did the fundraising, we would get two hotel rooms, and I got a list of calls that he had to make and the targeted amounts" from Dick Kline in the Brown administration, who had done the same thing for Brown. "Things were primitive in those days. We didn't have fax machines pumping things out. I'd get on a phone in one room and dial the person, then I'd get Alan to come in and take the call. We would spend an hour on this ping-pong calling. I'd try to keep track of the commitments, but getting information from him about who had committed was very tough. He'd say, 'Oh, yeah, they're going to give something – he's made a pledge.' 'How much, Alan?' 'Well, he has to think it over.' 'No, Alan, how much did you ask him for?' It was *impossible* in the beginning," Moore laughed of his frustration. "He got a little better at it as things got tighter, and I think he began to worry that this was not going to be a walk with Salinger."

Then there was the harrowing airplane flight to Northern California. "We had a press tour" to do, and Eleanor recommended "a couple of guys who had a small charter flying service. So, against all common sense and reason, we contracted with these guys to fly us on this tour. The plane was the most derelict-looking DC3 you ever saw! It did not look like it would get off the ground. And we were flying in the spring, with bad weather up north. There was a leak on something, they had to raise the landing gear with mechanical levers, and they landed at Red Bluff once, thinking it was Redding. It was the sort of trip that bonded Jack and Vicki Tomlinson because they didn't think they were going to survive it." The plane could not be kept in trim and had to fly with the wheels down to keep it from gaining altitude, Jack Tomlinson remembered. A number of reporters jumped ship after several legs, fearing for their lives. "Oh, God! – but in retrospect it was a lot of fun," Moore recounted with obvious amusement. [203]

Jerry Spingarn also offered help. He had seen a Drew Pearson column – "inspired, no doubt, by Mosk or Unruh" – that talked about Cranston's "vulnerability" because of his association with United World Federalists. Spingarn thought it more of a liability in the general election than the forthcoming primary, but he sent Cranston an "old file on Nixon, which may possibly contain a useful item." He also had told "a hard-working Democratic" friend, a neighbor of Salinger's in Virginia who had joined his California campaign, that "she was fighting against her own kind." [204]

Unruh indeed was strongly behind the Salinger campaign. "I expect a smear a day now that 'Big Daddy' Unruh has taken over active control of Pierre Salinger's faltering bid for the Senate," Cranston declared at a labor rally in Oakland. He likened Unruh's behind-the-scenes role to that of a "dictator," a word that Salinger had used for Governor Brown. "Pierre Salinger has made his biggest mistake of the campaign in accepting the public endorsement of Jesse Unruh," Cranston stated. "There isn't a Democrat in this state who doesn't recognize Unruh for what he is – a ruthless politician determined to become political boss of California. A vote for Unruh's man will be a vote for Tammany Hall politics in California – for absolute domination of the Democratic Party by Unruh and the special interests he represents." With Unruh's open endorsement of Salinger, people could now see the "deception and hypocrisy" they practiced. "Unruh backs Pierre and the fur flies," the *Los Angeles Herald-Examiner* headlined. [205]

Salinger retorted that the CDC was practicing "thought control" to thwart his candidacy and hinted that its leadership was corrupt. But Unruh had sent telegrams to assemblymen who were CDC delegates prior to the endorsing convention, asking them to support Engle while at the same time urging Mosk to run against him. Unruh also had drafted a bill to require that the Democratic State Central Committee, which Unruh's previous election bill had padded with pro-Unruh assemblymen, choose Engle's replacement if he resigned. Brown vetoed the bill, but reiterated that he did not think the speaker had "anything to do with Salinger's getting into the race." The CDC rallied to Cranston's defense and accused Unruh of "attempted mail fraud" in a postcard campaign for Salinger. In a publicized letter, Unruh stooped to calling Cranston – who had dubbed Salinger a "rookie" – "a bench-warmer in the minors, munching political peanuts but refusing to take his turn at bat on hard, tough issues." "I leave it to you to figure out which candidate Unruh is for, but I can figure out for myself which candidate he is against," Cranston had said at the National Press Club. They were "old combatants" and Cranston "enjoyed the jousts," but he had added, "right now, I feel as the Egyptians must have felt when some wily Assyrian decided to start using two horses for chariots instead of one. Happily, however, I anticipate that the complicated set of reins and lines in Jesse's hands will sooner or later snarl – and badly."

Cranston admitted to *Newsweek* just before the primary that if the election had been held two weeks after the well-known Salinger entered the race, "he'd have won it, no contest. Pierre had no place to go but down, and I had no place to go but up." Described as a "rangy (6-feet-2, 185 pounds) 49-year-old attuned to the long sprint," Cranston was said to "humor voters his way, in a dry, metallic voice, with gibes at Salinger's long absence from his native California." "I pay my taxes in California, I am against representation without taxation," Cranston would say to applause at rallies. "I promise that if I ever walk out on Lyndon Johnson, it won't be on one hour's notice," he quipped of Salinger's precipitous departure. Cranston had just gotten the California Federation of Young Democrats to overwhelmingly endorse him (84 to 12.3 percent for Salinger). Salinger in turn was sounding "more piqued than plucky," *Newsweek* said of that setback, although Engle's wife had endorsed him. [206]

A few days before the primary Cranston was cleared by a Los Angeles district attorney of O'Keefe's allegations of having "sold" ITA appointments. The D. A. stated disdainfully, "I do not look with approval on this attempt to use the D. A.'s office for partisan political" opportunism. He had found "no evidence whatsoever" of wrongdoing or criminal offense. Cranston had received contributions like other public officials. "It is clear that Mr. Cranston has not misused his office in making appointments or soliciting campaign funds toward his senatorial campaign." [207]

Cranston now felt as if he were winning. A Field poll in late May showed a reversal of public opinion and gave Cranston 33 percent to Salinger's 27. Ridder, however, wrote Governor Brown that a poll which his newspaper (the *Long Beach Independent Press-Telegram*) had just run put the race "far too close to be conclusive. As I told Alan sometime ago, I think that he is probably going to win; however…the appraiser situation cannot be casually brushed under the rug. The Republican party and the Internal Revenue Department probably won't let it be and I doubt that independents such as myself would want it brushed away either." Cranston, if he won, could "duck the questions that he thinks may hurt him" in the general election. Ridder thought that the "appraiser set-up definitely needs to be cleaned up…. Alan would have been better off if he had said that he would launch an immediate investigation instead of…'I didn't know anything about it,'" Ridder advised. [208]

Cranston and Salinger appeared on NBC television's "Meet the Press" a week before the primary – a news photo of them with moderator Lawrence Spivak showed both candidates smiling, Cranston towering over Salinger. Each candidate "fielded questions smoothly," a news report said, "and exchanged few criticisms." Cranston confirmed that he had accepted contributions from ITAs but denied pressuring them in any way. Such funds, he added, accounted for "far less than half" of his campaign contributions. He also had asked attorneys to determine if libel or slander had been committed by some appraisers attacking him. But a more daunting television confrontation was to be broadcast statewide four days before the primary. [209]

The candidates met at a San Diego television station May 29 in an hour-long format like the 1960 debates between the late President Kennedy and Nixon. Eleanor thought the debate revealed warts on both candidates. Cranston appeared humorless and reticent, Salinger uncharacteristically serious. Friends were quoted as saying that Cranston agreed to the debate largely because he let Salinger badger him into it. *Bee* newspapers publisher C. K. McClatchy nevertheless sent Cranston a note while aboard an airliner the next day, saying, "I want to take this opportunity before the votes are counted to say I think you were great. You fully justified the confidence so many people have in you. Win, lose or draw, you can look back on a campaign that will cause no regrets. Needless to say, I hope you win." [210]

Washington Post cartoonist Herb Block sent an encouraging telegram saying, "Alan Barth [*Post* editorial writer and civil libertarian] and I and lots of your old friends in Washington look forward to seeing you here again soon – this time, as United States Senator from California. You certainly deserve it, and we're for you." [211]

The Cranstons and Fowles flew to Los Angeles and waited for the primary results at the Biltmore Hotel. Early on a reporter asked Cranston if he were conceding. Certainly not, he replied, it was too soon, but Salinger was leading. As the night wore on, he continued to lead although at times the race grew closer. At one point, there was a question about a large bloc of votes in Los Angeles County, and Cranston continued to hold out. Toward midnight, however, before campaign supporters at a large hall, Cranston did concede. It was a blow that he genuinely had not expected. His sister recorded that "his words were as cheery as he could make them, but his friends, accustomed to his buoyancy, were stricken." He went off with Falk and Nebron to concede on television. "It's obvious he's won," Cranston admitted at seven a.m. Cranston's face showed fatigue and his eyes appeared dulled, his voice harsh and unsteady, despite an effort to put on a good front for Democrats. He offered Salinger support in his race against George Murphy who would be his opponent in November. The sixty-one-year-old hoofer still had "the same Irish twinkle and blarney" for which he was remembered in fifty films, one reporter noted. Goldwater also won the GOP presidential primary over more moderate New York Governor Nelson Rockefeller (backed by Senator Kuchel) in the California primary. At the hotel, Kim lay on the floor of his parents' room and cried himself to sleep. Lee Falk knocked on the door early in the morning, soon after Cranston finally had fallen asleep, to say that he was leaving. Everyone was despondent. [212]

The Senate seat had slipped from Cranston's grasp a second time, and he believed that Murphy, who had swept the Republican primary, probably would win the seat and possibly hold it for years. Kuchel remained popular as the state's other senator and would be hard to unseat in the next Senate race in 1968. Cranston now was fifty. He had not expected to lose, with the strong backing that he had from the governor down. It was the first time that a CDC-endorsed candidate had lost in a primary – ironically its first president and organizer. Brown by association also was a loser. Cranston's loss showed that Brown's advocacy was not strong enough to sway voters in his own party, thus killing any chance that he might be nominated for vice president. Unruh, by contrast, had emerged as a party leader and Don Bradley as a skillful strategist (he had concentrated on the Los Angeles area to swing the vote, recognizing that Cranston forces were well organized in Northern California). [213]

To Geneva's attempt to cheer Cranston up by reminding him that he usually saw the bright side of things, Cranston admitted that this time, he could not find a single good thing about his defeat. Eleanor saw that, "for a while, there was a depth of sadness that had not been there before" in her brother's eyes and face. "It was *terrible*," Ann Eliaser remembered of the upset, "it was just awful, losing that race. We couldn't *believe* it!" Cranston attributed his loss largely to Unruh, with whom he had not sought to fight but whose influence he believed had brought Salinger into the race and helped him to win. [214]

Initially considered the underdog, Salinger had won by 143,788 votes. Cranston called Salinger the next day and again offered support. "I want him to know that I stand ready to do whatever I can for him in the general election," Cranston's statement said. "Let me say that ours was not a losing cause," he added. "Our differences with the Goldwater-Murphy type of Republicans on the vital issues of our time are much more important than the differences we have among ourselves in the Democratic Party. I intend to work as energetically as I can between now and November to insure" Democratic victories. He also sent "feelers" to Salinger indicating that he might drop the suit because of a plea from President Johnson for party unity in the general election. Salinger reportedly told Cranston, "Let's leave the president out of this!" O'Keefe, however, counter-sued Cranston for slander, asking $1 million in damages for saying that O'Keefe, at Unruh's instigation, had made a "gutter attack," which O'Keefe called "a lie." That put Cranston in the uncomfortable position of having to proceed with his own libel action. The suit against Salinger and others would divide them until Salinger publicly apologized for making false charges. [215]

They also had made a "gentlemen's agreement," negotiated two days before the primary by Governor Brown and state party leader Eugene Wyman, that the winner would help the loser pay off his campaign deficit, an attempt to mend the rift between candidates and party factions. Brown acted as a peacemaker, even praising Unruh when signing a school finance bill that the speaker had pushed through the legislature. Brown told a press conference that he thought Cranston had made a mistake by repeated attacks on Unruh's role in the campaign. Cranston's "strategy was not my strategy," Brown stated bluntly, adding that he hoped Cranston would drop his lawsuit. As to the loss, Brown said, "There won't be home runs all the time, sometimes there'll be strike-outs." Cranston was pictured greeting Brown at the Sacramento airport, closely hugging Kim, dressed in suit and tie. The rift with Unruh, though, would continue through 1965, when Unruh and his backers disputed the use of funds raised by the party to help pay off both Cranston's and Salinger's campaign debts. [216]

After Salinger's apology, Cranston did drop the suit. There were rumors that President Johnson had persuaded him, but aides believed that Brown's top adviser Hale Champion had helped broker the deal. Cranston did work for Salinger's election, noting that Unruh's relationship with the candidate soon deteriorated. Senator Engle died July 30, and Brown appointed Salinger to fill the unexpired term to the end of the year. Unruh had recommended that Salinger turn it down, saying publicly that he should get to the Senate on his own by winning the election. That would make him look good to voters, as if he were going on his merits. Salinger, however, accepted the appointment. After meeting with Brown, Salinger walked across the hall into Cranston's office and told him that he knew how he felt but wanted to be his friend. Cranston could not help blurting out, "I had it in my hands! That's what hurt." [217]

"Unruh gave Salinger the only good advice he ever got," Cranston would say in retrospect. "It was, 'Let Pat Brown offer it to you but don't take it, and announce, 'I want to be Senator of California by a vote of the people of California – not by appointment of Pat Brown.' If he had done that, he might well have won the election and been the senator. But it was too easy to be nominated and then suddenly the senator by appointment. You can understand why Salinger took it," Cranston conceded. "It generally was thought to be an advantage on the ballot to be the incumbent. But he was not a full-fledged incumbent because of the way he got there."

Cranston himself had considered what he might do if offered the appointment, which many colleagues thought he was owed. But Cranston had considered that it would be a bad move to give up his controller job for a brief few months in the Senate, and had decided that he would not accept the appointment. "Oddly enough, Pat Brown was criticized widely by CDC-type people for not appointing me," he remembered. "They didn't realize that I didn't want it, and that it wouldn't make sense."

Cranston said that he was not bitter about the loss – "I don't get bitter about things." But he did feel cheated out of what he believed he had had in his pocket. He nevertheless was grateful to Brown for loyally supporting him "all the way."

Again he would find an unexpected advantage to the loss, rationalizing, "If I had gotten elected then, I think the odds were that I would have been a one-term senator.

Bob Finch would have run against me in 1970 at the height of his popularity. He was very strong and very popular for a brief time. He had been lieutenant governor [under Reagan] and was then HEW Secretary, one of Nixon's top people while Nixon was on top. He surely would have been my opponent in 1970, had I won in 1964, and might well have beaten me." In the end, Finch "couldn't run that year because George Murphy held the Senate seat, and Murphy was a colleague and friend." [218]

Looking back on the campaign, Tom Moore reflected that Cranston "was considered a shoe-in until Salinger got in." That had forced Cranston to "practically genuflect before wealthy and powerful people" to raise money. There also was "bitter infighting" in Cranston's camp, particularly between Hale Champion and another campaign aide, a former Kennedy under-secretary of state. Tomlinson saw the campaign as "really pathetic, tinted with paranoia and weird folk. You either had to be a complete died-in-the-wool Cranston slave and believer, or you ended up" being upset. "'The only good thing that came out of the campaign' – quoting Alan – was our marriage. Alan attended, and was a superstar at the reception." And in spite of campaign problems, Cranston did remarkably well, given the "unlucky break" of Salinger's entry, Tomlinson thought, believing that Cranston "would have *creamed* George Murphy." [219]

Old friends commiserated with Cranston. Lars Skattebol sent a long, rambling, sometimes unintelligible telegram reading, "No cause to fret, let alone grieve, if you be stopped at least temporarily," ending with hope "that justice…[was] merely delayed." "I ache and rebel at the thought of your effort having been aborted by Salinger's really quite reprehensible coat-tail venture," Ted Waller wrote. "The general impression in my circle is that you did everything just precisely right," which "you have done…for fifteen years. I know of nobody in American politics who has more thoroughly earned – and prepared himself for – a Senate seat. The whole bloody business is infamous. It reflects no credit on Pierre. Depressing." [220]

Falk wrote more humorously, taking Cranston down a peg or two. After a telephone call, Falk was glad that Cranston "no longer sounded like Jehovah talking into a power megaphone, but more like the flesh-and-blood Cranston of old." He also hoped that, with the primary now four months past, "the blind glaze of the potential senator has left your eyes and that you can find your way to the men's room without being led by your deputy and three public relations men. Are you able yet to go to a friend's house for dinner without automatically rising after the dessert to ask for contributions? Are you still wearing the same frozen grin even when you're shaving, or has your face relaxed enough for you to scowl or frown when necessary? Do you still run around your track every morning, even without the TV cameras? Do you still change shirts three times a day, as during the campaign, or have you returned to your old loveable ways of wearing the same shirt for a month?" As to his shoes, "It would never have occurred to the pre-candidate Cranston to waste time and money on a ridiculous and wasteful thing like a shoeshine. But during the campaign! – the amount of energy put in by shoeshine boys over your size-20 gunboats could, if properly harnessed, provide power for Eureka for six months. How about the haircuts? During the campaign, every time you spotted a barbershop, even from a speeding car or plane, you'd jump right out, race to it with your 440 stride, settle down happily before the mirror, with that blind senatorial glaze in your eyes and the frozen grin, announce in a mighty voice that you wanted a trim and would be pleased to accept all contributions to defeat Bossism in California. For a man with your amount of hair, this was obviously carrying things too far. All the poor barber could do was snip his scissors foolishly in the air, pretending to cut non-existent hair, then put on the powder, accept a Cranston button, sign a pledge card, shake your hand, and rush out and vote for Salinger. After all, he couldn't refuse to cut your hair, not after the Civil Rights bill and all that. It must be pretty dull in that controller's office," he ended, "after all those happy days of suing Salinger, hurling daily blockbusters at Unruh, etc." [221]

Chester Bowles wrote from his post as Ambassador to India, saying that he could put Cranston to work on a project like heading the $1-billion U. S. economic development program there if Cranston should "ever decide to step out of public life in California." "You would be the ideal person to tackle it," Bowles said, but he added, "I earnestly hope you stick with what you are doing and one day succeed Pat Brown or move into the Senate." [222]

"You are like Adlai Stevenson, who lost to a national hero" Raymond Gram Swing put it poignantly. "You lost to Kennedy, not to Unruh or anybody else. It was bad luck on a colossal scale to be bucking Kennedy, who is far stronger dead than he was alive." [223]

"Alan Cranston has learned to smile again" amid rumors that Brown might get a job in Washington and Cranston might run for governor, *Examiner* political reporter Sydney Kossen wrote in September. "Cranston, an affable egghead, is willing to get bruised again. He abhors fellow Democrat Jesse Unruh," and "went down swinging" in the primary when "most pollsters said Salinger would finish second. They were wrong. Cranston was stunned. His wife and two teenaged sons took the defeat hard, and this depressed Cranston further. It was a long, gloomy summer for the tall, bald controller who, less than two years ago, piled up more votes than any other California Democrat. Nobody rallies around a loser, and phone calls and mail fell off" from many who had turned to Cranston for help in the past, Kossen reported. "Some believed that he no longer had any political muscle." But as Cranston began to get invitations to speak, his "old ebullience returned." Salinger, Kossen concluded, had derisively referred to Cranston as a "tax collector – it probably stuck." [224]

One editorial suggested that Cranston's down-slide was caused by "his sour remarks about the manner in which Mr. Salinger got into the race. It was further hurt by the debate in which both parties exchanged "thinly-veiled insinuations…as to the integrity of each," which was "beneath the dignity of the two men" and the office they sought. "We hope that Mr. Cranston, an extremely able man, studies what happened in this campaign, profits therefrom and returns some day to try again." [225]

At first, political speculators assumed that Salinger would win the November election. Murphy was "hardly serious competition." Salinger, though, quickly began to lose ground after the primary and appointment to the Senate – as Unruh had foreseen. Murphy exploited the carpetbagger image, and dodged appearing as hard-line conservative. "His old footwork hasn't failed him," the *Life* magazine reporter wrote, and Murphy's films kept turning up on late-night television, giving him lots of free exposure to California voters. [226]

In the November election, President Johnson trounced Goldwater. But in California, Republican Murphy beat Salinger by 200,000 votes, despite the fact that there were one million more Democrats in California than Republicans. In an autobiography, Salinger blamed his loss on the controversial ballot proposition (14) to repeal the Rumford Fair-Housing Act, which caused a White voters' backlash against liberals (the fair-housing law, which Brown, Salinger and Kuchel all supported, was repealed by a two-to-one margin). But Cranston attributed the loss to Murphy's use of the carpetbagger image and ability to evade controversial issues. Murphy's show-biz experience helped him look senatorial in a widely-watched television debate with the overweight, strident Salinger. Salinger's "style, more than any single issue, was the measure of his failure," a *New Republic* analysis stated. "For the sorry truth was that the more Salinger exposed himself, on television and in public, the more voters soured on his candidacy. The glamour of his eleventh-hour cross-country dash to file for the June primary had long ago tarnished. His cavalier treatment of the grass-rootsy Democratic clubs was unseemly, and his quickie appointment to the Senate had the look of a shotgun affair." Salinger had the bravado to put on his billboards, "Retain Senator Pierre Salinger," which even his own staff predicted would backfire. Murphy, by contrast, ran a "soft-shoe, no-issues, honey-smooth campaign against Salinger's jarring, almost punchy effort. If Murphy was just another song-and-dance man, Salinger began to look more and more like an untrustworthy used-car salesman; worse, the portly Salinger had the problem of 'fat-lash.'" Cranston saw also that Democrats had been badly wounded and divided by the bitter primary, causing many to defect to Murphy in November. Asked if he thought he might have done better than Salinger, Cranston diplomatically said, "Having lost the primary, I don't think I should comment on what I could have done." [227]

Many, however, including Brown, thought that Cranston would have defeated Murphy. "I don't see any reason to doubt that," Tom Moore believed. "I don't think George Murphy could have made any kind of issue against Alan the way he did Salinger. Pierre began to look like a sort of ugly troublemaker. His personal style was testy and belligerent, and he never got out from under the carpetbagger cloud. That was a case of 'ego uber allis.' He just saw an opening and tried to go for the touchdown when it was only good for about five yards. [His candidacy] was a big mistake." And Cranston's popularity was still high. A Field poll after the primary showed him leading other possible candidates for governor if Brown did not run for a third term. Unruh, on the other hand, was again in disgrace for having master-minded Salinger's primary win only to cool to him in the general election, contributing to his loss. Murphy and other Republican candidates had used "Big Daddy" as an issue. Even the *Chronicle* had endorsed Murphy. [228]

Political columnist Dick Nolan observed that "In the ordinary course of events, Cranston would have been given that senatorial appointment, had Engle retired. And there would have been no primary fight." Cranston would have been "a far stronger candidate than Salinger" against Murphy, Nolan thought. But Unruh's strategy had proved that, with out-of-state backing, he could divide and beat Brown's "regular" Democrats and "even up old scores with Cranston." Nolan also blamed "amazingly inept campaign tactics engineered by Los Angeles professionals in the Cranston camp, not the least of which was an idiotic libel suit against Salinger." Salinger, though, ultimately lost to the "personable" Murphy because lots of Democrats did not "buy" the Salinger candidacy. [229]

Ralph Raymond wrote a consoling letter to Cranston, calling his old friend "a gentleman of sterling character" who should have been senator. Raymond had been tempted to write many times "since Fat Pierre appeared on the scene," and ended with encouragement: "I don't know what your present plans are, but I do know that *our* state *needs* men of your ability in the political world, and I hope you stay with it." [230]

Apparently as a joke intended to ease tension between them, Salinger sent Cranston a request for a job in January, 1965. "I have what I believe is an unusual combination of experience in newspaper work, public relations and politics," he said. "As your administrative assistant, the next time you run for office I would not only throw all my energies into your campaign but also by that time I would be able to vote for you. If you want to extend your interests in Washington, I know how to open the doors there, and I would be proud to speak for you." He could provide letters of recommendation from national figures like the Kennedy family, he added, and "from such Democratic leaders in California as the Honorable Stanley Mosk and Speaker Jesse Unruh." In seriousness, Salinger wrote Cranston in April, 1965, "I am grateful to you for dropping that libel suit, and I want to express to you once again the concern that I have felt over the accusations which were made during the heated final days of May about your conduct, both as an individual and as an officer-holder. For the record" Salinger said that he had not repeated anything other than facts about inheritance-tax appraisers' contributions, "but I at no time charged, and after further investigation, do not believe, that any…appraiser positions were sold or promised by you in return for contributions, or that improper pressures were ever utilized by you…. These charges were made by others – not by me – and were neither solicited by me nor by any person in my campaign…. Your reputation for honesty and integrity is and should be beyond reproach." [231]

The apology may have been orchestrated to get Cranston to drop his libel suit.

Cranston realized that the ITAs issue had hurt him, and considered ways of making the system more open by releasing appraisers' gross-income figures and other changes. Ridder again advised Brown on the matter, suggesting that he and Cranston initiate the changes rather than have them forced on them "by possibly unfriendly sources" like Unruh. Cranston in July did issue gross-income figures, saying that requests for the data "in the closing days of the recent primary" allowed no time to gather the information. The figures were made available in advance of an Assembly Ways and Means Committee hearing on the ITA system. Cranston noted that the increased number of appraisers, to 148, allowed for better distribution of the work. But the fallout continued. The analyst for the legislature testified that the system was a "remnant of the old-fashioned political spoils system," and the Assembly Elections Committee, whose chairman had supported Salinger, subpoenaed appraisers to provide detailed information about their political contributions. One of Cranston's campaign managers suggested that Cranston call for a non-partisan commission to look into the matter in order "to give the people of California an honest" picture of the system. Cranston was lauded by a columnist in Ridder's paper for "instituting reforms that his predecessors failed to adopt," including the reporting system to keep track of appraisers' incomes. In November Cranston declared that he would not accept contributions from his appointed appraisers in future. He also made a point of showing that ITAs had contributed to both perpetrators of the investigation, Unruh and Assemblyman Don A. Allen, and released a list of appraisers who had contributed to Kirkwood's campaign. But Unruh would continue to attack Cranston and the ITA system. [232]

Cranston found other ways to channel his energies after the election. He bought two properties in the Sierra Nevada mountains, one with his sister and another with his wife and sons, for which he signed an agreement to keep the land in a natural state. They named the latter (230 acres near Bridgeport) "KRAG Ranch," using the first initials for Kim, Robin, Alan and Geneva. Cranston also took up oil painting, turning out simple, primitive pictures that he used for Christmas cards. And he went back to running on a regular basis. [233]

The fundraising aspect of the primary had been eye-opening for Cranston. He wrote a bitter but prescient article about the losing campaign and the money that he had had to raise, published in *Fortune* magazine in November, 1964. Abraham Lincoln, he noted, had managed to raise $200 when he ran for Congress in 1846. After he won, he gave back $199.25, saying that he did not need money from others, having canvassed on his own horse and entertained at his own house, for which his only outlay was "75 cents for a barrel of cider, which some farmhands insisted" he should treat them to. "I ran in the United States Senate primary this year," Cranston said, "and my supporters spent approximately $1 million on my candidacy," of which $823,307 had been spent directly on the campaign. He had a $332,000 deficit, for which he was still raising money. Salinger had reported spending $481,000 for his campaign. "How much does money influence the actions of the winner after he takes office?" he asked, predicting that at least $100 million would be spent annually on campaigns in the near future, twice that amount in presidential elections. [234]

Little of the money spent on his Senate race had been his own, he noted. Only millionaire candidates like Kennedys and Rockefellers could afford to dip into personal fortunes for such purposes. The fact that much campaign money had come from outside sources was troubling, and existing laws did not require "full disclosure of all that is really spent in a campaign.... Yet in an intensely competitive situation, to spend much less than Salinger and I each did to reach the voters in a state like California would be to face almost certain defeat." He was "distressed by the fact that a great part of the money" was "not to communicate the candidate's ideas and convictions...but to create an image of what his managers think the voters would like him to be." The candidate became "a commodity." Then there was the allocation of funds – Cranston had spent $96,000 on billboards, but "you really can't say anything of substance on them." The same applied to broadcast media. Little could be said in ten-second TV and radio spots on which Cranston had spent $250,000, more than a quarter of his budget. He bemoaned that a second of silence at the beginning and end of such spots, and the required political announcement, actually reduced the content from ten to six seconds – "you pay for" dead time. Then there was the cost of mailings – "the 5-cent stamp is bank-breaking, but if you don't go first class, your literature is all too apt to land unopened in the wastebasket." [235]

But the reasons behind donations to candidates were what bothered Cranston the most – "ranging from those who…give only in return for a candidate's promise to vote or perform…in a certain way to those who expect 'access.'" In years past, contributors often sought patronage jobs. That now applied largely to people seeking diplomatic or high-level appointments. Cranston admitted that contributions from "my appointees was one of the issues in my race," if not the decisive one. Candidates had to ask themselves how obligated they were if they accepted money. Cranston warned against taking cash unless witnesses were present to avoid charges that the candidate pocketed the contribution for personal use. He had told fundraisers in all three of his campaigns that he would not tolerate any commitments in return for contributions. He also had voluntarily set a limit on the amount that he would accept from individuals – the same as in the federal Hatch Act, $5,000. But the fact remained that there was little public reporting of contributions.

Cranston favored full disclosure, but not if he were alone in agreeing to that. "If I did it and my opponents did not, I would be voluntarily handing them a strategic advantage." Far-reaching reforms were necessary. He proposed two alternatives, which appeared contradictory but could be combined. One was to remove all limits on contributions while requiring the fullest possible disclosure of them. The other approach would set low limits on contributions while encouraging public funding of campaigns, e.g., from income-tax deductions, something that both Theodore Roosevelt and Harry Truman had advocated. Americans had to realize that modest, across-the-board donations to political parties could only "strengthen our free institutions." *Fortune* paid him $1,000 for the article, but he listed the same amount as expenses (for "promotional fees") on his income-tax returns, thus showing no profit from the article. He subsequently had the article reprinted and would distribute it widely over many years. He took particular notice of the British system, which at the time permitted candidates to spend up to 2.5 cents per voter on campaigns, and required accounting for every shilling. [236]

"The problem of money in politics is really a serious and immense one," Cranston said in an interview, "and I hope that…we can achieve at least some corrections." At the time, he was speaking in favor of Governor Brown's "purity-of-elections" bill, which called for full disclosure of what was given and by whom. [237]

Cranston prior to the primary had publicly disclosed his tax returns, setting a precedent as the first major public official in California to voluntarily do so. (State law did not require such disclosure by elected or appointed officials.) "Cranston – an outspoken advocate of the principle that taxpayers have a right to know about the finances of their elected officials – now has gone even one step further," the *Los Angeles Times* reported of his giving the newspaper complete financial statements of assets and liabilities as of November 1, 1965. They revealed that he apparently was the wealthiest state official, thanks to real-estate investments prior to his first election in 1958. His taxable income for 1964 was $34,312. His and Geneva's assets totaled $488,861, liabilities (mostly mortgages) $108,700, leaving a net worth of $380,161. Among liabilities was the note to his mother for $10,000, which he was paying off . He owned property and buildings in San Bruno, Los Altos, Fort Bragg, his residence in Sacramento, Krag Ranch in Nevada County on which someone ran cattle, paying the Cranstons about $300 a year (the ranch house was rented). His salary was $22,050 (scheduled to rise to $25,000 in 1967). He still retained a real-estate license but had "put it on ice." [238]

Revealing his returns caught Governor Brown and other public officials off guard, and put them on the spot to follow suit. Brown even curtly told reporters that a public official's financial affairs were private unless a "valid political issue." He did not intend to expose his private life to public view merely "to satisfy the curiosity of another individual or the news media," he was quoted as saying. [239]

Back in the controller's office, Irwin Nebron again had taken offense at something that Cranston had said, which threatened to cause another rift in their relationship. "Friday last you asked a question which so astonished me, I thought at first you surely meant to be joking," Nebron said in a handwritten note to Cranston. His answer was "stated from the bottom of my heart."

"Alan, I am a human being who has weaknesses as well as strengths.... I happen to believe that you are an exceptional person – and have given of myself as much as I possibly could over a long period of time.... I am truly emotionally involved in the successful advancement of your career. If I am disturbed by what I see and hear, it is because of concern for your own welfare....

"I read once that a true friendship is like a fragile flower – hard to grow, more difficult to sustain, and easily destroyed. For my part, I hope the flower continues to flourish in the years ahead.

Affectionately,
Irwin" [240]

That was the last straw, and Nebron, at Cranston's request, was appointed a municipal court judge in Los Angeles by Pat Brown shortly after the disastrous Salinger campaign. In January, 1965, Cranston hired a former newsman who had been press secretary and speech writer for Hubert Humphrey, Winthrop Griffith, as chief deputy controller. The move was considered "significant" by political reporters who noted that replacing lawyer Nebron with writer Griffith was "taken in Capitol quarters as indicative of Cranston's future political plans" and a move to strengthen his image. (A book by Griffith, *Hubert Humphrey, Power and Purpose*, was published soon after the appointment.) Cranston's plans might include running for governor if Brown got a Supreme Court appointment or ran for the Senate, or for lieutenant governor if Brown ran again. [241]

Cranston's mother was increasingly frail, and Cranston visited her before Christmas, 1964, when the family would be in Mexico for the holiday. She warned in advance that he would "get a sniff of what life in a home turned into an infirmary is like. I shall never cease to be grateful that I was able to help Father through his long illness without all this turmoil – and expense!" she wrote in an unsteady hand. She had been thinking of telephoning to thank Cranston for all his messages but decided to save money and write instead – it "fit into my old-time frugal up-bringing. I note the carpetbagger is going to settle down here," she added about Salinger. "Do you suppose he can live down that title?" [242]

She asked if he could manage the interest payment due on her $10,000 loan "while you are under such heavy expenses? I don't care how long you take to pay it, for what I want most is to help you along. Still, I do appreciate your keeping it up in a businesslike way."[243]

Pat Brown meanwhile was saying openly that, even if reelected in 1966, he was interested in a U. S. Supreme Court appointment or running against Senator Kuchel in 1968. President Johnson had indicated that he expected Brown to run again for governor. But Brown's announcement that he had other objectives led to more active speculation of who else might run. Cranston still was considered a stronger candidate than Unruh or Lieutenant Governor Glenn Anderson.[244]

Brown was plagued by the conservative right's unhappiness with the growing counter-culture that had begun to dominate the University of California at Berkeley, beginning in the late 1950s when many faculty and liberals objected to the requirement that they sign a loyalty oath. University President Clark Kerr sided with the intellectuals against the anti-Communist right, who wanted to clean up the "mess" at Berkeley. It would provide fodder for attacks against Brown by a future opponent.[245]

"I hope that the current trouble at the University of California will not hurt Pat," Drew Pearson wrote Cranston in December, 1964. "I might tell you in passing that the president has come to be very fond of him." Pearson and Cranston, though, had had a tiff, prompting Cranston to ask whether he had lost Pearson as a friend. "You have not lost a friend," Pearson said. "Probably I should not have written you as abruptly as I did, though I confess I have been disappointed with a lot of well-meaning people who pose as friends of late, among them your pal Hubert Humphrey."[246]

Riots erupted during the summer of 1965 in the Los Angeles area of Watts, and charges of police brutality followed. Calling the disturbance a "symbol" of poverty and "lack of opportunity and hope," Cranston predicted that such problems would be campaign issues in future elections.[247]

He also became extremely vocal about "extremism" in political views, like those of the right-wing John Birch Society. Pat Brown shared those fears, particularly the potential of a rightist gubernatorial opponent in 1966. Brown wanted somebody to attack the extremists and Cranston agreed to do it. His new press aide Wes Willoughby drafted a hard-hitting, dramatic speech that Cranston first delivered to a Los Angeles Town Hall meeting in July, 1965, despite cautions from Willoughby that it might have repercussions because it was so outspoken. "Please read that speech carefully – maybe you shouldn't give it," Willoughby told him. "But is it *true*?" Cranston asked, and assured that the facts were as written, Cranston went ahead. He opened by describing two "bulky pieces of mail" that recently had landed on his desk. One envelope contained a publication from the Progressive Labor Party, the other, material from the John Birch Society. *Progressive Labor* "told me that we Americans live in a fascist state, that President Johnson and Walter Reuther are among its conspiratorial leaders and stooges, and that President Kennedy was assassinated by the big-business, police-state machine." The second packet told him exactly the same things, except that "President Kennedy was assassinated by the Communists for not being a good enough Communist."[248]

"There is a highly contagious virus in our land," Cranston warned. Proponents of extremism, some 3,000 groups, were "flooding Californians and Americans with their propaganda at an unprecedented rate. To the extremist, this is simply patriotism of the highest order – well meant, but deadly dangerous," because it thrived on fear, bigotry and hate. Extremist views could not be "removed surgically" like a cancer – "they are only as strong as we permit them to become" in a free and open society. "The prescription, I believe, is a massive and constant dose of the strong serum of truth," and speaking out. "The greatest ally of extremism is indifference. Silence is not golden, my friends. Silence is darkness." Hitler's "greatest early allies were ignorance and indifference," he told a B'nai B'rith group in another speech. "I saw it happen there. I never want to see it happen here." Cranston also put his name on a white paper attacking the Birch Society ("The John Birch Society: A Soiled Slip is Showing"), condemning it as fostering neo-Fascist, anti-Semitic and anti-Catholic "Nazi theses." [249]

The speech, "Who's an extremist?," was entered into the *Congressional Record* by liberal Democratic Senator Eugene J. McCarthy of Minnesota, reprinted and reported or excerpted in newspapers across the nation. "It could not have been easy for State Controller Alan Cranston to make his recent important speech on extremist groups in California," *Los Angeles Times* columnist Max Freedman wrote. "Had someone from outside California spoken in those harsh and challenging terms, he would have been charged with maligning the state as a paradise for extremists. Cranston accepted that risk because he believes that the extremists make their greatest gains when moderate and responsible people are silent or timid." "Few politicians are willing to stick their necks out in a good cause," *The Nation* editorialized. "Alan Cranston is one of the few. He has just released a 26-page blast at the John Birch Society. This is the more remarkable in that California is a hot-bed of the society, and Cranston is Controller of California." Membership in the Birch Society at that time was estimated at 100,000 nationwide and its budget $12 million to promote its views. [250]

The published attack documented the depth of bigotry and racism infusing the society, whose chapters met in secret to reinforce their belief that Jews were responsible for much of the world's problems and that Negroes were biologically inferior. Apparently from spies attending such meetings, Cranston wrote knowledgeably, "The dominance of racial hate and religious prejudice in [a] particular chapter [that met in a San Francisco apartment] is, in fact, part of an ugly pattern throughout the society, from top to bottom." It was "time someone in America pointed it out, clearly and straight-forwardly. My purpose is simply to sound an early warning to every American concerned about his country." [251]

Cranston next wrote a biting indictment of the man emerging as the likely Republican gubernatorial candidate in 1966 – actor Ronald Reagan – which was published in the magazine *Frontier*. Cranston couched it as a satirical subject for a play, prompted by "the sadly-serious foolishness that a popular movie star, without any background or experience in government or business whatsoever, becomes over night the leading Republican contender for one of the most challenging, demanding and toughest jobs in our nation – taking a cram course in California government en route." The central figure, "Reginald Rodgun," would be convinced by some "old wranglers" in a big Cadillac – "with an out-of-state license plate" – to seek the office in order to "save California from the evil, alien menaces of public roads and public schools – and the Post Office Act of 1797." All of the characters were caricatures of well-known right-wing extremists – "Billy James Hardgrass" (anti-Communist evangelist Billy James Hargis), "Dan Smooth " (conservative columnist Dan Smoot), "H. L. Hunted" (businessman H. L. Hunt who headed an anti-Communist Life Line Foundation). Another reality, though, was that former senator and presidential contender Barry Goldwater was suggesting Reagan for – "believe it or not – President of the United States! I still don't believe it. But I guess we'd all better believe it." Cranston thought that "Ronnie" would lose – "and lose badly" in a governor's bid, just as Knowland and Nixon had done when they had their eyes more on the White House than Sacramento. Reagan's nomination, Cranston felt, "would be a tragedy, not only for the Republican Party but for all of California." There was "nothing personal" in his attacks on Reagan, although he could "honestly find few characteristics or achievements in his background qualifying him to direct the fortunes of" the state. "And I think that most conservatives, on cold, clear reflection would agree, if silently, that…Reagan's gubernatorial and/or presidential aspirations are preposterous." But then, "maybe he won't recommend turning our state government over to central casting," Cranston ended sardonically. [252]

Cranston was speaking a lot around the state in the non-election year. To the Commonwealth Club of business and civic leaders in San Francisco he suggested that Californians take a hard look at themselves and the state, which outsiders continued to ridicule as "a sort of outsized and zany adolescent, sprawling and brawling along the shores of the Pacific, and not quite civilized politically or socially." In truth, Cranston said, "California is an uncommonwealth," disunified, "a jigsaw puzzle of social, economic and political segments…fragmented by…conflicting interests." Californians did not have a "sense of state citizenship." They needed an awareness of *common* concerns to solve statewide problems rather than dwelling on north-versus-south, urban-versus-rural, cities-versus-suburbs, majorities-versus-minorities, and "people-versus-automobiles. I seriously wonder if California today is geared more to satisfying the demands of automobiles than to serving the needs of the people," he mused. [253]

Three personal experiences had jolted him "into taking a new look at the role of the automobile in California." The first was a telephone call at midnight one Saturday – "the kind of call every parent dreads." It was from a hospital emergency room. Robin had been in an accident, riding in the back seat of a car that rolled over three or four times after an intersection collision. Cranston rushed to the hospital to find Robin lying on a gurney, "barely conscious, covered with blood, broken glass protruding from wounds in his face, neck and arms, waiting his turn for care." The emergency room experience was horrifying, and the picture of his son and other "battered, bleeding and broken human beings" was still vivid in his memory. Then he had seen a disturbing incident on a freeway in which two cars just ahead of him had collided, but "incredibly, continued on at 60 miles an hour or more without pause," the drivers merely glancing at each other, shrugging their shoulders, as if things like that were not out of the ordinary. And in Los Angeles he had heard a news broadcast stating, "in a matter-of-fact voice, 'There will be no eye irritation today.' Bully for us, I thought."

The extent to which the automobile caused pollution and the paving over of the environment was alarming, Cranston felt. Some 5,000 people had been killed in auto accidents in California in 1964, equal to wiping out the population of a small town like Sausalito. New cars outnumbered new babies, and the state spent $1.25 billion on highways and car-related costs, $70 per person. Californians need to "examine all the implications of the automobile" as merely one type of transportation, "one of many compelling problems" the state faced. "I want to see California become the scene and the standard of all that is best in America." It represented "the greatest hopes" of the nation with its endowment of "natural resources and skilled and talented human resources." They needed to be protected and developed with care. "If we do not see to it that our ever-more complicated, ever-more intricate technology serves to enhance man's dignity and freedom rather than to ensnarl and enslave him in its web…then hope must diminish throughout the land and, indeed, in all the world." [254]

"I would not stay in politics," he stated, "with all its merciless demands on privacy and family life, if I believed that this state was fated to endure endless internal feuding and infinite parochial conflicts. I am in public service because I do believe that beneath the surface of the uncommonwealth, there exist the foundations and elements of what I call the California Community." Its people had "a youthful spirit, a respect for individualism, an intelligent resourcefulness, a restless instinct for progress, a hunger for education and an eagerness to take on new and difficult tasks." After all, he pointed out, in the next census, California would have "the greatest voice in the affairs of our nation" and necessarily the world. Californians had a challenge to "set a standard" for America and all human beings.

On a lighter note, Cranston got amusing publicity describing how Robin taught his father the "new math." "It's so easy, the claim goes, that a child can do it," Cranston related in a speech to a group of businessmen. "So the other night, I struggled hard and long, under the patient guidance of my teenage son. He asked me, for example, to solve this one, as quickly as possible: 'What is 13 times 88 plus 13 times 12?' The ready answer, naturally, is 1,300 – a figure that I reached ultimately and painstakingly, by multiplying 13 times 88 and 13 times 12, and adding the results. 'Not very quick,' huffed my son Robin. 'You can get the answer much quicker by adding 88 and 12 (that's 100) and multiplying by 13. See?'" The press had fun with headlines like "State controller gets math lesson from son," "Son's math embarrasses A. Cranston," "Cranston gets a 'C.'" [255]

After the attacks that he had suffered during the Salinger debacle, Cranston became consumed in 1965 with reforming the appraiser system. At the same time, he could claim savings in his office of up to $500,000, thanks to the expanded use of computers and a tight rein on staff increases. His efforts to make the department more efficient again came in for amused press attention, this time from *San Francisco Chronicle* humorist Art Hoppe. Cranston had begun a speech with a story about a symphony orchestra that was in financial straits and hired efficiency experts to help it out. They reported "the four oboe players often had nothing to do; all twelve violins were playing identical notes – unnecessary duplication; there was too much repetition – no useful purpose is served by repeating on the horns a passage that has already been played by the strings; the concert time of two hours could easily be reduced to twenty minutes; excessive effort was used by players of wind instruments – one portable air compressor could supply adequate aid for all instruments; the leading violinist's instrument is already several hundred years old – more modern equipment should be purchased." Hoppe could not contain his delight: "Never have we…heard a more pithy indictment of the universally-accepted argument that efficiency is always to be admired. And our hats are off today to Mr. Cranston, truly an intelligent, courageous and witty public official. Of course, in all fairness, it should be noted that some say he runs a superbly efficient office. But our hearts are so full at this moment that we can't bring ourselves to hold it against him." [256]

Cranston's efficiency notwithstanding, the legislature now was close to approving a bill to abolish appraisers and go to a system of assessment in which estate administrators would file statements with the State Board of Equalization without using fee-collecting appraisers. It was "no secret," a reporter wrote, that Unruh, who was in a San Francisco hospital for treatment of an injured knee when the Assembly voted on the bill, "wanted badly" to get it passed, although it was Republican-sponsored. Unruh worked from his hospital bed and a number of Democrats were persuaded to vote for it rather than for one containing reforms proposed by Brown and Cranston. Their bill would transfer ITA collections from the controller to a new department of revenue under the governor, leaving appointment of appraisers in the controller's office. [257]

Editorials were calling for changes, saying that Cranston was not the first controller with appointive power subject to abuse. An Assembly Ways and Means Committee report called it an "unhealthy element of political patronage," and wasteful of public money. Eliminating appointed tax appraisers, one editorial quipped, "would help save the state controller from his friends." But another editorial noted that "it is not always clear…whether those who are assailing the system are anti-patronage or anti-Cranston." [258]

To counter the bills moving through the legislature, Cranston in May, 1965, offered his proposed reforms for consideration, saying the other bills "would create grief for all heirs, choke the probate courts with chaos, and result in bigger tax bills for all Californians. I cannot stand back any longer and watch a politically-inspired effort to wreck a basically sound, efficient and economical system, which provides protection and equity for widows, orphans and creditors alike." Conceding that changes were "necessary and appropriate," he wanted to repair, not "burn down, a fundamentally sound structure." His reforms would make future appointees subject to court confirmation, give them staggered terms, cut fees and require experience. If the revenue department and other ITA-reform bills were not enacted, Cranston noted, his proposal "can stand or fall on its own merits." But pressure was building to eliminate appraisers altogether. By 1965, there were 154. (The system ultimately would be abolished by the legislature.) [259]

Cranston nevertheless continued to get high marks for his performance. "I read a recent Field poll which revealed some very good information about my friend Alan Cranston," Hubert Humphrey wrote him from the vice president's office in September, 1965. "I'm very proud of you, Alan. You've proven yourself not only to be an extremely able public official and a loyal Democrat but, above all, a gentleman who commands respect and admiration." [260]

Another accomplishment, which Cranston wrote about for *Police* magazine, was enactment of legislation that he drafted permitting the state to pay the cost of damages or injuries suffered by someone helping prevent a crime or capture of a criminal – a Good-Samaritan law. It was the first of its kind in the nation, and received national publicity as a "pioneering bill, a timely response to the growing big-city fear of 'getting involved,'" *Time* magazine stated. Good-Samaritan claims, under the bill, had to be recommended by law-enforcement agencies, the state attorney general and Board of Control. The first payment was to a San Diego man who had fractured his right hand while capturing a prowler in a neighbor's yard where he held him until police arrived. He received $269.60 to pay medical bills not covered by insurance. "No one expects California's…law to change human nature," Cranston wrote, "but I believe that it is, at least, a step forward in helping to create an atmosphere all too often lacking in our modern society –concern and compassion for one's neighbors and fellow citizens." It reinforced California's responsibility to promote "progressive and creative social legislation." [261]

Life was looking bright again for Cranston, who was pictured with Geneva and the boys, now tall teenagers, on the occasion of their parents' twenty-fifth wedding anniversary in November, 1965. Robin and Kim had presented them with twenty-five white doves, which were added to the farm collection, now including a raccoon and geese named "Lewis" and "Eunice," pictured on one of their Christmas cards. [262]

In December, 1965, Cranston spent three weeks in Ghana doing an evaluation for the Peace Corps of its aid program to the potentially communist African nation. The personal references on his application for federal employment were impressive – Governor Brown, Vice President Humphrey and Congressman John M. Moss of California. He also listed a number of clubs and organizations to which he belonged – Rotary, Elks Lodge 6, Loyal Order of Moose and the American Legion, as well as the Sierra Club, Overseas Press Club, World Affairs Council and the American Association for the U. N. [263]

Calling the experience "one of the most pleasantly memorable" of his life, Cranston wrote his impressions for an article that ran in California newspapers on his return. "In Ghana, you don't just climb a mountain," he began, "you often wriggle up one – slithering under heavy growth, poling ahead with a forked stick to break huge spider webs while watching overhead and under hands and knees…for deadly snakes." He praised Peace Corps volunteers like geologist Dave Ripley from Illinois who was searching for bauxite to build a new industry, one of 122 American men and women (including six Californians) who were helping "enrich" Ghana and move it forward. "I have seldom been prouder of being an American," Cranston stated after seeing what Peace Corps volunteers confronted in the backward, Marxist-led (under President Kwama Nkrumah) nation where tribal chiefs and fetish priests still presided in villages. "Nkrumah's fears of neo-colonialism rule out innovation" by the Peace Corps, Cranston wrote in his evaluation. "The principal task in Ghana is to survive and surmount the political challenges." [264]

The diverse challenges facing the Peace Corps ranged from dealing with the ruthless, strong-man president to acclimating the people to sudden "doses of education, medicine and hope." It was a country with great riches but conflicting Marxist, socialist and capitalist doctrines. (A British atomic physicist, Alan Nunn May, who had vanished from London in the midst of an espionage exposé, was managing Ghana's Soviet-built nuclear reactor; one of Hitler's personal female pilots was training a glider force; and the widow of W. E. B. Dubois, founder of the NAACP and an avowed Communist, ran the president's television network.) The American volunteers had to "carefully avoid politics" while doing their jobs. "When you do all this and much more through the Peace Corps, you are accomplishing something that must be preserved, despite all provocations," Cranston concluded for the Washington bureaucrats. The only complaint that he heard from Ghanaians was that there were not enough Peace Corpsmen. [264]

Cranston arranged to have the head of a school send him snake skins to sell to raise funds for it. "My boys are thrilled about the snake skins and urge you to send as many as you can as soon as you can," Cranston wrote the school director. "I suspect that the boys can sell them for at least $10.00 apiece – splitting fifty-fifty with you and your students.... Is it possible to treat them in some way so that they will be more durable?" he asked. He also had arranged with another contact for the skins to be sold at a market in Accra. "I think you could develop quite a business there for your students," Cranston suggested, ending that he was impressed with all that the school and "many other members of the Peace Corps are doing." [265]

Cranston himself now was looking ahead to another election.

Notes

Introduction

1. Wallace Stegner, Forward, January, 1980, to Eleanor Fowle, *Cranston, The Senator from California* (Los Angeles: Jeremy P. Tarcher, Inc., 1984), second edition, xiv-xv.

2. Maya N. Federman, "Cranston: Making a Difference," San Marcos High School 10th-grade English paper, May, 1986, AC "Souvenirs, Miscellaneous Years to file," AC Personal Papers.

3. Eleanor Fowle, "A Day with Alan Cranston," [April, 1978], *California Living Magazine*, *San Francisco Examiner*, September 7, 1980, 27.

4. Douglas C. Rigg (1913-2004), Berkeley, California, to author, May 1, 2002.

5. Fowle, "A Day with Alan Cranston," 27-28.

Chapter 1 "*A dent in the world*"

1. Cranston Family Tree, Alan Cranston Papers, MSS 88/214c, The Bancroft Library, University of California, Berkeley, hereafter cited as AC Papers.

2. Herb [?] to "Will" Cranston, from 271 Sixth Street, Midland, [Canada], February 11, 1951, Pictures Collection, AC Papers, hereafter cited as Pics, AC Papers.

3. AC handwritten notes in "Early politics (CDC)" file, Carton 2, Pics, AC Papers.

Notes begin, "Jessie Bolt, born 1819, Edinburgh, age 18, alone, came to Canada, on ship met William MacGregor, who was traveling with his mother and two old maid sisters. Got married in Toronto, lived for a while with his family, she didn't like set-up, so lived in own place."

4. Ruth Eleanor Cranston Fowle Cameron (1909-2008), hereafter cited as REC, draft manuscript for biography of AC, "May 2, 1903, wedding of William MacGregor Cranston to Carol Dixon," page 15, AC Papers.

Dixon had an extensive cattle-raising business and brought a prize-winning herd of polled Angus to California, not seen before in the West, which resulted in financial losses. Carol Dixon was a "special student" at Stanford. Cranston's older sister, Eleanor Cranston, remembered her maternal grandmother, who spent summers with the Cranstons after she was widowed about 1932. AC claimed that his mother's ancestry qualified her as a Daughter of the American Revolution whose ancestors were early colonists. Oral history of AC, January 8, 1998, interviewed by Paul Nyberg, publisher, *Los Altos Town Crier*, transcript courtesy of Los Altos History Museum, hereafter cited as Oral history of AC, January 8, 1998.

5. Eleanor Fowle, *Cranston, The Senator from California* (Los Angeles: Jeremy P. Tarcher, Inc., 1984), second edition, 7.

6. *Ibid.*

Dixon's future son-in-law, William MacGregor Cranston, by 1904 backed the liberal Republican movement led by Theodore Roosevelt.

7. The Dixon house, no longer standing, faced the future site of the Senator Hotel.

8. REC draft manuscript for biography of AC, 16-17; R. E. Cranston Cameron interview with author September 28, 2000, hereafter cited as REC interview with author. A second interview March 28, 2003, is cited with that date.

9. REC draft manuscript.

10. Fowle, 7; Chris Nelson, Ph.D., architectural historian, Foundation for San Francisco's Architectural Heritage, "Robert Cranston, Builder in the Haight," letter and memo to Carolyn Fulton, office of Senator Alan Cranston, October 1, 1986, AC Papers; Mildred Hamilton, "Grandpa Cranston's gingerbread legacy," *San Francisco Examiner*, January 4, 1987.

11. Nelson, *ibid.*

Between 1874 and 1889, R. D. Cranston was listed in S. F. city directories as working for various companies. In 1889 when he began building houses in the Haight district, he was listed as an architect and builder with residence at 1032-1/2 Folsom Street. In 1893 the family lived at 1550 Page, which Cranston had built in 1891. They moved to 1414 Masonic Avenue in 1896, 502 Cole Street in 1897-98, 1777 Page in 1899, 649 Ashbury in 1907, 1418 Waller in 1908, and 635 Ashbury by 1916, the year of R. D. Cranston's death.

12. REC interview with author; R. E. to A. C., August 28, 1972, AC Personal Papers. R. D. Cranston was one of four children, including Florence, Jessie and Robert, Eleanor and Alan Cranston's aunts and uncles. Their mother Carol Dixon's sister Grace was married to William Sheets.

13. Janet S. Covan, "Thou shall want ere I want," poem, Pics, AC Papers; file, "Misc. to file, etc.," cards for R. G. Cranston, W. H. Cranston to AC, April 5, 1965, AC notes, "Home-Do," October 28, [1966?]; AC order for Cranston family crest to Highlands Inn Gift Shop, Carmel, March 26, 1965, Carton 14, AC Papers.

14. AC handwritten account, AC "Souvenirs 1930s-'40s," AC Personal Papers.

15. REC interview with author, September 28, 2000; Murray Flander interview with author, March 17, 2001, hereafter cited as Flander interview with author; Alan Cranston interview with author, October 25, 2000, hereafter cited as AC interview with author; Fowle, 8; Oral history of AC, 1995, interviewed by Erin Finnegan, transcript courtesy of Los Altos History Museum, hereafter cited as Oral history of AC, 1995.

Eleanor Cranston recorded that she and Alan were born at 1357 Cowper Street, Palo Alto. "Important events in my life," R. E. Cameron personal papers. Although also known as "R. E.," Eleanor is the name used hereafter to identify her.

16. Irma Goldsmith, "Scenes of Cranston's boyhood," Mountain View *Sun*, July 18, 1979, AC Personal Papers; Oral history of AC, January 8, 1998; Anna Knapp Fitz painting of Cranston mustard field and orchards with AC and REC, Los Altos History Museum (image 1995.013.131).

Anna Knapp Fitz (1913-95) painted local scenes and exhibited in Los Altos. A terra-cotta bust that she made of AC as an adult (1995.025) and a portrait of AC as a young boy holding a football (oil-on-canvas, 1978, 1995.013.159) were part of the Los Altos History Museum collection along with other Cranston materials including oral-history interviews with AC and Eleanor, photos, letters.

17. REC interview with author; R. E. Fowle to Florence [?], December 23, 1977, stating, "Alan remembers a carving on one of the oaks, 'Red Belt,' an Indian name, he was told," courtesy of Los Altos History Museum (1981.744.342 -561KB).

Tanaka remained with Mrs. William Cranston for the rest of her life. Eleanor wrote in 1977 of the site, "The small old ranch house that we think was built by the Mesas is on the right. To the right of it was an old shed where a man was said to have 'bled to death out of window' in the 1800s." The Villa Warec property, now on Cypress Drive, ran north off Edith between Foothill Expressway and Adobe Creek; the house, previously owned by families named Whitehead and Greenwood, was built about 1918 and was still standing as of 2007.

18. *Ibid.*

19. "William Cranston recalls old-timer's story, in the days before 'Los Altos,'" account of stories told by L. E. Walter to William Cranston, [circa late 1930s-early 1940s], unidentified newspaper article, no date; Harry Kallshian, "Los Altos Yesterday, the saga continues," Los

Altos *Town Crier*, July 3, 1991, AC Personal Papers.

The Cranston family sold Villa Warec in 1955; it was divided into some twenty residential properties. A cul-de-sac off Cypress Drive was named Warec Way. William Cranston in 1923 sold his interest in University Realty to Norwood Smith but they continued to jointly hold real-estate properties. John Ralston, "William Cranston, Son, Husband, Father, Businessman," presentation to Los Altos Hills Historical Society, December, 2007, courtesy of Los Altos History Museum.

20. "Story written by father, 'A Glance into Crooked Street,'" AC "Souvenirs 1914-1920," AC Personal Papers.

21. Joan McKinney, "Cranston no dull man, insists his author sister," *Oakland Tribune*, November 20, 1980; Oral history of AC, January 8, 1998.

22. AC interview with author; Fowle, 9; Oral history of AC, January 8, 1998; AC handwritten notes on yellow pad for speech December 1, 1977, at Los Altos 25th anniversary celebration, courtesy of Los Altos History Museum (20-page manuscript, 1978.037), hereafter cited as AC Los Altos 25th anniversary speech, December 1, 1977.

23. REC interview with author.

24. Fowle, 9.

25. Fowle, 9-10, 12-13; AC interview with author; Harry Kreisler, "Alan Cranston interview, Conversations with History," Institute of International Studies, University of California, Berkeley, web site, http://globetrotter.berkeley.edu, Regents of University of California, 2000, hereafter cited as Kreisler interview.

26. Fowle, 6; REC interview with author; Oral history of AC, January 8, 1998.

27. AC interview with author; Alan MacGregor Cranston, *Current Biography*, February, 1950, 15-16.

28. Fowle, 6-7; REC interview with author.

Eleanor believed that her grandfather was the first Congregationalist minister in Wisconsin.

29. AC interview with author; Ellen Hume, "Cranston Goal…: 'To make a big dent,' or a 'happy, Bohemian life,'" *Los Angeles Times*, nd, [1980?], Carton 550, and San Pedro *News Pilot*, August 16, 1975, Vol. 39, 1975, #2, AC Papers; notebook of drawings and writings by AC, file, "Comics and Writings, early '20s," and "Decathlon" record, "Souvenirs, '20s, Grammar School," AC Personal Papers.

30. Notebook of drawings and writings by AC.

31. *Ibid.*

32. "Perscription Johnston, By Alan Cranston, Chapter 1," typed story, " "Comics and Writings, early '20s," "Souvenirs, '20s, Grammar School," AC Personal Papers.

33. AC to Mr. William Sheets, October 25, 1922; AC to Uncle Willie, May 24, 1922; AC to Aunt Grace, June, 1922; AC to "Dear Sister," "from his camp in 1924, age 10," AC Personal Papers.

34. REC to AC, nd, "Souvenirs, '20s, Grammar School," AC Personal Papers; REC interview with author March 28, 2003.

Eleanor attended Girls' Collegiate school in Glendora near Pasadena for her last year of high school (1927) in order to improve her grades and enter Stanford in the fall of 1928; she completed two years before marrying in June, 1929.

35. REC to AC, nd, on Tahoe Tavern stationary, "Souvenirs, '20s, Grammar School," AC Personal Papers.

36. Gale Cook, "The old pro, Alan Cranston runs hard for reelection," *San Francisco Examiner*, *Image* magazine, October 19, 1986, 20-25; AC Los Altos 25th anniversary speech, December 1, 1977; Oral history of AC, January 8, 1998; "Mr. William Cranston's special role in the opening of Los Altos Scout Hall, April 20, 1922," by Edgar A. McDowell, president, Palo Alto Historical Association, October 29, 1978, and "Troop 37's reunion," *Town Crier*, June 5, 1968, courtesy of Los Altos History Museum.

37. Carol D. Cranston to AC, from Union Line ship, [1921], AC Personal Papers.

38. William Cranston to Ruth Eleanor and Alan, from ship leaving San Francisco Bay, and to "Dear Alan Boy," no dates, AC Personal Papers.

39. William Cranston to AC, from St. George's House, Hong Kong, December 8, 1921, "Souvenirs, '20s," AC Personal Papers.

40. William Cranston to AC, postcard from Paris, 1923, and Carol D. Cranston to AC, postcard postmarked Paris, 29 VIII, 1923, "Souvenirs, '20s," AC Personal Papers.

41. Memorabilia from Cunard Line *R.M.S. Franconia* around-the-world cruise, 1925, saloon passenger list; programme of entertainments; log advisories on stops at Balboa, Panama, and Havana, Cuba; menu for June 14, 1925, "Souvenirs, '20s," AC Personal Papers.

42. Letter to AC, July 11, 1928.

43. Ralph Raymond to AC, July 11, 1928, "Souvenirs, '20s," AC Personal Papers.

44. Raymond to AC, August 13, 1928, same.

45. "Jr. D. Skunk" Dutton to AC, August 27, 1928, same.

46. Raymond to AC, August 27, 1928, same.

47. "The Chatterbox, Published by the students of the Los Altos Grammar School," June, 1928, PICs, AC Papers. For Japanese friends see AC Los Altos 25th anniversary speech, December 1, 1977, and Oral history of AC, January 8, 1998.

48. Fowle, 10; Hume, "Cranston Goal…"; Oral history of AC, January 8, 1998.

49. AC, "Science slows aging," *Runner's World*, May, 1981, 37-40.

50. Dutton to AC, August 22, 1923, "Souvenirs, '20s, Grammar School," AC Personal Papers.

51. Dutton to AC, September 18, 1926, same; REC interview with author March 28, 2003.

52. Dutton to AC, September 27, 1926, AC Personal Papers.

53. Ralph Raymond to AC, September 21, 1926, same.

54. Raymond to AC, October 6 and 16, 1926, same.

55. Dutton to AC, October 10, 1926, same.

56. REC to AC, September 24, 1926, same.

57. *Ibid.*

58. REC to AC, postmarked 192[6?], same.

59. Fragment, AC "Souvenirs, 1930s-40s," same.

60. REC to AC, postmarked October 8, 192[6], same.

61. William Cranston to AC, handwritten, January 7, 1927, same.

62. William Cranston to AC, typed, January 26, 1927, same.

63. Dutton to AC, January 25, 1927, same.

64. AC to mother, October, 1929, same.

65. *Current Biography*, 15.

Cranston attended Castelleja private grammar school for kindergarten; Los Altos Grammar School, 1920-26; Tamalpais School, 1927; Menlo School, Menlo Park, Ca., 1928-29; Mt. View, Ca., Union High School, 1929-32. "Security Investigation Data for Sensitive Position," AC application, circa 1945, and "Personal History Statement," July 28, 1942, AC Papers.

66. "Personal History Statement," 1943.

67. Fowle, 10; Oral history of AC, 1995; Hume, "Cranston Goal…"

68. AC, "Alan Cranston saw the games," unidentified news clipping, [1932?], Mountain View *Register-Leader*, AC Papers.

69. Alan Cranston, '32, "Prophecy of the Senior Class," *Blue and Gray*, Mountain View High School, 33-36, AC "Souvenirs, 1930s-40s," AC Personal Papers.

70. AC interview with author; Hume, "Cranston goal…"

71. REC interview with author, and "Important events in my life."

Fowle (died 1982) was a consulting engineer who designed a diesel engine for the U. S. Navy that was placed in the Smithsonian Institution collection. He was a member of the

Los Altos Hills city council for fourteen years and the town's second mayor after World War II. The Fowles were married for 55 years until Jack's death in 1982 and adopted two children, Michael and Linda. Eleanor met her second husband, Donald Cameron, through tennis friends; he died in 1996. "Ruth Eleanor Cameron," (99 years old), obituary, Los Altos *Town Crier*, June 11, 2008.

72. AC interview with author.

Fremont Older (1856-1935) was editor of the *San Francisco Bulletin* (1895-1918) and the Hearst-owned *Call* (1918-29) and *Call-Bulletin* (1929-35).

73. "Autobiog. - Heredity, California and Pioneers," Index card notes, 1935-36, AC Papers.

74. "Autobiographical - the paper telling of T.R.'s death," "Aut.-first elections memories-why I for Hoover," Index card notes, 1935-36; Fowle, 7; AC interview with author.

75. *Ibid.*

76. Fowle, 5.

77. "The Long View Cycle," index card notes.

78. "Autobiog, I was close to Victorianism," index card notes.

79. Bill Peterson, "A pragmatic crusader tilting at the arms race," *Washington Post*, January 12, 1984, AC Papers.

One account said that it was William Cranston who went with Older to San Quentin, which he recounted to AC (John Ralston to Los Altos Hills Historical Society, 2007, see note 19). Tom Mooney (1882-1942) and Warren K. Billings (1893-1972), Socialist labor radicals convicted of the 1916 bombing in San Francisco, ultimately had their sentences commuted and were pardoned after Older showed that testimony against the two men had been perjured. Their case became an international *cause célèbre*. (Felix Frankfurter (1882-1965), a future Supreme Court Justice appointed in 1917 by President Woodrow Wilson to a Mediation Committee investigating strikes, argued that Mooney had been framed and deserved a new trial. Michael Alexander, *Jazz Age Jews* (Princeton: Princeton University Press, 2001), 84-87.) Mooney was pardoned by "the first Democratic Governor of California in the century, Cuthbert Olson; it was his first act as governor," Cranston noted. He drove Cora Older to the ceremony in Sacramento. Billings served 23 years in prison before the State Supreme Court in1939 recommended parole and he was released; he was pardoned by Gov. Edmund G. Brown in 1961. Johnny Miller, "Wayback Machine," *San Francisco Chronicle*, December 24, 2011, citing *Chronicle* December 22, 1961. See also Chapter 2.

The Olders' ranch "Woodhills" had a pool and extensive gardens, and they often took in paroled convicts to work on the ranch. The Midpeninsula Regional Open Space District acquired it and a publishing family, Levine, agreed to help restore the house, completed in 1979. In 1980 it was listed on the National Register of Historic Places. "Welcome to Woodhills," brochure, AC Personal Papers.

80. AC interview with author.

Jack Black (1871-1932?, possibly by suicide) was a hobo, professional burglar and sometime opium addict. Older hired him to work on the *San Francisco Call*. His autobiography *You Can't Win*, first published in 1926 (Macmillan) and a best-seller, influenced later Beat writers. It was republished in 2000 (Nabat series, AK Press) with an introduction by William S. Burroughs who said it influenced his book *Junkie*.

81. Index card notes.

82. REC, "Excerpt from Chapter 1," "Chapter III," biography manuscript drafts, AC Papers; Fowle, 10.

AC kept diaries in 1932, 1935, and possibly other years. On the cover of the one for 1932 he wrote: "Memo Book, Property of Alan Cranston, 1932, Keep Out, (Yes), (You.)." Typescript of AC 1932 diary, R. E. Cranston Cameron Papers.

83. *Ibid.*, "Chapter III."

84. *Ibid.* Doris was the daughter of John Atkinson's older half-brother, Lynn Atkinson.

85. *Ibid.*

86. *Ibid.*

87. *Ibid.*

88. "Short story - women of the world take charge of the world," index card notes.

89. "Ode to my Love," index card notes.

90 Fowle, 11.

91. AC to mother and father, September 21, 1932, AC "Souvenirs, 1930s, AC letters from Pomona," AC Personal Papers. All letters cited hereafter as AC letters from Pomona are from this source.

92. William Sheets to Carol Cranston, signed "with much love, W," no date, AC letters from Pomona.

93. AC to parents, September 23, 1932.

94. AC to parents, October 6, 1932.

AC was referring to H. G. Wells, *The Outline of History* (1919), and James Harvey Robinson, *The Mind in the Making, The Relation of Intelligence to Social Reform* (1921).

95. AC to parents, October 13, 1932.

Cranston would have been drawn to the book and illustrations depicting Josiah "Si Klegg," a fictional Indiana Civil War Union soldier, created in a series by the editor of the *National Tribune*, Washington, D. C. In 1897 an illustrated book was copyrighted by the editor's assistant without the editor's consent, authored by John McElroy (1846-1929) entitled *Si Klegg, His Transformation from a Raw Recruit to a Veteran*, issued in paperback in 1910 (re-issued 2009 by Cambridge Scholars Publishing). In 1895 veteran Wilbur Fisk Hinman published *Corporal Si Klegg and his 'Pard'- How They Lived and Talked, and What They Did and Suffered, while Fighting for the Flag*. Hinman, a major with the Ohio 65th Volunteer Infantry who fought in the South and was severely wounded at Chickamauga, based his fictional account on real experiences to tell the story of an average soldier. The books (subjects of copyright controversy) became the most popular fictional accounts of the Civil War.

96. AC to parents, October 20, 1932.

97. *Ibid.*

Scripps College was a neighboring women's school.

98. REC to author November 28, 2000.

99. AC to parents, October 27, 1932, AC letters from Pomona.

Robert A. Blaisdell (1867-1957) was the fourth president of Pomona College 1910-27, and founder (in 1925) of the Claremont Colleges consortium that expanded from Pomona to include four other colleges and two graduate institutions (as of 2010). Blaisdell, a minister and theologian, was no longer Pomona's president when Cranston met him in 1932 but headed the consortium, patterned after Oxford University with separate colleges sharing common facilities and library. Blaisdell authored words inscribed on Pomona's gates: "Let only the eager, thoughtful and reverent enter here," and "They only are loyal to this college who, departing, bear their added riches in trust for mankind." Courtesy of Kristin Fossum, Assistant Dean, Pomona College, e-mail letter to author, July 28, 2010.

100. AC to parents, November 1, 1932; AC Pomona transcript with grades for years 1932-34, courtesy, Pomona College.

In his second year at Pomona (one semester), AC's courses were: English composition; history (North America since 1763); philosophy (introduction to logic); psychology (elements of); sociology (elements of), in all of which he received the grade "W." Cranston entered no church preference at Pomona.

101. AC to parents, November 9, 1932, AC letters from Pomona.

102. Alan Cranston, "The funny side, the election," newspaper column, no identification, [November, 1932], AC Papers.

103. AC to parents, November 9, 1932.

104. *Ibid.*, and AC letter, November 16, 1932.

105. *Ibid.*, and AC letter, November 23, 1932.

106. AC to parents, November 21, 1932.

107. AC to "Pop & Mom," November 28, 1932.

108. AC to parents, December 6, 1932, same.

109. AC, "Quips and Slips," *The Daily Student Life*, December 14, 1932, AC Papers. Cranston was listed as a reporter on the masthead.

110. *Ibid.*

Cranston said in interview with author that although he could not remember his attitude toward the Klan in 1933, "I'm sure it was negative."

111. AC to parents, "Monday evening, 5:45 p.m., [December?, 1932], and January 18, 1932[3?], AC letters from Pomona.

112. *Ibid.*, January 18, 1932[3?].

113. AC, "Quips and Slips," *The Daily Student Life*, January 7, 1933.

114. AC to parents, January 25, 1932[3?], AC letters from Pomona.

115. AC to parents, February 15, 1932[3?].

116. AC to parents, March 3, 1933.

117. AC to parents, March 13, 1933.

118. AC to parents, no date, before Easter, [1933?].

119. *Ibid.*

120. *Ibid.*

The major earthquake occurred Friday, March 10, 1933 at 5:55 p.m. The Reconstruction Finance Corporation, one of President Hoover's cures for the economic Depression, established a government lending agency with authority to issue tax-exempt bonds and extend credit; within six months of enactment in February, 1932, it had authorized $1.2 billion in loans to life-insurance companies, agricultural credit corporations and other financial institutions.

121. AC, "Quips and Slips," March 18, 1933.

122. AC to parents, "Monday," [April?], 1933; AC, "A first-hand account of the Southern California earthquake," Mountain View *Register Leader*, April 14, 1933.

123. AC to parents, "Hello, Day Aft," [March 11, 1933], and April 14, 1933, AC letters from Pomona, 1933.

AC was referring to *The Making of the Modern Mind* (1926) by John Herman Randall, Jr.

124. AC to parents, spring, 1933, and "Hello, Day Aft"; Harry Dutton to AC, April 20, 1933.

125. *Ibid.*, AC to parents, spring, 1933, and "Hello, Day Aft."

126. AC to parents, "Monday evening," [1933].

127. *Ibid.*

128. AC to parents, "Monday," and no date, 1933.

129. AC to mother, "Happy Birthday, Mother!", May 16, 1932.

130. *Ibid.*, and AC interview with author.

Peter Nekrasov, Cranston said in an interview October 16, 2000, "became Peter [Van Orden?]." Targeted "by Communists for being too independent-minded, he left the Soviet Union somehow as a young man, because he didn't like the system.... [I]n San Francisco, he was... talking negatively in the Russian-American community about communism, and was kidnapped by Soviet agents.... He helped educate me about how Communists weren't so nice."

131. AC, "Russia to the Right? A Refugee's Tale," typescript, [circa 1936], AC Papers.

132. AC to Mother, May 16, 1932[3?], AC letters from Pomona.

133. AC to parents, "June 6th, 5:32 p.m."

134. Alan Cranston, "Radio police!" Mountain View *Register Leader*, June 30, 1933.

135. AC to parents, September 26, 1933, AC letters from Pomona.

136. *Ibid.*, and AC to parents, October 11, 1933.

137. AC to parents, October 4 and 11, 1933.

138. AC to parents, October 11 and 16, 1933.

139. AC to parents, October 23, 1933.

140. AC to parents, October 16, 1933.

141. AC to parents, October 29 and November 9, 1933.

142. *Ibid.*, November 9, 1933

143. AC, "Quips and Slips," *Student Life*, dated by AC "November 16, 1933," Pomona College, 1933, AC Papers.

The masthead listed Cranston as Feature Editor.

144. "Alan Cranston home from college visited friends," Mountain View *Register-Leader*, circa 1932-33; and "High School - Alumni," January 12, 1934, AC Papers.

145. AC interview with author; Fowle, 12-13.

The spy film *Foreign Correspondent* bore little resemblance to *Personal History* (1935) by Vincent Sheean (1899-1975) although the memoir was credited as its basis. At the end, as bombs are dropping on London, the American reporter hero, foretelling Edward R. Murrow's broadcasts, tells radio listeners, "Keep those lights burning [in America].... They're the only ones left on in the world."

146. AC to parents, November 9, 1933, AC letters from Pomona.

147. *Ibid.*, and AC to parents, November 14 and December 14, 1933.

Betty Bond was cited as reporter on the masthead of *The Daily Student Life*, January 7, 1933.

148. AC to parents, November 15, 1933.

149. AC to parents, November 21, 1933.

150. AC to parents, December 7, 1933.

151. AC to parents, December 14, 1933.

152. Frank Anderson, "Trackman Cranston runs on," Long Beach *Independent Press-Telegram*, September 9, 1968, AC Papers.

153. Fowle, 11-12.

154. AC interview with author; "Cranston ineligible; track row looms, technicality hits Card[inal] star, protest due," unidentified newspaper clipping [*Stanford Daily*?], AC "Souvenirs, 1930s-40s," AC Personal Papers.

Quad yearbooks for 1935 and 1936 referred principally to Cranston's track achievements.

155. AC interview with author; Charles "Chuck" Hurley, memorandum to *Fresno Bee* reporter Tom Meehan on AC's track and athletic prowess, May 7, 1963, for article on AC, "Cross country run, dip in pool launch day for Controller Cranston," *Fresno Bee*, May 11, 1963, AC Papers.

Robert Lyman ("Dink") Templeton (1897-1962) attended Stanford where he played football and rugby and received both undergraduate and law degrees. He was on the U. S. Olympic team in 1920 in rugby and the long jump. Also a high jumper, he was credited with inventing the "roll" as opposed to the "scissors" style of jumping, then illegal in the Olympics, which prevented his competing in that event but which prompted new records, according to Cranston. Templeton served as Stanford's track coach 1922-39 during which Stanford won the men's NCAA Outdoor Track and Field Championship 1925, 1928 and 1934. He was known for holding daily intensive practices, unusual at the time. He was inducted into the USA Track & Field Hall of Fame in 1976.

156. *Ibid.*, memorandum and newspaper article.

157. Bill Leiser, "Dink Templeton determined to quit Stanford," unidentified clipping [*Stanford Daily*?], circa 1940, AC "Souvenirs, 1930s-40s," AC Personal Papers.

158. AC notes, "After college," [circa 1935], index card notes, AC Papers.

159. AC interview with author; Fowle, 12, and Chapter III, draft MS; Hurley to Tom [Meehan]; AC, "Science slows aging," *Runner's World*, May, 1981, 37-40, AC Papers; "Archie Williams is dead at 78; won a gold medal at Berlin Olympics," obituary, *New York Times*, June 25, [1993?].

Cranston at one point said that he pulled an upper right leg muscle in 1935, which prevented his going to Olympic trials in the 400-meter. Vol. 38, #1, 1975, AC Papers.

160. *Ibid.*, Chapter III, draft MS, and Fowle, 12.

Cranston continued sprinting competitively for many years, running in senior track meets in his early eighties and jogging for exercise well into his eighties. He set a record for 55-year-olds in the 100-yard dash (18.6 seconds) but boasted, "My world record was 12.6 seconds." By then he had given up the longer sprint because he "couldn't get in shape to run the 400," admitting that "each year takes its toll." His track records would be good publicity in reelection bids over the years. AC interview with author.

161. *Ibid.*, Chapter III, draft MS; AC and REC interviews with author; Michael Barone, "Alan Cranston: Daring and Caution," profile of Democratic presidential candidates, *Washington Post*, September 15, 1983, AC Papers.

162. *Ibid.*, and AC notes, "Most vivid California memory of Ethiopian War," index card notes, AC Papers.

The League of Nations did not act on sanctioning Italy's invasion of Ethiopia in 1935.

163. AC notes, "Year-Day Program, June 1, 1935," index card notes.

164. "Year-Day Program, May, 1936," index card notes.

165. AC notes, "Once every 6 months...," no date, index card notes.

166. Index card notes.

167. Same.

Anatole France (pseudonym of Jacques-Anatole-François Thibault,1844-1922) won the Nobel Prize for literature in 1921. *At the Sign of the Reine Pédauque* was his second novel, published in 1893; *Penguin Island*, published in 1908 and translated in 1914, had a chapter on the French Dreyfus Affair. *Sabine*, a novel by Mikhail Petrovich Artzybashev (1878-1927), was condemned by the Soviets after the author emigrated to Poland following the Russian Revolution of 1917. Edward Powys Mathers (1892-1939), was the English translator (in 1923) of J. C. Mardrus's French version of *The Book of the Thousand Nights and One Night*, also known as *Arabian Nights* and *Coloured Stars: Fifty Asiatic Love Poems*, among others Some of his translations were set to music by American composer Aaron Copland (1900-90). Mathers also was known for advanced cryptic crosswords composed for the London *Observer* between 1926 and 1939 using the pseudonym Torquemada under which name he also reviewed detective stories.

168. Same.

169. AC, "Tryoutee - Laguanita rising rapidly," and "Another tire cure, March 1, 1934," AC Papers.

170. AC, "Mexican madness," Mountain View *Register-Leader*, March 2, 1934.

171. Fowle, Chapter III, draft MS, AC Papers.

172. Mountain View *Register-Leader*, June 14, 1934, AC Personal Papers.

173. AC, "Travelogia," "Souvenirs, 1930s, AC's Travelogue, '34," AC Personal Papers.

174. "Travelogia," draft letter July 24, 1934, to "Mr. Smith"; AC, "Alan Cranston writes from Paris, gets a taste of life in the celebrated Quartier Latin and tries out his French," Mountain View *Register-Leader*, [August?] 17, 1934.

175. "Alan Cranston writes from Paris...."

176. AC, "Speedy court action in Vienna, Alan Cranston, student journalist sojourning in Europe this summer, attends the trial of the murderers of Chancellor Dollfuss of Austria and writes a dramatic account for the *Register-Leader*," Mountain View *Register-Leader*, August 31, 1934, and unidentified reprint, September 7, 1934, AC Papers.

Dollfuss (1892-1934), a Christian Socialist appointed chancellor in 1932, assumed quasi-dictatorial powers in 1933 but was threatened by the powerful Austrian National Socialist party, backed by Nazi Germany. He dissolved the party in 1933 and allied with fascists and Italy's dictator Mussolini. Austria subsequently was brought under Hitler's Nazi Reich.

177. *Ibid.*, preface; David Hoffman, Washington Bureau, "Seasoned leader at political peak," *San Jose Mercury*, January 27, 1980.

178. *Ibid.,* "Speedy court action...."

179. AC, "Vienna after Dollfuss' Murder, Alan Cranston describes the Dollfuss funeral and also gives some impressions of Budapest and Germany," Mountain View *Register-Leader*, September 7, 1934; and "Derelict's Diary, Vienna, Austria," typescript version, AC Papers.

180. "Travelogia," and "Vienna after Dollfuss' murder."

181. "Vienna after Dollfuss' murder."

Between June 30 and July 2, 1934, a year after Hitler came to power, he ordered the execution of leaders of the three-million-man SA (Sturmabteilung) to thwart a feared coup and placate industrialists, the army and public who feared violent attacks of the "brown shirts." SA leader Ernst Röhm, who had helped put Hitler in power, was suspected of plotting to take control. The actions (code-named "Operation Hummingbird") became known as the *Röhm-Putsch* although Hitler referred to it as the "night of the long knives" (a phrase from a popular Nazi song) in a speech July 13 justifying his actions. Rohm's and other SA leaders' homosexuality also was cited as an excuse for the purge. Between 85 and 400 were believed shot and more than 1,000 arrested; fewer than half of the murdered were actually SA officers (one was Munich music critic mistaken for another man), although the actual number was lost with Gestapo records. It was a turning point in solidifying Hitler's power, enforced by the SS (Schutzstaffel, Hitler's personal body guard) and Gestapo (Geheime Staartspolizei), abolishing legal recourses. "The Night of the Long Knives," The History Place, web site http:// www.historyplace.com/worldwar2; Jewish Virtual Library, web site http://www.jewishvirtuallibrary.org.

182. "Travelogia."

183. "Hitler's astounding outburst," *Literary Digest*, December 31, 1931, copy in AC Personal Papers.

According to the article, Hitler claimed that his objective was destruction of communism. But he "flabbergasted Berlin" by declaring that, once he assumed power, Germany would pay its private debts, like those to American bond-holders, but repudiate paying reparations to France, which Hitler called "extortion." Many wondered if "Hitler's dramatic gesture was pure bluff," *New York Times* correspondent Harold Callender wrote. David Lawrence, Consolidated Press Association correspondent, reported that in Washington "there is a disposition to regard Hitlerism as worse in its bark than its bite." Other American newspapers editorialized that he was "strutting his stuff" which one called "clever ballyhoo."

184. AC, "Our jolly vagabonds," Mountain View *Register-Leader*, September 28, 1934.

185. "Travelogia," expense accounts and list of "Correspondence."

186. AC, "Adolf Hitler's Germany," November 16, 1934, and "Alan Cranston in Mexico," June 14, 1935, Mountain View *Register-Leader*.

187. "Adolf Hitler's Germany."

188. *Ibid.*; and "Derelict's Diary, Stein-am-Rhein," typescript version, AC Papers.

Cranston often related that he "got very close to Hitler one night in the streets of Munich and got a real good look at him." Kreisler interview.

189. "Derelict's Diary."

Hoover's book, *The Challenge to Liberty* (1934), expressed his economic theories based on "rugged individualism."

190. "Adolf Hitler's Germany" and "Derelict's Diary."

191. "Do college students think?" – Lars Skattebol, "The Foundation of Fascism," and

AC, "Fascism in America?", Mountain View *Register-Leader*, October 18, 1934, copy in AC Papers.

192. Fowle, 16; "Alan Cranston in Mexico," Mountain View *Register-Leader*, June 14, 1935.

193. AC notes from trip to Mexico, 1935, "AC Souvenirs, 1930s-1940s," AC Personal Papers.

194. *Ibid.*, "This is the story of three great gripes..."

195. *Ibid.*, "It is rumored that Johnnie and I are attending the University of Mexico summer school. We have thus far been unable to verify the rumor..."

196. *Ibid.*, "Altogether at Random."

197. "T. Garrido Canabal, Mexican leader, 52," obituary, *New York Times*, no date, AC "Souvenirs, 1930s-40s," AC Personal Papers.

198. AC, "Dictator in Mexico-1, Mexico City, July 18, 1935," AC "Souvenirs, 1930s-40s," AC Personal Papers; AC, "*Register-Leader* correspondent in Mexico joins a crusade to try to wipe out Tabasco tyrant," Mountain View *Register-Leader*, July 26, 1935, AC Papers.

Cárdenas was president of Mexico 1934-40.

199. AC, "Journey to Revolution, Mexico City, July 25, 1935," handwritten manuscript, AC "Souvenirs, 1930s-40s," AC Personal Papers; AC, "A journey to a revolution which did not revolute," Mountain View *Register-Leader*, August 2, 1935, AC Papers.

200. Fowle, 17-18; "Stanford boys join in revolt in Old Mexico," unidentified clip, AC Papers.

201. "Journey to Revolution," and "The punitive expedition to Tabasco," typescript, AC Personal Papers.

202. "Punitive expedition...," and "A journey...which did not revolute."

203. "A journey...which did not revolute," and AC segment, "Cuban bomb thrower," AC "Souvenirs, 1930s-40s," AC Personal Papers.

Machado was president of Cuba 1925-33. An abortive revolt in 1931 spurred student groups to rebel; Machado retaliated with oppression by secret police, causing the U. S. to intervene. He was forced to flee after a general strike and loss of army support.

204. "Punitive expedition..."; Fowle, 20.

205. "Punitive expedition...", "Cuban bomb thrower" and "Altogether at Random."

206. Fowle, 21.

207. *Ibid.*

208. AC, fragment, "Forty-eight hours to leave Mexico!" AC "Souvenirs, 1930s-40s," AC Personal Papers.

209. AC, "Derelict's Diary, Number 1, Mexico City," circa 1936, AC "Souvenirs, 1930s-40s," AC Personal Papers.

210. "Derelict's Diary, Number 2, and Number 6."

211. AC, "Two pictures of Mexico," Mountain View *Register-Leader*, September 13, 1935; AC handwritten note, no date, citing "Harold D. Lasswell, 'Propaganda Technique in the World War,' p. 145 – Hearst's *Chicago Tribune*'s editorial urging the USA to conquer Mexico," AC Papers.

212. AC notes, "University of Mexico summer school experience," index card notes.

213. Fowle, 11, and Chapter III, draft MS; Hume, "Cranston Goal…"

214. REC interview with author; REC, "Important events in my life."

At the time of the Depression, William Cranston's office was at 901 Alexander Building.

215. Fowle, 13.

216. Fowle, 13-14.

217. AC, "Super-Drama Reviewer," "The great Lamson show," *The News Letter and Wasp*, September 21, 1935, vol. 70, no. 38, copy in AC Papers; AC notes on trying to sell the article on Lamson, and notes on plays, novel ideas and outline for science fiction story, November

2, 1936, Carton 616, AC Papers.

David Lamson (1903-75) was accused in 1933 of murdering his wife, found dead in their bathtub, seemingly bludgeoned. A guilty verdict was overturned; a second trial ended in a deadlocked jury and two subsequent ones as mistrials. Charges were dropped in 1936. Lamson wrote an account after the first trial, *We Who Are About to Die* (1935).

218. AC notes, "Undoubtedly my article showed…bias against Lamson…," index card notes.

The Wasp, a satirical weekly founded in San Francisco in 1876, merged with the *S. F. News-Letter* in 1928 and continued until 1941. Its greatest period was under editor Ambrose Bierce (1881-86).

219. AC interview with author.

220. AC, "The revenge of Aduwa," Mountain View *Register-Leader*, November 8, 1935, copy in AC Papers.

An Italian expeditionary force first crossed into Ethiopia from Somaliland December 5, 1934. The League of Nations refused to intervene, and Italians invaded Ethiopia beginning October 2, 1935, taking Aduwa a few days later. Ethiopian Emperor Haile Selassie (1891-1975) personally led defending troops but in 1936 was forced to flee to England for protection and his regime collapsed. He appealed unsuccessfully twice (1936, 1938) to the League of Nations to act against Italy, and in 1940, after Italy entered World War II, returned to Africa with British aid, re-entering Ethiopia in 1941 and regaining his throne. He ruled with progressive policies but was deposed in 1974.

221. Fowle, 22; Oral history of AC, 1995.

Cranston attended Pomona College 1932-33, Stanford University 1933-36. At Stanford, he belonged to Sigma Nu fraternity and an informal "Block S" society of athletes who were awarded varsity letters for achievements. Pat White, Archives Specialist, Department of Special Collections, Stanford University Libraries, e-mail communication to author, August 27, 2010.

222. AC, "School versus Education," 1936, with return address "c/o Howard P. Davis, 6 Park St., Boston, Mass.," AC Papers; *Current Biography*, 15.

223. The professor whom Cranston cited as having been removed in 1936 was not identified. Stanford had a history of reaction to faculty firings going back to 1901 when sociology professor and political activist Edward A. Ross, forced to resign, was defended by history professor George E. Howard who argued that Ross had been forced out by corporate influence. Given the option of apology or resignation, Howard and several other faculty resigned in protest. Karen Bartholomew, '71, "Century at Stanford," *Stanford*, March/April, 2001, 51.

224. "Parents - accompanying note," index card notes, AC Papers.

225. AC typescript, "Crimson Purge," citing *Harvard Progressive*, no date, AC "Souvenirs - 1930s-40s," AC Personal Papers.

226. AC, "Memories: Vintage '36," Edith R. Mirrielees and Patricia F. Zelver, eds., *Stanford Mosaic* (Palo Alto: Leland Stanford Junior University, 1962), 180-182.

227. J. E. Wallace Sterling (1906-85) was President of Stanford 1949-68. He was a doctoral student in history at Stanford 1932-38 (while Cranston was an undergraduate), and served on research staff at Hoover Institution. During his 20-year tenure as president of Stanford, he oversaw its largest growth to date financially, in student body, faculty and campus facilities, and launched Stanford Industrial (later Research) Park which, together with government grants to the university, sparked the development of "Silicon Valley"; he also built up the medical school and created an undergraduate overseas study program.

Chapter 2 Realizing Dreams

1. Kreisler interview.

2. "Alan Cranston writes from Rome to the Register-Leader," Mountain View *Register-Leader*, October 30, 1936.

The editor prefaced the account by saying that Cranston "one day will be one the world's best-known, and most eagerly-read writers." Two of AC's articles from Rome also were published by the paper.

3. *Ibid.*

Amster Spiro (born 1894), dubbed "sharp-witted" by *Time* magazine in 1938, was a legendary city editor, beginning in 1927, of W. R. Hearst's largest newspaper, the *New York Journal-American*. In 1937 Spiro launched a newspaper game, "Flash News," the object of which was to complete the make-up of a newspaper front page to attract the greatest circulation. The next year he secured rights to other games, building a profitable business, and bought two-thirds interest in Ely Culbertson's *Bridge World* and *Games Digest* publications. "The Press, Flash News," *Time*, April 19, 1937, and "The Press, Spiro Games," *Time*, March 28, 1938.

4. Fowle, 24; "Alan Cranston writes from Rome."

William Hillman (1895-1962) was a veteran journalist when Cranston met him in 1936 when Hillman was Hearst newspapers' chief of staff for foreign correspondents (1934-39). In 1939 Hillman resigned from Hearst to become European Manager/Foreign Editor for *Collier's* magazine (1939-40) and Washington representative for the magazine. From 1941 to 1945 he was a radio news commentator with NBC and the Blue network; 1945-62 he was roving correspondent for North American Newspaper Alliance. A longtime friend of President Harry S. Truman, Hillman (assisted by advertising executive David Noyes) edited and helped write *Mr. President* (Farrar, Straus and Young, 1952), a collection of Truman's letters, diaries and personal papers. Hillman also assisted Truman in writing his *Memoirs* (1955-56) and *Mr. Citizen* (1960), and acted as agent and advisor to Truman on literary and television projects. He died in New York City in 1962; Truman attended his funeral.

Hearst's London bureau at 72-78 Fleet Street served the International News Service, Universal Service, King Features, American Weekly and International Photos for Europe.

5. "Alan Cranston writes from Rome"; Fowle, 25.

6. "Alan Cranston writes from Rome"; AC interview with author; Fowle, 25; Will Connolly, "It's 'James Cleveland' Owens and not 'Jesse' - and he can still beat a horse," column, unidentified news clipping, [Cleveland newspaper?], AC Personal Papers.

James Cleveland "Jesse" Owens (1913-80), born in Alabama the son of a sharecropper and grandson of a slave, grew up in Cleveland. He gained fame at Ohio State University by setting five world records in broad jumping, hurdle and flat racing (:09.4 seconds for the 100-yard dash) and tying another in one day, May 25, 1935, despite severe pain before the meet. At the 1936 Berlin Olympics he won four track-and-field Gold Medals in the 100- and 200-meter sprints, broad jump and 400-meter relay, setting records that lasted more than 20 years. Hitler left the stadium after his wins, a snub to Black athletes, but Owens was lionized in Germany and given a ticker-tape parade in New York. He later did exhibition stunts like racing against a horse in the 100-yard dash. In 1937 he lent his name to a chain of cleaners shops but was left bankrupt by partners. He promoted physical education for African-Americans, was director of minority employment at Ford Motor Co., and advocated improved race relations. Olympic teammate Archie Williams later said that "Jesse Owens might have been snubbed by Hitler but he was a hero in the eyes of the Germans. They followed him around the streets like he was the Pied Piper." Owens was given a Medal of Freedom by President Gerald Ford in 1976, a Living Legend Award by President Jimmy Carter (1979) and honored posthumously with a Congressional Gold Medal (by President G.

W. Bush, 1990) at the urging of Congressman Louis Stokes (D-Cleveland). "Archie Williams is dead...," citing 1981 interview with *Oakland Tribune.*

7. Fowle, 25-26.

8. AC, "Brenda," "Vaga-London," typescript, AC Papers.

The subject was Brenda Irene Isabelle Dean Paul (1907-59), daughter (and third child) of Sir Aubrey Edward Henry Dean Paul (1869-1961), 5th Baronet, descendant of the 1st Duke of Marlborough, and Belgian-born composer and pianist Régine Wieniawski (daughter of a Polish violinist and composer) who used the pseudonym Poldowski. Brenda Dean Paul became a well-known actress frequently arrested for drug addiction. She spent time in Holloway Prison and died of an overdose in her flat. The web site Wikipedia.org noted claims that both Brenda and her mother, also addicted to morphine, were lesbians, and that Brenda's brother, Sir Brian Kenneth Dean Paul, 6th Baronet (1904-72), painted by Lucian Freud, took opium. Brenda Dean Paul was depicted in *The American Weekly*, January 16, 1944, as a beautiful "leader of London's patrician set" before a broken love affair and illness resulted in addiction to alleviate a painful internal ailment that in three years left her "a trembling wreck," with photographs that Cranston saved. Paul was quoted as saying, "I am convinced there is no suffering on earth compared to that endured by the narcotic addict," referring to her efforts to stop addiction to morphine. Gobind Behari Lal, Science Analyst, "Prescription says 'dope,'" *The American Weekly*, January 16, 1944, copy in AC Personal Papers.

9. Fowle, 27.

10. AC notes, "Authors to read," "Read Thoreau's *Walden*," and "Start political quote section…," index card notes.

11. AC notes, "Survival of the fittest…"; "Wells - Man may yet be…," citing H. G. Wells, *The Idea of a World Encyclopedia*, dated May, 1937, index card notes, 1935-36, AC Papers.

12. AC notes, "Facial experts upsetting…," and "Best example today of sexual selection…," citing Dr. Ernest A. Hooten (1887-1954), Professor of Anthropology (1930-54), Harvard University, quoted in Paris *Herald*, September 25, 1936, index card notes.

Hooten, a physical anthropologist, was known for work on racial classification based on a correlation between anatomy and social, cultural and racial factors, exemplified in such books as *Up From The Ape* (1931).

13. AC notes, "B. Shaw - Man's imperfectness…," citing "Preface to *Back to Methuselah*, 10," index card notes.

Élie Metchnikoff (1845-1916) succeeded Louis Pasteur as head of the Pasteur Institute in Paris. *Nature of Man, Studies in Optimistic Philosophy* was translated into English by P. Chalmers Mitchell (London: Heinemann, N. Y.: Putnams, 1903).

14. AC notes, "Wells - There can be no perfect man…," citing "God the Invisible King, 147"; "What science has given me - ideal, evolution"; "The alert and progressive man…," index card notes.

The Outline of Man's Knowledge by Clement Wood was published in 1927 and 1930.

15. AC notes, "Britain, France, Japan arms budgets, *Newsweek*, December 5, 1936," and "Naval budgets - U.S., Japan, France, Newsweek, Jan. 9, 1937"; "Russia's arms preparation, statistics, army size, etc.," citing "Bill Reed in NYK *[New York] American*, March 17, 1937"; "Europe to spend 13 or 14 billion $$$..," citing "Hillman, NYK *American*, March 15, 1937"; "The greatest arms race begins," citing "Dorothy Thompson, Paris *Herald*, March 11, 1937"; under "War" category, "Pacifists cost...to incarcerate…," index card notes.

The Walsh-Healey Public Contracts Act of 1936 (named for its sponsors, Massachusetts Democrats Senator David I. Walsh and Arthur Healey) was a New Deal law requiring that employees of government contractors be paid a minimum wage and overtime beyond 8 hours per day and 40 hours work per week; it also set standards for child and convict labor, job sanitation and safety. It led to enactment of the Fair Labor Standards Act of 1938 affecting most workers in manufacturing.

16. AC note, "The World War was fought…", index card notes

17. AC notes, "Gabriel W[hite] H[ouse], World Peace by armament abolishment except world and domestic police," citing "*Gabriel Over the White House*, 229"; "Thompson - Bases of our Constitution, gov't of law, not of men," citing "Thompson, *Political Panaceas*," index card notes. See also Chapter 11, note 72.

Gabriel Over the White House was a pre-code film released a few weeks after Roosevelt's inauguration. It was adapted by Carey Wilson from the novel *Rinehard* by Thomas Frederic Tweed, an adviser to Liberal British Prime Minister David Lloyd George who advocated Bismarck's German welfare programs for the United Kingdom. The film featured a U. S. president (Judson C. "Judd" Hammond played by Walter Huston) changing, after a near-fatal automobile accident, from a passive Herbert Hoover-like leader to an activist FDR-like politician taking temporary control of government like a quasi-dictator. His objectives were to re-start the economy with public-works jobs and promote world peace by international control of military arms. W. R. Hearst initially supported Roosevelt and backed his election with his media empire. A large stockholder in Hearst-Metrotone News, half-owned by MGM, Hearst withdrew from MGM in 1934, allegedly because it refused to cast Hearst companion Marion Davies as Elizabeth Barrett in *The Barretts of Wimpole Street*. The same year Hearst turned against FDR and New Deal policies. N. M. Schenck, president, MGM, to Stephen T. Early, White House press secretary, March 11, 1933, citing "before the picture is released it will be free from all objectionable features"; FDR to W. R. Hearst, April 1, 1933, citing "how pleased I am with the changes which you made in GABRIEL OVER THE WHITE HOUSE. I think it is an intensely interesting picture…," Franklin Delano Roosevelt Library, President's Official and Personal Files; Ferdinand Lundberg, *Imperial Hearst, A Social Biography* (N. Y.: Equinox Cooperative Press, 1936), 199, 302.

18. AC notes, "Capitalism - Property is robbery, *Erewhon*, Sam. Butler, pp. 114, ch. XII"; "Would we be happy in a perfect state…"; "World state incompatible with capitalism"; "In the World State"; "Why capitalism is basically against internationalism"; "Internationalism is the thing of the future…"; "Is internationalism possible..."; "The weakness of all world conferences"; "No nation has retained strength with unemployed; method of other nations," citing Jerry Voorhis and Maury Maverick, "Don't sell out prosperity," *Nation*, May 15, 1937; "Laws may make corrupt business, but there must be laws to protect the helpless, dumb people," index card notes.

Cranston at the end of his life wrote *The Sovereignty Revolution* published by Stanford University Press, 2004. See Chapter 14, note 94.

19. AC notes, "B. Russell - politics interfere…," and "Darwinism as an argument…," citing *Freedom versus Organization* (N. Y.: W. W. Norton, 1934), 144; "Whole point of Russell's *Freedom versus Organization*"; "B. Woolf - The upper-crust that has always so far destroyed its own civilization," citing "Quack, quack! 22-4," index card notes.

20. AC notes, "[Upton?] Sinclair - campaign funds win presidential campaigns"; "A political man…," citing Thomas Mann, "I Stand with the Spanish People," *Nation*, April 17, 1937, index card notes.

Cranston may have been attracted to socialist Upton Sinclair (1878-1968) in part because of his 1923 book *Goose-Step* discussing harmful effects of capitalist economic pressure on educational institutions.

21. AC notes, "Our great United States Presidents…," index card notes.

22. AC notes, "Democracy is not so much an end…," "The [institute?] surprised the fact upon me that there's an awful lot of talking…," "Democracy is a racket," "B. Armstrong - Dem[ocracy] - Based on competition between parties," citing *We or They*, 102-03; "Democracy not used for the right purposes," index card notes.

23. AC notes, "Best methods of influencing public opinion"; "Capital worsens under burden of unemployment…," citing Carl Dreher, 'The American Way,' *Harper's*, March, '38;

"Big business must be preserved over small business, but its profits must be spread out," citing *Nation* editorial, July 3, 1937, index card notes.

Lewis's *It Can't Happen Here* (1935) dealt with a future fascist revolt in the U. S.

24. AC notes, "P. Thompson - Marxian theory of liquidation of middle class…," citing "Thompson, *Political Panaceas*; "B. Russell - Marxian class-warism killed 19th cent. liberalism…," citing *Freedom vs. organization*, 220; "Sinclair - communist fear in America," citing *100%*, 238, index card notes.

25. AC notes, typed on two cards, "Capitalism - man's way, thru poverty, to insure himself of plentiful, easily-made women, Nov. 9, '36," index card notes.

26. AC notes, "Does a man who visits a prostitute…"; "Year-round sex urge creates family," citing John Hodgon Bradley, "Sex Freedom and the Family," *Forum*, April, 1937; "Non-physical reasons for homosexuality," index card notes.

27. AC notes, "Jews - Looking down on someone idea (Negro)"; "Jew persecution question one of world's liberty - not confined to Jews," citing *Nation* editorial, Dec. 4, 1937; "Project - Visit Liberia, write up what Negroes can do by selves," index card notes.

28. AC notes, "Tolerance - I try my hardest to be a world cosmopolitan," index card notes.

29. "Alan Cranston writes from Rome"; Fowle, 28; AC to Frank Gervasi, handwritten on U. S. Senate memorandum note paper, July 25, 1974, AC Papers; Kim Cranston to author, August 24, 2005, on AC's learning Italian.

Frank Gervasi (1909-90), who started as a reporter with the *Philadelphia Record* and the Associated Press (1932), began his career as a foreign correspondent with Universal Service in 1934 covering the Spanish Civil War. He joined Hearst's International News Service as Rome bureau chief shortly after that and *Collier's* weekly magazine at the start of World War II, covering the fall of Holland, Belgium and France. He also witnessed the long march of the British Eighth Army across the Libyan desert and landed with American forces in Southern France. He later was a correspondent for *The Washington Post*, a syndicated columnist and from 1950 to 1954, chief of information for the Marshall Plan in Italy. He authored 10 books, including a memoir of 1935-45, *The Violent Decade* (W. W. Norton, 1989). Frank Gervasi obituary, *The New York Times*, January 22, 1990.

30. "Alan Cranston writes from Rome"; Fowle, 29.

31. AC notes, "Berlin, September 15, 1937," citing signer as Pierre J. Huss, index card notes.

32. "Alan Cranston writes from Rome"; Fowle, 30, 37.

33. Fowle, 31.

34. Fowle, 31; AC interview with author; AC to Dan Carson, *The Journalism Report and Review*, Journalism Department, San Francisco State University, March 14, 1975, AC Papers.

Lee Falk (1911-99) was in college when he sold the idea for the comic strip "Mandrake the Magician" to King Features in 1934; the name was inspired by John Donne's poem, "Goe, and catche a falling starre…Get with child a mandrake root." Falk worked as an advertising executive and copywriter in St. Louis, owned theaters, produced and wrote plays. In World War II he served in the Office of War Information (with Cranston) and headed the foreign-language radio division (before Army service). "Mandrake" was drawn by Phil Davis (1906-64). "The Phantom," drawn by Ray Moore, was created in 1936. Mel Heimer, "Lee Falk," King Features Syndicate, biographical series no. 2, no date, AC Papers; web-site biography of Lee Falk by Bryan Shedden, 2003. See also Chapter 7, note 111.

35. Fowle, 32-33.

Cranston, in notes under the subject "Books," proposed doing an "Introduction to book on Europe – 'We three and Civilization - A Search,' to be co-authored by himself, John Atkinson and Lars Skattebol. Atkinson as a United Press reporter covered Italy's entry into Libya with so-called farmer-colonists who actually were part of the Italian army. "Italy's place to be revealed by John Atkinson, famed news writer," San Diego *Club Life*, May 1, 1940, copy in

AC personal papers.

36. AC notes, "The phone listeners," "Tremendous speed sometimes necessary for a story," note regarding office boy (Orlando), index card notes.

37. AC notes, "The phone listeners," index card notes; Fowle, 34.

38. Fowle, 34.

39. AC notes, "Autobiog. - Apologies to all the poor people…," index card notes.

40. AC notes, "Autogiob. - Lars' morbid fears stanza," index card notes.

41. AC notes, "Autobiog - Journalism, in news work…, Oct., 1937, Rome"; "Description of a big gun ready for action," separate phrases, index card notes.

42. AC notes, "September 18, '37 Sun. I commit an error which sabotages Peace…," index card notes.

43. AC notes, "Hearst has hired the higher intellects…," "Hearst, without consent of the owners, 'made' the American mind…," "Biting the hand that fed me," "Hearst's orders to G. on Italy…given August 24, 1936, Rome," "He's inevitably a Fascist…," index card notes.

Cranston and William Randolph Hearst had more similarities than Cranston realized in 1936-37. Hearst began his anti-communism crusade after traveling through Europe in 1934 and witnessing, as Cranston had, the rise of nazism and fascism as antidotes to communism. Hearst met with Hitler that year and made a personal appeal for Jews. Also like Cranston, Hearst feared the rise of a fascist movement in the United States among labor movements. Hearst commissioned both Mussolini and Hitler to write columns for the Hearst papers (Mussolini was paid $1,500 but could not write properly for the media, and Hitler always missed deadlines). Harold Evans, "Press Baron's Progress," review of *The Chief, The Life of William Randolph Hearst*, by David Nasaw, *New York Times*, July 2, 2000.

44. AC notes, "Autobiog - Fear of becoming conservative…Mar. 29, '37 - Rome (for Jefferson and Hamilton, see note from Russell, *Freedom versus Organization*, comparing them)," index card notes.

45. AC notes, "When we say great men…," index card notes.

46. AC notes, "A brilliant thought trickles…," index card notes.

47. AC notes, "Einstein, *The World as I See It*, 237, Ideals," index card notes.

48. AC notes, "Autobiog - Fear and promise if idealism turned to cynicism," index card notes.

49. Fowle, 34-35; AC notes, "Article on fascism (first read Strachey's book)…"; "Bang-up article on fascism, 'Two Murders'," index card notes.

Ernest Roehm (1887-1934) was a Nationalist Socialist leader who helped Hitler launch his political career and organized the storm troops, over which he and Hitler vied for control. Roehm was imprisoned for participating in the abortive "beer-hall putsch" in 1923, reappointed as commander of the storm troops but executed by Hitler in a purge, ostensibly for plotting a coup. Ernest Giacomo Matteotti (1885-1924) was the leading Socialist opponent to fascism; his murder by fascist hirelings furthered Mussolini's dictatorship.

50. AC notes, "Article subject - radio & revolution, the rise of radio as a political weapon," and "Violin - I knew then…," index card notes.

51. AC notes, "Article - Italy and Germany are communist nations!!!!!", index card notes.

52. AC notes, "September 4, '37 Sat. - Tremendously interested tonight, in finishing...," index card notes.

John Herman Randall, Jr. (1899-1980), American philosopher and historian, was author of *The Making of the Modern Mind: A Survey of the Intellectual Background of the Present Age* (1926).

53. Fowle, 35-36.

54. *Ibid.*

55. *Ibid.*; Frank Gervasi to AC, July 19, 1974, and AC to Gervasi, July 25, 1974, AC Papers.

INS merged with Universal News Service in 1937. Gervasi subsequently was with *Collier's* magazine, noted by Cranston on a 1945 federal job application. See note 29 and Chapter 10, note 24.

56. AC to Gervasi, July 25, 1974.

After repelling an Italian invasion, Ethiopia in 1895 won independence led by Emperor Menelik II and Ras (Duke) Makonnen, Ethiopian general and diplomat whose son Ras Tafari was crowned Emperor Haile Selassie I in 1930. Italian Fascists in 1936 occupied Ethiopia until it regained independence following an Allied offensive in 1941. The Ethiopians, when invaded by Italy, adopted W. C. Handy's famous song, "The Saint Louis Blues," as their battle hymn. Rick Bromer, "'Saint Louis Blues' is big hit song for W. C. Handy," *Old News*, December, 2002, & January, 2003, 9.

57. Kreisler interview; Fowle, 37-39.

58. Fowle, 39.

59. *Ibid.*; AC typescript, "A young censor...," in file labeled "Ethiopian Articles, 1938," AC Papers; AC notes, "Press ministries' file on correspondents - Today I asked Jack Bosio if he'd finished my Adowa article, which I gave him as evidence I could write picturesquely and fairly about Ethiopia. He said: 'Do you want it now? I can give it to you tomorrow. It's in your file.' Jan. 25, '38[?]," index card notes.

60. AC typescript, "Massaua, Italian Eritrea, (INS), Gray ships choking a cramped harbor...," March 27, 1938, and "Asmara, (INS), Scorned and neglected for more than...," April 10, 1938, "Ethiopian Articles, 1938," AC Papers; AC notes, "Massaua, March 17, Mushroom city springing from nothing on 3 islands...," index card notes

Beneath his name on INS story drafts, Cranston typed "Alan Cranston, International News Service Correspondent."

61. AC notes, "AOI, April 5, Tues., '38 - Asmara," index card notes.

62. AC typescript, "Addis Ababa, (INS), Ten thousand stout-hearted...," June 29, 1938, "Ethiopian Articles, 1938," AC Papers; Fowle, 38.

63. Fowle, 39; "Haile Selassie, libel suit settlement," *London Sunday Express*, July 31, 1938, copy in AC Papers.

General Ruggero Santini (1870-1958) was a major Italian general who commanded troops in Ethiopia (1935-36) and Somalia (1936-38), both of which Italy invaded. See photo of AC with General Santini in Ethiopia, 1938.

64. *Ibid.*

The article in the *Evening Standard* that prompted Selassie's first libel suit had been published September 7, 1936. The exiled Selassie stayed for a time at Dunham Massey, ancestral home near Manchester, U. K., of Roger Grey (1896-1976), 10th Earl of Stamford, an ardent supporter of the League of Nations, who, contrary to British government policy, received Selassie in 1938. Grey had a special roof garden installed for Selassie to walk in. Dunham Massey staff to author, Feb. 11, 2011.

65. Fowle, 40-41, citing Pierre Van Paassen, *The Days of Our Years*.

66. "Haile Selassie, libel suit settlement," *London Sunday Express*, July 31, 1938; Fowle, 39.

67. Fowle, 41.

68. AC to Gervasi, July 25, 1974; Fowle, 39, 42.

"I left INS after my Ethiopia trip – around July or Aug. of '38," AC wrote Gervasi in 1974. Cecil Brown became well known for World War II coverage, including an account of being rescued from a British battleship, *H.M.S. Repulse*, after it was sunk off Malaysia.

69. AC interview with author; AC notes, "Journalists - amateurs of great events," and autobiographical note, "I suddenly saw the dull perspective...," index card notes.

70. AC to James Heiler, Italian Division, Foreign Economic Administration, Washington, D.C., August 7, 1945, AC "Souvenirs, World War II," AC Personal Papers.

Cranston in one application said of his work in the Rome bureau: "Due to censorship regulations making it difficult to cover political news in Italy adequately, I specialized in covering economic news as a more subtle and less censorable way of exposing the Mussolini regime." Application for Federal Employment, July 5, 1945, AC "Souvenirs," World War II, AC Personal Papers.

71. Skattebol to "Folks," from London, September 4, 1938, AC Papers.

Cranston later recorded that he was in London at the time of the Munich appeasement when Neville Chamberlain returned with "a piece of paper that was supposed to mean peace in our time." Kreisler interview.

72. Skattebol to "Dear All," September 19, 1938, AC Papers.

73. Skattebol to "Dear All," September 24, 1938.

74. *Ibid.*; and Skatebol to "Dear All," September 28, 1938.

Cranston listed his 1938 London address as 44 Mecklenberg [*sic*] Square. Supplemental Sheet for Standard Form 57, Application for Federal Employment, 1945, AC Papers. The square in the Bloomsbury-King's Cross area of London is notable for gardens (two acres) and historic houses facing it. A blue plaque marks number 21 as the residence of economic historian R. H. Tawney (1880-1962), University of London professor (1931-49) and socialist who helped formulate British Labour Party positions, explaining the library that Skattebol described. House numbers may have changed after WWII, accounting for the difference from his and Cranston's citing 44 as their address. Virginia and Leonard Woolf lived at number 37 where they ran the Hogarth Press 1939-40 until bombing forced them to evacuate. Number 44 bears a plaque identifying it as the residence (1917-18) of American poet H. D. (Hilda Doolitle), wife of Richard Aldington, a friend of D. H. Lawrence who lived there in 1917.

75. Skattebol to "Dear All," October 2, 1938.

76. "Italy and Jews," 1938, typescript draft of book proposal, 202 pages, AC Papers; Fowle, 42.

Cranston built a large file, "Anti-Semitism, 1939," of pamphlets and writings on the subject.

77. *Ibid.*

Cranston referred to several books as resources, both of which he called "propaganda": Gioacchino Volpe, *History of the Fascist Movement;* Mussolini, *Political and Social Doctrine of Fascism (1932).*

Time magazine July 24, 1939 (p. 18) reported a rumor that Edda Mussolini Ciano was not the daughter of Mussolini's wife Donna Rachele but of a Russian Socialist with whom he had an affair as a youth. Edda was credited with facilitating the Rome-Berlin Axis and advocating unpopular Nazi views, including anti-Semitism, in Italy. Dino Alfieri succeeded Ciano as Under Secretary for Press and Propaganda. Mussolini ordered Ciano (1903-44), who voted against Mussolini in a Fascist Grand Council, shot by firing squad for treason January 11, 1944.

Achille Starace (1889-1945) was a leader of the Italian Fascist Party of which he was secretary 1931-39. Fanatically loyal to Mussolini, Starace staged parades, proposed anti-Semitic measures and expanded Mussolini's personality cult. He increased party membership but failed to build a fascist youth group patterned on Hitler's. He participated in the Italian invasion of Ethiopia. In 1939 he was dismissed as party secretary and at the end of Mussolini's regime in 1943, was arrested, imprisoned and released but, recognized during a morning jog in Milan by anti-Fascist partisans in 1945, was executed as was Mussolini.

78. Skattebol to "Dear Folks," November 11, 1938.

79. Fowle, 42; William Hillman, London Correspondent, Hearst Newspapers, to "Dear Alan," October 12, 1938; and John Jobson, London Editor, *The Yorkshire Post*, December 6, 1938, AC Papers.

80. Clipping quoting Mark Twain, in "Souvenirs, 1930s-1940s."

81. Fowle, 42-43.

82. Fowle, 42; Skattebol to "Dear Pop, N.Y.C.," no date, AC Papers; typed note, "It is my wish that my grandnephew, Alan McGregor [*sic*] Cranston, attend an eight months' session of the School of Journalism...," dated July 12, 1938, (signature not legible), and Marsh Maslin, "This is the Life," unidentified newspaper article, no date, "Souvenirs '30s-'40s," AC Personal Papers; "Palo Altan plans book on travels as news writer," *Palo Alto Times*, August 30, 1938, AC Papers.

The relative who offered to send Cranston to journalism school may have been Ilbert or Ebert Cranston, William Cranston's cousin, according to Fowle. Cranston had visited the Royal Palace at Naples, according to notes in which he described the apartments of Belgian Princess Marie Jose (born August 4, 1906). Notes in file marked "Ital. Misc.," AC Papers.

83. Fowle, 45-47; Adventurers' Club Meeting announcement for March 9, 1939, 311-1/2 South Spring Street (postmarked Los Angeles, March 6, 1939); AC guest pass signed by Rupert Hughes to The Authors Club, Hollywood, California, January 18, 1939, and February 10, 1939, "Souvenirs '30s-'40s"; guest pass to University Club of Los Angeles, January 18, 1939; handwritten note to Bill Leiser, President, San Francisco Press Club (no date, signature unclear), introducing "Allan [*sic*] Cranston, European correspondent (I.N.S.) & a Stanford man. Treat him rough!" AC Personal Papers. For Mooney see also Chapter 1, note 79.

84. Fowle, 47; Joan Lisetor, "Mrs. Alan Cranston honored at Marin luncheon yesterday," *Marin Independent-Journal*, October 10, 1968, AC Papers.

85. S. Freifeld, "Information regarding Alan Cranston," June 14, 1939, AC personal papers.

Sidney A. Freifeld was with Seven Arts Feature Syndicate for which AC did reporting in New York. Freifeld, of Rockville Center, Long Island, New York, is listed on one of AC's job applications as a character reference. He later worked as information officer for the Canadian delegation to the United Nations, and served as Canadian Ambassador to Mexico and Colombia. AC job application "Personal History Statement," 1943; AC to Lee Falk, January 29, 1969, citing Freifeld as reference, AC Papers.

86. AC note on clipping, Jonathan Yardley, "Titan of American Realism," *Washington Post*, (no date), review of Richard Lingeman, *Theodore Dreiser, An American Journey, 1908-1945* (Putnam); AC notes, "U. S. fascism, 1939"; memo [from AC?] to Ethel Phillips and Sidney Freifeld, "RE: McClure Syndicate, Richard Waldo, James McMullin," November 6, 1939; Walter E. Roloff, Professor of Economics, Colorado School of Mines, *Chickens are Nordic, Too*, copy in AC Papers.

Cranston in 1939 identified eleven organizations, some with pro-fascist leanings, including: Citizens National Keep-America-Out-of-War Committee; National Defenders of Democracy ("anti-Semitic," according to Cranston's notes); Women's National Committee to Keep U. S. Out of War; Women's Investors in America, Inc.; World Peaceways; Keep America Out of War Congress ("socialist"); Committee for Neutrality Preservation; Emergency Council to Preserve Neutrality; German-American Conference of Greater New York; German-American Republican League (headed by a "Nazi organizer and chairman of the Citizens Protective league, he is definitely a Bund member," according to Cranston); Committee for Neutrality Preservation; American Coalition of Patriotic Societies; American Fellowship Forum; American Citizens Committee; Emigration Conference Control Board.

87. Draft of play, "Realists Who Analyze," and "The Death of God, A Novel by Alan Cranston," typescript, AC Papers.

88. AC typescripts, "Matrimonial Masquerade," by Tony Beacon and Alan Cranston, and "Prelude"; "Rejects, '39-'40" - "The Dictator's Daughter & the Crown Princess," two versions, one co-authored with Edward Kleinlerer; "To speak of many things," *New York Post*, September 10, 1940, column quoting AC article, "Crown Princes to the Dictators - Count Galeazzo Ciano," *The American Mercury*, September, 1940, 61-63, AC Papers.

The physician was the most noted gynecologist in Italy, Baron Arton di Sant'Agnese, a Catholic convert of Jewish ancestry.

89. Martha Anderson, National Bureau of Economic Research, Incorporated, to Rudolf Modley, December 7, 1938, citing *Modern Age*; March [Marshall?] Maslin column, "Young Alan Cranston, Stanford graduate…is now connected with a new publishing house in New York City, headed by Amster Spiro, formerly city editor of the *New York Journal*…," *San Francisco Call-Bulletin*, May 9, 1939, AC Papers; Fowle, 46-47.

The nickel that Cranston found was issued in 1883 with a bust of Liberty on one side, "V" for five on the back and lacking the word "cents." People gold-plated it and passed it off as a $5-gold piece until the mint stopped issuing it and put out one with "cents." The latter coin would have been more valuable because fewer were issued that year with the word "cents." In 2004, an 1883 liberty nickel *without* "cents" was worth $7.00, *with* "cents, $25.00. Roy Greenaway, a coin collector, to author, October 4, 2004.

90. Skattebol to "Dear Folks," December 15, 1938, AC Papers. See also note 3.

Cranston lived from March, 1939, until February, 1940, at 135 or 136 Perry St., Greenwich Village, and at various New York City hotels; he also gave his address as c/o Amster Spiro, Bridgeport, Connecticut. AC, "Attachment to Loyalty Investigation Questionnaire," AC "Souvenirs 1930s-40s," AC Personal Papers; "Personal History Statement," 1943, AC Papers. In New York Cranston joined the Overseas Press Club and the Dramatists Guild, and in Washington, the United Nations Club. "Personal History Statement," July 28, 1942.

91. Fowle, 47.

92. "Johannes Steel and A. Spiro (former city ed. at the Journal) start that new Brooklyn tab Nov. 15. One rumor is…," *Daily Mirror*, October 27, 1939, in "Brooklyn Express" file; "Brooklyn Tabloid," no date; Amster Spiro, editor, *The New York Express*, "To Whom It May Concern," March 25, 1940, identifying the publisher as David Garrison Berger and Cranston as a "representative" of the paper; memo, "*QUICK* will be a complete New York daily newspaper…," no date, AC Papers.

93. "QUICK will be…"

94. Memo, "A new paper is expected to announce its basic policies, but if this means we should utter a philosophy of life, of government, of economics, we don't think that is so important because we are not out for any one cause…," no date, AC Papers.

95. *Ibid.*

96. Skattebol, typescript, "a sports editorial - football injuries for cash," no date, in *Brooklyn Express* file, AC Papers.

97. Fowle, 47.

98. Skattebol to "Dear Alan," from "American Broadcasting Company, Inc. newsroom, April 21," [194?], ending, "Heard you have a baby: congratulations to you both...," AC Papers.

99. George W. Joel, managing director, Seven Arts Feature Syndicate, to Collector of Customs, January 3, 1940; AC memorandum to Sidney Freifeld, "Re: Refugees," AC Personal Papers.

100. *Ibid.*, AC memorandum to Freifeld.

101. S. Freifeld to D. Bernstein, memo, "Refugees," no date, AC Personal Papers.

102. AC typescript, "Four refugees from Nazism are sealed aboard the Italian liner Vulcania at the docks…," AC Personal Papers.

103. Fowle, 49; AC memorandum to Sidney Freifeld, "Re: Refugees," and memo dated "Dec. 11 - The Sunday papers report…," presumably from S. Freifeld, AC Personal Papers.

104. "With the *Vulcania* of the Italian Line has just arrived in New York the Baroness Lisette de Kapri, who is the first aviatrix in Switzerland…," typed press release[?], AC Personal Papers.

105. Dorothy Thompson, "The Example of England - III, The Great Miracle of Dunkerque," [*Washington Post*?], September 27, 2940, copy in AC Papers; AC note on "Dunkerque" file, Carton 133, AC Papers.

106. AC, "Darts and Shafts," *The Voice for Human Rights*, Vol. 1, no. 4, January, 1940, re: Congressman Martin Dies (Demoract of Texas), chairman, Special Committee to Investigate un-American Activities, AC Papers.

107. Typescript, "Nuts," no signature, AC Papers.

108. AC interview with author; *Program Revue*, "Before Broadway premiere, Gilbert Miller presents a new comedy, 'The Big Story' by Lee Falk and Alan Cranston with Donald Cook and distinguished Broadway cast," no date [circa September, 1940]; "Mandrake, Phantom author, aids Cranston," Humboldt, California, *Standard*, November 3, 1962, AC Papers.

The Big Story would be produced many years later, in Palo Alto in 1975 (see Chapter 10, note 48). By then, Cranston was a U. S. Senator and the authors' names had been reversed to read, "by Alan Cranston and Lee Falk," which Falk "needless to say, pointed out, and laughed about," Cranston joked. AC interview with author.

109. Kreisler interview; Celeste Fremon, "Alan Cranston," *Playgirl*, March, 1983, 34, AC Papers.

110. Fowle, 47; Anthony O. Miller, "Court halted dime edition of 'Mein Kampf,' Cranston tells how Hitler sued him and won," *The Los Angeles Times*, February 14, 1988, in which Cranston claimed being in the same room with Hitler in Munich.

AC claimed to have read the original in German and to have been "reasonably fluent" in German when traveling there, according to a 1998 oral history (transcript in Los Altos History Museum archives). *Mein Kampf*, written in prison, was first published in two volumes in 1925 and 1926, and in English translation in 1939. In the political manifesto, Hitler decried the terms of the Versailles Treaty as they adversely affected Germany, advocated re-arming, economic self-sufficiency, suppression of trade unions and persecution of Jews, which policies Hitler began to implement after becoming Führer in 1934. Miller in his article reported that *Mein Kampf* by 1939 was a best-seller in Germany and "earned the pauper-turned-dictator, once rejected by Austrian art schools, about $3 million."

111. *Ibid.*, 48; AC to Ronald E. Wade, Gilmer, Texas, May 15, 1975, AC Papers.

112. Fowle, *ibid.*; "Legal fight looms over *Mein Kampf*," *New York Times*, January 2, 1939; Maya N. Federman, "Cranston: Making a Difference," 10th grade English paper, San Marcos High School, May, 1986, AC "Souvenirs, Misc. Years to file," AC Personal Papers; "Adolf Hitler's Own Book *Mein Kampf* (My Battle), A new unexpurgated translation...," tabloid newspaper, Noram Publishing Company, Inc., Greenwich, Conn., AC Papers. One article about the tabloid said that AC produced it "in collaboration with the liberal-oriented *New York Post*." Frank Anderson, "Trackman Cranston runs on," *Long Beach Independent Press-Telegram*, September 9, 1968, AC Papers.

Germany seized Austria by force in 1938, Czechoslovakia in March, 1939. The invasion of Poland September 1, 1939, triggered war with Britain and France; Germany invaded France in 1940, Greece in 1941, then attacked Russia. Hitler became supreme military commander in 1942, escaped a plot to kill him in 1944 and died during a Russian attack on Berlin April 30, 1945.

113. "Legal fight looms over *Mein Kampf*," *ibid.*; *Readers' Digest*, March, [1939], copy in AC Papers.

Hitler refused to authorize a complete translation of *Mein Kampf*, thus only expurgated versions were available in English until 1939. A condensed edition published in London, which Cranston may have seen, omitted most of the passages attacking France and a section justifying war, and softened the tone of the book, making it false and misleading, according to a 1956 analysis. Hitler in 1936 had successfully sued and restrained publication of a full translation in France on grounds of copyright infringement. Stackpole Sons (still in business as Stackpole Company as of 2011) argued that Germany in 1939 no longer was the same government with which the United States had signed a copyright treaty in 1892, and that reciprocity was denied many American authors under new German decrees, thus further abrogating the treaty. Stackpole planned a first printing of 15,000 copies, and Houghton, Mifflin, 250,000 copies, both to sell for $3.00. By the outbreak of World War II, five million copies of *Mein Kampf* had been distributed in Germany alone. Norman Cousins in retrospect called it "by far the most effective book of the twentieth century.... For every word in *Mein Kampf*, 125 lives were to be lost; for every page, 4,700 lives; for every chapter, more than 1.2 million lives." Typescript excerpts from Robert B. Downs, *Books that Changed the World* (Chicago: American Library Association, 1956), AC Papers.

114. Flyer, "Mr. News dealer: You can do your bit to STOP HITLER!," AC Papers.

115. *"Mein Kampf* for a dime," *Los Angeles Times*, May 16, 1939; "I heard: Our bookman Luther Meyer tells me that those two fat editions of Hitler's *Mein Kampf*...," *San Francisco Call-Bulletin*, May 24, 1939.

116. Fowle, 48; Benjamin R. Epstein to Richard E. Gutstadt, April 27, 1939, AC Papers; Anthony O. Miller, "Court halted dime edition'Mein Kampf'..." *The Los Angeles Times*, February 14, 1988, noting that Epstein headed the Anti-Defamation League for 30 years and quoting him as saying, "I was shocked" that Spiro, also Jewish, was involved in publicizing Hitler, but "once I realized he was really on our side, I opened our files and we worked very closely together."

A columnist writing about Cranston's book *Killing of the Peace* stated that there were riots in "Yorkville, St. Louis and elsewhere" as a result of the tabloid publication. Clip Boutell, "Authors are like people, Cranston's warnings - history's stepchildren," *New York Post*, September [6?], 1945, copy in AC Papers.

117. Decision of Hon. Edward A. Conger, U. S. District Judge, in Southern District of New York, July 19, 1939, in case of Houghton Mifflin Company, Plaintiff, against Noram Publishing Company, Inc., Caslon Publication Service, Inc., Interborough News Company, Milton Spiro, Sam C. Markus, and Harry A. Sterne, Defendants, file no. civ. 3-344, copy in AC Papers; AC to Irving Wallace, February 25, 1981, AC Papers; "Stackpole loses *Mein Kampf* suit," *New York Times*, datelined October 23, 1939; AC to author, May 26, 2000.

Noram defendants in the judge's decision were cited as company "directors, officers, agents and employees." Stackpole Sons continued to argue that Hitler was a "stateless person when he wrote *Mein Kampf*," thus invalidating any copyright that he held because he was not a citizen of a state having reciprocal copyright arrangements with the United States. Hitler had identified himself as stateless when filing one copyright application in Austria in 1927.

Benito Mussolini, *The Cardinal's Mistress* (New York: Albert & Charles Boni, 1928), first American edition.

Cranston got a "working press pass" to attend a trial of Fritz Kuhn, possibly for attacks on news vendors of the tabloid. AC pass to press table, "People v. Fritz Kuhn," AC Personal Papers.

118. Corporal Blaine Davis, "Crofter was sued by Hitler over take on *Mein Kampf*," *The Spartan*, Camp Croft, U. S. Army, March 21, 1944, AC Personal Papers; AC to Ronald E. Wade, Gilmer, Texas, May 15, 1975, AC to Irving Wallace, February 25, 1981, AC to Jim Schendel, Golden Valley, Minnesota, February 18, 1975, AC Papers; Tuck Shepherd, "Biography traces Cranston's colorful career," Los Altos *Town Crier*, July 30, 1980, scrapbook entitled "Presidio Press," REC Papers.

Cranston's version of the story was mentioned in a book by John Toland, *Adolf Hitler, The Definitive Biography* (1976), p. 528, with a note quoting Cranston. Toland wrote that "Hitler was outraged by the recent appearance in the United States of an unauthorized condensed version of *Mein Kampf* which included passages omitted from the authorized American edition as well as editorial comments by Alan Cranston calling attention to Hitler's distortions."

119. Chester Kerr, chief, Book Division, Office of Facts and Figures, to Amster Spiro, Booktab, Inc., New York, May 12, 1943, AC Papers.

120. Paul Brooks, Lincoln Center, Massachusetts, to AC, August 15, 1983, AC Papers.

121. Murray Flander, memo to AC and members of staff, September 12, 1983, AC Papers.

122. Roy Greenaway to author, July 26, 2002; Biographical Sketch of U. S. Senator Alan Cranston of California, January, 1987, AC Papers.

123. Mrs. Charles G. (Helen) Gardner, Administrative Assistant to President, Hofstra University, to AC, [circa 1968?], "1969-72 ancient friends" file, Carton 129, AC Papers.

124. AC to Don Harris and Warren Wilson, KNBC, Burbank, California, May 22, 1975, AC Papers.

125. Kreisler interview.

126. *Ibid.*

Chapter 3 Marriage, Aliens and Army

1. Common Council for American Unity, description of purposes, 1939; "One Nation, indivisible," brochure of Common Council; "Memorandum to Council Members, summary of activities from Pearl Harbor to date," March 4, 1943, AC Papers; "New unity urged for citizens of U. S.," *New York Times*, June 13, 1940.

Cranston worked for the Common Council from February, 1940, to December, 1941. The Council was a non-profit organization that sought to prevent discrimination against aliens and foreign-born people in the United States. It was an opponent of anti-Communist deportation policies in the 1930s-40s and the internment of Japanese-Americans during World War II. "There is an America that bombs cannot reach…an America that all people share…where hate and intolerance are not masters…the America of the Declaration of Independence and the Constitution," one of the Council's brochures advertised. In 1959 the CCUA merged with the American Federation of International Institutes to form the American Council for Nationalities Service, still operating in 2006. Web site for Records of the American Council for Nationalities Service, 1921-1971 (www. lexisnexis.com/Academic2upa/Ai/AmericanCouncilNationalities Service.asp).

George Creel (1876-1953) was an investigative journalist and active member of the Democratic Party who ran against novelist Upton Sinclair for governor of California. He served on the San Francisco Regional Labor Board (1933) and as chairman of the National Advisory Board of the Works Progress Administration (1935). As head of the U. S. Committee on Public Information during World War I, he organized some 75,000 public speakers and distributed millions of pamphlets in support of the war effort; his memoir, *How We Advertised America* (1920), was one of 14 books that he authored. He lived in San Francisco (on Pacific Heights, at Divisadero and Green Streets), and was a member of the Bohemian Club. George Creel, Wikipedia; Geoff Whittington, SF.Blockshopper.com, *San Francisco Chronicle*, February 28, 2010, H18.

2. Common Council for American Unity, description of purposes, 1939; Common Council brochure, "Prelude to Victory."

3. Fowle, 49-50; AC résumé as chief, Foreign Language Division, Office of War Information, January 2, 1942, citing previous jobs and salaries; AC to James Heiler, Italian Division, Foreign Economic Administration (FEA), Washington, D. C., August 7, 1945; AC "Supplement to Application and Personal History Statement," December 18, 1941, application for job with U. S. Office of Facts and Figures; Common Council for American Unity, Inc., budget statement for 1940, AC Papers.

Louis Adamic (1899-1951) published *My America* in 1938. His book, *Two-Way Passage* (1941), proposed that European-Americans return to their homelands to educate Europeans in democracy, which led to a conference with Roosevelt and Churchill, described by Adamic in *Dinner at the White House* (1946).

4. Fowle, 51.

5. *Ibid.*, 51.

6. *Ibid.*, 50-51.

7. *Ibid.*, 50; Read Lewis to "Members and Friends of Common Council, February 19, 1941"; Lewis, telegram to AC, June 21, 1940, concerning the Alien Registration Act of 1940; AC passes to Senate and House of Representatives, May, 1940; American Political Science Association, nomination of AC for membership by President Robert C. Brooks, postmarked October 9, 1940, AC Papers.

John J. Dempsey (1879-1958) was New Mexico's lone representative, 1935-41, 1951-58, and governor 1943-47.

8. Phoebe [?] to AC, "Sunday," [March, 1940?], "Hell's been popping around here…"; AC to Lewis, 30 March, 1940, AC Papers.

William T. Schulte of Indiana and Charles Kramer of California were Democrats who served in Congress 1933-43.

9. Lewis to AC, April 1, 1940, and January 14, 1941, AC Papers.

10. Unidentified man [Kleinberg?], address 92-05 Whitney Ave., Elmhurst, L. I., New York, to AC, February 4 and 26, 1941; Ralph A. Reynolds, M.D., to AC, December 12, 1941, AC Papers.

Dr. Ralph A. Reynolds, a personal family friend, was listed as a character reference on one of AC's job applications. "Personal History Statement," 1943.

11. AC to "Dear Al," February 18, 1941, AC Papers.

AC ended the letter with, "It's 2:00 a.m. Geneva is getting sore at you and me both."

The case of Kessler (District Director of U. S. Immigration and Naturalization office) versus Strecker, 307 U. S. 22 (1939) concerned a Polish-born man who had entered the U. S. in 1912 and applied for citizenship in 1933 (to a U. S. District Court in Arkansas). He had joined the Communist Party in 1932 but dropped membership in 1933. The Sedition Act of 1918 authorized imprisonment and deportation of "aliens who believe in, advise, advocate, or teach, or who are members of or affiliated with any organization" that advocated the overthrow of the U. S. government. The U. S. Supreme Court in 1939 ruled that Strecker was not a member of the party at the time that he applied for naturalization, and thus should not be held or deported. Websites Justia.com, U. S. Supreme Court Center; and http://law.jrank.org.

12. "Memorandum to Council Members, summary of activities from Pearl Harbor to date," March 4, 1943, AC Papers.

Thomas Mann won the Nobel Prize for literature in 1929. He was deprived of German citizenship by Hitler and moved to the United States in 1938.

13. *Common Ground*, quarterly newsletters, Spring, 1944; Autumn, 1940; Spring, 1941; Summer, 1941; "Discrimination - Defense Bottle-neck," Autumn, 1941, 109; Winter, 1942; and *Magazine Digest*, November, 1941. AC to Frederick Osborne, War Department, re: "an acute labor shortage is developing in several states due to the hesitancy of employers to hire aliens...," February 18, 1941; AC to Collis Stocking, Social Security Board, Bureau of Employment Security, re: "state laws discriminating against aliens in employment," February 25, 1941; Read Lewis to Sen. William H. King, May 2, 1940, re: discrimination against dentists, AC Papers.

14. AC, "The American foreign-born and the war," *The Journal of Educational Sociology*, September, 1943; AC, "The Drive against the Alien," *Hadassah Newsletter*, April, 1940; AC to Miriam J. Cohen, associate editor, *Hadassah Newsletter*, March 11, 1940; AC to Allen Lesser, American Jewish Committee, May 13, 1940; AC, "New Americans," *Jewish Tribune*, January 25, 1940; "In the magazines, official scapegoat," *The Hellenic Spectator*, July, 1940, citing AC in May-June, 1940, issue of *Contemporary Jewish Record*, AC Papers.

15. Federal Works Agency, Works Projects Administration for New York City, to AC, January 18, 1941, re: lecture December 18, 1940, AC "Souvenirs, 1930s-40s," AC Personal Papers.

16. John Edgar Hoover, Director, F. B. I., to AC, March 12, 1940; AC to Paul Richman,

B'Nai B'rith, Washington, D.C., March 16, 1940; Paul Richman to AC, March 21, 1940; Read Lewis to Will Chenery, re: article in *Collier's*, May 13, 1940, AC Papers.

17. Louis H. Beer to AC, analyzing L. B. Johnson election, November 9, 1942, AC Papers; Fowle, 51.

Lyndon Johnson (1908-73), Democrat of Texas, was first elected to the House of Representatives in 1937, reelected until 1946. He lost a special election for the Senate in 1941, and served 1941-42 in the Navy. He won a Senate seat in 1948, and became 36th President of the U. S. (1963-69).

Hiram W. Johnson (1866-1945) was elected governor of California (1911-17) as a Progressive reform candidate fighting the political power of Southern Pacific railroad. He ran for vice president on the 1912 "Bull Moose" ticket with Theodore Roosevelt, carrying California despite Democrat Woodrow Wilson's victory. Johnson served four terms in the U. S. Senate (1917-45), first as a Progressive and after 1920 as a Republican.

18. Read Lewis, Director, to Hon. Joe Starnes, February 3, 1940, and Starnes to Lewis, February 12, 1940, AC Papers.

Congressman Joe Starnes (Democrat of Alabama), a member of the House Un-American Activities Committee (HUAC), was a strong opponent of federal arts programs instituted as part of the New Deal's Works Progress Administration (WPA), calling an army arts program "a piece of foolishness" (resulting in its funding being cancelled in 1943). He famously interrupted a witness at a hearing, Hallie Flanagan, director of the Federal Theatre Project, who was defending the program against charges that it was infested with Communist Party members, using a quote from English playwright Christopher Marlow; Starnes demanded to know Marlowe's political affiliation.

19. AC to Read Lewis, May 15, 1940, AC Papers. Cranston addressed his letters to "Mr. Lewis."

Harry Bridges (1901-90) was an Australian immigrant seaman when he arrived in San Francisco in 1920; he became a longshoreman and militant labor organizer, leading a 1934 strike of maritime workers that expanded into a general strike. In 1937 he organized the International Longshoremen's and Warehousemen's Union (ILWU) and became West Coast director of the Congress of Industrial Organizations (CIO). An effort to deport him as a Communist 1939 ended when he was absolved of the affiliation. The House of Representatives did approve a bill to deport Bridges in 1940 but it was ruled illegal by the U. S. Supreme Court in 1945, when Bridges became a U. S. citizen. He was sentenced to a five-year prison term in 1950 for falsely swearing at his naturalization hearing that he had never been a member of the Communist Party; the conviction was dismissed by the Supreme Court in 1953. The Justice Department announced in 1958 that it had given up the long fight to deport Bridges, who continued to lead the ILWU.

Senator Tom Connolly (1877-1963), Democrat of Texas, served in the House 1917-29, and Senate 1929-53, and was Chairman of the Senate Foreign Relations Committee.

20. Read Lewis to "Members of Joint Conference on Alien Legislation," May 23, 1940; Lewis to James L. Houghteling, "Dear Lawrence," May 24, 1940; AC to Read Lewis, May 24, 1940, AC Papers.

Legislative concerns cited by Lewis were the "President's Reorganization Plan No. 5 transferring the Immigration and Naturalization Service to the Department of Justice; the House Immigration Committee's favorable action yesterday on the Poage bill (H. R. 9774) providing for the deportation of those who have been convicted of felonies; the new Dies bill [Rep. Martin Dies was chairman of the Special Committee to Investigate Un-American Activities]; Senator Reynolds' amendment to the LaFollette Civil Liberties bill, proposing to limit employment of aliens."

Houghteling, whose wife Laura Delano was a first cousin of Franklin Roosevelt, was an uncle of Joe Houghteling, a California newspaper publisher and political friend of Cranston beginning in 1948.

21. AC to Read Lewis, May 24, 1940, AC Papers.

22. AC to Harold Payson, Senate Office Building, re: "suggesting to Senator Mead that he seek a seat on the committee for this session...when it will consider much legislation of vital import to many New Yorkers," March 11, 1941; Marian Schibsby, associate director, Common Council, to AC, re: "two private bills you have just sent up...," March 15, 1941, AC Papers.

James M. Mead (1885-1964), Democrat of New York, served in the Senate 1938-47; he lost a race for Governor of New York to incumbent Republican Thomas Dewey in 1946.

Richard B. Russell (1897-1971), Democrat of Georgia, served in the Senate 1933-71.

23. AC to Rep. Emanuel Celler, June 13, 1940; Bee Bettings to AC, January 17, 1941, asking Cranston if he could get Celler's permission to quote his endorsement of *Common Ground*, AC Papers.

24. Bee Bettings to AC, January 17, 1941; AC to Bee Bettings, January 21, 1941, AC Papers.

25. AC to Sen. Francis T. Maloney (1894-1945, Democrat of Connecticut, Senator 1935-45; Congressman 1933-35), June 13, 1940, AC Papers.

26. AC to Lewis, June 18 and June 20, 1940, AC Papers.

Hatton W. Sumners (1875-1962), Democrat from Texas, initially Texas' Representative-at-Large, served in the House 1913-47; he was Chairman of the Judiciary Committee 1932-46.

Clarence E. Hancock (1885-1948), Republican of New York, served in the House 1927-47.

John A. Danaher (1899-1990), Republican of Connecticut, served in the Senate 1939-45; he subsequently was appointed by President Eisenhower a U. S. Circuit Court of Appeals Judge.

27. *Ibid.*

28. AC to Frank Morris, New York City, August 16, 1940; AC to Harold Payson, Senate Office Building, January 14, 1941, citing "findings of a recent survey in California [that] showed that 70% of the people belonging to families headed by aliens are American citizens!", AC Papers.

George H. Lysle, when Mayor of McKeesport, Pa. (1920-37), had refused in 1934 to grant a permit to the Young Communist League to hold a meeting against war and Fascism, resulting in the arrest of 25 people and convictions of three for rioting, including a young woman who chained herself to a pole, which convictions were fought by the Pittsburgh Civil Liberties Union and other liberal groups.

29. Fowle, 51-52; Geneva McMath to "Letters to the Editor Dept.," *New York Journal*, April 23, 1940, AC Papers.

30. REC interview with author; Fowle, 52; Joan Lisetor, "Mrs. Alan Cranston honored at Marin luncheon yesterday," Marin *Independent-Journal*, October 10, 1968; "Mrs. Alan Cranston, GOPacrats for Cranston," press release, [1968], Carton 617; note on news clipping, Sydney Rosen, "Mrs. Alan Cranston plans many-sided life for herself," *Sacramento Bee*, January 12, 1959, and on news clipping, Caroline Drewes, "New life of our freshmen senator's wife," *San Francisco Examiner*, February 7, 1969, Vols. 1 and 10, 1969, AC Papers.

31. Fowle, 52; Dave Bond, San Francisco, to author, January 25, 2011, re: draft numbers and classifications.

32. New York State Department of Health, marriage license application and blood-test result, dated October 30, 1940, AC "Souvenirs, 1930s-40s," AC Personal papers. "Alan Cranston is wed, flies from New York to claim bride in south," *Daily Palo Alto Times*, Friday, November 8, 1940, AC Papers.

Lee Falk told reporters when campaigning with Cranston in 1962 that he had been best man. "Mandrake, Phantom author, aids Cranston," Humboldt *Standard*, November 3, 1962.

A war-time revision of the Selective Service Act of 1940 made men between 18 and 45 years old liable for military service, and required all men between 18 and 65 to register for the draft. Cranston initially was classified 3A (hardship deferment, having a wife), but after going to work for the Office of War Information, was reclassified 2B by the Selective Service board, allowing deferment for occupation in a war industry, per a Department of State job application for Director, Foreign Relief and Rehabilitation Operations, dated April 17, 1943, AC Papers.

33. "Alan Cranston is wed," *ibid.*; "Cora Older sends you a happy 1941," greeting card to Cranstons, postmarked December 27, 1940, with inscription, "All good fortune to you both, C.D.," AC "Souvenirs, 1930s-40s," AC Personal Papers.

34. Calling cards inscribed, "From..., To..., And to...may they grow...," AC "Souvenirs, 1930s-40s," AC Personal Papers; card signed by Geneva Cranston to "Married Men's Protective Assn.," August 21, 1943, AC Papers.

35. AC to Lewis, January 7, 1940[1?], AC Papers.

They later moved to 120 C Street, N.E., closer to the Capitol.

36. Fowle, 53-54; Telfair Knight, director, division of Training, U. S. Maritime Commission, to David Niles, May 5, 1941, AC Papers.

37. Fowle, 53.

38. *Ibid.*, 55.

39. Fowle, 56; AC resume, as chief, Foreign Language Division, Office of War Information, January 2, 1942, citing previous jobs and salaries.

Cranston's $6,500 annual salary was cited on a resume dated February 16, 1943.

On his application for the job, Cranston stated: "I feel that my intimate knowledge of the mechanics of the work, my contacts with the government officials who would be most affected by this work, my understanding of the sentiments and problems of the foreign-born in this country, and my news and publishing background, qualify me for this position." "Supplement to Application and Personal History Statement," December 18, 1941, and résumé, AC Papers.

Archibald MacLeish (1892-1982), who had served in World War I, was a lawyer, journalist and three-time Pulitzer Prize-winning poet among whose best-known works is the verse play, "J. B." President Roosevelt named him Librarian of Congress (1939-44) during which time he took on other duties for the Office of Facts and Figures and Office of War Information. After serving as Assistant Secretary of State (1944-45), MacLeish was chief of the U. S. delegation to the organizing conference of UNESCO. He was instrumental in getting friend and fellow poet Ezra Pound freed from St. Elizabeth's mental hospital, and spoke out against the House Un-American Activities Committee. Gilbert Harrison, "Serving his muse and his country," review of *Archibald MacLeish, An American Life* by Scott Donaldson, *Washington Post Book World*, May 3, 1992.

40. AC to James Heiler, no date, AC Papers.

41. AC, memorandum to William B. Lewis, December 23, 1941, AC Papers.

42. AC, memorandum to Allen Grover, "A program for American unity," January 12, 1942, AC Papers.

43. AC, memorandum to Archibald MacLeish, "Department of Justice centers attention upon aliens," January 19, 1942, AC Papers.

44. AC, memorandum to William B. Lewis, "Foreign language radio programs," January 27, 1942, AC Papers.

45. Fowle, 57; Tom Clark, *Charles Olson, The Allegory of a Poet's Life* (New York: Norton, 1991), 83; Elmer Davis "To whom it may concern," O. W. I. memo, November 2, 1943 re: Lee Falk employed as associate chief of foreign-language division from February 17, 1942 to October 15, 1943, Carton 3, AC Papers; AC to Lee Falk, Stamford, Connecticut, January 29, 1942; AC, memorandum to Archibald MacLeish, "Employment of Lee Falk," February 9, 1942; AC to Lee Falk, King Features Syndicate, July 8, 1943, AC Papers.

46. "The administration, truth & trouble," *Time*, March 15, 1943; "He sells democracy, Elmer Davis' job is to tell the world about our war effort," unidentified clipping, AC Papers.

The O. W. I., part of the Office for Emergency Management, was created by Executive Order June 13, 1942, consolidating four agencies: the Office of Facts and Figures, Office of Government Reports, Division of Information in the Office for Emergency Management, and Foreign Information Service in the Office of the Coordinator of Information. O. W. I.'s mission was to formulate and carry out, through the press, radio, motion-picture and other facilities, information programs to give an informed and intelligent understanding, at home and abroad, of the status and progress of the war effort and aims of the government. One O. W. I. poster in AC Papers portrayed three raised arms holding a tool, gun and wrench with the slogan, "Strong in the strength of the Lord, we who fight in the people's cause will never stop until that cause is won." Press release, Presidential "Executive Order consolidating in one new agency the information functions of the government, foreign and domestic," June 13, 1942, and poster, "O. W. I. #8, 1942," AC Papers; and *Congressional Record* - House, June 17, 1943, pp. 6087-88.

Elmer Davis (1890-1958) was a well-known journalist, Rhodes Scholar at Oxford University, England, who had worked for ten years at the *New York Times* of which he wrote a history (*History of the New York Times, 1851-1921* (1921); he also was a novelist, essayist and (beginning in 1939) a popular CBS radio commentator. "When Franklin Roosevelt tied all his muddling, uncoordinated news and propaganda agencies into a single loose package last summer, Elmer Davis was the only boss that no one could have objected to.... He took over some 3,000 employees, scores of jealousies and quarrels, innumerable unsolved problems of policy and procedure," *Time* reported March 15, 1943. Milton S. Eisenhower, brother of General Eisenhower, was one of Davis' assistants. While director of O. W. I., Davis recommended to President Roosevelt that Japanese-Americans be allowed to enlist for military service and urged opposing Congressional bills to deprive them of citizenship and intern them during the War. Davis was credited with helping inspire the all-Nisei 442nd Regimental Combat unit. Wikipedia, citing Japanese-American Voice (www.javoice.com).

In Cranston's division, David Karr (hired February 3, 1942) handled liaison duties with other federal agencies and non-governmental organizations, dealing with foreign nationality groups in the U. S.; Constantine Poulos, Greek-born veteran reporter, was in charge of the foreign-language press work (Poulos later returned to Greece to participate in political struggles); exiled aristocrat Adam Kulikowski handled Polish affairs.

Karr, whose legal name was David Katz, had previously worked for the American Council against Nazi Propaganda and as a reporter for other publications; he had written articles critical of the House Special Committee to Investigate Un-American Activities and its chairman, Rep. Martin Dies, for Communist-front publications *Daily Worker* and *Equality*, and for columnist Drew Pearson. In 1943 he was called to testify before the Un-American Activities Committee, which cited his association with the American League for Peace and Democracy, identified by the U. S. Attorney General in the 1940s as a Communist-front organization. See *Congressional Record*, Appendix, February 18, 1944, p. A815, citing Karr's testimony to the House committee April 6, 1943.

47. Fowle, 58; Clark, *Charles Olson...*, 73-74, 76-78, 82; "Foreign Language Division, Office of War Information, Statement of Functions"; "Foreign Language Press," statement justifying activities, AC Papers.

The Foreign Language Division of O. W. I.'s News Bureau was in charge of getting war information to 4.2 million aliens, 8 million foreign-born citizens and 23 million first-generation Americans who depended on foreign languages for information; the division worked in some 30 foreign languages with 1,108 foreign-language newspapers and 150 radio stations.

Charles Olson (1910-70) was a leader of the Black Mountain school of poets in the 1950s. Olson met Cranston when both worked at the Common Council and wrote for *Common Ground.* Olson's political views were influenced by Louis Adamic's writings in support of the "American dream" and individual rights. (Olson recruited folksinger Woody Guthrie to write a short piece about his rambling life for *Common Ground* that evolved into Guthrie's autobiography, *Bound for Glory*.) According to a 1991 Olson biography, "Cranston and Olson conferred frequently and took a liking to one another in the spring of 1942 when Cranston moved on to head a new government propaganda bureau in Washington. One of the first to be considered as an aide was energetic publicist Olson.... [Cranston] confirmed [Olson's] appointment as assistant chief in the division, at a starting salary of $75 a week." Olson wrote an O. W. I. pamphlet, *Spanish Speaking Americans in the War*, for which artist Ben Shahn did the layout and design. Cranston is quoted in the Olson biography from a 1987 interview. Olson subsequently directed the Democratic National Committee's foreign nationalities division for F. D. R.'s 1944 reelection campaign. Clark, 73-74, 76, 78-79, 85.

48. *Bombs Away, the Story of a Bomber Team*, by John Steinbeck, government promotion, December 3, 1942, AC Papers.

49. AC to Local Selective Service Board #16, New York City, January 3, 1942; "O. W. I. language chief," *Stanford Alumni Review*, January, 1943, AC Papers.

Cranston joined the Office of Facts and Figures in 1941. He became chief of the Foreign Language Division, O. W. I., a year later, January 1, 1942.

50. AC, memorandum to MacLeish, "Americans-All rallies," April 3, 1942, AC Papers.

51. AC speech to Italian-American Labor Council and Mazzini Society, June 2, 1942, AC Papers.

52. "Foreign tongue radio and press 'behaving' - O. W. I.," unidentified news clipping; AC, memorandum to James Allen, "Statement of recommended O. W. I. view on foreign-language papers opposed to the war," citing speech by Assistant Attorney General Wendell Berge January 23, [1942?]; "For alien-tongue press, Stimson says it should not be suppressed indiscriminately," *New York Times*, May 22, 1942, AC Papers.

53. AC, memorandum to Ulric Bell, "A Fascist selling bonds for the Treasury," April 6, 1942, AC Papers.

54. "Foreign tongue radio and press 'behaving' - O.W.I.," unidentified news clipping, AC Papers.

55. AC, memorandum to Elmer Davis, "Work of Foreign-Language Division," January 26, 1943, AC Papers.

56. AC, memoranda to MacLeish, "Civil Rights Federation," August 13, 1942; "Statement for American Committee for Protection of Foreign Born for ceremonies commemorating 67th anniversary of Statue of Liberty," October 2, 1942; "Request from 'Soviet Russia Today,'" October 5, 1942, AC Papers.

57. AC interview with author.

Cranston credited Joe Facci, an Italian refugee from Mussolini "gangs," for generating the idea to end enemy-alien status for Italian-Americans. Charles Olson described Facci's facial profile as resembling Dante's. Cranston interceded to try to help Facci when the State Department asked for his passport in 1951 (see Chapter 5). Fowle, 61-62; Clark, 78.

58. AC interview with author.

The U. S. Department of Justice in February, 1942, had removed from the category of alien enemies all those of German, Italian and Japanese nationality already serving in the U. S. armed forces, providing they had enlisted prior to the U. S. declaration of war in December, 1941. After that, alien enemies were prohibited from entering the armed forces. Press release, Department of Justice, February 23, 1942, AC Papers.

59. Fowle, 62; A. Tarchiani, secretary, Mazzini Society, Inc., to AC, October 16, 1942; Bruno Foa, director, Bureau of Latin American Research, to AC, October 20, 1942; AC to James Heiler, stating, "I was the first official to push the plan for exempting Italian aliens from the enemy-alien classification," AC Papers.

Italy's post-war foreign minister, Count Carlo Sfroza, credited the change in U. S. policy with saving the lives of American soldiers when Allies landed in Italy. The refugee anti-Fascist leader and defense minister was Randolfo Pacciardi.

60. Fowle, 65; Alfred Kazin, "Who hired the assassin?", review of Dorothy Gallagher, *All the Right Enemies, The Life and Murder of Carlo Tresca*, *New York Times Book Review*, October 2, 1988, copy in AC Personal Papers

Tresca (1879-1943) was a leader in defending Sacco and Vanzetti (two Italian anarchists accused of killing and robbing a shoe-factory paymaster and guard in Braintree, Massachusetts, in 1920; their death sentence and execution in 1927 aroused public sympathy as unjustified, although later ballistic tests (in 1961) indicated that a pistol found on Sacco had been the murder weapon. The Italian fascist government tried for years to get the U. S. to deport Tresca. His son, Peter Martin (by the sister of American communist leader Elizabeth Gurley Flynn), in 1953 co-founded with poet Lawrence Ferlinghetti City Lights Book Store in San Francisco. Jack Foley, "City Lights Books: A long-ago North Beach that Smells like Words," *The Argonaut*, San Francisco Historical Society, vol. 12, no. 1, Fall, 2001, 26.

61. Fowle, 65-66; AC interview with author.

Luigi Antonini was president of the Italian-American Labor Council.

62. Fowle, 65-66; Elmer Davis, statement, January 22, 1943, AC Papers.

63. AC, memoranda to Elmer Davis, "Work of Foreign-Language Division," January 21 and January 26, 1943, AC Papers.

64. Elmer Davis to Norman Thomas, January 23, 1943, AC Papers.

65. Louis Adamic, night letter to Elmer Davis, January 25, 1943; Elmer Davis to Adamic, January 23, 1943, AC Papers.

66. Fowle, 67; AC, memo to Davis, February 2, 1943, AC Papers; Kazin, "Who hired the assassin?"

Gallagher's biography of Tresca in 1988 attributed Tresca's murder to Carmine Galante, instigated by Frank Garofalo, an agent of Generoso Pope, who had tried to silence Tresca beginning in 1934.

67. Fowle, 66, citing E. L James, aide to *New York Times* publisher Sulzberger, to Davis.

68. Nathan H. Seidman, president, The Inter-Racial Press of America, Inc., to AC, May 19, 1942, AC Papers.

69. Oda M. Beaulieu, assistant editor, *Le Travailleur*, the largest French weekly in New England, to AC, August 7, 1942, AC Papers.

70. AC interview with author; U. S. Department of Justice press release, "A $16,000 payroll for the former New York branch of the German Gestapo...," February 25, 1942, AC Papers.

71. Joseph Jaisch, Union Mills, Indiana, undated letter, copy in AC Papers; Gerhart H. Seger to AC, August 3, 1942; Walter Jacobs, Menasha, Wisconsin, to editor, *Lincoln Freie Presse*, July 28, 1942, AC Papers.

72. "U. S. ordered paper to shift editors, plaint," *Milwaukee Journal*, September 2, 1942; Memorandum, "The National Weeklies," September 3, 1942; report of meeting between Mr. Emil Leicht, publisher of National Weeklies, AC, Lee Falk and others, August 12, 1942, AC Papers.

National Weeklies published seven newspapers and had a readership of some 200,000, according to an O. W. I. memorandum dated September 3, 1942.

73. "Denies editor forced by U. S., O. W. I. official comments on charge made in German language paper," *Milwaukee Journal*, September 3, 1942.

74. Charlotte Rauschenberg to "The President," March 25, 1943; AC to Emil Leicht, Royal Palm Hotel, Fort Meyers, Florida, March 25, 1943, AC Papers.

75. AC to K. R. Keydel, Harmonie Society, Detroit, October 17, 1942, AC Papers.

76. AC, memorandum to Elmer Davis, "Proposed exemption of certain German-Americans from alien enemy classification," [1942], AC Papers.

77. Elmer Davis to U. S. Attorney General, November 16, 1942, AC Papers.

78. AC to Ambassador [Lituinoff?] of the Union of Soviet Socialist Republics, May 12, 1942, AC Papers.

79. AC, memorandum to Elmer Davis, "Chinese Exclusion Acts," July 25, 1942, AC Papers.

A policy of prohibiting immigration of Chinese laborers to the United States began in 1882, in the wake of a large Chinese influx to California beginning with the 1849 Gold Rush. They provided cheap labor, especially building the transcontinental railroads in the 1860s, and their numbers increased after the conclusion in 1868 of the Burlingame Treaty with China, guaranteeing the right of Chinese immigration. Anti-Chinese sentiment grew in California, culminating in riots in San Francisco in 1877. An 1879 bill banning Chinese immigration was vetoed as violating the Burlingame Treaty. In 1880 a new treaty was negotiated, allowing the U. S. to regulate and limit the entry of Chinese labor but not prohibit it. The Chinese Exclusion Act of 1880 banned their immigration for 10 years. Subsequent acts (1888, 1892) violated the 1880 treaty; a new treaty was signed in 1894 in which China agreed to exclusion of laborers for 10 years. Congress continued the policy and a law in 1924 excluded all Asians. The acts were repealed in 1943 with a new law that permitted an annual immigration quota of 105 and extended citizenship privileges to Chinese.

80. AC interview with author.

81. "Memorial to Lidice," editorial, *Chicago Sun*, June 17, 1942; "Lidice, in Illinois," editorial, *New York Times*, July 14, 1942; "Lidice Lives Forever," Nicholas G. Blaint, editor, Europa Books, copies in AC Papers; Fowle, 62; AC, memorandum, "Application to attend Special Service School, Orientation Section, Morale Service Division, Washington, D.C. (through channels)," May 15, 1944, AC "Souvenirs, U. S. Army, 1943-45," AC Personal Papers.

World Government News credited Cranston with the idea of renaming the Illinois city for Lidice. (*Current Biography*, 15.) Cranston stated on an application to the Army Special Services Orientation Section in 1944: "Two propaganda moves I initiated were particularly effective: (1) the naming of an Illinois town Lidice a few days after the Nazis obliterated the Czechoslovakian village (*Look Magazine* called this 'the master propaganda stroke of the war'); and (2) the exempting of Italian aliens from the enemy alien classification on Columbus Day, 1942 (Count Carlo Sforza, now a cabinet minister in Allied-occupied Italy, declared this action saved thousands of American lives when we invaded Sicily and Italy)." Lidice, located near Prague, was rebuilt. Edna St. Vincent Millay wrote a poem in 1942, "The Murder of Lidice," which was criticized as propaganda. Dinitia Smith, "Rediscovering a lost poet and a life led dangerously," *New York Times*, August 30, 2001.

82. Message from AC, chief, foreign language division, O. W. I. , to American Croatian Congress, Chicago, February 20-21, 1943; AC, memorandum to Col. William Westlake, "Stolen bomber," September 16, 1943, AC Papers.

83. Louis Adamic to Read Lewis, and memorandum, March 1, 1944, AC Papers.

A splinter Serbian group had begun its own organization and newspaper, *Free Expression*, which the Serb National Federation considered pro-Communist.

Adamic's complaints also included: "...acted in such divisive ways as to defeat, rather than promote, the interests of the foreign-language groups as a whole; followed a policy of 'avoiding controversial issues' in such a way as to obstruct, rather than promote, the cause of democracy in the United States."

84. Adamic memorandum, citing AC to Adamic; L. M. Peyovich, "American Serbs and America," *American Srbobran*, February 24, 1943; Chester Lukiyan, "Congress vote to liquidate O. W. I.'s domestic bureau seen as mortal blow to left-wing and Croat propagandists," *American Srbobran*, June 23, 1943, AC Papers.

85. AC, memorandum to MacLeish, "American Slav Congress," May 1, 1942, citing *Christian Science Monitor*, April 28, 1942, AC Papers.

86. Clark, 82; "The administration, truth & trouble," *Time*, March 15, 1943; Lukiyan, "Congress vote to liquidate O. W. I.'s domestic bureau...."

The attack on O. W. I. was led by Alabama Democratic Congressman Joe Starnes and New Jersey Republican J. Parnell Thomas. The House reduced the O. W. I. appropriation by $5.5 million. O. W. I. created in June, 1942, was abolished August 31, 1945. It had spent some $125 million since its creation, and had 10,375 employees, many of whom were transferred to the State Department and other government agencies, according to a *Chicago Daily Tribune* article critical of the agency. Willard Edwards, "New globalist leader comes to fore in U. S., he's Alan Cranston, late of the O. W. I.," *Chicago Daily Tribune*, November, 7, 1949.

Congressman J. Parnell Thomas (1895-1970), Republican of New Jersey, served in the House 1936-1950 when he resigned after being convicted of salary fraud and sentenced to 18 months in prison. He was a strong opponent of Roosevelt's agenda, which Thomas charged "sabotaged the capitalist system." Like Starnes, Thomas opposed the Federal Theatre Project as "sheer propaganda for Communism or the New Deal." When Republicans took over Congress in 1947, Thomas became chairman of the House Un-American Activities Committee, from which he accused members of the Screen Writers Guild of being "subversives" or Communists, dubbed the "Hollywood Ten." Those who refused to answer the committee's questions citing the First Amendment were imprisoned for contempt of Congress. In 1948 a secretary disclosed that Thomas had put a women on his staff as clerk in return for receiving her salary, resulting in charges of fraud. Thomas ironically took the same First Amendment defense, and was sent to Danbury Prison where two members of the "Hollywood Ten" also were serving time (Lester Cole and Ring Lardner, Jr.).

87. Lukiyan, "Congress vote to liquidate O. W. I.'s domestic bureau...".

88. AC, memorandum to Constantine Poulos, "Press work - translations," July 8, 1943; AC, memorandum to "The Gang," "budget," July 9, 1943, AC Papers.

89. Memorandum, "Summary of Cox Committee Charges," [1942], AC Papers.

90. Fowle, 68; "Voluntary code of wartime practices for American broadcasters presenting programs in foreign languages," [June, 1942]; David Sentner, "O. W. I. forced firing of radio aid, probers told," *San Francisco Examiner*, August 6, 1943, AC Papers.

91. Fowle, 69-70; "Cox Committee tries - and fails," *P.M.* [a New York tabloid], August 19, 1943, reproducing copy of cancelled check from Albany, Georgia, radio station WALB, made out to Cox dated August 18, 1941; "Publications display further interest as Cox hits foreign tongue activity," *Broadcasting*, August 16, 1943, and typed notations thereon; "Radio man's critic linked to Gestapo," *New York Times*, August 18, 1943; "Propaganda is Propaganda," editorial, *New York Herald Tribune*, August 12, 1943; "A public letter to Speaker Rayburn," editorial signed by Eugene Meyer, editor and publisher, *The Washington Post*, September 27, 1943, AC Papers.

Cox in 1943 was appointed chairman of the Select Committee to Investigate the Federal Communications Commission. The FCC had petitioned Congress to disqualify Cox from the committee for bias and personal interest on the basis of his having accepted the radio station's fee to represent it before the FCC. The House Judiciary Committee had not acted on the FCC petition at the time of the *Post* editorial but Cox was forced to give up his committee seat. Wikipedia.

92. *Congressional Record*, House, June 17, 1943, pp. 6087-88; AC to Read Lewis, September 22, 1943, AC Papers.

93. Read Lewis to Rep. Clarence Cannon, Chairman, House Appropriations Committee, September 27, 1943, citing article by Willard Edwards, *Washington Times-Herald*, July 29, 1943, AC Personal Papers; AC to Lewis, September 22, 1943, AC Papers.

94. *Ibid.*

Cannon was a Democrat from Missouri for whom one of the House of Representatives' office buildings was named.

95. Read Lewis to Hon. Clarence Cannon, draft (no date) and letter, September 27, 1943, AC Papers.

96. *Congressional Record*, House, November 4, 1943, p. 9146.

97. *Ibid.*, November 4, 1943; Judith Robinson, *Noble Conspirator, Florence S. Mahoney and the Rise of the National Institutes of Health* (Washington, D.C.: The Francis Press, 2000), 115.

Draža Mihailović (1893-1946) was a Serbian soldier-leader in the Balkans appointed in 1942 as minister of war by the Yugoslav government-in-exile, in opposition to the forces of communist leader Marshal Tito. He became a legend for his anti-German 'guerrilla' tactics and was featured on the cover of *Time* magazine in 1942. He also opposed the Communists and after the war was captured and condemned to death by Tito.

98. *Congressional Record*, House, November 5, 1943, p. 9335, citing statement by Admiral McCullough, U. S. Navy, security officer, O. W. I., AC Papers.

99. *Congressional Record*, Appendix, February 18, 1944, p. A815.

100. Earl G. Harrison, Commissioner, U. S. Immigration and Naturalization Service, U. S. Department of Justice, to AC, July 25, 1944, AC Papers.

Harrison served as a Special Assistant to the U. S. Attorney General and was later Dean of the University of Pennsylvania Law School.

101. AC to "Dear Jimmie," August 17, 1945, AC Papers.

Possibly President Roosevelt's son James Roosevelt (1907-91), Congressman from California 1955-65, a Democratic Party friend of Cranston's. He was defeated by Earl Warren for Governor of California in 1950.

102. Elmer Davis to Private Alan M. Cranston, August 26, 1944, AC Papers.

103. President Roosevelt issued Presidential Executive Order 9066 which directed that any persons considered a threat be removed from vulnerable coastal areas.

104. Phyllis [?] to AC, "Tuesday morning," no date, AC Papers.

Spies did exist in the U. S., as revealed decades later in Russian and American files which indicated that some 300 Americans acted as Soviet agents during World War II, in all government agencies. In the case of the Rosenbergs' trial (they were executed June 19, 1953), much was not revealed because of the desire to keep secret the American VENONA project, aimed at code-breaking Russian communiqués related to the development of the atomic bomb, and to prevent the passing of information by American spies to the Soviets. Thus Americans did not know the extent of spying in the U. S. *Nova* television documentary, "Code-breaking operation VENONA," KQED TV, San Francisco, January 7, 2003.

105. Fred Yamamoto to AC, January 3, 1942, and December, 1942, AC Papers.

From the outset, internees were allowed to leave the camps to provide needed labor, such as agricultural field work. As the war progressed in favor of the U. S., young internees were allowed to go to college or take jobs arranged for them inland.

Heart Mountain, a previously unpopulated area, became the third-largest city in Wyoming as an internment camp. One of its inmates was future California Democratic Congressman and Secretary of Transportation Norman Yoshiro Mineta, who was 10 years old when interned with his family. Heart Mountain was one of 10 Japanese interment camps built at the outset of the war. At the height of internment, the camps housed more than 120,000 inmates (about half were *Issei*, Japanese-born immigrants, and half *Nisei*, U. S.-born citizens of Japanese descent). Exclusion orders and military restrictions were revoked on September 4, 1945, two weeks after V-J day (Victory over Japan, August 15, 1945). In 1980 President Jimmy Carter created the Commission on Wartime Relocation and Internment of Civilians, which concluded in 1983 that the camps had been unnecessary, the result of prejudice and war hysteria, and recommended compensating internees. President Reagan signed an official apology, the Civil Liberties Act, in 1988 and each survivor received $20,000 in compensation. Cranston, then a Senator, was an advocate of both. Shirley Streshinsky, "Place of Infamy," *Preservation* magazine, National Trust for Historic Preservation, November/December, 2002, 38-43, 78, 80.

106. Fowle, 60; "Japanese-Americans may sell spuds here," *New York World-Telegram*, November 16, 1943, citing AC addressing "Emergency Conference on Food Fights for Freedom Program and the Foreign Born," New York City, AC Papers.

A friend, Gertrude Gardiner, wrote Cranston in August, 1945, that Villa Warec "surely took a beating when they were away," referring to the interned Japanese servants.

107. Yamamoto to AC, December, 1942.

The U. S. government in 1944 required *Nisei* men 17 and older to prove their loyalty by signing a pledge renouncing any allegiance to Japan, swearing loyalty to the U. S. and signing up for military duty. Inductees were sent to the all-Japanese 100th/442nd U. S. Army Regimental Combat Team, the most decorated of its size in U. S. military history, but with one of the highest casualty rates. Those who refused to sign were transferred to Tule Lake, California, maximum-security camp, or tried as draft resisters and if convicted, sent to federal prison. Heart Mountain had the largest number of dissenters, 85 of 267 who refused induction and were convicted of draft resistance. President Truman pardoned the draft resisters soon after the war. Streshinsky, 43.

108. Mrs. Michi Takaki to AC, December 5, 1942, AC Papers.

109. AC to Mrs. Michi Takaki, Heart Mountain, February 10, 1943, AC Papers.

110. AC to Mr. and Mrs. E. Fujimiya, c/o Dr. [Professor] Sewall, Stanford, California, March 26, 1943, AC Papers.

111. AC to Mr. and Mrs. M. Tanaka, Heart Mountain, giving regards to "Fuzzy and Kiku," May 7, 1943, AC Papers.

112. AC to Mr. Katsuji Ikawa, Gila Relocation Center, Rivers, Arizona, February 2, 1943, AC Papers.

113. Pfc. Fred Yamamoto, Camp Shelby, Miss., to AC, April 20, 1944; M. Tanaka to Pvt. Alan M. Cranston, March 30, 1944, AC "Souvenirs, U. S. Army, 1943-44," AC Personal Papers.

114. AC postcard to Mrs. Geneva Cranston with photograph of Puck statue, postmarked Washington, D. C., April 5, 1943, AC Papers.

115. GC to "Dear Marian," re: Population Division of Census Bureau, July 31, 1942, AC Papers.

116. Carey McWilliams, "Los Angeles' Pachuco Gangs," *The New Republic*, January 18, 1943; "Trial of 22 Mexican youths made Axis propaganda issue, foes call it example of mistreatment, O. W. I. sends official to make inquiries here," *Los Angeles Times*, November [?], 1942, copies in AC Papers.

Carey McWilliams (1905-80) was a Los Angeles lawyer, activist, journalist, historian who chaired the Sleepy Lagoon Defense Committee; he helped overturn the convictions and was active in helping to defuse the zoot-suit riots in the summer of 1943. He was credited with beginning Chicano advocacy in California, which he continued through political activism and books like *Factories in the Field* (1939), a bestselling exposé of farm labor conditions, and *North from Mexico* (1949). He criticized Japanese-American internment, and wrote a Supreme Court amicus brief (denied) for two of the Hollywood Ten (Dalton Trumbo and John Howard Lawson). He was appointed chief of California's Division of Immigration and Housing by incoming Governor Culbert Olson, serving 1939-42. Among many books he wrote *Ambrose Bierce, A Biography* (N. Y.: Albert & Charles Boni, 1929), and was editor of *The Nation* (1955-75). Peter Richardson, "Always in Fashion? Carey McWilliams, California Radicalism, and the Politics of Cool," (Preface by Kevin Starr), Cashin Lecture Series, Number Two, reproduced in 'keepsake' published by The Book club of California, 2008, 12-15; Wikipedia.

117. Orson Welles, Foreword, *The Sleepy Lagoon Case*, Citizens' Committee for the

Defense of Mexican-American Youth, Los Angeles, 1942-43, AC Papers.

Other Hollywood celebrities involved were socially-conscious film producer Walter Wanger, actors Constance Bennett and Anthony Quinn. Fowle, 60.

118. *Sleepy Lagoon Case*, "Summary of the Facts," "Short biography of boys convicted in Sleepy Lagoon case."

119. Guy Endore, *The Sleepy Lagoon Mystery*, illustrations by Giacomo Patri, introduction by Carey McWilliams, chairman, Sleepy Lagoon Defense Committee, 3-4, 24-27, 39, copy in AC Papers.

Sumner Welles was quoted from the *New York Herald Tribune*, February 16, 1944. At the time, according to National Resources Planning Board figures, some 3 million people of Mexican descent lived in the United States.

120. McWilliams, "Los Angeles' Pachuco Gangs"; "Trial of 22 Mexican youths...," *Los Angeles Times*.

121. James Allen, Assistant Director, Domestic Operations, O. W. I., to John C. Lee, Los Angeles, November 10, 1942, AC Papers.

122. AC, memorandum to E. Davis, "Activities in Los Angeles," November 28, 1942, AC Papers.

123. "Youth gang war effects fought, committee outlines plan to combat menace of Axis distortion of fights," with photograph captioned "Committee seeks rehabilitation of youthful gangsters," *Los Angeles Times*, November 25, 1942; "Officials act to end youth gang battles," with photograph, *Los Angeles Examiner*, November 25, 1942.

124. *Ibid.*

125. *Ibid.*, and "Trial of 22 Mexican youths...," *Los Angeles Times*.

126. AC, memorandum, November 28, 1942.

127. *Ibid.*

128. In the case (People v. Zammora), seven different lawyers initially represented one or more of the defendants. Indictments of two other boys charged in the same case were dropped on grounds of insufficient evidence although the evidence against them was the same as against the seventeen who were convicted. The lawyer for the two who were released was former district attorney Harry Hunt, who demanded and got the right to separate trials. The judge, Charles W. Fricke (1882-1958), former prosecutor and author of criminal-law textbooks, was considered by defense committees as biased; he refused to allow the defendants to change clothes or cut their hair, limited lawyers' contact with the defendants, and issued tough sentences. The case virtually ended mass trials in California. PBS website, pbs.org, citing American Experience, "Zoot Suit Riots" television documentary.

129. "Court also orders 'pachuco' garb be discarded," *Los Angeles Examiner*, March 7, 1943, AC Papers.

130. AC memorandum, November 28, 1942.

131. George Gleason, executive secretary to Committee for Church and Community Cooperation, County of Los Angeles, to Elmer Davis, December 2, 1942, AC Papers.

132. Charles Olson, Foreign Language Division, to "Dear Al," December 8, 1942, AC Papers. AC never wore a toupee for baldness.

133. McWilliams, "Los Angeles' Pachuco Gangs."

McWilliams was involved in Cranston's programs to correct problems in L. A.

134. "Platoons of servicemen comb city in hunt for zoot suiters," *Los Angeles Times*, June 6, 1943; "Sheriff's aides jail nearly fifty after night battles, *Los Angeles Examiner*, June 7, 1943.

135. AC, memorandum to George Lyon, "Assignment in Los Angeles," June 28, 1943, AC Papers.

136. *Ibid.*

137. *Ibid.*; "Mexican group donates blood to aid victory," *Los Angeles Times*, July 2, 1943.

138. AC, memorandum to George Lyon, "Assignment in Los Angeles."

139. AC to Miss Sheila Erskine, Committee for American Unity, August 26, 1943, AC Papers.

140. Fowle, 70-72.

141. Clark, 82-83, citing interview with AC, March 13, 1987; Application to O. S. S., Department of State, April 17, 1943; and "Personal History Statement," 1943, AC Papers; Michael Doyle, "FBI file paints shadow portrait of Sen. Cranston," *Sacramento Bee*, August 26, 2003.

In May, 1944, press and radio releases began to be censored at O. W. I. Olson and Poulos filed formal complaints, which were ignored; both resigned in protest.

142. Fowle, 57; Geneva May McMath Cranston (1912-85), "Continuation sheet," resume and job descriptions, no date, "Souvenirs, 1930s-40s," AC Personal Papers.

143. Unsigned letter, "Hello Dear!" from 2516 San Marcos Ave., on Marston Company letterhead, San Diego, Carton 5, Geneva Cranston correspondence, October, 1943-Feb., 1944, AC Papers.

Edgar McMath (born September 12, 1881 at Gladstone, Illinois) died December 9, 1941, according to one of AC's job applications, "Personal History Statement," July 28, 1942. May Amend McMath was born December 7, 1886 in Kansas; in 1943 she resided at 3851 42nd Street, San Diego, according to AC "Personal History Statement," 1943, AC Papers.

144. "Status of Public Bills reported by House Immigration Committee, 77th Congress," chart for legislation 1941-42; "Refugee physicians," memorandum, no date; "Émigré doctors - 'we need these men,' recent editorial comments," collection of newspaper editorials, 1942, AC Papers.

145. Geneva May McMath Cranston, "Continuation sheet," resume and job descriptions.

146. Geneva Cranston, hereafter cited as GC, to Richard J. Walsh, Pearl Buck's husband, editor, *Asia Magazine*, Perkasie, Pennsylvania, April 19, 1942; "Memorandum to Nathan Cowan from Monroe Sweetland, National Director, Re: Repeal of Oriental Exclusion Act," seeking recommendation for endorsement of repeal by C. I. O. Executive Board, May 10, 1943, AC Papers.

Leaders in Congress for repeal were pro-labor Congressmen Walter Judd of Minnesota, Warren Magnuson of Washington, and Jerry Voorhis of California. Other backers besides Pearl Buck included the National Catholic Welfare Council, Federal Council of Churches of Christ in America, *San Francisco Chronicle*, Wendell Wilkie, Eleanor Roosevelt, then-Under Secretary of State Ambassador Joseph C. Grew (recently returned from Japan where he was interned), Chinese writer-translator Lin Yutang, American author John Gunther.

147. Read Lewis to Miss Pearl Buck, Perkasie, Pennsylvania, March 6, 1943, AC Papers.

Pearl Buck (1892-1973) was raised in China where her parents and first husband were missionaries. Author of 85 books, her best-known novel about China was *The Good Earth* (Pulitzer Prize, 1931). She was awarded the Nobel Prize for Literature in 1938. A long-time advocate of better understanding and support of China, she founded Welcome House to provide care for Amerasian children; the Pearl Buck Foundation, Philadelphia, to which she consigned most of her royalties, aided in the adoption of such children. She married her publisher, Richard J. Walsh, president of the John Day Company, in 1935.

148. Read Lewis to GC, March 27, 1943, AC Papers.

149. William Cranston to GC, ending, "Your holiday sounds like it was a delightful one, and I wish that we could have been along," signed "Father," May 10, 1943, AC Papers.

150. Memorandum, "No doubt you know that hearings on the repeal of the Chinese exclusion laws will begin before the House committee on Immigration and Naturalization, probably on May 12," April 30, 1943, and Read Lewis to GC, April 30, 1943, AC Papers.

A Citizens Committee to Repeal Chinese Exclusion was formed, with Richard J. Walsh, Buck's husband, as chairman; literary figures like Louis Bromfield, Pearl Buck, Dorothy

Canfield Fisher, Carl Van Doren were among members. Humorist-columnist Will Rogers' son, briefly a congressman from California (1942), and missionary Dr. Lyman Hoover, Y. M. C. A. secretary in China (1930-49), "just returned from China," testified in favor of repeal; the American Legion and A. F. of L. testified against. "Witnesses heard before House Immigration Committee regarding Chinese Exclusion Repeal beginning May 19, [1943]," AC Papers.

151. Richard J. Walsh to "Mrs. Cranston, Saturday," [1943]; GC to Walsh, "Monday 31st, [1943], citing M. W. Meier; GC to Admiral Yarnell, Newport, R. I., May 28, 1943, re: testifying June 3, 1943; GC to Walsh, June 2, 1943; statement by Richard J. Walsh, editor of *Asia and the Americas* magazine, and publisher, John Day Company, at hearing before House Committee on Immigration and Naturalization, May 20, 1943; Walsh to William Green, President, American Federation of Labor, June 13, 1943; GC to Walsh, December 9, 1943, AC Papers.

Admiral Harry E. Yarnell (1875-1959) had been commander of the Navy's Asiatic Fleet; he was recalled from retirement in 1941 to the Secretary of the Navy's office as Special Adviser to the Chinese Military Mission; he returned again in 1943 as Head of a Special Section to the Chief of Naval Operations (1943-44). He was famous for holding war games in 1932 demonstrating how airplanes could attack Hawaii from carriers, and warned of such a Japanese threat. Wikipedia.

Arguments to gain the A. F. of L.'s support were that, under the proposed bill, only about 100 Chinese would be permitted to enter the U. S., and that the Chinese did not want their skilled workers to emigrate, thus reducing competition for American laborers. The C. I. O. backed the repeal.

152. GC to Walsh, June 2, 1943.

153. Walsh to Mrs. Mason, memo, June 26, 1943; GC to Jack Leighter, August 30, 1943; GC to Walsh, September 9, 1943; GC to Mrs. J. B. Yaukey, Bethesda, Maryland, September 16, 1943, AC Papers.

154. A. McKie Donnan, Brisacher, Davis & Van Norden, Advertising Engineers, San Francisco, to GC, October 22, 1943; [Walsh?] to "Elizabeth and Geneva," October 31, 1943, AC Papers.

155. Walsh to GC, June 3, 1943; GC to Walsh, December 9, 1943, AC Papers.

156. Elmer Davis, copy of deferment request for Selective Service Office, New York, and AC, memorandum to Charles Allen, O. W. I., re: "Selective Service," October 15, 1943; "Background statement, Corporal Alan M. Cranston, ASN 33 752 520"; Application for Federal Employment, July 5, 1945: "Biographical statement for Alan Cranston," 1945; *Current Biography*, 15; "How to get into the Army - fast," memorandum citing Private John W. Atkinson, Military Police Officers Candidate School, Fort Custer, Michigan, "Before induction see Capt. Sherry B. Myers, Provost Marshal General.... Tell him that you were a newspaper associate and friend of...Atkinson in Rome…," AC "Souvenirs, U. S. Army, 1943-44," AC Personal Papers.

157. AC to Davis, February 2, 1944; Davis to AC, February 4, 1944, AC Papers.

Constantine Poulos succeeded Cranston as head of the Foreign Language Division.

158. AC to Selective Service Board #16, New York City, November 10, 1943, AC Papers; Drew Pearson, "Washington Merry-Go-Round," to AC, February 10, 1944; Marsh Maslin, "This is the life," *San Francisco Call-Bulletin*, [January 19, 1944?] and typescript, "*Call-Bulletin*, January 19, 1944, For This and That," with handwritten note, not like AC's, "Can you drop the last sentence?" reading: "Associates told him there is no reason in the world for his enlisting as a private but his attitude was that there was no reason in the world why he shouldn't," which was retained in published column, AC Papers; John F. Cramer, "Veterans Bureau may recruit new N. Y. staff," *Washington Daily News*, October 25, 1943; Leonard Lyons, "Broadway Bulletins" and "Times Square Tattle," and Jerry Klurtz, "The Federal

Diary," no dates, copies in AC "Souvenirs, U. S. Army, 1943-44," AC Personal Papers.

159. Fowle, 73, 75-76; AC to "Dearest Gevy [Geneva]," February 23 and March 1, 1944, AC "Souvenirs, U. S. Army, 1943-44," AC Personal Papers.

160. *Ibid.*, AC to GC, March 1, 1944.

161. *Ibid.*; Lee Falk to AC, February 25 and April 11, 1944; Rep. Henry M. Jackson to AC, May 12, 1944, AC "Souvenirs, U. S. Army, 1943-44," AC Personal Papers.

162. Corporal Blaine Davis, "Crofter was sued by Hitler over take on 'Mein Kampf,'" *The Spartan*, March 21, 1944, and "Croft trainee has own feud with fuehrer," *The Spartanburg Journal*, March 25, 1944, AC "Souvenirs, U. S. Army, 1943-45," AC Personal Papers.

163. AC, memorandum, "Application to attend Special Service School, Orientation Section, Morale Service Division, Washington, D. C. (through channels)," May 15, 1944; AC application to Officer Candidate School, June 21, 1944; AC to Major Julius Schreiber, Orientation Branch, Morale Services Division, June 16, 1944; Major J. Schreiber to Colonel Farlow, War Department Army Service Forces memo routing slip, July 3, 1944, AC "Souvenirs, U. S. Army, 1943-45," AC Personal Papers.

Dr. Julius Schreiber, a Ukraine-born psychiatrist who attended medical school at the University of Cincinnati, then a lieutenant colonel, headed the programs section of the Army Information and Education division and helped edit *Army Talks*. In 1954 he was called before a Senate Internal Security subcommittee chaired by Republican William E. Jennings of Indiana, which was investigating the extent to which Communists sought to indoctrinate soldiers in that division. Schreiber denied being a Communist after 1941 but relied on the First and Fifth Amendments to the Constitution in testifying as to whether he ever had belonged to the Communist Party, insisting that he was a "patriotic citizen...throughout the war" and at the time of the hearing. "Doctor is silent at army inquiry," *New York Times*, July 8, 1954, AC Papers.

164. AC, "On the Ground," *The Spartan*, Camp Croft, June 14, 1944; AC Papers and AC Personal Papers.

165. AC, "On the Ground," no dates, and August 9, 1944, AC Papers and AC Personal Papers.

166. AC notebook, AC "Souvenirs, Army, 1944," AC Personal Papers.

167. AC typescript, "The Wind and the Leaf," no date, AC "Souvenirs, Army, 1944," AC Personal Papers.

168. Lee Falk to AC, June 17, 1944, AC "Souvenirs, U. S. Army, 1943-45," AC Personal Papers.

Alan Lomax (1915-2002), folklorist and oral historian, with his father John Avery Lomax discovered American blues singers like Huddie Ledbetter (Leadbelly) while collecting and recording songs in Southern penitentiaries. They compiled *Negro Folk Songs as Sung by Lead Belly* (1936) and produced books of American folk songs including *Our Singing Country* (1941). Many songs and performers were recorded for the Library of Congress, where A. Lomax was assistant in charge of a Folk Song Archive (1937-42). Lomax worked in the O. W. I. Bureau of Special Services producing morale-building programs for the Armed Forces Radio Service. He specialized in reaching minority and non-English-speaking groups, outlined in a proposal, "Plans for Reaching Folk Groups with War Information." A memo proposing a book of fighting and freedom songs from Allied countries was sent to Cranston and Lee Falk, dated February 4, 1943 (Lomax during the war compiled a 300-page collection of *Freedom Songs of the United Nations*). Like Cranston, Lomax was investigated by the F. B. I. and Rep. Martin Dies's Un-American Activities Committee, but found too independent to associate with such as the Communist Party. John Szwed, *Alan Lomax, The Man Who Recorded the World* (N. Y.: Viking, 2010), 197, 199-209, 409, citing Lomax "Plans" memo, October 27, 1942, and memo to AC and Falk.

169. AC to Elmer Davis, July 24, 1944; AC to [James] Lawrence Houghteling, Treasury

Department, Read Lewis, and Jonathan Daniels, Administrative Assistant to the President, White House, July 24, 1944, AC "Souvenirs, U. S. Army, 1943-45," AC Personal Papers; Dave Bond to author re: army intelligence.

170. Read Lewis to AC, July 26, 1944; James L. Houghteling, Director, National Organizations, War Finance Division, U. S. Treasury, to Adjutant General of the Army, July 27, 1944; Houghteling to Assistant Chief of Staff, War Department, July 28, 1944; Houghteling to AC, July 28, 1944; AC to Houghteling, August 20, 1944; AC to "George," August 20, 1944, AC "Souvenirs, U. S. Army, 1943-45," AC Personal Papers.

171. AC interview with author.

172. Cornelia Matijasevich, "The other half - Mrs. Alan Cranston is serious about politics, homemaking," *Daily Palo Alto Times*, July 20, 1954; Ursula Vils, "For Mrs. Cranston, victory of husband was frosting on cake," *Los Angeles Times*, November 8, 1968, AC Papers.

173. Fowle, 73, 75-76; AC to "Dear Schreib," from Fort Leonard Wood, September 28, 1944; "Restricted," transfer orders for Pvt. Alan M. Cranston from Ft. Leonard Wood, 70th Infantry Division, to Army Service Forces, 205 East 42 St., N. Y. C., by October 8, 1944; Major Jack W. Weeks, Acting Commanding Officer, Army Service Forces, memorandum re: Good conduct medal to Pfc. Alan M. Cranston, February 20, 1945, AC "Souvenirs, U. S. Army, 1943-45," AC Personal Papers; Lisetor, "Mrs. Alan Cranston honored...," and "Mrs. Alan Cranston," GOPacrats for Cranston, release, [1968], Carton 617, AC Papers.

174. Fowle, 76; Theodore Waller, interview with author, January 13, 2002; "Know Why We Fight, Planned Orientation Builds Mental Fitness for Combat," Fact sheet no. 7, AC "Souvenirs, U. S. Army, 1943-45," AC Personal Papers; Clip Boutell, "Authors are like people, Cranston's warnings - history's stepchildren," *New York Post*, September [6?], 1945, copy in AC Papers.

Army Talk, in a *Life* magazine format, also dealt with servicemen's post-war adjustment.

175. "Liberal Party Rally for Roosevelt-Truman and Wagner, Madison Square Garden, Tuesday, October 31, 1944, AC "Souvenirs, U. S. Army, 1943-45," AC Personal Papers.

176. AC, "Responses to interrogatories on behalf of the defendant," and "Reponses to cross interrogatories on behalf of the plaintiff"; Victor F. Ridder, *Duluth Herald and News-Tribune*, to AC, August 25, 1944, citing "the suit with Frederick William Foerster," AC "Souvenirs, Army, 1944," AC Personal Papers.

New Yorker Staats-Zeitung remained the principal German-language newspaper in the U. S. for many years. Founded by German immigrants in 1834, it was bought by Herman Ridder in 1900, who contributed to founding the Knight Ridder newspaper company, and remained in the Ridder family until 1953, when it was sold; it was still in publication as of 2011.

177. "A three-day Free World conference," pamphlet announcing conference in California sponsored by American Free World Association, [1944-45]; Orson Welles to GC, February 17, 1944, AC Papers.

178. AC to Welles, March 2, 1944.

The Cranstons lived from January to September, 1941, at 317 10th Street, N. E.; from September, 1941, to February, 1944, at 120 C Street, N. E. AC "Attachment to Loyalty Investigation Questionnaire," AC "Souvenirs 1930s-40s," AC Personal Papers; "Personal History Statement," 1943, AC Papers.

179. Jackson Leighter, Mercury Productions, to GC, April 4, 1944.

180. GC to Leighter, June 29, 1944.

181. Leighter to GC, telegrams, December 6, 8 and 11, 1944; Shifra Haran, secretary, Mercury Productions, to GC, December 13, 1944; Loletta Hebert, Welles' assistant, to GC, December 15, 1944; Welles to GC, telegram, May 15, 1945 and December 12, 1945, AC Papers.

182. Bob [?], Airport News Service, to AC, asking, "What will [Welles] pay me, will it be based on what I submit or what you submit or what Orson uses…?", December 23, 1944;

AC to Bob, "Thanx for the two neat contributions…$5 for the item about the employee in Liberia...both damn good," [1944]; Orson Welles to "Dear Alan and Geneva," December 26, 1944, AC Papers.

183. Orson Welles (1915-85) made New York stage and radio debuts in 1934. In 1937 he directed Federal Theatre productions and formed the Mercury Theatre company. He was the radio voice of Lamont Cranston in the popular crime drama "The Shadow," and had an interest in magic which he performed with the U. S. O. during World War II. In 1939 RKO Pictures hired him and Mercury Productions to star, write and direct *Citizen Kane* which premiered May 1, 1941. He married Rita Hayworth (died 1987) in 1942, their daughter Rebecca was born in 1944, and Hayworth sought divorce not long afterward. Welles changed the setting of *War of the Worlds* from England in 1898 to contemporary America (1939), used the names of real towns and institutions that audiences would recognize, and staged the novel as an actual radio broadcast. It was aired by *Mercury Theatre on the Air* October 30, 1938, to coincide with Halloween. In his lectures, Welles made a point of having a metronome ticking to signify the ticking of an atomic bomb, according to an attendee at one event in San Francisco. Robert Pence, Mill Valley, California, to author, June 18, 2002; Bob Lochte, "Radio broadcast describes Martians invading New Jersey," *Old News*, October, 2002.

In a BBC interview at Las Vegas in 1982, Welles blamed Cranston for dissuading him from running for the Senate in California. According to Frank Brady, *Citizen Welles, A Biography of Orson Welles* (New York: Anchor Books, Doubleday, 1990), p. 576: "Orson related the story of how he thought of running for the Senate, based on Roosevelt's suggestion. 'He was very anxious to have me run.' Although still only in his late twenties at that time, Welles felt he might be able to carry California because of his celebrity presence, his ability as an orator, and the possible overt backing by F. D. R. It was Alan Cranston who dissuaded him from running, Orson stated. 'He told me I couldn't carry southern California because the Beverly Hills Communist Party was against me – I was a dangerous revisionist, they thought. I only had northern California.' Later, Cranston became the senator himself, leading Welles to believe that the former's advice was not that all disinterested."

184. Dexter Teed, "Orson Welles' column starts in *Post* Monday," *New York Post*, January 19, 1945, AC Papers; Paul Mazursky, "After 'Citizen Kane' - How a fabled show-business career began to unravel in the 1940s," review of Simon Callow, *Orson Welles: Hello Americans* (N. Y.: Viking, 2006), *Wall Street Journal*, August 19, 2006].

185. References to moves on December 22, 1944, to 646 West End Avenue, N. Y., and to Mayflower Hotel, 15 Central Park West, apartment 209, in correspondence, Carton 5; GC to Leighter, February 7, 1945, AC Papers.

Cranston cited 15 Central Park West as his address on a federal job application dated July 5, 1945.

186. Jack Leighter to GC, telegram, March 9, 1945; Orson Welles to GC, telegram, May 3, 1945; memorandum, "For: Orson Welles, From: John Atkinson (for Alan Cranston)," "American-Russian relations," and other topics, March 7, 1946, AC Papers.

187. Welles to GC, telegram June 12, 1945; Welles to Passport Division, Dept. of State, January 22, 1946, re: "For the past two years, Mrs. Cranston has been on my regular payroll, gathering information for my newspaper and radio work," AC Papers; Matijasevich, "The other half..."; Lisetor.

188. AC to Shelby Thompson, Deputy Director, Office of Public Information, United Nations Relief and Rehabilitation Administration, Washington, D. C., May 21, 1945; Thompson to AC, May 29, 1945; AC "Souvenirs, U. S. Army, 1943-45," AC Personal Papers.

Eleanor Roosevelt was involved with U. N. R. R. A. and it was run at one point by N. Y. Mayor Fiorello La Guardia. AC interview with author.

189. Lt. Colonel, M.C., Julius Schreiber, Chief, Program Section, Army Orientation Branch, to AC, June 11, 1945, AC "Souvenirs, U. S. Army, 1943-45," AC Personal Papers.

190. Application for Federal Employment, July 5, 1945; "Biographical statement for Alan Cranston," 1945; E. E. Hunt, Chief, Italian Division, Foreign Economic Administration, to AC, July 9, 1945; AC to Major Beech, July 11, 1945; Lt. General LeR. Lutes, U. S. A. Commanding, to Leo T. Crowley, Administrator, Foreign Economic Administration, July [?], 1945; Lyman H. Cozad, Assistant Director of Personnel, U. N. R. R. A., to AC, August 1, 1945; AC to Commanding Officer, Information and Education Div., Army Service Forces, August 13, 1945, AC "Souvenirs," World War II envelope, AC Personal Papers.

190. AC, draft typescript, "There is considerable evidence that not only is the big brass…," no date, in file, "Article copy, 1944-45," Carton 5, AC Papers.

191. AC and Falk, "The Bomb," typescript, no date, AC Papers.

Chapter 4 Killing the Peace and Confronting the Atom Cloud

1. Kreisler interview.

Woodrow Wilson was influenced by a 1918 pamphlet, *The League of Nations: A Practical Suggestion*, by Jan Smuts, a Boer army officer and leader of South Africa who championed the British Empire and counseled conservative leaders including Winston Churchill. Many of Wilson's proposals at the Paris treaty conference were based on Smuts' work. Brian Urquhart, "Finding the Hidden UN," review of two books on the U. N., *New York Review of Books*, May 27, 2010, 26-28. (Urquhart was a former Undersecretary-General of the U. N. In 1945, after leaving the British army, he joined the secretariat of the U. N. Preparatory Commission in London as private secretary to its executive secretary Gladwyn Jebb.)

2. Clip Boutell, "Authors are like people, Cranston's warnings - history's stepchildren," *New York Post*, September [6?], 1945.

3. Fowle, 76.

The term United Nations was coined by President Roosevelt in 1941 to describe the countries fighting against the Axis. It was first used officially at a ceremony at the White House on New Year's Day, 1942, when 26 nations joined in a Declaration of United Nations, pledging to continue the joint war effort, not make peace separately, and to support the 1941 Atlantic Charter (to restore independence to nations overrun by Hitler, Mussolini, the Japanese). The need for an organization to replace the League of Nations was iterated officially on October 30, 1943, in the Moscow Declaration issued by the U. S., Great Britain, China and the U. S. S. R. Those four countries drafted specific proposals for a charter for the new organization at the Dumbarton Oaks Conference (August-October, 1944) and reached further agreement at the Yalta Conference (February, 1945). All states that had adhered to the 1942 declaration and declared war on Germany or Japan were called to the founding conference in San Francisco (April-June, 1945), where the governing charter was drafted and signed June 26, 1945. All participating nations had to ratify the charter, which was finalized October 24, 1945 (U. N. Day). Brian Urquhart, "How Great Was Churchill?", review of Max Hastings, *Winston's War: Churchill, 1940-45* (N. Y.: Knopf, 2010), *New York Review of Books*, Aug. 9, 2010, 41-43.

4. Fowle, 77; managing editor [J.A.M.], *Collier's* magazine, to AC, April 19, 1945; M. Helene Cruser, Harold Matson literary agency, 30 Rockefeller Plaza, N. Y., to AC, May 15, 1945, citing final advance due AC of $500, less 10% commission; contract between Sgt. Alan Cranston, c/o Harold Matson, agent, and Viking Press, April 23, 1945, citing due-date for manuscript of May 10, 1945, and publication within nine months; Cranston held the copyright, and was to receive 17-1/2 percent royalty on the first 5,000 copies, 20 percent thereafter or 25 percent on all copies after the first 10,000, if priced at more than $2.00. AC Papers.

Cranston renewed the copyright in 1972. In 1969 he signed an agreement to option the book (for $1) for possible motion picture or television rights, for which Cranston would receive a $15,000 fee and percentage of any profits. The agreement was with Les Goldsmith, described in a memo from Lu Haas to AC as one who had "proven his loyalty to you and to the Democratic Party." AC, newly-elected U. S. Senator, was urged to appoint Goldsmith a "special advisor" on the film industry who "would always provide you with a very objective and level-headed analysis of motion picture problems," according to Haas. Michele Medeoz, Viking Press, to AC, March 10, 1972, on which AC authorized publisher to renew copyright on book; Haas to AC, memorandum re: Les Goldsmith, [1969]; Allyn O. Kreps to AC, January 10, 1969 re: "Killing of the Peace" television documentary; AC to Hilary Productions, Inc., North Hollywood, Ca., option agreement, literary property, January 9, 1969, AC Papers.

5. Sgt. Alan Cranston to Professor D. F. Fleming, Political Science Department, Vanderbilt University, April 9, 1945; AC to Ruth Brown, Viking Press, September 1, 1945; Allan Nevins, "A backward glance at the League," [*Saturday Review of Literature*?], September 8, 1945, AC Papers.

Denna Frank Fleming (1893-1980) was a distinguished professor and author, self-described as having a "fifty-year advocacy of the League of Nations, the U. N. and any other form of world organization that may save us from the final folly of one more world war." (Fleming letter to editors, *The New York Review of Books*, March 27, 1969.) Cranston thanked Fleming in his acknowledgements "for his invaluable criticism of the entire manuscript, and for his monumental *The United States and the League of Nations, 1918-1920* [1932], indispensable background for the writing of this book." Fleming's other books included: *The Treaty Veto of the American Senate* (1930); *The United States and World Organization, 1920-1933* (1938); *Can We Win the Peace?* (1943); *While America Slept* (1944); *The United States and the World Court* (1945); *The Cold War and Its Origins*, Vol. I, 1917-50, Vol. II, 1950-60 (1961); *The Origins and Legacies of World War I* (1968). His papers were given to Vanderbilt University Library.

6. GC to Leighter, April 3, 1945, AC Papers.

7. Fowle, 77.

8. GC to "Dear Jack and/or Orson," [August?, 1945]; AC to Fleming, April 9, 1945, AC Papers.

9. Fowle, 77; Alan Cranston, *The Killing of the Peace* (New York: The Viking Press, Compass Books Edition, 1960, second edition, paperback), xi.

All cites to the book hereafter are to the 1960 edition, which was dedicated "For my sons – Robin and Kim." Cranston agreed to melting the original plates for the book in 1947, after considering buying and shipping them to California. AC to Marjorie Griesser, Viking Press, June 24, 1947, Carton 14, AC Papers.

10. Cranston, *Killing of the Peace*, 9.

Some historians in later years saw Lodge as "internationalist" rather than "isolationist," and Wilson as hateful of enemies, narrowly focused, unwilling to compromise. Some thought that if people had known more about the seriousness of Wilson's stroke during that period (hidden from the public), it might have engendered sympathy in the Senate for Wilson's goals and U. S. participation in the League of Nations. CSPAN TV discussion of Thomas Fleming, *The Illusion of Victory - America in World War I* (N. Y.: Basic Books, 2003).

11. AC to "Dear Judge," Hatton W. Sumners, August 4, 1945, AC Papers.

12. Cranston, *Killing of the Peace*, Preface to 1945 edition, ix.

13. *Ibid.*, 7-8.

Republicans accused California Senator Hiram Johnson of sabotaging Hughes' efforts by having deserted the party for the Progressive ticket in 1912 when he ran for vice president with Theodore Roosevelt, and for failing to support Hughes in the 1916 election, although Johnson also ran as a Republican.

14. *Ibid.*, 17, citing President Wilson address to special session of Congress requesting a declaration of war against Germany, April 2, 1917.

15. *Ibid.*, 28, 37-38.

16. *Ibid.*, 74, 94, 234-35.

The *Literary Digest* poll showed that 718 papers favored the League unconditionally, 478 were for it conditionally, and 181 were against it, notably those published by William Randolph Hearst.

17. *Ibid.*, 75-76, 82.

The resolution stated that it was the sense of the Senate that "the constitution of the League of Nations in the form now proposed to the peace conference should not be accepted by the United States," and that the League should be separated from the peace treaty.

18. *Ibid.*, 78, 82-83.

19. *Ibid.*, 85-88.

Wilson agreed to amendments that 1) protected the Monroe Doctrine (declaring U. S. opposition to European interference in the Americas) and 2) U. S. domestic rights, 3) provided for member nations to withdraw from the league, and 4) reserved the right for nations to refuse to conform to its mandates. All except the Monroe Doctrine provision initially were agreed to but both proponents and opponents in America insisted on that provision. Wilson saw it as unnecessary, envisioning the League as making the doctrine a world concept. But the amendment ultimately was approved after exhausting negotiations with other nations during which Wilson was suffering a severe bout of flu. In effect, all of the demands of the League's American opponents were adopted. *Ibid.*, Pp. 90-91, 95-97, 100-01.

20. *Ibid.*, 113-15.

21. *Ibid.*, 119-21, 125, 155, 175.

22. *Ibid.*, 128-29.

The Senate was made up of 48 Republicans, 47 Democrats with one Progressive Republican (Johnson). The only remaining member still in Congress of 1920 League opponents, Johnson was too ill in 1945 to vote against the United Nations Charter.

23. *Ibid.*, 151, 165.

In the end, a large number of amendments were adopted in the Senate, aimed at striking out provisions for American participation in carrying out the terms of the treaty except reparations from Germany.

24. *Ibid.*, 178, 181; Gaetano Salvemini, Lowell House, Harvard University, to AC, March 28, 1945, AC Papers.

Salvemini told AC: "What you write in the pages you have sent me is correct from the beginning to the end as far as facts go.... The Fiume affair was a document of immense stupidity on the part of the Italian negotiators at the Peace Conference.... And if Mussolini had not been half mad and half idiot, the relations between Italy and Yugoslavia would not have been poisoned by the Fiume question."

25. *Ibid.*, 183 (Villard), 189.

Oswald Garrison Villard (1872-1949), grandson of abolitionist William Lloyd Garrison and son of railroad magnate and newspaper publisher (*N. Y. Evening Post* and *The Nation*) Henry Villard, was a founder of the American Anti-Imperialist League and an early civil-rights advocate. He published and edited *The Nation* 1918-32.

26. *Ibid.*, 196-98, 201-02, 208, 282 (Wilson's last words).

A major issue was the voting power of the United States versus the six votes that Great Britain controlled.

27. May McMath to AC, no date, AC Papers.

28. "Charles" (H. Kendrick?, San Francisco Democrat, see notes 33, 38) to AC, Metropolitan Club letterhead, Washington, D. C., August 8, 1945, AC Papers.

Charles H. Kendrick had lost a son in World War II at Guadalcanal, writing AC September 27, 1945 (see note 33), "I am sorry that Charles is not here to play his part. Like yourself, he had accumulated and was accumulating a vast store-house of world knowledge, and with his great mental power, I am sure he would have played a worthwhile role," AC Papers.

Cranston gave a copy of his book to President Jimmy Carter in 1979 at a White House breakfast; Carter promised to read it as part of background material for a Strategic Arms Limitation Treaty (SALT). Fowle, 77.

29. Nelson A. Rockefeller to AC, August 2, 1945; V. S. Hurban, Czechoslovak Ambassador, to AC, August 2, 1945, AC Papers.

30. Senator Harold H. Burton to AC, August 7, 1945; D. F. Fleming to AC, August 8, 1945; AC to Ruth [?], September 1, 1945, and statement from D. F. Fleming, AC Papers.

Harold H. Burton (1888-1964) served in the Senate 1941-45, resigning to accept President Truman's nomination to the U. S. Supreme Court, where Burton served 1945-58. He had served with Senator Truman on the Senate investigative committee overseeing the WWII war effort.

31. Arthur Sweetser, president, Woodrow Wilson Foundation, to AC, August 9, 1945, AC Papers.

32. Harry Braverman to AC, August 12, 1945, AC Papers.

Braverman (1920-76), who sometimes used the pseudonym Harry Frankel, was active in the Trotsky movement and Socialist Workers Party, in which during the 1950s he joined the "Cochranite" faction that rejected revolutionary tactics. An editor for Grove Press in the 1960s, he was instrumental in publishing *The Autobiography of Malcolm X*. Braverman authored *Labor and Monopoly Capital: The Degradation of Work in the Twentieth Century* (1974). Wikipedia.

33. William L. Shirer, CBS, Inc., to AC, September 17, 1945; Drew Pearson, telegram to AC, September 25, 1945, stating, "This is the story of dramatic events.... Remainder quote okay"; Drew Pearson, column datelined Kansas City, Mo., October 6, [1945]; Charles Kendrick to AC, September 27, 1945, AC Papers.

34. AC to Frances [Kethian?], November 1, 1945; AC to John Anson Ford, November 1, 1945; AC to Dr. and Mrs. Ralph Reynolds, November 2, 1945, AC Papers; *Killing of the Peace*, 131; Clip Boutell, "Authors are like people...."

John Anson Ford (1883-1983), who had an advertising and public-relations firm, was an L. A. County Supervisor (1934-58) and Democratic Party activist (Democratic Central Committee, chairman, Citizens for Kennedy, 1960). He promoted a County Human Relations Commission to deal with racism (1943, when Cranston may have met him during the zoot-suit troubles), as well as cultural projects including restoration of the Hollywood Bowl. Pilgrimage Play Amphitheatre was renamed for Ford in 1978. He wrote an autobiography, *Thirty Explosive Years in Los Angeles County* (published by The Huntington Library, 1961, re-issued by University of California Press, 2010).

Vandenberg (1884-1951) was appointed, and then won election, to the Senate in 1928; he was chairman of the Foreign Relations Committee 1946-51. Vandenberg was considered an isolationist before 1945, but became a proponent of bipartisan foreign policy, serving as a U. S. Delegate to the U. N. Conference in 1945 and to the General Assembly in 1946. He was instrumental in securing Senate approval of the Marshall Plan and North Atlantic Treaty organization, among other foreign policies of President Truman.

35. Lorraine Fuller, from Villa Warec, to AC, August 31, 1945; AC to Fuller, November 1, 1945, AC Papers.

36. The Viking Press, advertisement for *The Killing of the Peace*, *New York Times*, September 4, 1945, quoting Rex Stout: "A good, useful and exceptionally timely book... urgent and essential reading"; "The shocking inside story of the costliest battle America ever lost!", Viking Press promotion, quoting Johnson review; AC to Gerald W. Johnson, *Baltimore Evening Sun*, November 1, 1945, AC Papers; Gerald W. Johnson, "The Fight against the League," *New York Herald Tribune Weekly Book Review*, August 12, 1945, 5. All reviews cited are from copies in AC Papers.

Rex Stout (1886-1975), best known for his series featuring detective Nero Wolfe, wrote propaganda and did radio broadcasts during WW II (one in 1942 with Elmer Davis and Jacques Barzun on Mark Van Doren's popular CBS radio program, "Invitation to Learning"). He chaired the Writers' Board (successor to the Writers' War Board) that included many well-known authors and playwrights (among them Clifton Fadiman, Oscar Hammerstein II, Edna Ferber, John Gunther, John P. Marquand, Clifford Odets, Eugene O'Neill, Marjorie Kinnan Rawlings, Mary Roberts Rinehart, Dorothy Thompson). Stout was on the original board of the American Civil Liberties Union, and helped start the radical magazine *The New Masses* (succeeding a 1920s Marxist publication). He supported the New Deal and was active in many liberal causes, ignoring a subpoena from the House Un-American Activities Committee. He headed the Authors League of America during the 1950s anti-Communist era. Stout had detective Nero Wolfe reply to a man from the Balkans, who had said, "*Your country has no discipline*": "*We like our cops…[but] are extremely fond of our civil liberties.*" Nero Wolfe mystery, A & E television network, July 8, 2001.

37. Gerald W. Johnson, "The fight against the League."

38. AC to Johnson, November 1, 1945. See note 28.

39. AC to Erma Fischer, November 2, 1945, stating, "I hope…that Steve is now enjoying the *Chronicle*," AC Papers.

40. "That peace may live," *Newsweek*, August 27, 1945, 85-86; Karl Schriftgiesser, "Books: A Survey of American Letters in 1945," *Newsweek*, December 17, 1945, 106; "The Killing of the Peace," *New Yorker*, August 11, 1945, 72; Edward H. Blanchard, "The Book Corner," *New York Sun*, August 11, 1945; Sterling North, "The murdered peace," *New York Post*, August 23, 1945, and "Cranston succinctly states political methods, motives which killed peace before," *Washington Post*, August 26, 1945, with photograph of AC in uniform.

41. F. Lauriston Bullard, "Behind headlines, your news books of the week," *Boston Herald*, August 15, 1945; Burton Rascoe, "War or Peace? Author asserts it is up to Americans to decide on realistic basis," *New York World*, August 24, 1945; E. S., "Tragic drama of the League of Nations, The Bookshelf," *Christian Science Monitor*, September 1, 1945; "The Literary Scene," Menasha, Wisconsin, *Cresset*, [1945], AC Papers.

42. Allan Nevins, "A backward glance at the League," [*Saturday Review of Literature*?], September 8, 1945, AC Papers.

43. Lewis Gannett, "Books and Things," *New York Herald Tribune*, August 10, 1945.

Another biography of Wilson published in 1945, *The Story of Woodrow Wilson*, was written by Ruth Cranston, no relation to AC.

44. Karl Schriftgiesser, "American Saboteurs of the League of Nations," *New York [World?] Book Review*, August 12, 1945, 3, with cartoon captioned, "The Bomb Maker" by Rollin Kirby in the *New York World.*

45. Robert van Gelder, "The world of books at war's end, in a booming season, Christmas lists reflect the creative trends of peace," *The New York Times Book Review*, December 2, 1945, 1, 24, 26.

The authors mentioned who had been in military service, and their books, were: Bill Mauldin, *Up Front* (Henry Holt & Co.); Karl Shapiro, *Essay on Rime* (Reynal & Hitchcock, poems); Walter Bernstein, *Keep Your Head Down* (Viking); Peter Bowman, *Beach Red* (Random); Charles G. Bolte, *The New Veteran* (Reynal & Hitchcock); Harry Brown [Peter M'Nab], *Artie Greengroin Pfc.* (Alfred A. Knopf, humorous sketches of the Army in Britain). Louis Adamic's *A Nation of Nations*, stressing the role of non-Anglo-Saxons in U. S. history, and Norman Cousins' *Modern Man Is Obsolete* (Viking Press), also were published in 1945, as were works by a number of well-known fiction writers including Sinclair Lewis, J. P. Marquand, Christopher Isherwood, John O'Hara, Rumer Godden, Upton Sinclair, and collected poetry of W. H. Auden and Ogden Nash. Smythe's book was published by Princeton University Press.

46. Helen Gahagan Douglas, "League cited as parallel, Representative Douglas quotes some history and sounds warning," letter to editor, *New York Times*, August 16, 1945.

47. I. N. S., "Literature and life, how a peace was wasted and another war assured by a little group of willful men," *Ottawa Evening Journal*, September 8, 1945.

The book was published in Canada by Macmillan. William Cranston to Commonwealth Club of California, January 24, 1946, AC Papers.

48. "The Killing of the Peace," *Current History*, Philadelphia, December 1945; Manfred George, "The Killing of the Peace," review, "Das Buch ist schon einige Monate heraus...," *Aufbrau*, November 30, 1945, (translation by Marianne Schroeder, San Francisco, July, 2002); Manfred George, editor, *Aufbrau*, *American Jewish Weekly*, to AC, November 30, 1945, AC Papers.

George was referring to Cranston's participation in the Dublin Conference (see note 57).

49. "Best sellers," *San Francisco Chronicle*, August 31, 1945.

50. "Robert van Gelder, editor of…included 'The Killing of the Peace' by Alan Cranston [class of '36] on his Christmas list of the ten best books of 1945," *Stanford Alumni Review*, January,1946; "'Killing of the Peace' on list of 10 best," unidentified news clip identifying AC as "son of the William Cranstons of Los Altos"; "Critics see Cranston's 'Killing of the Peace' as dramatic warning against dangers ahead," *Daily Palo Alto Times*, September 20, 1945.

51. Joseph Henry Jackson, "Bookman's notebook," *San Francisco Chronicle*, November 16, 1945.

52. Samson Trop, "The peace vigil," *Free World*, (published by the American Free World Association?), September, 1945.

53. Paul Waitt, "9th annual Herald Book Fair at Symphony Hall Oct. 15-18," *Boston Sunday Herald*, September 9, 1945, AC Papers.

54. William Cranston to Commonwealth Club of California, January 24, 1946, AC Papers.

Theodore Roosevelt and the Progressive Movement by George Mowry received a silver medal for nonfiction in 1946.

55. AC to John Anson Ford, November 1, 1945; AC to Harold Matson, November 2, 1945, stating that "7-1/2% of my share of the royalties during the first year of such payments is to go to Erma May Calventra Fischer, who helped me with the research"; AC to Erma Fischer, November 2, 1945, AC Papers.

56. Marjorie Griesser, The Viking Press, to AC, February 13, 1946, and AC to Viking, April 16, 1946, AC Papers; Ruth Brown, The Viking Press, to AC, December 17, 1946, with unidentified news article, "Subway attack by sailors told by Frenchman, interpreter seeking U. N. job protests beating by six as crowd looked on," AC "Souvenirs," AC Personal Papers.

57. "Invitation to conference to consider how best to remedy the weaknesses of the United Nations organization, October 11-16, 1945," September 14, 1945; Grenville Clark to AC, "c/o *Yank Magazine*," New York, referring to invitation, September 25, 1945, AC Papers; Fowle, 78.

Among other groups then advocating world union was Americans United for World Organization. In 1945 it consolidated several older societies, including the American Free World Association, Citizens for Victory, Committee to Defend America, Fight for Freedom, and the United Nations Association. Dartmouth President Ernest M. Hopkins was chairman of the board; industrialist Henry J. Kaiser headed the membership campaign. Thomas K. Finletter, one of its directors, was among participants at the Dublin Conference. A *New York Times* editorial April 15, 1945, said the new group hoped for 10 million members. The editorial noted that "All signs indicate that most Americans favor United States participation in some form of world union to prevent war. There is still a chance, however, that the will of this peace-minded majority may be thwarted…. Some United States Senators are on record as opposing any effective form of world organization. Others are doubtful." "Americans

United for World organization, Inc., 465 Fifth Avenue, New York 17, N. Y.," flyer with reprint of editorial, "Americans United," *New York Times*, April 15, 1945, AC Papers.

58. Charles S. Pearson Presents, "Alan Cranston, chairman of the Dublin Conference Committee, author of 'The Killing of the Peace,'" flyer, AC Personal papers.

The concept to make permanent an international organization, derived from the war-time United Nations group, to enforce peace and prevent nuclear war was considered a logical follow-up to the world war that had just ended in 1945. As former U. N. Undersecretary-General Brian Urquhart stated in a review of two histories of the U. N.: "At its founding the United Nations was widely perceived by the public as a fundamentally idealistic institution that would change the way nations behaved. This was not the primary objective of the three governments – the United States, the Soviet Union, and Britain – that had been most involved in drafting the U. N. Charter." The original purpose of the U. N. was to protect member states from aggression while allowing individual state sovereignty. Urquhart, "Finding the Hidden U. N.," *N. Y. Review of Books*, May 27, 2010, 26, 28.

59. Invitation and list of invitees; Fowle, 79; AC, "Memoir of a Man," written October 15, 24 and 29, 1973, in *Memoirs of a Man, Grenville Clark*, collected by Mary Clark Dimond, Norman Cousins and J. Garry Clifford, eds. (New York: W. W. Norton & Company, Inc., 1975), 253.

Clark's farm telephone number was #1 in Dublin, New Hampshire. AC memorandum to Henry Usborne, October 23, 1947, AC Papers

Other participants, according to the invitation list, were: businessman Henry I. Harriman; Dartmouth College president Ernest M. Hopkins and president-elect John Sloan Dickey; Princeton University president Harold W. Dodds; St. John's College president Stringfellow Barr; Beardsley Ruml of R. H. Macy & Co., subsequently chairman of the Federal Reserve Bank of New York; writers Louis Fisher, Edgar Ansel Mowrer and Michael Straight of the *New Republic* and author of *Let's Make This the Last War*; Charles Bolte, head of the American Veterans Committee; Leo Cherne, executive secretary of Research Institute of America, Inc.; Polish-born Louis B. Sohn, then a student at Harvard Law School who would collaborate with Clark on a book proposing revisions of the U. N. charter, emphasizing a system of world law, *World Peace through World Law* (1958, 2nd ed., 1960, revisions 1966, 1973). Sohn participated in the S. F. Conference that established the U. N., and was a legal officer with the U. N. Secretariat for two years; he joined Harvard Law School faculty in 1951.

60. Fowle, 77; Charles S. Pearson Presents flyer; *Current Biography*.

61. AC interview with author, and AC, "Memoir of a Man," 254.

62. AC, "Memoir of a Man," 254, 258; Fowle, 78, 80-81.

The Selective Service Act was enacted in 1940. Clark advocated it as chairman of a national emergency committee for Military Training Camps. Root, Sr., won the 1912 Nobel Peace Prize.

63. AC, "Memoir of a Man," 254.

64. AC interview with author; AC, "Memoir of a Man," 253, 260; AC to Ford, November 1, 1945; *Stanford Alumni Review*, December, 1945, p. 25, AC Papers.

65. AC, "Memoir of a Man," 253.

66. AC, "Memoir of a Man," 253; Tentative Program of conference, AC Papers.

67. Robert Sagendorph, publisher (the only representative of the press allowed to sit in the conference), "The Dublin Conference," *Yankee*, Vol. IX, No. 6, December, 1945, p. 9, AC Papers.

The few who did not agree with either report were Louis Fischer, author of *Soviets in World Affairs*; John Jessup, editor of *Life* and *Fortune* magazines; and Winfield W. Riefler, a professor at the Princeton Institute for Advanced Studies.

68. Chester Davis, "30 sign proposal for organization at Dublin parley," *Manchester* (N. H.) *Union*, October 17, 1945, with photograph captioned, "Dublin conference plan was

explained" and citing 53 attendees.

69. "Declaration of the Dublin Conference, United Nations inadequate for peace, world federal government proposed," AC Papers.

70. Chester Davis, "30 sign proposal..."; W. E. Playfair, "Dublin plan asks control of A-bomb, United Nations held powerless to save civilized peoples," *Boston Herald*, October 17, 1945; William M. Blair, "World government is urged to bar ruin in atomic war, thirty prominent persons meeting in New Hampshire ask scrapping of U. N. O. in favor of a Federation," *New York Times*, October 17, 1945; "World union-instead of U. N. O.-urged," *San Francisco Chronicle*, special from *New York Times*, October 17, 1945. All news accounts about the conference are quoted from copies in AC Papers.

The number of conferees varied in news accounts. Cranston identified himself with *Yank* magazine and used it for a mailing address. A Los Altos *News* item November 1, 1945, stated that Cranston was on the "staff of *New York Times* book reviewers" after his discharge.

71. S. Nathan, *Black Star* correspondent, "The first conference on world government in Dublin, N. H., exclusive pictures made for *Free World*," *Free World*, November, 1945, 1, 3-4.

72. "Killing 40,000,000 overnight," editorial, *Boston Herald*, October 18, 1945.

73. "Albert Einstein on the atomic bomb," Norfolk, Virginia, *Virginian Pilot*, October 29, 1945.

Einstein's fears about the bomb, expressed to President Franklin Roosevelt after revelations that the Germans were building their own bomb, had spurred creation of the "Manhattan project" on which many Jewish scientists who fled Nazi Germany worked – one of the reasons, Cranston believed, that Germany lost the war. One Jewish Polish-born, naturalized British scientist working on it, Sir Joseph Rotblat (1908-2005), a 1995 Nobel prize winner, resigned the day that Hitler's suicide/death was announced, believing the bomb no longer was needed to defeat Hitler. Rotblat then formed an anti-bomb peace group, mainly of scientists, named "Pugwash" for the Canadian town (on northern seacoast of Nova Scotia) where it was founded. Another scientist who worked on the bomb, German-American Nobelist (1967) Hans Bethe (1906-2005), in 1995 (then 89), circulated a petition to scientists dubbed the "Bethe Pledge," exhorting them never to work on production of weapons of mass destruction. Cranston, when visiting Moscow in the 1990s, found a Russian scientist serving on Soviet President Yeltzin's security council circulating the "Bethe Pledge." AC interview with author.

British spy Donald McLean, a Soviet agent who, while working at the British embassy in Washington for four years (1944-48), passed valuable information to the Russians on the American atomic weapons program, said that he did it not so much to give the Russians a lead in the arms race but because he was convinced that the United States was preparing to destroy the Soviet Union in a first-strike nuclear attack. As a reviewer for *The New York Review of Books* wrote, that was "not [an] entirely improbable belief in the latter half of the 1940s, an unprecedentedly dangerous period in world history." Cranston obviously perceived that danger. John Banville, "'Cowboys and Indians,'" review, Miranda Carter, *Anthony Blunt: His Lives* (Farrer, Straus and Giroux), 2002, *The New York Review of Books*, February 14, 2002, 8.

74. "Meaningless gesture," *Columbus State Journal*, October 15, 1945; editorials, "The Innocents of Dublin," Springfield, Ohio, *Sun*, October 18, 1945, "The Dublin Utopia," *St. Louis Globe-Democrat*, October 18, 1945, "The Wrong Approach," *Washington Star*, October 22, 1945; "A Far-off Ideal," Charlotte, N. C., *Observer*, October 28, 1945, AC Papers.

75. "The wrong approach," editorial, *Washington Evening Star*, October 22, 1945.

76. Major George Fielding Eliot, "World government proposal is traced to 'atomic jitters,'" *New York Herald Tribune*, October 19, 1945; "Astir with the atom," editorial, *Washington Post*, October 18, 1945.

77. Conrad Hobbs, letter to editor, *New York Times*, November 2, 1945; "Danger in world federation plan," *St. Louis Post-Dispatch*, January 12, 1946, statement signed by 20 people

(including Mary McLeod Bethune and George Fielding Eliot); Robert P. Bass, "The Dublin Declaration, A Response to Editorial Criticism of the *New York Times* and *Herald Tribune*," October 24, 1945, AC Papers.

78. AC, "Memoir of a Man," 254.

79. *Ibid.*, 255, 257-58; Fowle, 80.

AC addressed letters to "Mr. Clark," Clark addressed his to "Alan" through 1945-46. The first evidence that the author found in AC's Papers of his calling Clark "Grenny" was a letter dated November 17, 1946. AC-Clark correspondence in AC Papers continued through 1957.

80. AC, "Memoir of a Man, 258.

81. *Ibid.*; AC to Dr. and Mrs. Ralph Reynolds, November 2, 1945, AC Papers.

82. Marshall Field III, *The Chicago Sun*, to "Dear Marsh," Marshall Field IV., October 23, 1945; Marshall Field IV, to AC, October 25, 1945; AC to Marshall Field IV, October 31, 1945, AC Papers.

Marshall Field IV (1916-65) was heir to the fortune of his great-grandfather (1834-1906), founder of the Chicago department store by that name (from 1881), co-founder of the Field Museum of Natural History and the University of Chicago. Field III (1893-1956) founded the *Chicago Sun* (later *Sun-Times*) and created *Parade* weekly newspaper supplement. Field IV served in the U. S. Navy 1942-44 as a gunnery officer on the aircraft carrier USS *Enterprise* and was wounded; he was awarded the Silver Star, Purple Heart and Presidential United Citation. He had a nervous breakdown at the death of his father (1956 of brain cancer) and was institutionalized. He ran the newspaper and Field Enterprises until his death at age 49 in 1965, rumored to be from an accidental overdose but ruled as from natural causes. Two professorships at the University of Chicago were named for him.

83. Mary McGrory, "Throng packs Symphony Hall for *Herald* Book Fair opening," *Boston Herald*, October 16, 1945, copy in AC Papers.

Robert Casey had two current best-sellers, *Battle Below* and *This Is Where I Came In*. Sophie Tucker, who had written a memoir, *Some of These Days*, announced that $35,000 of proceeds from it had gone charity.

84. Raymond Gram Swing, Norman Cousins, telegram to AC, October 18, 1945, AC Papers.

85. G. Clark to Ulric Bell, November 8, 1945; American United for World Organization, Inc., program for "Atomic Age Dinner," November 28, 1945, Waldorf Astoria, N. Y. C., with board of directors listing AC as a member, AC Papers.

Clark hoped that Federal Union would consolidate or affiliate with Americans United, if not thwarted by Clarence Streit's "obduracy." Federal Union disbanded in January, 1946, and some of its directors joined the A. U. board. It included a number of Dublin conference participants as well as George Fielding Eliot, who had publicly criticized the declaration, and Sumner Welles, Roosevelt's former Undersecretary of State (1937-42). The Dublin group wanted to affiliate with A. U. "in order to demonstrate as much unity as possible in the field," Cranston wrote Robert Wheelwright, December 8, 1945. A similar affiliation was needed with the World Federalists, Cranston felt. "General Progress," AC Papers.

86. G. Clark to Hon. Anthony Eden, House of Commons, November 24, 1945; Clark to Rt. Hon. Ernest Bevin, Secretary for Foreign Affairs, November 24, 1945; Clark to Rt. Hon. W. L. Mackenzie King, Prime Minister of Canada, December 18, 1945; Bruce M. Weinhold, Youngstown, Ohio, to AC, December 26, 1945, citing questionnaire to be circulated to 500 families; "Action by Dublin," editorial, *Boston Herald*, February 10, 1946, AC Papers.

Ernest Bevin (1881-1951) was an anti-Communist trade union leader who served as Labour Minister (1940-45) in Churchill's wartime cabinet and as Foreign Secretary (1945-51) in Clement Atlee's postwar labour government; he supported the creation of NATO, the development of nuclear weapons, and British alignment with the U. S. in the Cold War. Bevin stated in a foreign-affairs speech in November, 1945: "I am willing to sit in with anybody of any party, of any nation, to try to devise a franchise or a constitution for a World Assembly." "One world, one government," *News Review*, June 26, 1947, AC Papers.

Anthony Eden was Conservative Party Prime Minister 1955-57.

The charter initially gave every nation the same voting power. As Clark explained to Bernard Baruch, "I am sure you must have come to the conclusion that the present setup, whereby Liberia has as big a vote in the Assembly as the U. S., and Luxembourg as the United Kingdom, together with the unanimity requirement for the Big Five in the Council, is an ineffective and unworkable plan." Clark to Baruch, June 12, 1946, AC Papers.

Weinhold was a businessman and writer on world affairs. AC in a letter January 2, 1946 referred to Weinhold's helping get him a lower berth on a train from Youngstown.

Others on record for some form of world government, according to Americans United as of January 22, 1946, besides Bevin, Eden, MacKenzie King and Einstein, included: American politician Harold E. Stassen, a potential G. O. P. presidential candidate in 1948, some U. S. Senators and members of the House of Representatives; in the media, *Reader's Digest*, *Saturday Evening Post*, *Saturday Review of Literature*, *Christian Science Monitor*, *Washington Post*, *Chicago Sun*; organizations like Freedom House, Writers' Board, Association of Oak Ridge Scientists. "General Progress."

87. AC to Bruce Weinhold, January 2, 1946, AC Papers; "General Progress."

Cranston joined A. U. directors Bell, Cousins, Finletter and Meyer meeting with Truman.

88. Bruce M. Weinhold, Youngstown, Ohio, to Ernest Bevin, Foreign Secretary, London, England, December 20, 1945, AC Papers.

89. Rep. Jerry Voorhis to AC, November 17, 1945; Rep. Estes Kefauver to AC, November 17, 1945, AC Papers; Fowle, 88.

Jerry Voorhis (1901-84) represented California's 12th District in Congress from 1937 to 1947 when he was defeated by Richard Nixon. When he died, Cranston gave him a warm tribute in the Senate September 19, 1984. Voorhis "was the first victim of Richard Nixon's campaign tactics," Cranston noted of Nixon's falsely accusing the popular congressman of being a Communist in a telephone smear campaign. Voorhis had been a "loyal friend, staunch in support of my efforts on issues of mutual concern," Cranston said (Voorhis served on the first national advisory board to the United World Federalists, 1947). "He cared deeply about the issues of war and peace, meeting the needs of the poor, and about insuring adequate health care for all.... He worried about the mad armament race...supported a moratorium on nuclear testing and a nuclear freeze." Over the years, Voorhis had written Cranston some 40 times a year, the last only three weeks before he died. AC, "In memory of Jerry Voorhis," *Congressional Record*, September 19, 1984, pp. 11447-48.

90. [Sumner Welles?], on Plaza Bank of St. Louis letterhead, St. Louis, Mo., to "My dear Friend," December 20, 1945, with handwritten notation, "Not for publication," carbon copy in AC Papers. It is not clear to whom the letter was addressed; blind copies were sent to eight other people, including Raymond G. Swing, Ulric Bell, Thomas H. Mahony, Norman Cousins, Harris Wofford.

Benjamin Sumner Welles (1892-1961) was a long-time diplomat appointed by F. D. R. in 1933 as Assistant Secretary of State; he served as Undersecretary 1937-42. He was credited as a major drafter of the U. N. founding at the San Francisco conference in 1945, when he also was a commentator for American Broadcasting Company and author on foreign affairs issues. In 1943 he gave an address calling for use of force to preserve world peace (*New York Times*, October 17, 1943). Welles was the subject of reports that he was homosexual, revealed in a biography by his son, Benjamin Welles, *FDR's Global Strategist: A Biography*, Eleanor Roosevelt Institute Series on Diplomatic and Economic History (N. Y.: St. Martin's Press, 1997). Wikipedia.

91. Charles S. Pearson Presents flyer, AC Personal Papers; "Town meeting to air world organization," [Wilmington?], Delaware, [*Morning News*?], 1945, with photograph of "Sergt.

Alan Cranston," AC Papers.

After the war, only the U. S., Great Britain and Canada had the atom bomb.

92. "To the Editor of the *New York Times*," typescript, no date, AC Papers.

93. *Ibid.*; AC, "Memoir of a Man," 259.

94. Kingman Brewster, Jr., to AC, December 26, 1945; AC to Brewster, November 24, 1945, and January 6, 1946; Brewster to AC, saying that he had "such admiration for your handling of both Dublin and Princeton, I am fully confident that you see things as they are far better than I," January 13, 1946; AC to Brewster, Cambridge, Mass., January 22, 1946, AC Papers.

Kingman Brewster, Jr. (1919-88) was president of Yale University 1963 to '77 when he was appointed by President Jimmie Carter as Ambassador to the U. K. (1977-81). At Yale he had been a strong isolationist, inviting its strongest spokesman Charles Lindberg to speak at Yale in 1940. Brewster was a founder with other students of the America First Committee, whose members included future leaders like President Gerald Ford; Sargent Shriver, first director of the Peace Corps; future Supreme Court Justice Potter Stewart. Brewster resigned from the committee when it became apparent that the U. S. would have to enter the war, writing Stewart, "I still believe it outrageous to commit this country to the outcome of the war abroad," but "whether we like it or not, America has decided what its ends are," and he did not want to be a part of an obstructionist group. He was a Navy aviator, flying patrols over the Atlantic (1942-46). Wikipedia.

AC files (Carton 8) for the Princeton conference include correspondence with the following people, many of whom could not attend but expressed interest: Helen Gahagan Douglas; Jerry Voorhis; John Foster Dulles; Rep. Christian Herter, D-Mass.; Franklin Roosevelt, Jr.; Mark Van Doren; Pearl Buck (unable to attend "in spite of my sympathy with its purpose," telephone message, December 28, 1945); Louis Mumford (unable to attend but "I would be happy to be counted as one of the signers of the statement the conference will prepare," December 29, 1945); Merle Miller, Magazine Corporation of America, a biographer of Harry Truman; author E. B. White; public relations executive Albert Lasker; Sen. Claude Pepper, D-Florida; Mrs. Morrow [Anne Morrow Lindberg's mother?]; Templeton Peck, a Stanford classmate of AC's, then chief, European Broadcast Section, U. S. Office of International Information and Cultural Affairs, later editorial writer for the *San Francisco Chronicle* (would attend, saying, "Your own role in this movement is one that commands my admiration," January 9, 1946).

95. W. W. Waymack, editor, vice president, *The Register and Tribune*, Des Moines, Iowa, to AC, December 28, 1945; AC to Waymack, January 7, 1946, AC Papers.

96. Rex Stout, chairman, Writers' Board, to AC, January 8, 1946; draft press release embargoed for January 13, "Conference on world government held at The Princeton Inn, Princeton, N. J., Jan. 11-13, 1946," January 9, 1946; list of "Those attending Princeton meeting called by Dublin Conference Committee, Jan. 11-12, 1946," AC Papers.

97. Albert Einstein to AC, saying that he had to go to Washington on Friday but would "come to the Saturday meeting," January 10, 1946; A. U. program for "Atomic Age Dinner," November 28, 1945.

Some 1,500 people attended the Atomic Age dinner and meeting, including scientists, military men and leading advocates of world government. "General Progress," memorandum re: "Americans United has played its part toward creating a situation…," January 22, 1946, AC Papers.

98. AC interview with author.

Einstein wrote AC: "I agree wholeheartedly with the proposed change concerning the composition of the U. N. O. Assembly. My only doubt is whether it is not dangerous to restrict the competence of the Council and its permanent instrument in favor of the Assembly – the latter being, of course, not always in function and too clumsy for quick and vigorous action." Einstein to AC, January 10, 1946.

99. Draft press release, "The principal proposed amendments include…," with release dated January 9, 1945; AC, memorandum "To those who attended the Princeton Conference," January 31, 1946; "World police or atom war is held choice," *Washington Post*, February 8, 1946; "Action by Dublin," editorial, *Boston Herald*, February 10, 1946, AC Papers.

The drafting committee consisted of Clark, Cranston, Mahony and Cousins; Leo Cherne, executive secretary of Research Institute of America, Inc.; Joseph H. Rush, a director of both the Federation of Atomic Scientists and of American Scientists; Gray Thoron, a Wall Street lawyer and veteran; and Wayne D. Williams, also a veteran and lawyer, winner of the American Bar Association's 1944 Rose Medal for an essay on world organization.

The U. N. initially had 50 signatory nations. As of 2010 it had 192 member states.

100. Lewis Mumford, memorandum, "Comment on a petition for amendment of the United Nations charter," June 7, 1946; Mumford to AC, March 2, 1946, with memorandum, "A group of us have started a local movement in Hanover, [N.H.] which we hope will spread to other communities and play a part in redressing the very serious mistakes we have made as a nation in the exploitation of the atomic bomb…," February 26, 1946, AC Papers.

101. AC to Brewster, February 6, 1946; AC to Clark, December 7, 1945; Edwin L. James, "World union disciples would build upon U. N. O. …," February 17, 1946, AC Papers.

102. AC, "Memoir of a Man, 262; O. Welles to Passport Division, Dept. of State, January 22, 1946; AC British national registration, temporary identity card valid to April 21, 1946, citing Savoy Hotel address; Clark, "Memo, to Signers of the Petition February 1, 1946…," February 15, 1946, AC Papers

103. "One world," editorial, Charleston, S. C., *Post*, February 14, 1946; "Alan Cranston in London to present Dublin plan to UNO," Los Altos *News*, February 14, 1946, AC Papers.

104. United Nations, London, 1946, ticket for Mr. and Mrs. Alan Cranston to meeting of General Assembly, Saturday, February 16, 5 p.m., and pass for AC to House of Commons, February 20, 1946; Clark to AC, London, February 13, 1946, AC Papers; "Bevin is hero of UNO meeting," *Life*, February 25, 1946, 43-46.

Bevin, "the Foreign Minister who loves a fight though he knows he has a bad heart," was called "the hero of the London meeting" in *Life*'s account, which read, "Bevin became the boldest, most open spokesman for the Western democracies," standing up to Russia, led by Andrei Vishinsky, which "took resounding slaps in the face [losing nine of ten Russian-backed proposals], but made political gains in the Security Council." *Life*, 43.

No references were found in Cranston's papers to his meeting with Eleanor Roosevelt, a leader of the American delegation, in London, although he apparently had met her while with the Common Council. Mrs. Roosevelt invited women at the conference to sign an open letter calling on women to take part in world affairs. *Life*, 44.

105. AC interview with author; Fowle, 81-82.

Paul Henri Spaak (1899-1972), a moderate Socialist, was a Belgian statesman and premier, chairman of the Council for European Recovery (1948-49), and secretary general of NATO (1957-61).

A. A. Gromyko (1909-89) was Soviet Ambassador to the U. S. 1943-46; chief permanent Soviet delegate to the U. N. (1946-48); ambassador to Great Britain (1952-53); Soviet foreign affairs minister (beginning in 1957). In the early 1970s Groymko was active in building détente between Soviet leader Leonid Brezhnev and President Nixon, and in drawing up a non-aggression pact with West Germany. He supported Mikhail Gorbachev, with whom Cranston would become friends, to be U. S. S. R. General Secretary.

106. Corporal G. Kraus, 7, Kensington Palace Gardens, to AC, February 15, 22 and 28, 1946, AC Papers.

107. Sgt. J. Keith Killby, board of directors, Federal Union, to AC, February 23, 1946; Elsa [Robin?], organizing secretary, Federal Union, to AC, February 27, 1946; "On speaking tour,

Cranston petition has wide publicity," [Los Altos *News*?, May?], 1946, reprinting "World Parliament: When Do the People Come In?", *News Review*, February 21, 1946, AC Papers.

108. Laurence Olivier, New Theatre, to AC, February 26, AC Papers.

109. Clark, telegram to AC, March 2, 1946; Clark to AC, April 17, 1946, AC Papers.

The U. N. Assembly was to meet again in New York City in September, 1946.

110. AC to "My dear Louis [Sohn?]," March 6, 1946, AC Papers; Churchill's remarks from speech May 13, 1945; Brian Urquhart, "How Great Was Churchill?", *New York Review of Books*, 43.

Churchill, after returned as Conservative P. M., would campaign in the 1950s against the nuclear arms race. In 1952 he proposed to President Eisenhower that the two go to Moscow to persuade Stalin that potential nuclear disaster was more important than any differences between the super-powers; his proposal was not taken up. Urquhart, same. See also Chapter 14 and note 19.

Clement Attlee (1883-1967) succeeded Churchill (1874-1965) as Prime Minister, 1945-51, when Churchill returned as Conservative P. M., 1951-55. He was succeeded by Anthony Eden (1897-1977), 1955-57.

111. Mary Seaton, Atlas Dispatches Limited-Reuters, to AC, referring to AC's failure to meet with Attlee or Rt. Hon. Herbert Morrison, Lord President of the Council, March 13, 1946, AC Papers.

112. Mary Seaton, typescript, "World Peace for 177 Dollars?" AC Papers.

113. *Ibid.*

114. AC, "To the Editor, Dear Sir," March 22, 1946; AC to Sydney Walton, Esq., May 3, 1946; "On speaking tour," reprinting "World Parliament: When Do the People Come In?", *News Review*, February 21, 1946, AC Papers.

115. AC to Miss Sophia H. Dulles, May 1, 1946; AC to William N. Warbey, M.P., May 7, 1946; "On speaking tour, Cranston petition has wide publicity," [Los Altos *News*?, May?,] 1946, citing *News Review*, February 21, 1946; Clark to Bernard M. Baruch, June 12, 1946, AC Papers.

116. Clark to Byrnes and Vandenberg, June 7, and to Bernard M. Baruch, June 12, 1946; Clark to Henry A. Wallace, Secretary of Commerce, September 20, 1946; "World government, letter by Grenville Clark," remarks and reprint of Clark's letter to *New York Times*, inserted by Senator Walter F. George into the *Congressional Record*, June 24, 1946; "Case history of one-worlder," *Chicago Daily Tribune*, July 4, 1946, AC Papers.

117. Douglas Fairbanks, Jr., to AC, August 17, 1946, AC Papers.

118. Fowle, 81; AC to J. B. Orrick, chief, U. N. Section for Voluntary Organizations, Lake Success, L. I., requesting accreditation pass, November 4, 1946; Robert W. Kenney, California Attorney General, to AC, August 10, 1946; H. Leavitt Horton to AC, November 23, 1946; AC to Horton, December 10, 1946; Mayor Roger D. Lapham to AC, December 18, 1946, thanking him for help with the U. N. delegation, AC Papers.

119. Fowle, 82.

Reform of the U. N. would be a continuous subject of debate from its creation in 1945. Its missions evolved, adding peacekeeping, not mentioned in the original Charter. Many U. N. works were awarded Nobel Prizes – 23 as of 2010. Brian Urquhart, "Finding the Hidden UN," *N. Y. Review of Books*, May 27, 2010, 27-28.

120. AC, "Memoir of a Man," 260.

121. *Ibid.*, 261, 163.

Clark was born in 1882, died in 1967.

122. *Ibid.*, 263-64.

Lao-tzu (in Chinese "old person" or "old philosopher"), born circa 604 B. C., traditionally is credited with writing a collection of evocative sayings known as the *Tao Te Ching*, although it probably was written in the mid-3rd century B. C., several centuries after his supposed lifetime. He was associated with founding Taoism and his influence was important to Zen Buddhism. He may have been librarian to the Chou court and met his younger contemporary, Confucius. Witter Bynner, translator, *The Way of Life According to Lao Tzu*, 1944, Capricorn Books Edition, 1962.

123. AC to Ray L. Morrison, Librarian, Pittsburg State University, Pittsburg, Kansas, June 4, 1981, AC Papers.

The biography by Louis Fischer, *The Life of Mahatma Gandhi* (1950), was the basis for a film.

124. AC to Marshall Field IV, October 30, 1946, AC Papers..

Truman successfully advocated a change in the line of succession after vice president to Speaker of the House rather than to a cabinet member (Secretary of State), which Truman disliked because it was not an elected post. Robinson, *Noble Conspirator*, 186, and note 6, 311.

William F. Knowland (1908-74), publisher and editor of the *Oakland Tribune* whose father had been in the U. S. Congress (1904-06), was appointed in 1945 to complete Hiram Johnson's term. Knowland was reelected until 1958, serving as both majority and minority leader of the Senate. He was known for his conservative, anti-U. N., anti-Communist-China views. Defeated for governor in 1958, he quit politics. For internal Republican Party disputes, see Chapter 6 and note 81.

Joseph W. Martin, Jr. (1884-1968), Republican of Massachusetts, served in the House 1925-67; he was Speaker 1947-49, 1952-55. He was preceded and succeeded by Texas Democrat Sam Rayburn (1882-1961).

125. AC to "Dear Lee," October 31, 1946, AC Papers.

Alan Lomax died July, 2002.

Chapter 5 World Government and Red-baiting

1. AC interview with author.

2. AC to "Dear Grenny" [G. Clark], February 21, 1947, from "Somewhere in Tennessee," AC Papers.

3. AC to Marjorie Eaton, West Los Angeles, February 7, 1947, referring to paying "first and last month's rent and water – a total of $210.00 for February of '47 and January '48"; AC to Ralph and Jean Raymond, Glenwood Springs, Colorado, July 26, 1947; AC to M. J. Hubbell, Washington, D. C., August 7, 1947, citing address for rental house as Route 2, Box 902 B, Los Altos, Ca., AC Papers.

4. AC to "Dear Grenny", February 21, May 9, 1947, and August 2, 1947; AC to Raymonds, July 26, 1947; AC to Falk, August 7, 1947, AC Papers.

5. AC to Falk, August 7, 1947, AC Papers.

6. AC to Raymonds , July 26, 1947, AC Papers.

7. *Ibid.*; AC to Falk, August 7, 1947; AC to "Dear Grenny," May 9, 1947, AC Papers.

8. Fowle, 83; AC to Raymonds, July 26, 1947; Michael Barone, "Alan Cranston: Daring and Caution," profile of Democratic presidential candidates, *Washington Post*, September 15, 1983.

Cranston's business card read, "The Cranston Co., 533 Ramona St., Palo Alto, Branch Office - Menlo Park," AC Papers.

9. Fowle, 83; The Cranston Co., advertisements in *Palo Alto Times*, April 10, February 7, and May 23, 1948, AC Personal Papers.

Eleanor Fowle recollected that Cranston's bargain-priced housing may have been built by developer Joseph Eichler (1900-74) but she could not remember if they were racially-integrated projects. REC interview with author, March 28, 2003. Eichler began building in the area in 1947 using various names based on partnerships and without using architects.

Buyer's contracts as late as 1950 forbade re-sale to minorities (Blacks and Asians specifically). Marty Arbunich, Eichler Network, to author, February 4, 2011. The Cranston Co. also sold, under franchise, Century Homes, as of December 4, 1948; the company had offices in Palo Alto and San Jose.

10. AC to May [McMath], October 19, 1948; McMath to AC, October 10, 1948, and December 3, 1949, saying, "I surely appreciate what you are doing for me and want to thank you.... I feel that this money you are making for me I may never use and it will go to my two girls but that gives me a happy feeling...," AC Papers.

At least two of the rental-investment homes were built with Federal Housing Administration (FHA) loans, per McMath to AC, February 28, 1949, and AC to McMath, August 25, 1949, AC Papers.

11. Fowle, 83; Tuck Shepherd, "Biography traces Cranston's colorful career," Los Altos *Town Crier*, July 30, 1980; AC to Marjorie Eaton, January 17, 1948, citing renewal of lease with provision to end it if the Cranstons bought land and built on it in 1948; AC to May [McMath], October 19, 1948, AC Papers.

12. Hal McKelvig to W. Byron Bryant, December 23, 1948; Charles Fl. Bulotti, Jr., secretary, Bohemian Club, to Darwin L. Teilbet, Los Altos, CA., November 29, 1951, AC Papers.

Cranston submitted information with his application citing his co-authorship of the play with Lee Falk, his book and free-lance writing as well as "numerous skits and sketches for use by United World Federalists," while on the national executive committee and Northern California Chairman. "Supplement to application for membership, Bohemian Club," [circa 1951], AC Papers.

13. Fowle, 84; AC statement before California Senate Judiciary Committee, June 27, 1949, citing national officers of U. W. F.; Vance Johnson, "World government, delegates from six groups meet to plan drive for popular support, Washington correspondent, *The Chronicle*, no date, citing meeting at Asheville, N. C., February 21, [1947?]; U. W. F., Inc., "Beliefs, purposes and policies, revised November 1-2, 1947; AC to "Dear Grenny" [G. Clark], February 21, 1947, AC Papers; Fowle text for *One World (Maybe None)*, AC Personal Papers.

Cord Meyer, Jr. (1920-2001) was the son of a diplomat and real-estate developer. He lost his left eye in a grenade attack as platoon leader at the Battle of Guam (his twin brother was killed at Okinawa). His war dispatches ran in *The Atlantic Monthly*. He would be the first national president of U. W. F. After 1949 he worked for the CIA, joining it in 1951, working with James Jesus Angelton, counter-intelligence chief (1954). Meyer came under attack by the FBI, which claimed he was a security risk for having been on a podium with a "notorious leftist," which the CIA dismissed. Meyer became head of Covert Action from 1962 and held other CIA posts including station chief in London; he was a strong anti-Communist. He wrote *Peace or Anarchy* (Little, Brown, 1948); *The Search for Security* (World Government House, 1947); *Facing Reality: From World Federalism to the CIA* (University Press of America, reprint, 1982). Harris Wofford characterized Meyer as "brilliant, a wonderful writer," whose statement in *Peace or Anarchy* Wofford remembered: "*If this hope is naïve, then it is naïve to hope*." He believed that AC had "strong disagreements with Cord." Wofford interview with author, May 4, 2011.

Other U. W. F. national officers were: W. T. Holliday, president, Standard Oil of Ohio; Harry A. Bullis, chairman of the board, General Mills; Duncan M. Spencer, chairman, Fiduciary Trust Co., New York; James B. Carey, secretary-treasurer, C. I. O.; the Reverend Edward A. Conway, Society of Jesuits, editor of *America*. Wofford pointed out that after the atomic bomb, "everyone was interested in world peace; the movement had a lot of support" from corporation heads and members of the "establishment," including the father of U. S. Senator John Heinz of the food company, whom Wofford would succeed after Heinz' tragic death in a plane crash. Wofford interview with author.

The six organizations forming U. W. F. were: Americans United for World Government; World Federalists; Student Federalists; World Republic, Inc., Committee; Massachusetts Committee for World Federation; and World Citizens' Committee of Georgia. U. W. F. later was renamed World Federalists U. S. A. C. Brooks Peters, *New York Times*, February 23, 1947, AC Papers. The cartoon booklet was illustrated by Warren Goodrich.

14. AC to "Dear Grenny," May 9, 1947.

15. Fowle, 84; Booker T. Easley, assistant secretary, "The Seekers," California Department of Corrections, San Quentin Prison, to AC, September 17, 1947, AC Papers.

16. AC to "Dear Grenny," February 21, 1947.

17. AC handwritten notes, "There are those who say…," AC Papers.

18. *Ibid.*

19. AC notes, "4,000 treaties and alliances…," quoting Isocrates, in Federalists materials, AC Papers.

20. *Ibid.*

21. "Demosthenes to Athenians, 315 B. C.," typed on small paper, in Federalists materials, AC Papers.

22. AC handwritten notes, "There are those who say…," AC Papers.

23. U. W. F., *Inside the Straw-man…*, AC Papers.

24. "A globalist glossary…," with AC note, "Sp[eech?] material," AC Papers.

25. "Opening radio announcement, (After Dawn's Early Light), Section III, The Causes of War - European," radio broadcast transcript, no date, with AC handwritten notations, AC "Souvenirs, 1930s-40s," AC Personal Papers.

26. AC to Raymonds, July 26, 1947.

27. Ralph Raymond to AC, June 10, 1947, and December 16, [1947?], AC Papers.

28. AC to "Dear Grenny," May 9, 1947; AC to Senator Glen H. Taylor, June 29, 1947; Taylor, telegram, to AC, July 8, 1947, AC Papers.

Glen H. Taylor (1904-84), Democrat of Idaho, served in the Senate 1945-51. He was considered the second most liberal member of Congress after Sen. Wayne Morse (1900-74) of Oregon, Republican (1945-52), Independent (1952-55), Democrat (1955-69). See also note 46. Taylor was an early advocate of racial integration.

29. AC to Mayor Roger D. Lapham, San Francisco, May 6, 1947, AC Papers.

30. AC to "Dear Grenny," May 9, 1947, AC Papers.

31. AC to "Dear Grenny," August 2, 1947.

32. "U. N. veto is attacked by Federalists," *San Francisco Chronicle*, September 11, 1947, AC Papers.

Only the Big Five nations of eleven Security Council members had veto power

33. "World peace - which road to achieve it?" *San Francisco News*, October 25, 1947, with photograph of AC on panel for broadcast by KPO; Willard Edwards, "New globalist leader comes to fore in U. S., he's Alan Cranston, late of the O. W. I.," *Chicago Daily Tribune*, November 7, 1949, AC Papers.

Easton Rothwell, vice chairman of the Hoover Library at Stanford University, was another member of the panel. Usborne twenty-four years later would write Cranston, "I don't notice any progress toward world government, do you?" Usborne to AC, postcard, January 2, 1971, Carton 129, AC Papers.

34. AC to "Dear Grenny," October 9, 1947, AC Papers.

35. *Ibid.*

36. AC, telegram to Mrs. John Fowle, St. Louis, November 1, 1947; R. E., Louisa, Mary, Tom, to Mr. and Mrs. Alan Cranston, telegram, November 3, 1947; newspaper front pages for November 1, 1947; "Births, at Palo Alto Hospital, Nov. 1, 1947," *Palo Alto Times*, November 3, and "The Alan Cranstons are parents of a son," November 4, 1947, AC Papers.

37. Kyle Chracipion to "R. M.," *Collier's* letterhead, January 5, 1948, AC Papers.

The letter was signed "Y'r uncle Kyle."

38. AC to Marjorie Eaton, June 10, 1948; May McMath to AC, December 3, 1949, Carton 617, AC Papers.

39. "World law - or world war?" invitation to Cord Meyer's talks (April 11-14), S. F. Bay Area, April 3, 1938; book promotion for *Peace or Anarchy*, by Cord Meyer, Jr., Little, Brown & Co., AC Papers; The Cranston Co., advertisement in *Palo Alto Times*, April 10, 1948.

40. AC to Harris L. Wofford, Jr., University of Chicago, January 30, 1948; "Atom 'bomb' to 'blast' city tomorrow," *Palo Alto Times*, February 18, 1948, AC Papers.

41. Herb Caen, "It's news to me," *San Francisco Chronicle*, January 13, 1949; "About United World Federalists," editorial, *Chronicle*, March 2, 1949; AC, "What can we do about world peace?" Palo Alto *Mail-Dispatch*, January 15, 1948, and "United World Federalists say…," *Mail-Dispatch*, April 15, 1948; "Sobering thought to all of us," editorial, *San Jose Mercury Herald*, January 18, 1949, AC Papers.

42. "Under the oak," Los Altos *Town Crier*, January 19, 1949, AC Papers.

43. "Candidates back U. W. F.; Los Altans pledge $8,000," unidentified news clipping, no date [1948?]; Robert C. Kirkwood to AC, April 23, 1948; AC to Kirkwood, April 27, 1948, and August 9, 1949, stating, "It was wonderful to have someone on the floor of the Assembly who understood the Federalists' program as thoroughly as you do," AC Papers.

44. AC to Robert J. Walker, chairman, U. W.F., Berkeley, California, June 3, 1948, and *Oakland Tribune* published letter to "Tribune Forum" from Mrs. Richard C. Bradley, Berkeley, May 28, 1948, AC Papers.

45. AC to Jesse H. Steinhart and Ben Swig, June 10, 1948, AC Papers.

Two Steinhart brothers, Ignatz (1840-1917) and Sigmund, were principal benefactors to the Steinhart Aquarium, opened in 1923 at the California Academy of Sciences. Jesse Henry Steinhart (1881-1966) was a member of the Academy in 1948. Academy archivist to author, October 26, 2004.

46. *Town Meeting*, Bulletin of America's Town Meeting of the Air, Vol. 14, No. 14, July 27, 1948, 6-7, AC Personal Papers.

Sen. Morse (1900-74) was a Republican (1945-52) at the time; he became Independent with Eisenhower's election (1952-55), and a Democrat (1955-69).

47. *Ibid.*, 21.

Cranston pointed out that Britain's House of Commons had a committee working for world government; France and Italy had written into their constitutions clauses authorizing them to enter world government, and Belgium and India supported it. *Ibid*, 19.

48. AC, "Suppose the United Nations ran (Los Altos)," typescript, no date, AC Papers.

The U. N. was composed of three branches: a World Court, Assembly and Security Council.

49. AC to Wofford, January 30, 1948, AC Papers.

Harris L. Wofford, Jr. (born 1926), inspired by Clarence Streit's advocacy of world government, founded Student Federalists while in high school and was active in forming chapters in college, saying that "almost every major campus formed a committee." He received a B. A. from the University of Chicago, and was the first White man to graduate from Howard University Law School; he also received a law degree from Yale University. He served in the Army Air Force during World War II. In 1949 he and his wife Clare had a fellowship to India and China, and co-authored *India Afire* (N.Y.: J. Day Co., 1951). He began a public-service career as attorney for the U. S. Commission on Civil Rights (1954-58). In 1960 he was an adviser to John F. Kennedy's presidential campaign and was instrumental in creating the Peace Corps in the Kennedy administration (associate director 1962-66). His book *Of Kennedys and Kings: Making Sense of the Sixties* (N.Y.: Farrar, Straus, Giroux, 1980) described his civil-rights and government experiences. He was president of State University of New York (Old Westbury) 1966-68, and Bryn Mawr College 1970-78. In 1991 he was appointed Democratic U. S. Senator from Pennsylvania to fill the unexpired term of

Republican John Heinz who was killed in a plane crash; Wofford, in a surprise upset over Republican Attorney General and former governor Richard Thornburgh, won election for the seat that November, and served until 1995. He subsequently focused on national and community service (C. E. O., Corp. for National and Community Service, 1995-2001). See also notes 185, 188; Chapter 13, note 198, for AC's recommending Wofford as Clinton's vice-presidential candidate; Chapter 14, note 8.

50. William Cranston, Villa Warec, to George Lievre, June 27, 1948, AC Papers.

Lievre sent the letter to Cranston in 1964, writing, "Too bad he isn't here to see you advance up the ladder. He surely would be proud." George Lievre to AC, [February, 1964], AC Papers.

51. AC, "Voter 'forgotten man' in convention deals," Palo Alto *Mail-Dispatch*, June 24, 1948, AC Papers.

52. AC, "World affairs," Palo Alto *Mail-Dispatch*, August 19, 1948, AC Papers.

Cranston had lobbied at Lake Success in 1946 for approval of a resolution by the American delegation that would have extended authority of the U. N. to world government; it was defeated "but got a good deal of support," Cranston told U. W. F. in 1949. AC to Dorothy A. Stout, publicity director, U. W. F., April 11, 1949, AC Papers.

53. *Ibid.*; Harris Wofford interview author, May 4, 2011; Waller, chief of mission, U. N. N. R. A., "Enroute from Minsk to Odessa, USSR," to AC, February 16, 1947; AC to Waller, March 13 and September 15, 1947, and January 12, 1948; Waller to AC, March 31, 1948, AC Papers.

Waller worked as Washington representative for U. W. F. for several years beginning in 1948.

54. Cord Meyer, Jr., to G. Clark, March 23, 1948, AC Papers.

Forrestal (1892-1949), a naval aviator in World War I, was Secretary of the Navy 1944-47 and the first Secretary of Defense 1947-49 after reorganization of the War and Navy Departments. Illness forced his resignation and he later committed suicide.

55. "Memo to Cord Meyer, Jr., as to procedure…in connection with possible petition to the President and Congress," April 2, 1948; Clark to AC, April 14, 1948, AC Papers.

George C. Marshall (1880-1959) was Secretary of State 1947-49 and Defense 1950-51. Robert A. Lovett (1895-1986) was Under-Secretary of State 1947-49, and Secretary of Defense 1951-53. James V. Forrestal (1892-1949) was Secretary of Defense 1947-49. Admiral William D. Leahy (1875-1959) was Chief of Staff to the Commander-in-Chief for the Army & Navy 1942-49. General Walter Bedell Smith was U. S. Ambassador to the Soviet Union 1946-48; 4th Director of Central Intelligence 1950-53. Truman Library.

56. AC to Clark, May 19, 1948, AC Papers.

57. Clark, Memo re: "Citizens Committee to explore…," Dublin, N. H., August 5, 1948; AC to "Grenny," November 1, 1948, AC Papers.

58. Richard B. Johnson, Berkeley, Ca., to AC, December 7, 1948, AC Papers.

Cranston had to contend with interests in California who wanted a statewide, rather than autonomous northern and southern U. W. F. organizations (he favored the latter, which was instituted). Another intercine debate was whether the U. W. F. should hold a People's Convention on world government that British U. W. F. leader Usborne advocated. AC to Max Thelen, San Francisco, September 27, 1948; AC, memo to members of administrative committee, U. W. F. of Northern California, and to Charles G. Bolte, Rhodes House, Oxford, England, October 20, 1948, AC Papers.

59. AC to Bolte, October 20, 1948; "Chuck" Bolte to AC, October 27, 1948; AC to Waller, Foreign Affairs Research Council, November 1, 1948, AC Papers.

Charles G. Bolte (1920-94) joined the British Army before Pearl Harbor and was injured in North Africa. He founded the American Veterans Committee in 1943, and worked as an adviser to the United States U. N. Mission. He joined Viking Press as executive vice president in the early 1950s; was a director of the American Civil Liberties Union and vice president (beginning 1966) of the Carnegie Endowment for International Peace. He authored several books, including *The Price of Peace: A Plan for Disarmament* (1956). *New York Times*, obituary, March 9, 1994.

60. AC to Waller, November 1, 1948.

The U. W. F. letterhead read, "For world government with limited powers adequate to prevent war." The controversy over the convention was complicated by Usborne's having received a large grant from a Blaine Foundation, to which Cranston referred when discussing "retreating" because of communist charges, writing, "I do not see that the Blaine Foundation relationship to World Government movement is potentially more dangerous to us than the Progressive Party relationship to the...movement, as evinced in the Progressive Party's platform adopted at Philadelphia."

61. Waller to AC, November 19, 1948; AC to Waller, November 20, 1948, AC Papers.

62. AC to "Grenny," November 27, 1948, AC Papers.

63. *Ibid.*; and AC to Cord Meyer, November 30, 1948, AC Papers.

Article V respecting amendments to the Constitution requires Congress to call a Convention to consider amendments if: two thirds of both Houses propose amendments; or two thirds of state legislatures request a Convention. Amendments must be ratified by three fourths of the states.

64. AC to Waller, "confidential," January 5, 1949, AC Papers.

65. Waller to AC, January 27, 1949, AC Papers.

Roosevelt was Congressman from California 1955-65.

66. AC to "Grenny," March 20, 1949, AC Papers.

67. Fowle, 84-85; AC interview with author.

Artie Samish (1897-1974) operated as a lobbyist in Sacramento from the 1920s to '50s. Known for his expensive dinners and lavish parties, he funneled political contributions to legislators who in the 1950s were paid only $100 a month. He was close to San Francisco Republican Assemblyman Thomas A. Maloney (who served eight years in the Senate, 24 in the Assembly), who sponsored the U. W. F. resolution and helped steer it through the legislature. Hollywood columnist Jimmie Tarantino called Samish the "most powerful, most influential, most attacked, most talked about, and most smeared person in the annals of California politics." He was convicted of income tax violations in 1953 and in 1955 began a 26-month prison sentence. A "good-government" faction led by San Francisco Assemblyman Casper "Cap" Weinberger subsequently arose in the legislature. Fowle wrote that Cranston, on first meeting Samish, appealed to him to help kill legislation that was unfair to minorities (the bill was killed). Judith Robinson, *"You're in Your Mother's Arms" - The Life & Legacy of Congressman Phil Burton* (San Francisco: Telegraph Hill Press, 1994), 116; Richard Harmon, "Artie secret boss? True, says Cramer," [*The Journal*], August 15, 1949, and Jimmie Tarantino, "The Artie Samish smear," *Hollywood Life*, October 12, 1951, 2, copies in AC Papers. See also note 165.

68. Waller to AC, "Personal and confidential," August 9, 1949, AC Papers.

69. "Assembly unanimously for World Federalist resolution," *San Francisco Chronicle*, March 25, 1949; "World Federation advanced by California legislative victory," and "Opponents fail to reverse passage Assem. Joint Res. 26," *United World Federalist*, Berkeley, California, Vol. 2, No. 11, April, 1949, 1, 3; AC to Waller, April 11, 1949; Waller to AC, April 18, 1949, AC Papers.

Joint Resolution 26 requested Congress and President Truman to call a Constitutional Convention for the "sole purpose of proposing an amendment to the Constitution to expedite and insure the participation of the United States in a World Federal Government, open to all nations." The motion to reconsider lost 22-13. Nineteen other states were considering similar resolutions which faced stiff opposition in some states.

70. Fowle, 84-85; AC to "Grenny," May 1, 1949, AC Papers.

71. AC to "Grenny," March 20, 1949, AC Papers.

72. *Ibid.*

Donnelly considered the resolution as "fostering…an un-American activity – whether the authors realize it or not." "Opponents fail…," *United World Federalist*, April, 1949.

73. *Ibid.*

74. The legislative fight continued, however, when Donnelly introduced a resolution to rescind the one that was approved, and on June 21, 1949, tried to hold the Senate in session through the night in an effort to bring it to a vote. Powers led the fight to thwart that; a subsequent Judiciary Committee vote tabled the Donnelly resolution. "World govt. forces defeat efforts to repeal AJR [Assembly Joint Resolution] 26," *United World Federalist*, Berkeley, Ca., August, 1949, AC Papers.

75. Senator Thomas F. Keating, Marin County, to AC, July 13, 1949, referring to testimony before the Senate Judiciary Committee, per previous note, AC Papers.

Keating was not related to real-estate mogul Charles Keating.

76. U. W. F. release, "A new drive for the development…of the United Nations into a World Federation…," April 7, 1949; "California in one world," editorial, *Chicago Tribune*, April 12, 1949, transcription in AC Papers.

Robert McCormick's (1880-1955) brother Joseph Medill McCormick (1877-1925) had been a strong opponent of the League of Nations while in the U. S. Senate (1919-25).

77. AC, "Safety Valve," *San Francisco Chronicle*, May 10, 1949, AC Papers.

The Atlantic Charter, 1941, which called for disarmament of aggressor nations, was contained in the United Nations declaration of January 1, 1942, to which Atlantic Charter signers agreed. The North Atlantic Treaty Organization (NATO), established under treaty signed April 4, 1949, was made up of northern European and North American nations plus Greece and Turkey (joined 1952) and West Germany (joined 1955).

78. AC to Clark, June 16, 1949, AC Papers.

79. "The great illusion," editorial, *Chicago Daily Tribune*, June 18, 1949.

80. AC interview with author; Fowle, 88.

81. AC to Norman Cousins, Editor, *Saturday Review of Literature*, April 11, 1949, AC Papers.

82. "World rule held way to cut taxes by 80%," *San Francisco Chronicle*, August 3, 1949.

83. Richard Bergholz, "Cranston prepares to meet an old attack," *Los Angeles Times*, May 1, 1983, AC Papers.

84. Mimi [Hubbell?] to "Dear Nookie and Crannie," November 11, 1947, AC "Souvenirs, 1930s-40s," AC Personal Papers.

The writer and her husband, a radio broadcaster, shared friends in labor unions with AC.

85. Spiro to AC, no date, Carton 617, AC Papers.

86. AC statement before California Senate Judiciary Committee, Sacramento, June 27, 1949, AC Papers.

87. AC to author.

88. AC statement before California Senate Judiciary Committee, June 27, 1949, citing Truman message to U. W. F. on October 2, 1948, and Taft letter to U. W. F. January 21, 1949, AC Papers.

89. *Ibid.*

90. AC to Senators Luther E. Gibson and H. R. Judah, July 11, 1949, and Judah to AC, July 25, 1949, AC Papers.

91. AC to Judah, August 2, 1949, AC Papers.

92. AC to editor, *San Jose Mercury Herald*, June 29, 1949, citing letter to editor from Martha A. Hadley, Palo Alto, June 15, 1949, AC Papers.

93. Waller to AC, April 29, 1949, AC Papers.

94. AC to Waller, May 8, 1949, AC Papers.

95. Waller to AC, May 20, 1949, AC Papers.

The rivalry between U. W. F. and other groups centered on whether to exclude communist nations in world federation. Differing resolutions were introduced in Congress in 1949, one backed by the World Federalists to strengthen the U. N., and one (introduced by Sen. Kefauver) backed by Clarence Streit, Justice Owen J. Roberts and those allied with the American Unity group and Atlantic Union Committee. They supported the North Atlantic Pact of only democratic nations, designed to militarily overpower the communist bloc and Soviet Union. U. W. F. argued that such a pact would polarize the world into two armed camps because 1) it limited participation to only powerful nations, and 2) abrogated attempts to assure peace through the United Nations' regulating disarmament. "The Atlantic Union plan promises only a permanent arms race which in all probability would end in World War III," a U. W. F. policy stated. That plan excluded nations like Greece, Turkey, Latin American, Near Eastern, African and Asian countries, and some in the British Commonwealth. "Communists would make capital" of such an exclusionary attitude, U. W. F. believed. "A resolution to seek development of the United Nations into a World Federation," and "Group formed to promote union free from Atlantic Pact," *United World Federalist*, Berkeley, Ca., Vol. 2, No. 11, April, 1949, 3, AC Papers.

96. Waller to AC, June 21 and 28, 1949; AC to Waller, June 23 and 24, 1949, AC Papers.

97. Fowle, 87.

98. "Pros and cons of U. W. F. Presidency as seen by Father," handwritten, AC Personal Papers.

His father also urged that Cranston at least insist on being paid as much as his predecessor. Cranston cited his U. W. F. salary as president as starting at $10,000. Application for Federal Employment to Peace Corps, AC Papers; Fowle, 87.

99. AC to "Grenny," May 25, 1949, AC Papers.

100. Waller to AC, June 28, 1949, AC Papers.

101. Waller, memo to National Executive Council and National Advisory Board, U. W. F., July 27, 1949, and Waller to AC, August 2, 1949; "The fundamental objective," editorial, *New York Herald Tribune*, June 9, 1949; "World Federation," editorial, *San Diego Union*, June 20, 1949, AC Papers. See also note 95.

Principal congressional sponsors of the U. W. F. resolution were Democratic Senator Claude Pepper (Florida) and Republican Senator Charles W. Tobey (New Hampshire). Some members signed onto both resolutions. Sponsors of the Atlantic Union Committee resolution included: Democratic Senators Estes Kefauver (Tennessee), J. William Fulbright (Arkansas), Walter F. George (Georgia), Lister Hill and John J. Sparkman (Alabama); Representatives Hale Boggs (Louisiana), George A. Smathers (Florida); Republican Senators Joseph R. McCarthy (Wisconsin), Edward J. Thye (Minnesota), and Representatives Walter H. Judd (Minnesota), James W. Wadsworth (New York). "A resolution to seek development of the United Nations into a World Federation" U. W. F.; Harold B. Hinton, "Truman urged to call parley to form Atlantic federation," *New York Times*, July 26, 1949, AC Papers.

102. Rep. Walter H. Judd, telegram to Waller, June 10, 1949; "U. N. and world government," editorial, *Christian Science Monitor*, June 11, 1949, AC Papers.

Judd was referring to an advertisement for a U. W. F. rally at Madison Square Garden in support of its resolution. Judd and Brooks Hays, Democrat of Arkansas, "Dear Colleague" letter, June 2, 1949, AC Papers.

103. AC to Sen. Kefauver, January 19, 1949, AC Papers.

104. Harold B. Hinton, "Truman urged to call parley to form Atlantic federation," *New York Times*, July 26, 1949.

A third resolution was introduced by Sen. John Sparkman, Democrat of Alabama, giving the U. N. power to establish an atomic arms security force, by-passing the veto permitted in the charter; it was touted by bridge-card-game champion Ely Culbertson.

105. AC to Rep. Helen Gahagan Douglas, January 19, 1949, AC Papers; Fowle, 89.

Douglas served two terms in the House but would be defeated in the 1950 Senate race by Richard Nixon.

106. Fowle, 88.

The firm subsequently was sold to James Hawley.

107. Norman Cousins to "Alan," handwritten note, no date, AC Personal Papers.

108. "Social Progress, state of the world," *Fortnight, The Newsmagazine of California*, August 5, 1949, 12; "Alan Cranston heads World Federalists," *Stanford Alumni Review*, October 1, 1949, 5-6.

Cranston also served on U. W. F. National Executive Council which included Connecticut Governor Chester Bowles, Canfield and Cousins.

109. Bennett Skewes-Cox, "Alan Cranston," *World Government News*, August, 1949, 11-14, AC Papers.

110. *Ibid.*; and *Current Biography*, February, 1950, 16, citing *World Government News*, August, 1949. The *Current Biography* profile filled two pages.

111. Skewes-Cox, "Alan Cranston."

112. "Cranston thinks U. S. will accept limited world government by '55," *Daily Palo Alto Times*, August 25, 1949.

113. *Ibid.*; "Information from the files of the Committee on Un-American Activities, U. S. House of Representatives, [1950], United World Federalists, Inc."; AC to William H. Wells, Executive Director, U. W. F., Inc., New York, August 25, 1949, AC Papers.

114. AC to Wells, *ibid.*; Fowle, 88; Supplemental Sheet for Standard Form 57, Application for Federal Employment, citing AC address for 1949-51, and Mildred Schroeder, "The unusual is the typical in the Cranston Family - California's leading ladies," profiles of wives of state constitutional officers, *San Francisco Examiner*, December 14, 1958, AC Papers.

115. "Un-American Activities in California," 11th Report of Senate Fact-finding Subcommittee on Un-American Activities to the 1961 regular California Legislature, Sacramento, 1961, 198-200; "[Stanley A.] Weigel [chairman, California Federalists] reveals withdrawal by Fagan of suit for slander," *Los Angeles Times*[?], July 18, 1950, AC Papers.

See also "Information from the files of the Committee on Un-American Activities, U. S. House of Representatives, [1950], United World Federalists, Inc.", citing AC, Cousins, Walter P. Reuther, Mrs. J. Borden Harriman, Ray Swing, Carl Van Doren, AC Papers.

116. *Ibid.*

117. "Communists control U. W. F., declares Fagan," *Daily Palo Alto Times*, September 22, 1949.

18. "Federalist leader denies Red domination," *Daily Palo Alto Times*, September 22, 1949.

119. AC to Harry Braverman, August 31, 1949, AC Papers.

Rep. Donald L. Jackson represented Santa Monica, 1947-61.

120. Richard Nixon, Member of Congress, to Edward S. Shattuck, chairman, Republican State Central Committee, Los Angeles, August 17, 1949, AC Papers.

121. AC testimony as president of U. W. F. before House Committee on Foreign Affairs on House Concurrent Resolution 64, October 12, 1949, AC Papers.

122. *Ibid.*

123. *Ibid.*; "House group hears world union plans," *New York Times*, December 14, 1949, AC Papers.

124. Willard Edwards, "New globalist leader comes to fore in U. S., he's Alan Cranston, late of the OWI," *Chicago Daily Tribune*, November 7, 1949.

125. "Extinction of America," editorial, *Washington Times Herald*, November 9, 1949.

126. "Alan Cranston, president of the United World Federalists, and Albert Einstein combined to draw a large crowd to Alexander Hall…," *Princeton Alumni Weekly*, November

24, 1950, 11; AC note, "Einstein doodling"; "World government debated by Alan Cranston and Elmer Davis," *New Republic*, May 22, 1950; "We Can Save the Peace," *Future, the Magazine for Young Men*, December, 1949; AC, "One World or None," from unidentified publication, copies in AC Papers.

127. Photo caption, "January, 1950, a panel discussion on world government is featured at the first meeting of the year for the Los Altos Chapter of the United World Federalists…," *Town Crier & Foothill Focus*, November 7, 1957, AC Papers; REC interview with author, March 28, 2003.

128. "Information from the files of the Committee on Un-American Activities, U. S. House of Representatives, [1950], United World Federalists, Inc.," 1-3, citing *The Worker*, March 19, 1950, AC Papers; Michael Doyle, "FBI file paints shadow portrait of Sen. Cranston," *Sacramento Bee*, August 26, 2003, citing AC testimony before House committee, 1952.

129. Peggy Dudley, U. W. F., to AC, January 4, 1950, AC Papers; United World Federalist manuscript papers, The Lilly Library, University of Indiana, identifying Dudley as possibly an employee of U. W. F.

130. "Statement by Alan Cranston re: allegations appearing in the *Chicago Tribune* on November 7, 1949," February 27, 1950, AC Papers.

131. "RE: Alleged FBI report," typescript with AC handwritten note, "RE: Kamp attack in '58," containing AC replies to questions about previous charges regarding O. W. I., etc.; "Eleventh Report – Un-American Activities in California, 1961," typed excerpts from pages 109 and 165, AC Papers. Also cited in 1959 report of State Senate Fact-Finding Committee on Un-American Activities, p. 145.

132. Joanne P. Sonnichsen, Menlo Park, California, to author, October 15, 2000.

133. "DAR and VFW are misled, World Federalist charges," *San Francisco Chronicle*, March 16, 1950; "World Federalist officers state position; organization bars Communists from membership," Lewiston-Auburn, Maine, *Evening Journal*, August 31, 1950, AC Papers.

134. AC to Jerry [Spingarn], November 28, 1951, AC Papers.

135. AC to Joseph Facci, C.R.E.F.A.L., Patzcuaro, Michoacan, Mexico, December 14, 1951, and February 15, 1952, AC Papers.

Centro Regional de Alfabetización Funcional en las Zonas Rurales de América Latino (C.R.E.F.A.L.) was a rural education and teacher-training community-outreach program started by UNESCO in 1951.

136. "Federalist chief says U. W. F. foes playing into hands of Communists," *Denver Post*, [1950]; "Joseph P. Kamp," no date, typescript account of contempt-of-Congress conviction, AC Papers.

137. "They hate Ike," *Time*, May 5, 1952, reprint in AC Papers.

138. "Stand Up and Be Counted!" handbill, March 29, 1950, signed by "Keep America Committee," Los Angeles, AC Papers.

139. "A handbill has been circulated in the Los Altos business district during the past few days which reflects upon the character of one of its citizens, Alan Cranston," April 6, 1950, quoting *Look* magazine article, "Joseph P. Kamp," April 11, 1950, citing Nazi World Service and Hitler News Agency, AC Papers.

140. William Cranston to AC, April 6, 1950, AC Papers.

William Cranston said that the handbill was circulated by an A. R. Fitzpatrick of Carmel and Paso Robles Avenues, Los Altos.

141. "Speaker warns of germ warfare," *San Diego Journal*, May 23, 1950; "Moving Boeing plant favored, *The Spokane Spokesman-Review*, June 7, 1950; "Federalist boss denies group linked to Reds," *Oklahoma Citizen*, August 9, 1950; "Offer better idea to beat Reds, advice of Cranston," Santa Barbara *News-Press*, October 25, 1950; AC, draft letter to Chairman George H. Mahon, Armed Services Subcommittee, December 12, 1950, AC Papers.

142. Ambassador Ernest A. Gross, Deputy Representative of the United States to the

United Nations, to AC, August 18, 1950, AC Papers.

143. William Cranston to AC, October 2, 1950; AC to Hon. Aldo M. Mazio, Italian Consul General, New York, February 15, 1951, re: award to AC of *Stella della Solidarieta Italiana*; photograph of AC receiving award, *Daily Palo Alto Times*, February 29, 1952, AC Papers.

144. "Federalists affirm aim," *New York Times*, October 15, 1950.

145. AC message, "Federalism at Christmas, 1950," AC Papers.

146. George Todt, "The people's choice," *Los Angeles Herald-Examiner*, August 15, 1962; "Red Print for U. S. Conquest," booklet accusing Cranston of Communist ties, page 18, [1962], AC Papers.

147. William Fulton, "U. S. globalists intensify fight on sovereignty," *Chicago Tribune* Press Service, January 15, 1951; "Peace Partisans scored," *New York Times*, March 30, 1951; "U. S. Federalists may quit world group over Reds," *New York Herald Tribune*, March 30, 1951; "World Federalists' leader defends MacArthur firing," *Rocky Mountain News*, April 13, 1951; Robert L. Davis, letter to editor, "Forum," cited by AC as "taken from a Palo Alto or Peninsula paper," no date, AC Papers.

148. REC interview with author, March 28, 2003; R. E. Fowle to AC and Geneva, July 13, 1951, AC Personal Papers.

149. "Truman strikes back at critics, pain in the neck," *Los Angeles Times*, June 8, [1951?], AC Papers.

Finletter, a New York attorney and adviser to the State Department, was known for his 1948 "Finletter report" from a commission that he headed which called for greater spending to create an Air force capable of meeting a possible atomic attack; he succeeded W. Stuart Symington as Air Force secretary.

150. Announcement, "The Myth that Threatens the World," February 18, 1951, AC Papers.

The show was performed in New York, San Francisco, Philadelphia, Chicago, Baltimore, Boston, Minneapolis and Detroit. Oscar Hammerstein II (1895-1960), whose musical hits included Pulitzer Prize winners *Oklahoma!* (1943) and *South Pacific* (1949), was a committed liberal, founding member of U. W. F., and wrote speeches for Adlai Stevenson. "Oscar Hammerstein II: Out of My Dreams," PBS documentary, March 6, 2012.

151. R. E. Fowle to AC, "Monday eve," [July, 1951], handwritten letter from Union Pacific Streamliner, with emphases underlined, AC Papers.

The Bible quote is: "They who live by the sword shall die by sword," Matthew 26:52.

152. AC to Mrs. John Fowle, Fairweather Inn, Virginia City, Montana, July 16, 1951, AC Papers.

The Bible quote is: "Eye for eye, tooth for tooth, hand for hand, foot for foot," Exodus 21:24; also in Matthew 5:38.

153. R. E. Fowle to AC, no date, AC Papers.

154. Waller to AC, "via airmail special delivery," August 20, 1951, AC Papers.

155. R. E. Fowle to AC and Geneva, July 13, 1951, AC Personal Papers.

The address of the house was 12370 Hilltop Drive, Los Altos.

156. Cord Meyer, Jr., to AC, September 17, 1951; AC to Peter Van Norden, May 5, 1955, AC Papers.

157. AC to Rex Stout, Writers Board for World Government, September 20, 1951, AC Papers.

158. Ada M. Field to AC, Guilford College, N. C., December 15, 1951; AC to Field, January 17, 1952, AC Papers.

159. Richard H. Parke, "Statistics cause world group rift - report shows Federalists in decline and evokes detailed denial," *New York Times*, September 21, 1951, typescript copy of article, AC Papers.

160. AC to Sen. Robert A. Taft, November 2, 1951, AC Papers.

161. AC to "Grenny," October 11, 1951; Cornelia Matijasevich, "The other half - Mrs.

Alan Cranston is serious about politics, homemaking," *Daily Palo Alto Times*, July 20, 1954; Schroeder, "The unusual is the typical…", AC Papers.

162. Birth certificate for Kim Christopher Cranston; "Second son born to Alan Cranstons," unidentified news article, AC Personal Papers.

163. Waller, assistant to the president, American Book Publishers Council, to AC, April 29, 1952, AC Papers.

164. President Truman to AC, February 11, 1952; AC 1952 renewal notice to U. W. F. members; "Cranston," typescript of AC remarks to audience in Michigan, no date, AC Papers.

165. AC to Sen. Kefauver, February 6, 1952, AC Papers; Cecilia Rasmussen, "Lobbyist's ego led to downfall, prison," *Los Angeles Times*, Feburary 3, 2008, re: Samish and Kefauver. See also note 67.

Estes Kefauver (1903-63), Democrat of Tennessee, Congressman 1939-49, U. S. Senator 1949-63, led investigations into organized crime in the 1950s as chairman of the Senate Special Committee to Investigate Crime in Interstate Commerce (the "Kefauver Committee"), televised live just as Americans began to acquire TVs. He also investigated corporate monopolies as chairman of the Senate Antitrust and Monopoly Subcommittee (1957-63), with emphasis on the pharmaceutical industry. His progressive stands against Democratic Party bosses in Tennessee prompted charges that Kefauver, likened to a stealthy raccoon, was pro-Communist. He countered by wearing a coonskin cap and gained popularity for integrity. He ran twice for president (1952, 1956). In the 1952 campaign he wore the coonskin cap and upset sitting President Truman in the New Hampshire primary. Although ahead in primary votes, he lost the party nomination to Illinois Governor Adlai Stevenson, who lost the election to Eisenhower. There were eight Democratic candidates in 1952, four of them favorite-son candidates (including Minnesota Democratic Senator Hubert H. Humphrey).

166. AC to "Dear Estes," May 18, 1952, AC Papers.

167. "Kefauver denies he backs World Federalists," *Tampa Morning Tribune*, May 5, 1952, AC Papers; Fowle, 88.

168. AC to Harold Matson and Don Congdon, memorandum and chapter outline of book, "Peace on Earth - How?", February 17, 1952, AC Papers.

169. Eleanor Roosevelt, "E. R. corrects a mistake," "My Day" column, circa May, 1952; acknowledgement for U. W. F. memberships, "We hope that you realize a keen, inner satisfaction over the investment you have just made in the cause of world government and a durable peace," no date; "Likely sponsors for world government advertisement"; Charles B. Edison, Edison Brothers Stores, Inc., St. Louis, to AC, February 20, 1952, AC Papers.

170. AC to Edison, March 6, 1952, AC Papers.

171. Randolph P. Compton, voluntary controller, memorandum to U. W. F. National Executive Council, March 15, 1952, AC Papers.

172. AC to Frank Church, Boise, Idaho, April 14, 1952; AC to Sen. Adlai Stevenson, May 2 and June 13, 1952, AC Papers; "Stevenson draft, p. 1," no date, AC Personal Papers.

In the letter to Church, AC said, "Geneva and I heard Senator Kefauver speak at a rally in San Francisco the other evening. I must say that we found much more to cheer about then than we did when we heard the esteemed Senator from Oklahoma," Robert S. Kerr (one of eight Democratic candidates in 1952).

173. AC to William C. Dickinson, U. W. F., Los Alamos, N. M., April 23, 1952, citing former Congressman and Secretary of State Cordell Hull's autobiography (1948); "Proposed plan on U. N. and disarmament for Democratic Party Platform," AC Papers.

174. Fowle, 89-90.

Waller ended as executive vice president of the Grolier Society, a bibliophiles' club in New York City.

175. Swing to R. E. [Fowle], April 25, 1952, AC Papers.

176. Cass Canfield, Chairman of the Board, Harper & Brothers, "Publishers since 1817,"

May 9, 1952, AC Papers.

177. Margaret Sanger to AC, June 2, 1952; AC to Sanger, June 11, 1952, AC Papers.

178. Norman Cousins to AC, June 24, 1952, AC Papers.

179. Andrew Crichton, editor, *The Federalist*, to AC, August 22, 1952; AC to Crichton, September 15, 1952, AC Papers.

180. Grenville Clark, telegram to Eisenhower, "On board campaign train, Huntington, West Virginia," [September 24?], 1952, AC Papers.

181. Kevin Starr, *Golden Dreams, California in an Age of Abundance 1950-1963* (N. Y.: Oxford University Press, 2009), 203-06.

182. "Cranston clarifies Mayer 'exoneration,'" AC letter to "Forum," Palo Alto *Times*, August 3, 1953, AC Papers.

A controversy ensued over misconstrued remarks by Professor Milton Mayer, University of Chicago, at a public meeting in Syracuse, N. Y., in 1947, in which he stated in jest that a world constitution like that advocated by U. W. F. and a number of leading intellectuals, including University of Chicago president Robert Maynard Hutchins and Stringfellow Barr, president of St. John's College, might cause some people to equate it with hauling down the American flag, stamping and spitting on it. A rebuttal to charges that he had suggested actually doing that, apparently sent to the American Friends Service Committee, stated: "My remarks… about the flag were intended to portray the most extreme and exaggerated way that anyone might misunderstand the real meaning of world law. I did not advocate disrespect for the flag. Obviously we are not going to haul it down. The unscrupulous use [that] opponents of world law have made of my remarks, however, indicate how right I was in believing that some would assert that world law means hauling it down." Undated typescript with handwritten address for American Friends Service Committee Institute, Pennsylvania, AC Papers; Fowle, 84-85.

183. U. W. F. memorandum, "Special Washington Report on Dulles Speech," August 31, 1953; AC to Dulles, September 3, 1953, with note, "(on 'Cranston of California' stationary)"; Dulles to AC, September 14, 1953, AC Papers.

184. AC to Robert van Gelder, editor, *New York Times Book Review*, February 5, 1946; copies of AC published reviews: "An Italian considers the future," *Italy and the Coming World* by Don Luigi Sturzo, *New York Times Book Review*, October 7, 1945; *Suitors and Suppliants: The Little Nations at Versailles* by [Colonel] Stephen Bonsal (New York: Prentice-Hall, Inc., 1946), *Political Science Quarterly*; "Checking on your Congressman," *Handbook of Politics* by Lowell Mellett, *New York Times Book Review*, August 3, 1947; "Paradise Unlimited," *Southern California Country* by Carey McWilliams, *New York Times Book Review*, April 7, 1946; "A voice of eloquence, a manner of grace," *The Politics of Honor* by Kenneth S. Davis, [Riverside, California] Sunday *Press-Enterprise Diversion*, March 3, 1968, AC Papers.

185. Typescript copies of reviews by AC: *It's Up to Us* by Harris Wofford, Jr.; *The Coming Crisis* by Fritz Sternberg; *World on My Doorstep* by Harriet Eager Davis, no dates, AC Papers; Wofford interview with author, May 4, 2011.

Wofford told the story of his "bathtub" enlightenment in his book. He had written it while in the Army Air Corps (1944-45) to which he volunteered after his eighteenth birthday, hoping to become a pilot. He was sent to basic training in Selma, Alabama, and wrote the book while awaiting assignment. Wofford marched in the 1965 Selma-to-Montgomery Civil Rights demonstration. Federal Union, parent organization of Student Federalists, disbanded soon after Hiroshima.

186. AC review of *The Coming Crisis* by Fritz Sternberg.

187. Richard Bergholz, "Cranston prepares to meet an old attack," *Los Angeles Times*, May 1, 1983; AC to the Rev. G. G. Grant, S. J., council chairman, World Association of World Federalists, July 30, 1981, and "Dear Federalist friend," fundraising letter; AC to Edward Labrum, July 26, 1984, AC Papers.

188. AC to Edward Labrum.

Cranston particularly cited Reagan's membership in the Federalists during debate over Reagan's military budgets while he was president (1980-88).

Harris Wofford when campaigning for the U. S. Senate in 1991 also was confronted with innuendoes from opponent Richard Thornburgh, implying that association with Federalists branded Wofford a left-wing liberal. Wofford's campaign manager James Carville "at first was alarmed that there would be growing damage. But the next thing we knew, letters to the editor of the Pittsburg newspaper were saying, 'The Federalists was not a super-liberal organization. Our first [Pennsylvania] chapter was headed by [the late Sen. John] Heinz' father,'" of the food corporation. Wofford interview with author, May 4, 2011.

The World Federalist Movement remained active as of 2011, involving a number of organizations internationally. U. W. F. continued to advocate changes in the U. N. Charter, and by the 1960s had offices near the United Nations. As of 2011, the Movement claimed 30,000 to 50,000 supporters. U. W. F. in 1969 changed its name to World Federalists U. S. A., which evolved into Citizens for Global Solutions in 2003. The World Federalist Association of Northern California in 2004 split off into an independent organization, Democratic World Federalists, part of an 18-member Coalition for Democratic World Government. The Democratic World Federalists website cited Cranston's role as national president and the California chapter's work convincing the State Legislature to pass the world-government resolution. Democratic World Federalists website (http://dwfed.org), 2011.

189. Robert A. Bernstein to AC, June 12, 1990, with bylined article, "Cranston predicts Democratic upswing in '54 election contests," [1953], AC Personal Papers.

Chapter 6 "*'Politician' - a term of honor, not of scorn - the noblest of man's works*"

1. AC Application for Federal Employment, for position to evaluate Peace Corps in a foreign country, [1961-2?], and Supplemental Sheet for Standard Form 57, AC Papers; "Cranstons will put up 3-storey edifice on Main," Los Altos *News*, September 5, 1952, AC Personal Papers; AC to Frank C. Galli, owner of adjacent building, May 16, 1953, AC Papers.

Cranston listed as references on federal employment applications Vice President Hubert H. Humphrey, Governor Edmund G. Brown, and California Congressman John M. Moss; on a federal Security Investigation Data for Sensitive Position form, he cited his acquaintanceship with each respectively as 17, 15 and 12 years.

2. William Cranston to Mrs. Edgar McMath, and AC to May [McMath], June 14, 1953, AC Papers.

3. "$315,000 project," caption to map outlining proposed Los Altos assessment district, *Daily Palo Alto Times*, October 28, 1954, AC Papers.

4. AC to Mr. and Mrs. Earl C. Berger, April 22, 1955; "Parking plan for Los Altos being revived," no date, and "Expanded parking district move launched in Los Altos," *Daily Palo Alto Times*, May 14, 1955; "Los Altos parking plaza project approved, opponents found to be in minority," *Daily Palo Alto Times*, March 28, 1956, AC Papers.

5. Helen V. Broekhoff, Los Altos, to AC, April 4, 1956; AC to Broekhoff, May 1, 1956; Los Altos Board of Realtors, memorandum to Planning Commission and City Council, February 14, 1957; Oral history of AC, 1995, and AC Los Altos 25th anniversary speech, December 1, 1977, courtesy of Los Altos History Museum; "Civic and business figures shared the amused appreciation of Alan Cranston," caption to photograph, Los Altos *News*, October 16, 1958, AC Papers; Fowle, 91-92.

6. Robinson, *'You're in Your Mother's Arms' - The Life & Legacy of Congressman Phil Burton*, 43-44.

7. Lionel Steinberg, chairman, Committee for the Hosts, YDs of Fresno County, to Convention of Young Democrats of California, to AC, 533 Ramona Road, Palo Alto, March 22, 1949; invitation to Young Democrats of California convention, Fresno, 1949, AC Papers.

8. Frank Snyder, president, YDs of Fresno County, to AC, April 9, 1949, AC Papers.

9. The California YDs pre-dated formation of the California Democratic Council (CDC). YDs were part of a national organization that FDR formed, YDs of America, chartered by the National Democratic Committee. The California YDs chapter was formed in 1949 by party dissidents led by Lionel Steinberg, Phil Burton and others. That created controversy because Californians were considered by some to be "soft" on communism. Steinberg convened a meeting to apply for the charter that inadvertently coincided with the international communist celebration, May 1, resulting in a delay of six months before the national party was convinced to recognize the new CDC. Robinson, 44-45; Roy Greenaway interview with author.

10. Robinson, 44; Fowle, 90; AC to Drew Pearson, January 15, 1957, AC Papers.

Earl Warren (1891-1974) was district attorney of Alameda County and state attorney general prior to election as governor (1943-50) for an unprecedented three terms. President Eisenhower named him Chief Justice of the U. S. Supreme Court where he served 1953-69.

Knowland (1908-74) was appointed in 1945 to complete the Senate term of Hiram Johnson, and reelected until 1958, serving as both majority and minority leader.

Thomas Henry Kuchel (1910-94) was the son of an Anaheim, California, newspaper publisher who campaigned against the Ku Klux Klan. Elected chairman of the Republican State Central Committee in 1940, Kuchel served in the Navy (1942-45). He had been Assemblyman (1937-41) and Controller (1946-53) before being appointed U. S. Senator (1953) by Gov. Warren in 1953 to fill out the final years of Nixon's seat when he was elected vice president with Eisenhower in 1952. Subsequently elected, Kuchel served until 1969, defeating Sam Yorty in 1954 and Richard Richards in 1956. Kuchel consistently maintained moderate positions, attacking the John Birch Society. As minority whip (1959-69), he helped enact the Civil Rights Act of 1964 and Voting Rights Act of 1965. He was among a few Republican senators who backed Medicare health insurance for seniors, the Nuclear Test Ban Treaty and conservation measures. He declined to endorse conservative Republican candidates including: Nixon for governor (1962); Barry Goldwater for president (Kuchel backed Nelson Rockefeller) and George Murphy for senator (1964); Ronald Reagan for governor (1966). Thomas Kuchel, biographical sketch, Wikipedia; David Binder, "Thomas H. Kuchel Dies at 84; Ex-Republican whip in Senate," *New York Times*, November 24, 1994.

11. Fowle, 90-91; AC to Peter Van Norden, May 5, 1955; AC, "A voice of eloquence, a manner of grace," review of *The Politics of Honor* by Kenneth S. Davis, *Press-Enterprise Diversion*, March 3, 1968, AC Papers.

12. AC Application for Federal Employment, for position to evaluate Peace Corps in a foreign country, [1961-2?], supplemental sheet for Standard Form 86, page 2; AC to Van Norden, May 5, 1955; "Trip to India - Notes," AC notes on "Interviews in India and Japan - Summary," AC Papers.

One note listed fourteen names of people whom he met, including Gandhi and R. K. Nehru.

13. AC "Trip to India - Noteés"; Morikatsu Inagaki to AC, December 4, 1952, AC Papers.

14. AC to Van Norden, May 5, 1955; Cornelia Matijasevich, "The other half - Mrs. Alan Cranston is serious about politics, homemaking," *Daily Palo Alto Times*, July 20, 1954; "Los Altos resident heads new California Democratic Council," *Daily Palo Alto Times*, November 30, 1953, Carton 2, Pics, AC Papers, citing Cranston as heading the importing company, "Cranstons of California."

15. Elizabeth Hillier Witkin, architect, CDC treasurer, Berkeley, to Hon. George Miller., Jr., February 4, 1953; Miller, chairman, Democratic State Central Committee of California, to AC, April 9 and 24, 1953, AC Papers; Fowle, 93-94.

The Asilomar meeting was held January 30-31, 1953. Miller called a follow-up meeting for club leaders at Stockton in May, 1953, when Cranston presented a blueprint for coordinating the organization; it "met little opposition and was unanimously approved by the delegates," according to Francis Carney, *The Rise of the Democratic Clubs in California, Case Studies in Practical Politics* (Holt, Rinehart and Winston), 1958. Cranston and Wyatt wrote a book, *The California Democratic Council.* Frank Anderson, "Cranston: A man at war for peace," *Long Beach Independent Press-Telegram*, September 10, 1968.

16. Greenaway interview with author; AC to Drew Pearson, January 15, 1957, AC Papers.

17. Robinson, 43.

Samuel W. Yorty (1909-98) was a long-time L. A. politician and mayor. He served in the State Assembly 1937-41, 1949-50; as U. S. Congressman 1951-55; and Mayor of L. A. 1961-73. He started as a liberal Democrat but grew conservative over the years and switched to Republican in 1972 when George McGovern was the Democratic presidential candidate. Yorty had been called a Communist for getting support from the U. S. Communist Party in 1936 when running for the State Assembly. As a Democrat he supported the war in Viet Nam and opposed civil rights although he was the first mayor to hire different ethnicities. He ran for office numerous times, losing a 1940 bid for U. S. Senator against progressive Republican Hiram Johnson. Yorty lost a special election for the Senate in 1954 to Thomas H. Kuchel (appointed in 1953 to fill Nixon's seat), and endorsed Nixon for president in 1960. He defeated James Roosevelt for mayor in 1965 but was criticized for his administration's lack of attention to conditions that prompted L. A.'s Watts Riots August 11-17, 1965. Yorty challenged incumbent Gov. Pat Brown in 1966, then celebrated Republican Ronald Reagan's defeat of Brown. In 1968 Yorty refused to endorse Democrat Hubert Humphrey for president, hoping for a Cabinet post from Nixon, which was not offered when Nixon beat Humphrey. Yorty ran again for governor in 1970. In 1973 African-American Tom Bradley beat Yorty for mayor in a second run.

18. Fowle, 94-96.

19. Robert A. Bernstein to AC, June 12, 1990, with bylined article, "Cranston predicts Democratic upswing in '54 election contests," [1953], AC Personal Papers.

20. Robinson, 44-46; CDC files, AC Papers.

John Atkisson, who made the statement about the CDC's revolutionizing the party, was executive director of the California Democratic Party, 1971-72.

21. Greenaway interview with author, December 11, 2002; Greenaway résumé, Carton 140, and Vol. 10, 1969, AC Papers.

Greenaway (1929-2010) was elected chairman of the Fresno Democratic Council in 1955 and received his M. A. in 1956. He taught English and was high school debate coach at Kerman High School 1955-59 when he was appointed by AC as an inheritance tax appraiser (1959-67). He was an instructor at Fresno State College 1967-68. Greenaway served on the California delegation to the Democratic National Convention in 1956 and 1960. For the CDC he served as regional vice president 1957-60; state chairman of its political action committee 1961-65; Northern California vice president 1965-67. He also was a member of the Democratic State Central committee. He would become AC's administrative assistant throughout his Senate career, gaining a reputation for intelligent, creative political and legislative strategies and ability to hire bright, dedicated staff with commitment to public service.

22. "Los Altos resident heads new California Democratic Council," *Daily Palo Alto Times*, November 30, 1953, AC Pics, AC Papers.

23. "Democrats open S. J. office," *San Jose Mercury*, June 3, 1953, AC Personal Papers; "S. C. County central committee election winners are reported," *Daily Palo Alto Times*, June 16, 1964, Pics, Carton 2; AC to Attorney General Edmund G. Brown, March 23, 1953, AC Papers.

After being elected state controller, Cranston was made a member of the Central

Committee's executive committee in 1959. AC to Edith Seros, secretary, Democratic State Central Committee, April 8, 1959, AC Papers.

24. Envelope postmarked May 21, 1953, addressed to "Ye Alan Cranstons" with return address, "MBC, 2120 Staunton Court, Palo Alto"; AC to Van Norden, May 5, 1955, AC Papers.

25. GC to AC, December 8, 1952; letter from physician to Santa Clara County re: jury duty, April, 1954, AC Papers.

26. Eugene Katz to AC re: treatment for leukemia, May 22, 1953; "William Cranston, P. A. realty man, passes away at 74," *San Jose Mercury*, Central Coast edition, August 27, 1953; "Funeral held for Cranston," Los Altos *Times*, August 26, 1953; "Funeral Services held for pioneer developer, William Cranston, 74," with photo of him with dog, Los Altos *[News? or Times?]*, August 28, 1953; Ralph A. Reynolds, M. D., to "My dear Carol, R. E. and Alan," 4 September, 1953, AC Papers.

27. Florence [?], Los Altos, to R. E., August 28, 1953, Lorraine Fuller to R. E., Capitola, California, August 29, 1953, Pics, AC Papers and AC Personal Papers; AC interview with author.

28. AC interview with author; Fowle, 91; "Controller Cranston, wealthiest official sets a precedent," [*Los Angeles Times*?, November ?], 1965, AC Papers.

The landscape architect was Larry Lawrence of San Francisco. The property was 13 acres.

29. AC and REC interviews with author; Dewey Anderson, Public Affairs Institute, Washington, D. C., to AC, April 23, 1953, AC Papers.

If the same man with whom Cranston was corresponding, Dr. Hobson Dewey Anderson (1897-?), an economist, was Executive Director of the Public Affairs Institute at the time of the 1950s correspondence. Anderson was chief of field operations for the U. N. Relief and Rehabilitation Administration, 1943, according to *Who's Who in America* (1952-53 edition). He was a Stanford graduate (B.A. in education, 1929, "with great distinction," M. A., 1930, Ph.D., 1932, Phi Beta Kappa). After World War I he worked with Young Men's Christian Association organizations to aide prisoners in Poland, and from 1921-24 with the American Relief Administration in Russia and Baltic States. He served in the California Assembly (as a Republican) from the 30th district, Santa Clara Co. (1935-37), from which he resigned. In 1939 he was named head of the California budget department by Governor Culbert L. Olson and subsequently Administrator for Relief of California. He was executive director of the Temporary National Economic Committee (1939-41), appointed by President Roosevelt to investigate problems caused by the Depression; and chief of the American Hemisphere Division, Board of Economic Warfare (1942). He advocated public health insurance while in the legislature, and authored books on economic, occupational, tax, health and environmental subjects (including: *Health Service is a Basic Right of all the People* (1956?), and *Natural Resources, Their Protection and Development* (ca. 1959), published by the Public Affairs Institute, Washington; and *Taxation, Recovery and Defense* (U. S. Government Printing Office, 1941). Cranston may have known Anderson as a neighbor (see below) as well as politician and government official. Anderson considered running for the Senate in 1964, as Cranston did. Tammy Kelly, Archivist, Truman Presidential Library, to author, March 14, 2011; Dewey Anderson biographical sketch (no date), Oscar Cox Papers (box 1) and Official File 4966, U. N. Relief and Rehabilitation Administration (1943, box 2), courtesy of Matthew Hanson, Archives Specialist, Franklin D. Roosevelt Presidential Library.

Anderson wrote AC January 10, 1956, "We have begun to sell off the Los Altos property, two lots are gone and more are going soon. You ought to buy over there. It's an ideal place." Cranston agreed and bought property there.

30. AC to Anderson, June 22, 1953, AC Papers.

31. AC to Waller, 501 Madison Avenue, N. Y. City, January 26, 1954, AC Papers.

32. Eric Brazil and Vicki Haddock, "Alan Cranston: a career built from grass roots, a look

back at the pragmatic senator's long, contradictory political life," *San Francisco Examiner*, November 9, 1990, AC Papers

33. Fowle, 96-97; Michael Doyle, "FBI file paints shadow portrait of Sen. Cranston," *Sacramento Bee*, August 26, 2003.

34. Anderson to AC, February 4, 1954, AC Papers.

35. Fowle, 96.

36. Stanley Mosk, Superior Court of California, Los Angeles, to AC, February 13, 1954; Peter H. Odegard, Berkeley, to AC, February 17, 1954, AC Papers.

Stanley Mosk (1912-2001) in 1939, just out of law school, became executive secretary to California Gov. Culbert Olson, the first Democratic governor in the 20th century. He appointed Mosk in 1942 to the Los Angeles Superior Court (at 31, the youngest such judge in the state). In 1958 Mosk would be elected Attorney General on the wave that elected Pat Brown as Governor. He appointed Mosk to the Supreme Court in 1964. A consistent liberal, Mosk coined the phrase "little old ladies in tennis shoes" to characterize members of the John Birch Society in a report to Gov. Brown, published in the *New York Times* August 3, 1961 (p. 3), cited in "Celebration Session Honoring the Record Service of Justice Stanley Mosk, California Supreme Court (1964-Present)," January 7, 2000. See also Chapter 7, note 157, and Chapter 11, note 141.

37. AC to Anderson, May 16, 1954, AC Papers.

38. AC to Jerry Spingarn, Washington, D. C., April 21, 1954, AC Papers.

39. Dr. W. B. Townsend, Colton, Ca., to AC, with AC's note, "Re: June '54 memos for Demos," [1954], AC Papers.

Paul Ziffren (1914-91) was a leader of the Democratic Party beginning in the 1950s and National Democratic Committeeman from California (1953). He helped reactivate the Western States Democratic conference to elect liberals. He led the lobby to bring the Democratic National Convention to Los Angeles in 1960 but Gov. Pat Brown removed him as a national committeeman because Ziffren backed Sen. John F. Kennedy while Brown was himself a favorite-son contender. In 1979 Ziffren became chairman of the L. A. Olympic Organizing Committee that sponsored the 1984 Summer Olympics. "Paul Ziffren, Democratic Leader in California in 1950s, Dies at 77," *New York Times*, June 3, 1991.

40. AC to Spingarn, July 19, 1954; AC to Paul Ziffren, April 28, 1954; AC to Waller, Katonah, New York, July 17, 1954; Assemblyman George D. Collins, Jr., San Francisco, to AC, December 3, 1954, re: by-law committee, AC Papers.

Richard P. Graves (1906-89) in 1954 was seeking Democratic endorsement to run against incumbent Governor Goodwin Knight. See also note 81.

41. "S. C. central committee election winners are reported," *Daily Palo Alto Times*, June 16, 1954, Pics, Carton 2, AC Papers.

42. Peter H. Odegard, memorandum, July 24, 1954, Ac Papers.

43. Fowle, 98.

44. AC to Paul Ziffren, Beverly Hills, California, December 29, 1954, AC Papers.

45. Matijasevich, "The other half - Mrs. Alan Cranston is serious about politics, homemaking," *Daily Palo Alto Times*, July 20, 1954.

46. Typescript dated February 1, 1955, with excerpts from *Congressional Record*, re: AC activities with O. W. I. and Common Council for American Unity, citing *Congressional Record*, July 11, 1950, and The Katyn Forest Massacre, hearings before a Select committee, Part 7, 1952, pages 2174-75, AC Papers; "Moscow paper blames Soviets in Katyn deaths, wartime records said to implicate N.K.V.D.," Associated Press, [*New York*?] *Times*, and "Stalin ordered massacre of Polish officers in 1940, Soviet paper says," United Press International, [*Los Angeles*?] *Times*, March 22, 1990; Frank Anderson, "Cranston: a man at war for peace," copies in AC Personal Papers.

Stalin was revealed to have ordered the massacre because he feared Poles would lead an uprising and upset the 1939 secret pact that he had signed with Hitler. The 2010 Russian resolution acknowledging the murder did not satisfy Polish government requests that the Russians compensate victims' families. A 2007 film *Katyn* by Polish director Andrzej Wajda depicted the event. "Jazz pianist and World War II veteran Dave Brubeck's history lesson," *Wall Street Journal* editorial December 1, 2010.

The 1952 congressional committee chaired by Ray Madden, Democrat of Indiana, concluded that Soviet security police were responsible for the massacre; it was critical of U. S. handling of the issue but did not single Cranston out for censure. The Senate subcommittee conducting the 1954 inquiry was chaired by William E. Jenner, Republican of Indiana. "'45 praise of Reds is laid to Army," *New York Times*, July 7, 1954, and "Doctor is silent at army inquiry," *New York Times*, July 8, 1954.

47. AC to Peter Van Norden, New York City, May 5, 1955, AC Papers.

48. AC, "President's Report," *The California Democrat*, April 15, 1955, citing AC's report to 1955 CDC convention, AC Papers.

49. AC to Honorable Samuel W. Yorty, February 9, 1955, with handwritten response, "Dear Alan..."

50. AC to A. T. Lunceford, secretary-treasurer, Greater L. A. C. I. O, January 16, 1955, AC Papers.

51. AC to Paul Ziffren, March 25, 1955, AC Papers.

52. Kefauver, telegram to AC, chairman, CDC Council, March 18, 1955; Hubert H. Humphrey to AC, March 17, 1955; AC to Paul M. Butler, chairman, Democratic National Committee, April 1, 1955; Butler to AC, April 6, 1955, saying, "…delighted to meet you. I look forward to… exchanging ideas," AC Papers.

Humphrey in 1948, with backing of the Farmer-Labor party, became the first Democrat from Minnesota to be elected to the U. S. Senate and gained a national reputation for his stand for civil rights. He had just been reelected in 1954. He would narrowly lose the 1968 presidential race against Nixon.

A negative *Time* magazine story on Butler's visit to the convention was "apparently written by some sort of a vulgarly-brainwashed Hans Christian Anderson," Cranston told him, asking if he would like California party leaders to complain to *Time*. Butler agreed that the story was "one of the most distorted pieces of reporting I have encountered in a long time," but shared Cranston's concern that a rebuttal might give the magazine "further opportunity for twisting the facts." They did not respond to it.

53. Harriman to AC, telegrams, March 18, 1955, and January 28, 1956, AC Papers.

54. Rep. Clair Engle to AC, marked "air mail, personal stamp," January 21, 1955, AC Papers.

55. AC to Dan Kimball, February 14, 1955; Sen. Richard L. Neuberger to AC, October 25, 1956; Swig to AC, January 27, 1956; AC to Swig, October 1, 1956; AC, "A million-dollar loser looks at campaigning," *Fortune*, November, 1964, 280, AC Papers.

Neuberger also referred to going to Los Angeles with Truman in November, 1957.

56. Greenaway interview with author.

57. Greenaway to AC, March 13, 1955; AC to Greenaway, March 15 and 25, 1955; Greenaway to AC, March 28 and June 14, 1955, Carton 10, AC Papers.

58. Rep. B. F. Sisk to AC, April 15, 1955, AC Papers.

59. AC to Sisk, "Dear Tex," July 11, 1955, AC Papers.

60. AC to Senator Richard Richards, May 16, 1955, AC Papers.

61. Sisk to AC, telegram, October 1, 1957, AC Papers.

62. AC to Rep. Shelley, July 1, 1955, AC Papers.

63. Rep. John F. Shelley to AC, August 1, 1955, AC Papers.

George Christopher (1907-2000), Greek-born businessman (he owned a dairy) was elected to the S. F. Board of Supervisors in 1945, becoming its president in 1949. He lost a 1951 run for mayor (to the incumbent) but won the 1955 mayoral election with the biggest majority to date. During his eight years as mayor he presided over extensive building in the city, much of it controversial, expansion of the airport, and in 1957 lured the N. Y. Giants baseball team to San Francisco, building Candlestick Park, which opened 1960. He supported civil rights and offered his home to baseball star Willie Mays when it was reported that a realtor refused to sell to the Black player. Christopher was mayor during HUAC hearings at City Hall in 1960, supporting the committee and fire-hosing of protestors. He ran unsuccessfully for lieutenant governor and U. S. Senate, and lost the 1966 GOP primary for governor to Ronald Reagan. Carl Nolte, "George Christopher 1907-2000: Big-thinking S. F. Mayor of '50s and '60s is Dead," *San Francisco Chronicle*, September 15, 2000

64. AC to Shelley, November 10, 1955; Shelley, form letter, to AC, January 18, 1956, AC Papers.

65. A. Phillip Burton to AC, re: "Suggested items to be added to agenda, CDC Board of Directors meeting, San Francisco, September 17, 18, 1955," August 17, 1955, AC Papers.

66. AC to editor, *Time*, August 23, 1955, AC Papers.

67. AC to Jerry Spingarn, November 10, 1955, AC Papers.

68. AC to Marshall Field, Jr., *Chicago Sun-Times*, November 27, 1955, AC Papers.

69. Assemblyman Augustus R. Hawkins to AC, November 29, 1955, AC Papers.

Augustus "Gus" Hawkins (1907-2007) served in the California Assembly 1935-63, and the House of Representatives 1963-91.

70. Harold F. Taggart, San Mateo, to AC, December 23, 1955, AC Papers.

71. AC to Kefauver, December 23, 1955, AC Papers.

72. AC to Ben Held, Beverly Hills, California, December 26, 1955, AC Papers.

Cranston also asked Sen. John F. Kennedy to keynote the 1957 Long Beach convention but he was unable to do so. AC to Kennedy, February 9, 1957, AC Papers.

73. Art Hewitt, "Rival factions agree, Cal. Dems find way to convention unity," *Los Angeles Herald & Express*, January 3, 1956, AC Papers.

74. Rep. Clair Engle to AC, February 7, 1956, AC Papers; Fowle, 99.

75. AC to Greenaway, May 15, 1956, Carton 10, AC Papers; Greenaway interview with author.

76. Leo Ziffren, Beverly Hills, to AC, quoting portion of Governor Stevenson's press conference on February 6, February 8, 1956, AC Papers.

77. AC to Paul Ziffren, March 8, 1956, AC Papers. See note 17 for Yorty political biography.

78. AC to Engle, March 8, 1956, and April 19, 1956, AC Papers.

79. John E. Thorne, San Jose, to AC, March 8, 1956, AC Papers.

Yorty himself was infamous for litigiousness.

80. Fowle, 99; Steve Merksamer, "Who killed Alan Cranston? Flournoy win attributed to Democrats," Claremont *Collegian*, January 13, 1967, 8-9, AC Papers.

Phil Burton was among liberal YDs who worked to keep Yorty from getting the Senate nomination in 1956. Burton himself also considered running for U. S. Senate. Robinson, 43.

81. Frank Anderson, "Cranston, CDC toppled GOP control," *Long Beach Independent Press-Telegram*, September 11, 1968; AC to Dorothy Wilson, Beverly Hills office of Paul Ziffren, April 27, 1956, AC Papers.

Goodwin J. Knight (1896-1970) sought the Republican nomination for U. S. Senate in 1944 but dropped out to back candidate Fred Houser. Considered moderate and pro-labor, Knight was elected lieutenant governor in 1946, serving under Governor Earl Warren, reelected in 1950. He became Governor of California when Warren resigned to become Chief Justice of the Supreme Court (1953), was elected in 1954 and served until 1959. During those years, Knight fought for control of the state Republican Party against conservatives U. S. Senate Majority Leader William Knowland and Vice President Richard Nixon. A so-called Knight-Knowland alliance ended in 1956 when Knowland supported Nixon for renomination. In

1957 Knowland announced that he would challenge Knight in the 1958 primary for governor. Knight was induced by Knowland, Nixon, President Eisenhower and others to run for Knowland's Senate seat instead of governor. Both Knight and Knowland were defeated in 1958, Knight to Clair Engle, Knowland to Pat Brown.

82. Harry Farrell, "Wrangle over Richards, angry exchanges mark Yorty speech," *San Jose News*, May 11, 1956, AC Papers.

The issue of whether the United States should recognize Communist Red China was a major one at that time.

83. AC to Engle, April 19, 1956.

John McFall (1918-2006), Democrat, was Mayor of Manteca (1949-50); State Assemblyman (1951-56); Congressman (1957-63, 11th District; 1963-75, 15th District; 1975-79, 14th District. He served as Majority Whip in the House 1973-77 during which he was reprimanded for influence peddling in a scandal dubbed "Koreagate." In 1956 Bill Bidick, city attorney of Stockton, ran for McFall's Assembly seat.

84. AC to Drew Pearson, January 15, 1957, AC Papers.

85. Fowle, 100; Senator Richards to AC, with handwritten postscripts, June 19 and [no date] July, 1956, AC Papers.

86. Robinson, 62-63; AC to Assemblyman Phillip Burton, March 25, 1957, AC Papers.

87. AC to Assemblyman Gus Hawkins, April 21, 1956; AC to Hon. Carlos Bee, June 14, 1956, AC Papers.

88. AC to Engle, June 14, 1956; Engle to AC, June 30, 1956, AC Papers.

Engle had risen to chairman of the House Interior and Insular Affairs Committee in 1956.

89. Rep. Harry R. Sheppard to AC, June 19, 1956; Rep. Cecil R. King, 17th District, to AC, June 21, 1956; Assemblyman Charles H. Wilson to AC, July 5, 1956, AC Papers.

90. Senator John F. Kennedy to AC, October 23, 1956, AC Papers.

91. Robinson, 45.

92. Stevenson to AC, March 12, 1956; Stevenson to Mr. and Mrs. Cranston, May 12, 1956; Charles H. Wilson to AC, July 5, 1956, AC Papers.

93. AC, "A voice of eloquence, a manner of grace," review of *The Politics of Honor* by Kenneth S. Davis, *Press-Enterprise Diversion*, March 3, 1968; AC to Assemblyman John J. McFall, April 17, 1956; McFall to AC, April 18, 1956, AC Papers.

94. Ward Winslow, "Palo Alto crowd cheers Adlai, cultural trend seen by Demo candidate," with front-page photo captioned "Farewell to Palo Alto, Adlai Stevenson is bid farewell as he leaves on his campaign bus from Palo Alto by Alan Cranston…president of the California Democratic Council, holding aloft his son Kim…," *Daily Palo Alto Times*, May 8, 1956, Pics, Carton 2, and Herb Caen, "A little child shall lead them," *San Francisco Examiner*, January 25, 1956, AC Papers. See also Chapter 10 re: Robin and Pat Brown story, and note 161.

95. Lyndon B. Johnson, Office of the Democratic Leader, to AC, July 28, 1956, AC Papers.

96. AC to Mrs. Carmen H. Warschaw, Los Angeles, August 23, 1956, AC Papers.

97. Roger Kent, Democratic State chairman, Memorandum on Division of Limited State Funds, citing committee consisting of AC, Don Bradley and Libby Smith having to "divide the very small amount of state money available for candidates," September 23, 1956, AC Papers.

98. AC to Waller, October 15, 1956, AC Papers.

99. Robinson, 42; Senator Richard Richards to AC, with handwritten postscript, December 26, 1956, AC Papers.

100. Thomas K. Finletter, New York, to AC, November 9, 1956, AC Papers.

Stevenson lost the popular vote 57.4% to 42%, and carried only 7 southern states.

101. Waller to AC, November 16, 1956; AC to Waller, December 4, 1956, AC Papers.

102. AC to Judge Mosk, October 31, 1956; AC to Mrs. Daniel M. Tolmach, March 13, 1957, referring to his sons' being "involved with Little League," AC Papers.

103. Fowle, 100-01.

104. AC to Pearson, January 15, 1953.

105. AC to Pearson, February 6 and 20, 1957, AC Papers.

106. AC to Glenn Anderson, April 10 and June 17, 1957, AC Papers.

Cranston also urged that clubs raise contributions for the party. The State Central Committee could raise money as the official party organization appointed by elected legislators, but clubs could not officially raise money.

107. "Both suggestions are dangerous," unidentified editorial dated December 24, 1956, and typescript, "It is incredible and intolerable…," no date, AC Papers.

Some 190,000 refugees fled Hungary following the revolt.

108. Fowle, 101.

109. Reprint, Cranston for Controller Campaign Committee, "(Not printed at government expense)," Rep. James Roosevelt, Extension of Remarks, *Congressional Record*, 85th Congress, with "Statement on Civil Rights by Alan Cranston to Western Democratic Conference," February 15, 1957, AC Papers.

110. AC, Statement on Civil Rights, *ibid.*

111. The reference to "Eastlands" was to Mississippi Senator James Eastland (1904-86), a conservative "Dixiecrat" Democrat and segregationist. He served in the Senate 1941-41; 1943-78.

Cranston's proposal was to have federal administrators oversee elections in states where fewer than 50 percent of the population voted in federal elections. Voter participation in the 1956 presidential election averaged 60.4 percent nationally, from a high of 77.3 percent in Idaho to a low of 22.1 percent in Mississippi; in California it was 65 percent.

112. Release, Cranston for President, quoting excerpts from 1957 speech, [1983]; "Resolution (by Mr. Brooks) re: Federal Elections Commission," adopted by CDC in caucus, March 10, 1957; AC to Mrs. Carmen Warschaw, March 21, 1957, stating, "The Federal Elections Commission idea was approved by the resolutions committee but we lost our quorum and the convention adjourned before it and quite a few other resolutions were acted upon. I trust that our Board of Directors will act on it shortly"; AC to Sen. Wayne Morse, and Rep. Emmanuel Cellar, February 20, 1957; Sen. Humphrey to AC, February 25, 1957, AC Papers.

The Voting Rights Act of 1965 prohibited states from imposing any qualifications that denied the vote on account of race or color, like those used in southern states (e.g., literacy tests) to prevent African-Americans from registering and voting. The Act established federal oversight of elections and required states wanting to implement voting rules to first obtain federal pre-clearance. Enforcement applied to states that used anti-voting devices and in which less than 50 percent of the population was registered to vote in 1964. It was signed by President Lyndon Johnson with Martin Luther King, Jr., Rosa Parks and other civil-rights leaders present. The Act was extended for 25 years in 2006. A separate law in 1975 established a Federal Election Commission to oversee campaign-finance laws.

113. AC to the Rev. Ralph Abernathy, February 28, 1957; the Rev. M. L. King, Jr. to AC, May 3, 1957, AC Papers.

Prof. di Grazia, Cranston noted, was author of "many popular and textbook volumes in the political science field."

114. AC to Pearson, February 20, 1957; Hawkins to AC, March 1, 1957, AC Papers.

115. Senator Herbert H. Lehman, New York and Palm Springs, to AC, March 4, 1957; AC to Lehman, March 8, 1957, AC Papers.

116. AC to Mrs. Patsy Thompson, Pasadena, May 20, 1957, AC Papers.

117. AC to Glenn M. Anderson, Hawthorne, California, January 21, 1957; "Cranston urged for Demo post again," *San Jose Mercury News*, March 11, 1957, AC Papers

118. Edmund G. Brown, Attorney General, to Albert J. MacDonald, February 6, 1957, AC

Papers; Greenaway interviews with author

In addition to the CDC, there were some 50 local/regional councils of clubs, organized by county, congressional, senate or legislative districts, that made endorsements.

119. AC interview with author.

120. Brown *et al* to AC, February 25, 1957; "Cranston draft under way," *Daily Palo Alto Times*, March 11, 1957, AC Papers.

121. AC to Brown, March 11, 1957, AC Papers.

Cranston wrote similar thanks to Nicholas Petris, CDC vice president, later State Senator from Oakland-Alameda County, and to other signers of the letter. AC to Nicholas Petris, noting "also to Catherine Everett…Admiral Ross T. McIntrye" (Eisenhower's former physician), March 11, 1957.

122. "Cranston urged for Demo post again," *San Jose Mercury News*, March 11, 1957; AC to Robert K. Barber, president, Kensington Democratic Club, March 11, 1957, AC Papers.

123. Sen. Albert Gore to John M. Ball, executive secretary, Orange County Council of Democratic Clubs, March 23, 1957, AC Papers.

124. AC to Gore, March 25, 1957, AC Papers.

125. AC to Sen. Paul Douglas, August 7, 1957; Douglas to AC, November 1, 1957, AC Papers.

126. Release, CDC, Glendale, Ca., August 16, 1957, AC Papers.

Cranston's call for Johnson to step down would be echoed in December, 2002, when Mississippi Senator Trent Lott, expected to be re-elected Republican Majority leader, was forced to step down after praising segregationist Senator Strom Thurmond (1902-2003) of South Carolina, a presidential candidate in 1948, at his 100th birthday party.

127. Release, CDC, Tulare, Ca., August 23, 1957, AC Papers.

President Roosevelt appointed Henry A. Wallace (1888-1965) Secretary of Agriculture (1933-40), a post that his father had held (1921-24). His Depression order to slaughter pigs and plow up cotton fields to drive up commodities' prices and help farmers financially was not popular. He was Roosevelt's vice president (1941-45) and Secretary of Commerce (1945-46), fired by President Truman; Progressive Party presidential nominee (1948).

128. Trevor Thomas, Friends Committee on Legislation, San Francisco, postcard to AC; AC to Thomas, June 10, 1957; AC to Rep. Chet Holifield, June 19, 1957; Holifield to AC, July 2, 1957, AC Papers.

129. AC to Republican Assemblyman William A. Munnell, August 1, 1957; Carton 500, file, "Tight $," AC Papers.

Arc lights produce light from electric (or voltaic) arcs.

130. Fowle, 104.

For Goodwin J. Knight political history, see note 81. Nixon, who also had designs on being governor and president, had urged Eisenhower to appoint Warren to the court to remove him from California politics, and reportedly encouraged Knowland's retirement from the Senate to run for governor. Fowle, 103-04.

131. Fowle, 104; "Cranston urged for Demo post again," *San Jose Mercury News*, March 11, 1957; leaflet, "Cranston serious Demo U. S. Senate contender," with copies of news articles including Lawrence E. Davies, "California hums political tunes," *New York Times*, August 17, [1957?], AC Papers.

132. Fowle, 104-05.

133. Fowle, citing AC speech July 9, 1957, 105-06.

134. AC to Waller, Grolier Society, New York City, July 11, 1957, AC Papers.

135. Jerome H. Spingarn, Washington, D. C., to AC, September 9, 1957; AC to Spingarn, October 21, 1957, AC Papers.

136. Helen (Mrs. Ware) Myers, on Los Angeles County Democratic Central Committee letterhead, to AC, October 3, 1957, AC Papers.

137. AC to Myers, October 21, 1957, AC Papers.

Scudder (1888-1968), Republican of Sebastopol, was not a candidate for reelection in 1958; Miller succeeded him for the House seat.

138. AC to Anderson, October 18, 1957, AC Papers.

139. Joseph C. Houghteling, publisher, Sunnyvale *Standard*, to AC, October 18, 1957; AC to Houghteling, June 14 and November 13, 1957, AC Papers.

140. AC interview with author.

141. AC interview with author; Fowle, 106.

142. Fowle, 106.

Elinor Raas Heller (1904-87) was Democratic National Committeewoman 1944-52; alternate delegate to the 1944 Democratic National Convention, delegate in 1948 and 1956. In 1952 she was a candidate for Presidential Elector on behalf of Adlai Stevenson. She was a Regent of U. C. 1961-76, chair 1975-76. In 1964 during Free Speech Movement agitations at U. C.'s Berkeley campus, another Regent, Edwin Pauley, cooperating with the F. B. I., tried to have Heller removed from the board. She was married to financier Edward Hellman Heller, who died in 1961. Wikipedia.

143. Fowle, 107-08; AC interview with author.

144. Greenaway interview with author.

145. Fowle, 107-08; press release issued by Northwood & Associates [public relations firm?], San Francisco, December 4, 1957, AC Papers; Robert Blanchard, "Two Democrats to seek high state-wide office," *Los Angeles Times*, December 5, 1957, AC Personal Papers.

146. Typescript, "Early in 1952…," [1957?], AC Papers.

147. AC to Harry Farrell, *San Jose Mercury-News*, December 17, 1957, AC Papers.

148. AC interview with author.

149. Fowle, 107; "The people's voice, Cranston answers charges in *Daily Journal* editorials," AC letter to editor, Willows *Daily Journal*, May 26, 1958, AC Papers.

150. Fowle, 109; Harry Farrell, "Kirkwood seeks vacated seat," *San Jose Mercury-News*, January 8, 1957.

Kirkwood had been in the legislature for six years and controller for four, having won election in 1954 over Democrat George D. Collins, Jr. The Republican slate included: Knight for U. S. Senate, Knowland for governor, Harold J. Powers for lieutenant governor, Kirkwood for controller, Patrick J. Hillings for attorney general, A. Ronald Button for treasurer, Frank M. Jordan for secretary of state.

151. Citizens for Good Government, campaign flyer, [1954], "Who will speak for you as state controller?", AC Papers.

152. Fowle, 109; Farrell, "Kirkwood seeks vacated seat,"; "January, 1950, a panel discussion on world government…," caption to photograph, *Town Crier & Foothill Focus*, November 7, 1957, AC Papers; AC interview with author; Sonnichsen interview with author.

Kirkwood (1909-64) received a law degree from Harvard in 1933 and had served on a number of county and local school boards while maintaining a ranch in Saratoga. He was chairman of the Assembly Finance Committee 1947 to 1953 when he was named controller to succeed Kuchel (who succeeded Nixon as U. S. Senator). Kirkwood had been chairman of the California GOP platform committee (1951-51) and a delegate for Nixon in 1952. If Kirkwood had been elected Senator, both California Senators would have been former controllers.

153. Fowle, 109-11, citing *Los Angeles Mirror-News* editor Dick Bergholz, "the raucous 40,000-member CDC," and headline January 13, 1958, "Demo group backs Brown, Engle, amateur politicos…"; Harry Farrell, "Demo Council OKs Engle for Senator," *San Jose Mercury-News*, January 12, 1958; Peter Odegard to AC, announcing candidacy for Senate, December 4, 1957, AC Papers, AC Papers.

154. Earl C. Behrens, political editor, "Demos pick Engle for Senate race; Brown endorsed,

voting at Fresno," *San Francisco Chronicle*, January 12, 1958, AC Papers.

155. Fowle, 110; Farrell, "Demo Council Oks…"; Greenaway interview with author.

156. Farrell, *ibid.*; Clint Mosher, "State Demos pick slate," *San Francisco Examiner*, January 13, 1958, AC Papers.

Water rights was a divisive issue in the 1950s when abuses of the 1902 Reclamation Act, the federal law restricting to 160 acres the size of farms eligible for irrigation subsidies, came to light. Large growers wanted to increase the size of farms that qualified for the water-assistance program, which Cranston supported in 1977. Greenaway and Phil Burton favored maintaining the 160-acre limitation, for which they successfully lobbied Congress at the time. Robinson, 46. See also Chapter 9, note 271.

157. Fowle, 110-11; Mosher, "State Demos pick slate"; Behrens, "Demos pick Engle…," *San Francisco Chronicle*, January 12, 1958, AC Papers.

158. AC interview with author; Fowle, 113-17; Cranston for President, [1982?], release quoting excerpts from 1957 speech.

Cranston would cite the civil-rights speech in his 1982 presidential campaign as an example of his early and forceful stand on the issue.

159. Fowle, 113-17; AC interview with author.

160. Fowle, 118-19; "Los Altos provides a candidate, Cranston confident he will be state controller," *Daily Palo Alto News*, May 29, 1958, caption to photograph, "It was kids' day in the Alan Cranston family…," AC Papers.

161. Fowle, 113-18; AC interview with author.

162. Memorandum to AC, "Thoughts and questions and information," no date, [1958], AC Papers.

Cranston headquarters were located at 256 Sutter St., San Francisco, and at 401 South Vermont Ave., Los Angeles 5. Marta Teilhet was northern manager, Stanley M. Felix, treasurer; Teddy Mueller was southern manager, Claude E. Young, treasurer.

163. Fowle, 114-15.

164. Replica currency bill, campaign flyer, Cranston for Controller, AC Papers.

165. Memoranda, "Suggestions for Planning and Executing a Visit to your Community by Candidate Alan Cranston," and "A Sample Perfect Day, a Visit to your Community by Candidate Alan Cranston," [1958], AC Papers.

166. Cranston for Controller, "Draft of letter to be addressed by a local merchant to another or by a statewide leader to merchants in his group," [1958]; "Cranston says merchants are state helpers," *Fresno Bee*, September 21, 1958, AC Papers.

167. AC memo to Cranston Campaigners, re: retail merchants, AC Papers.

168. Files, "Campaign Literature," letter from two retired L.A.P.D. officers, and "Form letters," AC Papers.

169. Sample letter from attorneys, AC Papers.

170. W. Byron Bryant, San Francisco, to Frederick Walker, San Francisco, no date, [post-primary], AC Papers.

171. Releases, 1957, AC Papers.

172. "Democratic controller candidate suggests 4-point water program," Placerville *Mountain Democrat*, September 11, 1958; "Cranston raps Kirkwood bill as PGE windfall," *Sacramento Bee*, September 22, 1958, AC Papers.

The bill that Kirkwood sponsored in 1949 as a state assemblyman was known as "Chapter 1466"; it forced adjustment in state assessments to the advantage of utility companies. Implementation was delayed pending studies of government assessment practices.

173. Cranston for Controller Committee, release, October 13, 1958, AC Papers.

174. File, "Clips," Carton 501, AC Papers.

175. Leaflet, "Cranston serious Demo U. S. Senate contender," with copies news articles: "Cranston calls for ouster of Sen. Johnson," Glendale *News-Press*; "Cranston raps Richard

Nixon," Pleasant Hill *Sun*; "Cranston blasts Dulles for banning U. S. newsmen from Communist China," Anaheim *Bulletin*; "New inflation tactics urged by Cranston," *San Francisco Chronicle*, no dates [1957-58], AC Papers.

176. "Rider of the purple phrase," editorial, *Chico-Enterprise Record*, February 19, 1958, AC Papers.

177. "Cranston baloney," Willows *Daily Journal*, in Corning *Observer*, February 26, 1958, AC Papers.

178. "The people's voice, Cranston answers charges in *Daily Journal* editorials," AC letter to editor, Willows *Daily Journal*, May 26, 1958, AC Papers; Cranston for Controller Committee, release, February 27, 1958, AC Papers.

179. Memorandum from Marta and Teddy, April, 1958, AC Papers.

180. Memorandum from Teddy Mueller, "item #III. Special Project," no date, [1958]; memorandum, "Vote on State Constitutional Offices, General Election, November, 1954," AC Papers.

181. AC "To my friends in the Democratic Clubs of California"; release, August 14, 1957, AC Papers.

182. Marta Teilhet, "Memo to all coordinators, Cranston for Controller Campaign," April 4, 1958; memorandum from Teddy Mueller to "All Cranston Campaign Committee Members," May 22, 1958, AC Papers.

183. AC fundraising form letter, no date, AC Papers.

184. Memorandum from Marta and Teddy, April, 1958; memorandum from Rudy Nothenberg, July 24, 1958, concerning billboard availability, AC Papers.

Nebron was appointed field coordinator in the southern coastal region July 23, 1958.

185. Carton 500, file, "Budget"; Carton 499, memorandum, April, 1958, AC Papers.

186. Memorandum from Marta and Teddy, April, 1958, AC Papers.

187. "Los Altos provides a candidate, Cranston confident he will be state controller," *Daily Palo Alto News*, May 29, 1958, caption to photograph, "It was kids' day in the Alan Cranston family…,"

188. Mildred Schroeder, "The unusual is the typical in the Cranston family, California's leading ladies," profiles of wives of new state constitutional officers, *San Francisco Examiner*, December 14, 1958, AC Papers.

189. Fowle, 115; Greenaway interview with author.

190. Cranston for Controller Committee, release, June 3, 1958; release, "Alan Cranston won more votes in the primary…," no date, AC Papers; Fowle, 116-17.

191. *Ibid.*, "Alan Cranston won more votes…," and Fowle.

192. Cranston for Controller Committee, release for speech in Los Angeles, August 11, 1958, AC Papers.

193. Cranston for Controller Committee, releases, August 21 and 29, 1958, AC Papers.

194. Greenaway interview with author; Joseph B. Williams interview with author, February 21, 2003.

195. Williams interview.

196. "Cranston claims PGE used false Trinity figures," *Modesto Bee*, September 19, 1958.

197. Fowle, 119-20; Cranston for Controller Committee, two separate releases, October 23, 1958; "Cranston 'ignorant,' says Kirkwood," *San Francisco Examiner*, October 23, 1958; "Kirkwood hits Cranston record," unidentified newspaper clip, AC Papers.

198. Carton 500, Press releases, 1958; file, "Scout report," Carton 501, AC Papers.

199. Photograph with caption, "Good advice! Allan [*sic*] Cranston…presents the new Democratic slogan at the party's convention…well aware that a victory for the Democrats means a decisive defeat for the 'employer-employee relations' initiative petition," unidentified, AC Papers.

200. AC to William F. Peters, Los Angeles, form letter to appraisers, August 15, 1958, AC

Papers; Fowle, 120.

ITAs were not civil servants but appointed by the controller to county panels. When probate of an estate was required, a judge named a panel member to appraise the estate and compute inheritance tax owed, for which the estate paid. The intent of the law was to give courts independent, expert witnesses.

201. "Appraisers given 'no-politics' hint, Cranston writes to estate men," Watsonville *Register-Pajaronian*, September 19, 1958, AC Papers.

202. "Letter better not sent," editorial, Ventura County *Star Free Press*, September 30, 1958, AC Papers.

203. Typescript, AC statement/letter to editors, [1958], AC Papers.

204. Edmund G. Brown to AC, October 2, 1958; hand-drawn card, "Clair Engle and Pat Brown prefer Alan Cranston for State Controller because…," with photo of Brown, AC and Engle, AC Papers; Fowle, 121-22.

205. "Brown Biography," typescript, [1958], AC Papers.

206. Fowle, 121-22.

New York-born attorney J. F. Neylan (1885-1960) went to California in 1910, worked on Hearst's *San Francisco Call* and *Bulletin* and later was publisher of Hearst newspapers in San Francisco as well as Hearst's legal counsel. Initially a liberal, Neylan had been persuaded by Fremont Older to defend (in 1925) well-born philanthropist Anita Whitney, who had shared Older's view that Mooney and Billings were wrongly convicted and, as a member of the American Communist Party, had been convicted (1920) under California's Criminal Syndicalism Act of belonging to a group advocating unlawful violence to accomplish political change. After her conviction was upheld by the U. S. Supreme Court, Whitney was pardoned by Gov. C. C. Young (1927). Neylan subsequently turned conservative and opposed Roosevelt's New Deal.

University of California President Robert Gordon Sproul on March 25, 1949, proposed a loyalty oath for faculty. On September 26, 1950, the California legislature passed a bill requiring state employees to sign a loyalty oath.

207. Jack S. McDowell, "California Fact and Comment, Ghosts spook McCarthy," column, *San Francisco Call-Bulletin*, October 31, 1958, AC Papers.

208. Cranston for Controller Committee, Fresno County, form letter to "Fellow Democrat," October 10, 1958, AC Papers.

209. "Memo to all Cranston Coordinators," signed Marta and Teddy, no date; Associated Press, "Still used, says Brown," unidentified news clipping citing *New York Times* story, and smear clippings, Carton 9, AC Papers.

210. Reprint from "Headlines," December 31, 1951, with order form for additional flyers and address, Box 333, Westport, Connecticut, citing book *Ally Betrayed*, AC Papers.

Walter Reuther (1907-70), a powerful labor leader and Democratic Party activist, was anti-Communist and pro-civil rights. He had been a Socialist Party member and with his two brothers worked at a Gorky auto plant in the Soviet Union 1933-35. He was accused of being a Communist and did cooperate with them in the late 1930s. He supported the war effort, and in the 1940s purged the U. A. W. of Communists. He became president of the Congress of Industrial Organizations (C. I. O.) in 1952, negotiated a merger with the A. F. L., effective in 1955, and supported the United Farm Workers in California. A leader of liberal causes, he survived two assassination attempts, and one plane crash before dying with his wife and others in a plane crash in 1970, both of which were suspicious. Reuther was posthumously awarded the Presidential Medal of Freedom by President Bill Clinton in 1995.

211. "Democrats' candidate for state controller," unidentified editorial, [1958], AC Papers.

212. Fowle, 21.

213. Fowle, 122; Cranston for Controller Committee, release, "Statement by Alan Cranston on Joseph Kamp's letter to newspaper editors," [1958], and release, August 9, 1958;

typescript, "Alan Cranston…disclosed today that he was the target of a smear sheet prepared by hate-monger Joseph Kamp and distributed in the Sacramento area," no date; typescript, "Alan Cranston…today called upon his opponent…Kirkwood to repudiate the use by his campaign supporters of material published by Joseph Kamp, a New York pamphleteer with a criminal record," no date [1958], AC Papers.

214. Associated Press, "Still used, says Brown," unidentified news clipping citing *New York Times* story; "Old 'Red issue' again?" editorial, Ventura County *Star-Free Press*, July 21, 1958, AC Papers.

215. Harry Farrell, "Cranston silent on 'smear,'" *San Jose Mercury-News*, August 29, 1958, AC Papers.

216. Richard Nixon, Office of the Vice President, to Goodwin J. Knight, Governor of California, marked "Personal," March 12, 1958, AC Papers; Fowle, 123.

217. Reprint, letter to editor, *Los Angeles Times*, October 14, 1958, signed by Catherine A. Thorp, Santa Monica; Anne F. Redfield Heaver, Beverly Hills; and George R. Jordan, Major USAF (Ret.), Bel Air, AC Papers.

218. "More Kamp-following," editorial, Sunnyvale *Standard*, October 28, 1958, AC Papers.

219. "Form letters" file, Carton 500, and AC letter, August 29, 1958, AC Papers.

220. Republican Party, San Francisco, memorandum to "All GOP Leaders" from Chairman Bob Steele, Fact Memo No. 5, October 29, 1958, AC Papers.

221. "Kirkwood clips" files and "Endorsements," Carton 501, AC Papers.

222. Fowle, 124.

223. AC letter to campaign workers, "Hi! From the very start...," AC Papers.

224. Ann Alanson Eliaser, San Francisco, interview with author.

225. Fowle, 124.

226. *Ibid.*; Greenaway interview with author; scrapbook, Vol. 1, 1959, AC Papers.

227. Fowle, 125.

228. Teddy and Marta, memorandum, "Dear Constant Cranston Campaigner," AC Papers.

229. "Controller Kirkwood refuses to concede, 'pretty slim chance,'" *Daily Palo Alto Times*, Friday, November 7, 1958; AC Papers.

230. "State controller Robert C. Kirkwood dropped into the *Sun-Herald* office this morning…after a highly successful duck hunt…," Colusa *Sun-Herald*, November 19, 1958; "Kirkwood still hasn't conceded," *Daily Palo Alto Times*, November 26, 1958, AC Papers.

231. "Kirkwood may seek recount of November vote returns," special to *The Tribune*, datelined December 3, unidentified news article, AC Papers.

232. Fowle, 125.

233. "Kirkwood clips" files, Carton 501; "Record vote revealed in official state tally," Hayward *Daily Review*, December 16, 1958; scrapbook, Vol. 1, 1959, AC Papers.

Cranston's reported contributions and expenditures were: in the primary, contributions, $32,874, expenditures, $30,849; in the general election, contributions, $178,340, expenditures, $181,880, for a deficit of $3,540.

Kirkwood died of a heart attack at age fifty-four on May 5, 1964. He was S. F. Public Utilities Department manager. Cranston was quoted as saying that he "knew him as a neighbor and friend for many years in Santa Clara County." "Robert Kirkwood rites tomorrow," *San Francisco Examiner*, May 7, 1964, scrapbook, Vol. 7, 1964, AC Papers.

234. Fowle, 126; Teddy and Marta, memorandum, December, 10, 1958, AC Papers.

235. Mildred Schroeder, "The unusual is the typical in the Cranston family…," *San Francisco Examiner*, December 14, 1958.

236. AC interview with author; Carton 501, AC Papers.

237. Fowle, 126.

238. *Ibid.*, 126-27.

Chapter 7 Triumph and Defeat

1. AC to Mrs. Carol D. Cranston, 391 Cypress Drive, Los Altos, January 14, 1959, AC Papers.

2. Fowle, 131.

3. AC to Edith Seros, April 8, 1959; AC to Mrs. Liz Heller, State Central Committee-Northern California, April 8, 1959, AC Papers.

4. Fowle, 129, citing La Quinta Hotel.

5. Fowle, 130.

6. Fowle, 130-31, citing Brown's attendance at Los Gatos Novitiate, and *Sacramento Bee*, January 6, 1959.

7. Fowle, 141-42; David Dow, "Peaceful coexistence is a way of life on Cranston farm," *Sacramento Bee*, August 29, 1965; Dorothy Lindsey, "State controller's wife, she visits while he works," Sunnyvale *Standard*, November 14, 1961; Jeannette Branin, "Wife of state treasurer revisits girlhood scenes," *San Diego Independent*, July 29, 1962, AC Papers.

8. Fowle, 142; Dow, "Peaceful coexistence is a way of life on Cranston farm"; Jack and Vicki Tomlinson, San Francisco, interview with author, March 21, 2001.

9. Fowle, 142; Dow, *ibid.*

10. Sydney Rosen, "Mrs. Alan Cranston plans many-sided life for herself," *Sacramento Bee*, January 12, 1959, AC Papers; REC interview with author.

11. Dow, "Peaceful coexistence is a way of life on Cranston farm"; Eloise Dungan, "'It's part of the game,'" *San Francisco News-Call Bulletin*, October 24, 1962; "Controller Cranston, wealthiest official sets a precedent," unidentified news article, [*Los Angeles Times*?, November ?], 1965, scrapbook, Vol. 8, 1965, AC Papers.

12. Fowle, 143; Kim Cranston to author, August 24, 2005.

13. Kim to "Dear Mom, Happy Mother's Day," [no date], AC Personal Papers.

14. Robin M. Cranston, 5th grade, Marconi, "The Horse," April 2, 1959, AC Personal Papers.

15. Robin "To Alan," note, [no date], AC Personal Papers.

16. Robin Cranston, English class essay, October 17, 1961, AC Personal Papers.

17. AC to Mr. and Mrs. John Fowle, c/o American Express, Marseilles, France, October 3, 1963, AC Personal Papers.

18. Fowle, 132; "The State Controller," by Alan Cranston (no date), AC Papers; AC to Mrs. Carol D. Cranston, January 14, 1959.

Cranston was the state's 24th controller, an elected independent fiscal officer provided by the state's constitution, responsible for overseeing both collection and disbursement of state funds. No funds could be withdrawn from the treasury without the controller's approval/warrant. He was tax collector (serving on the Board of Equalization that collected sales, gasoline and business taxes, and the Franchise Tax Board that collected income and corporate taxes). He oversaw the sale of bonds to raise money for such things as school districts, veterans' home loans, capital investments in state properties. He managed state oil-producing tidelands and some 500,000 acres of other state lands on the three-member State Lands Commission, and a Pooled Money Investment Board that invested state funds. According to a brochure (circa 1961-62) that Cranston issued describing the controller's duties, 50 cents of each general-fund dollar went to local government, thus the controller examined local programs and expenditures. "Alan Cranston, Controller," brochure, circa 1961-62, AC Papers.

Friends like Greenaway were astonished that Nebron was appointed rather than Teddy Mueller.

19. Fowle, 132-33.

20. Nebron to AC, July 19, 1960, AC Papers.

21. "One of the boys," unidentified appraiser to AC, January 17, 1959, AC Papers.

ITAs' fees were fixed by law and paid by estates: 1/10th of one percent of the value of the estate up to $500,000, 1/20th, above that. Thus fees for a $5,000 estate would be $5, for $1 million, $750.

22. "Appraisers system, '58-'59" file, Carton 15; Martin E. Rothenberg, attorney, Pittsburg, CA., to AC, December 29, 1958, AC Papers.

When Cranston became controller, there were 125 ITAs.

23. Fowle, 139, 147; "Demo Lopez gets plum as appraiser, Cranston reaffirms patronage system," *San Francisco News*, February 16, 1959; "Salinger, Cranston trade insults," Huntington Park, Ca., *Signal*, May 21, 1964; Harry Farrell, "He'd 'turn rascals out' quick enough!" *San Jose Mercury-News*, March 11, 1962, AC Papers

Greenaway served as an ITA 1959-1967, when he was fired by Cranston's successor, Republican Houston Flourney. The appraiser system was abolished when the legislature abolished inheritance taxes in California, although appraisals continued to be done of real property for probate purposes.

24. Fowle, 139.

25. AC to Ziffren, May 6, 1959, AC Papers.

26. Williams interview with author.

27. Fowle, 127, 134.

28. Fowle, 133.

29. Fowle, 133-34; scrapbook, Vol. 1, 1959, AC Papers.

30. "Oil platform rule stays - Cranston," *Santa Barbara News Press*, August 26, 1960, AC Papers.

The Lands Commission halted further leases of state off-shore tracts after the 1969 oil spill. See note 33.

31. Paul Nissen, "Searchlight, Alan in Wonderland," Costa Mesa *Globe Herald*, April 26, 1961, AC Papers.

32. "State Controller once booted off train here," Barstow *Desert Dispatch*, March 9, 1962, AC Papers.

33. Press release, "State Controller Alan Cranston was elected chairman of the State Lands Commission today…," July 24, 1962; Palos Verdes *News*, November 2, 1961, Carton 15, AC Papers.

Cranston succeeded Lt. Gov. Glenn Anderson as chairman of the Lands Commission; Director of Finance Hale Champion was the commission's third member.

Off-shore oil-drilling rigs in the Wilmington Oil Field in Long Beach Harbor in 1965-68 were camouflaged to appear as islands, designed by landscape architect Joseph Linesch (1924-96) with palm trees, waterfalls and night-lit colored walls. Four platforms, called "THUMS" after the Texaco, Humble, Union, Mobil and Shell oil consortium, were named for astronauts who died (Virgil I. Grissom, Ed White, Robert B. Chafee, Theodore Freeman). California owned and controlled mineral resources within three nautical miles of shore, managed by the State Lands Commission. It halted further leasing of off-shore tracts after a Santa Barbara coast spill in 1969 and in 1994 California codified a ban on new leases with the Coastal Sanctuary Act. The federal government managed off-shore lease sales until 1984 when Congress banned additional leases off California, continued until 2008 when the ban was lifted although no federal lease-sales subsequently were proposed. As of 2011 there were nine active off-shore drilling sites in state waters.

34. "Does anyone have an old Indian war bond to cash in?" *San Jose Post Record*, September 21, 1959; "State still has funds to redeem Indian war bonds," South Gate, Ca., *Press*, September 20, 1959; scrapbook, Vol. 1, 1959, AC Papers.

35. Fowle, 134-35; Al Johns, "CREA ends 55th annual convention," [*Los Angeles*?] *Times*

Real Estate Editor, October 11, [1959]; scrapbook, Vol. 6, 1963, AC Papers.

36. Kirt MacBridge, "Good Morning," column, *Sacramento Union*, February 23, 1962, scrapbook, Vol. 4, 1962, AC Papers.

37. "Kate Hukill," Redondo Beach *Record*, May 2, 1963, scrapbook, Vol. 6, 1963, AC Papers.

38. "Over the fence gossip," *Sacramento Bee*, January 17, 1959; AC notes re: cars, [1965-66?], Carton 14, AC Papers.

39. Fowle, 135.

40. Fowle, 135-36; Carl Greenberg, "Time out to right an injustice," *Los Angeles Times*, July 24, 1962, AC Papers.

41. Fowle, 136-37; "Cranston halts pension for W. G. Bonelli," Associated Press, January 30, 1959, and "Over his live body," editorial, Redwood City *Tribune*, February 13, 1959, AC Papers.

42. Robinson, '*You're in Your Mother's Arms' – The Life & Legacy of Congressman Phil Burton*, 17.

43. Ward Winslow, "Unruh sealed own political doom," unidentified news article, [1963?]; "Capitol quotes," Capital News Service, December 1, 1964, scrapbook, Vol. 7, 1964; Dr. Fred Kugler, CDC Historian, "CDC's progressivism gains influence," California Democratic Council publication, February, 1973, 11, reviewing CDC's 20-year history, citing series on how Unruh built power by Harry Farrell, *San Jose Mercury News*, 1963, AC Papers.

44. Gene Marine, "Ode to Daddy," *California Feature Service*, August 12, 1963, AC Papers.

45. Scrapbook, Volume 5, 1963, AC Papers; Fowle, 144-45, citing AC testimony to Assembly Ways and Means Committee.

46. Fowle, 146.

47. Herbert L. Phillips, "Controller's auditors save $1 million for state by examination of claims," *Sacramento Bee*, October 20, 1959, AC Papers.

48. Fowle, 146.

49. AC interview with author; Fowle, 185.

50. "Drudgery of paying income taxes cut," Redwood City *Tribune*, December 5, 1959; news clippings in scrapbook, Vol. 1, 1959, AC Papers.

51. "Cranston says state once more has fiscal responsibility," *Palo Alto Times*, December 10, 1959, AC Papers.

52. Fowle, 149-50; Robinson, 131.

California was the third state in the nation to have a consumer watch-dog agency; it was headed by economist Helen Nelson who would become a nationally-recognized consumer advocate.

53. Vivian Batman, "State controller visits Montebello," Montebello *News*, May 12, 1960; "State Controller once booted off train here," Barstow *Desert Dispatch*, March 9,1962, AC Papers.

54. Fowle, 152.

55. Fowle, 150-51.

Caryl W. Chessman (1921-60) was a convicted robber and rapist with a long criminal record. After being paroled from a California prison, he was convicted in 1948 on 17 counts of robbery, kidnapping and rape (as the "Red-Light Bandit" for appearing to be a police officer). He was condemned under the "Lindbergh Law" allowing the death penalty for kidnapping with bodily harm. His case gained international attention at a time when many states and Western countries were abolishing the death penalty. Through 12 years on death row and dozens of appeals in which he claimed innocence or trial irregularities, Chessman authored four books and avoided eight executions (his life would be the subject of a film). Notable authors including Ray Bradbury, Robert Frost, Aldous Huxley, Norman Mailer as well as Eleanor Roosevelt and evangelist Billy Graham wrote Gov. Brown appealing for clemency. Brown stayed execution for 60 days on February 19, 1960, claiming that he was concerned for President Eisenhower's safety in South America where the case stirred anti-American feelings. The stay ran out in April and Chessman was executed at San Quentin Prison May 2, 1960.

56. Fowle, 150-51; Governor Brown to AC, May 25, 1960; AC to Brown, May 26, 1960; AC to Joel Blain, University Stevenson for President Committee, Riverside, California, June 13, 1960; AC to Clarence E. Heller, San Francisco, June 21, 1960; AC to Mrs. Wilma Merrill, Los Angeles, re: Johnson, July 8, 1960; AC to Mrs. Ray D. Owen, Pasadena, re: Sea Cliff Democrats for Bowles, July 8, 1960, AC Papers; Eliaser note to author, 2003, re: Bowles' half delegate vote.

Chester Bowles (1901-86) was Governor of Connecticut (1948-50), Ambassador to India twice (1951-53, 1963-69), Congressman (1959-61) and Under Secretary of State (1961). As chairman of the Democratic platform committee in 1960, he fought for a strong civil-rights plank and policy of foreign aid.

57. Jack S. McDowell, "Demos' Paul Ziffren is odd man out," *San Francisco News-Call Bulletin*, June 14, 1960; *News Call-Bulletin*, April 13, 1954; "The coup that failed, Ziffren's enemies tried to purge him with a scandal," *Fortnight*, May 19, 1954, 12, AC Papers.

For biographical information on Paul Ziffren, see Chapter 6 and note 40.

58. Greenaway to author, May 19, 2003, and November 2, 2004.

59. Fowle, 150-51; AC tallies for 1960 presidential nomination, Carton 13; Carl Greenberg, "Democrats are keeping wary watch on Unruh," *Los Angeles Times*, May 8, 1963, AC Papers.

60. Herman H. Ridder to Fred Dutton, Washington, D. C., April 11, 1961, and Hank Ridder to AC, April 11, 19, 20, 1961, Carton 14, file "Nixon"; AC Papers.

Fred G. Dutton (1923-2005) was a long-time Democratic strategist who served in Gov. Brown's administration and as Assistant Secretary of State in the Kennedy administration. He was active in Democratic presidential campaigns 1960-72. FredDutton.com website.

61. Philip Reiner, affidavit dated April 19, 1961, Carton 14, file "Nixon," AC Papers.

L. Sherman Adams (1899-1986) was a close friend of Eisenhower's and White House Chief of Staff 1953-58; Republican Governor of New Hampshire 1949-53; U. S. Congressman 1945-47. Vice President Nixon said in interviews that he regretted having to ask Adams to resign in the absence of legal proceedings, ending his political career. *Time* magazine May 16, 1977, reported that Connecticut lawyer and Republican National Committee Chairman (1957-59) H. Meade Alcorn, Jr. (1907-92) actually fired Adams.

62. Ridder to Fred Dutton, Washington, D. C., April 11, 1961, file "Nixon," AC Papers.

63. Ridder to AC, April 19, 20, 1961.

64. Canfield to AC, July 31, 1961, and files, "Nixon," "Nixon article" with AC notes, Carton 14, AC Papers; Hughes, Nixon and the CIA, http://www.democratic underground.com website; Trivia on President Richard M. Nixon, http://www.trivia-library.com website.

Shortly after making the loan in 1956, Hughes' Medical Institute was granted tax-exempt status by the IRS, previously refused. The loan also was controversial because Hughes was a defense contractor with the U. S. government.

65. Fowle, 152-53, citing Willows *Daily Journal* September 15, 1960, Ruth Finney, *San Francisco News-Call-Bulletin*, February 24, 1961, and Harry Farrell, *San Jose Mercury*, September 5, 1960.

66. AC, "Alan Cranston views," *Democratic Council News*, January, 1961, AC Papers.

67. Bob Wells, "Bob Wells' nightcap, no longer unknown," *Long Beach Press Telegram*, October 23, 1961; news clippings, scrapbook, Vol. 3, 1961, AC Papers.

68. Dorothy Lindsey, "State controller's wife, she visits while he works," Sunnyvale *Standard*, November 14, 1961; photo of GC weeding yard, *Sacramento Bee*, January 1, 1961, Carton 15; news clippings, scrapbook, Vol. 6, 1963, AC Papers.

69. Jack and Vicki Tomlinson interview with author, March 21, 2001.

70. Jeannette Branin, "Wife of state treasurer revisits girlhood scenes," *San Diego Independent*, July 29, 1962, AC Papers.

71. Eloise Dungan, "It's part of the game," *San Francisco News-Call Bulletin*, October 24, 1962, AC Papers.

72. Jack and Vicki Tomlinson interview with author, March 21, 2001.

73. Bert Clinkston, "Race for controller - problem in frustration," *Sacramento Union*, October 12, 1962, scrapbook, Vol. 5, 1962, AC Papers.

74. File, "Press releases," Carton 502, AC papers; AC to Mr. and Mrs. John Fowle, Hotel Grande Bretagne, Athens, Greece, January 30, 1962, AC Personal Papers.

75. "Cranston differs with Demo unit on probe stand," *Sacramento Bee*, August, 23, 1962; "CDC embarrasses candidates," editorial, *San Diego Union*, January 30, 1962, scrapbook, Vol. 5, 1962, AC Papers.

76. Press release announcing candidacy for reelection, March 13, 1962; AC notebook, scrapbook, Vol. 3, 1961, AC Papers.

77. Photo, AC milking cow, *Portuguese Journal*, January 11, 1962; photo of man registering to vote on AC's back, *Fresno Bee*, September 9, 1962, and Hayakawa article, Tiburon *Ebb Tide*, April 24, 1962, scrapbook, Vol. 5, 1962; file, "'62 mailings" and matchbooks with caption, "Re-elect Alan Cranston," Carton 502; "Vote with confidence, Re-elect Alan Cranston, your State Controller, Democrat," campaign brochure, [1962]; "Alan Cranston has been a life-long friend of Italy and of people of Italian origin," typescript, [1962?]; R. A. "Bones" Hamilton, Van Nuys, to "Dear Classmate," October 26, 1962, AC Papers.

Samuel Ichiye Hayakawa (1906-92) was an English professor at S. F. State College 1955-68, president 1968-73. In 1968-69 he quelled student demonstrations led by the Third World Liberation Front, pulling out speaker wires to end one rally. He was elected to the U. S. Senate in 1976, defeating John V. Tunney, and served one term until 1983, during which he got a reputation for snoozing at his desk on the Senate floor.

78. Fowle, 155.

79. "State Controller once booted off train here," Barstow *Desert Dispatch*, March 9, 1962, AC Papers.

California then ranked 27 among the 50 states in bond indebtedness but had the lowest debt of the nine highest-indebted states.

80. File, "'62 mailings." Carton 502; "Vote with confidence, Re-elect Alan Cranston, your State Controller, Democrat," campaign brochure, [1962], mailed to 117,000 people, AC Papers.

John Anson Ford was long-time L. A. County Supervisor 1934-58, a member of the Democratic Central Committee and chairman of Citizens for Kennedy, 1960. For biographical information, see Chapter 4, note 34.

81. Aileen C. Hernandez, memorandum "Personal and confidential," to AC and Irwin Nebron, April 20, 1962, AC Papers; Eliaser note to author, 2003.

82. Re-elect Cranston Controller Committee, "Cranston voter-appeal," campaign flyer, July, 1962; George Todt, "The peoples' choice," *Los Angeles Herald-Examiner*, August 15, 1962.

83. "Cranston voter-appeal" campaign flyer.

84. "State controller rescued," Redondo Beach *Daily Breeze*, October 31, 1962, scrapbook, Vol. 4, 1962; files on 1962 election, Carton 502, and scrapbook, Vol. 4, 1962, AC Papers; REC interview with author March 28, 2003.

85. Bob Frantz, "The Chowder Pot," Pismo Beach *Times*, October 18, 1962, AC Papers.

86. Craig C. Lee, Los Angeles, to AC, postcard with cartoon drawing postmarked October 31, 1962; AC to Lee, November 13, 1962; unidentified writer to AC, November 7, 1962, file "Postcard responses," Carton 502, AC Papers.

87. Fowle, 155; "The Kuchel Family," photo-postcard addressed to AC, 27060 Old Trace Road, Los Altos Hills, postmarked November [?], 1962, AC Papers.

Nixon beat conservative Republican Assemblyman Jose Shell in the gubernatorial primary. Actor Ronald Reagan (1911-2004) was known for portraying George Gipp in the film, *Knute Rockne - All American*. He had gone to Hollywood in 1937 and supported liberal groups until the Cold War promoted fears of communist conspiracies, prompting Reagan to run for Screen Actors Guild president. He subsequently became a frequent informer to the F. B. I. with names of actors and Hollywood figures whom Reagan suspected of communist sympathies. Reagan gave more than 200 speeches as a "Democrat for Nixon" in the 1959-60 presidential race against John F. Kennedy. Reagan became co-chair of California Republicans for Barry Goldwater for President in 1964 and gave a televised speech, "A Time for Choosing," that gave him national political attention. Seth Rosenfeld, "The F. B. I.'s secret U. C. files," *San Francisco Chronicle*, June 9, 2002. See also Chapter 8, note 18.

88. File "Suit," Carton 502, citing Herbert L. Phillips, McClatchey Newspapers, AC Papers.

89. Fowle, 156; file "Pat Brown red smear," Carton 502, AC Papers.

90. Fowle, 156-57.

92. Fowle, 157; *Palo Alto Times*, September 17, 1962, Carton 502, AC Papers.

The John Birch Society's anti-Communist stand was an election issue in 1962. The Cuban missile crisis also occurred in October, just before the 1962 elections, after photographs showed Soviet missile bases under construction in Cuba. The U. S. blockaded the island and Soviet Premier Khrushchev agreed to remove the missiles if the U. S. removed them from Turkey. On April 17, 1961, 1,500 Cuban émigrés, with U. S. training and support, unsuccessfully attempted an invasion at Cuba's Bay of Pigs.

92. Robinson, '*You're in Your Mother's Arms,*' 70.

93. Karl Prussion, 596 Panchita Way, Los Altos, CA., "Candidates not qualified to combat communism," political advertisement, circa 1962, AC Papers.

At a press conference, Prussion conceded that he had not actually been an F. B. I. agent but a former Communist and "counterspy" providing the F. B. I. with information. It was his booklet that depicted Governor Brown apparently bowing to Khrushchev with the caption, "Brown is a Red appeaser." The CDC bulletin said that the actual picture showing Brown with clasped hands was taken when he was making a Buddhist gesture of greeting, "Sambai," to a Laotian girl.

94. "GOP chief denies 'smear' booklet," Bakersfield *Californian*, October 11, 1962; CDC newsletter, "Special Campaign Bulletin, Nixon: Anything to win," October 23, 1962, AC Papers.

95. "Distribution of booklet barred," *Los Angeles Times*, October 30, 1962; "California suit names Chotiner," *New York Times*, western edition, October 31, 1962; file "Suit," Carton 502, AC Papers.

Three court orders in eight days were issued against Republican campaign literature.

96. "Red Print for U. S. Conquest," booklet, [1962], AC Papers.

The booklet promoted a book, *Toward Soviet America* by William Z. Foster, a former chairman of the Communist Party, U. S. A., which had been given plugs by commentators like Dan Smoot and George Todt, whose columns were critical of Cranston.

97. CDC newsletter, "Special Campaign Bulletin, Nixon: Anything to win," October 23, 1962, AC Papers.

The U. S. and Soviet Union had resumed atmospheric nuclear weapons tests in September, 1961, both underground and above ground.

98. Fowle to AC, April 25, 1962, citing "a leaflet attacking ACLU…enclosed with the Reich letter"; Wendell L. Reich to "Residents of Los Altos Hills," April 3, 1962, AC Personal Papers.

Jack Fowle, a businessman, on the Los Altos Hills City Council for fourteen years, led a push to incorporate Los Altos Hills in 1956. His father Arthur E. Fowle was elected the first mayor; Jack filled out his term when his father resigned for ill health, was elected for a full term in 1958, reelected in 1960. The Fowles' home was described in a *San Jose Mercury* feature story August 23, 1962, scrapbook, Vol. 4, 1962, AC Papers.

99. William K. Coblentz to John M. Fowle, April 19, 1962, AC Personal Papers.

100. President Dwight D. Eisenhower to Ernest Angell, chairman, American Civil Liberties Union, Chicago, April 18, 1960, AC Personal Papers; *San Jose Mercury*, April 6, 1962, scrapbook, Vol. 5, AC Papers.

101. Bruce Reagan political advertisement for controller, [1962]; George Todt, "The peoples' choice," *Los Angeles Herald-Examiner*, August 15, 1962; "Speakers at rally link Cranston to Samish, lash Betts on appointments," *Sacramento Bee*, August 31, 1962, AC Papers.

102. "Cranston differs with Demo unit on probe stand," *Sacramento Bee*, August, 23, 1962; "CDC's Cranston - what he thinks," United Press International, *San Francisco Examiner*, March 1, 1964; "CDC embarrasses candidates," editorial, *San Diego Union*, January 30, 1962, scrapbook, Vol. 5, 1962; Frank Anderson, "Cranston, CDC toppled GOP control," *Long Beach Independent Press-Telegram*, September 11, 1968, quoting AC statement of February, 1964, AC Papers; Greenway to author, May 19, 2003.

103. Bert Clinkston, "Race for controller - problem in frustration," *Sacramento Union*, October 12, 1962, scrapbook, Vol. 5, 1962, AC Papers.

104. "Area press fetes Cal. official here," Paramount, California, *Journal*, August 30, 1962, AC Papers.

105. Roger Kent to Stanley A. Weigel, San Francisco, August 27, 1962, AC Papers.

William Donlon (Don) Edwards (born 1915) of San Jose was elected to Congress in 1962 and served from 1963 to 1995. He was chairman of the House Subcommittee on Civil Liberties and Civil Rights for 23 years. The Don Edwards San Francisco Bay National Wildlife Refuge at the south end of S. F. Bay was named for him.

Roger Kent (1906-80), son of California Congressman William Kent (1911-17), was an unsuccessful candidate for Congress in 1948 and 1950. He served as General Counsel for the U. S. Department of Defense during the Joseph McCarthy attacks in the 1950s. In 1958 he became chairman of the Democratic State Central Committee and supported Brown's gubernatorial election, serving until Ronald Reagan's election over Brown in 1966. Kent co-chaired L. B. Johnson's 1964 presidential campaign and was a close friend of Johnson's Vice President Hubert Humphrey. William Kent (1864-1928) was a Progressive Republican who sponsored the bill that created the National Park Service, signed by President Wilson in 1916. The Kent family were early settlers (1870s) and large landowners of Marin County, north of San Francisco; the town of Kentfield was named for them. Kent's father A. E. Kent funded the Mt. Tamalpais & Muir Woods Railway. William Kent donated one of the last stands of coast redwoods in the county to the federal government for a park, declared a national monument by President Theodore Roosevelt in 1908. William Kent rejected naming it after him and suggested calling it Muir Woods to honor naturalist John Muir.

106. Letter to editor, *San Diego Union*, October 6, 1962, AC Papers.

Previously, couples who moved from another state to California, which had community-property laws, could by will or agreement, convert and declare all property community property, a taxable event because one was transferring half the property to the other. The legislature in 1961 made conversion non-taxable.

107. Mike Jackson, "Check machine locks when money runs out," *Los Angeles Herald-Examiner*, October 12, 1962, AC Papers.

108. Lee Ettelson, memorandum re: "Press Calls," October 13, 1962, AC Papers.

Lee Ettelson (died 1988) was a well-known journalist, former executive editor of Hearst's *Seattle Post-Intelligencer* transferred to the *San Francisco Call-Bulletin* as editor in 1951 by W. R. Hearst, Jr., after he took over the newspaper on the death of his father. Ettelson subsequently was editor of the *San Francisco Examiner*. His wife Suzanne (1913-2005), a founder of the S. F. Chamber Music Society and Composers, Inc., endowed a composers' award in memory of her husband.

109. Lee Ettelson to AC, memorandum, October 25, 1962; "Cranston cites feat in state's financing," Hanford *Sentinel*, October 4, 1962, scrapbook, Vol. 5, 1962, AC Papers.

California in 1962 ranked 7th of the 50 states in per-capita taxes, 31st in relation to income, second in bonded indebtedness.

110. File "Press endorsements," Carton 502; "Re-elect Cranston," editorial, *San Francisco Examiner*, October 24, 1962; "Cranston's surprise performance," editorial, *Palo Alto Times*, October 31, 1962; press release, typescript iterating endorsements, November 1, 1962; Bert Clinkston, "Vote-pulling stature suggests question of Cranston's future," *Sacramento Union*, November 14, 1962; *California Eagle*, April 26, 1962, scrapbook, Vol. 5, 1962, AC Papers.

The *San Francisco Chronicle* endorsed Republicans Nixon for governor, George Christopher for lieutenant governor, Kuchel for Senate and William Mailliard for Congress; it endorsed Democrats Mosk for attorney general, Shelley for Congress and Cranston. The *San Francisco Examiner* endorsed Brown for governor.

111. "Mandrake, Phantom author, aids Cranston," with photograph of AC and Falk in city room, Humboldt *Standard*, November 3, 1962; Jerry Belcher, "A busy plot spinner," *San Francisco Examiner*, October 28, 1962, AC Papers.

Falk was author of the two comic strips, syndicated by King Features, each of which had different artists, a 100-million audience worldwide in 1962, and was translated into 26 different languages (it appeared in every country except Africa and China, according to Falk). Falk also was a producer and director, and owned summer-stock theaters in Massachusetts and Nassau, The Bahamas. See also Chapter 2, note 34.

112. Lu Azevedo, "Politics rate high for R. E. Fowle," Los Altos *News & Guide*, May 25, 1961; RE to AC, May 5 and August 21, 1962, AC Personal Papers.

113. Fowle, 158; *San Francisco Examiner*, November 8, 1962, front-page story, Carton 502; Forrest Black, "California controller visits here; he got more votes than Gov. Brown," *Honolulu Star-Bulletin*, November 23, 1962, scrapbook, Vol. 5, 1962, AC Papers; Ethan Rarick, "Kicking Nixon around some more, Tricky Dick's career marked a stark change in press-politician relations," *San Francisco Chronicle*, December 1, 2002.

Nixon unexpectedly had appeared at his concession press conference originally intended to be conducted by his press secretary Herb Klein, grabbing the microphone from Klein to make his defensive statements, accusing the press of being "delighted that I have lost." Rarick pointed out that Otis Chandler had taken over the *Los Angeles Times* by 1962 and instituted reforms in its reportage and editorial style to be more balanced than the blatant pro-Republican stance for which it had a reputation in the past. For the 1962 Nixon-Brown gubernatorial race, Chandler ordered reporters to be fair, covering both candidates equally, a surprise to Nixon who had been lauded from the beginning of his career by the *Times* under former political editor, Kyle Palmer. Ethan Rarick, *California Rising: The Life and Times of Pat Brown* (University of California Press, 2005)

114. Fowle, 158; memorandum, vote totals, citing Cranston's unofficial final as 3,290,839 to Reagan's 2,034,483, a margin of 1,256,356, Gov. Rockefeller's total of 3,083,560, Javits' margin of 975,000; "Totals on State, Congress," *Citizen News*, San Fernando Valley edition, November 7, 1962; Henry MacArthur, "Cranston for governor?" Capitol News Service, Roseville *Press-Tribune*, November 12, 1962; Jerry Gillam, "Cranston backers spent $390,655 in campaign," *Los Angeles Times*, December 11, 1962, AC Papers.

Final results were: Cranston - 3,372,691, Reagan - 2,114,377. Cranston got the largest vote in a contested statewide election in U. S. history, to date, winning by a margin of 1,258,314. Mosk, the biggest vote-getter in 1958 with 1,150,000 votes, beat Tom Coakley by some

600,000 votes in 1962. Glenn Anderson won reelection by only 200,000 over S. F. Mayor George Christopher. Cranston staff claimed that his vote had been exceeded in the past only by those received by Knowland when running for U. S. Senate in 1946 and by Pat Brown when reelected attorney general in 1954, both of whom had benefited from cross-filing and the fact that neither had no major opponents when they set those records.

Cranston reported spending for his 1962 campaign: in the primary, contributions of $133,726, expenditures of $79,577; in the general election, contributions of $377,754, expenditures of $390,655. Contributors included numerous appointed tax appraisers and state officials as well as leading Democratic Party financial backers and a number of savings-and-loan corporate contributors. "Controller Cranston, wealthiest official sets a precedent," unidentified news article, [*Los Angeles Times*?, November ?], 1965.

115. Leonard V. Finder, office of the publisher, *The Sacramento Union*, to AC, November 8, 1962, AC Papers.

116. Joseph B. Williams, state inheritance-tax appraiser, San Francisco, to AC, [1962], AC Papers.

117. Harry Farrell, "Unruh, Cranston duel shapes," *San Jose Mercury*, August 30, 1962; Frank Anderson, "Cranston, CDC toppled GOP control," *Long Beach Independent Press-Telegram*, September 11, 1968, AC Papers.

118. Henry MacArthur, "Cranston for governor?" Capitol News Service, Roseville *Press-Tribune*, November 12, 1962; Bert Clinkston, "Vote-pulling stature suggests question of Cranston's future," *Sacramento Union*, November 14, 1962, AC Papers; Herbert L. Phillips, "Politicos see Cranston as year's state and U. S. vote-getting champ," *Sacramento Bee*, November [?], 1962, AC Personal Papers.

119. Robinson, *"You're in Your Mother's Arms,"* 47, 146-47; Ralph Bennett, "Big Daddy defends actions on 'purity,'" *San Diego Evening Tribune*, June 14, 1963; Daryl Lembke, "Strict election purity bill filed in Assembly," *Los Angeles Times*, May 30, 1963, AC Papers.

Burton was running for Jack Shelley's congressional seat while Shelley was running for mayor of San Francisco.

120. Robinson, *ibid.*, 147, citing *San Francisco Chronicle* editorial, June 6, 1963; Fowle, 147.

Institutes to foster the understanding and study of politics were established in both Brown's and Unruh's names after they retired. Brown in 1987 created an Institute of Public Affairs at California State University at Los Angeles. An Institute of Politics at the University of Southern California was named for Unruh. Edward Epstein, "Willie Brown's school for dealmakers," *San Francisco Chronicle*, January 26, 2003.

121. Able Dart, "Politics inside out," *The Liberal Democrat*, January, 1963; "When big shot Demos lose in CDC, everybody wins - including the big shots themselves," Valley *Labor Citizen*, April 5, 1963, AC Papers.

The incumbent CDC president was Tom Carvey.

122. Dick Nolan, "Rousing cheer for a rebellious CDC," *San Francisco Examiner*, April 4, 1963, AC Papers.

123. Harry Farrell, "Unruh, Cranston square off," *San Jose Mercury*, February 12, 1963; Earl C. Behrens, "Cranston on carpet for CDC session remarks, criticism by Demo caucus," *San Francisco Chronicle*, April 2, 1963, AC Papers.

124. Fowle, 131-32, citing interviews in 1973; Earl C. Behrens, "Cranston on carpet for CDC session remarks, criticism by Demo caucus," *San Francisco Chronicle*, April 2, 1963, AC Papers.

125. "Cranston's blast on withholding," editorial and cartoon, *San Francisco Chronicle*, April 12, 1963, AC Papers.

126. Carl Greenberg, "Democrats are keeping wary watch on Unruh," *Los Angeles Times*, May 8, 1963, AC Papers.

127. Tom Meehan, 'Cross country' run, dip in pool launch day for Controller Cranston," *Fresno Bee*, May 11, 1963, and Charles Hurley to Tom [Meehan], AC Papers.

128. Hurley to Tom [Meehan].

Hurley resigned from Cranston in 1965 to become executive secretary of the Episcopal Diocese of Northern California; he joined Rep. Burton's staff as administrative and legislative assistant in 1966.

129. Mrs. William Cranston, 391 Cypress Drive, Los Altos, to "Dearest Alan," September 6, 1963, AC Papers.

The address of the relative was for Mrs. Herbert Cranston, 271 Sixth Street, Midland, Ontario.

130. Richard Rodda, "Cranston finds Europeans optimistic over chance for peace," with photograph of family unpacking, *Sacramento Bee*, August 19, 1963, and *Modesto Bee*, August 29, 1963, AC Papers.

131. "AC trip list," Carton 14, [1963], AC Papers.

132. Richard Rodda, "Cranston finds Europeans optimistic over chance for peace," *Sacramento Bee*, August 19, 1963

133. *Ibid.*

134. "Cranston asks probe of fair bribery rumors," *Los Angeles Herald-Examiner*, September 20, 1963, AC Papers.

135. Memorandum, "Telephone conversation 9-24-63 between Alan Cranston and Cy Gains," AC Papers.

136. "Troubles pile up in Long Beach, hunt mystery man in fair wrangle," *Los Angeles Herald-Examiner*, September 21, 1963; "Mystery tape discloses no wrongdoings," Van Nuys *Valley News*, September 24, 1963, AC Papers.

137. Hale Champion to Attorney General Mosk, September 19, 1963; Statement of State Controller Alan Cranston at Lands Commission Meeting, September 30, 1963; "Controller questions World's Fair books," Van Nuys *Valley Times*, October 1, 1963, AC Papers.

Fair commission manager Fred Hall resigned when the district attorney began an investigation.

138. Hale Champion, Director of Finance, to state Senator Virgil O'Sullivan, Williams, California, October 14, 1963, AC Papers.

139. Fowle, 161.

140. William Sumner, Washington Bureau, "Will Unruh take Controller's job? Musical chairs for Sen. Engle's post," *San Jose Mercury*, October 1, 1963, AC Papers.

141. Fowle, 162; Eric Brazil and Vicki Haddock, "Alan Cranston: a career built from grass roots, a look back at the pragmatic senator's long, contradictory life," *San Francisco Examiner*, November 9, 1990, AC Papers.

142. William Gruver, Beverly Hills *Times*, October 25, 1963, AC Papers.

143. Gruver, *ibid.*; *San Francisco Examiner* clipping, October 9, 1963, Stanley Mosk file, Carton 14, AC Papers.

144. Gruver, *ibid.*, and photograph of AC with caption announcing his speaking at Friars Club; Jack Rannells, "Cranston assails Goldwater," *Palo Alto Times*, November 8, 1963; "Forum Letters," AC letter to editor, *Palo Alto Times*, November 23, 1963, AC Papers.

The Friars Club was started in 1947 by comedian Milton Berle. Known for celebrity "roasts," it numbered as members many well-known entertainers. In 1961 it moved into a modernist building designed by architect Sidney Eisenshtat and operated until 2004 when declining membership forced it to be sold to a for-profit corporation. It lost a suit by the New York Friars Club for trademark name infringement, changed its name and closed in 2008. The building was demolished in 2011 against objections from the Los Angeles Conservancy. Wikipedia.

145. Fowle, 162, citing Arthur Caylor, column, *San Francisco News-Call Bulletin*, October

2, 1963.

146. Fowle, 163.

147. AC, "The Watchdog of State Funds Tells His Trade Secrets," *PC* magazine, Ventura County *Press-Courier*, Vol. 1, No. 18, November 23, 1963, AC Papers.

148. Louis Lurie, alphabetical file, Carton 14; Louis R. Lurie to AC, "Personal, please," December 13, 1963, with brochure, "Rules" for membership in "Coronary Club," AC Papers.

Chicago-born Louis R. Lurie (Sept. 8, 1888-Sept. 8, 1972, his 84th birthday), a self-made man, was called the "last of the Horatio Algers" in a *San Francisco Examiner* feature story July 22, 1962. He rose from selling newspapers on the streets of Chicago to become a major real-estate developer of downtown San Francisco, Broadway play producer (of hits like *South Pacific* and *Fiddler on the Roof*) and philanthropist (establishing the Lurie Foundation). He and George Killion once sold newspapers on Market Street, S. F., with Mayor George Christopher to benefit the March of dimes. Lurie was famous for lunching daily at historic, Gold Rush-era "Jack's" restaurant in the city's downtown. "Louis Lurie dies - colorful tycoon," *San Francisco Chronicle*, September 7, 1972.

149. Mrs. William Cranston to AC, January 29, 1964, AC Papers.

150. AC to Assemblyman Burton, January 20, 1964, AC Papers.

151. Greenaway to author, May 19, 2003.

152. Fowle, 164-65; Democratic State Central Committee, press release, "California Democratic Party leaders today told Senator Clair Engle…," January 11, 1964, AC Papers.

153. Fowle, 165; AC statement to Board of Directors meeting, CDC, release, January 19, 1964, AC Papers; R. E. Fowle to AC, "Friday afternoon," [no date, 1964], AC Personal Papers.

154. Fowle, *ibid.*; AC to R. E. Fowle, February 4, 1964, AC Personal Papers; "Behind-the-scenes maneuvering revealed, Brown backs Cranston for Senate," *Long Beach Independent-Press-Telegram*, February [7?], 1964, AC Papers.

For Dewey Anderson see Chapter 6, note 29.

155. Fowle, 166; "Behind-the-scenes maneuvering…"; Herb Caen, "Some like 'em short," *San Francisco Chronicle*, February 12, 1964, AC Papers; Greenway to author, May 19, 2003.

The civil-rights issue would enflame people throughout the nation after President Johnson signed the Civil Rights Act on July 2, 1964, guaranteeing voting rights and ensuring equal access to public accommodations and education. Urban riots erupted in New York City and Rochester, New York, July 18, the first of many to follow. President Kennedy, campaigning and fundraising at a $1,000-per-couple Democratic dinner in San Diego in June, 1963, during a parade had been confronted by civil-rights advocates planning demonstrations in San Diego and Los Angeles. News clippings, scrapbook, Vol. 6, 1963, AC Papers.

156. Fowle, 166; David Broder, "Salinger 'plot' his own doing," *Washington Star*, March 24, 1964; "Engle spurned, Cranston given CDC support," headline, *Los Angeles Times*, February 24, 1964, Carton 506, AC Papers.

157. Fowle, 167; "Controller Cranston, wealthiest official sets a precedent," [*Los Angeles Times*?, November ?], 1965; "Despite Engle plea, liberal Democrats support Cranston," Associated Press, Marin *Independent Journal*, February 24, 1964; Broder, "Salinger 'plot' his own doing"; Mosk release, March 4, 1964; Richard Rodda, "Unruh falls off horse in jousting with Pat Brown," *Sacramento Bee*, March 8, 1964, AC Papers.

See Chapter 11 for revelations about photographs of Mosk with a girl friend. Mosk, a few months after the 1964 CDC convention, was appointed by Brown to the State Supreme Court and served until his death in 2001, the longest-serving justice to date. Ethan Rarick, *California Rising: The Life and Times of Pat Brown* (University of California Press, 2005), 280, 437, n. 29.

158. Fowle, 167-68, citing Kimmis Hendrick, *Christian Science Monitor*, January 13, 1965; Richard Rodda, "Unruh falls off horse in jousting with Pat Brown," *Sacramento Bee*,

March 8, 1964; "Despite Engle plea, liberal Democrats support Cranston," Associated Press, Marin *Independent Journal*, February 24, 1964, AC Papers.

159. "No hairpiece, Cranston decides to stay bald," Associated Press, February 13, 1964; "Back Fence Gossip," *Sacramento Bee*, February 16, 1964; Jud Baker, "'I'll make my own decisions' - Cranston," *Los Angeles Herald-Examiner*, February 26, 1964, AC Papers.

160. "CDC's Cranston - what he thinks," United Press International, *San Francisco Examiner*, March 1, 1964, AC Papers.

161. Fowle, 169; *San Francisco Examiner*, January 16, 1964, re: Lucretia Engle denies interest in Senate, Carton 506, AC Papers.

162. "CDC's Cranston - what he thinks," United Press International, *San Francisco Examiner*, March 1, 1964; files in Carton 508; clipping, *San Francisco Examiner*, May 9, 1964, Carton 506, AC Papers.

King had given his "I have a dream" speech at the Lincoln Memorial in Washington before some 250,000 civil-rights supporters August 28, 1963.

163. Fowle, 170; Robert Ajemian, "Salinger swings for Senate - there's bedlam in California," *Life*, April 3, 1964, 43; David Broder, "Salinger 'plot' his own doing," *Washington Star*, March 24, 1964, AC Papers; AC interview with author.

There also was speculation that Salinger's race was part of a plan to test the "carpetbagger" possibility for Kennedy forces to run in other states.

164. Fowle, 169-70; Ajemian, "Salinger swings for Senate..."

165. Fowle, 172; AC statement on Pierre Salinger's candidacy, release, March 19, 1964, AC Papers.

166. Fowle, 171; David Broder, "Salinger 'plot' his own doing," *Washington Evening Star*, March 24, 1964.

167. Statement by Pierre Salinger, release, March 20, 1964, AC Papers.

168. Fowle, 172; Ajemian, "Salinger swings for Senate…"; Time, May 8, 1964, 25; Patricia Yollin, "Pierre Salinger - press secretary to presidents," *San Francisco Chronicle*, October 17, 2004, AC Papers.

Salinger (1925-2004) in 1964 had a wife and three children including a 15-year-old son Marc. Born in San Francisco, Pierre Emil George Salinger was the son of a Jewish-American father who worked as a mining engineer and a French-born Catholic mother who ran a daily newspaper for San Francisco's French community. He served in the Navy during WWII and ended commanding a 110-foot sub-chaser. He worked for Robert Kennedy as an investigator for the U. S. Senate's select committee on racketeering in the late 1950s and became JFK's campaign press secretary in 1959, moving to the White House during that administration and staying on with LBJ until March, 1964. He returned to the news business after his brief Senate stint and lived for many years in France. Salinger, who had four wives, reportedly suffered from Alzheimer's disease for several years before his death.

169. Fowle, 171; Broder, "Salinger 'plot' his own doing," with handwritten note on margin, "Dick [Nevins], I have no idea of where this came from - not true, Glenn"; "Salinger's surprise," *The Economist*, London, March 28, 1964, AC Papers.

Andrew Hatcher had worked with Salinger on the *San Francisco Chronicle* and in managing the 1952 Stevenson and 1954 Richard Graves campaigns.

170. Fowle, 175; "The Salinger gambit," editorial, Ventura County *Press-Courier*, March 23, 1964. See also note 157.

171. Fowle, 173; AC statement on court decision, March 27, 1964; Governor Brown, release #262 re: Bradley's decision to manage Salinger campaign, March 31, 1964; Robert Ajemian, "Salinger swings for Senate - there's bedlam in California," *Life*, April 3, 1964; "Salinger's surprise," *The Economist*, London, March 28, 1964; Lou Grant, cartoon, "Bare knuckle brawl, *Palo Alto Times*, April 30, 1964; "Cranston not concerned about Salinger in race," *San Luis Obispo Telegram-Tribune*, March [2?], 1964, and "Cranston not afraid of

Salinger," Lompoc *Record*, March 23, 1964, AC Papers.

172. Michael Harris, "Cuties vs. issues, Cranston's wife bets on latter," *San Francisco Chronicle*, [1964], AC Papers.

173. Fowle, 174; Salinger buttons, Carton 506; "Cranston pledges all-out effort for world peace," *San Luis Obispo Telegram-Tribune*, March [2?], 1964; "Cranston not afraid of Salinger," Lompoc *Record*, March 23, 1964, AC Papers.

174. AC release re: Salinger's debate challenge, March 30, 1964, AC Papers.

175. Fowle, 174; Jacques Levy, "Cranston's secret weapon combines charm, enthusiasm," *Santa Rosa Press Democrat*, April 19, 1964; Michael Harris, "Cuties vs. Issues," AC Papers; Eliaser interview with author, January 13, 2004.

176. Thomas G. Moore interview with author, February 10, 2004, hereafter cited as Moore interview with author.

Moore was director of the California Department of Social Welfare, director of press for the Johnson campaign (1964) and worked on Governor Brown's 1962 and 1966 campaigns. He would work on AC's successful 1968 Senate campaign (see Chapter 8).

177. Levy, "Cranston's secret weapon…"; campaign buttons, Carton 503; "Mr. Salinger and Mr. Cranston," Santa Monica *Evening Outlook*, May 13, 1964, scrapbook, Vol. 7, 1964, AC Papers.

178. Fowle, 174, citing AC appearance at National Press Club April 22, 1964; AC text of address to National Press Club, April 22, 1964; George Dixon, "Cranston a hit in D. C.," *Washington Post and Times Herald*, April 27, 1964, AC Papers.

179. Mary McGrory, *Washington Star* column datelined San Francisco, May 29, 1964, scrapbook, Vol. 7, 1964; Elena Bell, Ukiah, Ca., "Colorful Cranston," letter to editor, *Newsweek*, April 13, 1964, AC Papers.

180. Fowle, 174-75; Hutchins letter, August 19, 1964, AC Papers.

181. Photographs, AC milking cow, Vallejo *Times-Herald*, May 2, 1964, and with mother, *San Jose Mercury*, May 9, 1964; Controller Alan Cranston, press release, "Boaters refund," May 18, 1964, with photograph of AC handing check to woman on boat, Carton 3, AC Pics; "Cranston on esthetics," editorial, *San Francisco Chronicle*, April 28, 1964, file "'64 Misc.," Carton 506, AC Papers.

182. Richard Bergholz, "Cranston uneasy with small talk," *Los Angeles Times*, May 22, 1964, AC Papers.

183. Fowle, 175, 177.

184. "People of the week, a Democratic battle with big stakes," *U. S. News & World Report*, May 11, 1964, 19; Morrie Landsberg, "Cranston has never stopped running," Redding *Record-Searchlight*, May 18, 1964, AC Papers.

Twelve candidates were vying for the Senate nomination, including Cranston and Salinger.

185. Jack Tomlinson interview with author, March 21, 2001.

Tomlinson was Gov. Brown's travel secretary, 1965, executive secretary to the Democratic State Central Committee, 1965, and Northern California campaign manager for Brown, 1966.

186. Jack, Vicki Tomlinson and Moore, interviews with author; Fowle, 177.

Falk joined the campaign in the last two weeks and periodically went back to producing his cartoon scripts, typing them at the Fowle's dining-room table, using one to three fingers, to Eleanor's amazement.

187. "'Dirty politics' slap hurled by Salinger," Hollywood *Citizen News*, May 26, 1964; "Cranston, Salinger trade blows," Associated Press, Ventura *Star Free Press*, May 21, 1964, AC Papers.

188. "Legal road-block fails," CDC Newsletter no. 6, May 22, 1964, AC Papers.

189. Fowle, 176.

190. "Welcome change," editorial, *Santa Rosa Press-Democrat*, May 12, 1964, AC Papers.

191. "Unruh admits part in Cranston attack," Pittsburg, Ca., *Post-Dispatch*, May 21, 1964;

Bob Houser, "Ex-appraiser says job bought 'in effect,'" *Long Beach Independent Press-Telegram*, May 23, 1964; John C. O'Keefe, Azusa, to AC, January 10, 1962; AC release, re: O'Keefe's affidavit, May 20, 1964; "State Controller Alan Cranston's opponents…," unidentified statement, AC Papers.

192. AC release, re: O'Keefe's affidavit, May 20, 1964, AC Papers.

193. Bob Houser, "Ex-appraiser says job bought 'in effect,'" *Independent Press-Telegram*, May 23, 1964; "Salinger bombshell, Assembly probe of tax job buying," *San Francisco News Call-Bulletin*, May 23, 1964, AC Papers; Kim Cranston to author, August 24, 2005.

194. "Salinger, Cranston trade insults," Huntington Park, Ca., *Signal*, May 21, 1964; Frank Anderson, "Cranston, CDC toppled GOP control"; Jerry Gillam, "Unruh joins attack on appraisers," *Los Angeles Times*, May 14, 1964; "Cranston 'probe' nets only yawns," *San Francisco Examiner*, May 14, 1964, AC Papers.

195. Jack Schrade, "Senate Resolution 140," May 15, 1964; "Cranston contributions by appointees charged," *Los Angeles Times*, May 13, 1964; "Cranston - 'I welcome a probe of appraisers,'" *San Francisco Examiner*, May 24, 1964; Dick West, "Appraisers' strange role," Turlock, Ca., *Journal*, June 2, 1964, AC Papers.

The investigation in the Assembly was pushed by Don A. Allen, Democrat of Los Angeles.

196. "Cranston contributions by appointees charged," *Los Angeles Times*, May 13, 1964; Senator James A. Cobey, release, re: Schrade's resolution, May 20, 1964; "Salinger, Cranston slugging," United Press International, *Long Beach Independent Press-Telegram*, May 22, 1964; Jim McCauley, "Cranston appraiser probe set," *Long Beach Independent Press-Telegram*, May [?], 1964; "Assembly appraiser probe on," *Long Beach Independent Press-Telegram*, May 23, 1964, AC Papers.

197. "Unruh admits part in Cranston attack," Pittsburg, Ca., *Post-Dispatch*, May 21, 1964; "State Controller Alan Cranston's opponents…," unidentified statement; AC release concerning ITAs, May 22, 1964, AC Papers.

198. Greenaway, Williams, Moore interviews with author.

199. Fowle, 176-77; "Candidate Cranston proves to be the sensitive type," editorial, Bellingham, Wash., *Herald*, May 29, 1964, AC Papers.

200. "Bluff and baloney time arrives in campaign," editorial, Redding *Record-Searchlight*, May 28, 1964; AC release re: information on ITAs, May 22, 1964; "Cranston's honor remains unsullied," [Ward Winslow], editorial, *Palo Alto Times*, May 30, 1964, AC Papers.

201. Myran C. Fagan, Cinema Educational Guild, Inc., "A vital message for C.E.G. members and all Americans in California," [1964], AC Papers.

202. "New charge hits Cranston political aide," Associated Press, Santa Monica *Evening Outlook*, May 23, 1964, AC Papers.

203. Moore interview with author; J. Tomlinson to author, November 4, 2004.

204. Spingarn to AC, May 19, 1964, AC Papers.

205. Fowle, 176; "Brown doubt Unruh pressed Salinger to run," *Los Angeles Times*, May 13, 1964; Vallejo *Labor Journal*, re: Salinger calling Brown "dictator," May 18, 1964; "Salinger, Cranston slugging," United Press International, *Long Beach Independent Press-Telegram*, May 22, 1964; "'Big Daddy' takes slap at Cranston," *Los Angeles Herald-Examiner*, June 1, 1964; AC text of address to National Press Club, April 22, 1964, AC Papers.

206. "Democrats: 'No place to go but up,'" *Newsweek*, May 25, 1964; "Cranston's honor remains unsullied," editorial, *Palo Alto Times*, May 30, 1964, Ac Papers.

207. "[D. A. William B.] McKesson clears Controller Cranston," *Los Angeles Herald-Examiner*, May 29, 1964, scrapbook, Vol. 7, 1964, AC Papers.

208. "Democrats: 'No place to go but up,'" *Newsweek*, May 25, 1964; H. H. Ridder to Gov. Brown, June 1, 1964, AC Papers.

209. "Salinger, Cranston meet on television," United Press International, Fontana *Herald & News*, May 25, 1964, with photograph captioned "Television appearance," AC Papers.

210. Fowle, 176-77; *Newsweek*, May 25, 1964; Richard Bergholz, "Cranston uneasy with small talk," *Los Angeles Times*, May 22, 1964; C. K. McClatchy to "Dear Alan," handwritten note on United Air Lines stationery, "Saturday" after television debate, [May, 1964], AC Papers.

211. Herb Block telegram to AC, May 31, 1964, Carton 503, AC Papers.

Alan Barth (1906-79), editorial writer at the *Washington Post* for 30 years (until 1972), also authored books on history and civil liberties (including *The Rights of Free Men: An Essential Guide to Civil Liberties*, 1984).

212. Fowle, 178-79; Robert Ajemian, "Salinger swings for Senate - there's bedlam in California," *Life*, April 3, 1964; "Democrats nominate Salinger for Senate," United Press International, *San Luis Obispo Telegram-Tribune*, June 3, 1964, AC Papers.

213. Fowle, 179; Henry D. MacArthur, "Backing defeated Cranston," Huntington Park, Ca., *Signal*, June 5, 1964; "The Observer," "Behind the scenes for Pierre Salinger," Woodland, Ca., *Daily Democrat*, June 4, 1964, AC Papers.

214. Fowle, 179-80; Eliaser interview with author, January 13, 2004.

215. Fowle, 182; AC release re: congratulate Salinger, June 3, 1964; Jack Baldwin, "Countersuit filed against Cranston," *Long Beach Press-Telegram*, July 3, 1964, AC Papers.

216. "Salinger, Cranston 'share the deficit plan' revealed," Huntington Park *Signal*, June 9, 1964, citing *Los Angeles Times*; "Brown moves to patch up party feuds," Associated Press, Napa *Register*, June 4, 1964; "Pierre will aid Cranston on deficit," United Press International, Modesto *Bee*, June 13, 1964; "Brown moves to end Democrats' feuding," Associated Press, June 4, 1964, with AP Wirephoto captioned "Losing 'team'" showing Brown, Kim and Cranston; Richard Bergholz, "Humphrey fete threatened by feud in party," *Los Angeles Times*, June 20, 1965, and "Democrats see dinner as success," *Los Angeles Times*, July 11, 1965, AC Papers.

217. Moore interview with author; Fowle, 182-83.

1964 was a year of scandal for LBJ also, involving congressional aide Bobby Baker. That June Senator Ted Kennedy was injured in a plane crash. *Los Angeles Times*, editorial, December 15, 1964, Carton 14, AC Papers.

218. AC interview with author.

Robert H. Finch (1925-95) was a close friend of Nixon, an aide when he was vice president, manager of the 1960 presidential campaign against Kennedy, and adviser for the winning 1968 race. Finch was Secretary of Health, Education and Welfare (HEW) in the Nixon Cabinet, 1969-70 and more moderate than Nixon on domestic issues. A Marine in the Korean War, Finch was elected Lieutenant Governor of California in 1966 (serving to 1969), receiving more votes than Ronald Reagan did for governor.

219. Moore, Jack Tomlinson interviews with author.

220. Skattebol to AC, 4-page telegram, June 3, 1964; Waller to AC, June 15, 1964, AC Papers.

221. Falk, 7 West 81 St., New York City, to AC, September 28, 1964, AC Papers.

222. Ambassador Chester Bowles, New Delhi, India, to AC, October 3, 1964, AC Papers.

223. Swing to AC, June 3, 1964, Carton 503, AC Papers.

224. Sydney Kossen, "Cranston's smile," *San Francisco Examiner*, September 20, 1964, scrapbook, Vol. 7, 1974, AC Papers.

225. "Cranston-Salinger race a sour show," editorial, Corona, Ca., *Independent*, June 3, 1964, AC Papers.

226. *Ibid.*, "Cranston-Salinger race a sour show"; Fowle, 183-84; Robert Ajemian, "Salinger swings for Senate - there's bedlam in California," *Life*, April 3, 1964.

Murphy's films included *For Me and My Gal* with Judy Garland and Gene Kelly, *Tom, Dick and Harry* with Ginger Rogers.

227. Fowle, 183-84, citing Salinger autobiography, *With Kennedy*; Special California

Correspondent, "Anything can happen in California - and did," *The New Republic*, November 14, 1964; "Salinger post mortem, Cranston: Primary wounds didn't heal," *Santa Rosa Press Democrat*, November 4, 1964; Jackson Doyle, "Democratic losses in the election," *San Francisco Chronicle*, November 15, 1964, AC Papers.

228. Moore interview with author.

Unruh associate Tom Bane also lost a race for Congress in Los Angeles in 1964, another set-back for Unruh, while two liberal Democrats who were decidedly not Unruh supporters won Assembly seats from San Francisco – Phil Burton's brother John L. Burton and African-American Willie L. Brown, Jr.

229. Dick Nolan, "Gov. Pat Brown's quick fox," *San Francisco Examiner*, November 6, 1964, AC Papers.

230. Raymond to AC, November 4, 1964, AC Papers.

231. Salinger to AC, January 14, 1965; Salinger to AC, April 21, 1965, AC Papers.

232. Ridder to Gov. Brown, June 26, 1964; AC releases re: ITAs gross incomes, July 2 and 7, 1964; "Gross incomes of tax appraisers to be made public, Cranston says," *Long Beach Press-Telegram*, July 3, 1964; "State inheritance tax called 'political spoils,'" *San Francisco Examiner*, July 9, 1964; "106 appraisers under subpoena," *San Francisco Chronicle*, July 24, 1964; memorandum, Martha to AC, re: KNX-CBS broadcast editorial, "Political patronage," August 17, [1964?]; Jim M'Cauley, "Morality in state offices high," *Long Beach Independent, Press-Telegram*, December 20, 1964, 1964; Jackson Doyle, "Unruh attack on appraisers," *San Francisco Chronicle*, January 8, 1965; "Inheritance tax appraisers," editorial, *Los Angeles Herald-Examiner*, June 6, 1965; file "ITAs," Carton 15, AC Papers.

233. Fowle, 184; "Controller Cranston, wealthiest official sets a precedent," [*Los Angeles Times*?, November ?], 1965.

The ranch purchased with Eleanor, about 880 acres, later was sold. Kim still owned some 20 acres of Krag Ranch in 2005. The 1965 article quoted AC as saying that they might sell off some ranch property to augment income.

234. AC, "A million-dollar loser looks at campaigning," *Fortune*, November, 1964.

Cranston's officially-reported campaign expenditures totaled $823,307. The CDC mailing had cost $100,000, which with other funds had not been paid from the campaign organization and therefore were not reportable. He listed all campaign contributors but not the amounts given; they included a number of ITAs, members of Gov. Brown's administration and their wives. He reported receiving contributions of $490,930 and loans of $219,343. He later told the *Los Angeles Times* that he considered the loans his own obligation although the Democratic Party was helping pay them off. Reimbursement for campaign expenses were reported to, among others, Nebron and James Roosevelt, then an official with the United Nations. "Controller Cranston, wealthiest official sets a precedent," [*Los Angeles Times*?, November ?], 1965.

235. *Ibid*., 124, 278.

236. *Ibid*., 280; reprint of *Fortune* article, AC Papers; "Controller Cranston, wealthiest official sets a precedent," [*Los Angeles Times*?, November ?], 1965; James J. Kilpatrick, "Regarding elections, the British are camp," *Los Angeles Times*, March 31, 1966, with AC note, "campaign $," AC Papers.

237. Lee Merriman, "Editor's Diary," Pasadena *Independent*, December 2, 1964, scrapbook, Vol. 7, 1964; James Wrightson, "Cranston decries role of money in politics," *Fresno Bee*, October 16, 1963, scrapbook, Vol. 6, 1963; "Campaign contributions compound problems of top elected officials," *Los Angeles Times*, December 30, 1965, AC Papers.

238. "Controller Cranston, wealthiest official sets a precedent," [*Los Angeles Times*?, November ?], 1965; Gene Blake and Paul Beck, "7 state officials' financial survey," *Los Angeles Times*, December 30, 1965, AC Papers.

239. Jackson Doyle, "Cranston put officials on the spot," *San Francisco Chronicle*, May

23, 1966, AC Papers.

240. Nebron to AC, September 20, 1964, AC Papers.

241. "California job for HHH aide," *San Francisco Examiner*, January 21, 1965; news clipping re: Winthrop Griffith, 1965, Carton 14, AC Papers; REC to author, March 28, 2003.

Griffith, 34, a Stanford graduate, had been a reporter for the *Examiner* until 1960 when he became Humphrey's press secretary.

242. "Mother" to AC, December 12, 1964, AC Papers.

243. "Mother" to AC, January 3, 1965, AC Papers.

244. Michael Harris, "Anderson's job now a prize post," *San Francisco Chronicle*, December 29, 1964, AC Papers.

245. Lisa Rubens, "When freedom wasn't just a word, Free Speech Movement's great impact," review of *The Free Speech Movement, Reflections on Berkeley in the 1960s*, Robert Cohen and Reginald E. Zelnik, eds., (Berkeley: University of California Press, 2002), *San Francisco Chronicle*, December 29, 2002.

U. C. President Clark Kerr had been accused in 1961 of opening "the campus gates to Communists" in a report by a California Senate subcommittee. Brown overruled Kerr by ordering police to clear Sproul Hall on the Berkeley campus after a sit-in by some 800 demonstrating students December 2-3, 1964. At issue was whether students could conduct political advocacy on campus. After Free Speech Movement leader Mario Savio was manhandled by police, many U. C. faculty voted to back the movement's demand to rescind a non-advocacy rule. U. C. Regents conceded that the university should follow U. S. Supreme Court decisions on free speech. Kerr in March, 1965, announced his intention to resign but Gov. Brown and the Berkeley faculty backed him and a divided Board of Regents persuaded him to stay. By then, Vietnam anti-war protestors also were using the campus for demonstrations. Seth Rosenfeld, "Trouble on campus," *San Francisco Chronicle*, June 9, 2002.

246. Pearson to AC, December 14, 1964, AC Papers.

247. News clippings, scrapbook, Vol. 8, 1965, AC Papers.

248. Greenaway to author, May 19, 2003; Wes Willoughby interviews with author, May 11, 2004, and July 25, 2005, hereafter cited as Willoughby interviews with author; AC text, "Who's an extremist?" for speech to Town Hall, Biltmore Hotel, Los Angeles, July 13, 1965, scrapbook, Willoughby Personal Papers.

Willoughby joined Cranston's staff as assistant deputy controller in March, 1965, succeeding "Chuck" Hurley. Willoughby had been a research and writing aide to Senator Kuchel while an American Political Science Association congressional fellow (1961-62) when he also worked for Sen. Humphrey; he also had worked on the Johnson-Humphrey presidential campaign and for N. Y. Governor Nelson Rockefeller's primary race in 1964. "Humphrey, Kuchel ex-aide named Cranston's deputy," *Long Beach Press-Telegram*, March 12, 1965, Willoughby Personal Papers.

249. "Extremism - its definition and prescribed antidote," *Los Angeles Times*, July 13, 1965, scrapbook, Vol. 8, 1965; Los Angeles B'nai B'rith *Messenger* article, August 5, 1966, AC Papers.

250. Reprint, Sen. Eugene McCarthy, "Alan Cranston's answer: 'Who's an extremist?'" *Congressional Record*, July 19, 1965; "Cranston on Birch," *The Nation*, editorial, August 2, 1966, scrapbook, Vol. 9, 1966, AC Papers; Max Freedman, "Cranston shows responsibility, courage in attack on extremism," *Los Angeles Times*, July 22, 1965, Willoughby Personal Papers.

The speech also was covered by the *St. Louis Post-Dispatch*, August 15, 1965; *Christian Science Monitor*, August 7, 1965; Orange County *Sun*, September, 1965.

251. AC, "John Birch Society, 1966: Seed-bed of bigotry, hate, neo-fascism," Ventura County *Star-Free Press*, July 28, 1965, AC Papers.

Birch Society leader Robert Welch, a retired New England candy manufacturer, in 1956 had started the organization with a book-length letter to wealthy friends, "The Politician," accusing President Eisenhower of being a "dedicated, conscious agent of the communist conspiracy" and thus of "treason."

252. AC, "Death Valley Daisy, starring Reginald Rodgun with Billie James Hardgrass, H. L. Hunted, Dan Smooth," *Frontier*, August, 1965, 7-8, AC Papers.

Billy James Hargis (1925-2004) preached political activism against communism and support of conservative politicians. His tax-exempt status was revoked in the early 1960s for political activities by his $1-million-a-year ministry. False information about a journalist's work led to a request for equal time and the U. S. Supreme Court's codifying the broadcast "fairness doctrine." His American Christian College in Tulsa was shut down in the late 1970s after allegations of sexual approaches to both sexes from Hargis who stated evasively, "I am guilty of sin, but not the sin I am accused of." Adam Bernstein, "Evangelist Billy James Hargis Dies; Spread Anti-Communist Message," *Washington Post*, November 30, 2004.

253. AC address to S. F. Commonwealth Club, "Legally California may be a single state; actually it is cruelly splintered," *Fresno Bee*, August 15, 1965, AC Papers.

254. *Ibid.*

255. News clippings re: AC speech to Peninsula Manufacturers Association, *Palo Alto Times*, Vallejo *Times-Herald*, Eureka *Humboldt-Times*, March 26, 1965, Willoughby Personal Papers.

256. Controller release re: fewer staff with 30% workload increase, March 2, 1966; news clippings, scrapbook, Vol. 8, 1965, AC Papers; Arthur Hoppe, "Fearless foe of efficiency," *San Francisco Chronicle* , June 27, 1965, Willoughby Personal Papers.

257. Jackson Doyle, "Appraiser system gets an uppercut," *San Francisco Chronicle*, February 14, 1965; Tom Arden, "Assembly votes to revoke controller's appraiser power," *Sacramento Bee*, June 9, 1965; "Bill to end tax appraiser patronage goes to Senate," June 10, 1965, AC Papers.

One GOP bill was sponsored by William T. Bagley of San Rafael; an earlier Bagley bill to make ITAs civil servants had been defeated in the Assembly Ways and Means Committee in 1963. Bagley joked when he introduced the second bill in 1965 that Unruh smiled at him for the first time since the legislative session began. A different bill was sponsored by S. F. Republican Assemblyman Milton Marks and supported by Gov. Brown. Bert Clinkston, "Cranston has door of patronage locked for another 2 years," *Sacramento Union*, June 7, 1963, scrapbook, Vol. 6, 1963, AC Papers.

258. "Inheritance appraisal system is discredited," editorial, *Long Beach Press-Telegram*, February 16, 1965; "Tax appraisal reform due," Stockton *Record*, February [25?], 1965; "Fuss over appraisers," Pasadena *Star-News*, February 25, 1965, Willoughby Personal Papers.

259. AC Controller release, re: reforms of ITA system, May 11, 1965, AC Papers.

Cranston's package was introduced by Sen. James A. Cobey.

260. Vice President Humphrey to AC, September 11, 1965, AC Papers.

261. AC, "California makes first use of unique Good Samaritan law," *Police*, September-October, 1966, reprint, AC Papers.

State Sen. George Miller, Jr., sponsored the bill and Gov. Brown signed it July 15, 1965. The first recipient was Clifford G. Miller, Jr., and payment was made by the Board of Control. Other states soon enacted similar laws.

262. "Fluttering occasion," caption to photograph of Cranstons on 25th anniversary, *Sacramento Bee*, November 6, 1965; "Holiday greetings from the Animal Farm," Christmas card, [1960s], file "Misc. to file," Carton 14, AC Papers.

263. AC application for federal employment for evaluation of Peace Corps operation in a foreign country, [1965]; material in scrapbook, Vol. 9, 1966, AC Papers.

His application stated that he accepted "0" as pay.

264. AC, "We need more like Dave Ripley," *San Luis Obispo Telegram-Tribune*, January 4, 1966; AC, "Ghana overseas evaluation," December, 1965, AC Papers.

265. AC to James Landewe, Nkwatia-Kwaha, Ghana, Africa, December 22, 1965, AC Papers.